On the Theory
of Social Change
How Economic Growth Begins

THE DORSEY SERIES IN ANTHROPOLOGY AND SOCIOLOGY

EDITOR   WILLIAM FOOTE WHYTE   *Cornell University*

ARGYRIS   *Understanding Organizational Behavior*

ADAMS & PREISS (eds.)   *Human Organization Research*   (Published for the Society for Applied Anthropology)

HSU (ed.)   *Psychological Anthropology: Approaches to Culture and Personality*

BELL (ed.)   *The Sociology of Education: A Sourcebook*

HAGEN   *On the Theory of Social Change: How Economic Growth Begins*

A Study from the Center for International Studies
Massachusetts Institute of Technology

On the Theory
of Social Change

How Economic Growth Begins

Everett E. Hagen Ph.D.
Professor of Economics
Senior Staff Member, Center for International Studies
Massachusetts Institute of Technology

1962   THE DORSEY PRESS, INC. *Homewood, Illinois*

First Printing, May, 1962
Second Printing, January, 1963
Third Printing, March, 1967

Library of Congress Catalogue Card No. 62–16517

PRINTED IN THE UNITED STATES OF AMERICA

In the traditional manner, I offer this book as a token to my wife, Ruth Alexander Hagen, whose tolerance of a rival during the past six years has been very modern.

Foreword

ONE OF THE DOMINANT CONCERNS OF THE CENTER FOR International Studies over the past decade has been to improve our understanding of the complex economic, political, psychological, and social forces at work in the nations emerging from tradition into the modern world. We were aware from the beginning that research on these forces posed unusually difficult problems because of the variety of separate disciplines that would somehow have to be harnessed together in the analysis. We were skeptical of the fruitfulness of the procedure usually suggested in such cases of assembling a team of specialists each of whom would apply his particular analytic machinery to a part of the problem. The history of interdisciplinary research is littered with the failures of such teams to emerge with the kind of synthesis that goes beyond partial insights. But we were not sure how else to proceed.

We had the great good fortune of having Everett Hagen associated with us almost from the start of this program. For Professor Hagen, who had already established a notable reputation as an economist, was convinced of the need for interdisciplinary work and was not content merely to associate with representatives of other disciplines. He concluded that to understand economic growth he would himself have to master the literature of psychology, anthropology, and sociology. This he set about doing, with a degree of success that can be judged from this book, which embodies the results of some years of both concept formation and empirical investigation into the origins of economic growth.

The Center's debt to him goes beyond the contribution this book makes to the development literature. As a man at home in each of a number of usually rather isolated ivory towers, he has made possible a degree of communication amongst us that would have been much more difficult in his absence. His insights have influenced a good many Center books that have already appeared over other names. We are happy to be able now to present this fuller statement of his own analysis.

Max F. Millikan

Preface

THE STUDY ON WHICH THIS BOOK IS BASED AROSE OUT OF the attempt to answer a question which puzzled me during two years as economic advisor to the government of the Union of Burma. The officials of Burma avowed their intense desire for economic development, and there was no reason to doubt the sincerity of their statements. Why then did they not use the resources at their disposal more effectively toward that end?

On my return to the United States late in 1953 to join the staff of the Center for International Studies at the Massachusetts Institute of Technology, I let that question lie fallow in my mind for two years or so. However, since 1956 my energies have been devoted primarily to evolving an answer to the general question implicit in that specific one: Why have the people of some societies entered upon technological progress sooner or more effectively than others? Since it seemed clear to me that the differences were due only in very minor degree to economic obstacles, lack of information, or lack of training, I turned my attention to other possible causes of differences in human behavior—to differences in personality, and hence personality formation and the social conditions affecting it.

This study led, in turn, to a general theory of social change.

A fuller account of the origins of my interest in personality formation would have to go back to various pleasures and traumas in childhood and as I grew up. The total narrative would indicate a process much less logical and systematic than is suggested by the summary account above. But that brief statement may provide an introduction sufficient to orient a reader.

A study such as this requires the knowledge and insights of those most practical students of personality formation, the psychoanalysts, of anthropologists, and of sociologists. My own formal training in economics could contribute little but a conception of the requirements for the analysis of theoretical models or systems and a sense of the inadequacy of economic theory to answer the question at hand. The theory, it would seem, should have been worked out through interaction among the members of an interdisciplinary team. However, while I owe a great deal to three social scientists who were my associates in the research, I attempted to organize in my own mind the principles of personality formation and societal

functioning necessary for the evolution of the general theory. For that I
have two justifications. One is an intense interest which led me to devote
my energies to the problem more completely than I could expect other
individuals to do. The other is a principle of research expressed in a statement by Hanns Sachs: "The best interdisciplinary research is that which
goes on within one skull."

My indebtedness to a variety of published materials is indicated in the
footnotes. The number of scholars to whom I owe thanks for more personal counsel is great. Pre-eminent are my obligations to the Center
for International Studies and its director, Max F. Millikan, whose philosophy of administration of an academic research organization has provided
an environment highly conducive to effective professional work; Professor Erik H. Erikson, from whose discussions at a graduate seminar and
a faculty seminar at M.I.T., during the period when the ideas of this book
were being formed, I benefited greatly; the late Professor Clyde Kluckhohn, who read two early drafts of half of the manuscript and contributed
greatly of his intellectual riches, as he did with such generosity to a host
of students and colleagues; Dr. Samuel Bojar of the Harvard Medical
School, who communicated so effectively his insights into the processes
of personality formation; and my students during the past five years in my
course, Economic Growth as Social Change, whose questions, objections,
demands for evidence, and analytical suggestions have contributed more
to the shaping of this manuscript than any one group of them may realize.

The research was not merely library philosophizing. Field work as well
as my freedom to devote full time to the study for three years were made
possible by a grant to the Center for International Studies from the Rockefeller Foundation. I am grateful for the breadth of interest which led to a
grant to support this unconventional project, organized in an unconventional manner.

Formal work on the project began in the spring of 1956 with a two-day
discussion by an advisory committee composed of Professors Jerome
Bruner, Cora DuBois, Bert Hoselitz, Alex Inkeles, David C. McClelland,
and Edward A. Shils, together with Professors Daniel Lerner, Max F.
Millikan, and Ithiel Pool of the Center for International Studies staff. The
ideas generated at that meeting provided valuable leads for later work.

My initial associates in the project were James C. Abegglen and Jean
MacKenzie Pool. After a year Dr. Abegglen resigned his position to accept one elsewhere and was replaced by Louis C. Schaw. Mrs. Pool is
broadly trained in social psychology and Abegglen and Schaw in that
interdisciplinary complex referred to as "culture and personality." I could
hardly have had a group of associates who could have provided greater
intellectual stimulus. Dr. Schaw worked on the project over the longest
period, and I must express my especial indebtedness for the brilliant insights which he provided throughout that time. In addition to his general
analytical co-operation he was responsible for psychological studies in

Colombia, and he rather than I was the senior author of the analysis of Sioux personality and society which is reflected in Chapter 19.

Interestingly, in his approach to the study of personality Abegglen stressed world view, Mrs. Pool values, and Schaw motivations, though of course each recognized the role of the other two qualities. Each of the three thus served as an exponent of one of the three elements which enter into the model of personality presented in the text.

Abegglen field-tested research instruments and design in Mexico. Later, Howard V. Perlmutter carried out an analysis of the results of this field work, and Oriol PiSunyer did a study of social and personality change in a Mexican town. I regret that it was not possible without delaying the publication of this book to reflect the results of these pieces of research in a chapter on the transition to economic growth in Mexico. They provided suggestions which are reflected in other chapters of the book.

Professor William E. Henry served briefly as consultant in the analysis of thematic apperception test protocols, and I gained aesthetic pleasure as well as intellectual benefit from the wisdom and art of his interpretations.

To three colleagues, Professors Richard S. Eckaus, Ithiel de Sola Pool, and Lucian W. Pye, I am indebted for a critical reading of a draft of all chapters other than those summarizing the case studies. Their judicious general comments and their penetrating detailed criticisms both contributed to improvement of the manuscript.

Professor Elting Morison read and criticized the manuscript of Chapter 13, Professors Masasada Inoue and Masatoshi Nagatomi that of Chapter 14, and Dr. Diego Tobón Arbeláez that of Chapter 15. While these men read these manuscripts without benefit of knowledge of the theoretical framework of the book as a whole, and rightly refused comment on the nature of the general analysis, they made thoughtful comments which are reflected in the final versions of the chapters, and which saved me from various errors of fact and interpretation.

My obligations to many persons with whom I had discussions during my two-year period of residence in Burma are so diffuse that I cannot specify individuals.

The names of the many individuals who helped in the study of the Sioux are given in E. E. Hagen and Louis C. Schaw, *The Sioux on the Reservations* (Cambridge, Mass.: Center for International Studies, Massachusetts Institute of Technology, 1960), and I shall not repeat them here. However, I have not elsewhere referred to a number of individuals in Colombia whose information was of great value to me in my study of that country, and it is a pleasure to do so here:

In Bogotá: Salvador Camacho Roldán, Hernán Echavarría, Roberto de J. Herrera, Señor Peñalosa, Jorge Restrepo Hoyos, Julio Samper Ortega, Luis Soto. In Cali: Ernesto Arango Tavera, Manuel María Buenaventura, Hernando Caicedo, Manuel Carvajal, Harold H. Eder, Alfredo Lloreda. In Medellín: Luis Echavarría, José Gutiérrez-Gómez (then in

Washington, D.C. as ambassador to the United States), Pedro Nel Ospina, Daniel Peláez, and Gonzalo Restrepo Jaramillo. I must acknowledge also my great indebtedness to the National Association of Industrialists, whose aid in guiding me to helpful individuals, in arranging for their co-operation, and in other ways was invaluable.

I must express indebtedness of other sorts to three members of the Center for International Studies staff. My secretary, Gabrielle Fuchs, in addition to doing research on English innovators, compiled and arranged the bibliography under my supervision from the footnotes and my files, and exercised a responsibility for the entire manuscript far beyond the call of secretarial duty. Richard W. Hatch, with that talent for which every writer on the Center staff is grateful, improved the arrangement and clarity of the text and removed many infelicities of substance and expression. And Mrs. Jean Clark felicitously performed an editorial function in the final stages of preparation of the manuscript for the press.

None of the individuals mentioned above shares responsibility for the final form of the manuscript. Final decisions concerning both details and the general architecture of the structure were mine, and I am responsible for errors that remain. In particular, in the discussion of personality formation, the decision to pay very little attention to the periods of latency and adolescence is solely mine. The various individuals who have counseled with me concerning personality formation all recognize the importance of these later periods, as do I, and I would not wish to burden any of them with responsibility for my decision to simplify reality by concentrating on the first half dozen years of life.

Everett E. Hagen

CAMBRIDGE, MASSACHUSETTS
        March, 1962

Contents

PART IV. TRANSITION TO ECONOMIC GROWTH: SOME CASES IN POINT

BIBLIOGRAPHY

INDEX

part **I**

The Nature
of the Problem

The Purpose and Structure
of the Book

chapter 1

THIS BOOK EXAMINES THE FACTORS WHICH CAUSE A TRA-
ditional society to become one in which economic growth is occurring.
The hypotheses presented to explain this change seem relevant to the
analysis of other types of social change, and it is my hope that I have been
able to make some fruitful comments concerning the problem of social
change in general. Briefly, then, the book attempts to contribute to knowledge of the process of economic growth, and in doing so to make some
additions to the content of social theory and suggest some changes in its
method of analysis.

The world is undergoing rapid social change, but while we social scientists give names to some of the manifestations—nationalism, the disruption of traditionalism, the revolution of rising expectations—it must
be confessed that we know very little about the forces that cause the
process of change and govern its course.

In part this is because the process of social change is exceedingly complex. The problems of the physical sciences are absurdly simple compared with those posed by the behavior of groups of human beings. In
part it is because the social sciences are very young. It was only 120
years ago that Comte first suggested that the phenomena and structure
of societies are subject to systematic classification. Except for Frazer's
Golden Bough, all of the major writings of anthropology are of the
twentieth century, and until well into that century it was widely believed
even among social scientists that personality is predominantly determined by biological heredity. At the beginning of the century Freud
was still unknown outside of a narrow circle.

Lastly, in part the inadequacy of our understanding is due to the fact
that until very recently the three major social sciences have gone their
separate ways. (It is also true that they have gone their separate ways
partly because of the inadequacy of our understanding.) The study of
culture and of primitive societies by anthropologists, of the social structure of societies by sociologists, and of personality formation by psy-

3

chologists have been largely separate disciplines.[1] They have reached a point at which they should be brought into interaction to form a theory of societies and social change.

In the process of integration, important advances in method and content can be made.

The Need for System Analysis

It seems to me that social theory has reached a point at which it is possible and will be increasingly fruitful to use the method known in the physical sciences as system analysis.

As I have said in another place, "As judged by the history of the physical, biological, and social sciences, study in any field is apt to begin with a none-too-ordered description of phenomena in the field, followed by a cataloguing of them on bases that seem to make sense. As understanding grows, the systems of classification become more closely related to the functioning of interacting elements. Gradually, generalizations about functioning are reached which are useful in predicting future events. As the generalizations gain rigor, they take the form of analytical models of the behavior of the elements being studied."[2] They take the form, that is, of systems. When they do, a great increase in rigor and power is achieved. I discuss system analysis in Appendix I; here let me merely note the commonplace fact that it involves breaking down the elements of the system into simple measurable ones and noting the functional relationships among them. The functional relationships do not consist of effects vaguely described as "the consequences of an item for the system in which it is implicated"[3]; rather, they are defined as alternative magnitudes or states of one element associated with alternative magnitudes or states of another. When a complete set of such relationships has been defined, one can analyze the results of any changes that affect the system.

Analysis in the physical sciences has been formulated in terms of models for several generations, an initial landmark being the work of Willard Gibbs in mathematics and the physical sciences some three quarters of a century ago. Recently theoretical analysis in economics has reached the stage of system analysis. Still more recently much analysis in some branches of psychology has done so. The analytical model is still not prominent in the other social sciences. The reason is probably not merely their lesser contact with mathematics, the general science of relationships among magnitudes, but also the greater complexity of their subject matter and hence the later development of understanding of it. Students of

---

[1] I do not mention political science. The newer school of political science integrates the three social sciences in the study of some aspects of social behavior, but it should not be listed as a fourth discipline.

[2] E. E. Hagen, "Analytical Models in the Study of Social Systems," *American Journal of Sociology*, Vol. LXVII (September, 1961), pp. 144–51.

[3] See Appendix I for definitions of function by Merton and Parsons.

any field of knowledge cannot formulate an analytical model until, as their understanding grows, their images of the phenomena begin to resemble elements connected by functional relationships.

I suggest that the understanding of causal relationships among phenomena in the social sciences has reached a point at which there is no longer any excuse for not employing the power of system analysis.

The Need for Integration of Social Science Theory

An important component of system analysis in the study of societies must be a theory of personality, for the analysis of societies is analysis of human behavior, and such analysis which omits the clues provided by current personality theory is unnecessarily crippled.

Until fairly recently sociologists and anthropologists might have claimed with some plausibility that they were in better position to analyze human behavior than were psychologists since the latter analyzed only small bits of total human behavior. Now, however, social and clinical, or "depth," psychology has contributed analysis of great power concerning the functioning of personality as a whole. While there are still important controversies and uncertainties in personality theory not only illuminating insights but also hypotheses of some rigor have emerged. The student of society or culture who does not have thorough professional competence in the psychology of personality is obsolescent.

The possible contribution is not entirely unidirectional. The clinical psychologist tests his theory of personality only with respect to separate individuals in a very special situation. While the social psychologist studies groups in less artificial situations, he does not study their total functioning. The student of society considers human behavior in its broadest context. I suggest that thoughtful analysis which comprehends both social or cultural theory and personality theory may contribute insights to all that may escape the separate analysis of any one of the three. However, it seems likely that the major flow of benefit will be from psychology to the other two disciplines.[4]

The Need to Relate Childhood to History

Moreover, it is possible, I think, to state something about the nature of the functional relationships between elements of social structure and

---

[4] The argument applies also along the third side of the triangle. The study of social structure and personality is unnecessarily crippled if it does not take advantage of the evidence concerning the functioning of both provided by present anthropological knowledge of the circumstances in which certain cultural phenomena—for example, certain changes in religious ethic—tend to appear. So also is a model which comprehends culture and personality without taking advantage of the knowledge concerning the functioning of both provided by evidence concerning the circumstances in which certain changes in social structure tend to appear. However, because the relating of the psychology of personality to the other two disciplines seems the most urgent order of business, in the text I have stressed its contribution to the other two.

elements of personality which need to be introduced into models of society.

Erik H. Erikson has discussed with great perceptiveness and suggestiveness the impact of childhood on society. Giving greatest attention to this relationship in the case of reformers, he has suggested that a reformer is an individual who learned when a child a pattern of solution of a personal problem that caused him intense anxiety. An example of such a problem is the tyranny of an arbitrary father. When the individual faced in adult life a social force (for example, authority which abuses its power) parallel to the deeply troublesome force of his childhood, his anxiety was re-aroused and he reacted as he had learned to react in childhood.

If the evil discerned by an individual who has thus been sensitized in his childhood is also perceived by enough fellow members of his society as an evil, they will follow his lead and he may accomplish a great social change and become an historic figure, for good or ill.

Erikson has traced the relationship most fully in his study of Martin Luther's struggle first against a father who exercised harsh and arbitrary authority without considering the welfare of his son, then against a Church that abused its authority in a Pike manner.[5] Similar parallels between childhood and adulthood exist in the lives of many, perhaps every, reformer.[6]

I would make explicit a broader generalization implicit in Erikson's discussions of personality formation (and which he might not wish to make as precise as I do). A relationship between childhood and adulthood somewhat like that in the lives of reformers exists for all men. The tenor of any age is powerfully influenced by the pattern of relationships which the members of a society have found satisfactory as children. If a hierarchical authoritarian social structure persists for centuries (as it has in traditional societies), it must be concluded that the members of the society found it satisfactory, and did so because in childhood they found such a structure of relationships the best solution to a problem they faced. When the people of Hitlerian Germany acquiesced in brutal anti-Semitism, or many people of the United States after World War II in McCarthyism, it must be concluded that the fear of some faceless threat which led them to feel security in Hitler's or Senator McCarthy's actions echoed a similar fear which they experienced in their childhood. When a society which has found satisfaction in authoritarian government changes to democratic government, it must be concluded that childhood environment has changed so that the need of a hierarchy above and below one is no longer felt in childhood and instead exploration without authoritarian guidance of one's relations with one's peers seems safe and satisfying, and therefore seems safe and satisfying in adulthood as well.

---

[5] *Young Man Luther* (New York: W. W. Norton & Co., Inc., 1958).

[6] See Chapter 11.

Similarly if a society transmits elements of its culture essentially unchanged from generation to generation—such as religious ethic, folk tales, or historic accounts extolling the virtues of the group—it must be concluded not that each generation learned and believed them merely because it heard the words from its elders but that the view of the world embodied in these cultural elements satisfied deep needs which arose in the development of personality.

Of course personality is not fully developed in childhood; it changes throughout life. Moreover, the relationship between childhood and adulthood is far more complex than this brief reference suggests. Some of the complexities are discussed in later chapters. Nevertheless, the impact on adult behavior of patterns learned in childhood is always great. A model of society which does not take it into account is of limited usefulness. The motivations of the adult which lead him to seek a pattern of relationships paralleling those which were satisfying in his childhood are of course unconscious. Perhaps no other single step in the broadening of their analytical tools will increase the power of sociology and anthropology as much as to incorporate in their analysis of human behavior informed analysis of unconscious processes.[7]

I suggest that the social sciences must recognize also the converse relationship between society and childhood. If changes in childhood environment are required before there can be any basic change in a society, it is also true that something must have caused the changes in childhood environment. And the most likely cause of change in childhood environment in a society which has hitherto been reasonably satisfying to its members (so that one generation has repeated the one before) is the appearance of some new tension in the social structure.

If a new social situation causes the members of some group who were previously reasonably content to be anxious about their lives, the anxiety will affect their behavior in the home and hence the environment in which their children grow up. I suggest that such tensions, existing over a period of generations, are a fundamental cause of social change, and that a model of society which incorporates such tensions and their impact on childhood environment may be fruitful in the interpretation of history.

The tensions may be due to either the impingement of outside groups on the society (for example, colonialism or the Norman conquest of England) or to the inner workings of the society itself (for example, the imposition on Japan by the Tokugawa of measures designed to counteract earlier governmental weaknesses and perpetuate their power). They are

---

[7] The need to do this may be one of the barriers which has retarded the integration of the social sciences. It is difficult for many individuals, in the social sciences as elsewhere, to admit unconscious processes into their analysis, simply because many of one's own unconscious processes are painful and it is just as well to deny that they are of importance.

of course not an ultimate cause, for ultimate historical analysis must go behind them to ask why the events which led to new tensions occurred. But if we can take such historic situations as starting points and construct models which explain the ensuing sequences of social change, we shall be doing well enough.

The Structure of This Book

It is necessary not merely to agree that such relationships exist but to sketch their nature. Indeed, until their nature has been sketched, and has given rise to models which have greater explanatory power than previous theories, there will be no general agreement that the relationships exist.

To give insight into the interrelationships involved, study of social change may be more useful than study of a society in equilibrium, for in a society in equilibrium, it may not be certain whether one generation is simply imitating the preceding one or whether some much more complex stabilizing factors are present. If we observe the process of change, we may be able to note the repercussions among personality culture and social structure that deter change as well as the forces causing it.

The transition of societies from a traditional state[8] to one characterized by continuing and rather rapid technological progress (economic growth) seems an especially promising subject for such analysis. In a number of societies the transition is now in process; in others it has been completed so recently that a fairly generous volume of historical evidence is available. These societies had varying characteristics before the transition began, and in them the transition has followed differing courses. Yet they have some common elements. Hence they provide fruitful cases for analysis. Moreover, this transition is of great importance to the world as a whole at present.

For this reason, as an approach to a general theory of social change this volume presents a study of the transition from a traditional social state to continuing technological progress.

Because there may still be some lingering feeling among not only economists but also some other scholars that the determinants of economic growth are mainly economic barriers and opportunities, Chapter 2 surveys the historical circumstances in which economic growth has begun in various countries and Chapter 3 surveys the economic theories of growth. The conclusion is drawn that economic theory has rather little to offer toward an explanation of economic growth, and that broader social and psychological considerations are pertinent.

The following chapters then evolve, piece by piece, a fully defined model of society, a model which stresses the chain of causation from social structure through parental behavior to childhood environment and then that from childhood environment through personality to social

---

[8] The term "traditional state of society" is defined precisely in Chapter 4.

change. The model is applied first to traditional society and then to the process of transition from a traditional state to economic growth. Six case studies attempt to show its relevance to life.

Like any theoretical discussion, the analysis abstracts from many complexities. It is hoped that it is sufficiently faithful to the basic features of life so that it contributes to both the understanding of economic growth and the body of social theory.

Historical Bases
for a Theory of Growth

chapter 2

GROWTH AND ABSENCE OF GROWTH

VIEWED IN THE BROAD SWEEP OF HUMAN HISTORY, IM-
provement in technology and resulting rise in per capita income have
always been occurring everywhere. If we had information for points in
time perhaps 10,000 years apart, we would probably find that the standard
of living of the world's human inhabitants had increased between each
two points. But the rising trend was so slow until recent times that examination even at thousand-year intervals might not show progress during
every interval.

In the eighteenth or early nineteenth century, however, following a
number of important improvements in methods in western Europe during
the Middle Ages, there began in England a series of advances in technology and a rise in per capita output rapid enough so that marked change
occurred within each generation, and indeed during each decade. Change
at such a pace may be termed *economic growth.*

In the nineteenth century economic growth spread from England to a
group of countries of western Europe culturally related to England and
to each other, stretching from the Scandinavian Peninsula to Italy and
from the Atlantic to Germany, but not including Spain and Portugal. Also
in the nineteenth century it was carried, partly by emigrants and partly
by cultural diffusion, from Britain and western Europe to North America,
Australia, and New Zealand. Well before the end of the century, economic growth had also begun in Japan, and at about the same time, but
with a slower pace, in Russia. In the twentieth century the virus of
growth spread within Europe to Poland and Czechoslovakia, and mar-
ginally to Spain, Portugal, and Greece. Continuing growth also seems to
have begun in Argentina, Chile, Mexico, Brazil, and Colombia, and may
have begun in several other Latin American countries, elsewhere in eastern Europe, and in some of the Middle East countries. Most recently, it is
almost certainly under way in China and may have begun in India.[1]

---

[1] During the Renaissance there occurred a technological flowering in Italy. For
example, ships were constructed in Venice by an assembly-line process. But the technological progress was not widespread, and the scientific and sociological basis for
its continuance did not exist.

Altogether, in countries containing approximately 30 per cent of the world's population and producing almost 80 per cent of its income, the process of technological progress now seems so firmly built into behavior patterns that, in the absence of military catastrophe, continuing rapid rise in productivity may confidently be anticipated throughout the foreseeable future. In countries having another 34 per cent of the world's population, fairly rapid technological progress is occurring, and it is plausible to assume that it will continue. Still another 20 per cent of the world's people live in countries where changes in techniques in recent years may herald the beginning of a continuing process. The rest of the people of the world —one of every six—live in countries where the available facts do not give clear evidence of an appreciable rate of technological progress.

Geographically, the distribution of countries among the four groups is not random. If on a map one were to shade the countries in which growth is long and solidly built in, crosshatch those in which it had probably taken root, dot those where it may have begun, and leave blank the others, then, as one moved from Europe and North America to Latin America to Asia to Africa, one would move from an area solidly shaded to ones that are crosshatched, find the hatching shrinking and dotted areas replacing it, and then see larger and larger blank patches. Economic growth is universal among the countries of Europe and North America, less common in Latin America, and least discernible in many countries of Asia and Africa. But there is some evidence of growth in some countries of every continent.[2]

What is this technological progress which is the cause of rising income? In essence it consists of two steps: the discovery of new knowledge which makes possible an increase in the output of goods and services per unit of labor, capital, and materials used in production; and the incorporation of that knowledge in productive processes. It includes the devising of more satisfying products as well as of more efficient methods of production. It includes the entire process of innovation, from an advance in pure science to its adaptation in engineering and its application in production.[3] Within the realm of methods it includes not only scientific and technical advances but also the devising of new forms of organization or methods of procedure which make the society more efficient in production.[4] To term all these somewhat varied activities "technological progress" is not to use the term as a catchall. They have in common the de-

---

[2] For a detailed presentation of the facts summarized here, see E. E. Hagen, "Some Facts About Income Levels and Economic Growth," *Review of Economics and Statistics*, Vol. XLII (February, 1960), pp. 62–67.

[3] If the creation of a new form in music or the arts increases human satisfaction, this too is technological progress, much though the artists or musicians might dislike being bracketed with engineers and technicians.

[4] Insofar as the spread of a new method throughout a society after it has appeared in one place is mere imitation, this is not technological progress; but since in fact the spread of a method throughout an industry or a society involves a degree of creative adaptation, elements of technological progress are present here too.

vising of new concepts, which is the essence of technological progress.

Income in a society may rise because of capital formation, that is, the production of additional instruments for use in production, even in the absence of technological progress.[5] But if capital formation consists solely of the construction of instruments already known and does not embody new ideas, the rise in income will gradually come to a halt. Continuing rise in income—that is, continuing economic growth—is obtained only by continuing improvement in techniques or products. There is no other road. But this road is an enchanted one, leading to an ever-expanding landscape. If steady technological progress is occurring in any given society at a rate sufficient to more than compensate for increase in population, and if the behavior pattern of the society is such that the technological progress promises to continue, then in a sense the fundamental economic problem has been solved. Technological progress may also grasp the social fabric roughly and warp it this way and that. If the resulting stresses are the cause of the neuroses of modern life, then perhaps the game is not worth the candle; nevertheless the process inexorably spreads.

SOME PLAUSIBLE EXPLANATIONS

I shall term the process of change in any society from technological advance so slow that it is hardly noticeable from generation to generation to continuing advance so rapid that it is conspicuous from decade to decade the transition to economic growth. This essay is devoted to the question: What are the causes of the transition?

Accelerating Cumulation and Spread of Knowledge as the Causes

In the broad sweep of history the answer is clear: Entry upon economic growth is a result of the accelerating cumulation of scientific and technical knowledge.

We shall see in later chapters that in traditional societies little human energy was devoted to the study of technology. For reasons arising from the structure of the societies, study of the physical world was repugnant to the members of elite groups. Yet occasional scientific or technological advance occurred in two ways. First, by more or less random discoveries by intelligent minds. Since the typical person felt antipathy to concerning

---

[5] Other possible forces are receipt of income from a rich natural resource such as oil, decision of an increased share of the population to enter the labor force, decision to work more hours per week, or, in densely populated countries, a catastrophe which decreases the population, leaving more resources per person. Thus the bubonic plague in Europe in the fourteenth century may have raised per capita income after the initial period of chaos. Receipt of income from a natural resource implies technological progress either by the society in which the resource exists or by individuals of some other society. These possible causes of rise in income are exceptional and limited; their effect must soon reach a ceiling.

himself with science or technology, this effect was not important. Second, however, variant and deviant individuals appear in any society, and the specific circumstances of their individual lives that caused such individuals to be different undoubtedly caused some of them to turn their energies to problems of technology. From time to time, therefore, new truths about the physical world were discovered, and new techniques of production devised. Some of these, which might threaten the position of powerful groups, or whose use ran counter to values held in the society, might not be adopted, but others, which ran into no such obstacles, were adopted.

These advances in technology cumulatively increased the ease of further advance, for each successive addition to the base of knowledge increases by an accelerating amount the number of further possible additions.[6] Moreover, when, ultimately, the advance per century or per generation had accelerated sufficiently so that the change was noticeable to human observation, the acceleration itself probably stimulated the devotion of increased energy to the study of science and technology precisely because such study had become more rewarding. The social changes resulting from the technological advance might of course generate increased pressures against it, which might negate the tendency to acceleration and even cause regression. Barring this, however, it was objectively certain centuries ago (though men did not necessarily realize it) that the trickle of technological progress would become a rivulet, a current, and ultimately a rushing tide, overcoming social obstacles, disrupting the traditional social structure, and bringing the changes in the social system necessary to support it.

History bears out this thesis. Following the scientific advances of ancient times, regression occurred through revulsion against the new ideas plus the disruption of wars, but advance began again in medieval Europe, and a long and accelerating cumulation of scientific and technological knowledge ensued. We know little about technological change during the

---

[6] It is probably illicit to argue that all advance in knowledge consists of combinations of previously existing ideas. Observation of additional data in the physical world is probably not appropriately termed a combination of old concepts, and some perceptive scholars would argue that in addition there are acts of mental creation that cannot correctly be termed combinations. (Clyde Kluckhohn argued this in conversation with me. While I am not convinced, on the other hand I am not prepared to assert dogmatically that this is incorrect.) However, combination is certainly a very important element in intellectual advance. And the appearance of each successive new concept increases by a larger amount the number of possible new combinations. Only one combination of two items is possible, but if they are combined to form a third, three additional possible combinations now exist (excluding the one by which the third item was formed). Similarly, there are nine possible additional combinations when a fourth item has been formed, 23 when a fifth has been formed, and so on. Mere quantity of scientific and technical knowledge is of course not the only relevant consideration. The quality of new concepts is important. The stimulus provided by the Newtonian synthesis or the conception of the theory of relativity was vastly greater than that provided by many other single new concepts. This fact, however, does not invalidate the thesis of a general tendency to acceleration of progress.

first few centuries after the nomadic peoples of western Europe had settled down to peasant life, but we do know that a thousand years or more
before the Industrial Revolution, and several centuries before the reopening of Mediterranean trade and the growth of cities, technology was moving forward. As early as the fourth century, water wheels were known in
Europe; their use spread rapidly during the next several centuries. The
making of soap was also discovered in the latter part of the fourth century. Apparently between the seventh and tenth centuries, the cultivation
of rye and oats was introduced, how to make butter was discovered,
and a three-field system was introduced, replacing the two-field system,
where summer rains made spring plowing advantageous. It kept two
thirds instead of one half of land under cultivation. In the tenth century
the method of making wire by drawing it was devised. The introduction
of the moldboard, apparently in the eleventh century, greatly improved
the efficiency of plowing in some soils.

In the twelfth to fifteenth centuries a number of other important technical advances occurred. Brickmaking was revived (beginning before
1200). The windmill was greatly improved. Means of heating iron to a
molten state and making it sufficiently free of impurities so that it could
be cast were devised. Improvements in steelmaking and working permitted the true needle, with fully enclosed eye. The spinning wheel doubled the amount of yarn one person could spin, the horizontal weaving
frame somewhat lessened work in weaving, and a fulling mill was devised
which was far more effective than the old method of fulling with the human foot. The use of two shafts in place of a single pole in harnessing
horses and the use of traces permitted harnessing in tandem, and the invention of the horse collar to replace the breast band, which had choked
horses when they pulled hard, increased by three or four times the load
one horse could pull.[7]

These inventions occurred before as well as after the reopening of
trade, and many of those that occurred later were not connected with
it. Thus the reopening of trade merely stimulated and did not initiate
change. The personality structure which these earlier inventions imply
probably facilitated the growth of cities in the twelfth century which the
reopening of trade in the eleventh occasioned. Following those developments, after a period which seems to have been one of relative stagnancy,

---

[7] Technological change during the Middle Ages is vividly described in Charles
Singer, E. J. Holmyard, A. R. Hall, and Trevor I. Williams (eds.), *A History of
Technology*, Vol. II: *The Mediterranean Civilizations and the Middle Ages, c. 700
B.C. to c. A.D. 1500* (Oxford: Clarendon Press, 1956). All of the information con-
cerning technical advance is from this volume (see also T. K. Derry and T. I.
Williams, *A Short History of Technology* [Oxford: Oxford University Press, 1961])
except that concerning the introduction of oats and rye and the three-field system.
Concerning early changes in crops and the system of fields the *History of Technology*
has a curious blind spot. Concerning these changes, see, for example, Carlton J. H.
Hayes, Marshall W. Baldwin, and Charles W. Cole, *History of Europe* (New York:
The Macmillan Co., 1950), pp. 172–73.

and after the great shock of the Black Death in the fourteenth century, came continuing acceleration of invention. Sarton's summary estimate that the "number of scientific events" of the fourteenth century doubled in the fifteenth century and tripled in the sixteenth is evidence of the increasing pace of events.[8] Then in the seventeenth century came the new concepts which Alfred North Whitehead has termed "the first physical synthesis."[9] That synthesis provided a qualitatively greatly improved base for scientific and technological advance. On this base the appearance of new fruitful scientific observations continued to accelerate. Concomitantly, technological progress spread, until in England it blossomed into the Industrial Revolution in the last half of the eighteenth century.

Once the tree had blossomed, its pollen was wafted afar on the winds of trade and carried into faraway lands on the boots of conquering armies. And with it were carried the seeds of radical social change. No one can doubt that the main source of change in societies in Latin America, Asia, and Africa during modern times is intrusion by the West and the parade of economic power and prowess by the West. If there are no serious internal stresses and no disturbing forces from the outside, cultural change in any society proceeds at a snail's pace. Virtually every social scientist would think it likely that except for Western intrusion and example the social structure and techniques that characterized traditional societies in say the sixteenth century would be little changed today.

Further, the logic of the effect seems so clear that anyone but a stubborn skeptic would have assumed it even if he had no historical knowledge. Income, wealth, and power are desired in every society.[10] Technological progress promises increase in all three. Is it naive to assume that contact by backward societies with technically advanced ones will more or less automatically lead to imitation of the more fruitful techniques?

Unanswered Questions

But these historical facts do not explain enough. They do not explain the pace of the advance of knowledge over the centuries. We tend to take the slow pace for granted; advance was slow, we suggest, because the base of knowledge was small. The explanation is not convincing. How

---

[8] "We may assume that the number of scientific events doubled in the fifteenth century [from the fourteenth] and trebled in the sixteenth (a moderate assumption; the increase was probably much larger)." George Sarton, *Six Wings: Men of Science in the Renaissance* (Bloomington, Ind.: Indiana University Press, 1957), p. vi. See also Charles Singer *et al.* (eds.), *A History of Technology*, Vol. III: *From the Renaissance to the Industrial Revolution, c. 1550 to c. 1750* (Oxford, Clarendon Press, 1957).

[9] Alfred North Whitehead, "The First Physical Synthesis," in his *Essays in Science and Philosophy* (New York: Philosophical Library, 1948). Galileo died and Newton was born in 1642. Whitehead suggests that this date may be taken as symbolizing the birth of modern science.

[10] With negligible exceptions. Anthropologists have described tiny isolated social groups of which these statements may not be true.

slow is slow? Some ancient Greeks knew that the earth is not the center of the universe. Why, when the advance of knowledge began again, was the same knowledge not again reached until the seventeenth century? Is there any objective reason why, earlier in history, advances separated by a century should not have occurred within a generation? I shall suggest in later chapters that until we understand the nature of the traditional societies based on peasant agriculture we shall not understand why advance in knowledge has been slow.

These questions may be of purely academic interest, but some questions concerning the modern world are not. Why has rapid technological progress appeared so spottily? Since at least the end of the eighteenth century technical knowledge adequate for economic growth has been available to any society in the world. Why have various societies differed so much in the degree to which they have taken advantage of it? We wish to know why, among the societies in the world that remained traditional longer than the West, some have made the transition to economic growth sooner than others. We would like to be able to forecast which of the societies that are still technically static will enter upon economic growth soon, and which less soon. We would like to understand the differential forces at work partly simply because we crave to understand the process of social change and partly because we would hasten the process if we could.

More Explanations

We do not suffer for lack of suggested explanations. The cause of differential performance among societies has been seen in race, geography and climate,[11] religion,[12] personality,[13] economic conditions, and resistances to cultural change, among other factors.[14] The several hypotheses have

---

[11] The most persuasive advocate of the influence of geography and climate was the late Ellsworth Huntington, distinguished professor of geography at Yale University. It has been noted, jokingly, but accurately, that he found the ideal climate for the stimulation of human energy and initiative to be that of New Haven. A late major book by him, which synthesizes and refines earlier writings, is *Mainsprings of Civilization* (New York: John Wiley & Sons, Inc., 1945).

[12] For the most noted thesis see Max Weber, *The Protestant Ethic and the Spirit of Capitalism* (New York: Charles Scribner's Sons, 1956). (First published in German in 1904–5.) The term *Puritan* ethic is more descriptive than Weber's term *Protestant* ethic, and is displacing it. Weber sometimes refers to Puritan dogma, and sometimes to the ethic or attitude of the individual, and at times seems almost to assert that one or the other is the central cause of material progress, but he carefully refrains from quite doing so.

[13] McClelland sees the difference in presence in high or low degree of the personality characteristic termed need achievement. See Chapter 6.

[14] For a somewhat more extended discussion of the arguments discussed in this section and some related arguments, see David C. McClelland, *The Achieving Society* (Princeton, N.J.: D. Van Nostrand Co., Inc., 1961), chap. i.

I shall not discuss here the general question of evolutionary versus diffusionist theories of social change, but Toynbee merits a brief reference. In his schema too severe a challenge crushes a civilization while too slight a challenge provokes no

varying degrees of force. The thesis that some countries have achieved faster or greater economic progress than others because the bloodstreams of some groups carry superior genes runs into the difficulty that some of the countries near the Mediterranean which made the first great economic and cultural advances of the Western world have since not merely failed to continue their advance but have retrogressed. To suggest that their peoples' genes have deteriorated is hardly persuasive.

The argument for geography and climate has been advanced most persuasively by Huntington, who suggested not merely that different climatic and geographic conditions were optimum at different stages of material advance, but also that slight but significant long-run changes in climate account for the advance and then retrogression of various human groups. Few authorities today, however, give full credence to Huntington's ingenious reconstruction from varied bits of evidence of climatic history.

Association of material progress with the Puritan dogma is no longer persuasive. By now we have had economic growth effectively led by Roman Catholics, Shintoists, Buddhists, adherents to the Orthodox Christain faith (in nineteenth century Russia), and avowed atheists (in twentieth century Russia), among others, and where not barred by social discrimination Jews have been conspicuous among the leaders. It seems true that a certain attitude of the individual which may be termed the Puritan ethic, like certain other personality traits, characterizes the innovating entrepreneurs in economic growth in whatever country. Yet this fact leaves unanswered the questions of how such personality came to appear in some groups and not others, and how it became channeled into technoeconomic endeavor.

Some observers find the explanation of the differential timing of entry upon economic growth largely in economic factors. The introduction of advanced methods, they note, requires the investment of a considerable amount of resources. They suggest that the traditional societies have too low a level of income to permit individuals to save enough to finance such investments,[15] or that the market is too small to make it advantageous for anyone to construct large plants embodying improved methods.

The first of these arguments would imply that no low-income country can develop without economic aid from the outside. Since we know that Japan began her development with virtually no external aid and Colombia

---

response, whereas a challenge of intermediate strength causes innovation; but there is no way to judge the strength of a challenge except by noting whether the response to it was successful. Until some independent measure of the strength of a challenge can be suggested, the thesis has no operational significance.

[15] In other terms, part of the nation's productive capacity must be used for the creation of what economists term capital goods—new structures, machines, and instruments for use in future production. It is suggested that all of the society's production is needed for consumption; the society cannot afford to divert say one tenth of its productive capacity to producing capital goods.

with very little, the argument is suspect on its face. Even without these cases to alert us, we would have no reason to assume without exploration that the individuals of low-income societies could not divert to economic growth sufficient resources to accomplish it if they wished to do so. We who have grown up in Western high-income societies could not save if we had the level of income typical of low-income societies, but to assume that this is true of the people of those societies is gratuitous. In even the lowest-income peasant societies the level of income is not so low that all of it is used for the necessities of life; this is true of only the lower-income classes. Other groups in these societies could typically save amounts equal to 10 per cent or more of the national income without hardship or physiological discomfort. This fraction is ample to finance economic growth. The relevant decisions are matters of social choice, not physiological necessity.

Likewise, we have no reason to assume without investigation that the markets in low-income countries are too small to justify the introduction of advanced methods. And when the necessary investigation is made, it suggests that they are not too small. (See Chapter 3.)

Individuals who are aware of the resistance of cultures to change sometimes vary the argument. They recognize that the members of low-income societies in their historical state—that is, before they have been disrupted by intrusion by Western powers—are not starving, suffering individuals longing for change; rather, they are happy with their life, which they find good. Simple contact with advanced societies may not be a sufficient force to bring economic growth because, valued by the standards of the traditional societies, their traditional condition is preferable to a changed one. It is suggested, however, that once intrusion by Western powers has broken the crust of custom, economic advance will occur.

However, on examination this argument too turns out to be ethnocentric rather than logical.

It is true that mere contact with advanced methods may possibly lead to desire for them. Since in virtually any society more income is preferable to less income, other things being equal, the example of a simple change in method of production which results directly in an increase in income, and which does not seem to imply change in traditional and valued behavior and relationships, probably leads to its adoption in a traditional peasant society as elsewhere. However, only very rarely do advanced techniques appear in this guise. Typically, the benefits asserted lie in the future and are uncertain. Typically, too, the advanced technology cannot be adopted while continuing a traditional way of life. The search for technological progress requires changing one's way of life, in some cases in some simple respect only, in some cases extensively. By the scale of values of Western culture the ways of living that are required are pleasant, or at least so little objectionable that they do not offset the material gain. However, when we investigate, we shall find that, by values which are present in probably all traditional peasant societies, the ways in which individuals must live in order to achieve continuing technological progress are improper, demeaning, and humiliating. Hence mere contact with a higher level of productivity does not usually lead to adoption of the ways of life necessary to duplicate it.

It is a *non sequitur*, however, to conclude that if the crust of custom is broken by Western intrusion, the ways of living necessary for technological progress will then seem desirable. Without investigation we have no reason to assume that when a traditional society is disrupted the disruption will leave it more desirous than before of adopting the ways of life of technologically advanced societies. It may instead become all the more antipathetic to those ways of life, especially if representatives of them were responsible for the disruption. We shall find that the latter is true; that the nature of colonial relationships created tremendously great psychological barriers to behaving in ways leading to technological progress. Indeed, the negative correlation between colonial control and the timing and pace of economic growth is striking, though it too leaves much unexplained.

The Purposes of a Theory of Growth

Of course the factors cited above may in combination explain the presence or absence of growth in various societies even though none of them taken separately does so. Their effect in combination may be more complex than can be appreciated by considering them singly. Certainly, except for the almost completely discredited idea that the biological heredity of some races or "kiths"—Huntington's term—is in some general sense superior to that of others, each of these factors has some influence on whether or when a country makes the transition to economic growth.

However, recognition of some connection between a factor and economic growth is not enough. A theory of growth, like any other theory, is to be accepted not in some absolute sense but only because it seems to provide a more comprehensive, accurate, and logically simple explanation of the facts of life than an alternative theory. In addition to having logical simplicity, a theory must meet two other tests. Do the outcomes it would lead one to expect coincide closely with outcomes so far observed? And do the component elements of the theory coincide closely with principles that have been verified independently? If the answer to both questions is "yes," one may hope that the theory will also predict future outcomes accurately.

In both respects the theories mentioned above, taken separately or as a group, score badly. On the basis of these theories we should have expected growth to begin in some countries where it has not, and we should not have expected it to begin in some countries where it has begun. Moreover, the theories ignore social and cultural factors which we now know to influence human behavior importantly. It is clear that to arrive at a satisfactory theory of economic growth we must abandon our preconceptions, examine the historical facts and the nature of human behavior once again, and ask ourselves what analytical considerations they should have suggested to us which we have overlooked.[16]

COMMENTS ON THE TRANSITION: FACTS AS A BASIS FOR THEORY

A theory or analytical model of the transition cannot be built up piece by piece by examination of historical facts. It must form a logical whole whose application to the problem is justified by its congruence to complex sets of historical relationships. Brief examination of some aspects of the history of countries which have entered upon continuing technological progress will suggest the general nature of a pertinent analytical model.

Agricultural Society—The Starting Point

So far in the world's history, economic growth has begun only in agricultural societies (or in new societies created by migrants from agricultural or industrial societies). It seems unlikely that it can begin in societies that have not reached the state of settled agriculture. Although there is no reason to believe in a rigid sequence of stages through which societal development must pass, peoples who are nomadic or pastoral cannot accumulate many cultural artifacts, and they will hardly make the transition to continuing technological progress until they do.

The Transition as a Gradual Process

Although the advent of economic growth has been sudden if one's viewpoint is the entire sweep of human history, it has been very gradual if measured in decades or even generations. Again, examples from selected countries will illustrate.

We are apt to think that growth in Russia began rather suddenly under the Communists, or, if we have somewhat greater knowledge of the data, early in the twentieth century. But a careful and competent investigator has estimated that Russia's national product rose by 2 per cent per year from 1860 to the early 1880's and by 3 per cent per year from then until World War I; and that output per capita rose by ¾ per cent and 1¼ per cent per year respectively during these two periods.[17] Detailed research

---

[16] I do not mean to imply that theories are formed only after looking at all of the facts. Without a tentative theory, formed on the basis of one's general impression of the nature of the facts, one would not know which facts to examine. In the process of forming a theory, examining the facts, revising the theory, and testing it, there is necessarily a movement back and forth between empirical study and abstract analysis, and between induction and deduction.

[17] Raymond W. Goldsmith, "The Economic Growth of Russia, 1860–1913," mimeographed, a paper presented to the Fourth Conference of the International Association for Research in Income and Wealth, September, 1955.

also indicates that growth did not begin in China suddenly with the accession to power of the Communist regime. Rather, the recent rapid growth is a culmination which takes advantage of steadily accelerating previous growth, interrupted by Japanese invasion, World War II, and postwar civil strife, which began at least as early as the 1870's.[18]

The generally accepted date for the beginning of economic growth in Japan is some year in the 1870's, after the reformers of the Meiji Restoration had consolidated their control of the economy. This dating, however, is associated less with the economic realities than with the fact that the standard series of economic statistics of Japan begin with the year 1878. A study of the history of the Tokugawa era, from 1600 to 1868, indicates clearly that technological ferment was great before the end of that period, and it suggests strongly that per capita income began to rise by at least 1700.[19]

The history of development in Latin America, and the misapprehensions about it, are similar. Colombian economists and businessmen state that rapid growth in Colombia began in the depression of the 1930's, when imports were cut off by lack of export earnings to purchase them and Colombia had to begin to make many articles she had previously been importing. But this too is an optical illusion arising from too casual observation. A study by the United Nations' Economic Commission for Latin America (ECLA) extending back to the early 1920's shows that the growth both in national production and in industrial output was more rapid in the 1920's than in the 1930's.[20] No comprehensive statistics are available for earlier periods, but study of the economic history of Colombia, some of it summarized in Chapter 15, suggests strongly that output per capita has been increasing at least since the spread of coffee cultivation began in about 1860. Industrialization began before 1900 and accelerated between 1900 and 1920. The more conspicuous industrial growth since 1920 is merely a continuation.

In Argentina, where economic growth is also often assumed to be recent, available data make possible estimates for a longer period. An ECLA study indicates that both national product and industrial output have been accelerating steadily since 1900, and no more rapidly after the 1930's

---

[18] Only scattered data are available, but in combination they are convincing. They are impressively marshalled in an unpublished manuscript, "External Trade, Foreign Investment, and Domestic Development: The Chinese Experience, 1840–1937," by Chi-ming Hou.

[19] An excellent summary, emphasizing the latter part of the Tokugawa era, is presented in Thomas C. Smith, *Political Change and Industrial Development in Japan* (Stanford, Calif.: Stanford University Press, 1955), chap i. For more general impressions of the Tokugawa era as a whole, see G. B. Sansom, *The Western World and Japan* (New York: Alfred A. Knopf, Inc., 1951), especially chaps. ix–xii, or E. O. Reischauer and John K. Fairbank, *East Asia: The Great Tradition*, Vol. I (Boston, Mass.: Houghton Mifflin Co., 1960), chaps. xiii and xiv.

[20] United Nations, *Analisis y Proyecciones del Desarrollo Económico, III: El Desarrollo Económico de Colombia* (Mexico, 1957).

than before.[21] The suggestion is strong that if data were available for still earlier periods, the beginnings of growth would be found well back in the nineteenth century.

The transition to economic growth, one may reasonably conclude from these several examples, typically occupies a period of several generations. A contrary judgment is sometimes drawn from the experience of England. According to the best available evidence, industrial production in England and Wales, after a brief spurt between 1710 and 1720, crept upward (with some fluctuations) until the mid-1760's, then remained roughly constant until 1780. Then it began that rather spectacular rapid rise for four decades which is often taken as marking the beginning of the modern economic period.[22]

This sudden acceleration of the rate of advance is associated, however, not with some basic underlying change in economic interrelationships but simply with the appearance of a remarkable group of inventions within a 20-year period. Between 1764 and 1784 there appeared in the textile industry Hargreaves' spinning jenny, Arkwright's water frame and carding cylinder, Crompton's mule, Cartwright's power loom, and Bell's method of calico printing; in the production of power Watt's several successive improvements in the steam engine; and in the iron industry Cort's improved method of removing impurities from iron. The incorporation in practice of this amazing cluster of inventions brought about the continuing rapid rise in manufacturing output.

Thus the abruptness with which the rise began was not due to some force which may be expected to be duplicated elsewhere. Neither, indeed, does it seem to have been matched by a correspondingly sudden change in the rate of rise of national production as a whole. One of the leading students of the economic growth of England estimates that national income in England and Wales grew by 0.3 per cent per year during the period from 1700 to 1740, 0.9 per cent per year during 1740–70, 1.5 per cent during 1770–1800, and exceeded 2 per cent per year after 1800. The acceleration of growth was long and cumulative.[23]

It should not be assumed that everywhere else the transition proceeded smoothly and steadily. Though we do not have sufficient historical information to be certain, the rate of economic growth in Russia may have

[21] United Nations. Economic Commission for Latin America, *El Desarrollo Económico de la Argentina, Anexo, Algunos Estudios Especiales y Estadísticos Macroeconómicos Preparados para el Informe* (mimeographed; Santiago, Chile: June 30, 1958).

[22] For statistical estimates, see Walther G. Hoffmann, *British Industry, 1700–1950*, trans. W. O. Henderson and W. H. Chaloner (Oxford: Basil Blackwell, 1955).

[23] The estimates, by Phyllis Deane, are cited by Simon Kuznets in "Qualitative Aspects of the Economic Growth of Nations, VI: Long-Term Trends in Capital Formation Proportions," *Economic Development and Cultural Change*, Vol. IX, No. 4, Part II (July, 1961). The precise estimates by 30-year periods are precarious, but that growth was accelerating during the first three fourths of the eighteenth century, and continued to accelerate in the nineteenth century, is clear.

accelerated fairly rapidly soon after the liberation of the serfs in the mid-nineteenth century. In Japan the energies which were partially confined by the social structure during the last generations of Tokugawa rule surged forth after the Meiji Restoration; and if we had data we should probably find that the rate of economic growth accelerated fairly abruptly during the two decades following 1868. Other instances of the bursting of barriers and probable discontinuity in the pace of economic change might be cited. Serious business recessions during the period of the transition have also affected the pace of change. But if we emphasize the moments of change, we shall be deceived by their apparent suddenness and apparent importance. Underlying them and preceding them were forces and sequences of change, operating over longer periods, which become manifest to the casual historical observer only when the pace of overt action changes. Their importance becomes apparent only when we ask ourselves what the mechanisms at work may be and construct an adequate theory of the functioning of the society.

Contact with the West

While economic growth requires some minimum contact with Western knowledge, the timing and pace of economic growth in low-income societies are not correlated with the amount of contact with technically advanced societies, the amount of investment in the low-income societies by the advanced ones, or the degree to which Western intrusion has disrupted the traditional social system. These are striking facts, which we have failed to see only because our preconceptions have blinded us.

Latin American countries in general have much higher income levels than the countries of Asia and Africa. It is sometimes suggested that the greater advance of Latin American countries in income levels is due to their greater contact with Europe during the past several centuries. Before that evidence is given too great weight, however, it should be noted that the phenomenon of Latin America is not one of societies which turned from traditional peasant cultures to continuing technological progress as a result of contact with Europeans. Rather, Europeans conquered the sparse indigenous populations, settled in considerable number, and lived their lives according to their own cultural patterns. Of course, the European cultures were modified by contact with the indigenous cultures and as an effect of intermarriage, but essentially the technological progress of the Latin American countries has been carried on by men of European blood who continued European cultures in Latin America, not by men of indigenous culture who absorbed technological progress into that culture.

(These facts raise the question why technological progress in Latin America has been so late to appear, not why it appeared so soon. The answer is dual. On the one hand, their conquest of the indigenous peoples gave many of the Europeans who came to Latin America positions of

income and power through exploitation of their dominance over the conquered peoples without the necessity of solving the problems of technological progress. Further, until new streams of migration set in during the
last half of the nineteenth century the Europeans in Latin America were
predominantly from the societies of Spain and Portugal, which the virus
of technological progress had infected only lightly. They were of only
weakly innovating stock.)

As soon as we leave the comparison of Latin America with Asia and
Africa, we find empirical evidence that indicates how little correlated the
transition to economic growth is with Western contacts, Western investment, or Western intrusion. Since only two dozen countries or so have yet
surely entered upon economic growth, not many comparisons are possible, but a few are pertinent. In Latin America, Colombia had very little
immigration after the eighteenth century and until recent decades had far
less contact than say Brazil or Mexico with Europeans and European
centers or the United States. And although Colombia had very little foreign investment until after World War II, it began a continuing advance
in technology and per capita income within a decade or two of Brazil and
Mexico. Growth has proceeded more vigorously in Turkey than in
Egypt, though Turkey hardly had more contact with Europe and her
traditional culture was probably less disrupted than that of Egypt. More
broadly, the entire Near East has failed to show any evidences of growth
until the middle of the twentieth century, and its failure to do so in spite
of its involvement in European history during the past several centuries is
strong evidence of the inadequacy of contact in itself to cause growth.
The most striking evidence, however, is that provided by the comparative history of the four major Asian nations—Indonesia, India, China, and
Japan.

The Portuguese had established contact with all four of these countries
during the first half of the sixteenth century. They established a few trading posts in both Indonesia and India between 1510 and 1535. They attempted to do so in China in 1520, but were expelled in 1522. In 1557 they
established themselves at Macao, and during the last half of the sixteenth
century Portuguese missionaries were active in China. Blown by a storm,
a Portuguese ship landed in Japan in 1542, and in 1549–51 Xavier began
missionary activity in Japan which continued during ensuing decades.

But the succeeding contact of the four countries with the West varied
widely. The Portuguese were succeeded in Indonesia by the Dutch and
English at the end of the sixteenth century. By early in the seventeenth
century the Dutch had established themselves securely. They continued
to rule the area, to invest in it, and to live in it in appreciable numbers
from then until the mid-twentieth century. In India the East India Company obtained its first trading concession in 1608. Thereafter, during the
seventeenth and eighteenth centuries, the British slowly expanded their
footholds on the subcontinent, but even by 1785 they controlled only

Bengal and strips of land along the east coast. Their conquest of the mass of the subcontinent occurred during the nineteenth century. In China, apart from the work of the missionaries, penetration never consisted of more than the establishment of a number of trading and manufacturing enclaves in coastal cities from which trade with the interior was forced on the country. Japan was too far away and too poor for the Western powers to press their attentions as assiduously as on the other three countries, and from about the 1630's on the Tokugawa were successful in enforcing a policy of no contact with the West except through a small Dutch trading group at Nagasaki, whom they permitted to remain as "a window on the West."

Thus, of the four countries, intrusion by and contact with the West were earliest and probably most extensive in Indonesia, next so in India, much less in China, and by far least of all in Japan.[24] The degree of disruption of the indigenous culture was probably in the same order, and certainly was much the least of all in Japan. The level of income in Japan in the seventeenth century was hardly higher than in the other three countries. Perhaps it was lower. Of the four countries, natural resources per capita were much the poorest in Japan, and it is probably justifiable to add that they were greater in both India and Indonesia than in China. Yet Japan entered upon rapid technological advance in the second half of the nineteenth century, China is now doing so vigorously, India has begun though at a slower pace, and retrogression rather than advance seems to be occurring in Indonesia. Clearly the effects of contact with Western knowledge, disruption of traditional culture, and availability of resources either were irrelevant or were nullified by other influences.

Economic, Social, and Political Change

Since the economic state of a society is closely related to its political state, and the forces that bring change in the one also bring some sort of change in the other, a model that explains economic growth must take into account noneconomic as well as economic aspects of human behavior. This is implied in the brief discussion above of the possible reasons why the peoples of some societies have failed to turn to technological progress, but further discussion will be useful.

A society whose technology is unchanging is unchanging in other elements of its culture as well. Lack of consistent progress in techniques is a characteristic of all traditional societies and only of traditional societies, except that during a period when forces for change are disrupting tradi-

---

[24] There may be some question concerning the relative degree of contact in India and Indonesia because of questions of the relative timing of penetration by the Dutch and British respectively and because of differences in administrative organization by the two powers, but there can be no question that contact was much less in China than in India or Indonesia, and far less still in Japan.

tional societies, technological change may become evident before social-political change becomes overt, or the reverse may be true.[25]

This generalization is stated here in sweeping terms to express the central point forcefully. The historical record underlying it is complex because of the presence in recent times over much of the world of colonialism, under which the political forms were neither traditional nor modern but rather imposed and not representative of the indigenous social structure beneath. The broad historical basis for the generalization made above is seen if one notes that the period preceding the industrial revolution is also the period of the divine right of kings, and that when the technically unprogressive societies of America, Asia, and Africa were conquered by Europeans, all were traditional. The political revulsions following the end of colonialism have obscured the relationship between traditionalism in techniques and traditionalism in other features of the culture; but it is a reasonable proposition that within a generation after independence, in each society the relationship will again be clear. In any event, the historical relationship is clear.

Conversely, in the countries in which the transition to economic growth has occurred it has been concomitant with far-reaching change in political organization, social structure, and attitudes toward life. The relationship is so striking and so universal that to assume that one of these aspects of basic social change is unrelated to the others is to strain the doctrine of coincidence beyond all warrant.

Glance at the historical record. In Britain the Industrial Revolution which gathered force gradually in the eighteenth century followed some centuries of social and religious tensions. Willingness to be ruled by a king and a small select group of nobles was replaced by a growing sense that such rule was wrong, and through their representatives in Parliament successive generations of townspeople progressively destroyed the hierarchy of political power. Concomitantly religious heterodoxy appeared. It culminated in the adoption of Calvinism by the Scots and the emergence of strong Protestant dissent among the townsmen of England. And the Dissenters and lowland Scots were present among the economic innovators in numbers out of all proportion to their numbers in the population at large.

In the countries of western Europe the industrial revolution got under way during or shortly after the series of upheavals in government and the social order which stretched from the French Revolution to the revolutions of the mid-nineteenth century. It is associated in time with the abolition of most elements of serfdom, with marked change in the ac-

---

[25] The term "traditional" is defined and the social circumstances accompanying traditionalism discussed at some length in Chapter 4. Because the term has a loose generally accepted meaning, it is used here without definition, in anticipation of the more precise discussion of Chapter 4.

cepted concepts of appropriate relationships among social classes, with extensions of representative government.

A simple reading of Japanese history is that after the restoration of the symbolic position of the emperor in 1868 the feudal leaders of Japan commanded economic modernization, and that, possessing intense feudal loyalty, the Japanese responded to the new national purpose and began to modernize. The facts, however, suggest origins of economic growth several centuries earlier—not later than in the fourteenth century.

In about 1600, after a period of disturbance and confusion, the Tokugawa and associated clans established an hegemony over the nation that was to last for more than 250 years. After their ascendancy to national power the Tokugawa enforced regulations whose purpose was to· freeze the social order and perpetuate the Tokugawa rule. Their result in fact was to create tensions which, economically, caused great pressure for expansion of income and, socially, inexorably undermined the traditional structure. During the seventeenth and eighteenth centuries discontented and frustrated social groups, after casting about elsewhere for satisfaction, turned gradually to study of the "barbarian books" of the West, which told how Westerners had become powerful. Early in the nineteenth century individuals of these groups began to build pilot plants using Western methods, and before the Meiji Restoration these economic shoots which had rooted in social discontent were flourishing. When the national government that came to power in 1868 took steps to remove the institutional barriers to economic innovation, the economic shoots burst into flower. But to assume that they were simply due to the new institutions is to ignore Japanese history.

In Russia in 1667 the Patriarch of Moscow, for the sake of diplomatic advantage, revised the Orthodox Church ritual and liturgical books to bring them into agreement with Greek practice. To many lower-class members of the Church the change seemed sacrilegious and a threat to their bond with God. These Old Believers were condemned as schismatics and were persecuted with varying vigor and harshness from the latter part of the seventeenth century until the early years of the twentieth. It surely is not coincidence that the Old Believers were prominent in the economic innovation which began to change the face of Russia in the nineteenth century.

These instances of associated social, political, and economic change are not unique. In Turkey economic growth began within a generation after Ataturk had seized the social order by the scruff of the neck and shaken it vigorously. Throughout Latin America political tension and the transition to economic growth are intertwined. In China the political upheaval associated with growth was as radical as in Russia. And so on. Can anyone doubt that there are causal connections which need to be explored?

If one classifies the underdeveloped countries of the world in three groups according to whether their political structure is authoritarian, semicompetitive, or competitive, and then ranks them according to their economic level as measured by objective indexes, one sees striking confirmation of historical association. By a "competitive political structure" is meant not necessarily a democratic one, but one in which the interests of various groups are considered before political decisions are taken. The dual classification referred to is most impressive if Latin America is considered separately from Asia-Africa, for which separation there is logical warrant. When this is done, one sees, broadly speaking, that the authoritarian countries rank low economically, the semicompetitive ones higher, and the competitive ones highest. There are exceptions to this correlation that testify to the complexity of history, conspicuous among them being that in some societies where the virus of innovation has been at work (in technology and elsewhere), but where the traditional despotism has been so repressive that it could be overthrown only by conspiratorial force, the rebels have themselves been authoritarian, after the manner of conspirators, and a new authoritarian rule has accompanied economic growth. However, the special nature of these circumstances, and the generality of the association between economic performance and political structure, is abundantly clear.[26]

The Concentration of Leadership

The foregoing sketches of the history of developing societies for a century or two before economic growth becomes conspicuous suggest that economic growth has been led not by individuals distributed at random throughout the society but disproportionately by individuals from some distinctive social group. The importance of such groups may be seen by considering again some of the countries whose history has been referred to just above. I shall add one other case, that of Colombia.

In the last half of the eighteenth century Nonconformists formed only about 7 per cent of the population of England and Wales. Probably the Scottish dissenters from the established Presbyterian church hardly formed a higher percentage of the population of Scotland. It is, I suggest, a fact of significance for social theory that, judging by a sample study of entrepreneurs reported on in Chapter 13 below, these groups provided

---

[26] Seymour Lipset indicated this correlation between economic growth and political structure in a professional article. Later, James S. Coleman assembled more data and elaborated the analysis. Still later, omitting colonies from the analysis, I presented a slightly variant analysis. See S. Lipset, "Some Social Requisites of Democracy: Economic Development and Political Legitimacy," *The American Political Science Review*, Vol. LIII, No. 1 (March, 1959); G. A. Almond, J. S. Coleman, *et al.*, *The Politics of the Developing Areas* (Princeton, N.J.: Princeton University Press, 1960); and E. E. Hagen, "A General Framework for Analyzing Economic and Political Change," in R. E. Asher, E. E. Hagen, A. O. Hirschman, *et al.*, *Development of the Emerging Countries* (Washington, D.C.: The Brookings Institution, 1962).

one half of the innovating entrepreneurs in Britain in the eighteenth and early nineteenth centuries. In proportion to their number in the population as a whole these dissenting groups provided more than 10 times as many innovators as did the rest of the society.

In Japan, leadership in economic change was concentrated among lower-class samurai and so-called "wealthy peasants." Although population estimates classified by social groups are not available, clearly these groups provided disproportionate numbers of leaders.

No study available to me indicates clearly whether the Old Believers were active in nineteenth century economic innovation in Russia in numbers greater than in proportion to their number in the population. Perhaps the historical research necessary to answer this question has not been done; but in view of the historical references to their activity, it is plausible that they were.

Consider finally the case of Colombia. The Spanish *conquistadores* came to Colombia during the 1530's. They readily conquered the Indians and occupied the high plateau around the present Bogotá (the Sabana), the valley of the upper Cauca river (known simply as "the Valley"), and the valley of Antioquia. They were in search of gold and adventure. They found little gold or silver on the Sabana or in the Valley, but they did find healthful fertile lands and set themselves up as gentry on large estates or ranches. The Indians, whom they took under their guardianship to save their souls, performed the manual labor. In Antioquia they found some gold and silver, and thereafter the continued quest for this form of wealth received much greater relative economic emphasis in Antioquia than on the Sabana or in the Valley. They found it impossible to keep their small mines manned with Indians and with the Negro slaves they brought from Africa, and, presently, increasingly they became mine workers themselves.

The *conquistadores* in all three areas were predominantly from the lower socioeconomic classes of Spain, not the higher. When the occupants of the other two areas became landed gentry or cattle ranchers, with the fervor of new insecure elite they felt and expressed contempt for their grubby neighbors in Antioquia who labored with their own hands, a feeling manifest in the literature and historical writings of the eighteenth and nineteenth centuries. The Antioqueños, conscious of their equal claim to Spanish blood and culture, felt resentment at the attitudes of superiority.

During Colombia's colonial period the central colonial city was Bogotá, and after independence Bogotá was the national capital. The Bogotanos had far greater contact with the various countries of western Europe than did the Antioqueños. Moreover, access from Cali, the main city of the Valley, both to Bogotá and to the Pacific was somewhat better than that from Antioquia and its main city, Medellín. Of the three areas, Antioquia was the most isolated. Yet as economic growth has proceeded in Colombia it has turned out that, out of proportion to their numbers, the Antioqueños are the innovating entrepreneurs.

These brief historical references indicate that leaders in the transition to economic growth were neither randomly distributed throughout the population nor drawn from the group that was most elite or had the greatest wealth or greatest opportunity for access to foreign knowledge and capital. Instead, they came disproportionately from some one or more less elite groups whose members had traditionally had a secure place in the social order but had lost the status they felt a right to expect and were now disparaged by the leading social group.

This common sociological aspect of the transition in these four societies is hardly coincidence. I suggest that similar phenomena would probably be found in other societies whose transition to economic growth was scrutinized carefully. Any analysis of the transition to economic growth must account for this phenomenon.

It is worthwhile to add, even in this introductory statement, that the phenomenon is not merely one of a group lacking complete acceptance in the society. The leaders in the transition were members of a group which had had a secure accepted status in the traditional society and then had lost it. They had been an integral part of a society and then, psychologically at least, had been rejected by it. This is a phenomenon of far more subtlety and significance than merely being an outsider.

Creativity as a Requisite

The last characteristic of economic growth which it seems useful to discuss in this introduction to the problem is that it always requires innovation.

I define "innovation" as arriving at a new mental or aesthetic concept and giving it reality in the world outside the mind. Since the term "innovation" is sometimes used as somewhat in contrast to creativity, it should be noted that as I shall use the term it always involves creativity.[27] A great amount of innovation, so defined, has gone and is still going into technological advance in the West. Innovation is of the essence of technological progress. Without it the progress would stop. But the advances which have already occurred in the West are here for all the world to observe. Underdeveloped economies can draw upon them. Therefore, it is said, they can advance simply by imitating; they need not create.

This, however, turns out not to be true. Previous technological advance abroad of course makes technological progress easier than otherwise for a present low-income society since the society has the alternatives of adapting methods from the West or devising methods itself, and without previous advance abroad it would have only the latter. Never-

---

[27] See Chapter 5.

theless, a tremendous degree of creative innovation is required for technological progress in any present traditional society, as it was in the societies where continuing technological progress first began.

It is required, surprisingly enough, for two purely technical reasons in addition to cultural and social ones.

First, the simple imitation of Western methods is typically impossible. Perhaps the most obvious problem is that the available labor force differs greatly. In the West the mass of men are literate and able to read instructions and information. Moreover, they have an understanding of the functioning of machinery, and thereby of its care and handling, which they have absorbed through their pores, so to speak, as they grew up in a mechanized civilization. Among them are many with varying degrees of training in engineering, scientific, financial, accounting, and managerial knowledge and techniques—and the elements of this knowledge acquired unconsciously from the entire world around one are as important as the elements learned in formal education. It is impossible to man an enterprise in an underdeveloped economy with corresponding individuals. Men anywhere can be trained rapidly in skills, for men everywhere are intelligent, but the broad background of other individual characteristics cannot be duplicated. A Western-type enterprise must be adapted to the human differences; indeed, a perceptive observer of an efficient industrial enterprise in a low-income society will note in how many ways both conspicuous and seemingly insignificant its operation differs from that of an enterprise in the West.

Equally important, every Western industry depends for its efficiency on other industries. It assumes the ready availability of materials, components, and tools. It depends also on auxiliary enterprises which can provide technical, financial, and managerial services on demand; on a complex network of communication and transportation facilities; and on an intricate system of business practices. A Western economy is a technical (and cultural) complex, not a set of isolated pieces of technology. In an underdeveloped society the auxiliary industries are missing and the framework of business practices is different. One piece cannot be detached from the complex and used efficiently elsewhere without skillful adaptation.

That such difficulties pertain to simple productive processes as well as to complex ones may be indicated by an example. In Burma and India, and no doubt elsewhere in South Asia and probably in most of Africa, the digging spade is almost unknown. Digging is done with a broad-bladed hoe. Though it is done with dexterity, it remains an awkward process in many circumstances. Surely, it would seem, the simple substitution of the spade would greatly increase productivity. But the ordinary digging spade cannot be used with sandals or bare feet, and it turns out that if the spade is constructed with a broad strip across the top, upon which the bare foot can press, then dirt sticks to this strip and the spade will not release its load. In Turkey and Iran, and perhaps elsewhere in the Middle East, though not in Arabia, the problem has been solved by a real act of creativity; a rod an inch or more in diameter, on which the bare foot can press with comfort, is thrust through the spade handle several inches above the blade, or a transverse strip which serves the same purpose is fastened on either side of the handle. The device is not new; the innovation was an ancient one. Even this arrangement must be somewhat awkward in some circumstances. Barring some further act of creativity, even so simple a tool as a spade cannot be imported into a low-income society with full efficiency until the level of living has risen sufficiently that it includes the wearing of shoes.

Thus the simple imitation of Western practices is usually impossible. Second, even the adaptation of Western methods, though both efficient and necessary for certain types of production and certain productive processes, may not be efficient for the undeveloped economy as a whole. Western methods use much productive equipment per laborer—machines, tools, buildings, roads, dams, power installations, communications systems. In the West this mass of equipment exists because for 150 years the West has been accumulating it. As more and more of such "capital" has become available, the energies of Western innovators have increasingly gone into the invention of methods employing little labor and much capital. Underdeveloped societies, on the other hand, have little capital per worker, even for the workers who are employed with full effectiveness. In addition many of them have many underemployed workers. In agriculture, for example, it is frequently true that if a fraction of the workers were removed from the land, after simple adjustments in methods of cultivation requiring little added capital, the remaining workers could produce as much as was being produced before. Figuratively speaking, and considering for the moment only the technical aspects of the problem, workers stand with empty hands available to be employed more productively.

Because the incomes of underdeveloped societies are low, the amount of capital they can accumulate per year, even with generous economic aid from the West, is small. Insofar as their method of endeavoring to increase productivity is to import (or construct) the system of productive apparatus which the West has elaborated over a century and a half, they will be able to afford only enough to benefit a tiny fraction of their workers. Indeed, a calculation of the amount of capital used per worker in the West indicates that an underdeveloped country could provide that much capital per worker for fewer workers per year than the growth in its labor force. Any increase in productivity in the remainder of the economy would have to be by improvements in methods involving no increase whatever in the equipment in use. This of course implies not only the devising of methods not known in the West but also an extremely high degree of creativity.

If the reader asks in surprise whether the importation of methods from the West by the underdeveloped economies, through their own efforts plus economic and technical aid, is not in fact the way they are proceeding, the answer is that this is the aspect of their efforts which is featured in the West. In fact, the countries which are developing rapidly are adopting Western methods only for selected purposes (such as steelmaking), even here adapting them so as to use more labor and less mechanization in auxiliary processes, but throughout the economy as a whole are devising ways of using Western principles with simpler tools and equipment, and in many cases are devising methods *de novo* to solve problems at hand.[28]

Moreover, the difficulty runs deeper than these technical problems. It is perhaps not an exaggeration to state that solving the technical problems is the easy aspect of technological progress for present-day low-income countries. Technological advance requires doing new things; it requires also the creation of new economic, political, and social organizations and relationships, or the adaptation to new functions of old organizations and relationships. But the things one does in a traditional society are not merely means to the end of living, means which one can readily discard in favor of others. They are symbols of one's identity and place in the world. As I shall note in Chapter 4, it is demeaning for a professional man or a member of the landed gentry in a traditional society to turn his attention to tools or machinery or become the manager of a business enterprise. Similarly, the organizations and relationships which exist in a society are not merely means to the end of production, subject to discard and replacement if problems of production change. They are a reflection of the beliefs and attitudes of the members of the society. Change which requires an alteration in social organizations and relationships is regarded as harmful.

A parallel will illustrate the point. American leaders desire a rapid rate of economic growth. The rate of economic growth in the Soviet Union and in Communist China is much higher than ours. Why do we not imitate Communist methods of mobilizing resources for growth in order to accelerate our growth? Even the question is shocking to us; the answer comes spontaneously and quickly. In several variants, it amounts to saying that we do not want a higher rate of growth at that cost; some

---

[28] An applicable principle of economics is that the increase in the country's aggregate output and income will be greater if the available amount of capital is spread over many workers rather than concentrated in a few capital-intensive projects. The necessary proof refers to the equating of productivity "at the margin" throughout the economy. The principle applies, however, only on the assumption that appropriate methods using little additional capital per worker are available. R. S. Eckaus has pointed out that, where appropriate methods are not available, aggregate output may be greater using capital-intensive methods for some workers and leaving others completely idle. See R. S. Eckaus, "The Factor Proportions Problem in Underdeveloped Areas," *American Economic Review*, Vol. XLV (September, 1955), pp. 539–65.

of the variants add that in our society it would not work anyway. The reader may select his own variant. The point in the present context is that, whichever variant he selects, in peasant societies there were and are parallel reasons for rejecting Western technology.

Consequently, changes in traditional social structure necessary for economic growth will be adopted only if considerable creativity is devoted to the task of making them acceptable or if there exist social tensions and pressures so great that they impel change even though it is painful.

Or, indeed, both conditions may be necessary. It may be that no society has begun technological progress in the past or will do so in the future without the exertion of great creativity in solution of the social problems as well as the technical ones, and that the necessary creativity will not be forthcoming except as severe tensions within the society impel the leaders of some group to new attitudes toward old institutions.[29]

Complementing technological innovation by a minority of the population, there must be acceptance of change and adaptation to it by other larger groups. This of course involves some degree of creativity on the part of the acceptors, but the difference in degree is sufficient to justify treating innovation and acceptance of change as distinct processes.

In this study I shall give primary attention to the innovational process. This I shall do not in the Schumpeterian belief that the true innovator can carry all before him, but rather because the appearance of a substantial stream of technological innovation in a society in which it has previously been largely absent seems by far the more difficult and more interesting of the two problems. I shall, however, discuss briefly the problem of acceptance of change.

A brief summary of these comments concerning the process of technological advance is in order. The transition to economic growth occurs rather gradually and over a considerable period of time. Although contact with the technologically advanced societies is a necessary condition

---

[29] I have labored the point that technological innovation requires creativity. The more general point might be made that any acceptance of a culture trait from outside the society is innovation; there is no such thing as passive imitation. See H. G. Barnett, *Innovation: The Basis of Cultural Change* (New York: McGraw-Hill Book Co., 1953), chap. xii.

The same type of problem, though in smaller degree, exists in the adaptation of technology even from one Western society to another, as numerous analyses of economic and social development in France and Germany vividly illustrate. For two concerning France which make the point convincingly and interestingly, see John Sawyer, "Strains in the Social Structure of Modern France," in Edward M. Earle, *Modern France* (Princeton, N.J.: Princeton University Press, 1951), pp. 293–312, and Jesse Pitts, "The Bourgeois Family and French Economic Retardation" (Ph.D. dissertation, Harvard University, 1958).

On the other hand, the requirements of industrial production are probably exerting a tendency over the long run to bring the cultures of all industrial countries closer together. This thesis is interestingly argued in the final chapter of Kerr, Dunlop, Harbison, and Myers, *Industrialism and Industrial Man* (Cambridge, Mass.: Harvard University Press, 1960).

for rapid technological progress (barring a long, slow process paralleling the technological history of the West), such progress does not occur merely because of this contact. In some countries it has not occurred after a prolonged period of considerable contact; in others with less contact it has proceeded. Low-income countries cannot simply imitate techniques in use in the West; technological progress in these countries requires a high degree of creativity, as it did in the West. The innovations required are not only technoeconomic changes but also social ones. The latter may be the more complex. The transition to economic growth is accompanied by major political and social change. The causes must be forces which affect many aspects of human behavior. Finally, the lead in the necessary innovations seems typically to be taken not by individuals at random but disproportionately by members of some one or more social groups, and not the groups who are in the best position to have contacts abroad or access to new knowledge and to capital.

A theory of economic growth must take into account these aspects of the process. They are not sufficient in themselves to suggest a theory, but, taken in combination with aspects of the current theories of personality formation and social structure which are spelled out in later chapters, they do indicate what the nature of the argument must be.

Inadequacy of Economic
Theories of Growth

chapter 3

THE FAILURE OF ECONOMIC GROWTH TO BEGIN IN SOME
low-income societies has attracted the attention of economic analysts in
recent years, and they have elaborated a number of theories of the barriers that have prevented growth. Those theories seem peculiarly fragile
or peculiarly removed from reality, and it seems desirable to present here
a brief critical review of a representative sample of them. The noneco-
mist reader who finds this discussion of little interest is advised to turn
at once to Chapter 4. The passing comments concerning economic theories of growth already presented in the preceding chapter provide adequate background for the reader who has no specific interest in the economic theories.

THE ECONOMIC APPROACH

The initial approach of economists, in the surge of interest after World
War II in the problems of growth of low-income economies,[1] was to assume that any barriers to growth that might exist are economic ones, and
that the process of economic growth is adequately dealt with by economic analysis alone.

The reasoning underlying this approach is as follows: Almost all individuals in every society seek higher income. Hence it seems natural that
everywhere individuals should seek improved methods of production.
Since knowledge of improved methods is now available, there seems no
reason why people everywhere should not be improving production tech-

---

[1] Of course there was earlier interest in economic growth. The German historical
school—later termed "institutional"—from List to Sombart evolved theories of stages
of economic or socioeconomic development. These, though in retrospect they
provide interesting suggestions, lacked analytical clarity, and their contributions did
not appreciably affect the recent analysis of the growth of low-income economies.
Later came the brilliant speculations of Professor Schumpeter concerning the future
of capitalism as a socioeconomic system. Interest specifically in the problems
of low-income or technologically static economies became conspicuous only after
World War II. One earlier article, a landmark in the analysis of those problems,
is P. N. Rosenstein-Rodan's "Problems of Industrialisation of Eastern and South-
Eastern Europe," *Economic Journal*, Vol. LIII (June–September, 1943), pp. 202–11.

niques—and rapidly. But they are not. Hence there must be some barriers which prevent them from doing so. Since these barriers do not lie in the nature of human desires, they must be external to humans. Therefore, except as individuals are blocked from technical progress by the vested interests of powerful groups, the barriers must be economic ones.

So runs the argument. Economists studying economic growth are less certain of it now than they were 10 years ago, both because with further knowledge the economic barriers seem less formidable and because other considerations have been forced on their attention.[2] Yet to most individuals not professionally concerned with the problem, the thesis that the economic conditions peculiar to the low-income countries are the primary barriers to growth still seems plausible.

THE ECONOMIC DOCTRINES OF PECULIAR BARRIERS

The Vicious Circle of Low Income and Inadequate Saving

All of the economic doctrines of peculiar barriers are stated in a paper prepared in 1948 by H. W. Singer.[3] The sources most commonly cited, however, are later sources which present fuller statements.

One doctrine, mentioned briefly in Chapter 2, is the theory of the vicious circle of low income and inability to save. Because income is so low that almost no saving is possible, capital formation is impossible. Therefore, methods remain primitive and income remains low.[4] In Singer's words, "There is, of course, the dominant vicious circle of low pro-

---

[2] Economists writing about growth, being sensible men, usually acknowledge the influence of noneconomic factors. As an example, note the following statement by Professor Kaldor: "In my view the greatly accelerated economic development of the last 200 years—the rise of modern capitalism—can only be explained in terms of changing human attitudes to risk-taking and profit-making. . . . The emergence of the 'business enterprise' characteristic of modern capitalism was thus the cause rather than the result of changes in the modes of production; and it was the product of social forces that cannot in turn be accounted for by economic and technical factors." Nicholas Kaldor, *Essays on Economic Stability and Growth* (London: G. Duckworth and Co., Ltd., 1960) p. 236.

Or this one by Professor Nurkse, following a statement that capital formation is at the heart of the problem of economic development:

"We shall do well to keep in mind, however, that this is by no means the whole story. Economic development has much to do with human endowments, social attitudes, political conditions—and historical accidents. Capital is necessary but not a sufficient condition of progress." Ragnar Nurkse, *Problems of Capital Formation in Underdeveloped Countries* (New York: Oxford University Press, 1953), p. 1.

But virtually without exception, the economists who make such acknowledgments in passing then proceed to present economic theories of growth as though they were the full and sufficient explanations.

[3] "Economic Progress in Underdeveloped Countries," *Social Research*, Vol. 16 (1949), pp. 1–11.

[4] Some primitive methods use much capital and some more productive methods use little, but in general little capital and low productivity are associated.

duction—no surpluses for economic investment—no tools and equipment—low standard of production."[5] Or, in the words of Nurkse a little
later: "On the supply side there is the small capacity to save, resulting
from the low level of real income. The low real income is a reflection of
low productivity, which in its turn is due largely to the lack of capital.
The lack of capital is a result of the small capacity to save, and so the circle is complete."[6]

The soundness of this hypothesis may seem axiomatic to a Westerner,
for he may feel that at the level of income which he visualizes in low-
income countries he could not live, much less save. At such low incomes,
he assumes, all income must be devoted to keeping alive. Empirical study,
however, suggests the absence of such a supposed physiological minimum
which prevents saving.

It is a matter of common judgment among economists acquainted with
the income statistics and the economic structure of low-income countries
that the distribution of income is more unequal in such countries than in
high-income ones, and especially so if the comparison is made after pay-
ment of direct individual taxes has been allowed for.[7] It follows that if the
mass of the population in low-income countries have a sufficient level of
income to live—which they do, and sufficiently well to increase steadily
in number—then the higher-income groups a fortiori are able to save if
they wish to. (Malnutrition is not so frequent a cause of death in low-
income countries as is commonly supposed by Westerners. The major
causes are tuberculosis, malaria, dysentery, venereal diseases, and certain
other diseases none of which except tuberculosis is closely associated with
lack of nutrition.)

It is also a matter of frequent observation by persons acquainted with
low-income countries that even the lower- (not necessarily the lowest)
income groups in many low-income countries either save some small
fraction of their incomes or spend it for purposes which are not remotely connected with physiological necessities. The saving referred to
may take the form of accumulation of gold or jewelry, or other forms;
the spending is for contributions to pagodas or temples, for village festivals during the idle season of the farm year, for neighborhood entertainment, and so on. Higher-income classes may save by investing in land or

---

[5] "Economic Progress in Underdeveloped Countries," p. 5.

[6] Ragnar Nurkse, *Problems of Capital Formation in Underdeveloped Countries*
(New York: Oxford University Press, 1953), p. 5.

[7] This judgment rests on incomplete data but on much personal observation, and it
is better established than most of our knowledge concerning low-income countries.
For a chart showing estimates of the percentage of income received by the highest-
income 10 per cent of the population in nine countries, see C. P. Kindleberger,
Economic Development (New York: McGraw-Hill Book Co., Inc., 1958), p. 8.
Among these few countries, the chart shows a strong negative correlation between
average per capita income of the country and percentage of income before tax received by the richest 10 per cent of the population.

in foreign assets; if they do not, they may spend lavishly on a luxurious landed life, maintaining a large number of retainers, or on a Western urban style of living.

W. Arthur Lewis says: "Least of all can those nations plead poverty as an excuse for not saving in which 40 per cent or so of the national income is squandered by the top 10 per cent of income receivers, living luxuriously on rents."[8] While only rough estimates are possible, Lewis's implied estimate that in a number of countries 10 per cent of the people consume 40 per cent of the output of the economy is reasonable. Reduction by one fourth in the level of consumption of those high-income families would provide resources ample for sufficient investment for economic growth. Indeed, economic growth usually starts with investment equal to 5 or 6 per cent of the national product, the percentage rising as profits are plowed back into the enterprises making them.

It is also pertinent to note that low-income societies angered at their neighbors have often mobilized resources for war. A society that can support a sizable army could if it chose devote resources to investment.

Economists who believe that inability to save perpetuates low income in the underdeveloped countries have failed to apply to the situation the theories of the determinants of consumption and saving developed by their fellow economists. Those theories themselves tend to discredit the hypothesis that saving is impossible in low-income societies.

Duesenberry has suggested that the ratio of its income saved by a family depends not on the absolute level of that income but on the position of the family in the income distribution of its group.[9] Brady has provided interesting empirical support for the hypothesis. With certain qualifications, families in a given decile of all families in an American community with respect to income save (or dissave) the same percentage of their incomes as families in the same decile of any other community regardless of the difference in average income in the communities.[10] The fraction of income saved in a low-income community is therefore as great as in a high-income community.

An alternative theory of the determinants of saving is presented in a recent volume by Milton Friedman, *A Theory of the Consumption Function*.[11] It is well known that the income of many and perhaps most American families does not remain constant or adhere closely to a foreseeable trend. There are good years and bad years, windfalls and unexpected

---

[8] *The Theory of Economic Growth* (London: George Allen & Unwin, Ltd., 1955), p. 236.

[9] James S. Duesenberry, *Income, Saving, and the Theory of Consumer Behavior* (Cambridge, Mass.: Harvard University Press, 1949).

[10] Dorothy S. Brady, "Research on the Size Distribution of Income," Part I, *Studies in Income and Wealth*, Vol. XIII (New York: National Bureau of Economic Research, Inc., c. 1951).

[11] Princeton, N.J.: Princeton University Press for National Bureau of Economic Research (General Series, No. 63), 1957.

losses of income. Friedman's thesis is that if transitory components of each family's income are separated from the permanent component, and similarly transitory components of expenditure are separated out from expenditure, the ratio of continuing or nontransitory flows of expenditure to permanent income is the same at all levels of income. Low-income families save the same fraction of their permanent income as wealthy families do.

The separation of transitory from permanent income or expenditure is a slippery business, and to make the separation Friedman uses ingenious statistical techniques and assumptions. The process is sufficiently complex that there is room for doubt as to its validity.[12] But at present no one can deny that Friedman may be correct. It should be noted that the Friedman and Duesenberry hypotheses are not necessarily inconsistent; both may be correct. According to both, the fraction of income saved is the same in low-income as in high-income communities.

It would be absurd to extrapolate Friedman's findings for the United States to other societies and assert that the fraction of permanent income saved is a universal constant. But if within the fairly wide range of incomes in the United States no one is too poor to save, this does suggest that careful empirical investigation is necessary before assuming that at lower incomes people are too poor to save. And if the percentage of total income (permanent plus transitory) saved by American families depends not on their absolute income level but on their position in the income distribution, why should not higher-income families in low-income societies also be expected to save significant fractions of their incomes —or be able to do so if they wish?

In the light of present knowledge, perhaps the best summary statement about saving in low-income societies is this: Of course there is a physiological subsistence level of living below which life is impossible. The term, if it is to have a precise meaning, refers to a level of living at which deaths equal births, so that the population remains unchanged in number. The mass of the people in a number of low-income societies must be not far above this level. Yet at present income levels, individuals in all but the lowest-income classes in these societies spend part of their income on products not at all related to the physical necessities of life. Higher-income classes dispose of a considerable fraction of their income in these ways. If sufficiently motivated, the people of the society could and would choose to save enough to finance the investment necessary for rising per capita income.[13]

---

[12] Objections by John Johnston in a review of Friedman's volume in the *Review of Economics and Statistics*, Vol. XL (November, 1958), pp. 431–35, seem to me to be well taken.

[13] Among the countries now experiencing technological progress, where the motivations to save which are one cause of such progress have taken root, the correlation between the level of income and the rate of saving may be negative; the lower-in-

The Demonstration Effect

An alternative to the too-poor-to-save argument admits that higher income classes in low-income societies could save but argues that, because they have seen the consumption levels of the West, they are driven to attain them and are psychologically unable to save. This assumed phenomenon is known as the demonstration effect.[14] In an American community, low-income families save nothing or spend beyond their income because they must keep close to the Joneses in their consumption standards. Just so, it is argued, even higher-income groups in low-income countries do not save because with increased international communication their standard of comparison is Western consumption standards.

The theoretical foundation for the demonstration-effect thesis is rather shaky. The much more intimate demonstration effect between communities within the United States does not work in the way indicated. A community in Arkansas or in Kansas surely has a far more intimate sense of the level of living in Hollywood or Chicago or New York than do the higher-income groups in India in general of Western standards. A number of individuals in those groups have lived in the West, but a number of Arkansas and Kansas individuals are also well acquainted with the big cities through personal contacts and many types of media. Yet as noted above, the percentage of income saved in the lower-income American communities seems to be much the same as in Hollywood, Chicago, or New York. These facts suggest that the comparison which most potently influences one is that with the fellow-members of one's day-to-day community. Why should the opposite be true across the world's oceans?

There is an answer to this question. Westerners, it is said, are a more important reference group to some members of elites in non-Western societies than are their fellow countrymen. If this is true, a demonstration effect probably occurs.[15]

In part, however, the demonstration effect has to do with the nature of

come countries may be saving higher percentages of their incomes than the higher-income ones. (The data are incomplete.)

It is pertinent to note that there is no discernible systematic difference between the "incremental capital-output ratio" in high- and low-income countries. In both it tends to be somewhere in the neighborhood of 3:1, varying in different circumstances between say 2.5:1 and 3.5:1, and ordinarily, except perhaps in cases of great population density and great paucity of natural resources, not much beyond these limits. This means that in both the United States and India saving of say 12 per cent of national income for one year will provide enough capital (some duplicating present capital and some embodying improved methods, as the case may be) to increase national income by 4 per cent, more or less. Of course the absolute increase in national income which equals 4 per cent of national income will be far greater in the United States, but so also will the amount of saving which equals 12 per cent of national income.

[14] See Nurkse, *Problems of Capital Formation*, chap. iii.

[15] See the discussion of the demonstration effect in Kindleberger, *Economic Development*, pp. 82–83.

consumption rather than with its level. There is no evidence that in the days of little or no communication with the West the highest-income groups of the traditional societies saved more than at present. There is general historical evidence of their lavish spending and low saving. Their spending then was on traditional objects; now to an appreciable extent it is on a Western style of living. The international demonstration effect obviously is responsible for this shift; it is much more difficult to find evidence that it has substantially increased the percentage of income consumed.

I am skeptical of the weight sometimes given to the demonstration-effect thesis because that thesis arises more from ethnocentric assumption by Western economists than from empirical evidence. But there is probably some demonstration effect on the level of consumption. The following, however, can be said with some certainty: Insofar as members of the Westernized elite of low-income societies do imitate Western levels of consumption rather than Western habits of saving and investment, they do so because they are not highly interested in participating in activities associated with technology. If they were motivated to strive personally for technological progress, they would find in Western entrepreneurs a model which might lead to a quite different demonstration effect.

The Vicious Circle of Inadequate Markets

A third barrier is sometimes found in another vicious circle: inadequate demand to justify investment in improved methods. More efficient plants, it is argued, have a minimum efficient capacity; because of the low level of income, the market is not large enough to provide a market for this minimum flow of output; hence there is little inducement for investment; without investment, productivity does not increase and incomes do not rise. "On the demand side," Nurkse writes, "the inducement to invest may be low because of the small buying power of the people, which is due to their small real income, which again is due to low productivity. The low level of productivity, however, is a result of the small amount of capital used in production, which in its turn may be caused at least partly by the small inducement to invest."[16] He spells out the minimum-size plant capacity argument and cites as examples shoe production in a hypothetical economy so low that few persons wear shoes, and steel production in Chile. He might have cited other examples: electric light bulbs, aluminum, automobiles.

However, his conclusion that the national market in low-income countries is not large enough to permit production on a scale necessary for reduction in cost is false, or at least grossly overdrawn. For while there is little demand for certain products in low-income countries, it is clear beyond question that in every country or colonial area of the world except

---

[16] *Problems of Capital Formation*, p. 5.

possibly a handful of the tiniest ones there are many other products commonly used in the area for which the demand provides a market amply adequate for productive units using modern methods. A few examples are sugar, rice or flour milling (depending on the tastes of the people), sandals, umbrellas, textiles, textile products, cigarettes, candies, and a considerable variety of agricultural products. Even economies of two or three million persons with very low income provide markets much more than large enough to justify technological progress in the production of these and a number of other commonly used products.

As an example, the first modern sugar refinery was established in one valley of Colombia and the first modern textile mill in another between 1900 and 1910, when the population of the entire country was not more than six million and the level of per capita income, as conventionally measured, probably less than $100; and each valley was so isolated from the rest of the country by barriers to transportation that the market for each enterprise initially was confined primarily to its own valley—at a maximum estimate, one fifth of the total national market in one case and much less in the other. Both flourished, as did a stream of other improvements.

Moreover, many investments not of a highly mechanized type are appropriate and advantageous. In sum, while many investments of a type which would be profitable in the United States would not be profitable in a low-income country, on the other hand many investments which would be profitable in the latter would not be profitable in the United States. There is no clear reason to assume the presence of a greater volume of investment opportunity in one, relative to the size of the economy, than in the other.

Kindleberger refines the argument concerning the size of the market as follows: In a traditional society much production is for a local market only. A very large percentage of the goods consumed in a village may be produced within 10 or 15 miles of the village. If there is a single producer of some handicraft item, reducing his cost of production will increase his sales very little. Even in a single village, for most commodities or handicraft products there are a number of producers; but the concept of production as a family affair, not an enterprise to be expanded by reducing costs and taking sales away from competitors, may dull any incentive to ponder ways of improving methods. If improvement in transportation and changes in marketing institutions have expanded the market to a region or the country as a whole, the situation is radically altered. The producer then faces an impersonal market. If he can reduce his price or improve his product, he can take sales from 100 or 1,000 other producers; hence the incentive to improve his methods is great.[17]

---

[17] Concerning the importance of expansion of the market from a community to a larger area, see C. P. Kindleberger, *Economic Development,* chap. vi.

From this set of facts the conclusion is sometimes drawn that if transport facilities were improved, production for a national market would begin and techniques would improve. No doubt there are circumstances in which this is true. With distribution costs reduced, the profitable operation of a large-scale plant is easier than otherwise, and there must be cases in which this change is just sufficient to induce someone to make the attempt and causes it to be successful.

However, to conclude that this is the central reason for failure of larger-scale plants to appear is a *non sequitur*. There may be other reasons. That there are seems likely. The developments in Colombia mentioned above suggest that a market sufficient in size to justify a large-scale plant may often be accessible to a local producer. Moreover, other obstacles, not economic in nature, are apparent.

Undoubtedly, if there were no barriers other than technical ones, for many products used in low-income countries increasing the size of the plant in which they are produced would considerably decrease costs or increase the quality of the product. However, if larger plants do not appear, a consideration apart from the size of the market or any other technical factor is probably the most important reason why they do not. The operation of a large plant involves rather radical changes in behavior, including that of the entrepreneur himself, and in interpersonal relations. A large plant will not be more economic until the management of new relationships has been mastered. I suggest that where larger plants have not appeared in traditional societies the most important reasons typically are that the community finds the change in behavior patterns involved somewhat repugnant, and entrepreneurs motivated to run against the social pressure (including their own inner reluctance) and capable of managing the nontraditional plants have not appeared. Clifford Geertz's discussion of the first budding of new entrepreneurship in two Indonesian towns, in Chapter 16 below, illustrates the difficulties vividly.

The Lump of Capital Argument

It is sometimes asserted that economic growth can go forward only when certain types of capital known as social overhead capital or infrastructure are present. By social overhead capital is meant those types of capital goods which serve not one industry but many, and which hence provide a springboard for advance in many industries. Examples are roads, railroads, and power installations, none of which, it is asserted, or at least neither of the last two of which, can be fully effective except in large and expensive units. Economic growth is blocked because low-income countries cannot afford the large lump of investment needed to complete large projects and because the large projects are a necessary base for other projects—so the argument runs.[18]

---

[18] See Singer, "Economic Progress in Underdeveloped Countries," p. 6. This thesis is most closely associated, however, with the name of Professor Paul N. Rosenstein-Rodan. He has stated it most fully and persuasively in his "Notes on the Theory of

When the expositors of this argument are asked how growth got under way in the first countries, which had no possibility of aid from the outside, they may suggest that in some, such as England and Japan, social overhead capital in transportation was provided free by the ocean; that other early investment in Britain was financed by income from her empire; and that Britain in turn, after it had begun to develop, financed transportation and other facilities in other countries.

In evaluating this argument it is necessary to distinguish among three statements: (1) that social and economic overhead capital may be fruitful in stimulating other development; (2) that at some stage in development some such projects are indispensable for further development; and (3) that the growth of present low-income countries is blocked through their inability to finance such indispensable projects.

Concerning the first proposition, there can be little dispute. The possible stimulus to other industries of transport and power facilities is beyond question. Concerning the second and third propositions, however, there is reason to be skeptical. The argument that absence of overhead capital facilities forms an insuperable or at least very serious barrier to economic growth violates the principle of continuity and flexibility in growth, which derives from general considerations of continuity in history. It is doubtful that any economic system is really so confined to only one course and order of development that its development is blocked, or even severely hampered, because very large-scale projects are not possible. There are always many alternative possible paths of change. Per capita income may be increased if a private entrepreneur or the state devises better spinning frames, introduces wheelbarrows, cultivates better seed, develops a more efficient division of labor in the production of sandals, and so on in infinite variety. An analytical model of an economy so rigid technologically that it cannot develop without some one or more large unitary projects seems too unreal to be a fruitful model for reality. It seems more realistic to assume that if a considerable group of individuals are exerting their energies imaginatively in technology, and if a large social overhead project is advantageous but not feasible, their energies will run to other small-scale improvements until, as income rises and the large-scale project becomes increasingly advantageous because of the increasing volume of activity, resources will be accumulated to carry it out, possibly with governmental support to mobilize the entire community's resources for the purpose.

Moreover, many transport and some types of power projects can in fact be built piecemeal. Roads can be and have been built or improved effectively by labor-intensive methods and a section at a time. So also have railroads, strange though this may seem to Americans. Again I cite the example of Colombia, where without exception railroads first appeared in

the 'Big Push'," chap. iii of *Economic Development for Latin America: Proceedings of a Conference Held by the International Economic Association,* H. S. Ellis and H. W. Wallich (eds.) (London: Macmillan & Co., Ltd., 1961).

stretches of a few miles out from the major cities, providing only local transportation within one valley.

Indeed, on cooler examination it appears that cases in which a lump of social overhead capital beyond the capacity of the economy to finance is of vital importance must be very rare indeed. The unique virtue of social overhead capital is supposed to be that it provides necessary facilities for other industries. On closer examination, this means only that the presence of social overhead capital will reduce the cost of production in the enterprises it serves. But so will the presence of those industries reduce the cost of production of the services of social overhead capital. The capital and service cost per vehicle using a modern road, if only a few vehicles per week do so, is enormous. In this respect the relationship between social overhead capital and other capital is symmetrical. Neither has a unique property. The special function of social overhead capital turns out to be largely an illusion.

No serious empirical evidence has been presented in print to support the social overhead capital hypothesis. The small amount of relevant research I have done contradicts it. In England, while the ocean always provided easy coastal transportation, the history of the eighteenth century gives no impression that construction of other social overhead capital preceded economic growth and permitted it. Rather, various types of investment proceeded *pari passu*. The construction of canals and roads within the country typically followed an increase in the demand for coal, timber, stone, and so on in urban centers. This demand of course is evidence of economic growth already proceeding. In turn, the roads and canals facilitated further progress.[19]

A study of economic growth in Argentina likewise suggests that social overhead capital "grew *pari passu* with the economy as a whole rather than being laid down prior to development in other sectors."[20] This is certainly also true in Colombia, and I venture to suggest that it would be found true wherever detailed historical studies are made.[21]

---

[19] For a moderately detailed study of economic growth during the century, see T. S. Ashton, *An Economic History of England: the 18th Century* (London: Methuen & Co., Ltd., 1955). Concerning transportation, see especially chap. iii.

[20] The quoted statements are from an unpublished study by Charles Cooper based primarily on an unpublished dissertation by Manuel Zymelman, "The Economic History of Argentina, 1933–52," Massachusetts Institute of Technology, 1958. Within the social overhead capital category, railroad construction began in 1857 and bulked large from 1891 to 1914, and other types of social overhead capital formation replaced it later. However, much of the early railroad construction did not serve multiple industries, the classic function of social overhead capital, but tapped the grain lands of the interior and, as Cooper says, was "somewhat like spur tracks leading to a gold mine."

[21] It should be noted, however, that if the social overhead capital thesis is refined to the statement that in certain circumstances investment in social overhead capital will yield greater returns than other investment, and for various reasons merits special attention in government policy, then the statement is indisputable. R. S. Eckaus has noted in an unpublished study that a high rate of railroad investment in South Italy

The Thesis of the Need for a Big Push

If it were true that income in underdeveloped societies is too low to permit saving and the market too small to justify investment, and in addition that large social overhead capital projects are a necessary base for technological progress, then it would follow that only a massive program to construct social overhead capital and to introduce income-raising projects all over the economy at once can get growth under way. To make this proposition consistent with the doctrine that income is too low to save, however, it must be held that the bar to saving is not physiological needs but rather merely a deep-seated unwillingness to save. Given this fact, and assuming that people may be aroused to a superhuman effort who would not be stirred to action by a smaller challenge, the thesis that a large comprehensive effort or "big push" is needed to start growth is internally consistent.

While the theory has been presented in an elaborate and attractive form by Harvey Leibenstein,[22] it was earlier advanced by Professor Rodan.[23] Professor Rodan presents it mainly as a prescription for getting growth started rapidly at present rather than as an historical explanation of how growth started. His suggestion put the theory in the most attractive light. One may remark that if technological creativity is absent in the society, the big push will be impossible, whereas if technological creativity is present in considerable degree growth will start gradually without a big push, but in the latter situation a big push might accelerate it.

In any event, the theory of the big push does not explain why growth has begun in some societies and not in others, for historically the presence or absence of a big push is not the distinguishing feature. One may reasonably ask: Has growth anywhere started with a big push?

POPULATION AND ECONOMIC GROWTH

It is sometimes assumed that incomes in low-income countries are low because technological progress which might have raised the level of income has been swamped by population growth. This view of the facts is incorrect. In many low-income countries the Malthusian problem simply has not appeared.

It is true that in a number of low-income countries population density is high. China, India, Java (not the other islands of Indonesia), Ceylon,

---

after the unification of North and South had relatively little effect on the rate of growth. See his "The Development of Regional Economic Differentials in Italy: North and South after Unification" (Cambridge: Center for International Studies, Massachusetts Institute of Technology, 1959).

[22] In his book, *Economic Backwardness and Economic Growth* (New York: John Wiley & Sons, Inc., 1957), chaps. viii and ix.

[23] See note 18 above.

Formosa, most Central American and Caribbean areas, and Egypt are the conspicuous examples. The small African countries of Ruanda-Urundi and Dahomey are also fairly densely populated, and there are pockets of high population density within Tanganyika, Nigeria, and Volta. In addition a few countries such as Libya, where the population density per square mile is low but the land is unproductive, belong on the list. In a much larger number of low-income countries, however, population density is not high. This is true of the several countries of Southeast Asia, the Middle East other than Egypt and the special case of Israel, all of Africa except for the areas named above, Mexico, and all of South America. In general, in these countries there is available to most peasants as much land as they can cultivate with the primitive methods to which they are accustomed. Land is not the factor limiting their level of income. In a number of sparsely or moderately populated Latin American countries economic growth has begun, but to attribute this fact to their lesser population density would be gratuitous. And except in Latin America, among the present low-income countries economic growth has proceeded no farther in the sparsely than in the densely populated countries.

It is true that even where land is plentiful population growth might prevent rise in income if the beginning of technological progress and rise in income resulted in a rate of population growth sufficient to offset it. In fact, however, this has not been the difficulty. It is apparently true that nowhere in the world has population growth *induced by rising income* been sufficient to halt the rise in income.[24] Where population is rising rapidly, it is doing so not because rise in income stimulated its growth but because modern public methods imported by means of technical aid from abroad have sharply reduced death rates. The historical record indicates that rise in income in these societies has failed to occur not because something thwarted it but because no force has been present to cause income to rise.

Thus the facts offer no basis for associating presence or absence of economic growth with differences in population density. Indeed, of the low-income countries outside of Latin America, two which give the most marked signs of entering upon continuing growth are the two huge densely populated countries of Asia—China and India.

At this point it is worthwhile to pause for a moment to note the fallacy of a belief frequently encountered. The densely populated countries, it is felt, have little chance to develop because they have such a small amount of natural resources per person; they are using their natural resources to capacity just to keep their teeming millions alive. This view implicitly assumes either that natural resources have some certain maximum capacity beyond which an increased flow of product cannot be extracted

---

[24] For an examination of the historical record, see E. E. Hagen, "Population and Economic Growth," *American Economic Review*, Vol. XLIX (June, 1959).

from them, or that unused natural resources must be tapped in order to increase the level of output per worker. The pertinent fact is that however low the quantity of resources per person, the present level of living is being obtained from them with primitive techniques and instruments. With improved technology the same resources will yield greater output —higher yields per acre, more water power, more tons of coal per man-year, more raw materials for industry per year. A resource-poor country may at each stage of its history have a lower level of living than a richer country can enjoy with the same ingenuity; but to conclude therefore that the resource-poor country cannot steadily improve its income per person is to indulge in confusion.

ORIGINS OF THE DOCTRINES OF PECULIAR BARRIERS

The doctrines of peculiar barriers have two elements in common: They all assume that the central problem in growth is capital formation, and they all assume that sufficient technological creativity to carry forward economic growth is present in all societies.

Now it is clear beyond any question that technological creativity is responsibile for a far greater share of increase in productivity than is capital formation. This was apparent to the first great modern student of economic growth, Schumpeter, who wrote:

> The slow and continuous increase in time of the national supply of productive means and savings is obviously an important factor in explaining the course of economic history through the centuries, but it is completely overshadowed by the fact that development consists primarily in employing existing resources in a different way, in doing new things with them, irrespective of whether those resources increase or not.[25]

Schumpeter's statement is true not merely in some vague qualitative way but also in a definite quantitative sense. Robert Solow has estimated that of the increase in output per man-hour in the United States from 1909 to 1949, not more than 13 per cent was due to increase in capital. Between 87 and 90 per cent was due to other changes, which may be lumped under the broad heading of technological progress (though some of them may not belong there).[26] This statistical estimate implies

---

[25] J. A. Schumpeter, *The Theory of Economic Development* (Cambridge: Harvard University Press, 1949), p. 68. See also A. K. Cairncross, "The Place of Capital in Economic Progress," in Léon H. Dupriez (ed.), *Economic Progress* (Louvain: Institut de Recherches Economiques et Sociales, 1955).

[26] If net capital formation is used in the calculation, the share of increase in productivity attributed to increase in capital is 10 per cent. If gross capital formation is used (equivalent in this calculation to assuming that capital retains its efficiency to the end of its useful life and then wears out at once like Oliver Wendell Holmes' wonderful one-hoss shay), the share attributed to capital is 10 per cent. Robert M. Solow, "Technical Change and the Aggregate Production Function," *Review of Eco-*

that if there had been no increase in the quantity of capital used per worker, and changes in productive equipment had been made only by replacing equipment as it wore out with new equipment embodying new ideas, we would have had at least 87 per cent of the increase in output per man-hour that we actually had; only 13 per cent or less is attributable to increase in the quantity of physical plant and equipment used per worker.

This statement must be qualified by the recognition that in practice plant and equipment would not have worn out fast enough for all of the new methods to be introduced economically by mere replacement of capital; without an increase in the quantity of capital in use per worker the introduction of some new methods would have had to be delayed. The converse statement, however, may be made without qualification. Solow's estimate suggests that if the quantity of capital in use per worker had been increased as much as it actually was but without the introduction of new methods, the increase in output per man-hour would have been only 13 per cent or less of what it actually was. Indeed, if creativity ceased, and capital formation in the United States were limited to producing additional machinery and equipment embodying methods already known, it is a reasonable guess that increase in output per man-hour and the accompanying steady rise in our level of living would probably decline almost to zero within two decades. And there is no doubt that these observations apply not only to this period of United States progress but also more generally. Improvement of human skills will of course increase productivity quite independently of capital formation; but if improvement of skills is restricted to the learning of skills already known—that is, if creativity in devising new elements of skill is ruled out—then the advance possible through education is also strictly limited.

This being so, why is technological creativity taken for granted in the economic theories? One reason no doubt is ethnocentricity. In Western societies we see technological creativity at work around us and assume that it is a fact of human nature rather than a culturally acquired trait. Therefore we assume that if technological progress is not going forward it must be because there are barriers to the capital formation in which it will be embodied. But there is another and perhaps more important reason. For reasons which were valid in the context in which they were first applied, economic thought since the second quarter of the nineteenth century, in which present-day economists are steeped, has ignored not only creativity but also the process of technological change itself.

nomics and Statistics, Vol. XXXIX (August, 1957), pp. 312–20; but note correction of arithmetical error in a "Note" by Warren P. Hogan in the November, 1958, issue and a further comment by Solow in the same issue.

Moses Abramovitz came to a similar conclusion in a statistical analysis of a longer period in the United States. See his Resource and Output Trends in the United States Since 1870 (National Bureau of Economic Research Occasional Paper 52) (New York, 1956). His statistical methodology, however, is more open to challenge than is that of Solow.

The first modern economist, Adam Smith, appreciated the importance of technological change and concerned himself with it.[27] His successors also issued shrewd and sensible *obiter dicta* about it, but in their formal theorizing they gradually turned their attention away from it so that by limiting the complexity of their analysis they could reason with more certainty about the remaining factors. By the time of Alfred Marshall this tendency was complete.[28] In virtually every book of neoclassical economic theory from Alfred Marshall to J. M. Keynes one will find a careful explicit statement about as follows: "Assuming for simplicity a constant state of the arts, let us see. . . ." A constant state of the arts; that is, absence of any advance in technological knowledge. By this simplification, more penetrating thinking about the remaining problems was possible. Those problems included questions of relative prices, competition and monopoly in the production and marketing of goods and services, international economic relations, the distribution of income, the level of employment, and inflation. Concerning them, economic theorists have formulated increasingly keen analytical tools and have contributed importantly to policy decisions. In doing so, as a practical matter they have taken into account the effects of technological change; but in their formal theory, technological change is absent.

As a result, in the formal body of neoclassical theory income per capita rises only because of capital formation. I suggest that in their discussions of economic growth many economists have applied this principle of capital formation as the only source of rise in per capita income for one principal reason: They have forgotten that they think of it as the only source merely because during the nineteenth century economic theory was gradually shaped in such a way as to rule out other and more important forces. As has happened to scientists in other fields, economists have been led astray by applying their conclusions to reality without recalling the assumptions on which the conclusions are based.

CONCLUSION: CHOICE AMONG THEORIES

The doctrines of peculiar barriers are the most conspicuous economic theories of growth. They are more or less representative in the sense that other economic theories are also particularistic and subject to somewhat similar objections.

---

[27] He regarded technological progress as consisting of increase in the division of labor. One of his most famous dictums is that "the division of labor . . . must always be limited . . . by the extent of the market." Edwin Cannan (ed.), *The Wealth of Nations* (London, 1904), Vol. I, p. 19.

[28] An interesting exception to the prior trend toward exclusion of technological advance from analysis is provided by John Rae, who discussed economic development and stressed the "accumulative principle" and the "inventive principle" as relevant forces. See Joseph J. Spengler, "John Rae on Economic Development: A Note," *Quarterly Journal of Economics*, Vol. LXXIII (August, 1959), pp. 393–406. Unfortunately, Rae's analysis did not affect the main stream of economic thought.

My analysis of these economic arguments does not lead to the conclusion that economic factors do not influence the timing or the pace of economic growth. Indeed, some of the arguments discussed above may be not so much wrong as greatly exaggerated. May it be, then, that while individually they are not weighty, in combination they do account for the important deterrents to growth?

It may indeed. If as a group they are given great weight, it would follow that economic growth requires and can be brought about by the injection of capital from outside the system, or by an expansion of markets because of some outside events (or perhaps by a technological change regarded as accidental which expands the market and causes a sequence of change). However, the analysis above of the separate arguments suggests that their importance, even taken in combination, is much less than might be supposed from less critical examination of them.

The weight to be given to the economic arguments must ultimately be decided by placing them beside alternative or additional explanations of why growth does or does not occur and then considering their appropriate place in the total explanatory network. It may then be decided that the most fruitful simple hypothesis of how growth begins may omit them. Any more elaborate or complete explanation obviously must take the economic circumstances into account, though perhaps only as parameters (elements assumed to remain constant, which affect the impact of variation in other elements). They have of course been regarded only as parameters in this volume.

part **II**

Personality and the Stability of Traditional Societies

The Traditional State of Societies[1]

chapter 4

TRADITIONAL SOCIETIES IN HISTORY

IT IS CLEAR FROM THE HISTORICAL INSTANCES I HAVE cited that to understand why some traditional societies enter upon economic growth sooner than others we must understand the internal structure and functioning of these societies, for both the barriers to growth and the causes of growth seem to be largely internal rather than external. We must ask: What differences among these societies themselves have caused some to enter upon economic growth sooner than others? First, however, in this chapter I shall lay a foundation by analyzing the characteristics which cause a society to be termed traditional and those which cause traditionalism, if it exists, to persist for a long time.[2]

A society is traditional if ways of behavior in it continue with little change from generation to generation. Where traditionalism is present, certain other characteristics are also found. Behavior is governed by custom, not law. The social structure is hierarchical.[3] The individual's position in the society is normally inherited rather than achieved. And, at least in the traditional state so far in the world's history, economic pro-

---

[1] For the description of traditional peasant-based society in this chapter, I rely partly on my own observations of peasant society in Burma and more casually in India, Colombia, and Egypt, but mainly on the many "village studies" and other anthropological discussions of peasant or primitive life plus the much smaller number of studies of personality and its formation in traditional societies. I have tried to ask what structure must underlie the facts described in these works rather than merely to summarize typical facts. A number of these works are referred to later in this chapter, but I am indebted to many that are not for the evolution of a matrix of concepts in my mind.

[2] For a discussion of the characteristics by which one distinguishes among types of societies, see the Appendix to this chapter.

[3] Where the society consists of a number of local communities possessing some common cultural traits but only very loosely bound together, the social structure may not be hierarchical simply because it is minimal in any event. However, where a clearly defined structure binds the local groups together, with extremely rare exceptions it is hierarchical. For evidence of both facts, see George Peter Murdock, "World Ethnographic Sample," *American Anthropologist*, Vol. LIX (1957), pp. 664–87.

ductivity is low. A traditional society, in short, tends to be custom-bound, hierarchical, ascriptive, and unproductive. If ways of behavior tended to continue unchanged, the society should be termed traditional even if these other characteristics were not present; but it will be suggested in this and the following chapters that there is a causal connection among these characteristics. A society will hardly continue to be traditional unless its basic behavior patterns are hierarchical and ascriptive and custom governs behavior. Of course every society is traditional, hierarchical, ascriptive, and governed by custom in some aspects of its behavior in some degree; but the differences in degree and scope are such that without undue distortion of reality they may be thought of as differences in type.

There have been traditional hunting and fishing societies, traditional pastoral societies, and traditional societies based on peasant agriculture, for example, agricultural production on small plots by rather primitive methods. Traditional peasant societies will be of especial interest here, for people of hunting and pastoral societies, not having settled habitations, can hardly accumulate artifacts and enter upon continuing technological progress. Although fishing societies might do so, they form a special case of less empirical interest.

In Africa below the Sahara desert, and in America, some societies were at the hunting and gathering stage until their conquest by Europeans. Elsewhere in these continents and in Europe traditional agricultural societies had existed for centuries when the industrial revolution began in western Europe. In Asia and around the Mediterranean, societies had taken this form millennia before that event.

These various societies characterized by traditionalism varied greatly in other features. Some were small tribal groups largely isolated from all other societies. Examples are certain tribes in Africa and America, the nations of Southeast Asia, the Greek city-states of the archaic period, and Italy before the expansion of the Latins. Others consisted of local communities only loosely connected politically but with a good deal of cultural interchange, such as the various areas of Europe in the Middle Ages, India during most of its history before the British conquest, and Indonesia before the Dutch. During long periods of its history China also belongs in this class, but during other long periods the central control was greater. In some other areas a large empire was superimposed on a number of traditional societies and partially integrated them. The Khmers, the Mongols, the Persians, the Romans, the Mayas, and the Incas formed such empires.

Traditional peasant societies existed thousands of years before the Industrial Revolution, but they did not remain traditional throughout those millennia. Repeatedly, bursts of innovation occurred, lasting in some societies for a century or so, in others for longer periods, but in none for as long as a thousand years.[4] The formation of an empire constituted such innovations. In most of the empires the dominating group developed elaborate urban life (supported by tribute levied on the subject peoples). The empires also developed elaborate political organization and far-reaching administration, built and maintained extensive public works, and evolved complex methods of record-keeping and communication.

Empire-building, however, was only one of the types of social and cultural innovation. Cumulative advances of other sorts occurred. Culture growth around the rim of the Mediterranean went on step by step from pictorial to syllabic to phonetic writing, each step being accomplished by a different society after the ability of another society to innovate in this respect had come to an end. In similar step-by-step progress, societies advanced from crude methods of record-keeping to the decimal system of notation, and from primitive art to the achievements of Greece. The Phoenicians became merchants, shippers, and colonizers. Scientific advance of note occurred in the several large countries of Asia, in Greece, and in Rome. Noble philosophies were evolved in India, in China, in Greece, in Judea, and elsewhere. During the Middle Ages in western Europe a series of technical advances in agriculture successively raised its productivity. In a few small societies the base of peasant agriculture was largely or wholly abandoned; economic activity consisted largely of trading. This was true of Phoenicia and, during the Middle Ages, of Genoa, Florence, and some cities of the Hanseatic League.

Great creativity was needed to achieve these changes; in each case, for a time tradition ceased to rule. In most and perhaps all periods of change the social structure also ceased to be purely hierarchical and inheritance was no longer the sole determinant of social position. In every case productivity, broadly defined, increased.

Perhaps the only characteristic that these preindustrial departures from traditionalism have in common is that they all ended. In some cases the society preserved its new techniques but became traditional in their use; in many others, the society lapsed into its old ways. In either event, the dependence on hierarchy, ascription, and tradition, which had disappeared for a time or had been concealed under the superstructure, became overt again. Often a political collapse occurred under the impact of attack from without, but in many of these instances a sort of ossification had occurred internally which made the nation unable to resist the external pressure or make an adjustment to it. That is, the return to traditionalism had already begun.

Traditional peasant society, in short, has been a stable situation from which departures have occurred, departures that in the long view were

---

[4] The most notable attempt to isolate, measure, and analyze periods of innovation is that of A. L. Kroeber in *Configurations of Culture Growth* (Berkeley and Los Angeles: University of California Press, 1944).

temporary. Many persons think that the present period of innovation is different in this respect. Continuing technological progress, it is thought, has caused permanent alteration of the basic characteristics of traditional societies. However, to state with assurance that this is true is unwarranted. It is true that up to the present time there have been no traditional industrial societies. This, however, may be merely because the burst of innovation that brought industrialization has not had time to run its course. A train of events that will bring a return to traditionalism may even now be pursuing its inevitable sequence. Barring a cataclysm, the higher level of productivity will presumably remain; but a few centuries must pass before it would be safe to conclude that technological progress will go on without an end, or that the other characteristics of traditional society, hierarchical social structure, the inheritance of position, and the rule of tradition, will not reappear.[5] Like all earlier periods of innovation or "culture growth," the present one may be temporary. But even if the transition to economic growth has destroyed traditional society forever, we may conclude that that transition parallels earlier historical phenomena in many respects, and that to be adequate an explanation of the recent event must probe forces that are also relevant to understanding of other sequences of social change. The discussion has another corollary of importance. Traditionalism, it is clear, is a state that may characterize any society. Its presence or absence distinguishes two states of a given society, rather than setting one society apart from others. While for brevity I shall occasionally use the term "traditional society," this must always be understood as an abbreviated reference to the traditional state of society.

In many societies of the present day the full traditional complex is still present or has given way to a sequence of change so recently that the old outlines are still visible. Since these are the societies in whose future behavior we are especially interested, I shall describe traditional societies in the present tense. As a basis for creating a model of the relationships which cause the traditional state of society to persist century after century, resistant to change, a rather detailed though generalized description of some relationships within traditional societies will be useful.

TRADITIONAL SOCIETY AS DUAL (OR TRIPLE) SOCIETY

A traditional (agricultural) society does not consist merely of peasants or of villagers. Every traditional society of any importance is a dual society. It consists on the one hand of villages and on the other hand of some larger towns plus one or more central cities. The cities are the king's court, the center of government, regional strong points, or commercial

---

[5] There is no technical reason why technical progress should not go on forever. If it ends, the reasons will be sociopsychological, not technical.

centers.[6] The society consists of peasants and other occupational classes on roughly the same social level and on the other hand various socially superior groups. There is no traditional society, unless some very tiny one consisting of hardly more than a single community, which does not have various elite groups socially far removed from the peasantry. Following a modern minstrel, I shall refer to the peasants, artisans, craftsmen-shopkeepers, and menials collectively as the simple folk,[7] and following anthropologists, I shall term all other classes elite,[8] sometimes separating out the great trader-financiers as a distinct third group.

Of course neither the elite nor the nonelite are undifferentiated. The core of the elite is typically an economically and politically powerful class of landowners, such as still exists in every Latin American country except Cuba; in every Middle Eastern country, though shorn of political power in Egypt and Iraq; in Ceylon; even in India as it shuffles off tradition. Around or under this central core are the bureaucrats, the doctors, lawyers, and other professionals; the writers, teachers, and other intellectuals; the religious officials; and the military. Religious officials, while they bolster the traditional social structure, typically form a class apart, having a status not directly comparable to secular status. Religious life often provides a role for individual deviants from all classes, but in most countries the higher church bureaucracy is of elite origin, aristocratic and traditional—except that in some colonial or ex-colonial Catholic countries it is an imported elite which was not necessarily elite in its home country. The learned are in a detached position which in lesser degree is similar to that of the religious. Until recently the landed class itself provided the military officers or had controlling ties with them. The simple folk provided only the foot soldiers. Within the elite groups there are gradations extending down to the local school teacher and the local representative of national political authority.

The landed elite and their families may constitute only a small fraction of 1 per cent of the population, and the total national elite, excluding the lowest members of the religious hierarchy and excluding most government employees, with their families may constitute only say 1 per cent of the population; or these percentages may be five or six times as great, depending on the cultural and social history of the country.

Below the elite are the peasants, the menial laborers, the artisans, and craftsmen who maintain shops where they sell their products but whose

---

[6] Sjoberg has noted how greatly the cities of low-income societies today resemble those of the other traditional societies of history. See Gideon Sjoberg, *The Preindustrial City, Past and Present* (Glencoe, Ill.: Free Press of Glencoe, Inc., 1960).

[7] Guinevere: "What do the simple folk do, when they're bored?" Arthur: "They whistle. . . . They sing. . . . They dance. . . . They wonder what the royal folk do—as I'm told." Alan Jay Lerner and Arthur Loewe, *Camelot*, Act II.

[8] See, for example, Robert Redfield, *Peasant Society and Culture* (Chicago: University of Chicago Press, 1956).

role is regarded as that of craftsmen, not traders. The peasantry, of course, far outnumber the others combined. The relative social ranking of these groups, in their own eyes and those of the elite, varies somewhat among traditional societies, but the conspicuous fact is that of rough equality in social status among them and great distance between all of them and the elite groups.

The Great Traders

I have mentioned the great traders. In traditional societies except small isolated ones there is a class of large-scale trader-financiers. The trade they conduct is importing and exporting and domestic trade divorced from production. Their loans may be to peasants and to princes. In spite of their economic power, almost nowhere are the trader-financiers accepted by other elite groups as equal in worth or as occupying a natural and proper place in the society. Napoleon's sneering reference to the English as a nation of shopkeepers, the attitude of the German Junkers toward money-grubbing upstarts, and the desire of Jesus to drive the money-changers from the temple are repeated the world around. In medieval Europe the Church condemned profit from trade as severely as it did usury. In Asia, Africa, and Latin America the great traders are often aliens—Chinese, Indians, persons from the Near East, Jews, and so on. In many countries they come from the trading group of their home country; in others they pursue in an alien society an occupation they would not pursue where their own folkways prevail. The local trader too (as distinguished from the craftsman who sells his own products) is typically set apart from the rest of the community. Often he too is an outsider in some sense. In India he is usually of a separate, and low, caste; in Japan, before industrialization, he was of a separate group forbidden to turn to other occupations; and so on.

An anthropologist has suggested that one's products are naturally thought of as part of oneself, and that until new folkways have legitimized it, making a living by buying and selling other people's produce is deemed like profiting from selling dignity or honor, or extorting a price for one's friendship.[9] This perhaps is one reason why trading is typically looked on in traditional societies as a not quite proper occupation. Another is that the trader-financiers do not have the same values, the same morals, as the other members of traditional society. In the villages of almost all traditional societies great weight is placed on the duty of mutual self-help and on group solidarity. This sense of mutuality also runs vertically: between the simple folk and the successive layers of the elite there is a sense of reciprocal obligation, of mutual dependence. We shall see how the circumstances of traditional society breed these relationships. The trader-financiers do not accept these obligations. They are lone wolves, or, if

---

[9] I remember reading such a suggestion, but I am now unable to locate the source.

you choose, the first economic men, looking out for themselves first in a way that is not true of other members of the society and which other members of the society regard as antisocial and immoral. No doubt this is why in some societies there are no indigenous trader-financiers. The ethics of the society's members would not permit them to stomach this activity. In societies where they are indigenous (England, Japan, China) the trader-financiers must originally have been social deviants led to amoral ways by their atypical personalities.

Because of the traditional attitude toward them, perhaps trader-financiers should not be termed elite, and traditional society should be regarded as triple, not dual, in its major class divisions. But in their economic power and often in their political power the trader-financiers are elite, and for many purposes it is justifiable to emphasize merely the duality of class structure.

The Cultural Brokers

While there is a great social distance between the elite and the simple folk, in every traditional society they are linked, socially and culturally, by a connection, established by certain of the lower-level elite, known variously to anthropologists as "the bridge," "the link," "the hinge," or "the brokers." The broker may be a regional or local lieutenant of the national government, the headman of the village, a monk or priest, the village school teacher, or a local member of the landed gentry. Through these persons the "little tradition" of the village and the "great tradition" of the elite intellectuals merge.[10] Through them the values of the elite and of the simple folk interact and influence each other.

THE PEASANTS

The simple folk of a society possess neither the capital nor the knowledge and other personality characteristics necessary to be innovators of technological progress. But we shall understand the elite better if we first understand the simple folk, especially the peasantry.

Robert Redfield, an anthropologist who perhaps more than any other has attempted to analyze the essential nature of peasant life, has noted how universally to historians, anthropologists, and novelists in recent times, in Rome in the fourth century after Christ, and in Greece in the eighth century before Christ peasants have seemed the same. Critical analysis has pointed out some variation in this sameness, as Redfield himself has noted,[11] but the common central characteristics are found the world around. They no doubt derive from characteristics of peasant life that are common to almost all traditional societies.

---

[10] These terms are from Redfield, *Peasant Society and Culture.*
[11] See *ibid.*, chap. iv.

The Village

The peasant village consists typically of a few dozen or a few hundred houses clustered along a single dirt street or a group of intersecting streets. Isolated homes on separate holdings apparently existed only in a few small areas until the settlement of the Western hemisphere, and they are a marked exception in traditional societies today.[12] The typical house consists of one room. Except in cold country, the floor is the dirt of the ground. Where bamboo grows, the house probably consists of walls and a roof hung on a frame of bamboo poles. The walls are made of panels woven from bamboo split and flattened into strips 2 or 3 inches wide. The roof is thatched. In other areas the walls may be made of mud, crude brick, straw, logs, or perhaps tall reeds tied into thick bundles. The houses of the headman, local representatives of the elite such as landed gentry, and a few of the wealthier peasants may have a wooden floor and walls partly or wholly of wood or brick.

Somewhere along the street—perhaps in the center, perhaps at the edge of the area covered by houses—will be the village pagoda or temple or shrine. There may or may not be a school. If there is, it teaches only the rudiments of literacy and devotes its main efforts to the sacred writings and the traditional virtues. Literacy is not one of the conspicuous characteristics of traditional society. The village meeting place will be the school or religious place. In the center or at the edge of the cluster of houses may be a village well and a tank which hold the village water supply. Nearby may be the village threshing floor, the grazing ground, and wood lot. On the acres around the village are the fields. Approximately half of the people of the world at present live in villages such as these.

The Village Economy

In most traditional societies virtually every village family except that of the teacher, if there is one, and the priest or monk cultivates the land, though in some societies small landlords who do not cultivate may also reside in the village. In every village there is need for occupations other than cultivation: weaving, sandal making, carpentry, candle making, pottery making, and the like. These as well as the maintenance of a tiny village store or shop, if there is one, are usually the part-time occupations of families whose primary position is that of peasants; but in some traditional societies, for example, the feudal society of the European Middle Ages and the caste society of India, full-time craft occupations develop. And in larger villages and towns there develop shops maintained by persons who are not craftsmen and who have no occupation but shopkeeper.

---

[12] See Robert Redfield, *The Little Community* (Chicago: University of Chicago Press, 1955), chap. i.

Techniques are everywhere rude, Biblical. The vehicle for carrying small burdens is the pan on the head. Digging is done more widely with the broad-bladed hoe than with the spade. Preparation of the soil is with a single-share wooden plow, possibly with a steel tip, or a hand hoe, followed, if the crop demands, by a harrow consisting of a heavy log or board in which wooden sticks project downward. These instruments are drawn by an ox, a water buffalo, or a camel; the horse as beast of burden has not yet reached most peasant societies. The crop is harvested with a hand sickle or pulled by hand, threshed out by being trodden upon on the threshing ground by oxen or other animals, or by having a threshing sled drawn repeatedly over it, and winnowed by pouring it repeatedly from head height to the ground so that the wind may blow away the chaff. In these as in other activities with few exceptions the members of traditional societies solve the problems of life by doing as their ancestors did before them.

One of our conceptions of the common characteristics of peasant life is that of teeming millions struggling for subsistence on plots of land one or two or three acres in size. This is true of China, India, Korea, and Japan; and of Java, Ceylon, and Egypt. In all but a few other peasant societies land is relatively plentiful, and the peasant family's landholding is as large as one family can cultivate with the techniques and tools in use, for most crops between 10 and 15 acres, or double that if the land must lie fallow every second year.

Because land is central in his life, the ownership, or if this is not possible the proprietorship, of land is more vital to the peasant than perhaps any other aspect of his material life. In some peasant societies, such as pre-British Burma, the right to use land was held by the individual peasant family, with no overriding claim in the land from above except the right of the king to collect customary taxes. Elsewhere the tribal chief or feudal lord collected his due. In societies where land was in communal tribal use by now it has commonly passed into the individual possession of the tribal chieftains or military elite and thence to their descendants. (In some areas of Africa and parts of Saudi Arabia this transition has not yet occurred.) In Latin America the Spanish and Portuguese conquerors simply took guardianship of the land, which became *de facto* and then legal ownership. Where land was held feudally it has passed into the ownership of either the feudal lords or the peasants, depending perhaps on who had the greater political power as feudalism broke up.[13]

Feudal or tribal land institutions did not imply economic or emotional insecurity concerning the land. In most traditional societies (but excluding China and ancient Greece and Rome) before Westerners introduced alienability of land in the name of progress the peasant had what anthro-

---

[13] Concerning Europe, see Doreen Warriner, *The Economics of Peasant Farming* (London: Oxford University Press, 1939), pp. 7–17.

pologists term "inherited use-ownership" of it.[14] Residence in the village implied holding a plot or plots of land. One had family land as one had one's name. It was held not by an individual but by the family, past, present, and future. A family might not have enough land, but its tenure on that which it had occasioned no concern; it was an incident of life. As long as the family remained in the village it had the land; if for some catastrophic reason it left the village, it left the land, which others occupied. The feudal lord, if there was one, had the right to his dues, but the land was not his.

Westerners introduced alienability of land and in the process established title to it. Peasants found that others now had complete claim to the land, or, if the peasants possessed the title, they lost it through the new-found ability to obtain money by mortgaging it. The resulting vacuum in their lives has led to the bidding for land which typically leaves them only subsistence above the rent they pay. The literature of the economics of traditional societies is full of references to the high rents which drive the level of living of the peasant down to subsistence. The literature often attributes these rents simply to the greed of monopolistic landlords. No doubt the greed is an observed fact. But it is only one blade of the scissors. The other blade is the intense unconscious urge of the peasant to be a proprietor of land, an urge undoubtedly arising in the past because of the economic importance of land but now reinforced by the symbolic social importance of land which drives the peasant in ways he does not understand. Associated with this sense of the importance of land there probably is commonly a feeling of fondness for the land. It may be mixed in varying proportions with bitterness at the dominant influence of land in one's welfare, but the bitterness may be prominent only where the peasant has lost control of the land and is a renter under modern institutions.[15]

The typical peasant village is not entirely self-sufficient. A group of villages join in periodic markets—typically at intervals ranging between five and 10 days—and through interlocking market areas there is exchange of specialized craft products over a considerable area. If the peasants of the village produce staple products for a foreign market, these are purchased by representatives of the great traders, and with the proceeds thus obtained the villagers purchase imported manufactured products and a few staples from abroad or from the central commercial city of the country. All of this trade may be over the rudest of transportation

---

[14] In India, although land was alienable before the advent of the British, apparently in fact occupants were not dispossessed, and owners to avoid loss of status did not sell the land except to kinsmen. Hence (undoubtedly with qualifications) in practice inherited use-ownership prevailed. The same may have been true in the earlier periods of Chinese history and in ancient Greece and Rome.

[15] See Redfield's discussion in chap. iv of *Peasant Society and Culture*. It is possible both that in his initial statement Redfield romanticized the peasant attitude somewhat and that he conceded too much in response to Friedman's comments.

facilities; unless colonial rulers have improved them, there may be few roads over which automobiles or heavy wagons can travel except within a limited radius of the main cities.

The Impotence of the Peasant[16]

It seems likely to me that a key causal force shaping both the pattern of social relations and the personality of the peasant is his awareness of the limited extent of his power. To the peasant, life is a mystery in a profound sense in which it is not a mystery to modern man. There is favorable weather, and his crops flourish. Or drought or excessive rain comes, and they fail. Or storms destroy them. His cattle live, bringing moderate prosperity; or they die, bringing disaster. Above all, his wife and his children live or die for causes he cannot clearly understand (though he spins webs of explanation concerning all of these things). Half of the children he begets die before the age of five years; or, if he lives in a less favorable environment, half may die before the age of one. The birth rate of his society is close to the biological maximum except as poverty delays marriage, yet until the recent introduction from abroad of modern public health and medical measures barely two of his children survived through the years of parenthood to perpetuate the race. Before all of these events he is helpless unless he can induce the spirits to help him. To state that he feels impotent may give a wrong connotation, for it may imply that he feels that his position is not as it should be. He probably does not. He merely takes for granted that the phenomena of the world around him are arbitrary and not amenable to analysis, and that they control him unless the spiritual authorities which control them can be persuaded to favor him. The major aspects of his personality, and the relationships within his community, I hypothesize, are closely related to this sense of impotence.

Interpersonal Relationships in the Village

In such a world, in a nuclear family the number of children left as orphans by the death of their father would be large, for death strikes frequently at adults as well as at children. Hence the logical family unit is the extended family of several generations, in which all feel responsible for all. In the extreme form of the extended family the economic resources of the family are pooled and available to every member subject to the judgment of the family patriarch—constituting a rude but effective sort of social security. Such a thing as an individual business venture is virtually unknown. Every economic act is taken in the name of the family and the associates in economic activity are members of the family.

---

[16] For a classification of personality types that is pertinent to the discussion of peasant personality, see Florence R. Kluckhohn, "Dominant and Variant Value Orientations," in C. Kluckhohn, H. Murray, and D. M. Schneider (eds.), *Personality in Nature, Society, and Culture* (2d ed.; New York: Alfred A. Knopf, Inc., 1955). Dr. Kluckhohn's classificatory scheme is a general one, not limited to peasant societies, but from her scheme sets of characteristics relevant to peasant societies emerge.

Even where the extended family does not exist in extreme form, the family group is usually larger than the nuclear family of husband, wife, and children and extends to kin of the several generations of living persons descended from the patriarch, breaking up into smaller groups only when the patriarch dies and each son becomes a head of his own group of descendants.[17]

The peasant depends for help against the hazards and difficulties of life not merely on the feudal relationship but also on a system of mutual self-help among members of the village or of the clan group in several villages. Members of the group help each other at planting time or harvest, or perhaps in maintaining irrigation ditches or paths, in some societies in house-building, usually at births, deaths, weddings, and other ceremonial occasions, almost everywhere whenever disaster strikes. The form of organization for the purposes and the scope of the reciprocal aid vary from society to society, as do the forms of organization for all of the functions described in this chapter. In Japan the village is the unit of mutual aid; in China the clan within the village; in India an intervillage clan group; in Indonesia complex networks of voluntary associations for various purposes.[18] Life depends on this mutual help; many economic functions, and many religious ones of great emotional import, could not be carried out without it. No sanction of peasant social life is more compelling than the sanction of refusal of co-operation by the group to an individual who has violated the customary relationships.

The relationship among the members of the group is diffuse. Because no one has labor or goods to spare, there is indeed the most scrupulous observance of reciprocity in the exchanges of mutual help. The half-days

---

[17] But Yang noted in 1947 that even in China, where the diffuse family responsibilities and diffuse clan relationships pertain, at the time he wrote frictions sometimes caused families to separate before both parents of the oldest generation died. "Quarreling about dividing a large family is almost everyday news in the village." M. C. Yang, *A Chinese Village, Taitou, Shantung Province* (London: Kegan Paul, Trench, Trubner Co., Ltd., 1948), pp. 236–39. The quotation is from p. 239. This trend probably should be interpreted as a step in the breakup of peasant society.

Banfield noted that in a village in southern Italy which he studied the nuclear family prevails. If both parents or perhaps only the father dies before the children grow up, they usually become beggars. He suggests that the prevalence of the nuclear family may be due to the fact that before the feudal system broke up, the typical landholding had become so small that it would support only one nuclear family. See Edward C. Banfield and Laura Fasano Banfield, *The Moral Basis of a Backward Society* (Glencoe, Ill.: Free Press of Glencoe, Inc., 1958), pp. 153–54. This explanation is obviously incomplete, for there is as much land per person whether the family is patriarchal or nuclear. The explanation of the decay of traditional society which led to this situation (I assume that it did not pertain in the traditional society) must be complex.

[18] See John F. Embree, *Suye Mura: A Japanese Village* (Chicago: University of Chicago Press, 1939), concerning Japan; Yang concerning China; various chapters of McKim Marriott (ed.), *Village India: Studies in the Little Community* (Chicago: University of Chicago Press, 1955), concerning India; and Clifford Geertz, "Form and Variation in Balinese Village Structure," *American Anthropologist*, Vol. LXI (December, 1959), concerning Indonesia. Or see a summary account by Geertz in Chapter 16 below.

of labor rendered, the number of cakes presented at a family occasion, are carefully noted in order that precise reciprocity may be rendered on occasion. But these are matters of building up a treasury of favors due; they are not a contractual exchange. In case of greater need, so that extra services are received, the family may feel an almost unbearable burden of obligation to the village, but the family is never sued. (Worse, however, if unco-operative it may be ostracized.)

One way to put the matter is that the obligations do indeed have the force of contract, but of a contract which is always renegotiable to prevent undue burden. Because the members of the village (or other group) must live in life-long intimate contact in the insecure world, the rigidity of the law and of contract is impossible. The enforcement of a rigid contract which turned out to bear harshly on a village member might endanger social relationships in the village throughout his life and even in coming generations. Similarly the application of rigid rules of civil or criminal law which in the name of uniformity worked inequity on a village member might endanger the structure of relationships on which the village life depends. Hence in the typical traditional society there is no contractual arrangement and there is no legal code. In many traditional societies each case of discontent with regard to an agreement among individuals and each grievance of one individual against another (whether civil or criminal in the Western frame of reference) is decided by the elders, not merely on grounds of equity but also with a keen sense of the relative power and social connections of the parties, the resentments aroused, and the implications for life in the village of the decisions reached. Equity enters primarily because a sense of unnecessary inequity will disturb future village relationships. When consensus has been reached concerning the action which best reconciles the interests involved, the village headman (or clan head) formulates the consensus as his decision, and his authority seals the decision.

It should not be supposed, however, that for the individual family, village interests have priority over its own. In many cultures the family submits to the common village good only if this is the way it can best get along. Village relations are everywhere carefully considered, but they are not everywhere idyllic. Perhaps they are hardly anywhere idyllic except to a casual observer. And in a few societies where the aggressiveness has become dominant, we have an atomistic dog-eat-dog existence with no pretense of group solidarity.[19] Even in cultures where the most scrupulous respect for interpersonal and interfamily relationships appear on the surface, the punctilious mutual considerateness may be a protection against jealousies and hostilities which are so dangerous that care must be taken to avoid giving any provocation. This seems to be the case in Japan; Japanese ritualized politeness is a protection against repressed aggressive-

---

[19] See, for example, Banfield and Banfield, *The Moral Basis of a Backward Society*.

ness. In Mexico the aggressiveness is slightly less carefully concealed. In Redfield's *Tepoztlán: A Mexican Village* one will find a description of near-idyllic village life; but in Oscar Lewis' account in *Life in a Mexican Village: Tepoztlán Restudied* one may note the hostility and rage seething through the same village; and there is little doubt that Lewis' more penetrating tools revealed a lower layer of truth. Sometimes the aggressiveness is still less concealed; consider Yang's picture of the degree to which a Chinese family observes village equities when dealing with other families of equal strength, but rides ruthlessly when it has the power. The account of interfamily relationships in Burma presented in Chapter 8 illustrates similar tensions and similar ruthlessness on occasion.

We must conclude that aggressiveness is basic in personality; that the simple folk of most if not all traditional societies find satisfaction in being aggressive when they dare rather than merely resorting to aggression in case of necessity. All this of course may be unconscious. In the typical instance the villagers probably are not conscious that they have aggressive tendencies.

In such an evironment the extended family is a close-knit defensive-offensive unit in other than economic ways. Each member is a representative of all. Each proper act of an individual casts credit on his family; each wrong act humiliates his family; and an act that offends the village will endanger his family.

The villager vents his aggression more freely outside the village than in it. Though he may feel a sense of national pride when a question of his nation versus others arises, his strong emotional tie is to his community, not his country. A person from outside the village or local group of villages is an alien. In many traditional societies, because he is an alien he is considered dangerous. As an alien he is fair prey for chicanery or robbery, and as a dangerous person he runs the risk of losing not only his property but also his life. This attitude prevailed in eighteenth century England as well as in many societies which come to mind sooner when the term "traditional society" is used.[20] Since there are travelers' accounts of journeying unmolested through strange peasant lands, attacks on strangers are not universal, but the limited social horizon of which they are one type of manifestation is probably nearly so.

The Hierarchy

The extended family is a logical unit for reasons other than the advantages of solidarity.

In the midst of great unknown forces the longest experience is the best guide. Hence it is wise to depend upon the eldest members of the family

---

[20] T. S. Ashton, in *An Economic History of England: The 18th Century* (New York: Barnes and Noble, Inc., 1955), chap. i, notes that a stranger in England was apt to be stoned purely because he was a stranger.

group (and in matters stretching beyond the family, the elders of the village) for advice and decision.

The eldest man rules the family and advises it. He rules an age- and sex-based hierarchy. In probably all traditional societies after the years of infancy, children are expected to accommodate themselves to the convenience of adults to a degree that is not true in any Western society unless it is the German. In many traditional societies, also, sisters submit to brothers and younger boys submit to older ones and in turn dominate their juniors and sisters. This set of family rankings is the base of a hierarchy that extends upward to an apex of authority and status at the top of the society.

The individual's primary loyalty may be to his family (this is the general case); it may be to his clan, as in China; or it may go to the higher hierarchical levels, as in Japan or any ideal feudal system, so that the individual must do what will benefit his lord or emperor (and if his lord or emperor is in danger glories in doing so) even at cost to his family.[21] Even though his primary loyalty is to family or clan, generally the family or clan in turn acknowledges allegiance to persons who are higher in the hierarchy.

The loyalty is more than ceremonial. Between the peasant and his superior in the hierarchical relationship there exists a relationship of mutual obligation. The inferior owes certain obligations to the superior— obligations of rent or taxation, or work and perhaps military service, or of following the superior's guidance in public matters. The superior owes protection, advice, help in emergency, action as judge or magistrate in translocal matters, support of village festivals, and, not least, ritual services such as blessing of the annual festival, service as godfather, and appearance on ceremonial occasions and family occasions of emotional importance. Not all of these obligations hold in any one society, but many of them—and others—do in any society. These are not quantitative exchanges whose magnitudes can be measured and contracted for but a much more diffuse obligational tie. In India this sort of relationship exists not so much between cultivator and landlord as between a member of the lower castes who is not a cultivator and some landlord who serves as his patron.

Rationality, Religion, and Magic

The dependence aspect of the hierarchy extends upward beyond the highest human to the spiritual forces that are seen to control the phenomena of nature. The peasant in the typical society is entirely "rational" insofar as "rationality" does him any good. He understands that there is a best time for planting, a best condition of the soil, the appropri-

---

[21] See Marion J. Levy, Jr., "Contrasting Factors in the Modernization of China and Japan," in S. S. Kuznets, W. Moore, and J. Spengler (eds.), *Economic Growth: Brazil, India, Japan* (Durham, N.C.: Duke University Press, 1955), pp. 496–536, for a discussion of contrasting cases in these two countries by Embree and Yang, respectively.

ate times and methods of irrigation, of cultivation, of harvesting, the best time and places to fish, the best design for a canoe. In all of these matters he exercises with craft, skill, and high rationality a learning accumulated throughout the generations.

But in other matters—storm, drought, the run of fish in the fishing grounds; death of his crops, his cattle, his kin—he knows that no direct actions of his will bring him security or save him from disaster. He knows that events have causes, and he attributes these events, whose causes are forces he cannot see, to the will of unseen forces. By magic or some equivalent he seeks to induce the spiritual forces to befriend rather than harm him. In some cultures great stress is placed on living in harmony with the universe so good may come; in others appeasement or bribing of the spirits is stressed. Whatever the precise approach, in every traditional (and primitive) society the relation to the spirits is important, and the attempt is made through that relationship to control uncertain events that are emotionally important.[22] The magic or equivalent does not control the event (except where the attitudes of the group have a causal influence), but it does serve the function of relieving the anxiety.

The Peasant View of the Social Structure

Just as it does not occur to the peasant that he can influence any of a wide range of phenomena of the physical world that are of great emotional importance to him, so it does not occur to him that the social structure is amenable to change. One should not conclude, however, that he is apathetic, despairing, and sullen. These he often is in the modern world, but the forces that bring him to this state are the forces that have disrupted his traditional society, not the circumstances of that society. In traditional society he seems to take both his physical environment and the social structure as data. Consciously, he neither grieves nor rejoices at them. They are simply there, and natural. He reveres the men who are learned concerning tradition and the invisible world—the humanistic-intellectual man and the religious functionary;[23] honors the elders of

---

[22] Malinowski was the first to note clearly how primitive peoples operate with great skill and rationality in areas where experience teaches them that they can control events by their direct actions, and with magic where they cannot. Other anthropologists and sociologists made explicit that emotional importance of the result is an added condition for the appearance of magic, and Parsons noted carefully that the result will be magic *or its functional equivalent*. See Bronislaw Malinowski, "Magic, Science, and Religion," in Joseph Needham (ed.), *Science, Religion & Reality* (1925), (reprint; New York: George Braziller, Inc., 1955); Talcott Parsons, "The Theoretical Development of the Sociology of Religion," *Essays in Sociological Theory* (rev. ed.; Glencoe, Ill.: Free Press of Glencoe, Inc., 1954); and Robert K. Merton, *Social Theory and Social Structure* (rev. ed.; Glencoe, Ill.: Free Press of Glencoe, Inc., 1957), pp. 32–34.

[23] When the religion has been imposed by invading elite, even though he has made his peace with it by blending his indigenous beliefs and rituals with the observances of the alien creed, his attitude toward religious officials may be rather one of half-

his community and the representatives of indigenous national authority; sees the top elite as in a world far beyond his ken; and respects himself as a peasant.[24] He looks on the statuses of these groups in his society as higher and lower, but also as not merely appropriate but proper. It never occurs to him to think that he might act so as to change things. The world is as it is. He thinks the concept of his trying to change it to be ridiculous, shocking, a little indecent, and immoral.[25]

Authoritarian Personality

The relationships, practices, and beliefs of a society are not accidental. In a society which has continued without basic change for a long time they are always seen to satisfy the purposes and motivations of the members of the society, conscious and unconscious, if only we can find what those purposes and motives are. If the basic elements of social structure and culture do not provide this satisfaction, the society changes.

In traditional society it is surely a mistake to picture the simple folk as held in a condition of grinding misery by the coercive power of the classes above them. This view is not consistent with the great stability of social structure of traditional societies. Powerful elite might hold a large mass of people in hated peonage for a generation or two, but that elite classes could have held their positions by force for centuries and even millennia, as has been true in many traditional societies, is inconceivable. One must conclude that the hierarchical structure of authority and power in traditional societies has been so stable because the simple folk as well as the elite accepted it. The simple folk must feel satisfaction in depending for decisions and direction on individuals above them, in submitting their wills to authority; and, conversely, they must feel uneasy about making judgments or coping with problems on their own initiative. They must feel anxiety in dealing with other persons if the relationship among them is not defined; and they must feel relief when

---

sullen awe and subservience. See Orlando Fals-Borda, *Peasant Society in the Colombian Andes* (Gainesville, Fla.: University of Florida Press, 1955), chap. xiv, pp. 215–30.

[24] Redfield, in *Peasant Society and Culture*, nicely expresses some aspects of this attitude toward his relationship to other classes in his society.

[25] Daniel Lerner comments as follows concerning interviews of Turkish villagers in 1950: "Late in the interview, after each respondent had named the greatest problem facing the Turkish people, Tosun asked what he would do about this problem if he were the president of Turkey. Most responded with stolid silence—the traditional way of handling 'projective questions' which require people to imagine themselves or things to be different from what they 'really are.' Some were shocked by the impropriety of the very question. 'My God! How can you say such a thing?' gasped the shepherd. 'How can I . . . I cannot . . . a poor villager . . . master of the whole world.'" *The Passing of Traditional Society* (Glencoe, Ill.: Free Press of Glencoe, Inc., 1958), p. 24.

James C. Abegglen has reported in conversation the inability of many Japanese factory workers (interviewed in 1955 and 1956) to visualize themselves in any job other than the one they held.

the relationship is defined by the simple rule that one is superior in authority and the other inferior.

Though the reaction of any individual in any society to new situations contains both some element of pleasurable anticipation at the possibility of using his capacities to deal with the situation and some element of anxiety at whether he can do so effectively, individuals differ in the degree to which they feel the one and the other. All persons may be ranged along a continuum with respect to their reaction. To individuals at one end of the continuum most such situations, at least within some one or more areas of activity in which they have chosen to operate, are seen as presenting an opportunity. By applying one's abilities, one may expect to master the difficulty in whole or part and to feel satisfaction at doing so. Hence the individual is drawn to problems.[26] Observing unexpected phenomena, which do not quite fit one's previous understanding of the world, causes a pleasant sense that here is something one can try one's wits on. Such individuals may be creative individuals; this reaction to problems is one of the requisites of creativity.

To individuals at the other end of the continuum almost all situations with new elements which must be dealt with are seen as holding the prospect of failure and frustration, and arouse anxiety. The anxiety of such individuals not only limits their actions; it also limits their awareness of problems. They wear blinders; they fail to see the presence of problems because by not doing so they avoid anxiety. They take the world about them as given and fail to see the possibility of new ways of acting, new modes of coping with the world, because to do so would raise the question whether they can successfully adapt to the new situation, and this would make them anxious.

Most individuals are probably closer to this end of the continuum than to the other. Everyone enjoys small problems in any area of activity familiar to him; but persons whose reaction to the prospect of facing a more difficult problem, one with more unknown elements, is primarily pleasure and includes little anxiety are probably relatively few in any society. But their number varies both among societies and during different eras in the same society. And they are not often found among the simple folk of traditional societies. In traditional societies more than elsewhere individuals feel anxiety in new situations.

The anxiety is avoided or relieved by two types of behavior characteristic of traditional societies. One is reliance on tradition. This indeed is perhaps the main reason why societies in their traditional state are traditional. Within traditional areas of behavior of course problems of skill and decision arise. There are questions of skill and judgment in cultivating, in negotiating in a market, in discussions within a group.

---

[26] He may be a person whose general state is anxiety, so that problem solving merely brings a temporary relief from or lessening of anxiety; or he may be a normally unanxious person to whom problem solving brings positive pleasure.

But these are skills gradually acquired within constricted areas of activity by observation of the elders. Only within those areas does one face problems without anxiety. Village problems may be settled by discussion and consensus among the elders, a process of patient probing of attitudes and consequences. Unless the headman is rash and arbitrary, only when he perceives the consensus does he announce a solution and give it sanction of his authority.

The other method of avoiding anxiety is decision by authority. When the decision of the appropriate authority is prima-facie right unless it flaunts tradition, testing of the goodness of the decision hardly occurs. Only if the decision conspicuously breaks down, will the matter of testing it have to be faced—and then the action will be to replace the authority who has failed by a new individual, by assassination if need be.[27] Questions of interpersonal relationships are also resolved when the relative authority rank of two individuals determines which shall control the contact. (In dealing with strangers relative authority is indeterminate; this is an important reason why the presence of strangers may arouse anxiety and therefore aggression.) Once the hierarchical system was established, it was reinforced by a further reaction. By independent decision, even in petty matters, one aroused anxiety in oneself not only through the process of making a choice oneself but also through one's challenge to the authority of a superior. By referring matters upward one avoids both.

Moreover, one of the corollaries of the rightness of submitting one's judgment to superiors is that it sanctions one's exercise of authority over inferiors. Every individual in the hierarchy of traditional society is aware of the duality of his position. Except in his very youngest days every male, even the son of the humblest peasant, has inferiors, whose number grows as he grows in age and status; and even his sister directs her younger sisters, in due time will become a mother directing a family, and one day will become a mother-in-law to whose wishes, in many traditional societies, her daughter-in-law must bow. If one does feel resentment at being ordered around by one's older brother, one can relieve one's frustration on one's younger brother. And where one has authority one need not be so anxious about the rightness of one's judgment; it is right because one has authority.

Satisfaction in yielding to the judgment and wishes of superiors and satisfaction in dominating inferiors are interwoven in the personality of the simple folk in traditional societies the world over. (We shall inquire presently concerning the members of the elite.) Personalities in which these traits are prominent may be termed authoritarian personalities. We may conclude that the structure of traditional society has lasted

---

[27] In China the ousting of one national dynasty by another was known as "obtaining a new mandate from heaven," a term which conveys considerable information about the culture.

as long as it has because the personalities of the simple folk are authoritarian. We shall find other reasons also.

The fact that authoritarian personality and authoritarian social structure are not chance qualities of traditional societies but parts of a system does not explain their origin. Although anxiety at using one's individual initiative and judgment makes an authoritarian social structure satisfying, we shall see that growing up in an authoritarian environment creates the anxiety. There is complex mutual causation. Rather than stating that one element is a cause and another the effect, we shall see that a number of interlocking functional relationships bring stability. Everything fits.

THE ELITE

Class Structure

At the center of the elite, as I have said, are the possessors of power in the society, the group of individuals who either by ancient conquest, by evolution from tribal chieftainship, or by evolution from feudalism control the country's land and are the recipients of a considerable share of the nation's income. The degree to which they are divided into clans or factions maneuvering or fighting for supremacy—as was the case in western Europe during the Middle Ages and in Japan before 1603—or on the other hand form a single group in control of the country is both a determinant and a result of the degree to which a national state has formed. In some countries of Latin America they seem to live largely separate lives, coming together only to decide the political administration of the country; in other countries they form a more closely knit social group. Some may live primarily on the land, visiting the city only occasionally to transact financial business or to exert political influence; others may live primarily in the city and engage primarily in political manipulation. They may be provincial and ignorant of the world, or educated in the West and widely traveled. In any case, so long as the society remains a traditional one they dominate it. If the country has a Western form of parliamentary government, they compose most of its members and dominate it, as in the Arab countries where they have not been overthrown, in India and Pakistan, and in a number of Latin American countries. They do not necessarily control by force; until new currents blew over traditional lands within the past generation, the elite controlled because the peasant, if he voted in national elections, automatically voted as his patron or his feudal landlord directed.

The Elite View of the World

Many of the elite wear Western clothes, drive Western automobiles, talk of Western art and literature, and to Westerners seem little different from themselves. Indeed, some of them are no longer traditional in their personalities. But in the main the elite of traditional societies, even today, and including those who are sophisticated visitors to Western centers, have values, motivations, a view of the world, and a sense of their identity which differ sharply from those of a typical member of the middle or upper classes of the technologically progressive societies.

In a sense the central elite are all-powerful. Their power, however, depends on their inherited position, not on individual achievement. It is worthwhile to note how greatly their view of the sources and limitations of their power resembles that of the peasantry. The absolute amount of the economic and political power of an individual member of the elite classes is not fixed. He may be able to gain in power at the expense of someone else. However, to each member of the elite this possibility is a threat as well as a promise; and apart from this possibility of shifts of power within the group, life seems greatly dominated by forces beyond their control, just as life does to the peasantry.

The physical environment exercises equally great control over them. Though they are more secure from starvation, their income, being derived from land, depends on the whims of the weather as does that of the peasants. In a sense they are more helpless than the peasants, since at least the peasants have skills which may influence the result somewhat, whereas the elite are barred by their concept of their role in life from paying any active attention to the plebian details of production. Of deeper emotional importance, their lives and those of their family members are as subject to sudden blows from forces that seem arbitrary and capricious; in a traditional society wealth provides no shield against disease and death. The hazard that a child will suddenly be stricken by disease is great for the elite, as it is for the peasantry, for among the causes of death in traditional societies the lack of community sanitation and the presence of malaria, dysentery, and other diseases not respectful of income or status rank high. Even though the incidence of disease is not as high as among the peasantry, the nature of the emotional hazard is the same. And except for the recently Westernized elite, who have some access to modern medicine, the sense that they have no control over whether the disease will cause death is as profound. Indeed, even for the Westernized elite this perception is not much relieved; even in the largest cities of traditional societies, except for the merest handful of doctors, the knowledge of modern medicine may be somewhat superficial.

To a member of the elite, in short, as to one of the simple folk, the phenomena of the physical world are a limiting and threatening force against which he is almost helpless. No more than the peasant does he think that his reason and the logical instrumentalities at his disposal can prevail against them. This is the great contrast between the elite of traditional societies and the middle and upper classes of technologically advanced societies, a contrast which it is difficult for a member of the latter to appreciate fully.

The Elite Sense of Identity: Differentiation from the Simple Folk

A number of other aspects of elite personality are closely related to the elite perception of the nature of the world.

One of these is an intense need of the elite to feel themselves different in essence from the simple folk. An individual must have some justification of his position in life. In a society in which one feels that one can manipulate the world one attains one's position in part by individual achievement. In such a society one can feel that one's superiority relative to someone else is due to a difference in capacity to achieve and is therefore morally defensible.

However, in a society in which one is almost helpless against the world, yet has prerogative and position, one must ascribe his position to some other cause. It is therefore necessary for the elite to feel that in essence—not because of what they can do, but in what they essentially are—they are different from the simple folk. For this reason it is necessary for them to feel repugnance to the distinctive features of the way of life of the simple folk. By feeling repugnance to what the simple folk do and like they persuade themselves that they are different and superior and that their superior status in life is justified.

One distinctive characteristic of the simple folk is that they work with their hands, with tools, and in the process become dirty. As a result, manual-technical labor, any work which soils the hands or clothing, or indeed any "labor" (unless, of course, it is "play"), is repugnant to the elite. Even carrying one's own brief case of papers from one's automobile into one's home when one arrives home from the office seems demeaning to a member of the elite; he has his servant do it. (This is an attitude which colonial administrators reinforced to impress their own class superiority upon the conquered people.) Peasants and craftsmen make physical materials and organisms function. Hence the elite are not interested in their functioning and would find interest in it demeaning and a sign of essential inferiority. The school teacher will find it distasteful, not interesting, to cut a cocoon from a bush and show her children how a butterfly emerges where a worm had sheathed itself. And when a typical member of the elite goes to college, for one reason or another he majors in some field other than engineering. Or, if under the pressure of verbal goals pressed upon him he turns to science or engineering, he will often select a very "pure" branch of science without direct practical application in his home country. He may value mathematics as a purely intellectual exercise.

In the last half-dozen years, in response to the call of governmental and social leaders for more technicians, enrollment in schools of engineering and business has risen sharply in many traditional societies. In part this response to the verbal values of the leaders may be expected to be accompanied by lack of effective academic performance in these fields because of the unconscious aversion I have outlined, but some of the new students are no doubt deviants who can effectively channel their energies into the new fields.

These considerations provide part of the explanation of the attitudes toward economic development of elite leaders in present-day societies that are still largely traditional. The leaders want economic development, for they want power and international respect. But those among them whose traditional attitudes have not been somehow disrupted and replaced in the course of their childhood development want it, so to speak, by magic. That is, they want it to occur because the state issues certain orders and through someone else's management. It is impossible for them to direct their own energies effectively to the management of material enterprises.

Trade and industrial activity have about them the aura of dirty or manual-technical work. Hence the typical member of the elite finds them distasteful. To be the manager of a business enterprise is good since this is a position symbolic of power, as the elite in ex-colonial countries have learned from their Western masters; but holding such a position does not imply any concern with the details of managing the business operations. For a member of the elite to be concerned with these grubby matters would destroy a major source of distinction between himself and the menials and thus threaten his very identity.[28]

With this background it is possible to understand better the attachment of the elite in traditional society to the land. Apparently without exception, in every traditional society there is no status higher than that associated with landed position. Control of land is important because it is a source of security in a perilous world. However, this is not the only tie. The landed life is good because it distinguishes one from the trader and the businessman. Love of the landed life marks one as being of a superior breed. Hence landedness has a value of deep emotional impor-

---

[28] An appropriate though limited comparison is with the attitude of an American of the temperance belt toward the occupation of saloonkeeper. The saloonkeeper in a small town may have double the income of other town businessmen; but it does not occur to them to emulate his occupation; to do so would demean them. To the member of the elite in traditional society all business activity is like saloonkeeping. Or—a case where the associated emotion is more overt—consider the need of the low-income poorly educated white man of the southern United States not to associate with the Negro. The poor white has no sense of achievement to give him emotional security, and his worth therefore depends almost solely on the fact that he is white, not colored, and therefore, as he persuades himself, essentially superior. He therefore maintains a distinction between himself and the Negro with an intensity and desperation that have no rational explanation. (Because he is forced to make a living by the same type of economic activity as the Negro, it is all the more vital to him to distinguish himself in other ways.) It is similarly vital for members of the elite to distinguish themselves from the menials by having a distaste for work with tools or the physical world.

tance even where it is no longer associated with economic security.[29]

Part of the discussion above has referred specifically to the landed elite. But all groups of the elite possess a view of the world which has important elements in common with that of the landed group. Other groups of the elite have supported the landed leaders not because of economic coercion but because their common culture has implanted common values (and a common opposition to change). The bureaucrats, the professionals, and the intellectuals, like the landed, preserve their significance in life by preserving the distinction between themselves and the peasantry. The intellectuals, while they may object to the nepotism and corruption of the ruling group, nevertheless oppose selection and advancement (in public or private affairs) on the basis of achievement; instead they expect appointment of individuals from the "proper" schools and the "proper" groups.

The need of professional personnel and the military to hold values differentiating them from the working class would seem to be less acute than that of the landed groups since their positions depend partly on achievement, not merely on social status. Yet to a considerable extent their position too depends on status. They succeed as professional men not merely because of ability but because of connections. Moreover, growing up in landed families, they absorb landed values. Most of the professionals are sons of the landed elite who have gone into the professions because it is proper to do so, the eldest son having inherited the estate. In the army of traditional societies, as I have noted, the officers are sons of the elite families, serving in the military both because the military life is good and to preserve the class position. Thus in these groups, though there are some variant individuals, most share fully the typical elite view of the world.[30]

The system of values of all elite groups includes qualified approval of humanistic, intellectual, or religious endeavors. These activities are untainted by indirect association with peasant or menial activities; hence there is no bar to considering them good. And there is positive warrant for doing so, for they are the study of the society's traditions, which are good, and of the spiritual forces underlying material phenomena that control destinies. Yet such study is a little queer, also. Perhaps there is unconscious uneasiness because these learned people dare to tinker, at

---

[29] In England even today it is said to be more disgraceful for a young member of the gentry to be a poor horseman than to fail in his college career. For a sympathetic description of this love of horses, incidental to a well-told murder mystery, see Josephine Tey's *Brat Farrar* (London and New York: The Macmillan Co., 1949). Today also, whatever the degree of urbanization, industrial activity, and cosmopolitanism of the elite in developing economies, many of them seem to feel rootless unless they have "a foot on the land."

[30] In recent years, where traditional society is disrupted and for various reasons armies have been expanded much beyond their traditional size, they have become ladders of ascent for able individuals of the nonelite classes. This, however, is a different story.

least in their minds, with the forces that control destinies. At any rate, while an occasional variant individual from the landed class is himself a humanistic-intellectual, or becomes a priest or monk or holy man, he is thereby looked upon as slightly odd even though he is highly respected.

The Elite Sense of Identity: The Role of Authority

Since it is necessary for the members of the elite to believe that they are of essence superior to the classes below them, it follows that positions of authority belong to them by virtue of who they are. Positions of authority are therefore granted in traditional societies not on the basis of the individual's ability to perform—to carry out a new administrative task, conduct a research project, or run a government enterprise well—but on the basis of his status. More accurately, perhaps it is assumed that a member of the elite has capacity to exercise authority that a member of the lower classes lacks. The king's sons and brothers, the relatives of members of his circle, the members of important landed families hold the national offices. In the conventional sociological terms, appointment is on the basis of ascription, not achievement. Today in Iran, in Thailand, in Taiwan, in new African countries where the tribal elite are in power, as in Korea under Rhee, Egypt before Nasser, Iraq before Kassim, office belongs to members of the elite on the basis of their ranking among the elite. To make selections except on the basis of position in the elite would be to question the innate rightness to be elite, to threaten the elite individual's sense of his superior essence without which he can have no justification for being elite. To grant position to a person of social inferiority would be offensive. By definition, such persons do not have the capacity to exercise authority. In ex-colonial countries in which colonial rule disrupted the traditional class structure, and where men of the lesser elite have become the national leaders, their intense need to prove their own eliteness often impels them to follow the same rules.

The use of initiative in resolving an indeterminate situation and the danger that one might be usurping the authority of a superior create anxiety in the members of the elite as well as in the simple folk. Hence even the pettiest questions for whose answer there is no clear precedent, or the handling of which indicates one's authority, will be referred upward and upward to the top official for decision. This tendency will be reinforced by his insistence on receiving them. For where authority is the symbol of one's identity the sharing of authority with one's subordinates constitutes an admission of their equality to one in status and raises a question concerning the rightness of one's status. Ex-colonial peoples sometimes blame the refusal of any but the top officials in their administrative systems to make decisions on precedents established by the colonial rulers, who insisted on concentrating authority in their own hands, but in fact the practice antedated colonial rule, which only coincided with and confirmed it.

The top officials are barred by another of their personality characteristics from using the most efficient method of approaching a decision. Obtaining opinions from one's subordinates, or even analyses of the facts on which to base the decision, might indicate the inadequacy of one's right to authority. Hence the top official will issue an order without staff help, depending on his authority to certify its rightness. Or, if the problem is a new one which makes him too anxious to settle even arbitrarily, it may simply lie on his desk, postponed.

In the traditional system the purpose of giving orders is to indicate one's status as well as to solve a problem or perform a function. In traditional activity, in which one knows the rules that work, the two purposes coincide. But in new activities, where the most effective decision has to be worked out anew, to analyze the problem would be to keep it before one for a period during which anxiety might rise. Further, if the problem is a technological one, one concerned with industry or with trade, then analyzing it has added repugnance. Hence the elite of traditional societies are uniquely unable to function effectively in technological innovation.

Even in a society based on tradition the effective prosecution of some functions must depend on judicious decision, and some way must be found to permit it. The solution worked out in traditional societies is twofold. First, in some spheres of action the constricting anxieties described above do not arise. Individual initiative is exerted, and decisions that are responsive to the problems faced are taken. It was noted above that in the circle of activity in which they have learned traditional skills—the time to plant, the way to cultivate, the time to harvest—the simple folk depend on their own skills, not on authority, to get results. Similarly, within their traditional sphere of activity the members of the elite operate with skill and decisiveness and are relatively free from the anxieties described above. Notable among the activities of which this is true are warfare and some types of governmental administration. But even here, it should be noted, the action is traditional.

Secondly, most traditional societies, struggling with the problem of the need for expertness, have created devices by which exceptions to the rule of ascription may be made. In medieval Europe a commoner might be made a knight for extraordinary service, and a knight promoted in court rank for conspicuous ability in the activities of traditional importance. In Japan the family responsibilities had to go to the eldest son, but a noble might adopt an eldest son if his own was conspicuously incompetent. In ancient Rome, as among some American Indian tribes, an individual might be made the leader of military expeditions on the basis of his prowess rather than his status—but removed from this authority when the fighting ended. (The refusal of Roman generals to be removed was one of the phenomena of the breakdown of the traditional system.)

Absence of Creativity

These, then, are some of the reasons for the relative absence of creative action, especially in technology, in traditional societies. There has always been some creativity in philosophy, literature, the arts, or religion which may have been predominantly the work of variant or deviant individuals, and always some creativity in other fields by individuals who clearly were not deviants. But examination of the history of traditional societies suggests that relative absence of creative activity was usually the case. The history books record predominantly periods of change, of innovation, or creative activity; but close reading reveals in virtually every society centuries or millennia which the history books fail to mention because they were uneventful, interrupted by bursts of activity that merit recording, bursts that I shall later try to explain.

Aggressiveness

Let it be noted, in concluding this discussion of the personalities of the traditional society elites, that their aggressiveness, like that of the simple folk, is typically high. International history is filled with wars and threats of wars, and the internal history of many traditional societies is filled with accounts of physical strife among groups of the elite for power. The argument hardly needs to be presented at length; a minute's reflection will probably convince the reader that a tendency toward aggression, sometimes repressed but always close to the surface, has typically characterized the elite groups of traditional societies (a trait which perhaps does not distinguish them from the elites of modern societies).

CLASS RELATIONSHIPS

The belief by the members of the traditional society in the essential superiority of the elite classes is one side of a coin. Its converse is belief by all classes in the nonimprovability of the simple folk and the fixity of their natural positions in life. Thus social classes are largely closed, and not necessarily by overt barriers. The member of each class simply knows of what class he is a member.

Though there is a certain amount of movement among peasant, artisan, and craftsman-shopkeeper occupations, and between them and the menials, the sons of each group normally expect to follow the occupations of their father. In the extreme cases, movement from any occupation to any other is interdicted.

Historically, this was true by legal decree in Japan and by social custom in the caste system of India and the feudal system of medieval Europe. Although similarly complete formal restrictions on occupational

movement have not received as much historical note as these, they may
have existed elsewhere as well.[31]

Yet almost everywhere in practice there were some exceptions. In
Burma the king might marry a commoner girl who caught his eye, and
with cunning and luck her son might become the next king. Receiving
knighthood for some extraordinary service or deed of value might bring
a rise in rank in medieval Europe, and adoption might do so in feudal
Japan. And so on. In China it was possible for a peasant family which
gained some wealth, perhaps through nonagricultural activity such as
trading, to buy its way into the landed gentry, and some movement
into and out of the gentry may have gone on at all times. In societies
where landownership by peasants existed, or was possible *de facto* whatever the legal presumption, a number of lesser economic elite or super-
peasants emerged. The kulaks of Russia, the individuals termed "big
peasants" or "wealthy peasants" in Tokugawa Japan, and some of the
yeomen of medieval England are examples. But it is doubtful that many
individuals in any traditional society moved upward from these positions
to become members of the true elite.

Historically, for individuals of either the elite or the simple folk who
were deviant in personality there were special career channels. Thus a
member of the nonelite classes, as well as a member of the elite, who
possessed exceptional interest might become a monk or holy man, and
if he also possessed exceptional capability and luck he might in other
countries become a priest. (In Burma every young man spent a rainy
season in a monastery, but this temporary acceptance of the role was
quite different from permanent monkhood.) With the same qualities, he
might possibly become a learned man; in many societies the career of
learned man was one variety of career as monk or priest. In China, for
the exceptional low-class individual who attracted such attention that a
career of learning was made available to him, a civil service career was
open. Entrance was based on erudition in the classic writings. These
channels for variance or deviance, however, were not a bridge into the
permanent elite. Typically, the careers in religious office implied
celibacy; indeed, sexual deviance or variance was one of the characteristics which led an individual into such careers. In any case, they carried
with them no inheritance of position.

Because his sense of identity depends so wholly on his position—because he sees no other evidence of his worth but his position in life—
a member of the elite feels a deep moral imperative to preserve that
position for himself and his family and next for his larger group. To preserve the status of his primary group, he may appropriate resources
which according to Western values belong to the nation. The corruption
and nepotism which the Westerner may criticize in a peasant society is

---

[31] J. S. Furnivall in *Colonial Policy and Practice* (Cambridge, Eng.: The University Press, 1948), p. 15, notes such restrictions in pre-British Burma.

the expression of this moral duty of the elite to his kin, his clan, and his class. The nepotism and corruption of the Chiang Kai-shek regime while it was in power in China, the corruption now being reported in the Congress party administration in India, the traditional financial performance of rulers in the Near East, the filching of the nation's wealth by the dictators or oligarchs of Latin America are all examples of this aspect of the culture of traditional society elite. They derive from the circumstances of the society as naturally as the more universalistic principles of Western society result from the conditions and history of the West.

The position of members of the elite is indeed frequently under some threat. Within the elite groups powerful individuals may not regard their place as fixed. The constraints on their aggressiveness are fewer than those which inhibit the simple folk, who must live in continuing face-to-face contact with each other. Elite aggressiveness therefore more often is unleashed; among the members of the elite there may be bitter competition for political and military power. Among the *daimyos* of Japan, the warlords of China, the feudal lords of medieval Europe, and probably the group possessing top economic and political power in most other peasant societies, conflict to force the allegiance of neighboring lords, enlarge one's territorial control, and ultimately gain national hegemony was frequent. When it was not occurring, it was always latent. Indeed, the national states of western Europe emerged as one or another lord was able to gain power ascendancy over all other lords (and became permanent as he gained not merely the acquiescence but also the loyalty of lesser nobles and the simple folk). In these struggles for power, or in measures by the dominant elite to prevent its displacement, might lie the seeds of social tensions that could lead to basic social change.

RECAPITULATION

In summary, societies in their traditional state are dual or in a sense triple societies; they consist of the peasantry and other simple folk, the elite classes, and, at one side, the trader-financiers.

The image of the world of the simple folk and elite classes alike includes a perception of uncontrollable forces around them that restrict and dominate their lives. The simple folk find protection from the material dangers in mutual aid within face-to-face groups and in dependence on elite individuals with whom they are related by material and symbolic bonds. The members of the elite find protection in their economic resources and their ability to levy (not necessarily by force) on the simple folk who owe allegiance to them. The lines of dependence extend upward to the spiritual powers, to whom the members of the society appeal for protection against the physical forces; in the appeal they gain relief from their anxieties.

The simple folk and the elite alike are aggressive. Interpersonal relationships whose nature is not clear are therefore dangerous; hence strangers are dangerous and may be attacked. Within the community the simple folk avoid the release of their aggression, which would endanger community life, by careful adherence to traditional relationships that provide for mutual accommodation. Moreover, each individual finds his place in the authoritarian hierarchy of human relationships. Conflict is obviated by submission to persons of superior status and domination of inferiors.

Domination over inferiors, like attack on aliens, also permits each individual to vent his aggressiveness. Even the lowliest peasant child may look forward to the exercise of dominance, increasing throughout his life as he attains the roles of older brother, father, and elder. Hence the simple folk find satisfaction in both submissiveness and domination; their personalities as well as those of the elite are authoritarian.

And members of both groups, fearing the world and fearing to attack its problems, preferring to avoid the issue of the rightness of solutions by letting them depend on authority, are by virtue of these characteristics uncreative.

In their values the members of the elite and the simple folk differ. The elite, needing to feel superior in essence to the simple folk to justify the privileged positions to which they are born, learn tastes which differentiate them from the simple folk, and in those tastes they see proof of their superiority. One element of these tastes is repugnance to manual labor, work with tools, or interest in the processes of the physical world, a repugnance which extends to all commercial and industrial work. Another is love of the landed life. They perceive also, as an element in their superior identities, the rightness of their greater authority. It follows that delegating authority, that is, sharing it with subordinates, is equivalent to sharing with them one's status, one's essential superiority. Thus in addition to their lack of creativity, the sense of identity of the elite creates peculiarly stubborn barriers to technological progress.

In these societies, except for struggles within the class of the elite itself, class relationships are fixed. Since the lower classes are of essence inferior, of course there is no way in which they can merit eliteness. But this class rigidity does not create a perception by the simple folk that they are bound or imposed upon, for they like both the avoidance of problems which the authoritarian hierarchy permits and the release of aggression which their own petty hierarchy of authorities permits. Traditional social structure persists because it is satisfying to all concerned. But some threat to its continuance lies in the struggles for power among the elite.

APPENDIX: DEFINING SOCIETIES

What are the basic characteristics by which one distinguishes one type of society from another? Sociologists describe the social structure of a society (the relationships among the individuals and groups of the society), anthropologists its culture (what the individuals and groups know, believe, and do), and social and clinical psychologists the personalities of its members (perhaps mainly their values, motivations, and the images they carry in their heads of what the world is like). All three take into account the physical environment, including the man-made artifacts possessed by the society's members. To a considerable degree, the facts by which the three disciplines characterize societies are the same facts seen from different viewpoints. The individual's image of what the world is like, plus his concepts of what he should and should not do, constitute what he knows and believes, that is, his culture. This culture, plus the nature of the physical environment, including the man-made material instruments of the society and the distribution of control over them, provide information from which one can deduce rather completely the relationships among individuals and groups, that is, the social structure. One can also deduce the values and motivations and images of the world of the members of the society. Conversely, if one knows what these physical circumstances of the society are, and the relationships among the individuals and groups, one knows or can deduce rather completely the culture of the society and the values and motivations and images of the world of its members. So also the society may be almost completely described purely in terms of values and motivations of its members and their beliefs concerning the nature of the world, plus the physical circumstances. From these one knows the culture and can deduce the social structure. I suggest that if the society is not changing, that is, is in equilibrium, then any one of the three descriptions provides sufficient information to permit deduction of the other two; specifying the other two is redundant. If, knowing the physical environment of a society in equilibrium including its man-made instruments and the distribution of control over them, plus any one of the three—personalities, culture, and social structure—an analyst cannot fully deduce the other two, this is not because there is any indeterminacy remaining, but merely because he does not yet understand sufficiently the principles which govern human behavior. No social scientist does, but the general nature of the interrelationships among social structure, culture, and personality are rapidly becoming clearer. In a society undergoing a process of secular change, information about one or more of the three elements in a previous period or periods will be necessary.

Similarly, a carefully selected set of facts including partial specification of personality plus partial specification of culture plus partial specification of social structure, or partial specification of any two, may provide a complete description of a society in equilibrium.

Also, because of the considerations indicated above, to refer to the structure and functioning of a society in equilibrium is redundant. If one knows either fully, one can deduce the other fully. However, because the assertions of this note are not yet fully accepted (or perhaps fully understood) by some social scientists, I have used both words in the text above to avoid ambiguity.

Innovational and Authoritarian Personalities

chapter 5

THE INTERRELATIONSHIPS BETWEEN PERSONALITY AND social structure are such as to make it clear that social change will not occur without change in personalities. We can more readily analyze changes in the personality type that is typical in traditional societies, authoritarian personality, if we probe that personality type further. We may understand it better if we delineate a contrasting case.

In discussing social change, Riesman has described tradition-directed and autonomous individuals, and in exploring the problems of colonial control Mannoni has referred to personalities dominated by a dependency complex and an inferiority complex respectively.[1] In the discussion below, the reader familiar with Riesman and Mannoni will be reminded of both pairs of contrasts, but neither seems to me to delineate fully the contrasting personality types that are typical of traditional and creative societies respectively. Hence instead of using the terminology of either author, I shall refer to "authoritarian" and "innovational" personalities.

I am using the term "innovational personality" rather than "creative personality" since the latter seems less descriptive. It will be well to begin the discussion by making clear the relationship between creativity and innovation.

CREATIVITY AND INNOVATION

Innovation consists of organizing reality into relationships embodying new mental or aesthetic concepts, the new relationships serving the purpose of the innovator better than the old. Analytically, and also in time sequence, innovation involves two steps: arriving at a new mental conception, and converting it into action or into material form.[2]

---

[1] David Riesman, *The Lonely Crowd* (New Haven, Conn.: Yale University Press, 1950), and O. Mannoni, *Psychologie de la Colonisation* (Paris, Ed. du Seuil, 1950), translated into English by Pamela Powesland as *Prospero and Caliban: The Psychology of Colonization* (New York: Frederick A. Praeger, Inc., 1956).

[2] The concept can hardly be put into overt form until after it has been conceived. The act of conception may be unconscious, however, and the innovator may not

In technological innovation the second step may involve only design or rearrangement of some items of physical equipment or it may involve the organization of a group of human beings into a going concern that carries out a new concept. In the latter case it is entrepreneurship; the concept of entrepreneurship seems always to include the management of other human beings.

In the limiting case the process consists of the first step alone; the individual may solve a problem mentally without any overt action. Perhaps the mathematician most closely approaches this limit, his only material craftsmanship being that of writing down his concepts. In technical innovation, however, putting flesh on the idea is of the essence of the process.

Arriving at the new conception may be termed the creative act, and sometimes the term "innovation" is reserved for the second step.[3] However, the implication that putting flesh on the concept is not creative is illusory, for a concept of new productive equipment or a new method of organization of human beings is hardly complete when it is only an idea in the mind. The purely mental concept probably virtually never anticipates correctly all the properties the human or physical material will exhibit when it is being reshaped. Creative adjustment and revision will be necessary as the idea is worked out overtly. Sometimes, of course, the further creativity required is very little. I have suggested that in the adaptation of Western technical methods to optimum use in underdeveloped economies it is great.

There is no such thing as innovation in the abstract. Innovation is always innovation in some specific field, involving some specific materials or concepts, or relationships of some sort to other persons. Some types of innovation will involve overcoming resistances by other persons; others will not. Some will involve managing a large organization; others, working in isolation. Some will involve experiencing smells or dirt; others will not. Some will have an aura of learned or sacred activity; others of practical work. And so on. An individual will enjoy one or another type of activity or relationship in the degree to which its various aspects satisfy his various attitudes. An individual will not innovate in a sphere in which, on balance, he finds dissatisfaction in working. Thus, in addition to creativity, attitudes favorable to working in one or another field are necessary for innovation in that field. In the present chapter I shall discuss

---

know that he has arrived at a new concept until he has produced a new artifact or a new organization. Conceivably, also, the innovator may arrive at a new result by trial and error, and only when he sees the results analyze the operation and realize the relationships responsible for the results. The statement in the text ignores this case.

[3] Either the first step or both may also be termed "problem-solving." Insofar as a problem has been solved previously and one merely repeats a known solution, one's activity is not problem solving. But any activity, mental or overt, that is not purely random is problem solving in some degree. Even walking down a familiar street involves some new elements. Innovation or creative activity, more strictly defined, is performing activity that involves problem solving in a high degree.

the general characteristics of creativity at some length and pay only brief attention to the added characteristics of personality that cause creativity to be exercised in one field rather than another.

INNOVATIONAL PERSONALITY

The Quality of Creativity

When it is stated that innovation requires creativity, the reader should not assume that the term "creativity" refers to genius. Creativity exists in varying degrees; the man who conceives of an improvement in a can opener as well as the man who conceives of the theory of relativity is creative. Technological progress results from the actions of men characterized by varying degrees of creativity. The discussion of creativity refers, therefore, not merely to the limiting case of genius but to the quality of creativity in general, in whatever degree it may be found in a given individual.

The major qualities that constitute creativity are easy to list imprecisely: openness to experience, and, underlying this, a tendency to perceive phenomena, especially in an area of life that is of interest to the individual, as forming systems of interacting forces whose action is explainable; creative imagination, of which the central component is the ability to let one's unconscious processes work on one's behalf; confidence and content in one's own evaluations; satisfaction in facing and attacking problems and in resolving confusion or inconsistency; a sense that one has a duty or responsibility to achieve; intelligence; energy; and, often, related to several of these, a perception that the world is somewhat threatening and that one must strive perpetually if one is to be able to cope with it. The type of creative personality that is driven by a sense that the world is threatening sometimes seems to belong to a different category from the person characterized by some of the other qualities listed. I shall discuss first the ideal or pure type of unanxious creative person, and then indicate how the sense of living in a threatening world qualifies the characteristics described.

Poincaré has suggested the "capacity to be surprised" and Carl R. Rogers "openness to experience" as essential to creativity.[4] I would judge that the meaning of the two is almost identical. What is referred to is an unconscious alertness that leads the individual to note that some aspect of an everyday phenomenon differs from the expected and to appreciate the significance of the difference. This is the capacity that leads an individual to note that, contrary to the body of scientific authority in his time and

---

[4] Poincaré's phrase is quoted by Erich Fromm in Harold H. Anderson (ed.), *Creativity and Its Cultivation* (New York: Harper & Bros., 1959), p. 48. "Scientific genius," said Poincaré, "is the capacity to be surprised." Rogers' phrase is in *ibid.*, p. 75. Several essays in this interesting volume are pertinent to the present discussion.

the conclusions of common sense, bodies fall at the same rate regardless of their weight if air resistance is the same; to have his curiosity aroused by the fact that iron filings adhere to a coil of wire as an electrical current passes through it; to observe that some men with paralyzed limbs handle them in ways that suggest that the paralysis of function begins at a point at which there is no physiological reason for it to begin—to note such a thing and say to himself, "What an interesting force must have caused that! I wonder what its implications are."

Basic to this quality of observation is assurance in one's own evaluation of experience, freedom from a tendency to take a generally accepted evaluation for granted and overlook facts inconsistent with it. Basic to it also is a tendency to assume that one can understand experience. The creative individual has a sense, deeper than any rational acceptance of cause and effect, that the world is orderly; that every phenomenon of life or of some large area of experience is part of a system whose operation can be understood and explained; that if he approaches the sphere of life in which he is interested it will respond dependably, even though perhaps in a complex fashion, so that if he has enough information he will be able to understand the response. If the world were not orderly, or if the individual were not confident and content in his ability to understand its order, he would not be unconsciously alert to unexpected aspects of phenomena, for they would contain no lessons for him.

Openness to experience, then, refers to a capacity to note phenomena that are starting points for new analyses. Creative imagination refers to a tendency to leap far afield from a starting point, to note relationships where others had not thought to find them. In part it is the product simply of superior innate intelligence, of a mind which can hold many factors in simultaneous consideration and analysis. But it is more than this. It embraces two kinds of mental activity. One is the capacity to use an interesting or unsatisfactory situation as a springboard from which one's imagination roams, apparently uncontrolled and seemingly undirected, in varying associational bypaths, regressions, and far reaches, then returns to the matter at hand either with a workable conception for the reconstruction or transformation of the unsatisfactory situation or with a novel analytical model of the significance of the observed fact. Conscious movement from one step of analysis to the next is at a minimum; the individual does not ask consciously whether the wandering is pertinent to the problem.

The other is the capacity to let one's purely unconscious processes work for one without any conscious awareness or acknowledgment of the activity and to admit the results to consciousness. Unaware that his mind has been working on the problem, the individual finds that a solution, an appropriate ordering, an explanation has come to him. Visualization occurs as he wakes from sleep, when he has been daydreaming, on rare occasions in a dream while sleeping, or perhaps while he walks his dog. "It came to me," the scientist sometimes says, or, "As the problem returned to my mind, I saw how it could be done." Subsequently he demonstrates to himself the logic of the solution. The solution was presumably reached by a sequence of logical steps or chain or association of thoughts (how else could it have been reached?), but these were unconscious, or, sometimes, in more precise psychological terminology, preconscious.

Such creative imagination is often stressed as a part of literary or, more generally, aesthetic creativity. But there is ample evidence from biographies of scientists that it is important in their creative achievement also.[5] There is less evidence concerning strictly technological creativity, but it is reasonable to suppose that this is because of absence of documentation rather than because of a difference in the creative process.

These two aspects of creative imagination have two important elements in common: the unconscious processes of the individual are productive rather than distractive in nature, and the individual is unafraid or little afraid of them. The aspect of a problem that some individuals react unconsciously to is a sense of frustration at not having an answer at hand. As a defense against that sense of frustration, the individual, if he lets himself go, experiences fantasies of magic achievement, crushing victories over persons who have slighted him, sexual conquest, the attainment of position so high that all of his wishes are gratified, and the like. Even if he does not let himself go, such fantasies occur in his unconscious processes. The unconscious processes of some individuals, on the other hand, react to the substance of a problem or surprising phenomena at hand, and aid in logical and imaginative analysis of it. When the individual "floats," his mind rearranges elements of thought in bold ways but ways which, when he returns to the details of reality, are fruitful. Every individual responds in some degree in both ways. Creative individuals are those who primarily respond productively.

The individual who responds with unacceptable fantasies may shut them out from his conscious mind, but he senses dimly the emotional surges within him and fears what is going on in his unconscious. Finding impulses in himself which he regards as evil or foul or dangerous, he is afraid of letting his unconscious processes come to the surface for fear that dangerous or evil or vile urges will appear. Hence his unconscious processes are not only primarily unproductive; even insofar as they are productive, they are unavailable to him. The results do not appear in his conscious mind. The creative individual, on the other hand, is not afraid of his unconscious processes, and their results appear in his conscious

---

[5] An interesting brief discussion of its presence in scientists is presented by Professor Donald W. MacKinnon of the Institute of Personality Assessment and Research of the University of California, in a paper delivered at a convention of the Western Branch, American Public Health Association, at San Francisco, June 2–5, 1959, which I have from him in mimeographed form.

mind. In the technical terms of psychoanalysis, he can "regress in the service of the ego."[6]

More than other individuals, he understands his unconscious motivations.[7] It is commonly recognized that ability to understand one's unconscious motivations is an important element in artistic and especially literary creativity; one understands others and can portray them only to the degree that one understands oneself. It is less well recognized that the same understanding of self may be conducive to understanding of the physical world as well. The man who understands something of his unconscious motivations understands his interaction with phenomena outside him as a system in which there is causality. He is self-conscious; he watches his own behavior as an observer. This understanding seems to be the model for the individual's perception of the external world as a system and subject to analysis, the perception which gives him openness to experience, which makes him wonder creatively why some everyday phenomenon is as it is.

Such an individual is somewhat detached from himself and from his society. To some degree all that goes on is something he watches from the outside. This detachment seems to be an integral part of creativity. It does not imply lack of interest in the world or of concern about it. In fact, it is often peculiarly associated with a sense of moral obligation, of responsibility for society and the world, to be discussed later.

This sense of detachment has often been observed in creative workers in science as well as in literature and art. It must also be associated with technological innovation. It is difficult to see how any person can manipulate the world about him, put its elements together in new ways to obtain new order, except as he sees it as a system outside himself, detached from himself. Even the tinkerer who merely improves a machine must see the machine as a system to be analyzed rather than simply taking it for granted as an instrument if he is to be free to conceive of changes in it. The business administrator, whose function is to manipulate other men, often gives little overt evidence of this detachment; yet his understanding of how other men function is evidence of such understanding of himself, which again is a symptom of this detachment.

Because the creative individual assumes that the world will respond dependably to his judicious initiative, he does not feel threatened by unresolved situations. He has no need to turn to the judgment of others for reassurance or relief from anxiety, for the facing of unresolved situations

---

[6] Ernst Kris, *Psychoanalytical Explorations in Art* (New York: International Universities Press, 1952).

[7] Which include passive, so-called "feminine" needs, needs to be dependent and to be nurtured, needs for aesthetic gratification. These needs are greater in him, as measured by psychological tests, than in the average person. Professor Donald W. MacKinnon, *op. cit.*, discussed relevant research at the Institute of Personality Assessment and Research.

arouses little anxiety within him. He trusts his own evaluations of them. His "locus of evaluative judgment" is within himself.[8] This does not mean that he is always sure that he is right, but only that he does not have anxiety about his own observations and evaluations. Knowing that the comments of others may suggest new avenues of approach or added relationships in a complex problem which has no one solution, he may turn to them, but as instruments to help him, not for reassurance.

He feels satisfaction at the prospect of testing his capacities against a problem and is drawn toward the attempt. If the solution does not readily appear, and the problem is of relevance to his interests, it remains a matter on a shelf in his mind, and he will anticipate the possibility of realizing a solution later.

Because he is not afraid of problems or of the world, he has a tolerance for recognizing apparently contradictory or discrepant facts. He will not unconsciously and conveniently ignore one of them because the discrepancy alarms him. But, because he perceives the world as orderly, he assumes that two discrepant facts, both having been verified as true, are not really contradictory but are part of a higher order whose nature he does not yet realize. Their apparent inconsistency, like any problem, is therefore a challenge to him, and he feels satisfaction in seeking a higher order within which they will both rest comfortably. He feels a need to place them in a logical or pleasing relationship. Too simple order is uninteresting and somewhat unpleasant to him.[9] He may have some fondness for disorder and conflicting logic since they suggest to him that a higher order is available.

As his experience and confidence in his ability grow, he will lose interest in simpler problems and will seek to attack more and more difficult ones, or sometimes merely different ones. The former trend is manifested by a painter who as his career proceeds passes from simple symmetry to balance of colors and forms so complex that the picture is confusing to the novice but brings the greatest aesthetic pleasure to the individual whose comprehension has grown until he can appreciate it, and the latter in a painter who moves from simple realism to impressionism to expressionism toward abstraction, as Rembrandt did. It is also readily noticeable in the other arts and in literature. In business the process is one of moving up the ladder to positions which are more difficult as well as more responsible.

In mathematics the peak of creativity usually comes early; almost all of the great mathematicians made their most original contributions before the age of thirty, whereas in some other fields creative activity

---

[8] Carl R. Rogers, in *Creativity and Its Cultivation*, p. 76.

[9] This is indicated by studies at the Institute for Personality Assessment and Research of the University of California of individuals from the arts and sciences whose careers demonstrate a high degree of creativity. See Frank Barron, "The Psychology of Imagination," *Scientific American*, Vol. CXCIX (September, 1958), pp. 150–66.

reaches its peak later in life. The difference seems to be associated with some degree of difference in the locus of the creative process. In mathematics the immediate creative act is more largely unconscious; the new concept presents itself to the conscious mind in largely finished form; whereas in many other fields a greater element of conscious judgment enters. Perhaps almost no one has within him more than one great new view of the world. In a field unrelated to the complex facts of life, one in which abstract logical relationships alone constitute the materials, one may encompass the known logic and realize his new view in his twenties. Then, his mind being drawn thereafter to the area which proved so satisfying, he spends the rest of his life tidying up and making minor advances here and there. However, in fields in which the complex details and relationships of real life are pertinent to the creative act, accumulation of knowledge by strengthening the basis for judgment provides increasing grist for one's unconscious (as well as conscious) processes to work on as the years pass, and creativity matures later in life.

The innovator not only feels pleasure in solving problems; he also feels a duty to achieve. The avowed goal of economic innovators, the purpose which they have felt it their duty to serve, has varied greatly among societies, but the sense of duty is a constant. Often this sense is religious in nature. The doctrine that the specific religious dogma of the Protestant Dissenters is peculiarly associated with innovational activity is obsolete,[10] but a number of scholars observing economic growth in various societies have noted that innovators in the early stages of growth seem to be characterized by a common ethic which is appropriately termed religious in nature, whatever their religious dogma. They feel a personal responsibility to transform the world that far transcends a profit motive.

To these qualities should be added intelligence and energy.[11] Intellectual capacity is in part inherited, and no doubt innate capacity is higher among innovators than among the population in general. In part, however, the intellectual capacity of innovators is due to the qualities described above. An individual with a given intellectual endowment will use it the more effectively the greater the degree to which he perceives the world as an orderly system, the greater his contentedness in his own judgment and reactions, the greater his satisfaction in attacking problems or in resolving inconsistencies, and the less the degree to which his energy has to be used to suppress unacceptable impulses within himself. The person with lack of these attitudes toward the world will be inhibited from attempting to use his capacities. But these attitudes are not simply the products of high innate intelligence; they derive primarily from conditions

---

[10] Perhaps it never was held by scholars. Max Weber in *The Protestant Ethic and the Spirit of Capitalism*, trans. Talcott Parsons (New York: Charles Scribner's Sons, 1956), at times seems to argue this thesis but then backs away from it.

[11] For an analysis of leading American business executives which stresses their energy, see Osborn Elliott, *Men at the Top* (New York: Harper & Bros., 1959).

of the individual's environment as he grows up, and especially in childhood, that are quite independent of his innate capacities.

Much the same factors determine the individual's level of energy. No doubt there are innate or, more broadly, constitutional determinants of energy just as there are of intelligence. The individual who is constitutionally endowed with an ampler than average reserve of energy stands a better than average chance of accomplishing creative deeds. But to a large degree the ability to draw on a great store of energy seems to depend on an individual's freedom from doubt and mistrust of himself, on his sense that the world is orderly and will respond dependably and pleasingly to his initiative. It is as though, not having to use his energy in conflicts within himself, he has it available to direct toward the world outside him.

The creative individual is not necessarily a happy man who faces problems with pure pleasure. Rather, most creative individuals are driven to creative activity by an incessant anxiety; their perception of the world as a threatening place leaves them only while they are active, then returns to drive them on again. Yet in other individuals anxiety is associated with rage that provokes urges and fantasies which persist in the unconscious and cause an individual to seal over his unconscious processes for fear of what he will find in them. (The anxiety is also largely unconscious; if questioned, the individual would probably deny its existence.) The two types of personality must be distinguished.

An individual acquires persisting anxiety if in his early life he faces a sequence of situations important to him that he cannot resolve satisfactorily or can resolve satisfactorily only by repeated attempts and with great difficulty—hunger, pressure on him to walk, and so on. The anxiety-creating situations may, however, be of two types which convey to the child differing perceptions of the world. He may become anxious because persons important to him, for example, his mother, seem willing to hurt him. If so, combined with his anxiety will be rage directed at her and fantasies of revenge. However, he must suppress these from consciousness since his mother is so important to him that he dares not admit that he hates her. He then seals over his unconscious processes, and their inaccessibility to him prevents him from being creative, or greatly cripples his creativity.

Suppose, however, that his experiences of infancy and early childhood give him a firm and satisfying impression of the loving nurturance of his mother, but that repeatedly he is unable to achieve as she seems to wish him to. He may then feel that the fault must lie in him, and there may become built into him anxiety that he may not accomplish enough, anxiety that drives him all his life to achieve in order to regain fleetingly that temporary feeling of security conveyed by his mother's praise and caresses. In this case, little rage and hatred may be provoked in him, and his unconscious processes will remain accessible to him. Given the other necessary qualities, he becomes the anxious creative individual.

Of course the perceptions sketched here as arising from his relationship to his mother may arise also in relationships to other persons important to him in early life.

He may not be quite as open to experience as the unanxious creative individual because he is more fearful of experience. The accessibility of his unconscious processes to him may be somewhat less than to the unanxious individual, since the tensions of his childhood may have caused some reactions in him which were fearful or unacceptable and had to be repressed permanently. But these handicaps to creativity are compensated for by his incessant scanning of the horizon and by the great energy which he is incessantly driven to exert in defense against his anxieties.

Indeed, innovational activity is always a reaction to some degree of anxiety. The individual who is not in the least pushed toward creative activity as a relief from anxiety but is only drawn toward it by the great pleasure it gives him is an ideal case; he does not exist in life. Creativity does not require complete access to one's unconscious processes, complete confidence in one's own judgment, and so on. It requires only somewhat more of these qualities than characterizes the average person. Moreover, some types of innovation may require only a moderate degree of creativity combined with dogged determination or a high degree of motivation to dominate other men. Thus the characteristics of creativity described may not be high in some economic innovators. Often, however, they are greater than appears on the surface, especially since in business it is often desirable to keep one's inner life to oneself and to cast an image of oneself as a highly conventional extrovert.

The Determinants of the Innovational Field

The discussion to this point has referred only to creativity in general. However, an individual is never creative in general; he is creative in some specific activity or activities. His being attuned to one or another sort of activity is therefore an element in his creativity.

Perhaps we may think of the characteristics which channel and release creativity into one field or another as being of three types: one's values concerning activities, one's anxieties or satisfactions in relationships with other men, and the scale of activity or influence in which one feels content or secure.

Perhaps there is, first of all, a rather direct attachment to one activity or another. In some sense an individual may enjoy for its own sake tilling the soil or tinkering with machinery or contemplating mathematical relationships. Second, one may have one or another attitude toward relationships with other men. One may find satisfaction in competition with them; the act of inner or outer aggression may give one pleasure or temporarily relieve one's anxiety. Or one may find a sense of security in being able to influence other men by one's logic or persuasiveness or in gaining a position of control over them. Or on the contrary one may feel uneasy in any close competition or co-operation with other men and may turn toward working in isolation. In combination these characteristics plus the alternatives objectively open to him will determine the occupation in which a man chooses to work. Third, if one is characterized by a drive to influence or direct other men, he may be content to do so on a small scale or, on the other hand, he may feel that he has not sufficiently proved himself or made himself secure so long as there are wider groups against which he has not tested himself. One may therefore be content to work in his own pond—perhaps intellectually or technically or socially a very important pond—or one may be driven to seek national influence in his profession or in society as a whole and reform all society.

The choice of technology as a field in which to innovate of course requires one or another of certain combinations of these attitudes. It was noted in Chapter 4 that the sense of identity of a member of the elite classes in traditional society makes him unable to function effectively in work which he associates with the menial classes. In general, the authoritarian personality of traditional society is uncreative. If, however, a deviant individual of the elite classes became creative, he would nevertheless be unable to innovate in technology so long as he retained the elite antipathy to manual labor, work with tools and machinery, and interest in the physical world.[12]

In recapitulation, then, the creative individual is unconsciously alert to new aspects of phenomena; he assumes that the phenomena of the area of experience of interest to him form a system that he can understand and manage, and that therefore encountering unexpected aspects will lead him to new understanding, not to frustration. He responds imaginatively to the stimuli that new observations provide; his unconscious mental processes deal with the substance of the problem rather than reacting to a sense of frustration with angry or aggressive fantasies or fantasies of magic solutions. And since he does not fear the content of his unconscious processes, their results are available to his conscious mind. He observes with detachment his own interactions with the world outside him; his recognition that both the reactions of the world to him and his reactions to the world have understandable causes, that he himself is a system, is probably the basis of his assumption that the larger world is orderly and understandable. He trusts his evaluations of the world. The prospect of resolving a problem therefore attracts him; he approaches rather than evades it. Many effective innovators are oppressed by a pervasive anxiety concerning life. Their anxiety, however, is not the result of conflicting urges whose balance creates paralysis; rather, it is a gnawing feeling that they are not doing enough, or not well enough. Repeatedly, they escape from their anxiety temporarily by crea-

---

[12] Of course the same forces in his immediate environment which caused him to become deviant in ways that made him creative would probably also impinge on some of these attitudes.

tive achievement. Effective innovators also typically feel a sense of duty to achieve.

AUTHORITARIAN PERSONALITY

Against the foil of this description of creative personality, it is possible to enrich the discussion of authoritarian personality presented in Chapter 4, for many characteristics of authoritarian personality are simply the negatives of characteristics of the creative individual. For that reason they may be outlined in a few paragraphs. Authoritarian personality is not the only type of uncreative personality; what is described here briefly is not uncreative personality in general but one specific type.

One gains an understanding of most of the facets of authoritarian personality if one assumes that as a child the authoritarian individual acquired no perception of the phenomena around him as elements in systems whose operation is amenable to analysis and responsive to his judicious initiative. Instead he must have gained two other impressions of the world that were overwhelmingly important in disciplining his later behavior. One of these is a perception of the world as arbitrary, capricious, not amenable to analysis, as consisting of an agglomeration of phenomena not related by a cause-and-effect network. The other is that the caprice of the world is not accidental but the play of willful powers far greater than his which serve their own purposes and disregard his unless he submits his will to theirs. These perceptions, we must assume, because the experiences which gave rise to them were very painful, have been pressed down out of his conscious mind; but he retains them in his unconscious, and they guide his adult behavior.

These perceptions breed in him a fear of using his initiative, an uncertainty concerning the quality of his own judgment, a tendency to let someone else evaluate a situation in order to avoid frustration and anxiety. Out of these perceptions also grows uneasiness at facing unresolved situations. Rather than rely on his own analysis to solve problems of the physical world or his relations to other individuals, he avoids pain by falling back on traditional ways of behavior that his parents and other earlier authorities taught him, and by relying on the judgment or will of individuals superior to him in authority or power.

To an individual guided by such perceptions it would seem to serve no satisfying purpose to be open to experience. Since phenomena and the forces that control them seem arbitrary to him, there are no useful deductions to be drawn from them. Moreover, a novel phenomenon would be disturbing since if it posed a problem it would arouse the anxiety associated with prospective initiative on his part. Hence for both positive and negative reasons he wears blinders to the interesting details of the world. He finds it safer to rely on traditional rules or on the judgment of older, wiser, and superior persons.

The painful experiences which gave rise to these perceptions must have created hatreds in him which shocked those around him. We shall see in Chapter 6 that they also tend to arouse in him both doubt of his manliness and homosexual inclinations and desires. He presses these fears and unacceptable urges out of his conscious mind and seals over his unconscious processes as best he can because he is uneasy about what thoughts and fears they include. Hence his unconscious processes are inaccessible to him. In addition, they would not be useful if they were accessible, for instead of reactions to the phenomena he has currently observed they consist of the inadmissible impulses and desires which he has repressed and which are activated anew by the anxiety created by facing a problem.

But rage and pain, though repressed, are still within him. He dared not express his rage against the superior authorities who early in life directed him arbitrarily, but once he is an elder in the community, or a father, or even an older brother, he can somewhat satisfy his aggressiveness by his dominance over his inferiors. Moreover, as he moves to successive positions of authority at successive stages in his life the anxiety he feels in ambiguous situations causes him to insist that his own authority not be questioned, just as it earlier required that he submit his judgment to superior judgment and will. Thus each traditional adult individual in traditional society presents strong resistance to the questioning of authoritative decisions or traditional ways. That resistance is an important obstacle to change.

In sum, then, the member of a traditional society is uncreative for several reasons. He perceives the world as an arbitrary place rather than an orderly one amenable to analysis and responsive to his initiative. His unconscious processes are both inaccessible and uncreative. He resolves his relationships with his fellows primarily on the basis of ascriptive authority. He avoids the anxiety caused by facing unresolved situations in the physical world by reliance on the judgment of authority.

The analysis is incomplete in two respects. It is based on an assumption concerning the authoritarian individual's early perceptions of the nature of the world and on a further assumption that he remembers these perceptions unconsciously and generalizes from them in ways that guide all his later behavior. Unless these two assumptions can be justified, the sketch is only a possibly interesting speculation.

Innovational and Authoritarian Personalities in a Formal Framework

chapter 6

INTRODUCTION

BEFORE ATTEMPTING TO JUSTIFY OUR ASSUMPTIONS about the perceptions of the authoritarian individual, we need to define the characteristics of both innovational and authoritarian personalities more precisely. Much of the preceding discussion of these personality types has dealt with the individual's perception of what the world is like, the types of activity that give him satisfaction or make him anxious, and the things he values in life. It will be useful to sharpen the definitions of these three types of personality characteristics and to ask what other sorts of qualities must be specified for a comprehensive description of the personality of any individual. When there has been sketched a standard framework sufficiently comprehensive to be used in outlining the nature of any personality type, innovational and authoritarian personalities may be delineated more precisely by locating them within that general framework. Later the framework will be useful when we identify the influences that cause an individual's personality to become what it does become.

"Personality" may be defined as the complex of qualities other than purely bodily ones which determine how an individual will behave in any given situation. If the differences in personality between two individuals have been completely specified, from them the differences in their behavior in all possible situations can be deduced. It would be futile to attempt a complete catalogue of personality traits, but it seems feasible to sketch a framework in which all differences that are important for an introductory model of social change can be indicated.

In the psychological writings there is no commonly accepted schema for the purpose. In the 1930's Murray and his associates listed and discussed a large number of needs and other concepts relevant to the study of personality without claiming to set forth a definitive or complete framework of personality.[1] Since that time social and clinical psycholo-

---

[1] The findings are set forth in Henry A. Murray and associates, *Explorations in Personality* (New York: Oxford University Press, 1938).

gists have in general turned away from the attempt to establish a frame of reference for a complete description of personality and toward the study of selected personality characteristics. For my purposes, however, a comprehensive rather than partial analysis of personality is necessary. Hence in this essay I am forced to run counter to the recent trend and present a model of personality as a whole and, in doing so, to establish my own set of constructs for the purpose.

The constructs I shall use have been derived by psychologists from observations of others and of themselves. They are not ultimate units of measurement. They are subject to the imperfections of empirical observation and introspective analysis. I believe, however, that they are sufficiently precise and comprehensive to bear the weight of the theory to be advanced here, and perhaps also of more general theories of social change, without being so complex as to be unwieldy.

THE CONSTRUCTS

There is fairly general agreement that among the constructs which are useful in differentiating among personalities are intelligence and energy level. Apart from these two characteristics some social scientists in describing personality specify the individual's needs (motivations)[2] or need-dispositions,[3] others describe his values or value-orientations,[4] and still others stress world view.[5] These concepts overlap, and where they do not some of the lines of demarcation are not clear. "World view," as usually defined, includes both the individual's concepts of what is good and bad, proper and improper, in life and his more purely cognitive conception of the nature of the world. That is, it includes values as well as cognitive concepts.[6] The term "value-orientation" has similar coverage, though discussion of personality in terms of value-orientations is often

---

[2] The classic discussion of needs is that in *ibid.*

[3] See Talcott Parsons, *The Social System* (Glencoe, Ill.: Free Press of Glencoe, Inc., 1951), p. 7, and *passim;* and Talcott Parsons and Edward A. Shils (eds.), *Toward a General Theory of Action* (Cambridge, Mass.: Harvard University Press, 1954), Part I, chap. i, and Part II, *passim.*

[4] See, for example, Charles Morris, *Varieties of Human Value* (Chicago: University of Chicago Press, 1956), and Florence Rockwood Kluckhohn, "Dominant and Variant Value Orientations," in C. Kluckhohn, H. Murray, and D. M. Schneider (eds.), *Personality in Nature, Society, and Culture* (2d ed.; New York: Alfred A. Knopf, Inc., 1955), chap. xxi. Or see Clyde Kluckhohn *et al.*, "Values and Value-Orientations in the Theory of Action," in Parsons and Shils, *Toward a General Theory of Action*, pp. 388–433, and the references cited there.

[5] See, for example, Robert Redfield, "An Outlook on Life," *The Little Community* (Chicago: University of Chicago Press, 1955), chap. vi; and "The Peasant View of the Good Life," *Peasant Society and Culture* (Chicago: University of Chicago Press, 1956), chap. iv.

[6] It is difficult to draw a line between the two. The statement, "This is a world in which it is desirable to behave in such and such a way," is cognitive in form, but it states values.

less comprehensive than that in terms of world view. The term "need-disposition" refers to a combination of need and value.

I shall suggest that the terms "need" and "value," given precise definitions consistent with customary usage, are mutually exclusive. I shall suggest also that a description of personality in terms of needs, values, and cognitive elements of world view, together with intelligence and energy level, is adequate in a simplified model of personality. For convenience I shall use the term "cognitions" to refer to the cognitive elements of world view. I shall define types of needs, of values, and of cognitions and shall suggest that, if the degree to which an individual is characterized by each of these is specified together with his intelligence and energy level, then no important ambiguity remains concerning how he will act in any given situation.[7]

INTELLIGENCE AND ENERGY

Obviously, there are marked differences among the members of any society with respect to both intelligence and energy level, somehow defined,[8] and obviously, too, an individual's intelligence and energy may affect his success in technological innovation. It has already been suggested that individuals with innate characteristics conducive to high intelligence and energy are more apt than other individuals to be creative and innovative. However, the differences in personality which are important for the theory of why one society enters upon economic growth sooner than another are those not among individuals but among national or ethnic groups or social groups within a society.[9] There is no evidence

---

[7] In discussing personality the preceding chapters have referred to anxiety and rage. In the terminology of system analysis, anxiety and rage are to be regarded as intervening variables, that is, variables which are hypothesized as links in causation without themselves having to be specified to have a complete specification of the system. Thus it is convenient to think of the arousing of anxiety or rage in the individual as a step in the formation of one or another need, value, and so on; but if his needs, values, and the like have been defined, the nature of his behavior in the presence of any external situation is determined without need to specify the degree of his anxiety or rage in addition.

[8] The concepts of intelligence and energy level are vague ones. The concept of intelligence perhaps refers not to a single characteristic but to a bundle of characteristics. However defined, it refers not to the capacity which an individual uses in intellectual endeavors but in some sense to the capacity which he might display if emotional factors did not get in the way. (Sometimes it seems to be intended to refer to an inherited component of intellectual ability, as though there were an inherited component not affected by environment.) The term "energy level" is not much more precise; it refers to the reserve of capacity to do work which an individual has at his command. By *to do work* here I mean *to act*. The concept includes capacity to play, to express oneself.

[9] While the individual members of almost any social group will differ in intelligence and energy level, it does not necessarily follow that the distribution of these characteristics among the members of one national, ethnic, or other social group differs from that among the members of another. As between different national and ethnic groups, we have no certain means of knowing whether differences in intelligence

to suggest differences in intelligence between members of societies which at this particular moment in history have entered upon economic growth and members of those which have not, or between those which entered earlier and those which entered later; and a great deal of historical evidence casts a strong presumption that there are no marked differences. Neither is there reason to believe that the members of a group within a society which takes the lead in introducing technological progress are distinguished from the members of other groups in the society with respect to intelligence.

With regard to differences in energy level among groups, we know so little that discussion is of little use.[10] Differences in climatic conditions may, both directly and through their effect on the constitution, cause differences in energy level. I shall not assume such differences in this essay; they seem of minor importance relative to other factors in explaining economic growth. As with intelligence, we have no need to assume differences in the distribution of innate or constitutional determinants of energy level among the members of different societies or of relevant groups within societies in order to explain differential performance in economic growth. Alternative explanations seem much more plausible. Differences in energy level or in intelligence among social groups will therefore be ignored in the theory of economic growth presented in this essay and in the discussion of personality presented in this chapter.

Let us turn then to a discussion of cognitions, needs, and values.

COGNITIONS

As interaction between the individual and his environment proceeds, increasingly clear and complex images of the factual nature of the relationships between himself and the world around him form in his mind. Unless he is an analytical and introspective individual, they are primarily unconscious frames of reference which he takes for granted as characteristics of the external world, not of himself.[11]

---

exist. We have no tests that will measure the relative level of intelligence or various components of it of individuals from different cultures. Tests of intelligence are almost necessarily culture-bound.

[10] In conversation, Clyde Kluckhohn offered as a basis for suspecting innate differences in energy level among different ethnic groups the results of tests administered to Mormon, Mexican-American, Zuni, and Navaho children less than 24 hours old. All were given the Moro Startle Response test, which is designed to measure differences in the innate activity level of infants. The differences found were highly significant statistically. No single Zuni child, for example, was within the upper quartile of Mormon children. If such differences exist, perhaps there is some presumption that among ethnic groups differences in the physiological basis of other characteristics of personality also exist.

[11] For an amusing and instructive illustration of limitations on belief imposed by the view of early twentieth century Americans concerning the nature of the world, see Fred C. Kelly's account of the refusal of sophisticated citizens to believe incontestably documented accounts of flights at Kitty Hawk by the Wrights (because every-

What are some of the important elements of any individual's understanding of the nature of the world? We shall not be much interested in his sense impressions of things as hard or soft, red or blue or green, large or small, round or cubic; but we shall be much interested in his cognitions of the world as holding promise or threat, benefit or harm, to him.

1. Every individual sees some elements of the world he lives in as threatening him in lesser or greater degree. The threatening elements may be men or women or children, or some classes or groups of each, in some relationships and circumstances but not in others, and some manifestations of the nonhuman world but not others. The world is bewildering to every individual as he grows through infancy and childhood and youth to manhood; and probably no individual ever escapes the sense that some elements of the world threaten him, though he may suppress the awareness of being threatened from his conscious thought processes.

2. To a greater or lesser degree he sees the phenomena of life or of some area of experience as causing one another in ways that are orderly, determinable, and capable of being managed and manipulated, ways that one may not understand on first observing them but can come to understand and manage by the use of one's abilities. In greater or less degree he sees life as an experience in which one encounters successive new bits of disorder and, if they interest one, can uncover the previously unrealized order in them. To this extent the phenomena are not threatening, or the threats can be met by analyzing and manipulating them. He views the world in this way only if he sees his own interrelations with phenomena as subject to causality, for his own interactions formed the model from which he initially generalized concerning other areas of experience. He as the viewer is more or less detached both from himself and from the world about him.

3. He sees some elements of the world as valuing him (loving him, having regard for him) in greater or lesser degree. This perception is so closely related to a view of the world as dependably responding to one's initiative that it may perhaps be considered a corollary of the view of the world just described, but perhaps in some degree it is independent and merits separate listing.

4. He sees power in the world and he acquires perception of its origins. He may see the amount of power possessed by each individual as wholly determined by his position in the social structure. In this case, in his image of the world to some degree the positions are arranged in a hierarchy, and all, some, or none of them are attainable by him either with the passage of time, by a sequence of events (for example, increase in his age) which he does not control, or by prowess of some sort. Or he may see power as a function of one's behavior, as something one can possess by one or another type of management of the environment.

one knows that men cannot fly) in "They Wouldn't Believe the Wrights Had Flown," *Harper's Magazine*, Vol. CLXXXI (August, 1940), pp. 286–300.

To the degree that he does not see physical phenomena as subject to causality and amenable to analysis he almost inevitably sees them as determined by forces that have wills like his own. The experiences of early life are virtually certain to give him the one perception or the other.

The individual's view of various aspects of the world as threatening or not threatening him, as orderly and manageable by him or not so, as valuing him or not valuing him, and his view of the nature of the power in the world dominate his life to a degree that many of us do not realize.

NEEDS

Just as the individual learns to view the world in one way or another, so he also learns to solve the problems of his relationship to the world in one way or another. He acquires various desires, wishes, preferences, urges, or emotional (affective) attitudes which impel him toward one or another type of action or reaction toward his environment. Psychologists term these elements of his personality his motivations, or, by a simple extension of a familiar term, his needs. It is important to note that the connotation of the term is much broader than that of need or necessity in the layman's sense.

"A need," Murray says, "is a construct (a convenient fiction or hypothetical concept) which stands for a force (the physico-chemical nature of which is unknown) in the brain region, a force which organizes perception, apperception, intellection, conation and action in such a way as to transform in a certain direction an existing, unsatisfying situation."[12] More concretely, to state that a person has a need for a certain type of action or behavior means that he feels an increase in satisfaction (or a decrease in pain or discomfort, which is equivalent) if he acts in that way, and that he will perceive and interpret the situation in a way that will yield him the maximum gain in satisfaction. The concept of a need relates only to a general tendency, such as a need to be aggressive, a need to organize order out of disorder, and so on. His values and world cognition will determine the objects against which he will direct his needs, for example, against whom or what he will be aggressive, what sort of phenomena he will be interested in putting in order.

An individual is often not conscious of his needs, especially of needs which he does not regard as admirable or respectable. Thus a person with a high need to be dependent on someone else may be amazed, and become violently angry, if told that he possesses this characteristic; an individual who feels keen anxiety if put in a position where he must face a situation with unknown elements will think of himself as imaginative and re-

---

[12] *Explorations in Personality,* p. 123. This definition should not be taken to imply that a need will dominate reality and of itself determine a course of action; but, given the external situation, a need will determine the individual's perception and interpretation of it.

For a suggested list of needs and extended thought-provoking discussion of them, see chap. iii.

sourceful; a highly aggressive individual will regard himself as never being aggressive unless he is unjustly treated. The operation of a person's needs, then, is often unconscious. His needs are to be ascertained not by his own conception of them but by deduction from his overt behavior, clinical observation, or so-called "projective testing."

In referring to needs, psychologists ordinarily use the preposition "for" followed by a noun, as in need for aggression, need for order; and for brevity they omit the preposition. I shall follow this practice.[13]

Some needs seem purely biological in origin—to breathe, to suck, to eliminate, to sleep, and need for skin comfort, for example. Others have no direct base in physiological requirements. We shall be interested in the latter rather than the former. Some of the needs defined below are standard concepts in the literature; others (need understanding, need aggression-in, need dependence) are not.[14] I shall discuss needs under four heads: on the one hand manipulative and aggressive needs, and on the other passive and succorant ones.

Manipulative Needs

If an individual has learned to find satisfaction in analyzing and manipulating some elements of his environment, we say that he exhibits one or more of a group of needs which may be termed manipulative: need achievement, autonomy, and order. All three were referred to but in different terms in the discussion of innovational personality.

Need achievement is ambiguously named. It is not a need to attain a certain station in life but rather satisfaction in the process of achieving. It refers to a quality which makes an individual find satisfaction (pleasure, or a lessening of discomfort) in the process of solving problems, in manipulating effectively by the exercise of his judgment and abilities a situation containing elements he has not previously dealt with, in attempting something difficult, in facing a test of his capability. It should be distinguished sharply from the feeling that one has a duty to accomplish something in life. This constitutes pressure on one to achieve, or, as social psychologists would say, *press achievement*. If one feels guilty at not having done enough in life, one is experiencing press achievement. If one likes to face problems, or feels a lessening of anxiety when one is attacking a problem, one is characterized by need achievement.[15]

---

[13] I shall avoid the still greater degree of abbreviation, *n ach, n aut*, and so on which is often used by psychologists.

[14] There is no agreed-on wording of definitions of needs; the concepts are not entirely clear or homogeneous. The definitions here which are not quoted are my own, and differ in detail from those of Murray or others.

[15] Neither is need achievement an aspect of the value-orientation which Parsons terms orientation toward achievement (or performance) as opposed to ascription (or quality). This is a conception (or its corollary in behavior) that one should treat a person or object in accordance with the results that will flow from his or its actions rather than in accordance with what he or it is; the other is a psychological disposition which causes one to gain satisfaction from problem solving.

Need achievement implies willingness to take risks, for in facing any problem there is a risk of failure. It does not, however, make an individual a gambler; it does not lend attractiveness to taking a chance on success or failure or on gain or loss when the individual cannot influence the chance by the exercise of ability. Indeed, McClelland has shown that individuals with high need achievement shy away from ventures with small odds of success even though they are somewhat amenable to being influenced by the exercise of ability. They prefer ventures in which judgment and capability play a larger role.[16]

Need autonomy is the quality which makes one prefer to be independent of control of one's judgment by others, to make one's own decisions. It implies that the locus of evaluation of one's efforts is within one. One does not have anxiety concerning whether others will judge that one has done well; one is satisfied with one's own appraisal. The individual with high need autonomy, while willing to follow directions from superiors as the occasion requires, will not tend automatically to assume that they reflect the best possible course. Neither will he tend to accept present concepts, procedures, or logic as correct or best automatically; he will tend to look at each situation for himself. Need autonomy does not, however, involve an aggressive desire to do something unconventional or different simply because it is different, as an act of defiance, rebellion, or hostility. The individual with high need autonomy will judge for himself whether others are wrong, but the need to attack them because they are wrong is a different matter.

Need order is the need "to put things in order; to achieve cleanliness, arrangement, organization, balance, neatness, tidiness and precision";[17] to achieve logical or aesthetic relationships within a whole. The person with high need order may make an efficient clerk or bookkeeper, or, if he also possesses high need achievement and certain other characteristics, may attain far more complex and creative synthesis. I include here both aesthetic and logical order. Whether they are essentially related is an interesting question. Certainly the creative scientist and mathematician are driven or led by an aesthetic as well as logical motivation. Logic is the most appropriate or suitable way of looking at a problem; an aesthetic formulation may be defined in the same words.[18] The difference between

---

[16] Among numerous writings on the subject by him and his students, see David C. McClelland, John W. Atkinson, Russell A. Clark, and Edgar L. Lowell, *The Achievement Motive* (New York, Appleton-Century-Crofts, Inc., 1953), and David C. McClelland, *The Achieving Society* (Princeton, N.J.: D. Van Nostrand Co., Inc., 1961).

[17] Murray, *Explorations in Personality*, p. 201.

[18] "In sum, then, we have been proposing that the difference between science and art is not as great as one may first imagine. Both aim to control percepts, but only science is concerned with the public validation of such attempts at control. . . .

"But we would suggest further that the similarity between art and science extends beyond their both being attempts to control percepts. For they both seem to involve systems of information organized by various rules. . . . Such rules . . . guide

the two lies in a difference in the axioms on which the order is based. Even if the two qualities are distinct, it seems highly probable to assume that the same motivation is related to both.

Some psychologists treat *need understanding* as a need distinct from those discussed above. Need understanding is the need to understand the logic of the events one observes; to "make thought correspond to fact."[19] It implies discomfort with explanations of phenomena in which one is interested which are not mutually consistent. "To acquiesce in discrepancy is destructive of candor and moral cleanliness," Whitehead has said; ". . . it belongs to the self-respect of intellect to pursue every tangle of thought to its final unravelment."[20] He was expressing need understanding. However, creating order is simply finding the order that exists in the universe, and I suggest that need understanding is simply a manifestation of need order and need not be treated as a separate characteristic.[21]

Aggressive Needs

If the individual who finds the world threatening finds his satisfaction more in striking back at it than in understanding and manipulating it, he may be characterized by one or another of two needs which may be termed aggressive needs: need aggression and need dominance (or, more fully, need submission-dominance). The substance of both was discussed in describing authoritarian personality.

Need aggression is the need to attack or injure someone or something, to overcome opposition forcefully. The person who has a high degree of need aggression may manifest it in physically belligerent behavior, in verbal behavior, or only in his thoughts and fantasies, depending on other aspects of his personality. He may enjoy reading news of conflict, viewing television programs or cinemas featuring fighting or sex, reading fiction of sexual or other violence, seeing or participating in competitive sports like prize fighting. He may resent being passed by another automobile when driving, may compete intensely in business or politics he may be the conversationally clever person at a party, with a tinge of viciousness in his cleverness.

An individual acquires need aggression because during a formative period his urges were frustrated by individuals around him and he felt rage. This happened enough times in emotionally important circumstances so that he came unconsciously to think of every contact with other persons

---

the construction of information structures designed to bring about certain sights or motive states." M. A. Wallach, *Journal of Aesthetics and Art Criticism*, Vol. XVIII, pp. 159–73.

[19] Murray, *Explorations in Personality*, p. 225.

[20] Alfred North Whitehead, *Science and the Modern World* (New York: The Macmillan Co., 1929), chap. iv.

[21] For a discussion of whether need understanding should be categorized as a distinct need, or as a need at all, see Murray, *Explorations in Personality*, p. 224.

(or at least with any of some class of persons) as involving the danger of conflict and pain, whereafter he rages unconsciously and is aggressive, at least inwardly, at every actual or prospective conflict. He may come to feel the same reaction at every contact with an object or problem which he must manipulate—to react, so to speak, as though someone had deliberately put it in his way to cause him pain.

In some circumstances (discussed in the following chapter) he will decide during a formative period that his own evil actions are the cause of his pain, and he will feel guilt and a need to punish himself. Even though he represses from consciousness the original causes of this feeling, he may be guilt-laden all his life. I term this personality characteristic "need aggression-in," to distinguish it from a tendency to be agressive toward others, which may be termed "need agression-out."

An individual who thus perceives each contact with other persons as involving a danger of conflict and a threat of pain may conceive of dominating others rather than merely attacking them as a solution to the threat and an outlet for the rage which is within him. This need will express itself as a need to obtain performance from others by command, to influence or direct the behavior of others, to affect others so as to obtain desired performance from them. Or he may conceive of avoiding the danger of conflict by yielding to the will of others, meanwhile repressing the rage within him. This tendency is *need submission,* the need to receive directions from others, to act under direction or instruction, to be told what to do, to feel that he is following a leader. This need and *need dominance* are solutions to the same problem; they are both alternatives to need aggression, the tendency to oppose and attack the person perceived as causing the danger. Need submission and need dominance are often fused, the individual desiring either to submit or to command as the circumstance makes possible. I shall refer to either need separately or treat of the two jointly as need submission-dominance as is convenient in the context. Both are also sometimes fused with need aggression; probably any person characterized by one of the three also has some degree of the other two.

Finally, the solution seen by the individual to some of the problems of life may be to obtain advice, protection, guidance, or help from others. He has one or both of two sets of needs termed respectively "passive" and "succorant."

Passive Needs

Need dependence is the need to receive guidance from another or others in order to avoid the risk of failure and frustration involved in making judgments and decisions oneself. It involves the need to have one's ideas and attitudes approved by another person or persons; to think what other persons think. The person with high need dependence does not consciously alter his judgment to coincide with that of someone else. He simply finds that he agrees with the other person. An unresolved situation creates uncertainty and some anxiety in his mind, and he waits for a person whose judgment he thinks is superior to his to speak. When that person has suggested an evaluation, it seems reasonable, and the individual with high need dependence finds that he now has an opinion and that his anxiety is gone. Such an individual feels uncomfortable when his ideas disagree with those of anyone else. He therefore feels uncomfortable in reasoning problems out with a group of peers, for differences of opinion may arise.

He feels a sense of loss or unease when he has no point of reference to lean on. While all of us consciously or unconsciously play to some audience, termed by sociologists our reference group, to a person with high need dependence the felt attitude of some reference group is especially dominating. The reference group may of course be different for different aspects of behavior; each of us carries not one but many reference groups around in our heads. For the individual with extreme need dependence the reference group is everyone else, and a judgment of anyone else which differs from his makes him anxious.

Need dependence should be distinguished carefully from need submission. Need submission is a need to be ordered about by someone else even in the routine matters of life simply because it is satisfying to receive orders. Need dependence is the need to receive guidance in the making of choices or decisions. Need dependence need not involve rage, or at least the exercise of it is not so closely associated with rage as is the exercise of need submission-dominance. It is perhaps true that need submission always includes need dependence, but the reverse need not be true.

High need dependence may take the form of a need to obtain the fruits of achievement without effort rather than merely obtaining guidance in how to attain them. The subservient person who repeatedly seeks for material or other help, and if it ceases to be forthcoming feels mistreated, is manifesting high need dependence, perhaps combined with need submission.

A person with high need dependence is apt to seek a career in which someone will make decisions for him which he has no occasion to question and indeed is directed not to question, for example, as a bookkeeper, where the rules of the profession determine the decision, or in a routine military role in peacetime. Yet he may have fantasies of being in a position of supreme authority. Then he has the ultimate in guidance and aid; his every decision is unanimously approved.

In a traditional society such a person may reach a position of high authority simply because he was born to it. Even in a democratic society he may do so if he is highly intelligent and ambitious. If he does, he will seek to avoid the painful process of reasoning out decisions with a group of advisers and instead is apt to delegate responsibility to others where possible and ask them simply to present decisions to him for ratification.

His own decisions, when he must make them, are apt to be hasty and arbitrary, to avoid the pain of prolonging conflict of judgment in arriving at
them.

If he also feels need submission-dominance, he will enjoy high position purely for the opportunity it affords to order other individuals
around.

Need affiliation has been defined as the need to draw near and enjoy-
ably co-operate or reciprocate with an allied other, an other who resembles one or who likes one; to please and win affection of a liked or loved
other; to adhere and remain loyal to a friend.[22] I suggest that need affiliation is a moderate form of need dependence combined with need suc-
corance-nuturance.

Succorant-Nurturant Needs

Need succorance has been defined as the need "to have one's needs
gratified by the sympathetic aid of an allied other. To be nursed, supported, sustained, surrounded, protected, loved, advised, guided, indulged, forgiven, consoled. To remain close to a devoted protector. To
have always a supporter."[23] *Need nurturance* is defined as the need "to
give sympathy and gratify the needs of a helpless other: an infant or any
other that is weak, disabled, tired, inexperienced, infirm, defeated, humiliated, lonely, defected, sick, mentally confused. To assist an other in
danger. To feed, help, support, console, protect, comfort, nurse, heal."[24]
Stated in less extreme form, need succorance is the need to have someone
love and value one and assuage one's loneliness, and need nurturance the
need to love, value, and assuage the loneliness of another. Love and valuation involve understanding. An individual can be characterized by either
need only if he has some degree of understanding of his own unconscious needs, and if he has this understanding, he is apt to be characterized by both needs, though of course they may be combined in different
degrees, depending on the emotional background that gave rise to them
in the given individual. I shall usually treat the two in combination, as
need succorance-nurturance, defined as the need to reciprocate love, valuation, and understanding with another.

The association of the two with understanding of one's unconscious
needs probably explains why high need succorance and need nurturance
are associated with creativity. The understanding of one's unconscious
processes makes those processes productive and available to one, and it is
their availability and productivity rather than the need succorance-
nurturance as such that contributes to creativity.

---

[22] This is Murray's definition, *ibid.*, p. 174, except that I have substituted words for
his abbreviations, have substituted the phrase "liked or loved" for the technical word
"cathected," and have altered the punctuation.

[23] *Ibid.*, p. 182. I have substituted the word "other" for Murray's abbreviation "O."

[24] *Ibid.*, p. 184. Here, too, I have substituted the word "other" for Murray's "O."

Noting the difference between the need succorance-nurturance of an innovational individual and the need dependence of an authoritarian individual may illuminate the nature of both needs. The innovational individual sees the other person with whom he comes in contact as an individual with his own needs, values, and image of the world. He empathizes with the other individual, enters into his skin, so to speak, and to some degree shares his needs and wants to help him satisfy them. In turn, he wants to be understood and to be helped in satisfying his own needs.

The authoritarian individual, on the other hand, sees the other individual merely as an object from which he may attain something. There is no empathy, no perception of the other individual as having his own system of needs, values, and world image—only a self-centered and unstructured view of the world as a place from which one receives impacts, and a desire to be relieved of the need of making decisions about those impacts.

How Needs Function: Concluding Comments

The classification of needs into manipulative and passive, aggressive and nurturant-succorant may be thought of as exhaustive; any needs may perhaps be listed under one or another of these four heads.

Needs are continuing elements in an individual's personality, forever demanding to be satisfied, or, more precisely, quieted for a brief interval by one experience of satisfaction, then arising to demand satisfaction again. Just as the individual must forever eat again and sleep again after he has at any given time satisfied his hunger or weariness, so he must forever resatisfy his other needs. The individual with high need achievement is forever looking anew for problems to use his abilities on; the individual with high need aggression is forever finding objects which ought to be attacked; the individual with high need autonomy is not satisfied with one pleasing exercise of his independent judgment and thereafter willing to take someone else's judgment, but perpetually makes his own evaluations; the person with high need dependence gains only temporary relief from evidences of support and must have more; and so on.

But the individual does not vigorously exert in every activity of his life each need which characterizes him. If he is characterized by need aggression, he may vent it on his wife and children or on business rivals or on members of a different social or economic group. He may vent it in murder, robbery, or business competition, or by empathizing with brutality in television "Westerns." He may vent it in some of these ways and on some of these objects and not others. Similar observations apply for apparently all needs.

There are limits, it is true, to the extent to which needs are thus contained and channeled. Many and possibly all needs, even though vented primarily in one area of behavior, diffuse over the personality to some extent. The tendency to diffusion is greater, the greater the degree in which the need exists. Thus, for example, the aggressive man is apt to manifest some touch of aggressiveness in all of his behavior. It is as though a general tendency was present but was curbed by pressures and constraints from moving in most directions, which curbs it could tolerate so long as it had one or more sufficiently large escape valves.

I suggest that the pressures and constraints consist primarily of conflicting needs.

Some needs of course conflict with others. In general, passive needs tend to conflict with manipulative ones, and succorant-nurturant needs with aggressive ones. It is tempting to think of each pair thus opposed as at the two ends of a continuum, one simply being a negative degree of the other. This, however, seems not to be correct. An individual may be characterized by both of two conflicting needs: thus they exist in him independently. Indeed, every individual is characterized by conflicting needs in some degree.

The individual with conflicting needs may be paralyzed, or he may oscillate between contradictory actions. But some individuals are able to avoid both of these results by satisfying one need in one type of activity and a conflicting need in another, and to keep the conflict between them minor and bearable. Thus John D. Rockefeller, who solved boldly and sometimes ruthlessly the problems of building a business empire, was conformist and conventional in his family and religious life. Similarly, Henry Ford, breaking boldly with the past industrially, reassured himself against the uneasiness this boldness caused him by attaching himself to old Americana.

Often the fact that the individual is satisfying one need in one area of activity and another in another is less obvious.

A scientist who is driven by high need order to eliminate all discrepancy in his scientific analysis and who intuitively notes inaccuracies in statements in his field may at the same time hold mutually inconsistent political or social beliefs without being aware of their inconsistency. A talented writer will demonstrate great autonomy in noting and vigorously affirming the infelicity of a phrase regardless of the opinion of those around him but yield meekly to group consensus in more utilitarian areas in which a little elementary observation could indicate to him that the group is wrong. I suggest that these are cases of expressing conflicting needs in different areas of activity. By expressing novel or unconventional beliefs in social or political matters the scientist may be indicating his contempt for social scientists and thereby venting the need aggression which he has to keep under control in his own field lest it invalidate his analysis. Or, tiring of the mental effort and continual alertness which he has needed to achieve in his field, he may satisfy his repressed need dependence by soaring to grand conclusions in another field without going to the pain of solid analysis. Similarly the writer, relaxing his self-consciousness when outside of his field, may be satisfying need affiliation or dependence which he guards against in his own professional work.

Not only is there "so much good in the worst of us, and so much bad in the best of us . . ."; there is some degree of every need in each of us.

VALUES

Even though conflict with other needs explains why the expression of any one need does not diffuse over all areas of activity, it does not explain why the individual chooses one area of activity rather than another for the satisfaction of any given need. The elements of personality which do determine where an individual will find it satisfying (worthwhile, safe) to express his needs are termed his values.

"A value," Kluckhohn states, "is a conception, explicit or implicit, distinctive of an individual or characteristic of a group, of the desirable which influences the selection from available modes, means, and ends of action."[25] That there is some question concerning the distinction between values and needs is shown by Kluckhohn's alternative definition of value in psychological terms: "Value may be defined as that aspect of motivation which is referable to standards, personal or cultural, that do not arise solely out of immediate tensions or immediate situations."[26] In this definition values are one type of needs.

Yet a distinction between needs and values can be drawn. Needs are inner forces causing general tendencies. Values are the standards which determine the type of action by which (including the objects toward which) one will give vent to one's needs. In the sentence, "The union ought to be destroyed," the predicate "ought to be destroyed" is a manifestation of need aggression, whereas the concept that the union, rather than the church, the corporation, or the political party, is the appropri-

---

[25] C. Kluckhohn, "Values and Value Orientations," in Parsons and Shils, *Toward a General Theory of Action*, p. 395. He discusses this definition on pp. 395–403.

Kluckhohn distinguishes between values, which, he suggests, have a moral content, and preferences, which do not. "It is a fact both of introspection and observation," he states, "that there are three fundamental types of experiencing: what is or is believed to be (existential); what I and/or others want (desire); and what I and/or others ought to want (the desirable)." (*Ibid.*, p. 394.) In another place he illustrates his inclusion of aesthetic and rational judgments within values as follows: ". . . if Smith justified his preference for spinach in rational or pseudo-rational terms of vitamins, mineral content, and the like, it then becomes by definition one of his values. If, however, he simply says, 'I just like spinach better than broccoli,' it remains a mere preference." (*Ibid.*, p. 397, n. 16.) I cannot see a clear line of demarcation here, although a distinction somewhat paralleling that between the superego and the ego-ideal is discernible. Further, the distinction, even if a clear one can be drawn, does not seem significant for purposes of this essay. Hence I shall include preferences within values.

[26] *Ibid.*, p. 425. Concerning the inadequacy of needs alone to explain human behavior or culture, see Dorothy Lee, "Are Basic Needs Ultimate?" *Journal of Abnormal and Social Psychology*, Vol. XLIII (1948), pp. 391–95, reprinted as chap. xx of Kluckhohn *et al.*, *Personality*.

ate target for destruction, or that the union is the more appropriate target, is a value judgment.

The separation of behavior into (1) a generalized tendency and (2) selection of an object is itself a construct, since the individual in reality never merely hates or loves in general; he hates or loves something.[27] But there is nothing in the nature of personality which causes a necessary association between certain needs and certain values. Not only are similar needs in different individuals channeled toward different objects. It is also true that within a given individual needs originally channeled toward one type of object may later be diverted toward another. Hence in defining a personality it is useful to specify needs and values separately.[28]

Parallel to the classification of needs as aggressive and succorant, manipulative and passive, values may be classified as moral values, those dealing with hate and love, and manipulative values, those dealing with the area in which one exercises one's capacities. While I am not sure that these classes include all values, they are the only types with which we shall be concerned.

Moral values relate to the individual's sense of what is good or bad, right or wrong, proper or improper—what anthropologists sometimes term the "oughts" of the society. They channel the expression of aggressive and nurturant-succorant needs. These needs, like all needs, arise initially in infancy and childhood, and the behavior by which one satisfies them relates at that time primarily to one's family members and playmates. The child hates his father for failing to succor him or for depriving him of his mother's attentions, feels a longing to be succored by his mother, gains satisfaction from dominating his fellow siblings or playmates or on the other hand gains security from sharing with them, and so on. But directing certain needs toward some of these objects (for example, hating his father) is forbidden and penalized, or it conflicts with important aspects of the child's perception of the world. He must find substitute objects. As his life unfolds he must also find substitute objects for other aggressive or succorant needs simply because the initial objects are no longer available. Toward whom will the process of personality

---

[27] Though sometimes the need is so intense and so widely diffused that the individual will vent it on almost any object available toward which it could possibly be directed.

[28] A solution which is different in form is to specify combinations of needs and values in such a way as to eliminate the need for one general class *needs* and another general class *values*. Thus we might if we chose divide the class need aggression into a number of subclasses, need aggression-union, need aggression-church, need aggression-alien, and so on, thus describing more specifically how the individual's contacts with his environment had taught him to behave. If we thus subdivided all needs in this way, we would eliminate the necessity for the two separate categories *needs* and *values*. This, however, is substantively not different from treating of needs and of values separately and relating the two to each other. It is more convenient to adopt the latter approach here.

formation (or, we may say, his culture) compel, permit, and induce him to direct these needs? More specifically, what manifestation of each aggressive or succorant need will he be permitted or induced to express toward groups in various degrees of relationship to him?

The values which answer this question are moral values; they form the society's moral code. The moral code of every society takes the form, "Thou shalt love," "Thou shalt not hate," but it qualifies these commandments. In the mythology of a society—in the utterances of its religious teachers—some moral values may be stated as universal. The idealized value is: "Thou shalt love thy neighbor as thyself; thou shalt even love thine enemy, and respect him that persecutes you." But the actual value, which the individual is required to obey, states that he need treat only a narrow circle of individuals with regard (almost) equal to that with which he treats himself. Within that circle he must respect the wishes and values of the individuals as (almost) equal in worth and importance to his own; he must perhaps share income according to need. But beyond that circle, in various circumstances and more readily with respect to individuals who are socially more and more distant, he may deceive, steal, reject and humiliate, attack, and kill. Indeed, in some circumstances he not only may do each of these things but is commanded to do so.

In any society the areas in which the expression of love is commanded and the expression of hate forbidden, those within which the expression of love is not required and the expression of hate permitted, and the bound beyond which the expression of love is forbidden and the expression of hate commanded differ for different types of activity. The moral code also allows for differences in behavior with different intensities of pressure on the individual. The entire system of areas differs from society to society. It is this question of the social area within which or outside of which values confine the expression of aggressive and nurturant-succorant needs that is of especial interest here. I shall refer to this dimension of moral values as their social scope.

We may think of the individual as being at the center of a series of social circles or ovals which are generally of increasing size, though the boundaries of some cross those of others. These areas are, for example, a nuclear family, a wider group of relatives (extended family, clan), his acquaintances, the people of a village, town, or city, of a group of villages, a region, a nation, a grouping of nations, the world. For each type of activity, inner or overt, that brings the individual into relationship with members of one or more of these groups the questions arise: What groups ought he to give the same consideration as he gives to himself? As we pass beyond this boundary of equal regard, what degree of subordination of treatment is applicable to groups successively farther removed? With social distance, the obligation imposed by a value becomes more and more tenuous: white shades into deeper and deeper gray, and gray into black.

The concepts stated in this abstract way may be illustrated. Although one's need achievement and need order might motivate one to select as one's associates or subordinates the most capable possible individuals, one's value system may indicate so conclusively that the only proper act is to select one's brother's son that one is not aware of any alternative. (In another society one may select the most competent individual from among all the members of one's business community or of one's religious faith; in still another, from among all members of the society.) Within some circle of persons one must share one's income according to economic need. This circle may be one's nuclear family, one's extended family, or conceivably a larger circle. Beyond that circle does one feel compulsion to contribute annually to relieve economic distress among the members of one's community, to contribute for relief of citizens of one's country in case of major disaster, but not to contribute at all in case of a major catastrophe in another continent? If one feels one has experienced due provocation, will one, without feeling compunction about the grief caused dependents, kill a member of an opposing army? A member of a conquered country? Any alien? Any stranger? These examples might be multiplied by drawing illustrations from every area of human behavior.

The relevance to the theory of social change of this way of conceptualizing moral values is this: It is not very fruitful to think of change in moral values as consisting of the disappearance of one moral value from a society and its replacement by another; such sea-changes in values do not occur. For example, it is not most fruitful to think of members of a traditional society as being untrustworthy in economic transactions while members of modern societies are honest, or as having diffuse relationships in economic transactions while members of modern societies have contractual ones. For every individual in any society is honest in some circumstances and dishonest in others; he has diffuse relationships with some individuals and contractual ones with others. It is more illuminating to think of differences among societies in moral values as consisting of differences in the areas within which certain types of behavior are commanded or permitted or forbidden, and to think of changes in a society's moral values as consisting of expansion or contraction of such areas.[29]

Vocation-Related Values

I shall not attempt a comprehensive discussion of manipulative values, those that determine where an individual will choose to exercise his ca-

---

[29] In discussing with me this way of looking at differences in values in different societies, Michael A. Wallach has pointed out its relevance to the question of cultural relativism versus absolutism with respect to values. My analysis of values would suggest that certain values (or types of value) may be universal, the great superficial differences among societies being in fact differences in the scope of application of the value.

pacities. Within this class of values the discussion will be limited to values that determine the economic activities and socioeconomic positions in which the individual spends his life. How does the individual rate, on a scale ranging from strong repugnance to strong attraction, the activities involved in work with his muscles and hands on the land, or handling objects, or with tools and machines; or work which keeps him clean or gets him dirty; killing animals; exchanging ownership of goods; studying the physical world versus studying concepts remote from the physical world (scientific versus humanistic areas of intellectual activity); and so on? How does he rank, from strong repugnance to strong attraction, social position as farmer, artisan, trader, manufacturer, professional, political, or military man, or scholar (as well as positions not associated with occupations, such as father, elder, villager)?

While the choice of economic activity and that of economic status are intimately associated, preferences with respect to one are separable from those with respect to the other. Neither sort of preference is a lifelong absolute one; an individual anticipates changing his status or activity as his life goes on. Certain activities and certain statuses are good and satisfying when one is a child but no longer fitting when one is adolescent; others become satisfying only when one is an elder. Preferences are also contingent on the general situation; for example, those in wartime differ from those in peacetime.

Important in determining the individual's choice of economic activity and position in life are his concepts of where he can most satisfactorily vent his manipulative needs. If it is possible to see order in the world, where is there the clearest order? If one feels it satisfying to solve problems, against what sort of problems does one feel most effective? Or where will one find the most challenging problems? Or, if one sees the world as threatening, and specifically as threatening to frustrate one's humble desires for order and for achievement, where will it least molest one and leave one to enjoy one's little triumphs and little arrangements of order? Can one till the soil with wisdom acquired from one's elders, plant seeds with craftsmanship, and enjoy the harvest, whereas one fears to venture other activities? Then one will be a farmer. And so for other activities.

However, there is no exclusive association between manipulative values and the channeling of manipulative needs, or between moral values and the channeling of aggressive and succorant needs. One's moral values also influence the activity and status in life in which one will choose to satisfy one's manipulative or passive needs; one chooses an activity partly because one thinks it important. And conversely one's manipulative values influence one's expression of one's aggressive and nurturant-succorant needs.[30] But for most individuals the central lines of relationship are between

---

[30] And one set of needs influences the expression of the other.

moral values and aggressive and succorant-nurturant needs, and between manipulative values and manipulative and passive needs, and it is useful to keep these associations of values and needs in mind.[31]

INNOVATIONAL AND AUTHORITARIAN PERSONALITIES IN THE GENERAL FRAMEWORK

The discussion has referred occasionally to innovational and authoritarian personalities. In summary, where may innovational and authoritarian personalities be located within the schema of cognitions, needs, and values? The two kinds of personalities shade into each other by degrees, but the pure types are sharply distinguished. There is no reason to assume innate differences among the two with respect to intelligence and energy, though I have suggested that the intelligence and energy of innovational individuals as a group are probably greater as a result of other differences. While in any given social situation a person with innovational personality will tend to choose a different occupational role from an individual with authoritarian personality, such choices are so dependent on the total social situation, which may make some positions attractive to an innovator at one time and others at another, that it is difficult to state in general that the vocation-related values of the one type of person will differ from those of the other. Concerning moral values, however, and concerning needs and cognitions, the two personality types contrast sharply.

---

[31] It is of interest to compare this schema for the description of personalities with that suggested by Dr. Florence Kluckhohn. ("Dominant and Variant Value Orientations," in Kluckhohn *et al.*, *Personality*, chap. xxii.) Dr. Kluckhohn categorizes personalities according to their "value orientations," as follows (*ibid.*, p. 346, except that I have reversed the position of the "Evil" and "Good" categories in the first line of the table):

HUMAN PROBLEMS AND TYPE SOLUTIONS

Innate predispositions	Good (mutable or immutable)	Neither good nor bad (mutable or immutable)	Evil (mutable or immutable)
Man's relation to nature	Man subjugated to nature	Man in nature	Man over nature
Time dimension	Past	Present	Future
Value personality type	Being	Being-in-becoming	Doing
Modality of relationship	Lineal	Collateral	Individualistic

This typology is partially self-explanatory; for precise definitions of the categories, the reader is referred to Dr. Kluckhohn's essay. The general relationship of the typology to the cognitions defined in the text above and to various needs will be apparent. Dr. Kluckhohn suggests that in the personalities of any given society one is apt to find a single complex of value orientations dominant, though one will also find variation along a considerable range.

In the terms of her typology, change in value orientations from those of the first two columns of her table as arranged above to those of the third would seem to be conducive to the appearance of continuing technological progress.

The individual with innovational personality views the phenomena of the world, at least in an area which he values highly, as forming systems whose operation is orderly and amenable to logical analysis. He regards this as true of both phenomena whose system he already understands and phenomena which at first observation run counter to any previously known system. He also views the world as valuing him, though this perception may be a qualified one which creates anxiety in him: he may see the world as valuing him only provided that he achieve effectively. His high need succorance, need to receive assurances of being valued, then drives him to achieve and is the source of that deep religious sense of duty to achieve that is so often present in innovational personality. He is also high in need autonomy, achievement, and order; and since he conceives of all phenomena, no matter how disorderly superficially, as capable of being understood, these needs cause him ever to be alert to new disorderly phenomena within his field of interest in order that he may have the pleasure of autonomously achieving discovery of the order that governs them. Moreover, because he understands himself and hence has empathy with the needs of others, he is high in need nurturance. Perhaps it is because of this need nurturance that the scope of an innovational individual's moral values is broad. He is apt to regard the welfare of individuals and groups over a wide area of his society and perhaps other societies as (almost) equal in importance to his own. The degree of his regard declines only slightly with respect to groups farther and farther removed from him.

The authoritarian individual, on the other hand, perceives the phenomena of the world as forming a system whose operation is not orderly and not capable of analysis. Hence he is high in need dependence. He also perceives the world as not valuing him highly, and sees power as residing in position rather than resulting from accomplishment. Because of the rage and the need to curb it which these perceptions generate in him, he is high in need submission-dominance and low in need succorance-nurturance. He is low in need autonomy and achievement and probably low also in need order, though he may be conceived of as high in need order but driven to satisfy it by evading recognition of inconsistencies or discrepancies in his perception of phenomena. He regards the welfare of very few if any individuals as (almost) equal in importance to his own, and outside of that limited group the degree of his regard for the welfare of others declines rapidly.

This specification of the two personality types in terms of needs, values, and cognitions encompasses all that was stated concerning them in Chapter 5. The summary above includes no explicit reference to two aspects of personality that were stressed in the discussion of Chapter 5, namely, the nature of an individual's anxiety and the productivity and accessibility to him of his unconscious processes. I suggest, however, that when the qualities listed above have been specified, these aspects of personality are also determinate. Thus when we have stated that an individual views the world as not orderly and understandable and as not valuing him, and views power as residing in position, and that he is characterized by high need aggression and submission-dominance and low need autonomy, achievement, and order, we have also implied that his anxiety is high and that in his unconscious processes there are urges and fantasies that he must repress, and therefore that those processes are neither productive nor available to him. And when we have stated that an individual perceives the world as orderly and as valuing him, and that he is high in need autonomy, achievement, order, and succorance-nurturance, it also follows that his unconscious processes are productive and accessible to him. If his perception of the world is as valuing him only if he achieves, then necessarily he is characterized by a high degree of anxiety, but of a nature that does not breed inadmissible fantasies and thus cause him to wall in his unconscious processes.

One qualification must be made concerning this sketch of the two personality types as dichotomous. As will be noted in Chapter 7, the childhood circumstances which cause an individual to feel a persistent anxious drive to achieve do not differ greatly from those which cause him to feel rage and a sense of not being valued. Many innovational individuals are driven not merely by the former but also by the need aggression that results from the latter. To the extent that this is true, they are presumably less creative than they might otherwise be, for their unconscious processes are partly occupied with rages and fantasies of revenge and domination. However, since not all innovation requires the highest degree of creativity, many individuals of this mixed type become very successful innovators.

APPENDIX: THE SCOPE OF MORAL VALUES AND PARSONS' PATTERN VARIABLES

The concept of moral values as determining the social scope for the expression of aggressive and succorant needs will be elaborated on in this appendix.

In the text we have pictured the individual figuratively as standing at the center of a set of concentric circles or ovals. The individuals in each successive area, moving away from him, are farther from him in social distance. His moral values permit him to treat each successively more distant group with less regard.

However, these areas with concentric boundaries are not fixed. In circumstances in which the intensity of one's need is greater one may show disregard for the interests of groups closer to one. On the vertical scale of the geometric representation one may locate increasing intensities of one's need, and at each intensity, plot a similar plane. The area representing any given degree of regard for others will draw closer and closer to one on higher and higher planes, forming a hollow cone. The cone may be truncated and appear rather like an inverted flower pot with a rather small base, for there may be individuals close to one whose interests one feels co-ordinate with one's own regardless of the intensity of one's need.

Or, instead of plotting on successively higher planes the change in one's areas of relationship with different intensities of one's need, we might plot the moral value systems of different individuals in circumstances of normal degree of need. If we arranged the individuals in appropriate order, we would again get cone-shaped or truncated cone-shaped surfaces.

Alternatively we might plot as concentric circles not groups of persons successively farther removed from the individual but different spheres of action in which different moral values concerning, say, lying pertain. By these various diagrammatics, in a multidimensional surface we may sketch a complete representation of a society's moral code.

This schema of concentric areas in various dimensions, by which moral values channel the expression of aggressive and succorant needs, serves the same purpose as Parsons' pattern variables of value orientation.

Parsons presents the pattern variables in *The Social System*, and Parsons and Shils elaborate the discussion of them and their relationship to action in *Toward a General Theory of Action*. Since these concepts were developed in a series of steps in Parsons' writings before *Toward a General Theory of Action*, it is perhaps appropriate to attribute them to him alone. The discussion by Parsons and Shils, however, carries the analysis of their relationship to a general theory of action further than it had previously been carried.

The pattern variables consist of five dichotomous choices which, Parsons suggests, define any situation for any individual—that is, define appropriate action. In fact, however, they seem to refer only to the choices I have termed moral ones. It is difficult, for example, to visualize an individual making a choice among occupations or economic positions in terms solely of the pattern variables.

The pattern variables may be defined loosely as follows: The individual must decide whether to grant gratification of his immediate impulses or to evaluate the various effects of action in the situation (affectivity versus affective neutrality); if he decides to evaluate, whether to give "primacy to interests, goals, and values shared with other members of a given collective unit of which he is a member or . . . [to give] primacy to his personal or private interests without considering their bearing on collective interests" (collectivity-orientation versus self-orientation; *Toward a General Theory of Action*, pp. 80–81); whether to "treat the objects in the situation in accordance with a general norm covering *all* objects in that class, or whether to treat them in accordance with their standing in some particular relationship to him or his collectivity . . ." (universalism versus particularism; *ibid.*, p. 81); whether to treat a person or object on the basis of the results which will flow from its actions or on the basis of its "qualities" (achievement versus ascription); and whether he should limit his involvement with the person or object to a restricted range or be concerned with all aspects of the person or object (functional specificity versus functional diffuseness).

This is a formal classification of great usefulness. But to state that the value system of a social group changes by the members of the group becoming universalistic rather than particularistic, self- rather than collectivity-oriented, and so on, or that they become more universalistic or more self-oriented, does not seem to me to give one a very useful tool for the analysis of social change. For example, it is sometimes stated that a traditional society is characterized by collectivity-orientation, functional diffuseness, particularism, and ascription, and that for economic growth or modernization in general to occur it must become (more) self-oriented, functionally specific, particularistic, and achievement oriented. But any such general statement, if not wrong, is either misleading or too vague to convey much information. There are

important elements of the qualities on both sides of each dichotomous choice
in both traditional and modern society. The significant change is that for some
values the area within which they are pertinent widens and for others narrows.
It conveys much specific information to state that the collectivity with respect
to whose interests one evaluates various types of situations has shrunk in size,
and for some has become the self only; that the circle of persons for whose
interests one has a diffuse regard has shrunk from the extended to the
nuclear family, but with weaker diffuse regard persisting for a larger group;
that the boundary within which one must preserve affective neutrality has
expanded for some types of actions, contracted for others; that the area within
which one exercises universalistic values has expanded, particularism still prevailing, however, as between that larger group of persons and outsiders; and
that similarly one chooses on the basis of achievement among a larger group
of persons than before, but applies ascriptive distinctions as between members
of that larger group and individuals outside it. Specifically, the widening or
narrowing of such circles will be seen to be of some importance for economic
growth.

Formation of Creative and Authoritarian Personalities

chapter 7

WE SHALL BE INTERESTED HERE IN HOW INNOVATIONAL and authoritarian personalities, to which so much attention has already been devoted, are formed in traditional society or elsewhere. A number of relevant influences of childhood have already been suggested, but we shall not be able to analyze how personalities may change from one generation to the next without a more systematic analysis of the process of personality formation. Since the elements of environment which determine whether personality becomes creative or authoritarian are also the elements which determine any other outcome of personality, our discussion of them involves consideration of the current theory of personality formation in general.

The study of personality formation since Freud has made clear the general nature of the influences and mechanisms involved, but the theory is not yet firm; in part it still consists of intuitions and insights rather than of fully tested hypotheses. The brief account below is arranged to a very limited degree under new organizing principles[1] but is consistent, I hope, with the best current materials. To readers who are not already acquainted with the theory of personality formation no brief sketch will bring conviction or complete clarity, yet it seems desirable to present an introductory account as a point of reference for later discussion.

The discussion will stress the impact of the environment rather than the differences among individuals caused by differences in inherited qualities. Of course the latter are also important. Each individual inherits biologically a set of qualities and capacities which reacts with the chemical environment in the womb and the social environment after birth to affect the process of his development, and these vary among individuals. Further, as he grows, the individual will undergo an unfolding of physiological capacities which is influenced by inherited tendencies as well as by his environment. In his progressive development the ways and degree to which the child himself reaches out toward his environment at each stage of his development (his proaction, in Murray's term) and the ways in

---

[1] In particular, my stress on whether the individual sees the world as orderly, that is, possessing dependable relationships which can be understood and managed.

which he reacts to the environment as it impinges on him depend on what he has become in his previous development up to each given moment. Thus the effect of his inherited characteristics and tendencies and his environment interact throughout his life and jointly determine what he becomes.

However, the differences among groups caused by differences in environment are of most interest here. The alternative ways in which the environment acts on the individual and reacts on him as he reaches out toward it powerfully affect the personality outcome. Though the environment which each child faces as he develops differs from that which any other child faces, the childhood environment within one social group has common elements which differ from those in other social groups, and all those within one culture typically have common elements different from those in other cultures. In the ensuing discussion of personality formation a foundation will be laid for analyzing the differential effects of these environmental differences.

CHILDHOOD GENERALIZATIONS AND ADULT BEHAVIOR

The discussion of personality in preceding chapters has assumed that from the experiences even of his earliest years the child draws conclusions which influence his actions during the rest of his life. It has assumed, indeed, that from a succession of childhood experiences the child unconsciously observes not merely the specific circumstances of painful or satisfying events but also the general nature of the relationship, and that thereafter he tends to match relationships against that general pattern and be guided by the anxiety or the anticipation which that matching arouses. The assumption is one of long-lasting and powerful effects of early impressions, powerful generalizations from them, and the use of the generalizations to guide later behavior. It is time to consider the justification for these assumptions.

They would be justified, even if we had no other evidence, by the fact that they provide a highly plausible explanation of variations in adult behavior for which we have no other satisfactory explanation. But there is also more direct evidence that even from his earliest experiences the infant and child generalizes broadly concerning the nature of the universe around him, and that these generalizations powerfully influence the nature of the individual he will become.

The Evidence of Social Psychology

A striking piece of evidence from overt childhood behavior concerning the child's power to generalize is cited by Professor Merton:

Not infrequently, *children detect and incorporate cultural uniformities even when these remain implicit and have not been reduced to rules.*

Language patterns provide the most impressive evidence, readily observable in clinical fashion, that children in the process of socialization detect uniformities which have not been explicitly formulated for them by elders or contemporaries and which are not formulated by the children themselves. Persistent errors of language among children are most instructive. Thus the child will spontaneously use such words as "mouses" or "moneys," *even though he has never heard such terms or been taught "the rule for forming plurals."* Or he will create such words as "falled," "runned," "singed," "hitted," though at the age of three he has not been taught "rules" of conjugation. Or he will refer to a choice morsel as "gooder" than another less favored, or perhaps through a logical extension, he may describe it as "goodest" of all. Obviously he has detected the implicit paradigms for the expression of plurality, for the conjugation of verbs, and the inflection of adjectives. The very nature of his error and misapplication of the paradigm testifies to this.

It may be tentatively inferred, therefore, that he is also busily engaged in *detecting and acting upon the implicit paradigms of cultural evaluation, and categorization of people and things, and the formation of estimable goals* as well as assimilating the explicit cultural orientation set forth in an endless stream of commands, explanations and exhortations by parents. . . . It may well be that the child retains the implicit paradigm of cultural values detected in the day-by-day behavior of his parents even when this conflicts with their explicit advice and exhortations.[2]

Certainly the child sees so clearly what his parents do, generalizes from it, and models his own behavior after it that he hears only rather indistinctly what they say—though the conflict of their words with their deeds, as one aspect of their behavior, makes its own impression on him.

It is clear, as Merton notes, that the generalizing process is not conscious. The child does not acquire a mental concept of language structure from which he generalizes by a conscious logical process, as from a syllogism. He does not say to himself, "Persons add 'ed' when they are talking about something that has already happened; therefore when I am talking about the past I will always add 'ed' to verbs." But we must conclude that in his unconscious thought processes he makes precisely such a generalization. There is no other way to explain his behavior. We must believe, therefore, that the ability of a very young child to generalize unconsciously is very great.

A child who can make these grammatical generalizations can also generalize in ways which, put into conscious form, are the equivalent of saying: "Sometimes people help you, but often they don't. One should be suspicious of all people." Or, if his environment were a happy and encouraging one as he learned to focus his eyes, to crawl, to walk, to control his grasping movement, to throw: "When one tries new things, one finds the most interesting and successful results. I must always look around for new things to explore." Or, on the contrary, if anxious parents restrain him from explorations he is capable of, or authoritarian ones force him to

---

[2] Robert K. Merton, *Social Theory and Social Structure* (rev. ed.; Glencoe, Ill.: Free Press of Glencoe, Inc., 1957), pp. 158–59. Italics in the original.

follow their pattern instead of his own: "If one sees new things and explores them, one experiences alarm, anxiety, and pain. I will do well not to look around for phenomena to explore. They cause trouble." Or, if his mother is shocked as he approaches her sexually during the fourth and fifth years of life, or his father abruptly pushes him aside and himself takes over intimate relations with the mother: "Approaching my mother is exciting but dangerous. Perhaps it is not safe for me to try to be a man. Whenever I contemplate approaching a woman sexually, I shall remember those things."

These illustrations imply very broad generalizations from the limited (but fairly extensive) experiences of say the first six or eight years of life. The few persons around the individual during his first years of life equal all persons; crawling, walking, throwing, eating equal all new experiences; approaching his mother during the period of infantile sexuality equals approaching any woman later in life; and so on. He forms patterns in his brain about the pain or satisfaction he may expect from situations of various types, abstracts from the specifics of the situation, and generalizes very broadly about the elements that caused the satisfaction or pain; and whenever thereafter he approaches a situation that seems to contain the same elements, he anticipates the same type of emotional experience and acts accordingly. He does not generalize in words or in logical syllogisms; he generalizes the emotional impact of experiences on him.

Persistence of the Patterns: Evidence from Psychoanalysis

What seems incredible about such patterns to laymen—especially to laymen who experienced fears and alarms in their own childhoods which they can best avoid remembering by insisting that such things do not exist—is that such patterns persist and influence behavior after the individual has become old enough and informed enough to use his conscious reasoning processes to resolve situations. That the brain has the capacity to carry an extremely large number of patterns throughout life and rapidly match any situation against all of them until it finds the congruent one is amply demonstrated by the researches of modern biophysics.[3] That

---

[3] Moreover, while biophysicists do not yet know in detail just how the brain does this matching, they know that the brain does carry throughout life a vastly larger store of records of life's events than ever appears in conscious memory—conceivably records of all events that ever impinged on the attention of the individual—and that these records seem to consist of electrical circuits or flows or at least propensities for a previous flow to be re-evoked by a stimulus related in some specific way to the one which initially created it. The most spectacular evidence is provided by experiments by Penfield. In a number of brain operations under local anesthesia, with the consent of the patients, he touched electrodes bearing minute currents to various exposed points of the brain. In certain sectors of the brain, these tiny electrical discharges evoked in the patient a re-experiencing of a passing bit of his previous life, often one so inconsequential that it would hardly be expected ever to be remembered in the normal course of recall. The patient was simultaneously also aware of the present; he experienced a double exposure, as it were. His recall of the past was somewhat like a

it actually tends to do so, and that the effect on behavior of early unconscious generalizations is amazingly persistent, are indicated not only by the light such an assumption casts on adult behavior that is not otherwise explainable but also by more direct evidence from psychoanalysis.

The evidence emerges from cases of compulsions or anxieties in adults. Examples are anxieties concerning contacts with persons of the opposite sex; great anxiety to be accepted in a group, associated with torturing feelings of being rebuffed whenever one is in a group; paralysis in the face of the simplest choices; inability to read, to spell, or to cook, even though the individual has superior intelligence and there is no physiological deficiency. In a large number of cases such incapacitating anxieties have been relieved when, in therapy, the individual relived or, so to speak, un-lived his life. Successively recalling the elements in a complex of anxiety producing events, the ability to tolerate the pain of each recall in the supporting environment of therapy enabling him to recall another, finally he arrived at emotion-laden remembrance of traumatic relationships in early childhood in which any possible alternative action or lack of action had brought him pain. In adulthood he had been avoiding actions or relationships that in some characteristic of emotional importance to him were parallel to ones which had produced great pain in infancy or early childhood (such as making a choice, or attempting some feat to meet his mother's desires and failing). Or he had been acting in ways that were unrealistic in the adult world but which were perfectly designed to avoid the pain he had suffered in early childhood. The proof that this generalizing process is typically at the root of neuroses is that after this process has sufficiently revealed the childhood parallels, and the adult has brought up to consciousness what he was doing unconsciously, in typical cases the anxieties are so softened that the individual is able to generalize more reasonably and to live more comfortably and effectively. The failures in therapy are those in which fear of the pain of recall is so great that the individual is unable to bring to consciousness his childhood tortures.

---

dream, and much more than a memory. Since among the cells of the human brain there are more than 10 billion neurons, each capable of exercising the functions of a tube or transistor of an electronic computer plus other functions useful for the purpose, the brain has the capacity to carry throughout life the vast store of records indicated.

For discussions of research concerning the physical process of memory and the related mechanisms and functioning of the brain and nervous system, see R. W. Gerard, "Your Brain and Your Behavior," *Saturday Evening Post*, Vol. CCXXXI, May 30, 1959, pp. 22–23; W. Penfield and L. Roberts, *Speech and Brain-Mechanisms* (Princeton, N.J.: Princeton University Press, 1959); Walter A. Rosenblith, "The Quantification of the Electrical Activity of the Nervous System," in Daniel Lerner (ed.), *Quantity and Quality* (New York: Free Press of Glencoe, Inc., 1961); and J. Z. Young, *Doubt and Certainty in Science* (Oxford: The Clarendon Press, 1951). I am indebted to Professor Rosenblith for oral comments as well, but he is not responsible for my nontechnical summary of the information.

Reasons for Persistence of Early Patterns

The persistence of early patterns is due in large measure to four influences they have on later behavior. First, and much the most important, if the individual has learned that explorations on his own are apt to lead to pain, he bars himself from observing new facts or unexpected aspects of familiar facts lest exploration revive the pain which is so well preserved in his unconscious processes. Thereby he bars his conscious processes from having materials to work with, and hence prevents new revised generalizations.

Second, by his early generalizations he anticipates the impacts which objects of various types (human and other) will have on him and acts in anticipation, inviting the expected impact if favorable and repelling it if unfavorable. His anticipatory action may so blur his perception of the phenomenon that unless there is a dramatically unexpected impact little correction of early patterns occurs. The reaction of individuals to him that counts is their inner attitude toward him as he perceives it, and his perception will be governed in large part by his expectation.

Third, by his own anticipatory attitude he often influences the impact so that it becomes what he had expected. Thus, if an individual is suspicious or aggressive in defense against pain he expects from other persons, his attitude will repel the friendliness that might otherwise have been exhibited and generate the hostility which he expects.

Finally, he does not know that he is reacting in a way that might be changed to his advantage. For he sees the friendliness, the hostility, the presence of interesting little deviations of phenomena from the expected, the absence of such deviations, the attractiveness of women, the danger that women will reject him, and all his thousands of other perceptions not as aspects of his interpretation of the world or as joint aspects of the external phenomena and his reaction to them, but simply as objective facts of the world outside him. Hence his conscious mind has no basis for assuming that he might behave differently. That is, it has no basis for such an assumption unless a favorable early environment kept him relatively free of fear of his unconscious processes and led him to perceive his own behavior as a system of causal relationships that can be understood as can any other system, in which case he is always open to new interpretations of the world. In being open he is extending early patterns of behavior, so that this case is no exception to the principle of high degree of persistence of early patterns. The case of every real individual is, of course, somewhere between these two extremes.

As a further reason for the tendency of early patterns to persist, it may be noted that the home environment from which the individual drew his early deductions, those of say the first half dozen years, typically continues to be a central part of his environment during the next dozen or more years. Moreover, in a stable society, the personality types he encounters even in adulthood will be like those he had earlier known in his parental home. His adult environment continues to reinforce the early patterns.

Nevertheless, some later experiences that contradict his earlier impressions are apt to penetrate this screen in some degree. If so, these later experiences will of course affect his perception of the world, but they will not eradicate deeply impressive earlier ones from which the individual has generalized. An individual who in early years has perceived important elements of his environment as arbitrary and incomprehensible may have that impression softened later, or may become bewildered by conflicting impressions, but his unconscious processes will nevertheless inhibit him from manipulating that experience as creatively as he otherwise might or even with any significant degree of creativity at all. On the other hand, if, after having learned to respond to the world as dependable and manageable, in adult life he is subjected to severe and continuing control, typically he will not cease to think intuitively of life as controlled by understandable forces and to seek for ways to escape from the situation that binds him.

THE CRISES OF INFANCY

With these observations, let us turn to discuss the stages of development of the individual's personality. The reader familiar with the writings of Erik H. Erikson will be aware how much my sketch owes to him.[4]

For convenience I shall term the first period of life, roughly the first year for the average child, babyhood or infancy; the second period, roughly the second and third years, late infancy; and the third period, roughly the fourth and fifth years, early childhood. The dating of the later periods of latency, puberty, and adolescence, and early, mature, and late adulthood must be much less definite.

Babyhood

A baby is born with a physiological mechanism that gives rise to certain needs: to breathe, to grasp, to suck, to eliminate, to sleep, for skin comfort, and others—needs in the psychological sense, some of them also requirements for physiological survival. His central concern, now that he is shifting from the chemical exchange system of his mother's body to a social exchange system, is to have these needs cared for. The sequence of tension and relaxation, building up and satisfaction of a need, is a pleasure-giving one (if the intensity of the need is not allowed to become too great before satisfaction) which presumably he did not experience before

---

[4] See his three works: *Childhood and Society* (New York: W. W. Norton & Co., Inc., 1950); "Growth and Crises of the 'Healthy Personality'," in Kluckhohn and Murray, and Schneider (eds.), *Personality;* and *Young Man Luther* (New York: W. W. Norton & Co., Inc., 1958).

birth. Some other needs emerge automatically with his physiological development, but he acquires many only by learning them. For example, he learns hunger as he comes to associate ingesting nourishment with disappearance of the gnawing feeling within him. He also learns dependence on his environment to satisfy his needs. In this way, and also perhaps because of innate needs to cling to another person and follow her with his senses,[5] he comes to have intense dependence on his mother or a mother-surrogate; he turns to her both to have his physiological needs cared for and to be loved. At first, and for a period of months, all events probably seem to him to go on within him. He does not distinguish between inner and outer; he is the world. Then, as he gradually makes a distinction between himself and the environment around him, he phrases the lessons he is learning in terms of relationships between him and the outer world.

Trust versus Mistrust

Erikson suggests that the central psychosocial problem of the period of babyhood is to what degree the baby acquires a sense of trust in himself and in the world, and to what degree a sense of mistrust. At times the infant has to feel a need more intensely than at others in order for its satisfaction to occur, and at times he has to cry out. He learns in greater or less degree that the connection between his initiative and satisfactory response to it is not automatic or certain. But the degree to which this is true varies greatly for different children, and from the degree the infant learns an important lesson. He either typically faces a problem (for example, hunger), attacks it (stirs or cries out), and solves it (nourishment appears within a reasonable period of time), or he faces it and lies in pain and anxiety during a period of time during which he fails to find a solution. (Perhaps his mother is too busy to feed him or thinks that waiting will teach him good habits.) Either he can depend on his initiative, the response being safe, dependable, comforting; or he cannot, and gains a sense that initiative is not followed by dependable response.

That he shall come to trust his ability to obtain a satisfactory response from the world requires not merely that his physiological needs shall be met dependably but also that their relief shall be accomplished in a manner that is comforting, reassuring, and loving. From his mother's confident, smooth movements, caressing touches, relaxed muscles, and easy and caressing voice he gains a feeling that the world is a secure place. Insofar as he is fussed over needlessly by an anxious mother, or handled abruptly by an impatient or irritated mother, or handled by a mother whose main interest at the time is elsewhere—in a conversation she is carrying on, say, or her complexion—he learns that the world does not respond to him, and thereby threatens him, even though his physiological care is adequate. If he is to trust, he must gain a perception that his envi-

---

[5] This is suggested by John Bowlby, in "The Nature of the Child's Tie to His Mother," *International Journal of Psycho-Analysis*, Vol. XXXIX (1958), pp. 350–73.

ronment, at this stage almost wholly his mother or her surrogate, is trust-worthy.

Of course to no baby and child are the responses of his environment to his urges entirely dependable. Even in the most favorable of environments a pin will prick, colic will develop, he will cut his finger, and so on. Inevitably during the teething period every child will experience pain for which he sees no cause and will feel that the world is arbitrary and hostile. The cases of general happy trust in one's relationship to one's world and of a pervading anxiety are extremes of a continuum. In Erikson's phrase, the infant gains a balance of trust and mistrust.

Separation

Inevitably the intimate nurturance of babyhood must be followed by a process of separation from the source of nurturance. The child is weaned from nourishment at his mother's breast. He is weaned also from cuddling or bodily contact, from the close response of his mother to his cries and smiles, from her physical presence whenever his attention turns to her. The time and the manner of this process of separation will vary. Each aspect of his intimate nurturance may be terminated early or late, and abruptly or gradually. In these ways, as in the partial failure of nurturance to appear, the child learns that the world is a somewhat dangerous and somewhat lonely place.[6] But the gentleness or severity of the lesson, and the sense on the one hand that it is a part of a safe and reasonable process or on the other that it is arbitrary and without regard for his needs, vary greatly among individuals and among cultures.

Demands for Self-Control

When his teeth begin to press sharply against his gums from the inside, the infant bites, perhaps partly in anger and partly because this is the only way in which he can get relief. When one or two teeth have appeared, if he is breast fed he tends to bite his mother's nipple. In almost any culture he then repeatedly and more or less suddenly finds it snatched from him; and he may be shaken, jerked, or even thumped on the head involuntarily in response to the pain, or deliberately in anger at the sudden pain or as a part of his training. He regains contact with the source of goodness only by extreme self-control countering his tendency to bite, control for which previously he has had little need and little practice.

At some stage he must learn to control his urination and bowel movements. The demand may come from his parents or from his siblings and

---

[6] "Our clinical work indicates that this point in the individual's early history provides him with some sense of basic loss, leaving the general impression that once upon a time one's unity with a maternal matrix was destroyed. . . . This stage seems to introduce into the psychic life a sense of division and a dim but universal nostalgia for a lost paradise." Erikson, in C. Kluckhohn, H. Murray, and D. M. Schneider (eds.), *Personality in Nature, Society, and Culture* (2d ed.; New York: Alfred A. Knopf, Inc., 1955), p. 193.

playmate peers. It may come early, before his physiological development has made it easy for him to exercise the necessary control, or it may come later when he is fully prepared physiologically. But it will certainly come. And these conventional examples of teething and toilet training are only the most conspicuous of a variety of ways in which the need is forced on him to control his urges in order to maintain contact with sources of nourishment, comfort, and companionship and to avoid some sort and degree of ostracism. He is coerced to control the timing of his expression of his urges, the object toward which he will express them, and the nature of his expression of them.

The timing, nature, and emotional tone of the coercion vary greatly. If the demands are made by individuals who give him the perception of having regard for his urges and desires, and at a time when he is physiologically capable of complying, the demands may not qualify greatly his perception that the world is an understandable place which responds in a pleasing way to one's initiative. If, on the other hand, the demands are made by individuals whose attention is centered on their own anxieties and compulsions, at a time when the demands bewilder him because his bodily system as yet has only the first weak undependable stirrings of the necessary capacities, then he learns that the world is a bewildering place, impossible to understand; and he learns also the tremendous importance of complying with arbitrary and inconsiderate demands of important persons around him.[7]

Physiological Development: Exploration

During this period of babyhood, as well as during the succeeding periods of late infancy and early childhood, physiological maturation occurs. A baby at birth is unable to do many things, not merely for lack of practice but also because his neuromuscular system has not yet developed the necessary connections and controls. For example, he does not yet have the necessary physiological equipment to focus his eyes, control his sphincter muscles, arch his body upward from a lying position, sit up, control his vocal chords, exercise the fine control over his legs needed for walking, or the fine control over his arms and fingers needed for throwing and handling. During the first several years of life, as myelination and other developments in his neuromuscular system proceed, he finds himself in possession of progressively expanding capacities. If he learns to use these capacities, an increasingly wide world will come within his reach. Walking and running will become automatic and can be forgotten about, and he will have an exhilarating ability to move about. Imitating sounds about him will lead to the ability to communicate, to express his wishes more meaningfully than before, to attack verbally. Through his increasing

---

[7] Concerning this effect of some types of toilet training, see Appendix 1 to this chapter.

muscular control he will become able to throw, to handle eating utensils and many other utensils, to build.

Because of his developing capacities, he exercises initiative (proaction) toward his environment, initiative which depends in part on his inherited physiological tendencies; he is by no means merely a passive reactor. But while he acquires capacities automatically, he does not automatically learn the activities. Even in the absence of other humans, the impact of his environment on him would teach him some simple activities such as to focus his eyes, but he does not come automatically to walk, talk, or use muscles in various precise ways. He learns these activities only as he observes other individuals using the capacities which he is finding in himself. Without models he would not learn to walk upright or to talk. Neither would he learn the manifold ways of thinking and acting that make him as an adult a normal member of his society.

He learns abilities, interests, and activities at the urging of the persons most important to him, from the models of action they provide even while they are trying to restrain him from action, and from their normal behavior which is not directed at him in any specific way but from which he generalizes about what he may do and become. Largely unconsciously, he learns from the adults and older siblings about him. But he does not blindly imitate them simply because their example exists. Rather, he responds to the stimuli presented to him by their relationship to him, and, within the limits of what their examples suggest to him as possible, he reacts in the ways that he thinks will best serve his interests. While he is learning physiological abilities he is also learning how to handle the increasing range of problems he encounters.

CONSIDERATE PARENTHOOD

At this point it will contribute to clarity to discuss separately the differing impacts on him of different types of parents.

Suppose first that in their own intuitive perceptions of the nature of the world his parents came to look on phenomena as forming understandable systems. They sense the nature of the interactions which are occurring between the child and his environment and understand their own reactions to their child's intrusion into their lives. If so, in his babyhood they may provide him with the more favorable of the alternatives suggested above, and in his late infancy and childhood may provide him with the aid, guidance, restraint, and nurturance he needs.

Parenthood and the Child's Explorations

In his explorations the child needs two types of aid. The process of learning to use his developing capacities is complex and uncertain. He needs encouragement, demonstration, and advice. Moreover, his exhilaration when the learning is successful may lead to exuberant and unrestrained action which is destructive and thereby provokes alarm or anger, punishment, and rejection. He needs guidance and restraint.

He also needs to gain a perception of being valued. If he is to learn to act effectively in relation to other persons, he must learn from nurturant models, models who have regard for his childish urges and purposes. It is difficult to overemphasize the degree to which learning both specific acts and complex interaction with other persons requires nurturance as well as demonstration. A child whose parents do not manifest an adequate degree of love for him is unable to learn effectively from their precept or example. It is as though, since they do not have regard for his needs and desires in life, he distrusts their advice and example and repels them. Indeed, the degree to which a child feels valued and responded to as he grows probably has an important effect on the level of intelligence he exhibits in later life.[8]

Parents who intuitively understand themselves and therefore their child may give him just the aid and guidance that will make the process of exploration most satisfying to him. They encourage his explorations without pushing him beyond his unfolding capacities. They close off areas of danger to him and move out of reach things that might damage him or that he might damage, so that as he ventures he does not suffer either the trauma of injuring himself or that of suddenly arousing alarm in his parents and thereby in himself. As he needs a bit of assistance, they provide it. As he succeeds, they reward him with love. They restrain him as his new powers go to his head, so that he neither harms himself or acts destructively. If this is the set of responses which meet his expanding capacities, he learns to trust his own evaluations, learns satisfaction in facing unresolved situations and trying to resolve them, and in general reinforces the perception he no doubt had gained earlier in such a home that the world responds dependably and satisfyingly to his initiative.

At first the mother's care was the centrally important element, but during this period the attitudes and acts of the father become increasingly important.

The parental behavior sketched above is in the sociological sense an ideal type. The individual may become more innovational if his parents' behavior is a somewhat qualified version of that sketched above—if, on a base of infantile security and nurturance, he gains the perception that his

---

[8] Experiments conducted by Professor Harry F. Harlow at the University of Wisconsin, in which monkeys who were reared by "mechanical mothers"—a wire apparatus which provided milk, and so on—are pertinent. Although adequately cared for physiologically, the monkeys became withdrawn, vacant, failed to care for their own appearance as normal monkeys do, could not learn to play although placed in association with play apparatus and with each other and normal monkeys after a period of babyhood, and in general failed to learn many interests and many abilities to perform and to interact, which before this experiment were commonly assumed to be instinctive for monkeys. See H. F. Harlow, "Mice, Monkeys, Men, and Motives," *Psychological Review*, Vol. LX (1953), pp. 23–32, and *The New York Times*, January 29, 1961, Section VI, pp. 62 and 64.

continued love and nurturance depend on certain standards of achievement by him. This case is discussed below in the section on The Anxious Innovator.

Rage

Many of his early experiences will arouse rage in him. The tendency to rage when one's desires are frustrated is probably inborn. When a need of the infant remains unsatisfied until it reaches an intensity sufficient to cause anxiety in him, he rages. He is apt to feel rage when he is separated from the intimate nurturance of his babyhood; at weaning and the other processes of separation he rages unless they are so long delayed that he chooses the separation himself and can regress to dependence whenever he chooses. Rage is unavoidable at teething. And he rages as successive demands for self-control are imposed upon him, the most important in early life being toilet training and the need not to bite while nursing.

If rage builds up in him, its results will be important elements of his personality. However, if his mother or a mother-surrogate responds to his rages with composure and love, and he gets a sense from her total relationship to him that the restraints and demands on him make sense and neither threaten him nor are attacks on him, less rage is aroused, and that which is aroused seems to diffuse itself.[9]

Infantile Genitality: The Identification Process

As his self-assurance grows, in say the fourth and fifth years, the boy wants to be big like his father. He may walk like his father, talk like him, and assume his other mannerisms. The boy dares to imagine that he can match his ideal, which is his father. He wants to be like his father because he has new capacities to try out and because he loves his father.

He wants to be like him also for another reason. The period of roughly the fourth and fifth years, as Freud observed and as is now recognized, is a period of real sexuality. The boy recognizes himself as a male, loves his mother, and, daring, as his capacities expand, to think of rivaling his father, wants to displace his father in every aspect of his father's relationship with his mother as he understands those relationships. But since his father seems to have special attractions for his mother, in order to rival his father he feels a need to *be* his father, except insofar as some aspects of his father's behavior have seemed to distress his mother or cause aversion in her, or do not serve the child's other purposes. And so he not merely imitates his father; he almost literally identifies himself with his father insofar as his father is acceptable to him as a model.

---

[9] "For no matter what we do in detail, the child will feel primarily what we live by, what makes us loving, cooperative, and firm beings, and what makes us hateful, anxious, and divided in ourselves." Erik H. Erikson in Kluckhohn *et al.*, *Personality*, p. 202. Erikson's statement directly relates to the question of weaning and toilet training, but the context indicates that he would apply it more generally.

There is a still more subtle and compelling reason for his partial identi-fication with his father. Along with his love and admiration for his father, the boy is jealous of him and hates him. But if he perceives that his father loves and values him, this hatred and jealousy cause the boy to feel guilt. He will sense rejection of him by his father at times, for example, when he attempts to come between his father and his mother. He seeks some explanation of this rejection. His father being loving, he cannot blame his father, and so he blames himself, and for this reason too feels guilt. To protect himself from this guilt and fear of rejection, he incorporates into his own personality standards of conduct which he believes to be those of his father. By doing so (*a*) he tries to prove to himself that since he is like (or is) his father, he cannot really hate his father, and so need not feel guilty, and (*b*) he tries to reassure himself that since he is his father, his father does not really wish to reject him.[10]

He tends to acquire not only his father's mannerisms and methods of physical behavior, so far as he can, but also his father's values and attitudes toward life, as the son understands them, insofar as they are satisfying to the son. If the father is conflicted and distressed, the boy is apt to reject one or more of his father's conflicting values unless all taken individually have corollaries which make him value them highly. If his father is caus-ing his mother distress, the son in his desire to be loved by his mother may reject the distressing attribute, again except as it serves some other function which is compelling. Whatever in the father seems unsatisfying to the father and therefore an unsafe guide to later life the boy will reject so far as he can find an alternative. Except for these qualifications (which in times of stress become important), the father's values and attitudes will be satisfying to the son, provided that the son can understand them, merely because they are satisfying to the father. If the father envies or admires the political leader or businessman—or on the other hand regards business as a grubby and unpleasant vocation—so will the son. If the father loves work on the soil, the son too will tend to find satisfaction and peace in it. So also with attitudes toward work with the hands, with tools, toward intellectual activity, gadgetry, tinkering with techniques, exploring the physical world. If the father preaches honesty and fair play but cuts corners to attain a pleasure without paying for it, the behavior, not the verbal admonition, will be learned. The process of identification with satisfying models has much to do with the transmission of a society's traditional values to successive generations. Above all, if the child has learned security and satisfaction in exploring the world, at this time he will observe his father's adult behavior and begin to turn his mind toward the problem of training himself to perform a man's occupational role.

Of course the model presented by his father is not the only model from which he learns. From observing his mother's behavior he also

---

[10] The process of identification, in Freudian terms, relates to both the ego-ideal and the superego.

learns many ways of behavior. More generally, both during this infantile genital period and later, he learns by imitating all of the models around him which are attractive and important to him and by behaving in ways opposite to models that are repugnant and promise ill results rather than good.

Moreover, the boy who is somewhat uncertain during the infantile-genital period of his ability to succeed in competition with his father for his mother's attention and nurturance is apt to find great pleasure in activity of a type which his father does not value highly but which his mother values and rewards. In this activity he can readily capture his mother's love in competition with his father. In many cases the initial inclination toward the career which he later follows in adulthood is provided by such a circumstance during the fourth, fifth, and sixth years of life.

As a girl passes through these years she goes through a parallel process. She wants to be big like her mother because she now dares to think of being big and because her mother is her ideal. She too recognizes her sex, prizes being attractive to her father, wants to be his sexual mate as she understands this, and, observing that her mother seems to have a special attraction for her father, wants to be identical with her mother for this reason too. And, hating her mother as a rival, she identifies with her the more to protect herself against this hatred. But, like her brother in relation to her father, she will identify with her mother only to the extent that her mother provides a satisfying model. And she too will find other models as well. They will in the normal case be models that lead her to attempt to be attractive rather than creative.

The World as Understandable

At this point it may be useful to focus attention on a theme which has run through the previous discussion. A centrally important aspect of the child's experience is whether he comes to perceive that the world is an understandable even though never fully understood place, and that achieving understanding yields satisfaction.

The child, it is clear, generalizes unconsciously from his early psychic experience to the nature of the external world. So to speak, he creates the world in his own image. Interesting relevant evidence is found in the work of Piaget. In his studies of what children believe at various ages from infancy to adolescence he found that at first the child assumes no distinction in behavior between animate and inanimate objects or between volitional and nonvolitional behavior. He applies the origins of behavior which he sees in himself to all objects. He assumes that the sun shines on him wherever he goes because, liking him, it follows him around, or because he wants it to; that the water holds up the boat because it likes the boat (or because it dislikes it), just as he holds things or lets them go for a similar reason. Gradually over the period of his childhood he comes more or less to distinguish mechanical cause and effect from willed action and response. As he does so, the one seems reasonable because the other seemed reasonable.[11] What I am suggesting here is that if the child finds the environment's response to his sequence of urges and initiatives in early life rather consistently understandable, then he will come unconsciously to feel that the world about him is governed by order and is susceptible to understanding. I use the word "feel" rather than "believe," for what is in point is not verbal assent to a formal doctrine that cause and effect operate, but an unconscious mind-set that causes one to sense that experience will respond to one's analysis, and to reach out toward it.

To state that the early response to urges and initiatives is understandable is equivalent to stating that it is satisfying. For that the environment responds to one's urges by giving one pain is bewildering; that one's urge yields satisfaction seems right. To any baby the world at first is, to use the trite, conventional phrase, "buzzing, blooming confusion." Then, as his experience causes him to focus his attention on some part of it, he may find that his urges and actions bring responses that seem appropriate. When he is hungry his hunger causes nourishment to appear; when he accomplishes the surprising new feat of sitting up in his crib, his evironment (his mother) expresses delight; when he is lonely, loving nurturance occurs and gives him security; as he tries out 100 new capacities in infancy and early childhood, harm or anxiety rarely results and pleasure and nurturance regularly do. If so, he acquires a sense that initiative meets with dependable response, that one can count on the world to make sense.

What is in point is far more than a static perception that the world one knows is understandable. It is a perception that as life proceeds one will repeatedly meet phenomena that do not fit in the schema one knows to that point, and that if they interest one, one can count dependably on being able both to deduce the system in which they do belong and on finding satisfaction in the process of discovering and exploring it.

This is the set of perceptions, I suggest, that creates in the individual the "openness to experience" or "capacity to be surprised" that is at the heart of creativity.

Dependability, it may be noted, is not enough to bring this set of perceptions. If, for example, the baby's mother feeds him dependably every five hours, while pains of hunger begin to arise in his body at four hours and cause him rising anxiety and terror until nourishment finally is given, he may perceive that the world is dependable in its infliction of pain, but he will not be able to understand it.

A perception that the world as one encounters it progressively will be a dependable and understandable place does not, on the other hand, require that all of the child's urges and initiative shall meet satisfying responses. It is impossible that they shall do so. Even under ideal circum-

---

[11] See Jean Piaget, *The Child's Conception of Physical Causation*, trans. Marjorie Gabain (London: Routledge & Kegan Paul, Ltd., 1951); *The Child's Conception of the World*, trans. J. and A. Tomlinson (New York: Harcourt-Brace & Co., 1929); and *The Child's Construction of Reality* (New York: Basic Books, 1954).

stances he will encounter some anxiety and some frustrations. Moreover, some whole areas of his experience may be rather painful and bewildering while others are satisfying. If so, shall he conclude that the world is arbitrary and incomprehensible or merely that its behavior is complex? Thus, if a boy's mother responds—dependably and consistently—to his urges while his father at times satisfies his needs for nurturance but more often is irritable and inconsiderate and causes him pain, does he perceive life as incomprehensible, or does he conclude that much of the world is understandable but somehow his father is different?

The answer probably depends on several factors. It must depend, firstly, on his intelligence. The higher his intelligence, the greater his capacity to see order rather than arbitrariness in complexity. It depends, secondly, on how secure a sense of basic trust he has acquired before he comes in contact with arbitrary behavior. If his needs for nurturance have been deeply and richly satisfied during the first year or two of his life, he is more apt than otherwise to respond to bewildering behavior later by assuming that the world is all right in general and that there merely is some aspect of it whose management is more difficult than he had assumed.[12] As a corollary, his reaction depends on how much experience he has had before the bewildering behavior impinges on him. He will be less likely to be shaken by arbitrary action if it occurs after he has had say three years of perception of the world as dependable.

Thirdly, the result probably depends on the degree to which there are present in his ken other models of the same general class as the one which is incomprehensible but whose behavior is more dependable. A child with an arbitrary father but who also has contacts with an uncle and grandfather whose behavior sustains his confidence in the reasonableness of the world is more apt than otherwise to perceive that something understandable lies behind the variability of his father's behavior even though the basis of variability is not yet within his grasp.

It is a reasonable speculation that the child becomes more resourceful and more creative the greater the number of differing understandable models he comes in contact with in emotionally favorable contexts. For example, he probably is more creative if his father and mother differ in their attitudes toward life, so long as the differences are not of a sort or degree that create tensions between them and cause him emotional problems.[13]

---

[12] J. W. M. Whiting and I. L. Child, *Child Training and Personality* (New Haven, Conn.: Yale University Press, 1953), cite research which suggests strongly that the degree of need autonomy in adulthood is positively correlated with the degree to which dependency needs were indulged at an early age.

[13] W. E. Henry has suggested, in conversation, the importance of the presence of differing models. He summarizes the suggestion very briefly in a different context—a discussion of the type of person who is apt to make the best interpreter of such materials as thematic apperception tests—in "The Language of Fantasy—A Problem in Instruction and Supervision," *American Journal of Orthopsychiatry*, Vol. XXIII, No. 2 (1953), pp. 315–21.

Within limits which depend upon these factors, it may be that variability of response of the environment, rather than making the world as a whole seem uncontrollable, aids the child in learning to master complex situations. However, those limits must be rather narrow in infancy, and, beyond them, variability of response probably makes the world seem threatening and unmanageable and checks development of need autonomy and need achievement.

If the child gains a perception that the world is understandable and can be managed, concomitantly he almost certainly gains a perception of being valued. For the same judicious loving unanxious care, responsive to his needs, that makes him perceive that the world is dependable will inculcate a feeling that he is valued. The child's conception of himself as a being of great or little worth seems to derive from his perception of the attitude of the important persons around him. If they indicate that they regard him as an individual of worth, he understands their valuation and believes it. And if they treat him as of little worth, he understands that too, and cannot be sure that they are wrong.[14] Of course, just as he understands some parts of his environment and not others, so he may sense that he is valued by some persons important to him and not valued by others. To acquire a self-valuation high enough for a high degree of creativity, almost certainly he must be valued highly—loved, nurtured dependably—by his parent of the opposite sex. Unless the attitude of the parent of the same sex is too adverse, this sex-satisfying valuation alone may be sufficient to convince him that he is important enough to be able to achieve.

If in his early development he acquires a perception that he is valued and securely cared for, he will be able without great anxiety to accept delays and minor frustrations. He will also be able to accept restrictions from the persons who value him, secure in the sense that the restrictions must be all right; and in the course of his exploration of the world he will come to understand that other persons have purposes and needs, as he does, and that reasonable adjustment by him or reasonable requirement imposed on him to adjust his purposes to theirs does not threaten him but gives him a more secure place in his expanding environment.

The perceptions by an individual that the world is dependable and that he has worth are probably the source of high need autonomy. If the individual feels that good results when he does what seems reasonable, and feels also that the environment values him highly, he need feel no anxiety lest someone else's judgment differs from his. Even if it does, there is no harm; this thought contents him. (For further comments on the

---

[14] One must distinguish sharply between the individual's sense of his own worth and his assertion to others around him that he is worthy, capable, superior. This assertion typically is evidence that he is not certain of his own worth and is trying to persuade himself, testing the opinion of those around, and challenging the low valuation by them which he half anticipates.

acquisition of need order and need succorance-nurturance, see Appendix 3 to this chapter.)

The Anxious Innovator

However, even though the innovational individual does not feel anxious at the exercise of autonomy or at facing unexplained phenomena, he is not necessarily anxiety-free. In Chapters 5 and 6 I suggested the presence of a type of anxiety that does not inhibit creativity but motivates it, and earlier in this chapter I referred briefly to circumstances that may create anxiety of this type. The presentation was overly simple; in practice, anxiety almost certainly contains a component which inhibits creativity in some degree. However, let us first consider the imaginary pure case where no such component exists.

Suppose that in the infant's period of complete dependence his parents' care of him gives him a secure feeling of love and nurturance. Suppose also, however, that his mother is somewhat anxious that he shall be a capable and effective person (for example, because her own father was not). As the infant's capacities develop, her love and considerateness keep her from making demands upon him that are too unreasonable; but she presses him to crawl, to talk, to walk, to throw, and so on just a little before each capacity is fully developed, so that each achievement is possible for him but somewhat difficult.

Her nurturance gives him the impression that she would not ask anything unreasonable of him. Therefore he tends to feel that neither she nor he but rather the intrinsic difficulty of the task is responsible for the initial difficulty with which he meets her requests. Because her love is important to him, and her sense of the importance of his actions communicates itself to him, he strives; and because her thoughtfulness keeps her from making the request too soon, he is able to succeed, though not with ease. The pleasure and nurturance which flow out from her at each success give him intense satisfaction, for anxiety followed by pleasure provides a powerful motivating force and makes a deep and lasting impression.[15]

On balance, the individual who has had this kind of experience in early childhood anticipates success each time he tries to achieve later in life, for this was the pattern of his early striving; but because success is not a foregone conclusion, he forever feels a need to try another task and reassure himself.

---

[15] A fact known long before the day of modern psychology, as is evidenced by Benvenuto Cellini's account of seeing a salamander in the midst of the flames in a fireplace—a symbol of great import—whereupon his father gave him "a great box on the ears" and said: "My dear little boy, I am not striking you for any wrong that you have done, but only to make you remember that lizard which you see in the fire is a salamander. . . ." So saying, he kissed Benvenuto and gave him some pieces of money. *The Autobiography of Benvenuto Cellini*, trans. J. A. Symonds (New York: The Macmillan Co., 1929), Book I, section 4, p. 7.

The results, then, are the inculcation of the following unconscious processes:

1. When he is not attacking problems, he is pervaded by restlessness (a manifestation of anxiety), which leaves him while he is striving and, only temporarily assuaged by each success, reappears as he relaxes.[16]

2. Often this anxiety takes the form of a deep sense of duty to perform —duty to his God (as in the Protestant Dissenters), to his emperor (as in Meiji Japan), or perhaps to his country or community. I shall try to show in later chapters that home environment such as that indicated probably existed among the groups named.

3. However, insofar as the individual came in childhood to blame not his mother or himself but rather the intrinsic difficulty of achievement for his anxiety, he does not feel rage and therefore experiences no inadmissible urges or fantasies. Hence he has no defensive need to seal over his unconscious processes, and they remain available to aid him in creative endeavors.

For simplicity, in sketching the circumstances which will have this effect on the child I have referred only to his relations with his mother. Various other conditions in the childhood environment may occasion the results sketched. For example, he may have an older brother or sister in whose achievements the parents often show pleasure. Even if they also manifest love for the younger child, he is apt repeatedly to become anxious to duplicate the performance of the older brother or sister which temporarily draws his parents from him. Hence he is apt to acquire the anxious need achievement sketched above.

The behavior within the individual which I have sketched is of course somewhat conjectural, but that such circumstances are apt to inculcate a higher degree of need achievement than will a more relaxed environment is both consistent with psychoanalytic theory of personality development and indicated by much experimental evidence.[17] The degree of need autonomy inculcated is probably lower than would have emerged in a more relaxed environment, for the repeated pressure on the child, driving him to attempt feats before he is quite ready to do so, must instill some uncertainty in him concerning his own judgment about his capacities and actions.

Further, as I suggested earlier, the case in which the child's anxiety is associated with no constriction whatever on his creativity is probably imaginary. A necessary element in the anxiety-producing situation neces-

---

[16] In this case the anxiety takes the form of guilt. In other cultures, in which the personalities of the parents are such that the pressure on the child is not to reveal inadequacy to others, the anxiety may take the form of shame. See Gerhardt Piers and Milton B. Singer, *Shame and Guilt: A Psychoanalytic and Cultural Study* (Springfield, Ill.: Charles C. Thomas, 1953), and Melford G. Spiro, *Children of the Kibbutz* (Cambridge, Mass.: Harvard University Press, 1957), pp. 407–8.

[17] See Appendix 2 to this chapter.

sarily is the pressure someone is putting on him to achieve, and, no matter how great the earlier sense of being loved and nurtured by that person, that pressure is bound to provoke some rage directed at her. If the child feels rage, he also feels urges and fantasies which he must repress from consciousness. His resulting fear of admitting the existence of those urges and fantasies must cause him to be somewhat guarded in accepting concepts from his unconscious processes and so must limit his creativity in some degree. However, the limitation may not be severe. Moreover, since much innovation may result from only moderate creativity combined with intense drive, a highly anxious individual may be a more effective innovator than an individual with high creative capacity but less incentive to use it.

To appreciate the role of anxiety in personality and behavior, it is important to note clearly a fact mentioned briefly in Chapter 5, that anxiety is often largely unconscious. The anxiety referred to here is due to early experiences which caused pain. To lessen the pain the individual repressed memory of the experiences from consciousness. Because he repressed the memory he is also forced to deny that the events caused him anxiety; hence he represses the anxiety as well. Overtly, he is a very quiet person, or an unusually voluble person; a touchy, aggressive person, or an acquiescent person; restless whenever he is not working intensely, as in the case of many anxious innovators; or, depending on the nature of the experiences which gave him pain and the patterns of behavior which he perceived to be the best solution of his problem, his defense may be of some other sort. But the fact that he is not aware of his anxiety or of the needs associated with it does not lessen the importance of those needs as determinants of his behavior all his life.

AUTHORITARIAN PARENTHOOD IN TRADITIONAL SOCIETIES

We have been considering parenthood that is considerate of the child's urges and needs. Suppose, at the other extreme, that the parents are authoritarian. They do not see the phenomena of the world as interacting in systems amenable to analysis. Rather, they perceive phenomena as fortuitous objects or events over which they have no control except in the narrow area of traditional craftsmanship, within which their control is gained by the learning of traditional skills. Since the available evidence suggests that such parents are typical in the traditional society, the essential characteristics of the generalized description below are probably a fairly faithful reflection of childhood environment in almost every such society.[18]

---

[18] Some of the relevant empirical evidence is presented in Chapter 8, together with reasons for thinking it is generally typical.

Early Indulgence and Later Control

Unconsciously remembering the arbitrary nature of the events which impinged on them during their own childhoods, against which their initiative led only to frustrations, such parents think of a child as capable of developing a skill and judgment in traditional areas of activity but as otherwise rather defenseless against the world and incapable of developing its own ability to act and react against the world. They think of the child as an object which as an infant is fragile and must be protected and perhaps indulged, and then as it grows older must be trained by detailed guidance in the way in which it ought to go.

Both of these apparently contradictory attitudes—early indulgence or toleration, later strict control—derive partly from the perception that the infant and child has no resources within himself and partly from another aspect of parental personality. Consider the indulgence first. The environment in which the parents grew up led them, especially the father, to fear the impingement of other persons on him rather than to welcome it, for in general he perceived other persons as tending to thwart and hurt him rather than help him. He intuitively reacts defensively when anyone impinges on his life, and, unconsciously, he regards the intrusion of a child with some annoyance, fear, and resentment. He thereby feels guilt, and to assuage his guilt he excessively indulges the infant. And, unconsciously wishing that the infant would come to harm or would disappear from his life, the father projects this fear onto the outer world and fears that the child will come to harm. In the light of infant mortality rates in traditional societies, that fear is easy to rationalize. The mother experiences these reactions only in lesser degree, for she has learned the feminine role of serving others and hence does not so object to the child's intrusion into her life. However, since her own personality is authoritarian in its way, she must experience the same reactions to some extent. In any event, in the early care of the child she follows the lead of her husband and of tradition. Hence the parents, fearing excessively that the child may injure himself or be injured, overprotect and restrain him even while in a sense they indulge him.

Weaning is often late and gradual, in some cultures as late as the child desires except as the arrival of another baby interferes. (In most traditional societies, however, such interference typically occurs rather soon.) Toilet training, too, is permissive in many cultures, or at least is imposed by the slightly older siblings and playmates rather than by the parents, the mother not indicating the least repugnance to her child's soiled condition or to the smell of urine or feces. Where the training is by one's mates, however, their demands for conformity and their ridicule and shaming of the child who does not behave as the group feels he should may be as cruel as the sternest training by an adult.

The small child is apt to be picked up instantly if it cries or is alarmed, since there is fear for its safety and welfare. In this case the child may not perceive tenderness, for the child sometimes seems to be treated almost as if it were to blame for its discomfort or alarm. It may also be allowed to babble or wander about as its parents engage in conversation, and to accompany its mother wherever she goes. It is not checked from its babbling or from interfering with the adult group, but it often finds no response to its initiative; it simply is not paid attention to. Even as the mother cares for the child's toilet needs, she may be talking with someone else, and she may put the child down without interruption of the activity she is engaged in.

The environment of early childhood in traditional societies, seen through Western perceptions of the nature of interpersonal relations, has often been described by Western observers as characterized by great permissiveness. Rather, it is indulgence or toleration combined with protective restraint. The difference is important. The child, being thought without resources of its own, is prevented from using its initiative. In word, tone, and bodily action adults may express fear and alarm of its ventures, and so may prevent it from using its growing capacities even though they are ready to be used and observation by the child of models around it creates urges in it to use them. At its slightest wandering, it may be picked up; if it begins to crawl, it may be seized and carried instead. It may be borne on its mother's hip or back throughout the entire crawling period, so that it is given almost no chance to propel itself about until it is fully able to walk. This treatment must breed in the child as strongly as would more positive controls a sense that the world is not responsive to its initiative but is arbitrary and unmanageable, a sense of being unable to understand why things are as they are and by what action one can get along.[19]

But when the child is no longer so fragile, the father's guilt no longer forces him to be indulgent. Moreover, as the child grows, if he is a boy he becomes more of a rival to his father. Hence the father finds that the time has come for training, and he consistently quiets, subdues, and represses the child. "A child," he says, in the traditional phrase, "should be seen and not heard." All this is in accord with the tradition of the culture, which is consistent with the world image of the parents, and which teaches that at a certain age the child's training should begin.

---

[19] A study at the Yale University School of Medicine showed that children of both "overpermissive" and rigid parents (and without significant difference between the two groups) developed problem behavior in areas of sleep, feeding, toileting, and socialization. See Ethelyn H. Klatskin, Edith B. Jackson, and Louise C. Wilkin, "The Influence of Degree of Flexibility in Maternal Child Care Practices on Early Child Behavior," *American Journal of Orthopsychiatry*, Vol. XXVI (1956), pp. 79–93, cited by Robert I. Watson in *Psychology of the Child* (New York: John Wiley & Sons, Inc., 1959), p. 110. I suggest that the "overpermissive" behavior may have included elements of constraint, like the behavior described in the text above, and in any case was not responsive to the child's needs.

It also is in accord with the need dominance of the parents. Their world image and their need dominance interact, each reinforcing the other.

Protectiveness becomes control. The prime duties of the child become to learn a certain set of rules: not to bother adults, but on the contrary to exhibit deference to them; to reflect the family's position in the community; not to get the family into trouble; to learn the traditional skills; to pay due respect to the spiritual powers. The parents subject him to a daily rhythm of directions. Except in the traditional skills of his class, there is no assumption that he has any organizing abilities within him and can learn to anticipate responsibilities or to resolve problems. He is a bottle into which directions are poured, not a developing organism. His parents do not guide or assist him; they control his development. They do this, however, not with any overt sternness or aggressiveness but simply because this is what the nature of the world as they see it requires.

The child's actions which spring from his own initiative will often seem irrelevant and will be suppressed. This suppression will cause him to feel a sense of failure and alienation, a sense, which he felt earlier in life, that he does not understand how one can proceed in life and must seek for direction. In the name of training, the parents unwittingly give him the perception that except in a few activities the interaction between his initiative and the world around him is necessarily an anxious process, and that the anxiety is to be avoided by submitting to authority. No doubt he has repressed his rage at his parents and simply feels obligation toward them.

He has no models which would teach him that differences among individuals can be reasoned out, understood, and reconciled or compromised, and so he sees domination by one individual or the other as the only solution. Since most of the persons who frustrate him are more powerful than he, he learns to avoid anxiety by submitting to them. He learns both need dependence and need submission.

But he also rages, and, observing that larger dominate smaller and senior dominate junior, he vents some of his rage by dominating his juniors and finds it satisfying. Thus he also learns need dominance. His parents, consciously or unconsciously, are aware of his rages and of the necessity of building a defense against the danger that those rages shall turn against them. Hence the extreme importance placed in probably every traditional society on deference by the child toward adults and especially toward his parents. (Again, the rule is applicable that there is a reason for every practice of any culture; it forms part of a system, even though sometimes not all the elements of the system are easy to perceive.

The Crisis of the Oedipal Period

In the crisis of the Oedipal relationship the impact of authoritarian parenthood reaches a climax. At the beginning of this period the boy may feel free to react to his new sexuality and to reach out to his mother

*Can diagram this Φ of tradytal fam. as fam constellog + relshps.
of M, F, S.*

as a woman, for the period of indulgence often extends to and into the Oedipal period. His father, however, is comfortable only in an authoritarian role, and as his son's new sexual rivalry for his mother's attentions arouses the father's anxieties and his need aggression and dominance, he pushes the boy aside. Severe training may begin abruptly. The boy has previously received a degree of nurturance from both his father and his mother. Now, besides finding neither as available as before, he learns with a shock the penalty for daring to think himself equal to his father. Even though he has previously been active and vociferous, at this time he may become quite subdued. The difference in degree between this experience and the Oedipal crisis with "considerate parenthood" is so great that the results are radically different.

The shock is often and even typically so great that never again will he be quite certain that he is able to be a man. The doubt will apply specifically to his relationships to women. However, because of another aspect of interpersonal relationships which he observes at the same time, the shock is typically not so great as altogether to prevent him from functioning sexually. This other aspect is the fact that females are subordinate to males; he sees all around him the fact that men call upon women to help and serve them, and that it is the role of women to respond. This perception will ordinarily cause him to feel capable of feminine conquests, but his traumatic rejection when he first tried to approach a woman will cause him throughout life to feel anxiety about that capability. The combination may cause him to reassure himself repeatedly of his virility throughout his adult life by means of repeated sexual conquests;[20] it will cause him also to be hypersensitive to any action that casts doubt on his manliness.

This seems to be the origin of the style of behavior observed among men of Latin blood both throughout Latin America and along the Mediterranean wherever traditional culture and personalities prevail— the style of personality termed *machismo*. It has two aspects: incessant sexual adventure and an intense need to defend one's honor against any slight. The male is ready to regard his honor as put in question by the inflection of a voice or the turn of a word; he must defend it, not really against the attack of the other individual, but against his own uncertainty. Although uncertainty concerning one's manhood does not express itself in quite the same way in non-Latin traditional societies, it manifests itself in analogous ways. The duels and knightly sensitivity of the Middle Ages were probably reflections of the same aspects of authoritarian personality. The multiple marriages in Muslim countries may reflect the same aspects. Extramarital adventure is common in many traditional societies in which it is not glorified in male lore as in Latin America. In Japan it is institutionalized. "Three steps down from his doorway and a married man is a

---

[20] Just as the anxious innovator must reassure himself of his ability to achieve by tackling another problem.

bachelor again" (and in search of sexual adventure), it is said in Burma. And in some other countries one difficulty in obtaining a reduction in the birth rate is that a man is regarded as not virile if he does not procreate a child every year.

If the trauma of the Oedipal period is especially acute, it may produce a reaction in the boy more extreme than *machismo*. The boy may feel that his aggressiveness has not only failed to gain his mother; it has also brought the danger of loss of his father. The boy may seek rather desperately for a model of behavior that will assure him his father's regard and may see it in his mother, who obviously is attractive to his father. His perception of a feminine role will heighten his earlier need dependence, and he will become a dutiful, obedient, constricted individual, all his life unable to exert normal initiative of action or thought. Or, in the extreme case, he becomes feminine even in his sexual behavior, that is, becomes homosexual. Since there is always an element of aggressiveness in homosexuality, by this device he also somewhat satisfies his rage. Short of homosexuality, he may avoid the sex issue in an asexual life. We shall see illustrations of this too in traditional society.

Of course individuals who repress such fears, anxieties, and urges into their unconscious processes do not have those processes available for creative work. Moreover, the needs inculcated during this period by an authoritarian environment are adverse to creativity. The foundations of uncreative personality are laid.

Sources of Satisfaction

From this description of authoritarian childhood, one might conclude that life is a pretty grim affair for the child in traditional society. This is not true. The child is probably no more unhappy than the typical child in American society. The circumstances of his childhood fit into the life pattern of his society, and on the whole he finds them good.

He finds three sources of satisfaction in his life. First, the one qualification to the expectation that he has no capacities of his own is that it is assumed he can learn traditional skills. Even though this learning involves closely following traditional models, for the child it requires the solution of a series of problems and the repeated testing of the capacities developing in him. His satisfaction in their effective exercise and in his parents' pleasure at his performance must give him considerable pleasure.

Part of this learning consists of imitating or participating in his father's occupation. That occupation being readily understandable even at an early age, he will follow his father about and will participate in the smaller tasks. In a landed family he may have his own pony and ride about directing the hired hands like his father. Because the exercise of traditional activities is the only area of behavior in which he is encouraged to use his initiative, he will turn to them the more eagerly, and he will find it the more satisfying as an adult to cling to them.

Many of his games will be versions of the activities he is expected to carry on when he becomes an adult. The others will embody in some way the skills or attitudes he must have as an adult. Since competitive achievement is not an expectation of his culture, his games will probably involve no scoring activity (until Westerners disrupt his culture and make scoring games attractive), and since need aggression is too threatening to be unleashed, his games will probably not involve competition of team against team.

A second source of pleasure lies in the fact that the child is provided with an outlet for his rage. Venting his need aggression on persons junior to him gives him just as true satisfaction as would the venting of need achievement, need order, or any other need.

Also, in many cultures, the boy is expected to be mischievous at times and to violate a little aggressively the rules laid down for him. This is only by way of testing slightly the aggression he will later be expected to exercise: serious infraction will bring pressures too great for him to resist; but his minor infractions must give him satisfaction.

Third, the behavior of his parents is not overtly angry or tense but seems a reasonable part of a way of life. It is an integral part of a set of relationships satisfying to them, which he may look forward to entering into when he becomes an adult. This perception reinforces the satisfaction he obtains in the sanctioned venting of his rage. His anticipation of successively senior hierarchical roles as his life proceeds is satisfying to him and compensates him for his frustrations because it seems satisfying to the models about him. Hence he represses his need aggression and need dominance; but they persist in his unconscious processes and he vents them, partly in childhood and partly all the rest of his life, in his relationships to inferiors.

He resolves any situation by structuring it in terms of domination by one of the individuals involved, who renders an authoritative decision. A situation that cannot be so resolved because there are no rules to determine who is superior creates anxiety which by its reminder of earlier anxieties due to frustration leads to rage. This, as I have suggested, is an important reason why the advent of strangers is so often seen as threatening in a traditional society and leads to aggression against them.

The childhood of the girl is not quite the same. She too finds pleasure in learning traditional skills, in her case the skills of homemaking, and in games which embody or symbolize those activities which will later in life be hers. Like her brother, she no doubt finds anxiety and pain in the repeated frustration of her urges and explorations as she grows; but these are not as great as her brother's because in the model of her mother's behavior, and in her own feminine sexual desire to be attractive to her father, she sees that the satisfying role of woman is to serve. In the satisfaction which her mother manifests in her serving, nurturant role the daughter's rages no doubt diffuse.

Religion and the Meaning of Life

Since the early initiative of the child led to alarm and pain, he learned a general fear of exercising initiative. Moreover, he was often snatched up by his elders in alarm as he explored the simple physical world immediately around him. Thus he probably learned a specific apprehension concerning the physical world. This, however, seems less important in inhibiting him as an adult from exploring the operations of the physical world than is another aspect of his childhood experience.

The individuals responsible for his early anxiety and pain were his parents. However, it is intolerable to him to hold them responsible; they are so important to him that he dares not harbor the thought that they do not hold his purposes and needs in high regard. Hence he represses from his conscious mind the knowledge that the behavior of his parents was the source of his bewilderment, anxiety, and pain.

Yet the pain and anxiety stay within him, and he asks himself why they exist. The question why pain exists haunts individuals in all cultures; it must haunt the members of authoritarian cultures in especially high degree. With this problem in his emotions, the child becomes aware during the infantile-genital period that his elders regard the physical world as containing forces that dominate life and are threatening and unmanageable. They fear for their crops, their health, the lives of their animals and of the members of their families. Their fears are obviously justified by the events that occur. They attribute those events to the actions of unseen powers that act arbitrarily or capriciously or at least without regard for the welfare of individual human beings. And they relieve their anxiety concerning such events by appeal to those spiritual forces. Humbly, they make offerings or perform magic rites in the plea that their crops or their animals or their lives may be spared. As they thus approach the spiritual forces, their anxiety is relieved.[21]

As he comprehends this behavior, the child sees an explanation of the problems that have been tormenting him. The source of his anxiety is the presence in the world of arbitrary forces that control his destiny. And he has been shown pain to teach him to bow humbly before these spiritual powers in order that they may bless his life, and to enable him to prove by enduring the pain that he is worthy of their favor. Moreover, he is to the powerful humans about him as they are to the spiritual powers. In these realizations he finds an explanation of his anxiety and pain. They gain meaning. He comes to believe in the rightness of authoritarian behavior, in the spiritual forces, and in the wrongness of transgressing on their authority with a belief that transcends reason and makes reason unnecessary. Thereafter, like the elders before him, he appeals to the unseen spirits only with the proper ritual (magic or its

---

[21] See Chapter 4, pp. 69–70 and n. 22.

equivalent) and with the aid of a religious practitioner (somewhat as in childhood he had approached his father with the mother's aid). In the technology of production his efforts become concentrated not on technical explorations which the modern world would term rational but on methods of appeasing the spirits and assuring their favor.

Having solved the problem of pain by this cognition of the nature of the world, the members of traditional society cannot conceive of the world as subject to management by their initiative and intelligence, for that conception, by denying that arbitrary forces rule the world, would destroy the justification for pain. Thus a supremely powerful sanction for not trespassing on the realm of the spiritual forces presses on the individuals of traditional peasant societies.

In this coincidence of belief and early unconscious perceptions lies much of the explanation of the transmission of culture from generation to generation. Culture is transmitted from generation to generation not primarily in memory but in personality.[22]

Let it be clear that this sanction presses on the members of the elite as well as the simple folk. The members of the elite too experience authoritarian parenthood, live within the same social structure, and incorporate the same attitude toward the forces which they conceive to control that world. They feel the same pain in childhood when their explorations lead to authoritarian domination of their activities by their parents; the conception that arbitrary forces which one must approach with respect and ritual rule the world fits their early experience as neatly as that of the simple folk; and in the maintenance of their relationship to those unseen forces they find the same justification for pain as do the simple folk. Even though in later historical times they may decry in words a simple animist formulation of that attitude, their conception of the world, beneath more sophisticated verbalizations, is the same. Their homilies concerning the virtues of humanism, the glories of the past, the wisdom of the old, and so on express the attitudes toward life which they have learned it is not quite stylish to hold in starker form.

The world's noble religions, which the members of the elite in some societies have accepted, are, it may be noted, reconcilable with this same view of the world and in peasant societies incorporate it. The Buddhist doctrine that to attain peace one must eschew worldly desires readily

---

[22] Illustrations of the tendency to rationalize one's emotions may be found closer to home. For example, I suggest that millions of persons in the United States believed Senator Joseph McCarthy's statements in the early 1950's about the sinister network of Communists that threatened American life not because of any evidence they read but because the concept of a mysterious force which threatened them matched and confirmed a sense of alarm they had felt in infancy and childhood at arbitrary threatening forces (perhaps authoritarian parents) in their lives, a sense which of course had been reinforced and deepened during the depression of the 1930's and World War II. The emotional attachment of millions of Americans to President F. D. Roosevelt and again to President Eisenhower reflects a similar process.

justifies the conception that the function of pain is to teach one to curb one's desires. The prohibition of Islam against practices not sanctioned by Allah through Mohammed is severe. The Christian religion teaches that the pain which Christ suffered on one's behalf earns one the grace of God and everlasting life. That conception is consistent with the revolutionary doctrines that every man is his own interpreter of the Scriptures and that one reflects God's grace by glorifying God through developing the earth to make it fruitful; but it is consistent also with the traditional doctrines that one learns from one's religious superiors one's duties to God and will not question the order of the universe. And so on. Thus these nobler views of the world are all interpretable, and are traditionally interpreted, as finding pain blessed because it leads one to the correct relationship to the Power that rules the universe (or, in the case of Buddhism, because it guides one toward peace). As a corollary, the religions command that one shall not have the arrogance to attempt to understand the physical universe out of one's own initiative and intelligence. Thus the members of the elite who partially abandon animist religions should not be thought thereby to have abandoned the cognition of the nature of the universe which the animist religions reflect.

OTHER TYPES OF PARENTHOOD

Considerate and authoritarian parenthood are of course not the only possible types, unless one defines all parental behavior that is not considerate of the child's needs as authoritarian. Parental behavior may be inconsiderate in ways not usually so classed. For example, parents who are anxious about their own inadequacies may relieve their anxieties by determination that their child shall achieve. Seizing upon the first tentative budding in him of each new capacity, they may press him to walk, to talk, to control his bowels, and so on before he has acquired the physiological capacity to do these things, the result being that he is repeatedly frustrated. Or, because of the same anxieties, they may feel such satisfaction at the deeds of an older brother or sister, turning their attention and love away from the younger child in the process, that he feels that his salvation lies in doing what his older rival is doing. In this case too he may try doggedly to do things he cannot yet do and fail repeatedly.

This case differs only in degree from that sketched earlier as inculcating high though anxious need achievement. The environments that will produce these contrasting results do not always differ greatly. If the parents are pressing for achievement too early, the very fact that they expect the child to achieve is apt to instill in him the (rather confused) perception that they value and love him. He is therefore apt to feel that his failure must be his fault, for loving parents would not require unreasonable things. His failure, he feels, must be due to some error in the way he is trying to accomplish the desired feat. He must not be doing it quite right. Yet since his body is not yet ready to perform the task, it is bewildering to him. Hence he will seek anxiously for external guidance, and he will try painstakingly and without understanding them to follow the details of the motions that his parents seem to be asking him to make. This effort, if he persists, will eventually succeed as his neuromuscular development proceeds to a stage that makes success possible. Thus he learns that painstaking rote following of external guidance is the way to find one's way out of anxiety and frustration. He learns a high degree of need dependence; a pattern of looking for rules; of being precise, bent on detail, and utterly unimaginative.

On the other hand, if the father is weak and irresponsible, his failure to exert authority in the home may permit the mother to be nurturant to her son and may permit the son to gain access to her attentions during the Oedipal period. Or, if the father is irritable and demanding but is erratic and often absent from the home or preoccupied with other matters, the son may learn that at times his initiative works and at times it does not and so may acquire a strained, anxious need autonomy and achievement. In both of these cases achieving and creative personalities may result. We shall have no occasion to consider further the first of these three cases, but the latter two will be analyzed further in later chapters in considering the transition from traditional society to technologically progressive society.

CHILDHOOD AND ADULTHOOD

As was recognized above, the formation of personality is not completed in infancy and early childhood. It proceeds throughout life. Every event until death has some impact on personality. However, the events of later life never cause the process of personality formation to begin anew, as though childhood had never occurred; rather, they reinforce or conflict with, and build upon, the personality traits inculcated in childhood. With the process of personality formation in infancy and early childhood analyzed as it has been above, the purposes of this book may be served by a rather brief discussion of later periods in life; for, although changes in personality from generation to generation will be of great importance in the discussion in later chapters, it will be suggested that in causing those changes the impact of altered adult *behavior* on the personalities of the next generation of children is of much more importance than is direct alteration in adult *personality*. A change in adult behavior may be illustrated as follows: without any basic change in their cognitions, needs, or values, adults will behave differently—for example, will experience new emotions or new intensities of emotion—if they face new circumstances. Thus adults whose occupations, once respected, are looked upon with contempt by a new ruling group may react with anger, anxiety, or fear of degrees they had not felt before. The new behavior implies no change in personalities. Some change in personalities will also certainly occur, but, to repeat, it is regarded as less important in affecting the personalities of ensuing generations than is the change in behavior.

It is important, however, to note briefly how the personality with which the individual emerges from early childhood plus the environment of his later life combine to determine his adult personality. First, the later stages of personality development may be sketched briefly.

Latency; Dealing with a Wider Group

During the period of roughly the sixth to the tenth or twelfth years the child's body is, so to speak, assimilating the physiological changes of the first five years and getting ready for the further changes of puberty and adolescence. During these years the neighborhood and in most cultures a school become important. The child comes into increased contact with playmates, schoolmates, and teachers. He sees them as additional models of behavior, but in addition he must interact with them. If he enters the period with high need achievement, autonomy, and succorance-nurturance, and with a view of new phenomena as potentially orderly and manageable, he will experiment in his relationships with his new peers and mentors and, unless they differ sharply from him in important ways, will achieve satisfying relationships and find his previous perceptions validated. If he is high in need aggression and submission-dominance and low in need achievement and autonomy, and views the world in ways consistent with these needs, he will establish submissive relationships to his mentors and elders, he will domineer over his juniors, and he will deal with peers on such terms of aggression as are expedient. Here too his earlier perceptions will be validated. In either case, if his society sanctions the social structure implicit in his view of the world, as it will if he is a typical member of the society, the elders he now comes in contact with will in the one case offer him, in the other impose on him, the relations deemed appropriate; and it is all the more certain that his development will be an extension of what he has already gone through.

This period is often termed the latency period because in most cultures the sexual activity of the period of infantile genitality subsides, to reappear only in adolescence. The latency, however, seems to be learned rather than merely physiological, for in some traditional societies it does not occur.[23]

The Problem of Identity

Then comes adolescence, the beginning of adult genitality, and the child is in a real sense a new person and all over again must go through

---

[23] See Watson, *Psychology of the Child,* p. 590, citing evidence from Malinowski and Devereux.

the process of finding out who he is. In a traditional society there is little problem. At the age of six he could understand most of the things adults do, especially in their work, and before he comes out of the period of latency the formation of his adult identity is fairly well along. In a society in which adult roles are not so understandable to a child he must hold his identity in abeyance. He wants to be like his father or some other adult model, but since he does not know just what his model does in life (and he realizes this more and more as he passes through the latency period) he must remain vague about himself until he can find what it is he wants to be. In adolescence, as he increasingly understands adult roles, he also encounters a much wider range of models in his teachers, in peers who have had different experiences from his, in the roles acted out in moving pictures and in the daily news which he learns by word of mouth or from newspapers or the radio, in television programs if he lives in an economically advanced country. Insofar as his previous models have been so unsatisfactory to him that he bears conflicting images of a satisfactory identity for himself, this period may either suggest new possibilities or crystallize for him the image of something he has earlier vaguely sought. Even if his sense of an identity is satisfactory as he enters the period, the image will become sharper now. His sexual role will now be different if he did experience latency. Unless his earlier development has made him afraid of substituting another female person for his mother, or deeply afraid of rivaling his father, he begins again to do both and seeks out companions of the other sex.

In early adulthood in the normal case he will no longer postpone the decision concerning who he will be as an adult. Perhaps with a "wander-jahr," a year of knightly deeds, or some other temporary withdrawal from his prospective community in order to gather the threads of his identity together (Erikson's social moratorium), he enters adulthood.[24]

During this period, as in the latency period, in a society in equilibrium the new experiences and the new models will validate his experience up to that point, and there will be no sharp break in his development. Rather, his earlier needs, values, and cognitions will be reinforced.

Intimacy; Adulthood

Thereafter, with whatever capacity his development to date has given him, he must solve (or evade) the problems of playing his role as an adult and of relating intimately with a person of the opposite sex not only in sexual activity but also in the full scope of his life. In the remainder of adulthood he works and loves with the capacities his complex develop-

---

[24] He may find that a self compounded out of the various aspects of him which have emerged to that time is satisfying, or he may have to contain somehow a struggle within him between inconsistent needs and values and views of the world. He may handle the latter problem by refusing to conceive a clear image of himself, instead holding in his mind a diffuse conception which avoids goals and roles except in impossible fantasy, and under which he suppresses anxiety and ambivalence.

ment up to his full adulthood has given him. Though the impress of his past life exerts a powerful influence on his remaining development, to some extent he changes with all succeeding experiences until he dies.

Childhood and Adulthood

In times of social tension the children of some group in society may not see the lives lived by the adults around them as satisfying. That situation is too complex to summarize here. The full meaning of this statement and its tremendous implications for social change are discussed later in this book. Here it may be useful merely to suggest summarily certain relationships to adult roles of the personality with which an individual emerges from childhood, relationships that will also be explored later.

An individual possesses as an adult a clear view of the nature of the larger environment within which he lives only if the relationships of that environment are consistent with those of the minuscule world of his childhood. If the two conflict, he will at best be confused. And no individual will be effective in any social role as an adult who has not found it necessary, effective, and satisfying to act in an analogous way in the little world of his childhood.

Thus no individual becomes a reformer of his community or society who does not feel both that the institutions of his community or society threaten him deeply and that they can be changed by his efforts; and no individual feels this who did not in childhood feel that the institutions which governed him in childhood threatened him, and also that he could and must escape from the childhood threat by changing those institutions through his own efforts.

Similarly, no man feels that a satisfying career lies in manipulating the elements of the physical world around him to make them serve him more productively who did not find as a child that he could attack problems of the miniature environment of his home with success and satisfaction. In these profoundly important ways the child is father to the man.

It does not follow that some important problem of the larger environment is always analogous to the problem which an individual solved as a child. Where it is not, the individual may live his adult life in little relationship to the larger world. But where it is, the tendencies created in him as a child may have important social consequences.

It is a corollary of the above, though until further explained it may seem to be a quite separate statement, that his life within his society is not satisfying to an adult unless it gives meaning to the problems he explored as a child and found it necessary to repress into his unconscious processes. That is, life is not satisfying unless it provides justification for the pains that were bewildering in childhood.

If it does, the result is not that he no longer feels the pains but that they are tolerable. I have illustrated this principle above in discussing religion in primitive society. Because the individual can interpret the pain he suffered in his authoritarian infancy and childhood as needed to teach him to be humble before the spiritual powers that rule his adulthood in an authoritarian fashion, that pain becomes tolerable, and indeed now unites him with his fellows (since he entreats the spiritual powers on behalf of his entire group) rather than isolating him. I shall illustrate the principle further below.

Moreover, I suggest that no social system will be satisfying and thereby stable which does not provide a sanctioned outlet for the rage which childhood pain provokes, rage which persists throughout life even though unconsciously. In traditional society that rage can be vented by dominating everyone below one in the social hierarchy. In most traditional societies it can also be vented in more overt form against outsiders. I suggest that in a culture which provokes rage (as all must) but provides no appropriate outlet the rage will burst forth in unsanctioned channels and the social system will change.[25]

APPENDIX 1
COMMENTS ON TOILET TRAINING

While toilet training is not the almost exclusive key to some aspects of personality which it was once thought to be, it is of considerable importance. The ability to urinate and defecate is probably a source of wonder and pleasure to every child. He has created his urine and his feces, and they delight him. He will play with them with rejoicing if he is not restrained by command or an expression of repugnance by a loved and needed person. Then the time comes when he is directed by his mother or a mother-surrogate or his playmates to control this activity, and to create his essences on request and only on request. Perhaps even in the most favorable context the request will seem somewhat arbitrary, a somewhat bewildering and rage-provoking interference by the environment with his behavior. Yet if it is made when he has the capacity to obey, it may seem rather reasonable because he has that capacity, because it is made in a way that makes it seem a sensible part of the

---

[25] The flux and insecurity of the highly mobile American society cause environments in many homes that frustrate childhood urges, create anxiety, and provoke intense rage that must be repressed but throughout life seeks release and justification. The society sanctions brutality in many of its television programs and much of its mass literature, and intense conflict in some of its sports, but none of these serves a social purpose and so they provide inadequate release. The circumstances of the society have not been conducive to a world view in which there is an external threat which can be rationalized as the cause of the anxiety and at which the rage can be released. In the present generation the Soviet Union, or, more generally, Communism, has come close to providing such a rationale and such a target. However, the sense of reality of the majority of the society's members prevents the uninhibited release of aggression at "the Communists," and so here too it finds no adequate release. It and the insecurity underlying it have wrought continuing social change and created continuing social tensions. If the rage-producing environment should become more widespread, or if certain external circumstances should heighten the latent anxiety and rage in people who now control it effectively, it might become a threat to social stability. It is not the only threat to social stability, and I do not intend by this passing comment to suggest that it is a crucial factor.

arrangements around him, and because it is made without anxiety by a person who loves and values him. Compliance carries the promise of reward (love, acceptance, pleasure) from a part of his environment of importance to him, his mother, a mother-surrogate, or a group of peers. If so, it may seem a part of a reasonable world.

However, the request may be made at a stage of his physiological development when he is incapable of complying, or is able to comply only by a tremendous effort to gain performance from a nerve-muscle system which can as yet respond only uncertainly and by means of great tension. The demand may be made with a tone (arising out of anxiety of his mother that her house shall be clean and respectable and her child capable, or out of her compulsive need to control this infant who has disrupted her life, or out of the pleasure of his peers in making him submit) which indicates to him that it is of great importance to the coercive authority making it but is made arbitrarily, for no comprehensible reason, and out of no regard for him. To the extent that this is true, again he feels rage, even though he may not dare to express it. In this case, depending on the outcome of his resistance to the coercion, he may learn with especial emotional intensity either the importance of complying with arbitrary demands that have no regard for his desires or the satisfaction of planning his own rigid scheme of when he will hold on and when let go, and become stubborn, obstinate, explosive—the "anal type." And he may learn such a mania for superficial order that his compulsiveness about neatness and regularity is matched only by his inability to think a bold thought.

APPENDIX 2
EVIDENCE FROM SOCIAL PSYCHOLOGY
CONCERNING PERSONALITY FORMATION

Much experimental evidence concerning personality formation is summarized by Irvin L. Child in "Socialization," Gardner Lindzey (ed.), Handbook of Social Psychology (Cambridge, Mass.: Addison-Wesley Publishing Co., Inc., 1954), Vol. II. He cites (pp. 675–78) research by Marian R. Winterbottom showing that high-achievement children had been subject to more restrictions at early ages than had low-achievement children (though restrictions were fewer than demands), but that demands had been made on them at an earlier age than on low-achievement children. Child (p. 674) cites research by E. Fales indicating that praise for achievement and mild reproach for failure in progressively more difficult tasks for nursery children (putting on own clothes) brought more persistence and achievement; and (p. 674) research by J. H. Grosslight and I. L. Child indicating that persistence at a task was favored by previous experience of failure followed later by success. McClelland stresses the influence of disapproval of not venturing as inculcating need achievement. See David C. McClelland et al., The Achievement Motive (New York: Appleton-Century-Crofts, Inc., 1953), chap. ix, section 1.2. But his statement needs to be qualified in that the disapproval of not venturing must not come before the child is physiologically capable of venturing successfully. Child (p. 675) summarizes research by Theta H. Wolf as showing (for young children) "that a high level of persistence is associated with a level of performance demand from adults that is properly adjusted to the child's ability, and that a low level of persistence is associated either with unreasonable demands or with insufficient demands." Pauline Sears, according to Child (p. 675), found: "that an important determinant of children's level of aspiration in a particular task is their history of success and failure in tasks of the same general kind."

Child concludes (pp. 674–75):

"First, the development of persistent striving for achievement is influenced by social approval of this behavior and disapproval of its absence. Second, the development of persistent striving for achievement is also affected by the pattern of successes and failures resulting from such striving in the past, and this pattern results not only from approval or disapproval but also from the child's capacities, his physical environment, and other aspects of his social environment. Thus, where persistence in striving for achievement is an objective of socialization, parents may fail to reach this objective, despite their approval of the child's striving and disapproval of his failure to strive, if they permit the child's interaction with his environment to be such that his strivings for achievement are uniformly unsuccessful."

It is to be noted that two of these studies relate to persistence at tasks rather than to creativity. Thus previous failure followed by success, reported by Grosslight and Child to be associated with persistence, is less apt (under some conditions) to be associated with high achievement. Concerning persistence, as associated with concern with achievement without fear of trying, see also the suggestions of Albert J. Caron and Michael A. Wallach, in "Recall of Interrupted Tasks under Stress: A Phenomenon of Memory or Learning?" *Journal of Abnormal and Social Psychology*, Vol. LV (November, 1957), pp. 372–81, and "Personality Determinants of Repressive and Obsessive Reactions to Failure-Stress," *ibid.*, Vol. LIX (September, 1959), pp. 236–45.

APPENDIX 3
FURTHER COMMENTS ON NEED ORDER AND NEED SUCCORANCE-NURTURANCE

Since these needs are important for creativity, and since insights about their formation are so uncertain, further brief speculations may be permitted here.

Need Order

Probably every child, when faced with the problem of whether the environment will respond adequately to his expression of his needs, asks himself: How can I best assure that my needs will be fulfilled adequately? What can I learn from my experiences? How can I find order in my universe?

Need order, I suggest, is inculcated by the perception on the part of the child that the important individuals in his environment expect that he will be able to achieve. That expectation implies that there is a path which he ought to be able to find, and so it becomes important for him to find it. If his environment has also instilled in him the perception that he can probe a confused situation and find the key to it provided that he assesses judiciously all of the elements, he will be characterized by what may be termed high need reality or high need understanding. He will make order out of complex situations. If, however, he has found it impossible to solve the situations that face him in spite of perceiving an expectation and desire that he shall do so, then he will fear to admit the existence of a problem. In this case his need order will be met by creating superficial order, or perceiving order whether or not it exists, and refusing to recognize inadequacies in it. He will delight in simple systems of order. His personality may be termed the bookkeeper type.

It seems justifiable to regard the need order component of personality as identical or similar in the two cases, the difference between them being in the degree of the needs for dependence, achievement, and autonomy. Between the two extremes sketched there lies of course a continuum of intermediate cases.

Contrasting with the effect of this expectation that the child will be able to achieve are the effects of authoritarian parenthood. In the extreme case the child finds the exercise of his initiative in searching for a method of understanding and meeting his parents' arbitrary demands of no avail whatever. The search for order becomes meaningless to him; he comes to have low (or zero) need order. He simply obeys. Between this extreme and the opposite extreme of high need order lies a continuum; in every personality there is some need for order and some disregard for order. The degree, I suggest, depends on the degree to which the environment manifested an expectation that order could be found.

Need Succorance-Nurturance

It is difficult to define the circumstances which inculcate high need succorance-nurturance. It may be suggested speculatively that it results when early nurturance was adequate, so that the individual gained need autonomy and achievement, but when subsequent nurturance was terminated not quite so traumatically as to produce need dependence but with sufficient pain so that the individual seeks throughout his life to assuage that pain by loving and being loved. If the early phase of nurturance was sufficient, or if the perception of being loved persisted because the interruption of nurturance could be understood, then the individual may be relatively free to admit to himself his unconscious expression of needs. Indeed, given adequate intelligence and adequate prior experience in successful problem solving, he may seek semiconsciously, and successfully, to examine his unconscious processes to find there the explanation of his pain. Whether or not this speculation concerning the processes involved is correct, need succorance-nurturance seems to be associated often with a drive to understand the world and with creativity.

It will be obvious from these comments that the inculcation of need order and need succorance-nurturance is closely related to that of need achievement.

Personality Formation and the Stability of Traditional Society

chapter 8

Illustration from present-day quasi-traditional societies of the process of personality formation will put flesh on the bare abstract bones of the discussion of Chapter 7 and provide a basis for some concluding generalizations concerning the stability of traditional societies. I have chosen accounts of childhood in Burma and Indonesia not because personality formation in those countries is closer to a pure traditional type than elsewhere but simply because they offer the most specific descriptions available to me as I write. With respect to each of the two countries I shall quote directly from the accounts of skilled observers. Later in the chapter I shall suggest reasons for believing that while the detailed methods of childhood training and the rationale by which practices are justified vary among cultures, the essential elements of parent-child relationships and the personality type that emerges are the same in all other traditional societies as in these two.

CHILDHOOD IN BURMA AND JAVA

Burma

The description of childhood in Burma is primarily that of Hazel M. Hitson, who spent some months in 1957 and 1958 studying personality in a village 20 miles from the capital city Rangoon. I shall also quote briefly from an account by Lucien M. Hanks, who spent part of a year at the end of World War II among the Arakanese, a people of western Burma closely related to the Burmese ethnically.[1] Miss Hitson writes:

The [Burmese] family is a unit created to serve the needs of the father. Obedience is required by mother and children alike. Children are subdued in

[1] Lucien M. Hanks, "The Quest for Individual Autonomy in the Burmese Personality," *Psychiatry*, Vol. XII (1949), pp. 285–300; Hazel Marie Hitson, "Family Patterns and Paranoidal Personality Structure in Boston and Burma" (Ph.D. dissertation, Radcliffe College, April, 1959). See also Margaret Mead (ed.), *Cultural Patterns and Technical Change* (Paris: United Nations, 1953), chap. iii. I also rely on my own observations in Burma. Hanks' interpretation of the meaning for personality of the facts he observed stresses aspects other than those presented here.

the presence of their fathers and are kept out of the way when guests are present. The father must protect the family in time of trouble. Wives are scolded and sometimes beaten if they place him in a position whereby he may have to become involved in an argument with the head of another family, i.e., if they gossip and there are witnesses to things she has said. Children must stay out of serious trouble to avoid his wrath and to prevent his becoming involved in fights with fathers of other children. In brief, the family functions well to the extent that its members meet the needs of the dominant parent and to the extent that its members keep out of trouble.[2]

After a mother has given birth, all of her energies are directed toward caring for the infant; while the next oldest child is placed under the care of an older sibling, aunt, or grandmother. The infant is with the mother constantly, being fed on demand, night and day. . . .

Indulgence begins early—in the feeding on demand. An infant must not be allowed to cry for fear he will have fits; so every attempt is made to quiet and comfort him, and since it is assumed that when a child cries, he is hungry, attempts to soothe usually involve nursing. After he is three months old he is permitted to cry a while without immediate attendance if the mother is busy, but not for long, for fear crying will become a habit and it will not be easy to comfort him. Again, comforting takes the form of offering the breast until the child begins to be alert and approaches the one year mark. People dislike crying, then, because it is so noisy and because they do not like to hear it. Comforting still involves food in the way of mother's milk, cakes, or sweets, but a new element is added. He is frightened to prevent his crying. He is threatened with being given away to strangers. He is frightened by being told that a big dog, an Indian, a stranger, a ghost, thunder, etc. will come and carry him away. When he is around three years and goes about in the care of an older sibling all efforts are taken to prevent his crying, for fear the older child will be punished. A child of three or four is viewed as "too young to understand," as "not knowing," and older siblings in charge of him must give in to him to prevent his crying, for he always has recourse to his mother, who will indulge him his wishes, and will admonish the older child. Indulgence and threats of harm are again the standard means of preventing his crying and calling out for mother.[3]

Toilet training is not compulsive, though the insistence and firmness and perhaps disregard with which the infant is sometimes held out from the body of the adult holding him when he evidences a tendency to urinate or defecate, the adult continuing her conversation with someone else, may constitute more pressure on him than would appear at first glance. (The fact that the baby is naked except for a short shirt facilitates this casual care of his toilet needs.)

Hanks notes:

The people who hold and laugh at the child are free of obligation to him. At any moment they may hand him to someone and depart as if he were a doll or pet monkey.

Although a child may experience few overt shocks by this treatment, there is a fragility in his relations to people. . . . Bathing, smearing with sandalwood paste, dressing, and guarding may be done by one of a number of mother substitutes. Males seldom tend to these affairs of the toilet; but at any other time of

---

[2] "Family Patterns," p. 121.

[3] *Ibid.*, pp. 73–75.

day the child may be with his father at a gossip session, cock-fight or wrestling match. All these attentions are voluntary, thus enhancing their warmth and enthusiasm; but since they are given without obligation, at any moment they may end like a cataclysm. There may be warmth and affection, but it lacks continuity and dependability.[4]

Miss Hitson's account summarizes parental attitudes concerning the ability of children to bear responsibility:

It is assumed that children will not figure things out for themselves. It is felt that they have to be taught to do everything. It is said that without being told, children will know only how to play and to eat.

There are no regular duties assigned to children that they are expected to do each day without being told. In the early years children are told what to do whenever parents want them to do something. Later, their tasks become more and more regular, but they are told every day, two or three times a day, to do the same job. Children say that if their parents do not tell them to do anything, they play. They say they do not know why they always wait to be told what to do but they do. Finally, after years of repetition, children come to know their own work and to do it without being told. It is expected that children will carry out orders given, but that, in the parents' absence, they cannot be trusted in this until girls are eleven, twelve, or thirteen years old and until boys are thirteen, fourteen, or fifteen years old. There is no suggestion that children should anticipate the wishes of their parents by going ahead and doing things without being told.[5]

The transition from seeming indulgence to insistence on docile submission to elders is traumatically completed for a boy at about the age of eight. After being treated with a day of ritual honor (the *shinbyu* ceremony) he is delivered to a monastery, where, performing menial tasks and drilled in rote learning for hours at a time, he is subjected to unrelieved harsh discipline. Though today the period in the monastery may be only two weeks, in precolonial Burma it was a full rainy season, three or four months.

He is not entirely unprepared for the arbitrariness of the treatment, since he has already learned that persons of authority treat one as an object without capability or responsibility. Yet the harshness of the regimen must drive the lesson home with a shock.

Rather than quote further details of Miss Hitson's account, it will be useful to cite a large part of her summary of the essential characteristics of the parent-child relationship:

FAMILY CULTURE
ATTITUDES TOWARD CHILDREN

In order to understand socialization processes, it is necessary to know the kinds of assumptions made about the nature of interpersonal relationships. Most importantly, it is necessary to know the attitudes of parents toward children.

In Burma the first basic assumption parents make is that children are to be used:

---

[4] "The Quest for Individual Autonomy," p. 290.

[5] "Family Patterns," p. 122.

a) They are to run errands for parents and elders and are to do things for them. Girls are adopted into families to work only. Boys are adopted to work and to earn merit for the adopting parents through the *shinbyu* ceremony.[6]

b) Children are to be teased as a form of enjoyment for elders, and a child's sensitive areas and special fears are used to make it more effective. Teasing means getting a child to cry for the enjoyment of all present. It means frightening a child to see his response. It means making him perform as a soldier paying respect to a superior officer.

c) Children are to be blamed instead of adults whenever possible. Because raising chickens for food is a sin, they are said to belong to children. Because elders engage in spiteful behavior, toward each other during disagreements, it is camouflaged as being directed toward children. . . .

Secondly, it is assumed that children are unimportant:

a) They are not completely formed human beings. They are not yet full-fledged members of this world and need not be treated as well as adults.

b) They are viewed as not knowing, not understanding, and are talked about as though they had no feelings. Anything is discussed before children as though they were not present.

c) They are believed to be dirtier than adults and are not permitted to sit on mats adults use.

d) They need not be thanked for doing things for elders. . . .

Thirdly, it is assumed that children will make no internal demands upon themselves:

a) It is assumed that children will have temper tantrums and will try to get what they want. They will steal, lie, take by force, argue, and fight with others.

b) They will do bad things in parents' absences if elders do not watch them and prevent it.

c) It is assumed that they are mischievous and will break things.

d) If they are out of sight, they will forget the elders' words and will do what they please. They will give in to temptation and be led astray by others.

e) It is assumed that children cannot be relied upon, cannot be trusted to carry out orders until about 12, 13, or 14 years old for girls and 14, 15, or 16 years old for boys.

Fourthly, it is assumed that children will be difficult to control unless they are made to obey through use of fear and force:

a) Parents like for their children to be afraid of them so they will obey.

b) It is felt that children who are praised directly will think too much of themselves and will grow lazy.

c) Boys are thought to be more difficult to raise than girls and must be beaten more.

d) Children who are pampered are naughty and become bad when they grow up. . . .

Sixthly, it is assumed that children are helpless and defenseless.

a) They do not know how to take care of themselves properly.

b) They do not know and do not understand cultural values and will unintentionally transgress norms; so they must be protected from outsiders who may try to punish them when they do, or who will try to take advantage of them in some way.[7]

---

[6] The *shinbyu* ceremony for young boys entering the monastery is a religious ceremony of greatest significance to parents. The merit gained enables them to go to the next existence carrying a golden umbrella—the symbol of kingly status and all things good.

An environment that reflects these assumptions of course creates frustrations and provokes rage. The parents treat temper tantrums with amusement or ridicule. As noted, they expect children to do things which are formally termed bad when the parents are not present to prevent them. Thus provided with a channel for their rage which is sanctioned by the parents' attitudes if not by verbal injunctions, children are highly aggressive, verbally and physically, in play.

The aggressive behavior of any child toward neighbor children or strangers is automatically right in the eyes of his parents unless it causes them trouble. If his aggressions are challenged, his parents support him whenever it is safe to do so regardless of the equities of the circumstance. The ethics of the situation seem to be that the status of the family is of supreme importance and is threatened if a child is admitted to have done wrong. Unless other powerful persons have actually seen the offense, denial is rather safe, since accusation without positive proof may be denounced as an act of aggression and an offense by the accuser. But if the aggression is exposed by a powerful other family, or causes coalition against a family whose child has offended, the parents may suddenly turn, and the child then receives a severe beating. His error lies not in having been aggressive, cruel, or dishonest but in having caused the family to lose status.[8]

The parents can hardly be said to train the children. Rather, they rule them, perhaps laxly, perhaps amusedly. However, against one manifestation of rage, rage toward one's parents, there is severe training. Great importance is attached to teaching the child deference toward his elders. It is at first enforced by coercion and then by extreme emotional sanction. The monastery experience of course reinforces it. The importance attached to it suggests unconscious awareness of a tendency toward hatred of elders so strong that powerful defenses must be erected against it. Boys become unable to function independently in the presence of elders or superiors, relying on the elders or superiors for judgment.

Miss Hitson summarizes some obligations inculcated by this childhood environment in a passage in which the reader will find reminders of various aspects of traditional society discussed in preceding chapters:

> They are oughts regarding respectful behavior to elders and to high status people. They are oughts to avoid offending anyone in the natural or supernatural realms for fear of harm to the self or the family. They are oughts about absolute loyalty to and protection of family members regardless of kinds of behavior engaged in. They are oughts to bring all things good to the family regardless of methods employed in doing so. They are oughts to avoid letting anyone get the best of you or your family, to avoid letting anyone place the blame for something at your feet, to avoid letting anyone show superiority over you through the slightest implication of lower status. To disregard these oughts is to place yourself in a position of shame, and above all you ought to avoid letting yourself be shamed by others.[9]

---

[8] *Ibid.*, chap. iv.

Java

A study of the early years of Javanese childhood by Hildred Geertz will be quoted more briefly.[10] Mrs. Geertz's account illustrates vividly how within gentle and seemingly nurturant care the characteristics which I have termed "authoritarian" may appear. Except for the italicized Indonesian words, the italics are mine.

Until the fetus is seven months old, it is not yet fully formed and is particularly susceptible to entry by evil spirits. . . .

The Javanese feel that a baby is extremely vulnerable, especially to sudden shock which can lead to sickness or death. . . . All the customs of infant care can be seen as attempts to ward off this danger.

The baby is handled in a relaxed, completely supportive, gentle, unemotional way. . . . A crying baby is rarely heard, mainly because no Javanese can bear to hear the sound without trying to do something about it no matter whose baby it is. . . .

The baby spends most of his time, especially after the first few months, cradled on his mother's hip as she walks here and there about her work. She carries him by means of a long, narrow shawl (*sléndang*) looped over one shoulder and down over the opposite hip, which gives a firm place for the baby to sit, conveniently adjacent to the breast. . . .

Carrying a baby is called *nggéndong;* and it is this action that is usually re-enacted as symbolic of the mother's total care—for instance at the wedding ceremony. . . . The *sléndang* represents total security. . . .[11]

A child, especially in the first two phases [infancy and early childhood, or until five or six years of age], is said to be *durung djawa*, which literally means "not yet Javanese." The same phrase is applied to mentally unbalanced persons and to adults who are not properly respectful to their elders. . . . This term implies that the person is not yet civilized, not yet able to control emotions in an adult manner, not yet able to speak with the proper respectful circumlocutions appropriate to different social occasions. Such a person is also said to be *durung ngerti*, "does not yet understand," and therefore it is thought that there is no point in forcing him to be what he is not or punishing him for faults which are incomprehensible to him. These two related notions, of being *djawa* and *ngerti* sum up for the Javanese their ideas of maturity and adult personal relationships, and they are the key to the whole complex of such ideas that are communicated to the growing child. But in the first phase of his life and for most of the second phase, these criteria for judging behavior are held in abeyance. . . .

When he is about 14 months old—or sometimes much later, if no younger sibling has intervened—the mother weans the child. Almost from the beginning of his life he has been given supplementary feeding, in the form of banana mush, rice, and other bland foods, so that there is usually little trauma associated with

---

[10] In order to quote Mrs. Geertz's precise words without undue length, rather than to summarize or paraphrase, I have intermingled quotations from two descriptions by her, one in an article, "The Vocabulary of Emotion: A Study of Javanese Socialization Processes," *Psychiatry*, Vol. XXII (August, 1959), pp. 225–37, and the other, more detailed, in her book, *The Javanese Family* (New York: Free Press of Glencoe, Inc., 1961). I shall refer to these sources as "Vocabulary" and *Javanese Family*, respectively, in later footnotes in this chapter.

[11] *Javanese Family*, pp. 87 and 92–94.

weaning. It is interesting, however, that *the mothers are much afraid of upsetting the child* by a too abrupt or severe weaning, and try to make it as gradual as possible. . . . Sometimes a mother's timidity and ambivalence about weaning are such that *the child goes through a long period of inconsistent treatment,* being weaned and then returned to the breast, and then weaned again. . . .

Walking is another significant transition, one which is given a peculiarly Javanese flavor, for until the child's muscles are developed enough for him to actually support himself erect, *he is not permitted to move about alone.* A Javanese baby misses the crawling stage entirely. All during his infancy he is carried about by his mother in a sling-like shawl on her hip. He passively hangs there, close to the breast where he may suckle at will, and is given constant attention by his mother. . . . His every wish is anticipated, and *he is expected to have no initiative of his own.* . . . The long period of being supported on the mother's hip must be related to the adult's tendency toward passive spectatorship rather than active participation in the world around him.[12]

Unlike weaning and politeness training, toilet training is a matter of little concern.[13]

With the accomplishment of weaning and walking, the main characteristic of the second phase is that the child now can move independently of the mother, and some sort of social rather than merely physical control of his actions is needed. The most common techniques used in this early period are first, detailed, unemotional instructions to the child, unaccompanied by threats of punishment from the parents; but, second, threats of horrible fates at the hands of outsiders or spirits if the child is bad. Actual punishment by the family members themselves is rare, and threats of withdrawal of love are never employed. No demands are made on the child until he is considered old enough to comprehend verbal instructions. These are delivered in a calm, steady stream by the adults: "Go around back of the house to urinate. . . . Fix your dress. . . . Don't run so fast. . . . Say good-bye." The assumption seems to be that the child is completely without resources of his own with which to face these little everyday problems. . . . *There is no attempt or desire to let the child develop initiative or independence.* . . .

During the period of weaning and learning to walk, the father begins to take an interest in the child. There are many moments of warmth, affection, and fondling between the father and child during this second phase, which are given heightened meaning by the fact that the father is frequently away from the house, or, if at home, preoccupied with his own thoughts or entertaining friends, and the further fact that the relationship changes radically after the child is about five. While mothers are described as "loving" (*trisna*) their children, *fathers are expected only to "take pleasure" (seneng) in them.* . . . It is the mother who instructs the child in social forms, *who makes countless decisions for him,* and who performs most punishments. . . . Only from the end of the child's first year to about his fifth year does he feel close to his father; the time then [gradually] comes when he can no longer play next to his father or trail along with him on visits, *but must respectfully stay away from him* and speak circumspectly and softly to him. At about this same time the child's behavior in general seems to undergo a change; once spontaneous and laughing, *he now adopts the docile, restrained, formal, controlled demeanor of his elders. The two events are somehow related.*[14]

---

[12] "Vocabulary," pp. 230–31.

[13] *Javanese Family,* p. 101.

[14] "Vocabulary," pp. 231–32.

The shift in the father's role from one of warmth to one of distance and re-serve, although it is only one step in the whole series of events by which the child learns the Javanese concepts of self-control and respect, is probably the most significant, both because of the crucial place of the father in the child's emotional life and because this transition period occurs during the period of the oedipal crisis.[15]

Common Elements: Parental Attitudes

There are marked differences between these two cases; yet, in spite of the lack of historical or cultural connection between Burma and Java, whose peoples came from different areas and one of which is Buddhist, the other Muslim, the underlying similarities are impressive.[16] Probably basic to the other common elements is a similarity in the view held by parents of the nature of children. In the view of adults in both societies, an infant is irresponsible and incapable, without power to resist or manage either his own impulses or any outside force; and he is also emotionally delicate, in constant danger of harm. Hence he is cared for rather anx-iously, and above all is prevented from crying. However, this is not be-cause crying is a sign of pain or anxiety which he should not be caused to suffer but because crying may harm him. When he is at an age at which threats may keep him from crying, threats are as satisfactory as accom-plishing the same end by indulgence. He is not an autonomous human being to be respected, but an automaton or toy. His mother, who bore the burden of creating him, cherishes him; his father's attitude is little more than taking pleasure in him.

Then, after babyhood, another aspect of the same view, the child is seen as having no inner resources for self-development. And so his train-ing does not consist of providing an environment in which he can develop, and in aiding his development; it consists of protecting, restrain-ing, controlling, directing, as if he were putty or a sponge or capable only of imitating.

Common Effects on Personality: Self-Doubt

In neither society, therefore, does the child receive enough or long-enough continued nurturance to relieve his anxieties. The apparent in-dulgence in infancy is not necessarily responsive to his needs. Infancy

---

[15] *Javanese Family*, p. 110.

A third description of childhood environment in a traditional (or in this case semi-traditional) society is found in David Landy, *Tropical Childhood* (Chapel Hill, N.C.: The University of North Carolina Press, 1959). This is an account of a village in Puerto Rico. The circumstances are much less unqualifiedly traditional than are those in the accounts of Java and Burma summarized in the text above, and Landy does not cover all of the aspects of personality formation discussed by Hitson and Geertz. Yet the reader will be struck by the parallels, for example, in the adult attitudes con-cerning the capabilities or lack of capabilities of young children.

[16] The Burmese came to Burma from Central Asia and in Burma were landlocked. The Javanese came from somewhere by sea. There seem to have been no inter-mediaries who might have created a cultural connection between the two.

and early childhood in Java seem to be more nurturant than in Burma, though this may be due to the colder psychoanalytic eye with which Miss Hitson viewed Burma. But even if there is an objective difference, the stream of commands described by Mrs. Geertz is certainly not nurturant. Of course the infant in both cultures senses some love and nurturance, but in both cultures very soon after babyhood he must often perceive the powerful persons around him as simply not responsive to his urges or initiative. Then, often in response to the intrusion of his initiative on them, they cause him pain (not in anger, or at least not in conscious anger, but with the sense that he must learn what is expected of him). As he passes through the Oedipal period, the screws are gradually or abruptly tightened. The reaction of his environment to his actions is bewildering and beyond his comprehension. Or perhaps it is more accurate to say that the world is perceived as a place in which events are determined by the wills of the powerful, and in which one finds security by submitting, unless one is in a situation of power and can command.

In both cultures, as elsewhere, the impact of authoritarian parenthood is perhaps most searing in the period of the Oedipal crisis. Though the accounts by Mrs. Geertz and Miss Hitson do not discuss the point (obviously they had no access to the necessary information), in view of adult sexual attitudes discussed below, it is as certain as a circumstantial deduction can be that the father gives his demands on the mother virtually absolute priority over those of his son and that the Oedipal crisis is severe.

As a result not merely of the sexual experience of the Oedipal period but also of all of the relationships of the first six or eight years of life, the individual must come to feel that it is dangerous to use initiative or to rival authority (his father) rather than submit to its guidance.[17]

Such a feeling is rather intense in the sexual sphere in both cultures. It does not lead to the extreme reaction of identification with the mother and to overt homosexuality. At least there is no evidence that it does. And it is likely that the males are saved from that extreme by two perceptions which counter that conveyed by the father's authoritarianism. One is the perception that women do offer nurturance, a perception gained in both cultures in infancy (though not with crystal clarity) that must persist in some degree in spite of the confusing evidence of later infancy and childhood. The second is the perception that the role of women is to support

---

[17] Miss Hitson interprets the Burmese case as verifying the hypothesis that "if pervasive attitudes, social acts, and verbalizations within the family imply that a child is the recipient of action by someone in authority, that he is subject to parental direction and rule, and that he, himself, has no initial responsibility toward others and no influence on the way others act toward him, the child's intrapsychic perception of the social and physical environment will be that it is physically threatening and not susceptible of management by him." ("Family Patterns," p. 32.)

and to submit, and that therefore one should be able to seduce and master them.

That homosexuality is not far off, especially in Burma, is indicated by two pieces of evidence. One is the strength of the humiliation and anger that Burmese men have learned to feel if they are put in a feminine position or if a woman is physically above them.[18] I interpret the strength of the feeling to be fear of a repressed desire to be in the feminine role.

The other item of evidence is the frequency of complete evasion of the sexual situation. Of the Burmese and closely associated ethnic groups of Burma (that is, omitting Karens and nonindigenous residents) about one of every 30 or 35 adult and young adult men in Burma is a monk and celibate.[19] In Java too some religious practices imply celibacy and even an intimacy among young men that has sexual overtones or overt homosexual aspects,[20] but the incidence is much smaller than in Burma.

The result even among men who do not find this extreme solution necessary is a perpetual anxiety about their manliness and an accompanying need forever to be testing it sexually. This is reflected in Burma in the commonness of extramarital sexual adventure, which has already been referred to, and in Java by various protections cast about women which are based on the assumption that the slightest approach of a man to an unmarried woman has sexual intent.[21] Also, in both countries there is found that touchiness, quickness to anger, and need to defend one's honor against the slightest question which is associated with men's doubt of their manliness. In short, the equivalent of *machismo* characterizes personalities in these societies even though the Latin term is not known.

The fear of sexual inadequacy, if it were an isolated fact, would be of little importance, but its context in personality makes clear that the doubt of one's capability as a man, the feeling that it is presumptuous to exercise initiative, pervades all personality. It leads to avoidance of any situation

---

[18] For an intimate piece of women's clothing to be passed over a man's head or to be hung above him is intolerably insulting.

[19] The figure excludes Chinese, Indians, Europeans, and Karens. Though the Karens are an indigenous ethnic group, they are culturally different in various ways from other ethnic groups in Burma. Buddhism is much less prevalent among them than among other ethnic groups in the country. The calculation is a rough one, based on the fact that according to the 1931 census, one of each 115 persons in Burma was a religious functionary, and a statement by a Burmese scholar that one of each 140 persons in Burma is a Buddhist monk. Somewhat more than 20 per cent of the population are Chinese, Indian, or Karen, and men above the age of 18 form perhaps 30 per cent of the population. (A number of hill peoples should also be excluded from the computation, but their number is too small to be significant in this connection.)

[20] See the description of the Javanese religious community known as a *pesantren*, in Clifford Geertz, "The Javanese Kijaji: The Changing Role of a Cultural Broker," *Comparative Studies in Society and History*, Vol. II (January, 1960), pp. 234–39.

[21] Unchaperoned contact ruins an unmarried woman's reputation, and the slightest contact between a man and a woman except under protected circumstances requires a male relative of the woman to address himself to the offending man with a demand for marriage.

in which one explores one's relationships with other persons as equals, that is, in which one attacks problems of human relations.

Common Effects: "Respect"

Rather, in a group of peers one cautiously explores until a workable consensus, a least common denominator, can be found; and if a ranking of power or authority can be established, one settles relationships in terms of that. One is inferior and submits, or one is superior and directs.

A person who discusses interpersonal relationships with Burmans soon finds a Burmese term used frequently which cannot be translated adequately into English because there is no corresponding concept in the cultures of Western societies. The term is *anadeh*.

Perhaps the concept in the English language with which *anadeh* has the greatest overlap is *respect;* but *anadeh* is not an attitude toward a man's achievement, his moral or intellectual qualities, or a stand he has taken. It is a reaction to his position or, more accurately, to the relationship between the two persons concerned. In some circumstances it has a little of the connotation of bashfulness or timidity and of reserve or modesty. There is a larger flavor of fear or shame, perhaps fused with anxiety. The concept refers to due observance of propriety, but to an inner observance and sensation, not merely to outward form, and the propriety involved is that of one's behavior toward a person superior in prestige and position. It is something which seizes one's mind, keeps one from thinking clearly, and freezes one's tongue. It is, in short, the proper inner attitude in the presence of superior social rank.[22]

Anadeh, I suggest, is an inevitable result of the environment in which personality is formed. It is therefore significant, though not surprising when one has recovered from the initial bit of astonishment, to find a similar concept in Javanese culture.

In discussing the adult values which the child must learn, Mrs. Geertz writes:

> The central premise which I shall discuss here is the concept of "respect" itself, a notion so peculiarly Javanese that it cannot be easily translated. The words for respect (*urmat, adji*) have complex meanings which only slightly overlap with the American notion of "respect." First, the respectful action is not evoked by the individual himself but by his status—as father, headman of the village, or educated government official. Further, unlike some usages in the West, "respect" does not necessarily refer to an attitude toward a person superior in power: in the Javanese family the mother exerts the real authority, but the father receives the "respect." A further difference from Western ideas of respect is that, for the Javanese, it does not matter whether a person actually "feels" respectful "inside" or merely acts as if he did. . . .

---

[22] A Burmese graduate student in a Western school, whose previous education had been in Burma, fainted when attempting to fulfill the requirement that he should give a seminar report to a group including more advanced students and his professor. He was afflicted with a severe case of *anadeh*.

It does not follow that there is no emotional aspect to Javanese respectful behavior; on the contrary, there may be a very acutely felt emotional accompaniment, a component of "respect" signified by the three Javanese words, *wedi, isin,* and *sungkan,* which denote three states of feeling that are considered appropriate to situations demanding respectful behavior. . . .

Wedi means "afraid" in both the physical sense and in the social sense of apprehension of unpleasant consequences of an action. . . .

Isin may be translated as "shame, shyness, embarrassment, guilt." A child even as young as three begins to *ngerti isin,* to "know *isin,*" which is thought to be the first step toward growing up; and when there are guests children usually withdraw into themselves with an intensely felt sense of shyness and become completely unresponsive. . . .

Wedi is a fear response, especially to strange things; *isin* is a complex anxiety reaction, involving not only fear but also a lowered self-esteem, and it concerns only social anxieties, most usually those having to do with social distance, including distance self-imposed through social transgression. . . .

Javanese children are *taught* how and when to be *wedi* and *isin;* they are praised for being *wedi* to their elders and *isin* to their betters. . . .

The child begins to learn *isin* even during early childhood, and he develops and elaborates the feeling and comprehension of the contexts in which it is applicable after he is five or so. As he becomes more adept at social intercourse and, entering adolescence, begins to be treated as a full-fledged member of society, he learns the feeling of *sungkan,* last of the three respect concepts of the Javanese.

Isin and *wedi,* although complex, are close enough to American ideas to be translated "shame" and "fear," but *sungkan* is peculiarly Javanese. Roughly, *sungkan* refers to a feeling of respectful politeness before a superior or an unfamiliar equal. "*Sungkan* is like *isin* only 'lighter.'" "*Sungkan* is like *isin,* only without the feeling of doing something wrong." "If a delegation of official visitors comes to my house and they sit at my table, I sit off in a chair in the corner; that's *sungkan*". . . .[23]

Obviously, while there are cultural differences between *anadeh* and the group of Javanese concepts, there is a core of identity. Both, I suggest, are the reflection of the cognitions and the need submission-dominance of traditional society. It will be surprising if closely related concepts are not found in other traditional societies.

The Handling of Rage

In both cultures the child must react with rage to the anxiety and terror repeatedly created in him during infancy and early childhood. This is inevitable in view of the nature of the childhood environment. Collateral evidence, if any is needed, is found in the compulsiveness of the "respect" relationships just described, which are consistent with the presence of repressed rage sufficiently intense so that it must be walled in by these strong sanctions.

Such rage must be diverted somewhere if the society is to be stable. In both societies it is directed against juniors, though of course with the restraints necessary for social cohesion. The methods of training

---

[23] *Javanese Family,* pp. 110–14.

children described above certainly reflect strong elements of need aggression and need dominance and serve to relieve repressed rage, and the more effectively because the dominance can be interpreted as serving a social purpose.

However, other outlets are found necessary in both societies. Like people everywhere, the Javanese give release to their rage by venting it against outsiders—verbally and in their inner mental behavior as well as in national policy. Like traditional people over a large area of the world, they justify aggression against outsiders by giving it religious sanction. The Muslim religion at the same time bolsters authoritarianism within the society and sanctions aggression without, though this aggression has been reduced from physical to symbolic form by the gentle rubbing of history. In the Javanese case and the Muslim case more generally, the outsiders against whom attack is sanctioned include all unbelievers. That exercise of aggression, which survives in tradition if not in present-day wars against the infidels, is one of the paths to the pleasures of Paradise. Among those pleasures, in turn, is assurance of that sexual virility concerning which the individual feels somewhat uncertain in this life.[24]

This seems to be the only special provision which the Javanese find necessary to handle their rage. The Burmese have a more serious problem. The rage built up in the individual by the frustrations of Burmese childhood is so great that it seems necessary to permit the child to vent it against anyone outside the family. This solves the immediate problem, but the sanction thereby given for aggressiveness leaves such a slender margin of self-control the Burmese man apparently continually or repeatedly feels a danger that he may lose control of himself and attack anyone around him. Burmese personality may be characterized as authoritarianism with a slight paranoiac streak. The intense Burmese fear of dysentery, not paralleled by corresponding fear of other causes of sickness and death, may arise from this dread of losing control of oneself.

The fear is not without basis. Dacoity (armed robbery by a small band, often with little regard for person) was rife in pre-British Burma, and, although it was perhaps declining during the generation before the British conquest,[25] it sprang up again as soon as the constraints of British rule were ended. The civil war of the immediate postindependence period degenerated in many parts of the country into armed robbery as a way of life, and up to the present time attempts to suppress lawlessness have not been highly successful. As another bit of evidence, observers of

---

[24] Perhaps, also, early childhood treatment is more nurturant than in Burma and creates a sense of guilt so deep that it is feared that rage will turn wholly inward and incapacitate the individual. That is, perhaps religious sanction seemed necessary to turn rage out from the individual himself toward someone outside him.

[25] J. S. Furnivall, in *Colonial Policy and Practice: A Comparative Study of Netherlands India* (Cambridge, Eng.: The University Press, 1948), suggests this.

Burmese history narrate (apparently rather rare) incidents of Burmese suddenly going berserk and killing without reason.

Against this aggressiveness which unconsciously he fears in himself a Burmese individual erects defenses of various kinds. One of these is the very characteristic which causes casual visitors to reject as ridiculous the suggestion that the Burmese are aggressive: a merry, happy-go-lucky, friendly cast of behavior. This, I suggest, is an attitude the Burmese individual adopts as a part of the process of repressing his dangerous rage.

Another defense is the stern injunction in the culture against asking for things for oneself. This injunction is so strong that even destitute Burmans do not beg.[26]

I have already suggested that extreme deference to elders is another defense. It extends to all persons in authority. It is coupled in Burmese history with references to anarchistic resistance to authority; to keep oneself from giving way to the latter, one is most scrupulous in suppressing any individuality in the face of authority.

And one of the strongest defenses is adherence to Buddhism. Buddhism preaches that peace (Nirvana) lies only in abandoning all desire, all lust, all aggression; only he who wants nothing can have peace. This happy injunction justifies at one stroke the individual's resistance to his need aggression, his avoidance of the problem of his relations to women and to other men, and his anxiety at attempting to explore the problems of the physical world. Other religions might serve the last two purposes equally well, but perhaps no other could so well aid the individual in his struggle against his need aggression. At least his previous animism could not, and the sanction given to aggression by Islam would accentuate his problem. However, at the same time that Buddhism sanctions submission to authoritarianism it sanctions the exercise of a superior role if it falls to one's lot. No wonder, then, that when the Buddhist doctrine reached Burma it was absorbed as a parched soil soaks up rain, and that later, when the disciples of Islam reached Burma on their way to their religious conquest of Indonesia, their doctrines were repelled. Among the people in Burma who are of Burmese and culturally similar ethnic groups perhaps 99 per cent or more are avowed Buddhists even today, after the disruptive events of colonial rule, and virtually none are or ever have been Muslim.

THE STABILITY OF TRADITIONAL SOCIETY

Let us now consider the ways in which the Burmese and Javanese societies and cultures are typical of all traditional societies and cultures.

---

[26] In spite of the destitution of tens of thousands of refugees from disorder in the countryside who settled in the outskirts of Rangoon, in two years in Burma I was never asked for alms by a Burman. There were many beggars, but they were hill peoples or Indians.

We are now at the end of the long process of posing the first of the central questions of this essay: What are the resistances to change from traditional social behavior to continuing technological progress?

Interacting Forces of Stability

It is clear from the accounts above that the childhood environments in Burma and Java do not result from deliberate rules or policies laid down by the parents which it would be possible for the parents to alter. Rather, they result from the parents' cognitions of the nature of the world and of children and from the unconscious needs of the parents. And the cognitions and needs which give rise to such childhood environments are the cognitions and needs of authoritarian personality. Childhood environments in Burma and Java are as they are not by some cultural accident unique to those societies but because adults in those societies are authoritarian. Wherever we find authoritarian personality in adults, we may expect that childhood environment and its effects on personality are fundamentally as they are in Java and Burma.

Although parental personalities are centrally important in childhood environment, other factors also affect childhood personality. I suggest that those other factors consist of a physical world seen as dominating human fortunes and a social structure that accommodates authoritarian personality and no other. In the way sketched in an earlier chapter in outlining the nature of traditional society, helplessness in the face of forces of the physical world provides the basis for religious sanction for authoritarianism; and as the growing individual emerges from his home into the larger community, its social structure fits perfectly his expectation of authoritarian relationships. Thus everything fits; and authoritarian personality, authoritarian social structure, and a physical environment perceived as dominating, threatening, and not manageable re-create themselves generation after generation. In all traditional societies, then, in the absence of rather powerful disturbing forces we may expect authoritarian personality and with it authoritarian social structure and the traditional image of the nature of the world to be perpetuated.[27]

---

[27] This hypothesis about the perpetuation of authoritarian personality in peasant societies will be most convincing if it is possible to point to some common circumstances in traditional societies which brought authoritarian personality initially. Speculatively, it is quite possible to do so. For the forces of nature are mysterious, powerful, and willful to primitive man (both members of the elite and the simple folk). When oppressed and frustrated by them, he may well have turned the rage provoked in him against those around him who were under his control. Whatever personality type we may hypothesize to have existed initially in various societies, this process may have resulted in a gradual convergence toward authoritarian personality in all. But all this is little more than fanciful, and hardly evidential. Hence I shall be content merely to assert the empirical observations that personality in all or virtually all traditional societies is authoritarian, and that childhood environment, where it has been observed, re-creates the same personality, and, taking these facts as given, to note their significance for the perpetuation of the equilibrium of the social system of a traditional society.

This is the generalization toward which the discussion of the several previous chapters has been moving. From the viewpoint of social theory, it and the concomitant circumstances which tend to prevent any deviation from this pattern are the most important characteristics of traditional society.

Weakness of Forces for Change

The stability of this system over time might be broken if there were, say, some slow cumulative change in the social structure or a steady increase in the understanding of natural phenomena which gradually tended to force a new perception of the physical world. Indeed, some past periods of culture growth, in which a society broke out of the mold of traditional social structure and personality, may have been brought about in just this way. We cannot be sure that other forces were at work in every historical instance of basic social change. The tendency to such slow cumulative change is slight, however, for several reasons.

One of these is that the forces for change are weak. The members of traditional society, unless something happens to affect their personalities, are low in need autonomy and need achievement. They have very little "capacity to be surprised," very little "openness to experience." Because their unconscious mental processes are inaccessible to them, they lack creative imagination with which to make the most of any unexpected phenomena which might come to their notice. Further, accepting roles in an authoritarian social hierarchy satisfies their need submission; and, conversely, in parenthood and other positions of authority in adult life they are able to exercise dominance over their subordinates and in that dominance vent their unconscious rage. Here they find further redress for the pain they suffered. Hence their needs are satisfied; they have no need to look for paths to technical or social change.

Resistances to Change

Some of these personality characteristics, looked at from another viewpoint, constitute positive resistances to change since they tend to bar even random mental activity from leading to change. The members of traditional society are barred from looking at either nature or the social structure with a fresh view because if they did they might find a problem to be explored, and the anxiety which any unresolved situation creates in them inhibits them. Its effect is reinforced by their need to believe the physical world dominated by arbitrary unseen forces in order that they may feel that their childhood pain was justified because it proved them worthy of the favor of the spiritual forces.

In addition, the values of the society create interpersonal sanctions against change. Such sanctions lie in the shame which falls on an individual who does not share his income with the members of his family group as they have need instead of using it for his own purposes; in the reaction of his kin if he subjects them to danger by not performing the familial obligations—economic, social, or ritual—within the community; and in the reaction of all the members of his community if he subjects them to difficulty by shirking his share in the customary exchange of services, or to danger by failing to respect the rituals and the submissiveness due the spiritual powers.

Among the elite an added factor operates, the compulsion to preserve an identity differentiated from that of peasants and menials. Failing to observe the proper rounds of landed life, or demeaning oneself by participating in manual-technical labor or exhibiting interest in the physical world or in business, threatens the entire group by weakening the symbols of differentiation between them and the simple folk. For these various reasons there is aversion in some degree to the activities of the individual, whether simple or elite, who steps outside the bounds of conventional behavior. He experiences social opprobrium—not merely conscious criticism, but also the perception by others that he is queer.

Probably more important, he exerts this same pressure on himself. The attitudes of the society are built into his own personality as well as into those of others. Like the needs of individuals in traditional society, the values of the society probably cause each individual to exert pressures on himself that are greater than those exerted on him by other persons. If by some chance he faces and becomes aware of a new situation which from the viewpoint of Western culture might be regarded as promising, a sense of unease at his unelite behavior must keep him from observing its significance and impel him to follow customary behavior.

Some sanctions reach between the members of the elite groups and the simple folk. Deviations from the traditional round of life interfere in various ways with fulfilling customary obligations of simple folk to members of the elite, whether they are intercaste relations as in the recent past in India, feudal obligations as in premodern western Europe or Japan, or obligations in other peasant societies that do not fit into either of these two patterns. Their status and vested interests thus threatened, the members of the elite may be expected to take preventive or punitive action. Such use by members of the elite of the instruments of power they possess has often been mentioned as a force preventing change in peasant society. It has undoubtedly been greatly overemphasized relative to the inhibitions and compulsions built into personality,[28] but it should not be ignored.

Deviations of the elite from the traditional economic relationships or other deviations from the traditional moral or ethical code likewise create interclass tensions (as well as resistances by other members of the elite). The simple folk have no physical or economic power to exert

---

[28] Present concepts of personality and personality formation are young. In the absence of understanding of them it was natural to seek elsewhere for an explanation and to stress the power structure.

against the elite short of the extreme measure of peasant revolt, which requires severe tensions indeed. However, their feeling of being wronged by violations of customary obligations or customary symbolic behavior no doubt manifests itself. Some sense among members of the elite of the obligations of eliteness, or some sensitivity to the attitudes of the common people, or both, is probably a deterrent to deviant elite behavior.

The Specific Case of Technological Change

Consider these aspects of the traditional social structure and culture in specific relation to a few illustrative cases of possible technological change. If some simple change in production methods is presented to a peasant under sponsorship which convinces him that it is intended to benefit him, and if the change promises an increase in material income and seems not to interfere with traditional behavior or relationships, it is probably adopted. But this is not the guise in which technological progress ordinarily presents itself. A change in the seed one uses perhaps requires change in the time of planting, the preparation of the soil, or the use of moisture, recommendations running counter to the precious rules of craft which have been diligently learned and successfully used and are blessed by the sanction of the elders and favored by the spiritual powers. The change, moreover, may prevent his fulfilling his co-operative obligations to the community. Even if it requires no such changes in practices, the advice for change was probably given by a member of the elite who does not work with his hands, who does not know much about peasant agriculture, and whose entry into this sphere of activity creates in one a certain sense of inappropriateness and a certain unease and suspicion. Altogether, attempting to gain the benefits which it is asserted will accrue involves running dangers and incurring anxiety which constitute high costs.

If in town a textile craftsman is to install an engine or motor and eight mechanized looms and become an entrepreneur, he will require credit from men who do not customarily look upon him as worthy of credit except on a pawnshop basis. Further, he must have the presumption to step up from his accepted role in the community and audaciously assume authority beyond that provided for him by the structure of his group. Perhaps he will be viewed as aiming at gaining equality with members of an elite group above him. He must organize workers, supplies, and a market beyond the scope of his usual activity. Engaged in the activity of doing so, he may perhaps perforce neglect familial duties or obligations within the community. And this assertion of himself, for future gains which are uncertain, will create the anxieties within him which self-assertion created from his earliest childhood. The risks he runs are far broader than merely the economic uncertainties.

If, on the other hand, a member of the elite is to set up such a textile enterprise, he will be demeaning himself in the ways which have been suggested above; the humiliation and sense of discomfort which would be entailed will probably keep the thought that he might benefit materially from such activity from ever entering his mind.

As for the introduction of larger-scale industry, that is experienced in traditional peasant society as an activity of foreigners and remote from the power or ken of members of the indigenous elite as well as the simple folk—an activity in which one no more expects to engage than one expects to occupy a house like the places which motion pictures present as the homes of the pictured characters. One's government may, if it becomes sovereign, introduce such symbols of power, and an individual official may be assigned the honor of being manager of the enterprise, but that he will demean himself, or can assert himself against problems, so that he will execute with effectiveness the practical and complex tasks of running the enterprise is asking him to shed his personality structure and become a different man.

Nevertheless, there must be some deviance at all times, both because the random play of human intelligence will cause some new ideas to seem attractive in spite of all the sanctions that exist and, more important, because random differences in family environment produce deviants of various types in any society.

Traditional societies prevent some types of deviance from spreading by providing special niches for deviants. In probably every peasant society the individual who cannot face the risk of testing his own capabilities in a role as father or in the power structure can assume a role as seer, medicine man, shaman, priest, monk, village fool, or learned man. The learned man and the religious man are often one and the same, and the learning sanctioned is in the traditional humanistic wisdom of the society, not in technological exploration. Thus such individuals serve the society and cause no strain on its structure.

The deviant with need autonomy, need achievement, and creative imagination offers a different problem. The social pressures may not rest so heavily on him as to deter him, and in spite of them he may explore the physical environment or, aware of information available from other societies, may avail himself of it. However, if he is produced by the random appearance of unusual circumstances within individual families, he is an isolated individual within a traditional community. The social pressures will certainly tend to create tensions in him which lessen his nurturance to his children and tend to cause authoritarian personality to reappear in them. Moreover, his children will observe the tensions in his behavior and reject those characteristics of his personality which cause the difficulty. Thus there are powerful forces tending against cumulative innovation and change.

I suggest that these pressures account for the historical tendency of the traditional state of societies to continue unchanged. Specifically, these pressures, more than the difficulty of scientific advance in some objective sense, account for the extreme slowness of development of scientific concepts and accumulation of knowledge of the physical world.

These facts do not, however, prove that basic change can never occur in traditional society. We know that it has occurred on a number of occasions. What the argument above, if it is acceptable, does demonstrate is that we must look for a force or forces of considerable power if we are to have a satisfactory explanation of the occasional historical disruptions of traditional society.

In conclusion, it may be well to repeat that no society is perfectly traditional. None, that is, is in complete equilibrium. It is almost certainly true that in every traditional society the members of some group or groups are somewhat dissatisfied with their roles, and seeds of change exist which would eventually disrupt the traditional structure, personality, and culture, even though no force for change impinged on the society from without. The sketch drawn here of a completely traditional society is a model which abstracts from the complexities of life. It is useful because it portrays basic elements and relationships present in every traditional society and hence the nature of the forces resisting change. Thereby it lays a basis for discussion of the sorts of forces that may initiate change.

APPENDIX: THE GENERAL QUESTION OF PERPETUATION OF PERSONALITY TYPES

As one discusses the perpetuation of authoritarian personality in traditional peasant society, the more general question arises: Does every type of personality tend to perpetuate itself? If creative personality comes into existence fairly generally within a society or within some social group, will it too tend to perpetuate itself?

Historically, the question is easily answered. Creative personality has not been as durable as authoritarian personality. Creative personality leads to progressive achievement and to change in culture and social structure; but, as Kroeber has shown in *Configurations of Culture Growth,*[29] the typical pattern in history has been for processes of culture growth to appear and to come to an end. The culture growth may be sudden and spectacular and the termination gradual, or both may be gradual, or both may be abrupt. The period of progressive achievement may be 100 years or closer to a millennium. It may be in governmental administration, in warfare, in colonization, in art or literature or philosophy. But, whatever the variation in its area and time pattern, an underlying fact is that it tends to end. Hence creativity too must tend to come to an end.

This fact, however, does not settle the question at issue, for creativity may have ended because of external pressures of some sort, not because creative individuals behave in such ways that over a number of generations creativity disappears. The broader question must therefore be asked: Why do periods of culture growth tend to come to an end?

---

[29] A. L. Kroeber, *Configurations of Culture Growth* (Berkeley and Los Angeles: University of California Press, 1944).

Kroeber explains the cessation of bursts of culture growth by noting that achievement tends to center in some field, and suggests that culture growth runs down as the possibility of progress in that field is exhausted. This explanation is attractive but not complete. It is necessary also to explain why the creativity that led to culture growth in one field does not turn to another field as the first one plays out.

One or the other of two developments must have occurred. Either a decline of creativity occurred and caused the cessation of culture growth, or some forces must have existed that prevented creativity from turning elsewhere when one field of activity had been played out, the resulting frustration thereupon affecting the family environment in such a way that creativity declined.

It is easy to visualize the forces which might hold creativity compulsively within one area of action. When creative action makes effort in one area of action successful, that area attains a high value in the culture, and that high valuation may make diversion of effort to other fields unsatisfying and impossible.

Thus we have two explanations to choose between. Did the Phoenician culture, for example, reach an apex and then decline simply because creativity declined in the colonies along the Mediterranean which Phoenicians had founded? Or did it decline because colonization had come to have such high value that, when it had been pursued until it had been extended beyond maintainable limits, turning to other fields was impossible and the frustration of further efforts in colonization led to a decline in creativity? Did the Khmer empire decline because creativity declined, or because the drive of each god-king to build a structure to serve his spirit greater than the greatest previous structure strained the society beyond maintainable limits, and the compulsions of the religious values prevented change in behavior? Did the glory that was Greece come to an end because personality steadily changed, or because the skein of advance in intellectual achievement had exhausted the possibilities for such advance until technical progress created a new base, whereupon the frustration of continued efforts in the same field caused alteration of personality? Did the Roman Empire disintegrate because insistence on the governmental and social pattern which had been satisfying in the early period of expansion made it inflexible, whereupon the frustrations altered personality in succeeding generations, or simply because the later Romans were less creative and not able to solve their problems as well as the earlier Romans had solved theirs?

Probably both forces have been at work. There is impressive historical evidence that persistence of value-patterns that have become outmoded has been an important element in the termination of some periods of culture growth. However, there is also impressive evidence that, apart from this development, creativity may fail to perpetuate itself. For example, E. R. Dodds, in *The Greeks and the Irrational*,[30] presents evidence that to me at least seems incontestible that progressive change in personality, quite independent of any compulsive retention of old values, occurred throughout Greek history and caused the end of its period of greatness.

It is easy to see how such change might occur during any period of creative activity. Successful attack on new problems brings change, and change, causing each generation to live in some respect or other differently from the previous generation, will change childhood environment and may be expected to cause change in personality. Only personality, physical environment, and social structure which interlock so as to prevent change, it may plausibly be argued, can be expected to perpetuate themselves. Specifically, then, only authoritarian

---

[30] Berkeley: University of California Press, 1956.

personality and traditional social structure (whether or not peasant) can be expected to be stable.

We need not pursue this thread of thought further. It is not central to our argument except as it illustrates the nature of the factors which determine social stability or change.

part **III**

The Transition to Economic Growth

Disturbing Events and
Reactions to Them

chapter **9**

SINCE THE STABILITY OF THE STRUCTURE AND FUNC-
tioning of traditional society is great, the forces which disrupt it must be
powerful ones. Waiving the case of slow technological change over many
centuries, what forces will cause a group to emerge which abandons traditional ways and turns its energies to the tasks of technological advance,
doing so with a creativity the groups of the society had not hitherto possessed? In other words, what influences will cause a group to emerge with
altered needs, values, and cognitions?

WITHDRAWAL OF STATUS RESPECT[1]

It will be argued in the following chapters that the basic cause of such
change is the perception on the part of the members of some social group
that their purposes and values in life are not respected by groups in the
society whom they respect and whose esteem they value. The satisfaction derived by an individual from his activity in life depends in part on
the status associated with it. That status shall be satisfying requires not
that it is high but merely that it is deemed appropriate by the person occupying it and is respected by others. The peasant as well as the lord,
the craftsman as well as the political leader or corporation executive, has a
status. One's status derives not only from one's economic function, however, but from all that one does and believes, all of one's relationships to
other persons and to the unseen forces in which one believes. One is a
person who tills the soil, believes in God, joins in pleasantries on the village green on Sunday afternoons, is greeted with courtesy by the mayor
and the sheriff. One's status, that is, is one's identity; it includes one's
purposes and values in life.

---

[1] In two previous publications, "The Process of Economic Development," *Econ-
nomic Development and Cultural Change*, Vol. V, No. 3 (April, 1957), pp. 193–215,
and "How Economic Growth Begins: A General Theory Applied to Japan," *Public
Opinion Quarterly*, Vol. XXII, No. 3 (Fall, 1958), pp. 373–90, I referred to "group
subordination" or "social subordination," and in early mimeographed drafts of the
present volume to "denial of expected status." These concepts are identical with
the one I now term "withdrawal of status respect."

185

Like other values, the value one places on one's status becomes internalized, and one regards that status as right. (In a nonstatic society, one's concept of status may be one of moving from position to position as one progresses in life.) For the inner satisfaction of the members of a society, as for social stability, it is essential that the status (the identity) of the members of each group in a society also be recognized by the other groups as appropriate and good. One cannot find satisfaction in one's adult pattern of behavior, including in this term one's beliefs, if one does not also perceive that the groups whose opinion one values (one's "reference groups") approve of such behavior. If the members of a group, having learned a role and status in infancy and childhood—role and status which their forebears learned before them—and having learned also to value certain groups in the society as reference groups, then find in adulthood that the members of their reference groups do not regard their role and status as worthy and proper, for example, disregard their beliefs and moral standards, the impossibility of believing (feeling) at the same time that their role and status are worthy and that the judgment of their reference groups is trustworthy creates tensions within them. They value both their position in life and the opinion of other social groups, but they cannot pursue the one and still have the other.

In a traditional society in which social disruption has not occurred the purposes, values, and activities of each group are respected. Each group in the society has its accepted place and feels that it is valued. To each group, therefore, not only its own status but also the structure of the society as a whole are good. Since the existing relationships are satisfying, changed ones have little attraction. By the yardstick of the values of the traditional society, alien values, including many aspects of the ways of living necessary to obtain higher income, are inferior and repugnant.

The effects of withdrawal from members of some group in such a society of respect for their status in life (for brevity, withdrawal of status respect) will be discussed at some length.[2] For the time being, the conditions which cause the members of a group to be looked upon with some lack of respect will be regarded as accidents of history. Although there are no true accidents of history, it seems justifiable not to push the causal analysis back beyond the point where such situations exist. To illustrate concretely the nature of the situations referred to, I shall suggest some incidents of history which seem to have been important in bringing withdrawal from some group of recognition of its traditional status in the so-

---

[2] Properly defined, the word "status" refers not merely to one's overt position in life as landowner, learned man, or peasant but also to the attitudes of others in the society toward that position. Thus if others do not respect one's position as much as previously, one's status has changed even though one's overt position has not. Hence the phenomenon referred to here should be termed simply "withdrawal of status" or "denial of status." To avoid ambiguity, however, I shall use the redundant term "withdrawal of status respect."

ciety. Four types of events will be of importance in the discussion of later chapters.

Withdrawal of Status Respect: Displacement by Force

One is the displacement of a traditional elite group from its previous status by another traditional group by physical force. In virtually every peasant society historically the position of the elite initially depended on physical force.[3] No matter how firmly that position was later protected by other sanctions as against nonelite classes, it might be subject to attack by other landed or warrior elites. Such attack itself was usually sanctioned until quite late in history. In most or all traditional societies the physical circumstances of life, the need aggression inculcated in children, and the public aspects of childhood environment interrelated to glorify fighting by the appropriate elite (and also to restrict warfare to these groups).

Often the fighting might be among themselves rather than against outsiders. In many societies, therefore, the power equilibrium was unstable. One group replaced another as controllers of the social order. There are numerous examples of such changes in Japan and western Europe during the Christian era. If the displacement was part of an expected game of conquest by force, in which status was politely left alone except for specific relations of political subordination, the displaced groups may merely have continued the game; but where the group newly in power created new rules or otherwise indicated their lack of regard for the status that had traditionally been respected, there undoubtedly resulted that anxiety, that sense of lack of equilibrium or of emotional incompleteness, which is in point here.

As one example of such a development, in Japan the Tokugawa, gaining nationwide hegemony at the beginning of the seventeenth century, imposed new political and social restrictions on the "outer clans" and maintained them for some 250 years. They imposed also a national peace under which the samurai of all clans quickly lost their traditional function and gradually lost their traditional status, and under which, because of a change in the role of samurai, the so-called "wealthy peasants" lost the close contact with important samurai that they had previously had.

The top elite may of course be displaced by force not by some rival group within the society but by invasion from abroad. The prominent pertinent examples are the conquests by Western powers of all of South and Southeast Asia, including Indonesia, except Thailand, and all of Latin America, Africa, and the Middle East. The social impact of these events differs greatly from that of domestic conquests. In the establishment of

---

[3] Concerning eight important societies, see Rushton Coulborn (ed.), *Feudalism in History* (Princeton, N.J.: Princeton University Press, 1956). In this work specialists discuss feudalism in western Europe, Japan, China, ancient Mesopotamia and Iran, ancient Egypt, India, the Byzantine Empire, and Russia.

colonial authority the conquering group which becomes the top elite in the society has values alien to the traditional culture, while in domestic conquests the new top elite has traditional values.

The difference is fundamental. The reaction of the subordinated groups is in some respects radically different. The colonial case and its special characteristics will be discussed and illustrated in Chapters 17 through 19.

Withdrawal of Status Respect: Denigration of Valued Symbols

Even without any such gross change in group relationships there has sometimes occurred, through some historical change in the attitude of the superior group, the prohibition of some activity or relationship vital to the sense of status of a subordinate group, or a milder variant of the same type of relationship—manifestation of contempt, scorn, or some other degree of psychological ostracism by a high-prestige group of a subordinate group because of distaste for some element in the role of the subordinate group.

An interesting case is the schism in the Orthodox Church in seventeenth century Russia.[4] After the period of national difficulties early in the century known as the Time of Troubles, new religious zeal appeared. The movement involved emphasis on traditional rituals and symbols. But in the seventeenth century the Patriarch of Moscow and the Tsar seem to have had little respect for either the traditional dogma or the sensitivities of the faithful. In the 1660's, for diplomatic reasons, they decreed a number of innovations in the Russian Church service to make it accord with Greek practice. These included making the sign of the cross with three fingers instead of two. This practice implied the full divinity of Christ the Son, a concept previously rejected and one that was shocking to many of the faithful. The traditionalists—later known as the Old Believers—refused to conform. A schism resulted which persisted until the Bolshevik Revolution in 1917. It has been estimated that, in spite of persecution, in the 1860's over one fourth of Great Russians were Old Believers, and in the late nineteenth and early twentieth centuries, one third.[5]

Religious suppression occurred also in seventeenth century England. The social tension, however, related not merely to religion. For centuries preceding the acute religious persecution, the aristocracy and landed gentry of England, infected by continental manners and values, had sneered at the values and the persons of the "good old English stock" and of the lowland Scots. In Russia disdain for the dissenters by the elite probably also accompanied the persecution. Indeed, religious suppression probably never occurs unless there exists a low social valuation of the group whose religious activity is suppressed.

---

[4] Serge A. Zenkovsky, "The Russian Church Schism: Its Background and Repercussions," *Russian Review*, Vol. XVI (October, 1957), pp. 37–58.

[5] *Ibid.*, pp. 51–52.

The denigration of valued symbols, like displacement by force, may occur internationally. Apparently the people of every society, so long as they were isolated from the rest of the world, thought of their country as the center of world civilization and the power of their rulers as all-encompassing. When Europeans first reached their soil, the rulers of Japan and Burma refused to treat with foreign nations as equals but instead expected their envoys to petition as inferiors. The Japanese referred to Dutch books as the barbarian books. Suppose, then, that a previously isolated country comes into contact with a more powerful foreign group, a group which does not intrude physically into the society and conquer it, but which by its acts forces the repeated perception of the unquestionable superiority of its power and of its condescension toward the elites of the society. Since virtually every people places a high valuation on power, the condescension of the powerful foreign group will be painful. The resulting tensions may be felt by individuals throughout the society; the entire society will experience withdrawal of respect. (Since an isolated society assumes that it is the whole world of any importance and therefore that the whole world respects it, the knowledge of a contrary attitude constitutes *withdrawal* of respect, not merely denial of respect.)

The purest example that comes to mind is Japan, on which Western nations impressed their power without otherwise appreciably disrupting the domestic social order. In a number of other countries—China, some countries of Latin America after they had gained their independence, some in the Middle East—we have mixed cases; along with the demonstration of unquestionably superior power there was some intrusion, but there was not complete displacement of the top elite by a conquering group. We shall be most interested in the case of Japan, where this relationship was superimposed on domestic tensions created earlier.

Withdrawal of Status Respect: Inconsistency of Status Symbols

A feeling of status displacement has often arisen from the development and long continuance of inconsistency between economic and other status relationships. Since the situation has most commonly arisen between a new trading group and an old elite, it may be discussed in that context rather than in general terms.

Small-scale intercommunity trading inevitably arises in a peasant society and comes to be an accepted activity for some group. If interregional or international trade expands, members of the merchant group may become large-scale traders and financiers of great economic power. The elite of the society are apt to find it advantageous to go to the trading-financial group for financial aid.

When they first do so, their status makes dealing with them flattering as well as profitable to the trading group. But that group now possesses one of the important status symbols, economic power. Yet other elements of recognition may be denied the traders all the more rigidly because the elite, forced to be suppliants economically, must cling the more compulsively to their other claims to social superiority. Social discrimination continues. The result is a dual frustration of values: the traders are denied the social status which traditionally has belonged to persons of the economic position they have now attained, and the old elite are denied exclusive possession of the economic status symbols which used to be part of the bundle of symbols setting them apart. Neither feels that its position is fully respected.

Withdrawal of Status Respect: Nonacceptance in a New Society

Social disaffection is almost certain to arise when a group migrates to a new society in which it does not have high prestige. In the new society the activity and mode of life of the members of the group are alien and are not accorded recognition. If they do not expect recognition, then they may continue indefinitely in but not of the society without feeling withdrawal of status; but if they expect their position to be respected, then they will experience tensions which will cause social change of some sort. Even if in the second or later generations they internalize in a distorted fashion the values of the new society, the problem is not solved; for, since they are still rejected in some degree because they are alien, performing the activities valued in the new society will not yield them status.

A related case that may be a very special one, or on the other hand may be found on investigation to be of more general applicability, occurred when Spanish armies migrated to Colombia and established a new Spanish society there. As has been noted in Chapter 3, the landed elite who developed in two valleys looked with condescension on those of a third, Antioquia, because in operating the mines of the area the Antioqueños found it necessary to work with their own hands.[6]

I suggest these four types of events as causes of withdrawal of respect for the status of some group in a society. To the specific events I have mentioned as examples of each type, other observers may add others. Stated generally, however, the four types of events, change in the power structure, derogation of institutionalized activity without change in the power structure, contradiction among status symbols, and nonacceptance of expected status on migration to a new society, are exhaustive. Any cause of withdrawal of recognition of status can be classed under one of the four heads.

The phenomenon, it should be noted, is not merely one of being regarded as inferior. In any society some individuals and some groups regard themselves as inferior to others in various respects without therefore feeling frustrated or improperly treated. The peasant regards himself

---

[6] The condescension may have been increased by differences in regional origin; a larger proportion of the Antioqueños may have come from the Basque provinces.

as inferior in social status to the lord, and a worker to the corporation executive. Neither thereby feels frustrated or humiliated. He feels humiliated and indecently treated if his function as a peasant or worker, which he has been led to believe is a useful and worthy element in the functioning of the society, is no longer accorded due respect. The phenomenon, that is, is one of withdrawal from a group of respect for a status which it has previously had in a society, which has been accepted, and which the group regards as a worthy part of a reasonable order of things. One has not necessarily experienced withdrawal of status respect simply because one is a member of a minority or alien group or a so-called "outsider." Something cannot be withdrawn which has never been extended or expected.

Respect for one's role and status in a society always involves respect for one's purposes and values in life, and withdrawal of status respect always involves lack of respect for one's purposes and values in life. Indeed, this is the central aspect of the phenomenon. Moreover, the impact is often made not by what the offending group does with intent to affect some other group but simply by its disregard of the values of the other group. Thus the withdrawal of respect by many of the rulers and higher nobles of England from Norman through Tudor times for the status of the lesser nobles and gentry and the simple folk consisted primarily of the following: During some periods the noblemen dressed and acted in ways which the lesser folk regarded as effeminate and unmanly. Their plays, dancing, gambling, and speech were of sorts which the lesser folk regarded as indecent and immoral. They often used their positions for personal gain, cheating, robbing, and killing in the process. They failed to preserve public order, because their concern for their own aggrandizement overshadowed their interest in the welfare of the classes beneath them. They violated solemn oaths when circumstances made this expedient, and their action in doing so was sanctioned by the religious officials who presumed to be the representatives of God on earth. And so on. In short, they did not think that lesser folk merited much consideration. Periods to which these comments apply were interspersed with periods of better rule, but the cumulative impact over time of the sorts of actions mentioned above was devastating. The withdrawal of status respect which such acts constituted was undoubtedly extremely important in causing anxiety, alienation from traditional values, and other changes in personality, probably much more important, for example, than acts specifically directed at the religious dissenters.

Whenever withdrawal of status respect appears in a society, it is a powerful solvent of the cement which binds the society together. It will be suggested in the following chapter that groups who feel that classes above them no longer have decent regard for the groups' purposes in life will lose their contentment with the traditional society. In their children and grandchildren personality changes will be bred that contain the seeds of social change—seeds that may push through the toughest crust of social controls and set the society on new courses.

The Social Revolution of the Present Age

Indeed, withdrawal of status respect is at the root of the world's turbulence today. The elites of traditional societies, as has been noted above, respected the positions and functions of the groups below them and served the interests of those groups economically, politically, and symbolically. Today, however, in many economically underdeveloped areas of the world the elites are self-centered groups who look with condescension and contempt on the classes below them, rule them rather than represent them, and perform little symbolic representational function. The resulting perception by the lower classes that their superiors have no interest in or regard for the purposes or values of those lower classes but rather, in the true sense of that much-abused word, exploit them—this perception is the basic disruptive force in these societies.

The attitudes of the elites have changed for two major reasons. One is that indigenous traditional elites have been displaced by European ones through conquest. The European elites thereafter showed contempt not only for the former top elites but also for the classes beneath them. This situation characterizes not only the areas of Asia and Africa that are still colonial or have been until recent years but also the countries of Latin America. Although the countries of Latin America have been free of colonial control for almost a century and a half, their independence early in the nineteenth century was the independence not of indigenous peoples from European elites but of European elites in the colonies from their mother countries. The European groups continued to rule the countries they had conquered, and even to the present day their disregard of the purposes of the simple folk has continued.

The second reason is that even in many countries where the present elites are indigenous ones, their attitudes have been corroded by the events of history. Landed classes and groups around them hold their traditional privileges and traditional rule while they have forgotten their traditional responsibilities to provide symbolic and material representation of the common people. They breed a deep feeling in the lower classes that their interests are held in condescension or contempt. This is true in Iran, just as it was true in Iraq before Kassim and in Egypt before Naguib and Nasser. It is true in Thailand, in Laos, and apparently in South Vietnam. The present popular feeling of resentment in such countries is often said to be due to new aspirations on the part of the people. No doubt there is truth in this, but in the main the feeling is probably due to the fact that a traditional sense of respected status in a meaningful society has eroded.

Perhaps the main influence eroding the traditional attitudes of the elite classes in these countries has been contact with the West. Finding themselves disdained by powerful European groups, the indigenous elites have reacted to this condescension by persuading themselves that it was directed not against them but against their humbler countrymen, adopting this attitude to convince themselves that they are as elite and superior in their attitudes as are the Europeans. As a result, they are as far removed from sympathetic understanding of the classes below them as any alien ruling group might be. The reaction of the groups below them to this attitude is the explosive force that is causing social revolutions throughout the underdeveloped world.

This indirect impact of the West, rather than its direct impact in disrupting traditional society or in imparting knowledge of Western goods, may be the most important way in which it has contributed to social change.

In this study the possible origins of withdrawal of status respect will not be pursued further. The discussion will take one of the four conditions sketched above as a starting point and will consider the effects.[7]

WITHDRAWAL OF STATUS RESPECT: MERTON'S TYPOLOGY OF ADAPTIVE MODES

Withdrawal of status respect causes conflict within the individuals who are subject to it: they value highly two conflicting goals and are frustrated in the attempt to attain both. I shall suggest that the anxiety and rage thus created in adults will alter the home environment in predictable ways that will in turn affect the personalities of the next generation, and that these effects, in one generation or cumulatively over several generations, are of great importance for the theory of social change.

The first effect seems to be the appearance after one or more generations of a type of personality which I shall term "retreatist"; or, if the social tensions are more severe, a type which I shall term "ritualist." Out of ritualism, in turn, retreatism may develop. Later, retreatist personality may give way to innovational personality, in some cases to a special type of innovational personality to be termed "reformist."

As a basis for analyzing the effects, it will be useful first to define these personality types: retreatist, ritualist, innovational, reformist. Behavior of these four types encompasses the main possible sorts of reaction to social stresses. The terms are not mine; I owe the last to Erik H. Erik-

---

[7] In the final chapter (xiv) of his book *Innovation: The Basis of Cultural Change* (New York: McGraw-Hill Book Co., Inc., 1953), H. G. Barnett suggests that innovations are accepted by the dissident (those "who have consistently refused to identify themselves with some of the conventions of their group"), the indifferent (those who "have not dedicated themselves irretrievably to a custom or to an ideal of their society"), the disaffected (those who have been "active participants in certain aspects of their culture but later acquire a distaste for them"), and the resentful (those who "are dissatisfied not because they object to the values of their group but because they are denied those that are esteemed the most"). His "disaffected" and his "resentful" correspond fairly closely to my groups denied status respect.

son and the first three to Robert K. Merton, who has presented a perceptive analysis of possible modes of adaptation to social tensions.[8] Merton implicitly assumes that the modes of behavior he classifies are direct reactions to the social pressures rather than the reactions of children, grandchildren, or great-grandchildren to the changed home environment caused by the tensions.[9] Nevertheless, his typology will be a useful point of departure for the present discussion.

He defines the source of social pressure on the individual as "independent variation of cultural goals and institutionalized means," and specifically discusses a society "in which there is an exceptionally strong emphasis upon specific goals without a corresponding emphasis upon institutional procedures."[10] Primarily, he discusses a situation in which "the channels of vertical mobility are closed or narrowed *in a society which places a high premium on economic affluence and social ascent for all its members.*"[11] He has in mind the United States, in which, he suggests, individuals are told by their culture that if they are to be regarded highly they must gain affluence but in which many individuals are not accepted into channels leading to affluence. Thus economic affluence or social ascent is the cultural goal, and diligent endeavor in a business career is the institutionalized procedure; but this procedure does not lead some individuals to the desired goal either because of their individual lack of capacities or because they are members of a group which is not accepted in the business community. A normal type of social behavior in a stable society is acceptance of both the culture's goals and its institutionalized means; but in the situation cited, since the means will not lead to attaining the goals, it is impossible for some individuals to accept both as good.

Merton's typology of individual adaptation is presented below.[12] To the extent that goals and means are consistent, conformity to both as indicated by line I of his tabulation is the common pattern of behavior. If, however, the two cannot be reconciled, one of the alternative methods of

A TYPOLOGY OF MODES OF INDIVIDUAL ADAPTATION

Modes of Adaptation	Culture Goals	Institutionalized Means
I. Conformity	+	+
II. Innovation	+	−
III. Ritualism	−	+
IV. Retreatism	−	−
V. Rebellion	±	±

---

[8] In *Social Theory and Social Structure* (rev. ed.; Glencoe, Ill.: Free Press of Glencoe, Inc., 1957), Part II, especially chap. iv.

[9] In part, Merton's discussion is an attack on the theory that social deviance is the result of "imperious biological drives." (*Ibid.*, p. 131.)

[10] *Ibid.*, p. 134.

[11] *Ibid.*, p. 146. Italics in the original.

[12] The tabulation is from *ibid.*, p. 140.

adaptation indicated on lines II–V will occur (+ indicating acceptance and − indicating rejection).

Merton defines innovation as "the use of institutionally proscribed but often effective means of attaining at least the simulacrum of success—wealth and power"; ritualism as "the abandoning or scaling down of the lofty cultural goals of great pecuniary success and rapid social mobility to the point where one's aspirations can be satisfied"; retreatism as abandonment of both the cultural goals and institutionalized norms of behavior; and rebellion as turning "outside the environing social structure to envisage and seek to bring into being a new, that is to say, a greatly modified social structure," or, alternatively, as "seeking to *institutionalize* new goals and new procedures to be shared by other members of the society," and "to *change* the existing cultural and social structure rather than to accommodate efforts within this structure." Rebellion, he adds, is hardly of the same nature as the other nonconformist adaptations. While they constitute adaptations within the society, rebellion attempts to change it. The typology, he notes, is one not of individuals but of modes of role behavior. Individuals may shift from one to another "in different spheres of social activities."[13]

He offers no suggestion concerning why individuals adopt one mode of adaptation or another. It will be important to us to consider the differential effects of different conditions, for we are centrally interested in only one result, creative social change, and, specifically, the appearance of economic growth. The analysis may be applied far more broadly than to certain conflicts within American culture.

NEW WINE IN MERTON'S BOTTLES

I shall find it convenient to augment the content of Merton's adaptive modes and to redefine ritualism and rebellion to some extent.

Merton's main example of innovation is the use of unscrupulous, "sharp," or illegal practice to gain financial success in American society. Although he does not limit his discussion to the nineteenth century, the ironical passages by Dickens and Bierce which he quotes, portraying the American scoundrel who is accepted because he is smart, center on that period. He could equally well have featured more recent American phenomena.[14] The racketeering of the 1930's, the ready acceptance by the Teamsters Union of corrupt, brutal, and criminal leaders so long as they gain results, and the corrupt urban political machines which flourish, sub-

---

[13] The definitions are from *ibid.* as follows: innovation, p. 141; ritualism, pp. 149–50; retreatism, p. 153; and rebellion, pp. 155 and 140, n. 13. The ensuing discussion is from p. 140.

[14] And he might have turned the tables on Dickens. "Get place and power, if possible with grace, but by whatever means, get power and place," was written of English society.

side or withdraw from attention, and then flourish again would serve as equally good texts for this discussion. Al Capone, James M. Curley, and Jimmy Hoffa would provide as good examples as the robber barons.

It is obvious that my use of the term "innovation" is broader than Merton's. My innovation shares with Merton's concept the use of low-valued activity, but the degree of creativity involved does not enter into his definition. Merton's usage, moreover, implies activity which in some objective sense is antisocial. My more general definition includes all activity contrary to the values of the society. The industrialist in a peasant society as well as the racketeer in the United States may usefully be termed innovators.[15]

The individual who is uncomfortable in the modal activities of his society often seeks a satisfactory identity in a deviant role that is socially sanctioned. The most notable cases perhaps are the seeking of attainment in intellectual life or in a religious role that involves some degree of withdrawal from secular life. Choice of such occupational roles is not innovation, but within them the individual may innovate.

A frustrated individual may turn his energies to science, mathematics, philosophy, or other learning when social discrimination has shut other doors to him. He presumably does so both because the intellectual discipline may satisfy alternative status values he carries within him and because it is a source of satisfaction in a more subtle sense. Knowledge of the universe is mastery of it. The man who can explore farther than had been done before the nature of the universe—moral or physical—has gained a mastery that neither armies nor landed gentry can take from him if his personality has been given a bent that makes this kind of mastery satisfying. The prominence of Jews first in philosophy and then in mathematics and science during the past 150 years is probably a case of innovation motivated in this way.

The innovator, whether he operates a political machine or engages in, say, technological exploration or the study of science in a peasant society, in some degree is "seeking to institutionalize new goals" and "to change the existing cultural and social structure." That is, innovation and rebellion shade into each other. Where the line between them is drawn is probably not a matter of great substantive importance, but there is a distinction to be made.

The persons who carry out rebellion as Merton defines it include reformers, men who are driven to make overt changes in the institutions

---

[15] Racketeering and crime as roads to satisfying the cultural goals of affluence are accepted procedures to many Americans. See Daniel Bell, "Crime as an American Way of Life: A Queer Ladder of Social Mobility," *The End of Ideology* (Glencoe, Ill.: Free Press of Glencoe, Inc., 1960), chap. vii. However, they violate the ideal values of the society and also the practical values of important reference groups, and their use to gain affluence should be regarded as rejection of institutionalized means. This rejection of institutionalized means is by entire social groups, not merely by individuals.

of their society. Woodrow Wilson and Martin Luther are classic examples. Reformers are men who cannot satisfy their needs and values—their need-dispositions—without imposing their changed values upon their fellows; reformers, of course, are innovators, but the term "innovator" also includes individuals who can satisfy their need-dispositions without directly disturbing greatly the relationships among their fellows. The difference, however, is one of degree, not of kind. For if any innovator is successful, the values of his fellows will be changed somewhat, and he knows it.[16]

Rebellion, however defined, includes the attempt to establish a new society. The pure example is Utopianism, establishment of a society of one's own, where good and right shall flourish. But migration to a going society must partake of this aim; the migrant moves only if he thinks he will do better in the new society.

Merton defines ritualism as the scaling down of lofty goals until they seem attainable. This description, it seems to me, does not fully connote the nature of the behavior. The ritualist goes through the motions called for by the culture with which he identifies himself without any real hope that his actions will attain the goals of the culture, and without initiative, imagination, or vigor. His behavior is a complex psychological defense to a threat to his identity; it will be examined in some detail in the discussion of colonialism, for it is frequent in colonial societies.

The retreatist is the person who during the process of personality formation has met the problem of being unable to satisfy conflicting values by repressing them from his consciousness without being able to replace them by others. He continues to function within the society, but without much interest either concerning his work activity or in the attainment of position. He is possessed of a high degree of *anomie*, or normlessness. But even he has only suppressed within himself the norms of the society and of his group in it, not eliminated them. If he had done the latter, he could live a successful autonomous life, but this he cannot do.

Merton suggests that retreatism characterizes "some of the adaptive activities of psychotics, autists, pariahs, outcasts, vagrants, vagabonds,

---

[16] Among writings specifically on the subject of rebellion or revolution, I have been stimulated by George S. Pettee, *The Process of Revolution* (New York: Harper & Bros., 1938). I read this before reading Crane Brinton, *The Anatomy of Revolution* (New York: W. W. Norton & Co., Inc., 1938). Albert Camus, *The Rebel* (New York: Alfred A. Knopf, Inc., 1956), is more philosophical, less sociological. My indebtedness to Barnett, *Innovation: The Basis of Cultural Change*, is apparent from references in earlier chapters.

Erik H. Erikson suggested, in a seminar at the Massachusetts Institute of Technology in 1958–59: "A social reformer is a man who has an account to settle, and who must settle it on the largest possible scale." I am suggesting here a difference between a reformer and a mere innovator which relates not merely to the scale of his activities. In a sense, an innovator must act on as large a scale as a reformer, but the reformer's area of operations must include all the fellows of his group or community or society, whereas the mere innovator's area of operation extends in a different dimension.

tramps, chronic drunkards, and drug addicts."[17] Charlie Chaplin's bum is a retreatist. Merton notes, however, that these individuals are not unqualifiedly retreatist. They "may retain some orientation to the values of their own groupings within the larger society or, occasionally, to the values of the conventional society itself."[18] The classic cases of retreatist groups in the American society are the Indians living rather listlessly on a reservation and the "shiftless" Negroes of the deep South of the past two or three generations.

These, then, are possible modes of adaptation by the individual to conflict within him caused by contradictory demands of his culture: he may become ritualist, retreatist, innovational, or rebellious. The classification seems to be exhaustive; any possible reaction lies within one or another of these classes. We shall use this typology in discussing the effects of withdrawal of status respect in succeeding chapters.[19]

---

[17] *Social Theory and Social Structure*, p. 153.

[18] *Loc. cit.*, n. 37.

[19] In the manuscript for *Economic Development and Social Change in South India* (Manchester, Eng.: Manchester University Press, forthcoming 1962), T. S. Epstein (Scarlett Trent) illustrates both the variety of possible specific sources of change and several of the principles suggested in this volume. In the mid-1950's Mrs. Epstein studied two towns in the Mandya district of Mysore State. One of them, "Wangala," is in the center of an area to which irrigation was brought early in the 1930's by the action of the state of Mysore. The other, "Dalena," lies on the fringe of the irrigated area, too high for irrigation to be brought to it. Irrigation increased the income of peasants in Wangala without requiring social change. As a result traditional social relationships continue in Wangala, with no major change except that economic symbols now are a greater element in prestige than before. Wives of the better-off farmers no longer work in the fields, since not doing so can now be afforded and brings higher prestige in the village. Caste relationships remain unchanged; a person's ascribed (or in Mrs. Epstein's terminology "ritual") characteristics are still the basic determinant of his prestige, and his relative income has little influence on his prestige; the homes still house humans and animals together; and only lineage elders form the village *panchayat*, even though formally the members are now elected.

By a process mentioned below, the change at Wangala caused men at Dalena to seek to increase *their* incomes. To do so they have gone to the town of Mandya to work in factories, have introduced some new enterprises in the village, and have rented wet lands in neighboring villages. Their widened nexus of relationships makes their prestige in the town more important to them than their prestige in the villages. Unlike in Wangala, therefore, the more well-to-do wear fine bought shirts over *dhotis* even on work days. Economic aspects of prestige (homes, clothing, watches, bicycles) are now more important than ritual ones. Well-to-do who are not lineage elders are now elected to the *panchayat*, and the functions of the *panchayat* are decaying; cases are now taken to courts in Mandya. Houses have changed; animals are now housed in a separate shed. Because of the widened contacts, English words not previously used have entered speech in Dalena; more have entered than in Wangala. Dalena men now participate in the politics of the district. Men working away from the village, no longer having use for the services of various untouchables, have terminated their annual "rewards," and the untouchables have terminated ritual services as well as economic ones. But wives still work in the fields; this is necessary, since someone must manage the workers there; moreover, prestige in the village does not have the relative importance it has in Wangala. And in spite of the economic changes, to be a farmer is still the ultimate aim of every Dalena man, even if at present he is a factory worker in Mandya.

I quote the author's judgment of the motivation for changes in Dalena. "In Dalena, too, villagers used to attach highest value to farming. But as they saw irrigation *making their neighbors richer, while their own lands remained dry,* they decided that they too would participate in the economic expansion of the region in whatever way they could." (Italics mine.)

This is a delightful illustration in minuscule of several of the principles discussed in this and later chapters. Status is a relative thing; when the men of Dalena no longer were on a par with their neighbors in Wangala, their status had declined even though their absolute condition had not changed. While to remedy this situation they moved outside of old valued occupations (and thus without intending it brought about a series of changes in social relationships), their ultimate occupational goal remained to achieve the old symbol of status, landedness, while achieving their old position of parity in other symbols as well.

In both villages conversion to a cash economy has led to a breakdown of the joint family.

We must assume that changes in traditional society had occurred in Dalena before the 1930's, for that the changes in personality necessary for the behavior noted in the 1950's could occur in one generation is contrary to much other evidence. The case merits further study.

Appearance of Retreatism

chapter 10

THE ANALYSIS OF EFFECTS OF CONDITIONS IN THE SO-
ciety at large on personality formation has been a no man's land of the
social sciences. Sociology and anthropology have considered (among
other matters) social structure, anthropology has analyzed culture, and
social and clinical psychology have considered, from somewhat differing
viewpoints, the impact of stimuli immediately touching the individual—
for example, his home environment—on his personality and, given a certain personality, on his behavior. But in their formal analyses the three
disciplines have made little contact with each other. Perceptive individuals in these disciplines have discussed the relationships among social
structure, culture, and personality and have noted that certain types of
change in one are often associated with certain types of change in the
others, suggesting, by means of this circumstantial evidence, that there
are causal relationships. In path-breaking studies, Erik H. Erikson has
discussed the relationships between an individual's childhood and his later
role in society. But hypotheses concerning the specific causal mechanisms
by which conditions in the larger society affect the personalities which
are being formed in successive generations are largely absent. Only the
most tentative footings have yet been laid down of a bridge connecting
the disciplines which deal with the behavior of society as a whole and the
psychology of personality formation. (David Riesman discusses the
broad causal relationships perceptively, and at a number of points he also
suggests specific mechanisms.)

In this chapter and Chapters 11 and 17 I attempt to build a bridge. I
shall suggest specific causal sequences by which it seems likely that the
pressure of withdrawal of status respect on authoritarian parents will create a home environment leading to progressively increasing retreatism
over a period of several generations. Out of this, still later, creative personality is apt to arise.

The argument of these chapters is admittedly a far reach from the facts
at our disposal, yet this aspect of the theory of social change is so fundamental, and the relevant facts which we now have so intriguing, that it
seems useful to cover the ground even though the margin for error is
great.

Analysis of this sequence of personality change must be speculative, or, to use the term loosely, intuitive. Sequences of action and of reaction within individuals are difficult to analyze, at least with tools yet devised by social scientists. In the main, the analysis must be by introspective examination and rearrangement of elements of behavior within oneself until one feels that one has arrived at a sequence that accounts for certain outer manifestations in other individuals. Moreover, the phenomenon involved is not a simple change in behavior or personality within a short time period but a complicated sequence of events extending over a period of, say, several generations. Construction of a fairly complex model is necessary, increasing the possibility of error. The justification of the model presented here is that it has broad applicability and over the wide area to which it refers seems to match the facts of social change and of human behavior better than do alternative explanations.

THE IMMEDIATE IMPACT OF WITHDRAWAL OF STATUS RESPECT

In considering the effects of withdrawal of status respect it is useful to distinguish between those on behavior and those on personality.

Immediate Reactions

The most immediate effect on the behavior of individuals will be resentment, or under severe disparagement some stronger form of rage, and anxiety. If the disparagement consists of the assumption of power in the society by a group which violates old values, the resentment will lead the disparaged group or groups to attempt to oust the aggressors, provided that they have sufficient power to make the attempt and that their system of values sanctions the action. Virtually without exception, this is the reaction to aggression from outside the society unless the power of the aggressors is overwhelming, for the culture of virtually every society sanctions resistance to aggression by aliens.[1] The indigenous population of probably every colonial area attempted to eject the foreign invaders by force when they first appeared.

Within a society, resistance by force also occurs at times. Various *hans* attempted revolt against the Tokugawa when the latter had gained hegemony over Japan and changed the rules of the game. The Great Rebellion in England may reasonably be interpreted as a similar resistance to change in the social structure. The withdrawal of status respect, however, may be by a group within a society, and the status of the group

---

[1] In the rare limiting case the culture of the society may have taught that the appropriate reaction to any aggression whatever is to submit or to flee. For such a case, see Elizabeth Marshall Thomas, *The Harmless People* (New York: Alfred A. Knopf, Inc., 1959).

may be so strongly sanctioned that rebellion is not morally acceptable unless the group grossly violates the society's most sacred values. Or the power of a ruling group may be unchallengeable.

Where possible, one reaction no doubt is to attempt to ignore the disparagement. Colonial conquerors cannot control all aspects of life, and to some degree indigenous peoples attempt to ignore them. Though the British forced their way into various ports of India from 1600 on, it has been estimated that 150 years later not more than 100 Indians had learned English. But, although ignoring them may inconvenience the conquerors, the disparaged individuals do not fool themselves. They must be well aware of their humiliation no matter how compulsively they attempt to ignore it.

So far as these forms of reaction are not possible, the course of behavior must be to continue to function while enduring the disparagement, observing old and valued rules of behavior where possible, paying inward tribute to them if outward observance is barred. Thus the Old Believers in Russia continued to worship by the forbidden ritual, openly where possible, clandestinely where necessary, and the Protestant Dissenters in England continued to meet in forbidden groups even in the face of the threat to harry them from the land; in Tokugawa Japan many samurai must have honored their old values in their hearts while unable to live overtly according to their code. Individuals continue to live or at least to believe according to the values they have learned, feeling continuing anxiety and rage and probably also some self-pity, hoping the while that the troubles will end and that the good old days in which they had their rightful place will return.

These new types of action in response to a new situation are changes in behavior but not in personality. Personality has changed only if one behaves differently from the way one would previously have behaved in the identical situation. The personalities of adults subjected to withdrawal of status respect will certainly change somewhat also. However, in adults the changes in personality will hardly be far-reaching since, by the time of adulthood, needs, values, and cognitions are so deeply ingrained that they are not apt to be notably changed thereafter except by the most drastic alterations in external circumstances. That, for example, a person of authoritarian personality should become markedly creative in adulthood because of the tensions created in him by withdrawal of status respect is hardly conceivable even in the most extreme or unique cases.

The major effects of withdrawal of status respect on personality must therefore be the effects on younger individuals, and especially on children in their most formative years. These considerations suggest that the major effect of withdrawal of status respect on personality will be the effect on young children of altered behavior in the home by adults who are denied the status they expect life to accord them. Verification in the larger society of the new perceptions of life which the infant and child gain in the home may then confirm and seal the new personality.

It should not be supposed that human behavior will necessarily be seriously affected, and a cumulative process of personality change begun, by minor disparagement, or even by rather severe disparagement if it is temporary. Men and women have adaptive capacity and can slough off signs of ill regard and interferences with their way of life without such marked reaction in their behavior that the home environment is materially changed. Indeed, some such buffeting is a normal part of any life. But we may reasonably suppose that continued ill regard for the way of life in which one finds satisfactory identity, or continued overt interference in some important aspect of it, if pronounced and if by groups whose good regard one values and expects, will have more serious effects. A considerable degree of disparagement persisted in over time is intended by the term "withdrawal of status respect."

The ways and degree to which adult behavior in the home will be altered depend on the severity of the withdrawal of status respect. It is convenient to divide the various cases into two types: disparagement by an elite group within the society which has traditionally had high place and is therefore an accepted and respected part of the social structure; and, in contrast, conquest and social disruption by an external group which does not share the society's culture and which therefore has little claim to respect or prestige in the society except for its one characteristic of overwhelming importance, its power. In the first case, because the elite group shares the society's culture, its violation of old values is apt to be limited. In the second case, because the conquering group is alien its system of values differs from that of the society and, whatever its deliberate policies of government may be, by its very pattern of life it will indicate contempt, repugnance, or at least a low valuation for a wide array of the characteristics of the society. The differences between the cases are thus two: in the degree of moral acceptance of and regard for the offending group by the groups being injured, and in the limitations or comprehensiveness of the aspersion cast on the society's culture by the offending group.

These two types of withdrawal of status respect are of course not fundamentally different in quality. Rather, they are at the ends of a continuum. When an indigenous group adopts attitudes which contravene the expectations of the culture, it loses some of its claim to respect and high regard, and, on the other hand, a conquering group has at least the one important claim to high regard—that it is powerful. Yet the differences between a group which is almost wholly accepted and traditionally has been accepted and a group whose behavior is almost wholly repugnant are so great that it is useful to treat these two limiting cases as differing types. The first will be considered in this chapter, the second in Chapter 17.

The authoritarian individual feels satisfaction in three overt aspects of authoritarian behavior: aggression, which satisfies the rage that simmers in him all his life, domination of others, and acceptance of a dependent role in relation to persons of superior position and status. These aspects of his satisfaction are integrally related; they are not separate items. There is a complex relationship among them.

When the exercise of initiative by a child in traditional society is frustrated by his parents' insistence on passive obedience, he feels pain and rage, yet paradoxically, submission to his parents' wishes causes him to feel security. For his parents' reaction to his initiative creates anxiety in him, and that anxiety is allayed by internalizing the rules of obedience they enforce. Further, in his father's domination he sees the promise of roles he himself will play in the statuses he will successively attain with the passage of time, roles that will permit the exercise of the need aggression which his rage instills in him. One of these roles, his aggressive relationship to his younger playmates, he can fill at once; in that aggression he experiences foretastes of the satisfactions he will feel all his life.

However, his security and satisfaction would be uneasy, because he also tends to hate the persons coercing him, if it were not for the fact that his father's treatment of him seems to be right. His father himself has no "locus of evaluative judgment" within him; he acts only according to the ready-made rules his culture provides him with, or after consultation with his elders who know those rules better than he, or by humble dependence on his human superiors or on the unseen spirits who exercise the highest power in the world. Because he himself has no sense of the possibility of autonomous judgment, he assumes as a fact of human nature that children cannot bear responsibility; because of his sense of the rightness of the dependence-dominance relationship, he feels as an axiom that the actions of his children should depend on his will. And so, with no sense of being harsh or aggressive, indeed, with no self-consciousness at all, but acting only in accordance with the way of the world, he vents his need dominance and need aggression on them, ensuring that as good children they shall be obedient and shall refrain from bothering him or competing with him.

In their father's sense that all this is right, the children, despite their pain, gain a sense that it is right. They come to feel moral rightness, as well as security and satisfaction, in yielding their wills to superiors. As they see in the rule of life by the spiritual powers an explanation of their anxieties, and in the need to placate those powers a justification for their pain, the moral rightness of their submissiveness is sealed and validated. Observation of authoritarian relationships in the community outside their homes provides further validation. Thus, because the enforced submission is right, it is not painful. Or, better, it is worth the pain. The child can afford to recognize the pain and rage in his unconscious processes, in a sense, and to live with them.

Without the father's sense of the rightness of domination and aggression, the son would not feel that it is right. The father's assumption that it is good and right depends on his sense of the rightness of his own need submission. In turn that sense depends in part on his sense of his inability to understand the world and in part on his perception that the social groups in the society who form his reference groups recognize the rightness of his place in the social hierarchy.

His economic role in the society is an important aspect of that place. The economic roles in a traditional society of craftsmen, shopkeepers, lesser landholders, and other groups of the lesser elite are not separable from their social roles, and the two in combination define their position in the social hierarchy. To every member of the society, the term "small landholder" or "craftsman-shopkeeper" means not merely someone who does a certain thing; it means someone who does a certain thing and has certain relationships to other groups. The individual's identity as, say, small landholder or petty manufacturer is fully satisfying to him only in relation to nobility or landed upper classes to whom he regards himself as inferior and who he knows look upon his function as an appropriate and good element of the social system.

Thus the sense of rightness of dominance-submission is intimately related to the value individuals place on the economic-social role they perform, their valuation of the roles of higher social groups, and their knowledge of respect for their roles by those groups.

THE IMPACT IN THE HOME OF WITHDRAWAL OF STATUS RESPECT

When a traditional and respected reference group indicates by its attitude that it does not have unqualified respect for the social role of the individual, when it ridicules some aspect of his role or forbids him to do some of the things that give him peace and security, some degree of anxiety pervades his psychic processes.

Attitudes such as the following may be conveyed in the home both verbally and by the tone of attitudes and actions:

In fifteenth to seventeenth century England, by a father, speaking of the Cavalier landed gentry: "The ladies with their immoral dresses and the men with their lace cuffs and long hair! There's no decency left in the land. They worship with Romish rituals that separate a man from his God. They have no respect for an honest yeoman any more. They are too powerful; a small man can't get anywhere on the land any more." And the mother: "Your father is a good farmer (or craftsman). There couldn't be better. But those city folk don't respect honest work."

In seventeenth or eighteenth century Japan, by a samurai: "Being a samurai is a noble position. But now they pay us too little to enable us to follow the customs which samurai should follow. Fighting for one's house was noble, but there's none of that any more. Our swords are sheathed. It is not our daimyo's fault; it's the way things are now, with the Tokugawa in power. Life is not good." Or by a wealthy peasant: "The daimyo's agent used to consult with my father about administering the district, but the samurai don't bother to help us country folk any more. They don't have any more contact with us than with ordinary peasants."

In eighteenth or nineteenth century Russia, by a member of the Old Believers: "The Patriarch and the Tsar and the officials under them command us to worship in ways and with symbols which do not convey the meaning of our holy faith. They ask us to assert the equal divinity with God of a son of man. Will I receive solace from my God if I approach Him with this blasphemy? They do this just for earthly advantage. How can they ask such a thing?"

In eighteenth or nineteenth century Antioquia: "Living on the land is good. It's a good life. But in Antioquia we can't compete with those snobs on the Sabana (or in the Valley). They've got rich flat land. Here the land is broken up by hills, and the soil's not as rich. That's why your father is a miner. He's of good Spanish blood. But those Bogotanos sneer at us just because they have more land and can afford to be lazy."

When such disparagement impinges on a man, his traditional occupation no longer yields the satisfaction it used to. This is true whether or not the withdrawal of status respect takes the form of direct disparagement of his economic role. Even if it does not, the disparagement demonstrates that that role is not sufficiently valued by the reference groups to validate other aspects of his traditional behavior. He may be as diligent a cultivator or petty manufacturer or shopkeeper as anyone could possibly expect, yet he is still disparaged. Diligence in his calling is no longer of as much use as it was in former times. Groups whose opinions he has learned to respect no longer respect his values (for if they did they would not act in ways that violate them) and no longer look on his role in life as entirely worthy.

For peace of mind he must feel that the position which defines his position in the social structure is worthy, and he must also defer to the attitudes of the reference groups. These two inner attitudes are now contradictory; he cannot do both.

He will call into question whether his reference groups deserve the respect he has paid them. He will criticize their actions, since these violate his values. And he will call into question whether his own old way of life is as good as it was, since it no longer serves the purpose of commanding social respect. But by his old values, his way of life *is* good, and by other of his values, the other social groups are worthy of respect.

These inner conflicts will cause him anxiety and frustration. And anxiety and frustration cause irritation and rage.[2] He cannot vent his rage

---

[2] This rage plus the reactions sketched just above in the text, and the rage of retreatist personality plus the attitudes toward society associated with it, are closely

freely on the individuals who are patronizing or disparaging him, both because they are too powerful and because of inhibitions within him; they are surrogates of his father or other seniors to whom he learned when a child to defer. At times, therefore, he will vent his frustration in other channels sanctioned by his culture. And in a peasant society, or virtually any society, the objects on which he is permitted to vent his irritation will include his children, provided that he keeps the manner of expression of his rage within acceptable bounds. More than before, he will be irritated at their play or their chatter and insist that they avoid being nuisances to him. Everyone is acquainted with the father in a Western society, coming home after a frustrating day at the shop or office, who, instead of enjoying or enduring his children's noisy play, startles and shocks them with his unwonted abruptness. What is contemplated here is the persistence of analogous action, in some degree, over a long period in traditional society. In a traditional society the father will also be more authoritarian toward his wife, and she will be even more heedful of his moods than before and will suppress the children more.

This change in home environment, I suggest, is a crucial effect of withdrawal of status respect. One may expect that children experiencing this changed childhood environment will come out of it with personalities different from those of their predecessors. Consider first the effect of the fact that the father's values have come into conflict with each other.

THE EROSION OF VALUES

With that marvelous capacity for generalization which has been noted, the son will make deductions from his father's behavior concerning the nature of the world in which the son and the father live. From his father's attitudes toward his work and the daily round of life and toward other persons and the symbols of his society the son will perceive in some unverbalized way that it is of great importance to his father to believe in the goodness of his occupation and class position and in the goodness of the attitudes of superior social groups. And he will perceive that his father's anxiety results from the fact that these things have become incompatible; he can no longer believe in both of them at the same time. Of course to a young child the meaning of occupation and class position will be a limited one, as will the significance to him of the attitudes of other social groups; but these aspects of his environment as he understands them are of great importance to him, and his emotional (affective) reaction to them may be expected to be strong.

The father is helpless. He values both things; he cannot change his values. But the son's values are not yet formed; and an important part of

related to the attitude termed *ressentiment* by Nietzsche and Scheler. See Max Scheler, *Ressentiment,* trans. William W. Holdheim (New York: Free Press of Glencoe, Inc., 1961).

his perception is that the situation causes his father to feel pain. Even while the son values his father's occupational position, he expects pain to result from it. And even while he must satisfy his need dependence by valuing highly the regard of groups in authority, he expects that they will not give that regard unqualifiedly and anticipates pain. As a result, he hates the members of the superior groups. He also probably envies them in a way in which his father did not. Previously persons of his class had no reason for envy except in the sense that everyone would like in fantasy to be a glorious prince or a fairy princess. One was satisfied with what one was in relation to what others were. But now that powerful others can cause one harm, one would like, in a new positive somewhat hostile sense, to be them, or at least equal to them, in order to be immune from their disparagement or to have such worth that they can no longer be critical.

He cannot solve the problem by simply ceasing to value one of the two conflicting elements highly, for the two cannot be separated. The goodness of the economic role depends partly on the regard for it by superior groups; hence he cannot obtain satisfaction in his role without obtaining the regard of those groups. And he cannot obtain the high regard of those groups by abandoning his traditional role, for his society and his own cognition of the nature of the world give him little chance of moving to another role. A small landholder has slight chance of becoming a member of the landed gentry, or a shopkeeper a member of the elite bureaucracy.[3] In any event, he is psychologically inhibited from abandoning either. In a static society, and because his high need dependence deprives him of bold imagination, he can discern no promising model of an identity in life except the one his father's role in life provides.[4] And, because of that same high need dependence, to avoid anxiety he must feel deference to the groups in positions of authority.

A possible solution lies in the nature of his need dependence. The structure of traditional society, as a child in such a society normally perceives it in his father's attitudes, includes a hierarchy of authority extending up to the spiritual powers. As has been noted, the concept of such a hierarchy normally gives the child a rationale for the pains he suffers

---

[3] If the derogation is of his religious faith, the society will permit him to change that; a Protestant Dissenter could become a member of the Church of England, and an Old Believer could adopt the prescribed ritual. But such a change involves abandoning dependence on powers whose regard is even more important to him than that of the social elite.

[4] Even in England, where class rigidity began to break down during the late Middle Ages, much sooner than on the continent, this statement applies with little qualification even up to the eighteenth century. The relaxation of class lines during the Elizabethan period was followed by greater rigidity later, partly because gentry whose families had risen through trade wanted to forget their past, partly because many of the middle-level landholders, the squires, had been squeezed out of existence, and for other reasons as well. These two historical changes are vivid examples of the resistances of traditional society to change in its structure. Concerning the Elizabethan period and the later reversion, see G. M. Trevelyan, *Illustrated English Social History* (New York: Longmans, Green, & Co., Inc., 1950), Vol. II, pp. 23 ff.

in an authoritarian childhood environment, and he finds it satisfying. However, now that he rages at the groups above him in that hierarchy, he may be able to defy those groups and still satisfy his need dependence by channeling it directly and exclusively into his relationship with God (or, in a more primitive culture, with the plural spiritual powers). If he does, he may also find sufficient comfort in the valuation placed by God on his socioeconomic role so that he does not need the good regard of the superior social groups.

However, such a shift in values would require an extremely high degree of creative imagination. For nothing in the model presented by his father and other adults suggests such a solution. What these models suggest are ambivalences, conflicting values existing side by side, important and irreconcilable. Hence it is extremely unlikely that he will arrive at this highly creative solution—the more unlikely because his environment does not tend to produce creative persons. The pain of this value conflict is far more likely to send him to another solution. This solution is to deny that either value is important. The more intensely the boy values his father's traditional social role, the more he will be pained. The more he cares about the opinion of the reference group, the more he will be pained. But if he can only deny that these things are important, deny that he has any high expectation for satisfaction or contentment in life, then he can avoid pain. Life does not offer the prospect of full happiness; it is best not to have too zestful anticipations. If one does not expect too much, one cannot be wounded by failure to achieve much. Hence the boy will repress his zeal for life; that way lies safety.

As he emerges from his home farther and farther into the larger community, in late childhood and after, he will find the wisdom of this choice confirmed. He will find that the facts of the outer world verify the reflection of it which he perceived earlier in his father's behavior, that the behavior pattern he learned earlier to meet the problems of conflicting values fits the larger scene, and that the best solution is not to expect too great satisfaction from his socioeconomic role and not to hope too highly for social acceptance.

The case we are considering is one in which an entire social group, rather than a single individual, is disparaged by the actions or attitudes of an upper class. In this case the same trend in personality will appear in a number of peers throughout the derogated group. Each boy will then find his attitude reinforced by the attitudes of his fellows. This is of some importance. If he is alone in his tendency not to struggle so hard to fulfill a position in society capably as the adults of the preceding generation did, the example of the greater striving and interest of the youths about him as he grows to adulthood will tend to temper his attitude in the direction of more vigor. But if other youths emerge with the same tendencies as his, a "youth culture" different from that of the older generation will probably appear, confirming the change in personality.

One need not expect a drastic change in values in one generation, but one may expect a cumulative change over a number of generations. In the first generation of withdrawal of status respect, the son perceived in his father a clear belief in the goodness of the traditional social position, and he perceived his father's pain and anxiety. *His* son will probably internalize the same social identity since he too has no alternative, but together with the expectation of pain he will see an aspect in his father's personality which was absent from his grandfather's, the suggestion that the road to safety lies in repressing one's values. It seems likely that this will be a convincing part of the model his father provides, and that the desire to avoid pain will propel him farther along that road than his father traveled. And *his* son still farther. Thus over several generations, if the external withdrawal of status respect continues, the safety of not hoping for satisfaction in any role is apt to become more and more appealing and apathy to increase.

THE REPRESSION OF NEEDS

A process of change in need structure may be expected to go on concomitantly with the change in values.

I have suggested above that the father will become more irritable, more demanding. In the case of comprehensive and severe disparagement, for example contempt by colonial rulers for virtually the entire culture of the society, the resulting shock of some individuals of the society at the humiliations and frustrations which overwhelm their lives may lead them to such intolerance of the little frictions of home life, such irritation at anything that further crosses or disturbs them, that the impressions they convey to their children of absolute inconsiderateness and complete authoritarianism swamp all other perceptions and dominate the atmosphere. If, however, as we are assuming, the disparagement is not so severe or comprehensive, then, while frequently the fathers will be more irritable and harsh than before, this effect will not dominate the atmosphere, and the children will be able to perceive other aspects of the situation.

They will perceive, as did their fathers, that their environment is unmanageable and threatening. Indeed, the perception will be heightened. However, the traditional dual solution to that perception, on the one hand the avoidance of anxiety by submission to authoritarian guidance, and on the other the release of the frustration and rage which authoritarian control creates in them by their own authoritarian behavior later, will not seem a fully adequate way of life. In the traditional case, undisturbed by withdrawal of status respect, the father's dominance over the children and his submission to the hierarchy of life provide a model for his sons which they look forward to following. But when the father is anxious and irritable, his behavior does not convey as a perception either that his authoritarian control is good and right or that his combined submissiveness and dominance are satisfying to him.

Because the authorities on whom the father must depend to escape anxiety now disparage him, the relationship no longer relieves his anxiety. In his behavior the children will perceive that fact. They therefore cannot look forward with unquestioning satisfaction to accepting authoritarian guidance as the good and right outcome of their present pain and anxiety. Neither can they feel that domination of someone else is a satisfying solution to the problem of rage, for it is not fully satisfying to their father. Even though he vents his frustration on his wife and children, he is still anxious and distressed. Dominating or aggressive behavior is never fully satisfying unless it is a meaningful response to a problem of life (as it was in the traditional situation). At times their father himself will probably recognize his new short-temperedness for what it is, a misdirected reaction to frustration and anger rather than an appropriate element in a good way of life. Certainly his children will do so. Perceiving this, they will perceive that rage is dangerous since it can find no satisfying outlet.

This does not mean that they will experience less rage than before. They will experience more, because their father's control of their initiative does not seem so fully justified to them as it did to their predecessors in the traditional situation. But they dare not release that rage by striking back, because their father is powerful, and they need him. Hence, since they also cannot anticipate fully satisfactory outlets for their rage in the future, it will seem especially dangerous to them.

It does not follow that the son will not internalize authoritarian behavior. The dominant behavior pattern he sees in his father is an authoritarian one. On the whole, his father still feels that the hierarchical structure of life, and the submission-domination relationships by which it functions, are good and right. Such satisfaction of his rage and frustration as he gets, he gets by venting rage through control of his children and other inferiors. His son will probably see no other solution to the problem of human relationships and will tend to behave likewise. But he will anticipate incomplete relief of anxiety and incomplete release of pain and rage in behaving thus. He will anticipate some danger as well as some satisfaction in this role.

As in the case of conflicting values, there is a possible solution. Since it is dangerous to feel rage, one will be safer if one buries it within one and does not respond to it. The son will not succeed in this very fully, for the models of authoritarian behavior around him will lead him in the contrary direction, but his sense of the unhappiness which results from rage will be sufficient so that his expression of his need domination and need aggression will be not quite free but a little suppressed and subdued.

Another force will put equally strong pressure on him to bury his rage and deny to himself that it exists. Any child finds that the manifestation of his rage at curtailment of his activities by his parents puts him in peril. For the shock and anger of his parents in return threatens him with complete loneliness and isolation. This is why every person buries his rage at his parents in his unconsciousness, and most persons later are shocked at the idea that a child might hate his parents; the idea is a dangerous one to admit. In the circumstances we are considering here the child's rage is greater than normal because of his perception that there is no justification for his father's irritable behavior. Hence the tendency is the greater for him to strike back, and it is necessary for him to put all the stronger constraints on his own action to prevent himself from doing so. So his behavior will be somewhat constricted, somewhat inhibited, in a way that his father's was not.

As he enters gradually into the outer world, he will find that the perceptions he received in the home fit. As in the home, the authoritarian nature of life will seem almost right but not quite. The groups he has learned to respect as reference groups, and to whom he must turn for guidance to satisfy his need dependence, in turn respect most of the aspects of his traditional role but not all. Hence the uneasiness he learned in the home, the desirability of not admitting his rage to himself and acting on it, is validated and strengthened.

As in the case of values, this glossing over, this encysting of authoritarian needs tends to cumulate, generation after generation. Like his own father, the son grown to be a father will no doubt expect his children to yield their initiative to him rather than to become responsible for themselves. That is, he will vent his need aggression and dominance within his home, and like his father he will do so all the more because of the gnawing effect of the denial of expected status. But his sons will note the constricted flavor of his behavior, his fear of his own actions. He is not more responsive to the needs of his children because of this diminished freedom to release his authoritarian needs. Rather, insofar as he is not authoritarian in overt behavior, he is somewhat withdrawn and inaccessible. He presents to his children, in some degree, a positive model of the safety of passivity as a solution of life's problems as well as a negative model of the danger of admitting the existence of rage within one.

His sons will therefore perceive more clearly than he did that the goodness of submission-domination is open to question and that rage is dangerous because there is no way to release it fully. Even more than he, therefore, they will tend to bury their rage within them. They will become more conflicted, more inhibited, more apathetic.

Without tracing these speculations further, I suggest that the initial change in personality creates a disequilibrium by which, over a few generations, an increasing trend toward denial of one's active needs, an increasing tendency to encyst them within one, is created. With respect to needs as well as values, the degree of retreatism rises.

THE WOMEN

In analyzing the effects of withdrawal of status respect I have discussed only the sons of each generation. The effect on personalities of the daughters differs from that on the sons. The passivity forced upon the son by his father's dominance is also forced upon the daughter, but for the daughter it is only an intensification of her normal social role, which is to be attractive and of service to men. The father's new moods increase the mother's need to serve and help him. The mother's behavior is therefore intensified, with new anxieties attached, but it is not as distorted as is her husband's, and the daughter continues to see a not unnurturant model. Moreover, the husband's domination over his wife, intensified by his tensions, may make the daughter see her mother as a suppressed fellow creature rather than merely as a superior. Any such inducement to wonder how another person is reacting increases one's awareness of how the world functions, and the experience is apt to lessen the girl's tendency toward constriction and apathy.

Hence women are not apt to become as retreatist as men, a fact that will be of importance in later analysis.

CONCLUDING COMMENTS

Energy and Rage in the Retreatist Person

This discussion of the way in which retreatism comes about illuminates the nature of retreatism. Needs and values are not nonexistent even in fully retreatist personality. But they are so conflicted, and, to solve the conflict, so buried, that the individual is immobilized. The need to repress conflict within one requires a continuing great expenditure of energy. Little energy is left for overt action. The retreatist individual is apathetic, not merely because he does not think it worthwhile or safe to exert energy toward any goal but also because he has little energy left over to exert.

The retreatist person is not free of rage. His rage is intense. But because he fears its violence, he denies that it exists and holds it within a constricting leash. In some circumstances it will break the bonds of its inhibitions and burst forth with shocking violence. One such case is individuals "running amok." Another is colonial uprisings. When the members of an indigenous society come to realize they can rise up, take their destinies in their own hands, and throw out the masters who have violated their culture, the violence of their reaction may be such that it startles people who have thought of them as apathetic creatures who ought to be grateful for the contacts with advanced customs that have been vouchsafed them.

Empirical Evidence Concerning Retreatism

The historical evidence that retreatism has followed extended periods of denial of expected status in the societies which are analyzed in this book is considerable. The Antioqueños are now vigorous, imaginative, and effective economic innovators throughout Colombia, but there is some evidence that in the eighteenth century they were regarded as shiftless and irresponsible.[5] American Negroes and Indians, who have experienced extreme denial of expected status, have passed through a period of retreatism from which Negroes are now emerging and Indians beginning to emerge. Descriptions of social conditions in Japan in the late seventeenth and eighteenth centuries suggest a withdrawal from contemporary Japanese culture by many samurai and then a rather frivolous life of abandon by many elite, both of which suggest retreatism.[6] It is also an interesting question whether the earlier acceptance of Christianity by a surprising number of Japanese (at the very end of the sixteenth century and the first decades of the Tokugawa era) is not a manifestation of the same personality traits.[7] English history provides some uncertain evidence of a parallel development in the towns and cities in the eighteenth century—witness, for example, the great increase in the consumption of gin. I shall not examine these historical facts at more length because at best they provide no direct evidence of the causal factors at work. They are worth noting, however, as evidence that the complex facts of history are, as a minimum, not inconsistent with the chain of causation described here.

Group Retreat into Fantasy

A variant development is the appearance in an isolated and beleaguered social group of behavior that somewhat resembles retreatism but is a different and perhaps more complex phenomenon.

Assume a relatively small social group, defeated and beaten down by more powerful invaders, unable to follow the life dictated by its former values simply because the conquerors have destroyed the material means for doing so, and isolated to considerable degree from the hostile outer world. The archetype is the American Indian tribe, their hunting grounds occupied, tribal power gone, living on a reservation as wards of the white conquerors. Tribal Indian values are preserved through mutual reinforcement in conversation, symbol, and fantasy among the adults of the closed

---

[5] See Emilio Robledo, *Bosquejo Biográfico del Señor Oidor Juan Antonio Mon y Velarde, Visitador de Antioquia, 1785–1788*, especially Vol. I (Bogotá: Publicaciones del Banco de la República, Archivo de la Economia Nacional, 1954), and James J. Parsons, *Antioqueño Colonization in Western Colombia* (Berkeley and Los Angeles: University of California Press, 1949).

[6] See George B. Sansom, *The Western World and Japan: A Study in the Interaction of European and Asiatic Cultures* (New York: Alfred A. Knopf, Inc., 1951), especially chaps. ix and x.

[7] See *ibid.*, chaps. vii and viii.

group. They may then continue to give enough satisfaction to be transmitted from generation to generation through the usual mechanism of identification. Of course the old values will be only partly satisfactory, and they will be introjected by the children with anxiety attached. But their vitality will be greater than if the closed group did not exist, and much greater than the conquerors realize.

To some extent, individuals in childhood will have contact also with the new models of the outer society. In adolescence they will then be faced with a cruel choice, to abandon their group and try to find an identity in the larger society or to retreat into their group. Insofar as they resolve the problem by the latter choice, the group will preserve its identity. Its members will be overtly apathetic, but their seeming apathy will be not quite the usual retreatism but retreatism blended with withdrawal from the larger society to continue living in fantasy a type of social life which is denied them in reality by the coercion of superior force.[8]

This phenomenon differs only in degree from that whose origin I have sought to explain above. Any retreatist, having withdrawn from reality, necessarily lives in fantasy. The added suggestion I am making here is that the fantasy may not be merely an individual world of the individual retreatist but a fairly well-organized inner life more or less common to the group, a preservation in fantasy of some aspects of an identity which was once real and satisfying.

This living of an older life in fantasy can hardly be true of apathetic American Negroes of recent generations; their earlier culture was too far removed to be preserved in major aspects even in fantasy. And of course even American Indians can preserve in fantasy only certain elements of their former culture. But in peasant society enough of the precolonial environment remains so that, partly in reality and partly in fantasy, peasants can live a fairly complete life which they do not reveal to the conquerors.

Retreatism in All of Us

Perhaps it is pertinent to note that some degree of retreatism appears in most of us, at least in the middle classes of modern Western society. Most of us continue in adulthood the search and struggle for an identity which we began as children, finding the situation in the larger society neither so hopeless that we become fully retreatist early nor so favorable that we gain the identity we seek. Still struggling for status through early adulthood and into middle age, we resign ourselves in middle age to the fact that life will not yield the complete identity we need, and then we retreat into passive and resigned old age. For some of us the disappointment is extreme and resignation to the facts of life bitter, and we spend

---

[8] This possibility was suggested to me by a study of two Dakota Sioux tribes now living on reservations under the control of the federal government. See Chapter 19.

the last decade or two of life as automatons. This occurs not as a necessary fact of life but only because status is not secure and traditional in our ever-changing society, and because the individual has learned goals which in middle age he is forced to recognize as impossible of attainment. In more favorable social conditions the individual might have been sufficiently successful to keep the retreatist component of his personality from ever becoming overt.

This is retreatism wearing a garb to which we do not usually give this name, but the garb, I think, fits.

Emergence of Technological Creativity

chapter 11

RETREATISM IS NOT A DEAD END. AS RETREATISM DEEPENS in successive generations, it creates circumstances of home life and social environment that are conducive to the development of innovational personality. The historical sequence seems to be: authoritarianism, withdrawal of status respect, retreatism, creativity. This seems to have been the sequence of events over a period of some generations in Japan, Colombia, England (where the retreatism was probably less intense), and Russia. Perhaps if the social history of other countries in which economic growth has emerged out of traditional society were studied intensively, the same sequence would be found there too. Sociological historical accounts sufficiently detailed to provide direct description of the causal sequence of events are not available, but from knowledge of the impact of home environment on personality a plausible explanation of the development may be constructed.

ALTERNATIVE DEVELOPMENTS WITHIN RETREATISM

The turnaround from increasing retreatism toward creativity presumably occurs because of progressive changes in the personality of the fathers and mothers of succeeding generations. As retreatism increases, the personality of the father may vary along two dimensions: his expectations concerning his position in the home, and his expectations concerning his son's behavior. Concerning the home, paternal attitudes may range from the one extreme of self-assured domination except in areas traditionally delegated to the wife to the other of abdication of authority and responsibility. Attitudes concerning the sons' behavior may range from simply expecting them to learn to follow directions to expecting untraditional achievement from them. The father's attitude in either area may become quite untraditional even while it remains highly traditional in the other: a stern father may expect high achievement of his sons, and a weak father may expect only that they learn to behave in the traditional manner. Consider the two types of variation in turn.

217

The first has been analyzed in the preceding chapter. The individual who, growing up under withdrawal of status respect, has lost the fully authoritarian view of the world may nevertheless be rather domineering, but with some tenseness, assertiveness, and irritation that were not present in the traditional situation. He vents in the home the rage resulting from his frustration at the community's refusal to grant him the regard he expects. He is assertive and domineering, or reacts with annoyance to being crossed. If the world refuses him adequate regard, at least he can control his wife or his children. By this anxiety, irritation, and lack of self-assurance, as has been noted, he conveys to the next generation more doubt than he himself internalized that the dependency-domination relationship is the natural way of the world.

A generation or two later, therefore, the father may be erratic: sometimes asserting his dominance, sometimes sympathetic, sometimes self-pitying, and at times withdrawing irresponsibly from the struggle and absenting himself from the home, drinking with his cronies or perhaps asserting his manhood and relieving his anxiety by mastering some woman other than his wife. Finally, the fully retreatist father may simply be weak. He has repressed his values, and attempts to meet few goals in life. He withdraws frequently from the home. When at home he may be pleasant company for his children, but he is ineffective. He is a Rip Van Winkle.

The sequence by which a change in expectation concerning the sons occurs is more complex. A prerequisite is the appearance in some generation of self-consciousness concerning one's unhappy lot. The adults who first experience withdrawal of status respect will hardly feel self-conscious, for, being fully authoritarian, they take relationships in the world as objective external facts and are probably not capable of the introspection required for self-pity. However, a son who observes his father's anxieties may carry into adulthood a self-conscious unhappiness concerning his lot in life, and, on becoming a father, he may convey to *his* son a sense that he regrets the son's lot as well as his own. If so, by this sequence of personality development a son of say the fourth generation may gain strongly a perception that is never conveyed strongly in the traditional situation, a perception that his father values him.

If a son does gain this perception, the authoritarian controls which bewilder him and cause him pain will not lead him to feel unmixed rage toward his father, for if his father values him, it will seem questionable to him that his father would cause the pain. But if his father is not responsible for the painful restraints and arbitrary commands which the son experiences, the son may feel that his own shortcomings must be. So he feels some mixture of shame (sense of inadequacy) and guilt (sense of wrongdoing) at not having somehow relieved his father's anxiety and thus enabled his father to love him more fully. He will not achieve in order to relieve this guilt, for his authoritarian childhood environment taught him to feel anxiety if he exercised initiative, but he will carry his sense of guilt and shame within him.

When he in turn has become a father, he will rationalize the guilt and shame by feeling that he is failing his son; and then, remembering that it was the son who failed the father, he will project his guilt onto his son and feel that his son is failing him. By this conclusion he satisfies and gives meaning to the need aggression and need dominance that his own childhood pain bred into him. He will not therefore free himself of a sense of guilt, but repeatedly he will somewhat relieve it temporarily— as by eating he temporarily relieves hunger.

At this point he has a golden opportunity. By insisting that as his son develops he shall meet successive standards of attainment so high that they will surely gain the social approval the father failed to gain, the father can simultaneously further assuage his guilt, further satisfy his need aggression and need dominance, and give meaning to the pain of his own life (which, caused by his own failure, was to teach him that his son must not fail). He finds reasons (which may be objectively valid) to excuse his own failure, but insists on the goal for his son's life that his son must attain social approval.

Whether such a father conveys to his son a perception of being loved depends on the balance of the father's personality. If the need aggression that resulted from his childhood pain dominates, then his harshness may give his son the perception of a father who, feeling that the son can achieve, must somehow value him, yet who is primarily tyrannical and self-centered, exercising a tyranny that threatens the son by posing near-impossible tasks. If the father's memory of his own father's concern for him dominates, he may be softer, yet demanding, and the son may acquire a perception that his father loves him and therefore that the demands must be right.

From the possible combinations of these dual elements in transitional personality—one of which ranges from stern to weak and the other from expecting traditional obedience to demanding high achievement—four cases may be selected for analysis:

1. The father who feels a sense of guilt and expects his son to achieve in his stead, but who is still close to authoritarianism. He demands achievement and dominates his son's life to this end, but he creates little perception of love or valuation of his son. Rather, his behavior, no longer traditional and assured, creates in his son's mind a perception of both the wrongness of this tyranny and the possibility of escaping it. Martin Luther's father, a transitional individual in the period when the religious-political system of the traditional past was disintegrating in Germany, was such a man.

2. The stern father, unsure of his own position in society and guilty in response to his own sense of failure, who imposes on his son the burden of achievement he was unable to carry, but who also manifests love for

his son. Woodrow Wilson's father, who lived as the traditional South disintegrated, was such a man.

3. The erratic father, who manifests little expectation that his son can achieve and who asserts his domination of the home when his irritations and frustrations goad him, but who is withdrawn or absent often enough so that his son regards his father's arbitrary control as a constant threat, but a threat often successfully evaded.

4. The weak father, who neither manifests such expectation that his son can achieve nor stands as a barrier to his son's childhood explorations.

The last two of the four situations are rather simple cases of retreatism. The first two are deviations from the pure retreatist trend. It seems almost inevitable that one or another of the four will appear in many families if denial of status respect persists for several generations. In all four situations the wife is probably somewhat warmer than the husband, and perhaps even somewhat nurturant, for, as has been noted, the father's behavior in the home under denial of status respect is apt to intensify his daughters' need to be attractive and to be of service to men. When these daughters have become mothers, their authoritarianism will be qualified by these changes in their personalities.

Each of these four situations tends to create one or another type of creative personality. The last two, the simpler cases of retreatism in the father, will be considered first.

CREATIVITY OUT OF RETREATISM

Because of her husband's erratic or weak behavior, the mother is less controlled by his expectations than was true in the traditional case and has somewhat more autonomy in her relations to her baby. If she felt rejected by an authoritarian father, and feels rejected again by a retreatist or erratic husband, she may hold her son compulsively to her as a substitute for the father to whom she could never get close, or for her husband, and may manifest such pain or alarm at her son's attempts at autonomy that he comes to fear autonomy and finds safety only in dependence (even while he feels rage at her). But if her own father was weak or erratic, as a child she may have felt humiliation at his weakness and may have tried in vain to give him the protection he needed and to help him to be strong. Again substituting her infant son for her father and husband, she may be trying once more to give him protection and to help him to be strong. Rather than cling to him she may give him nurturance but may require performance of him as his capacities develop. If she thus permits her son to develop initiative—to show promise of the achievement she sought in vain in her father—she will glow with love because of her own happiness, and that response will reward the child.

This sort of care is conducive to the sprouting early in life of high need autonomy and high need achievement. The sense of security and of being valued which will give a child boldness to explore the world are present, and so also are pressure to achieve and reward for doing so. During the first year or so of life the father may not interfere greatly, simply because in most traditional societies the baby is supposed to be the mother's concern. The important qualification exists in many cultures that the mother is to be available to serve the father when he desires it, but even this qualification will be softened in the homes we are considering by the fact that the father is weaker or less consistently demanding than the fully authoritarian father.

During the second and third years, as the boy moves about and ventures into new areas of behavior, the impact on him of his father's behavior is greater. If the father is domineering and demanding when he is at home, he may create various pressures on the boy—may insist that he act or not act, not according to the boy's urges and initiative but according to the father's conceptions of what a good boy should do and be. But if the mother is protective and stronger than the father, she will shield the child to some extent from these frustrating pressures; and in any event, if the father is somewhat apathetic or is erratic in his demands, her attitude rather than her husband's may have the determining effect on the child much of the time. Moreover, in many cultures even the authoritarian father is expected to be permissive during this period also, as the above accounts of childhood in Burma and Java indicate.

Thus the son may reach the period of the Oedipal crisis with a fairly good basis laid for creative personality. What happens during the period of the Oedipal crisis is of crucial importance.

The son has more access to his mother during this period than in the fully authoritarian home. If the father is fully retreatist, the son's victory is soon won. During periods of irritability and self-assertion the not quite fully retreatist father may demand priority over his son's needs for the mother's attention, and the mother may give her husband priority, for he needs mothering too. But except for these periods he yields to the insistence of his son. If the father is domineering and harsh in his suppression of rivalry when he is assertive, but is erratic, his periods of neglect or withdrawal create opportunities for the son. Thus the son can often gain access to his mother and get response from her by actions of various types, of varying cleverness and insistence, which he will not be slow to learn. She is still available to comfort and guide him, so far as a feminine model can, as he explores new areas of behavior.

However, victory in the attempt to gain access to his mother is never certain. At times the result of self-assertion will be the harsh or irritated interposition of a more powerful rival. Thus the son learns a constant anxiety about whether he can manage things, whether he can gain nurturance. But he has concomitantly learned that the best hope of gaining the satisfaction he seeks is by achieving, not by shrinking from the test. His anxiety forces him to test continually and forever whether he can manage affairs, whether the world will receive him. Always this compulsion is mixed with some degree of desire to retreat and not risk the attempt, but over the range of parental behavior that we are considering here the compulsion to achieve and the perception that one can achieve become dominant.

In the case of a harsh though erratic father these needs are mixed with rage which may give the son aggressive drive to surpass his father. If his father is weak, the son may come to feel instead a rather melancholy warmth and closeness to him, coupled always with an awareness of a lack of strength which ought to be made good. Especially, he may resent his father's inadequate care of his mother and may feel always a restless need to erase this unsatisfying model he carries in his mind by doing better himself. As a child he was never able to do well enough to keep his mother from discomfort and anxiety. The guilt that this inadequacy instills will never wholly leave him. It is perhaps the largest element in the insatiable need for success that such an individual manifests. All his life it draws forth his energy to fuel his drive for achievement.

Although the fully retreatist father may provide only slight interference to the mother's nurturance of her son, he likewise fails to provide one of the elements necessary for the formation of creative personality, an attractive model of at least a moderately resourceful and successful personality. The model perhaps need be successful within only a fairly narrow range of performance; the son, if his need autonomy and intelligence are high, may generalize fairly broadly from the limited example; but there must be some model.

In many instances the masculine qualities woven into the mother's personality may provide the model, for, if her father was weak, she may be strong and achieving in order to compensate. By good chance, some male relative may provide a model. In other cases it may not exist in the flesh, and the mother may provide it in her recollections of the achievements and personalities of father or grandfather or uncle in happier times. Conceivably, even the weak father may provide it in this way, though this is less likely, for to tell a story persuasively the individual must understand it. If the model is not provided in some way, the son's need achievement will not flourish, though if successful in his childish endeavors, he may be able to hold his identity in suspense in early childhood and to pick up adult models of successful management outside his home in late childhood and adolescence.

Provided that adequate models of successful achievement are somehow available, a rather weak father remembered with melancholy warmth is more consistent with high creativity than is the erratic father who is asserting and domineering at times. For the rage engendered in the latter case will provoke forbidden urges and fantasies, and the resulting necessity for the individual to seal over his unconscious processes will limit his creativity. As has been noted, he may nevertheless be an aggressive and effective innovator.

That such circumstances in the home are conducive to the emergence of innovational personality is indicated by sketches of typical successful American businessmen. Warner and Abegglen, in *Big Business Leaders in America*, quote the recollections of their childhood by typical individuals from among a number of men they studied who had achieved business success from humble starting points.

Said one:

My father used to like to drink, and spent little time at home. I can't remember my father ever doing anything for us. Yes, my mother had to work. She took in washing, and we were still delivering it until after we were married. Mother was always even-tempered, hard-working. She had a good home with what she had to do with. She was always serious but she was a good mother. . . . We were afraid of my father, and so was my mother. I never saw my father comb • his hair or tie his shoelace; my mother did it for him. Of course we didn't see my father much as he just wasn't around.[1]

Another:

[My father] was easygoing in one way. He had a wonderful sense of humor although he was very strict. A lot of German in him. My parents were divorced when I was about sixteen. I never did get along with him. He was too strict and stubborn. I just couldn't see eye to eye with him. I didn't have much to do with him when he was at home. I avoided him most of the time. My mother was a dynamic woman. Full of pep and never satisfied. She had plenty of drive. I always went to her for advice, and she wanted me to get ahead. She was always in favor of my doing whatever would help me to get ahead. I generally took advice from my mother.[2]

That the son was able to avoid his father as easily as this account indicates suggests a lack of dominance by the father which somewhat belies the son's characterization of him. Indeed, the father probably compensated by his verbal strictness for his lack of strictness in action. The nurturant nature of the mother in the son's early years is indicated by the son's readiness to turn to her for advice later.

A few of the authors' summary comments will indicate how closely the conclusions they drew parallel those sketched here. The unsatisfactory nature of the family's relationships with its society is indicated by the following:

Without exception, the mobile men in our study describe their [parental] families as not involved in community activities, and there appear to be but few instances where any substantial interaction took place with the wider circle of blood relations.

---

[1] W. Lloyd Warner and James C. Abegglen, *Big Business Leaders in America* (New York: Harper & Bros., 1955), p. 64.

[2] *Ibid.*, p. 77.

Within the home,

Generally the focus of energy on mobility derives from the mothers. At the same time, the TAT[3] indicates some negative feeling toward the mother as the figure who attempts to hold and control the son. The fathers seem in most cases to have been distant from the sons, and not at all supporting or reinforcing. The father is an unreliable figure. At the same time, there is this feeling of loss and deprivation, that the father is withholding something from the son that he might provide, and some of the process of mobility may be seen as an effort to gain this withheld support, and to prove oneself a worthy and able figure in the eyes of the father.

Certainly the nature of the mother is important, for apparently it is through her that these men learn to strive, to work hard today for rewards that may possibly be forthcoming at some future time, and deeply believe in this. Also, and unlike the typical history of social maladjustment, these men seem to have during their adolescent years positive experiences with male figures, and to have experiences that reinforce the training and life-view implanted by the mother.

Another element of central importance is the experience of some father-figure who gave them encouragement and aid, and thereby ameliorated their hostility toward males by fulfilling some of the functions they feel their fathers have neglected. These men seem most often to have been teachers.[4]

It is impossible to know how closely the circumstances in traditional society under withdrawal of status respect parallel those summarized by Warner and Abegglen, but that an increased level of creativity results from circumstances more or less like those sketched seems more plausible than any alternative explanation of its appearance.

For the reasons summarized at the beginning of this chapter, it is also highly plausible that circumstances of this general sort appear when withdrawal of status respect disrupts traditional society. These conditions will not necessarily appear in every family subjected to withdrawal of status respect for a number of generations. With respect to any single family chosen at random, one would be rash to predict that creative individuals would appear somewhere in the course of deepening retreatism or after full retreatism existed. But in any large number of families one would expect that favorable circumstances would appear in many. Withdrawal of status respect creates forces which, so to speak, move the personalities of a group inexorably down a slope of retreatism, but that movement itself creates counterforces which, gathering strength as the flow proceeds, may disturb, interrupt, and divert it, until finally a current of creativity emerges sufficient to turn the social flow in a new direction.

THE REFORMER: TWO VARIANTS

The influence of the stern and demanding but loving father and that of the harsh and demanding father who creates little perception of love

---

[3] Thematic apperception test, a test designed to reveal unconscious attitudes.
[4] These four quotations are respectively from *op. cit.*, pp. 78, 77–78, 78, and 79.

have one element in common: each may induce in a son a personality type that may cause him to be known as a reformer. But apart from the reforming zeal the sons of the two men will differ, and the nature of their reforming efforts will differ. The two cases must be considered separately.

The Stern, Demanding, Loving Father

The father's need to have the son achieve what the father could not achieve may be so compulsive that he insists on performance before the child is physiologically ready to perform. If he does, he will create in the son a perception that attempts to achieve bring failure, and a fear of trying. But he need have no such impact. Even though he is demanding, he may harbor the traditional notion that the proper time for training to begin is the age of five or six. Earlier in the child's life the traditional father, regarding the infant as having no potentialities within him, is apt to restrain him to keep him from harm and to direct that the mother shall do so. The father who regards his son as worthy and capable is apt to refrain from this extreme restraint, so that the child's early life is more conducive to happy and successful exploration of his environment than would otherwise be true.

When the father does assert his demands for achievement, the impact is quite different from that of authoritarianism. The authoritarian father insists mainly that his son be obedient; he thus indicates little expectation that his son can achieve or can bear responsibility. The loving father we are discussing now determines a field of achievement and sets hard standards in it. By doing so he indicates a deep conviction that his son can achieve, that the son is responsible for his own success in life. Even if the son feels rage at his father's arbitrary demands on him, he also gains a perception of warmth, or, if not of warmth, at least of being felt of high worth; for only from a worthy individual would so much be expected.

The father's requirements are hard to meet, and so the son will feel persistent anxiety. He will also feel rage at his father's arbitrariness. But he cannot turn his rage against his father or against authority in general. For the father's high valuation of him and his earlier nurturance suggest to the son that the father would not make impossible requests of him, and therefore that he, not his father, must be at fault if it requires extreme effort for him to achieve as expected. And yet perhaps he is not at fault either, for would his father have expected so much from him if he were not capable of achievement? But his anxiety forever drives him to seek some explanation. The only satisfactory explanation is that there is some flaw in the environment that prevents his complete success. In that conception he will find a satisfying explanation of the problem of his life; it will make life seem logically complete to him, just as the traditional child sees the explanation of his anxiety in the arbitrary actions of the unseen spiritual powers.

In remedying the flaw in the environment the son will temporarily satisfy his need achievement, need aggression, and anxiety. And so he will seek some flaw, and attack it; and if he has innate intelligence and energy, he will perhaps succeed in remedying it. But in spite of each success he will find that he still has the gnawing feeling of not having achieved enough for unqualified praise and complete security. Therefore in the successive circumstances of his life he will find other flaws to remedy—again and again, all his life.

The circumstances in his environment which he perceives as flaws and as dangers to him will be ones against which some talent he developed as a child is effective. It would be wrong to say that either the choice of talent to develop or the choice of flaw to attack was the cause of the other; the two choices were made concomitantly over a period of years, and each influenced the other. The most appropriate thing to say about the relationship of the two is that they fit. The talent will be one in whose development, as a child, he achieved repeated temporary release from anxiety because its development was valued by his father. It is not likely to be a talent which was central in his father's personality, for to develop that talent would be to rival his father too directly. In a number of cases which have been observed the capacity the individual found it exciting to develop as a child was one that was somewhat peripheral in his father's activities and one in which his father was not highly competent. Perhaps in this activity the son stood the best chance of doing enough, or well enough, to satisfy his father and gain release from anxiety. Perhaps in this activity also he could satisfy his rage at his father's harsh commands by rivaling his father while avoiding the danger of admitting to himself that this is what he was doing.

He will turn away from following in the central pathway of his father's career, not so much because of a fear that disaster will strike him if he dares to try to surpass this model as because guilt at his desire to challenge his father will inhibit him. Yet he will choose a career somewhat related to his father's talents.

As I have noted, each success he gains will prove inadequate. If his capacities are great, after each success in one arena he will strive to achieve in a broader one, always using the same range of talents, trying to reshape the same sorts of elements in the environment, satisfying the same inner needs. If his needs happen to be parallel to those of his fellows so that his activity vicariously satisfies theirs, and if the type of problem he attacks on a larger and larger scale happens to be one concerning which his society as a whole feels anxiety, he may be acclaimed by widening circles in his society, gain a national stage, and become an historic figure.

The set of circumstances that produces such a man will appear not only in a group that has been denied expected status in a traditional society. It will appear in other societies as well, and perhaps the most telling example for an American audience is Thomas Woodrow Wilson.[5] Wilson's father, a pastor and professor in a theological seminary, expressed great love for his son and high expectations and demands concerning his son's career. During Woodrow's childhood and adolescence his father set him exacting tasks and exacting standards of performance in writing and in speaking. He was cruelly sarcastic at failure in any detail. But there is no record of any expression of resentment by Woodrow. Rather, his father's love overwhelmed him and his guilt turned inward. He expressed his sense of his own inadequacy at the same time that he expressed a sense of having a mission in life.

He tried to follow in his father's footsteps but collapsed in the attempt. Accepting his father's religious creed of Presbyterianism, he enrolled in a Presbyterian seminary, but during the first year at the seminary he underwent an almost complete physical breakdown, said to be from overwork, and he withdrew at the end of the year. He had been a poor student. He then enrolled at Princeton. After graduation he enrolled in law school, where he again collapsed and withdrew. In both cases, I suggest, guilt was the basic cause. The reason for guilt at entering the seminary is obvious; he was daring to aim at directly rivaling his father. The more complex reasons for guilt at contemplating a career in the law are discussed below.

After a brief (and unsuccessful) practice of law he entered graduate study of government at Johns Hopkins, completed this study, and began the career of teaching which led to the presidency of Princeton and his public career.

His tensions and the guilt which drove him manifested themselves in repeated periods of melancholy and physical illness occasioned by overwork, not only those cited above but at least two others which forced interruptions of his teaching at Princeton. Until he was 40 he made no important decision without his father's approval.

However, perhaps he was unconsciously defying his father when, at the age of 25, he abandoned the given name with which he had been christened and adopted the use of his mother's family name, Woodrow. And in effect all his life he competed with his father, though unconsciously, in safe fields and in those in which his father had enjoined him to perfect himself. As a boy he had developed a taste for oratory and for

---

[5] The conception of the reformer as being a product of childhood environment was suggested by Erik H. Erikson in a graduate seminar and a faculty discussion group at the Massachusetts Institute of Technology in the academic year 1958–59. I derive it from those discussions. My summary of the life history of Wilson is taken from a report made by a member of the seminar, Robert Jones, rather than from my own research. Corroboration of the general thesis was found in a number of other biographies, for example, those of Bolivar, Nasser, Kierkegaard, Marie Curie, and Eleanor Roosevelt. However, the specific interpretation in the text is my own; while I am greatly indebted to Erikson and the discussions referred to, neither Professor Erikson nor any other member of the group is responsible for any specific element in it.

writing, in neither of which his father was talented. Woodrow used these twin talents to attack the flaws he perceived in his environment.

The flaw he found repeatedly as the explanation of his anxiety and pain was lack of order in the society around him. Throughout his life he strove by the use of his eloquence and skill in writing to remake the structure of successive worlds he lived in. By his eloquence and persuasiveness he gained eminence both in a series of clubs throughout his school career and then of course later in his public life. He became president of a childhood club and later of two societies in his school and university career. In each of the three he rewrote the constitution of the club and then persuaded the group to adopt his revision. Later his criticism of the administration of Princeton led to his selection as president, and he then reshaped much of the framework of the university's activity. As President of the United States he envisaged a constitution of the world, participated in writing it (perhaps if he became executive of that he would be secure?), resisted proposals in the United States Senate for amendment in any detail, and collapsed of a stroke when it became evident that his oratory would not be sufficient to persuade the American people to support it. I suggest that again and again and again he had to find and remedy a flaw in the environment which seemed to be the reason he could not meet the standard of perfection he had internalized from his father's demands; each time he temporarily, but only temporarily, assuaged his guilty sense that he had not worked enough or capably enough. He became an historical figure because his capabilities were great and because his personal problem, the reordering of political structure, was also a problem of his era.

Why did his inner tensions bar him from a career in law but not from a career in government? I suggest that the practice of law requires debating, which constituted too direct a challenge to rival authority; that it constitutes also *ex parte* pleading, which violated the moral precepts his father had sternly laid down; and that it requires submission to the rules of the imperfect existing legal order and thereby constituted a threat which Wilson could not tolerate. A career in government, on the other hand, did not imply rivalry of his father, permitted the furtherance of the highest moral precepts, provided a far less restricted field for the exercise of persuasion and eloquence in writing and in speech, and permitted direct attack on the broadest scale on whatever imperfections in the structure of society he might perceive.

The Demanding Tyrant

If the father who feels guilty at his lack of success and expects his son to achieve what he could not is more resentful, aggressive, and harsh, and conveys little perception that he loves or values his son, he will produce a different result. The son cannot solve his problem by use of the authoritarian solution of submitting passively to domination, for the father rejects mere submissiveness. The father demands that the son do what the father values highly: school studies, athletic activity, the ways of the country gentry, preparation for a legal or business career, or whatever it may be. If the father's demands for achievement do not begin too soon, and if meanwhile the boy's mother has been somewhat nurturant, the boy will have experienced ability to meet problems and satisfaction in doing so. Then, even while he feels intense anxiety at his father's demands, he will also feel some relief from anxiety in successes at tasks his father values. In a sense, he will perceive that he is valued.

However, he will perceive more deeply his father's lack of respect or regard for him. To his father he is primarily an instrument to fulfill his father's desires, and the son will perceive this. As a consequence, he will feel little guilt at his inability or refusal to meet his father's demands and will be free to direct outward his rage at their arbitrariness. Since the father's harsh exercise of authority is not self-assured and natural, the son, despite fear of challenging arbitrary authority and guilt at doing so, may perceive the possibility of challenging it successfully and the need to do so if he is ever to escape the anxiety which pervades his life. If his father's tyranny is the dominant feature of his childhood, and if it does not seem inevitable, challenging it may become the central need of his life. If childhood defiance in the small brought a reaction which led to pain and terror, but also to some exhilaration, at some later time he may decide to defy his father's wishes concerning the central course of his life. The fateful decision is most likely to be taken in late adolescence or early adulthood, when he can no longer postpone the question of what his identity shall be in the adult world he is entering.

When he has made the decision, he will still suffer anxiety, but in accordance with the human tendency to find current forces that explain one's anxiety he will interpret it as the result of arbitrary power which threatens him in the adult world. His sensitivity to the exercise of power may be so diffuse that he perceives a threat in almost any positive act by any other person that affects his own actions. He may see the danger of arbitrary and unjust authority everywhere and denounce it.

He will denounce it the more intensely because he is attracted to its exercise. For he saw his father's exercise of power as evil, but he also saw gaining superior power oneself as the safest way of challenging it, and he had fantasies of satisfying his rage once he himself had the whip hand. His sense of wanting something evil causes him to repress the desire the more insistently and to look everywhere outside himself for it so that he can assure himself that the desire is outside him, where he can attack it, not within him. But to attack it he needs power, which he can assure himself is for good ends. Any man fights most intensely what he fears and represses in himself. Then, having successfully attacked it outside him, he often feels safe, relaxes his self-repression, and indulges in it.

If such an individual's sense of the presence of dangerous power causes no sympathetic reverberation in his fellows—if they do not share his sense of danger—then he will be regarded as a crank and will be suppressed or merely tolerated. But if there is arbitrary power in his society which is perceived as a threat by his fellow men, so that what he says and does satisfies their inner needs as well, and if his ability and the intensity of his need are great, then he may become a leader in social revolution and, like the less extreme reformer sketched above, may become an historic figure.

Such an individual, who sees a threat in any power outside himself, will feel security only if he himself is exercising supreme power over others. Having overthrown tyranny, he is apt to become a tyrant himself.

The more firmly a harsh and repressive ruler is installed in power, the more violent the effort needed to overthrow him, the more likely that the revolution will not succeed until someone with a fanatical hatred of power appears to lead it—someone who had a personal problem of arbitrary power in extreme form in his own childhood and who in his extreme hatred of power manifests that he is repressing in himself an extreme desire for power. This is why, when a violent revolution is successful, the form of old relationships is so often restored, though with new names and new symbols and on behalf of new social groups; why a revolutionary in the name of democracy and liberty, when he has attained power, is apt to act as a tyrant in the name of democracy and liberty; why the Bolsheviks, having overthrown Tsarist authoritarianism, set up their own in the name of democracy; and why Fidel Castro, having overthrown the tyranny of Batista, finds it possible to save Cuba only by being Batista-like in his methods even though his goals are different.

The career of Martin Luther may be cited by way of illustration.[6] Martin's paternal grandfather was a peasant. The younger brother of Martin's father Hans having inherited the land, after the German custom, Hans left the land to earn a better living as a mine worker and then a mine manager. Hans was intensely determined that Martin should advance farther in life than he had done. He decreed that Martin should become a lawyer—whereafter he might even become burgomaster of a city. Hans was not only stern but also brutally harsh to his son. Martin seems to have become driven by tremendous inner rage at arbitrary power such as his father exercised, but nevertheless to have felt guilt at his inability and unwillingness to act and achieve so as to satisfy his father. An almost crippling dread of disobeying his father was combined in him with a great compulsion to escape from his father's authority or more generally any authority such as his father symbolized.

Martin attended college, received bachelor's and master's degrees,

---

[6] I am indebted to the rich analysis of the relationships between personality and social action in Luther's case by Erik H. Erikson in *Young Man Luther* (New York: W. W. Norton & Co., Inc., 1958), and to Erikson's discussion in the graduate seminar mentioned in the preceding note.

and at the age of 22, at his father's direction, entered law school. He obtained leave to go home soon after the term began. There he must have discussed with his father and mother some matters that troubled him deeply. In any event, as he was on the way back to school, a thunderstorm occurred. A bolt of lightning struck the ground near him and threw him into a state of terror. Before he knew what he was doing, he relates, he had called out to his father's patron saint (the patron saint of miners), "Help me, St. Anne. . . . I want to become a monk." Thereafter, after debating with friends whether he had uttered a binding pledge, he entered a monastery. Only when he was safely within the monastery did he write to inform his father of his act.

He abandoned pursuit of the career his father had ordained for him, but he mitigated the danger of defying authority by finding heavenly sanction for doing so and by seeking a career under the church—a greater power than his father. But this authority's power apparently also threatened him. A few years after his ordination, and almost unwittingly, as though to avoid admitting to himself what he was doing, he attacked not the church but its abuses, by posting theses about its abuses. In the fashion of the time, these constituted a challenge to others to debate with him. In the resulting debate his criticism steadily broadened to an attack on the church itself, the greatest power of his time and one which in his time acted arbitrarily and corruptly. He attacked it at successively higher levels, and then established a rival authority. But he preached the necessity of respect for authority, and he spoke and acted in authoritarian fashion. And when social unrest for which his preachings were partly responsible led to revolt by peasants against the secular authorities, he allied himself with the princes and sanctioned bloody suppression of the peasants.

Neither Wilson nor Luther played a historic role merely because of the personal problem he faced in childhood. Rather, the opportunity which each found to pursue the solution to his problem on a wider and wider stage occurred because his personal problem coincided with a major problem of his society. But, conversely, that latter fact alone did not determine that either Wilson or Luther would arise to act as he did. Neither would have done what he did if his personal childhood problem had not created a pattern of behavior in him which he was driven with tremendous compulsion to follow all his life and which happened to fit the social problem of his age. Study of the life histories of a dozen other social reformers (for good or evil) suggests that in any reformer's childhood there will be found a history of a relationship to the authorities of his life like that of either Wilson or Luther. The more harsh the father or father-surrogate of the reformer, the more authoritarian is apt to be his own exercise of power if he gains power.

Although both the reforming personality and social circumstances which cause a reform career of great historical significance may appear in any type of society, appearance of this type of personality seems especially likely under denial of expected status in traditional society, for the presence in a father of authoritarian personality modified in the way necessary to permit a son to see the possibility of solution of his problem by defying the authority seems especially likely in these circumstances. The family, community, and larger social environment at this stage of societal disruption are also conducive to the perception by a son that this solution is possible, for the hierarchy of social authority is being questioned all about him.

The reformer of either the Wilsonian or Lutherian type, like the innovator, may play an important role in social change. The reformer must change the institutions about him. The innovator feels no such compulsion, but he has burst loose from some of the values of his society and is free to pursue an unconventional occupation.

THE EMERGENCE OF VALUES CONDUCIVE TO ECONOMIC GROWTH

If the social change that occurs is to be a transition to economic growth, it is necessary that values conducive to technological innovation and other activities pertinent to economic growth should appear in personalities. They are less apt to appear in reformers than in other innovators, for reformers are concerned with moral questions and power rather than with efficiency. Institutional changes favorable to economic growth are apt to be made by innovators who are not reformers, though these men may influence reformers and work through them.

I have suggested how the personality of a member of a group from which respect for its status has been withdrawn may become creative. How does he simultaneously come to hold new and radical values?

Identification and the Search for a New Identity

In the normal course of events, we say, a son identifies with his father. This statement, however, is elliptical. The son internalizes an image of a satisfactory role in life if he can find one. In normal circumstances his father's role as the son understands it serves this purpose. In the circumstances of withdrawal of expected status, however, his father casts an image of satisfaction in his role in life as conflicting with satisfaction in the regard other members of the society have for him. This conflict is the source of his father's anxiety. The son has the problem of deciding what is good in life in the face of this conflict.

As has been suggested, individuals of the first generation—perhaps the first several generations—that face this problem can find no better solution to it than to repress the conflicting values. From one generation to the next they become increasingly retreatist. But when an individual with a higher degree of creativity, and specifically higher need achievement and need autonomy, emerges, his creativity is conducive to a more effective solution to the problem.

Even the most self-reliant son will internalize his father's values in some degree. His father is so important in his life that this is inevitable. But if the son is creative, he may hold in abeyance a commitment concerning some of his father's values, questioning them because they lead to an unsatisfying identity in his father, but not yet knowing quite what to do about them. Later he will be able to observe models of behavior beyond his father, and, observing that they are more satisfying, he may be able to interpret them as extensions of certain of his father's values. If so, he may find in them promising paths to an appropriate role in life, and not an abandonment but rather a fulfillment of his early purposes.

Early in life, if he has high need autonomy, he holds commitment in abeyance, not merely because of a general sense that he must look for more satisfying models but for a specific reason: the rage and disappointment which he feels at his father's behavior.

His mother's nurturance and the image of his father's motivations which he receives directly and which his mother also presents to him create guilt in him at his rage. He can relieve his guilt by directing his rage not at his father but only at some quality of his father which does not seem an essential part of his father. By presenting the perception that he himself is not at ease about some of his values, the father invites the son to find this solution. Similarly, a little later in life the son feels rage at the aggressor group, yet he cannot reject their values outright and completely since that would leave him with an incomplete frame of reference for an identity in his society. He can solve his problem if he can denounce and abandon certain elite values yet take hold of some aspect of life which will satisfy other of their values and offer greater promise than does his father's life of giving him satisfactory status.

Looking around his universe, he may be able to find some group or individuals who do not threaten him, who have power or status recognized and respected by the group which does disparage and threaten him, and whose role in life is not closed to him. If he sees the possibility of proving his worth (to himself and to his society) by adopting the values and some aspects of the way of life of that group, then he has a promising solution. If the new values can be interpreted as extensions of values which are a part of his father's personality and thus of his childhood model, so that by superimposition he partly replaces the old values without really losing them, then he has the best of the worlds which are possible in his circumstances: He can reject the low valuation of him by his father and the aggressor group, divert his rage toward imperfections in them which are a permissible target, gain a new promise of security, and yet in intent act in accordance with the more general values of his society after all.

Indeed, if he is clever enough he can serve yet another purpose. With part of himself he identifies both with his father and with the aggressor group and knows that they identify with him. They presumably scorn some of the values of the group he has now adopted as his model, for if some of its values were not contrary to theirs, selection of the group as a model would not have satisfied his rage. If now he can safely reject values which his father and the society accuse him of not measuring up to, and adopt others which they scorn, he will have his revenge on them; for he will thus destroy his identity and, in his view of the world, by his identification with them destroy their identity also. This is the phenomenon, writ large, of the child who, angry at his mother for scolding him, injures himself to make her feel sorry. But he can safely do all this only if in the same operation he can also find some new values, extensions of old ones, which will promise him recognition and preserve his identity. Otherwise, in his view, he will truly destroy himself.

I trust it is clear that new values are not adopted by a process of rational choice either by children or adults. Rather, the process is a largely unconscious one of responding to needs and finding the mental model which will justify holding the values that promise to satisfy the needs. The environmental pressures which initiate the process of the adoption of new values are not those of the larger society but the complex of pressures which impinge immediately on the individual in childhood. I suggest, for example, that no individual in any underdeveloped country decides on a business career merely because of a mental judgment, after he has learned of Western technology, that such a career would be profitable and would yield economic power. (He may think that he decided on such a basis, but I would not take the individual's testimony as good evidence in the matter.) Rather, he turned in this direction only if the activity itself (not its results) gives him a sense of power and of a satisfying identity. This it will do only because of images he has in mind of the worthiness of the type of people who pursue such activity.

The Selection of Technology: Religious Ethic

There is nothing in the process of search for new values to suggest that groups who are under pressure of withdrawal of status respect will everywhere turn to prowess in technology to prove their worth. They will do so only if, among the models of activity they see in the world around them, this type of activity provides a more satisfying sense of identity, a better prospect of attaining regard and respect by the reference groups whose opinion one values, than any other. Throughout history groups whose status is no longer respected have chosen various new roles, usually roles which they thought would lead to social power. Once a model of technological progress and of the power it yields existed, it was inevitable that this course to proving one's worth would be sought by many groups denied status respect.

In Japan, to various unhappy groups in the population the occupations in which the warriors of the Western world found the sources of their military strength met the requirements perfectly. They promised status greater than that of the Tokugawa; they were an extension of the traditional military values of the samurai; and they defied the Tokugawa aggressors. In Colombia the technological prowess of groups in foreign countries served the purpose well. It was an extension of the manual-technical occupations of the Antioqueños; engaging in it flaunted the values of the other Colombians; and it promised economic status greater than that of the other Colombians. Indeed, it is obvious that groups in traditional societies who are at the present time rebelling against the lack of respect of elites for their purposes are apt to turn to the way of life in which foreigners (of West or East) have found prestige.

It is less obvious where the Protestant Dissenters and lowland Scots found a model which led them to technological prowess; the model was not so obviously at hand. The reasons why technological prowess was attractive are discussed in Chapter 13. Let it merely be noted here that these groups had earlier reinterpreted their religious beliefs so those beliefs first provided an acceptable channel for need dependence, and that when the devotion of energies to technological progress proved attractive it was possible to extend the religious reinterpretation to sanction the activity.

This dual result of a reinterpretation of religion occurred also in Russia. Although the Old Believers were formally the upholders of the old faith rather than sponsors of a new one, the schism undoubtedly led them to a closer personal responsibility to God than they had previously felt. The religious decree which brought the breach with the higher church authorities in the seventeenth century may reasonably be regarded as initiating the entire subsequent sequence of personality change.

Even if prior religious change has not occurred, the individual who has found a new identity will probably project it onto his religion and interpret his religion so as to provide sanction for his new purpose in life.

In Japan the change in interpretation of the role of the emperor, though not religious in form in the usual sense of the term, may reasonably be regarded as a reinterpretation of a religious ethic. In Colombia there has been neither any break with the established religious tradition nor any manifest reinterpretation of the meaning of religion, but inner reinterpretation may have occurred. Observers have noted that many Antioqueños seem to feel a special sense of their obligation in life.

Eating One's Cake and Having It

Following their success in economic prowess, unless the old social order has been largely disrupted, the innovators are apt to turn to acquiring traditional symbols of status which their economic affluence makes possible. For they have not rejected the general status values of their society. They have only temporarily abandoned the old values as not open to them. The economic innovators of Colombia make no attempt to conceal their nostalgia for the land and their desire to "keep one foot on it" when economic success in industry has made this possible. Satisfaction at landed status and titles of honor and nobility in England was felt by business leaders of the Industrial Revolution and their descendants as well as by the old aristocracy and gentry. In Japan the old feudal economic system broke down with revolutionary speed. By the time the economic innovators had succeeded, no place in that system could be sought because the system no longer existed. But their satisfaction at a place in a social hierarchy modeled after the old one in most essentials, though without the economic-military trappings, is obvious.

In these ways, then, creative and reformist personalities may emerge out of retreatism. In cultural circumstances in which creative individuals see technological prowess as a promising path to satisfaction of their needs, the values of the new generation will tend to turn in this direction. Innovations in production will then appear, innovational individuals will guide institutional reforms in favorable directions, and economic growth will gain momentum.

Further Observations on Technological Innovation

chapter 12

THE PRECEDING DISCUSSION HAS LAID STRONG EMPHASIS on change in personality. Other conditions have been assumed constant; change in personality, or, more strictly, a change in social structure leading to change in personality, has been treated as the prime mover in social change. This seems justified because of the great empirical importance of change in personality.

Nevertheless, factors which operate at a time when personality change occurs greatly influence the actions which the creative individuals who have emerged choose to take and find it possible to take. This book will not discuss these effects of other factors at length. In this chapter, however, brief comments will be drawn together in order to prevent loss of perspective concerning the interrelationships.

INFLUENCE OF THE STATE OF KNOWLEDGE AND OF ECONOMIC CONDITIONS[1]

The State of Knowledge

Given the individual's personality, his conscious choice of career and also his unconscious attraction toward one or another career because it suits his needs and values depend on a number of external factors, among them the state of scientific and technical knowledge. Whether or not a given set of changes in personalities in a society will lead to economic growth may depend on the state of knowledge at the time. It also influences somewhat the perceptions of the world which the child will gain and thus the formation of his personality.

The state of scientific and technical knowledge has been a very important determinant of whether economic growth has occurred in past periods. I have suggested in Chapter 2 that the scientific advances of the seventeenth century provided a new framework of theory that permitted a qualitatively different approach to the physical universe. The social rebels of the eighteenth and nineteenth centuries had a tool at

---

[1] In technical terms, I am here considering these factors as parameters rather than as variables.

hand not available to the rebels who left the manors in the twelfth and thirteenth centuries. However, since any society today has a great flow of scientific and technical knowledge available from other societies if it chooses to receive it, one may justifiably regard differences in the availability of knowledge as not a cause of differences in economic performance today, and turn one's attention to other factors.

Markets and the Supply of Capital

A summary discussion here will indicate the relationship to other factors of the two most important economic aspects, the size of markets and the volume of the flow of saving available for investment.

The more favorable these economic circumstances are, the more readily change in personality may bring about continuing technological progress. Too small a market is a barrier, though when the market has reached even a regional scale embracing a very few million persons of low incomes, market considerations may no longer be a limiting factor of great importance.

Opportunity is multiplied if the market, however large or small it is, is expanding since its expansion makes it possible for a lesser degree of innovational skill than otherwise to be successful. Many an enterprise entered into on an overly optimistic estimate of the market which a new product would capture or the cost reduction which a new method would contribute has been saved by an expansion of the total market for the product. An expanding market is important also because the expanding market provides greater profits, and thereby, if innovation is under way, more earnings to plow back into the innovational process.

In Japan the growth of cities and of interregional trade, mainly an unintended result of the political policy of Sankin-Kotai,[2] provided an expanding market that greatly increased the prospect of material gain from economic ventures. That expansion certainly facilitated growth, though it is difficult to measure its relative contribution.

Nevertheless, the independent influence of market size or market growth may not be great. Where innovational effort is present, size of the market is not apt to be a serious barrier, for an expanding market is created almost automatically if any considerable measure of innovational activity is present or if a vigorous national effort to induce new output to meet some national purpose is going forward. Japan's experience illustrates the point. The expansion process may run into the difficulty that an increase in output is apt to require an increase in the import of some types of equipment, raw materials, and other goods; and if the country cannot curtail other imports without crippling its economy, a shortage of foreign exchange may frustrate the effort to expand production. This problem will be the more serious, the more specialized the country's production and resources. But with this qualification, an expanding market not only can be created by the country

[2] See Chapter 14.

itself but will be created automatically if any considerable measure of innovational effort is exerted.

The volume of saving by consumers, business enterprises, and the government also influences the prospects for economic growth. Technological improvements usually (though not invariably) require the use of additional equipment for production. The greater the flow of saving that becomes available to men who are interested in obtaining and using such equipment, the greater the possibility of technological progress. A country's saving may be augmented by external aid, but the bulk of the saving flow must come from within the country, and the size of the domestic saving flow is an important factor. Though many successful innovators start from very small beginnings, expanding by plowing back their profits, yet in every country which has so far entered upon industrialization there had previously developed a class of large traders who had accumulated a considerable amount of liquid capital—stocks of goods in excess of those needed for the country's current consumption, plus in some cases bullion or monetary deposits abroad usable for the purchase of imports. The large traders themselves in some countries were not the industrial innovators, but they provided "fat" which could be purchased or borrowed by the persons who were. In England relatively few of the innovators seem themselves to have been large overseas traders who turned to industrial ventures. Colombia illustrates the other extreme. The few very successful importers to the country's three major inland cities at the turn of the twentieth century made great profits. The plowing of these profits into industry—as transportation improved and trading profit margins shrank—marked the beginning of accelerated technological advance, and in many cases the merchants themselves became the industrialists. Japan provides an intermediate case. Traders were important supporters of the new activity, but often the entrepreneurs were lower-level samurai or wealthy peasants rather than the traders themselves. But in both England and Japan the capital provided by the traders was of great importance after innovation was under way.

Change in Economic Conditions as the Force Initiating Growth

Although the size of markets and of the flow of saving available influence the pace of growth when innovators arise, change in these economic variables does not seem important as a force causing economic growth to begin. In a traditional society in which nothing else has yet occurred to change traditional personality and culture, an increase in the size of the market or in the flow of saving available is not apt to have a great effect in inducing continuing change in technology.[3]

---

[3] The economic models in which these variables seem important as initiating factors are ones in which, implicitly, creative personality and values conducive to effort in technology already exist, for the models assume absence of any problem of motivation or values. But if they did exist, the economic variables would probably not be of primary importance as bottlenecks; endogenous change in them would probably be going on.

Market expansion as a force initiating growth is a symptom of change more often than an initiating force. Expansion of the market probably has little effect in a sluggish society. In colonial societies the market expansion that followed Western intrusion did not result in continuing economic growth. Though the Industrial Revolution in England is often cited as the classic instance of the importance of market expansion in economic growth, an expanding market did not provide the initial incentive for improvement in the British textile industry—or at least there is no simple one-way causation. British textiles became able to undersell those of competitor producers after the first technological advances—notably Kay's flying shuttle—had markedly reduced costs of production. Once this first step had been taken, Britain's merchant fleet and her control of the seas opened a world market that would otherwise have been much smaller. The size and expansion of that market obviously greatly increased the profitability of further advances in textile manufacture and thereby the flow of funds available for still further expansion. It would be rash to assert that technological advance was thereby greatly stimulated, for the vigor of entrepreneurial activity in Britain during the relevant half-century was great, and obviously would have been great regardless of expansion in the textile industry. The market influence certainly was favorable, but one can hardly say more.

Similarly, there is reason to doubt that an increased supply of funds available for investment will stir a traditional society to economic progress. The funds are apt to be siphoned off into the pockets of the traditional elite if social and psychological changes conducive to economic growth have not already occurred.

If economic conditions change for the better at the same time that personality becomes more favorable, obviously the impetus for growth is increased. And it is possible to conceive of a state of personality in which, given other conditions, some economic improvement of external origin is just sufficient to bring continuing technological progress and should be termed the initiating force. But because change in personality seems empirically more important as the dominant factor initiating change, it is convenient to treat the economic situation, as we have treated the state of technological and scientific knowledge, as a given condition ("parameter" is the technical term) rather than as a variable, and to treat forces that bring about changes in personality as the factors that disrupt the stability of traditional society and initiate change.

THE PRINCIPLE OF RELATIVE SOCIAL BLOCKAGE

The General Principle

The fact that the availability of scientific and technical knowledge, the size of the market, and the size of the flow of saving at a time when creative personalities appear influence whether the creative energies will turn to technological innovation illustrates a general principle. Other influences being equal, creative energies within a group from which social recognition has been withdrawn will seek expression where the opportunity seems best to exercise one's talents, prove one's worth to oneself, and gain social recognition. To state the principle from the obverse viewpoint, the channel in which creative energies will flow depends in part on the degree to which other possible channels are blocked.

This principle should not be taken to imply that only the alternative availability of various channels influences the decision. Other influences are also present. The relative attractiveness of alternative careers to a certain group of individuals, as well as their relative availability, will influence choice of career. Not all individuals or groups find the same activities most attractive. Under the pressures of one social situation, need aggression will be high in a disparaged group; under the pressures of another, need affiliation and a tendency toward mutual support; under others, tendencies to deal with social frictions in various alternative ways; and so on. Because of these variations in need structure, the relative attractiveness of alternative careers to a group in one historical situation will differ from that to a group in another society and another period of history, and these differences will influence the individual's choice of a career. But in addition the relative availability of alternative careers will also vary and will influence one's choice of career. This is the point being made here.

It should not be assumed that the creative individual necessarily makes a conscious judgment that he can accomplish his purposes in life better in one area of endeavor than in another and chooses accordingly. More often the conscious thought process involved is simply that for undefined reasons the individual finds one type of activity more interesting than other types. The decision is an unconscious one, perhaps made in a series of steps fairly early in life. As a child the individual chose activities that satisfied his needs and his values, and in the course of formation of his personality his early choices of activities led him by a steady stream of consequences into his life career. Passing over discussion of the mechanisms of his choice here, since they have been discussed in previous chapters, we may say elliptically that the field in which he uses his energies is determined in part by the relative social blockage in the various possible fields.

It is frequently stated that social mobility is essential to or at least important for economic progress. That is, if individuals wish to ascend from one social level to another, the possibility of doing so is conducive to economic progress. Put in this unqualified way, the statement is false. It is not the mere possibility of social ascent but specifically the social recognition accorded to economic prowess that is favorable to economic progress.

If traditional sanctioned channels of gaining or maintaining status are open in a traditional society, then the opportunity for attaining status by means of these sanctioned channels will direct energies into them. For example, if young members of the elite can gain social acceptance by prowess in chivalry, humanistic-literary learning, or the inheritance of land, and if these activities satisfy their needs, they will tend to choose careers involving these activities. If the occupations of yeoman, craftsman, and merchant, and the ways of life of the individuals who follow them, are respected, then these occupations will yield satisfaction and there will be little stimulus for sons of families in them to seek new ways of life.

In a society in which the use of force to attain or retain social power is sanctioned, as was true in the Middle Ages in western Europe, in Japan until the twentieth century, and in many traditional societies today, it seems probable that a group that has been derogated by another group within the society will hold to the traditional values of the society and attempt to regain its lost status by force if force offers even moderate possibility of success.

However, if traditionally honored roles are not open to an individual, or if prowess in them does not win him recognition because his other characteristics bar him from being honored, and if armed rebellion is impossible because of the preponderance of strength of the new dominant group, then if migration is not a feasible solution the pressure of unsatisfiable values and frustrations may be expected over a number of generations to inculcate new values. If armed rebellion comes to be outside the social pale, the pressure of social sanctions against it becomes one of the forces making other channels of status attainment seem more available. In short, a requisite for economic growth in a traditional society is not merely that upward social mobility by new means is possible but also that upward social mobility by traditional channels is not possible.

The Case of Immigrant Groups

Conversely, in the United States at present some groups are led to the use of socially proscribed means of attaining social status because the widest conventional channel, economic prowess, is closed or at least difficult of access for them. This is most conspicuously true of immigrant groups.

Immigrants settling in a society in which they do not have prestige and power almost inevitably find themselves regarded by that society as queer, the usual group judgment concerning persons adhering to alien values and institutions. Hence they are not apt to be accepted into the usual channels of social ascent of the society. In the United States during the period of mass immigration, immigrants were accepted as hewers of wood and drawers of water, but they were not thought suitable for advancement within the business system. The Slav, the Greek, the Irishman, the Italian, the Negro, and other groups have in turn suffered this discrimination.

The immigrant is merely bewildered, but his son, born within a new society and subjected to humiliations during his formative years, rages at the established groups of that society. At the same time, he rejects his parents' values, because the peasant or menial-class qualities which were virtues in the old society—honesty, diligence, piety, respect for authority—gain him no acceptance in the new. Even though some of these qualities are also valued by the members of the new society, they are not valued sufficiently to offset the amusement, condescension, or contempt at his differentness.

While the boy's father is primarily bewildered, his mother, whose life is less affected by the outer world, may be nurturant, and so her son may acquire need autonomy and need achievement along with his need aggression. If his need aggression dominates his behavior, he becomes a common criminal. But if his determination to gain the status symbols of the new society is greater, he may satisfy his need aggression and at the same time follow the only channel open to him which may promise economic power and thus perhaps status by becoming a racketeer. Or organizing a corrupt political machine may give him both social power and money. His fellow immigrant sons who lack his need autonomy and need achievement but not his need aggression or his scorn for the moral values of the new society will not condemn him for his violation of the common moral values but will rather exult at his successful defiance of their disparagers.

These considerations explain both the powerful political machines based on the support of second- and third-generation immigrants which have sprung up repeatedly in our major cities and the success of such labor leaders as Hoffa and predecessors like him. The leaders of such movements are innovators, and often very effective ones. In other social circumstances they might have chosen technological innovation as a career, but in the circumstances in which they grew up such a career was barred to them and, moreover, did not provide sufficient satisfaction of their need aggression.[4]

When in a further generation or two the immigrants and the descendants of laborers are accepted, gain access to advanced education, and find social barriers lessened, they become respectable (that is, conventional) in their methods and are replaced as the users of unsanctioned methods by a newer group. American Negroes will have access to political processes and political influence before social discrimination against them lessens greatly. It is likely that the next generation of the Negro population in many areas of the United States, losing its apathy, will go through this phase of attainment of social goals by unsanctioned means, and at one stage will support unscrupulous leaders.

---

[4] See Robert K. Merton's discussion of political machines, not as part of his discussion of adaptive modes but within his discussion of manifest and latent functions, in *Social Theory and Social Structure* (rev. ed.; Glencoe, Ill.: Free Press of Glencoe, Inc., 1957), pp. 71–82.

Illustrations from China, Japan, and England

The histories of China and Japan respectively during the past several centuries illustrate negatively and positively the relationship of social institutions to the mechanism of relative social blockage.

In China high social prestige was associated with status as landed gentry. Trading was in low esteem, but members of a landed family under economic pressure sometimes left the land and turned to trading in order to improve the family's fortune. They were not thereby locked into trade. Land was alienable, and through its purchase landed gentry status could be attained or re-attained. Hence persons who made money in trade moved back to the land. This mobility probably deterred economic development by channeling energies back to "landedness." Further, the channel of local warlordism was often open and often siphoned off energies which, given other social circumstances, might have gone into technological innovation. The availability of these channels to achievement and status greatly lessened the relative attractiveness of remaining in trading or turning to technological advance in other fields.

In the frequently chaotic conditions of the eighteenth and nineteenth centuries, the position in the society of the simple folk had lost much of its ancient meaning; many of the simple folk became pawns in the struggle of local warlords for power and in the attempts of the landed to increase their security. It is plausible to assume that over a number of generations many of them became retreatist and then creative. The situation also provided the possibility of some social ascent; an individual with enough energy and creativity might become a petty and then a larger trader and wealthy enough to attain land. However, the opportunities were not great and the resulting social acceptance limited, and at the same time that the withholding of status respect from nonelite individuals caused some of them to be creative, it must have caused many of the same individuals to become disgusted with the entire social system. Since warlordism destroyed the security of elite life and the recognition accorded it, the same must have happened to some members of the elite. In spite of the possibilities for elites pushed from their traditional landed status to regain it, the pressures for drastic social change gradually accumulated. These pressures, plus the availability of advanced techniques and a model of revolutionary social structure made to order to satisfy the rage of the simple folk at the old elites, caused a social revolution and an acceleration of technological progress in the mid-twentieth century. Rapid technological progress must have been delayed from the nineteenth century to the twentieth by the existence of channels through which a resourceful person might become landed or might gain military power. These possibilities deterred discontented members of the elite from using their energies more constructively.

In addition, the social forces of the eighteenth and nineteenth centuries in China were probably not as conducive to the appearance of creativity as were those in Japan. In Japan, where a strictly feudal class structure existed and mobility between classes was not possible, the merchant class could not escape from its role. The peasant held land in feudal tenure, not in fee simple. Until the Meiji restoration there was no legal way in which merchants could buy any other social role. Even though during the preceding century some had become *de facto* landowners through mortgage arrangements, this did not elevate their social status. Locked into their economic role as traders, they continued to devote their energies to the expansion of trade and to related economic activities.[5] This devotion of energies was a significant force toward development even though in the final stage of the transition other groups assumed the more active roles.

England provides the other and more frequently cited illustration of the importance of social institutions. Much has been written about the importance for economic progress of the institutions of private property, contract, various freedoms of the individual, individual equality under law, and so on, and specifically of their importance in England. The stress is justified, but perhaps no one will still claim that these institutions are *the* causes of economic growth in England. Rather, they are factors which helped to determine into which channels deviant energies would flow. Not only did they prevent interference by the state or by leading social groups with technological innovation, once the motivation for it appeared; more than this, they affected the psychological milieu of deviant social groups in a way conducive to the development of innovational personality in them.

THE PRINCIPLE OF PROTECTION BY THE GROUP

Variant and deviant individuals appear not only in disparaged social groups. They may appear in families of secure status because of circumstances in the home that affect some one child idiosyncratically. Some such individuals may reject traditional values and be motivated to turn their energies into channels repugnant to their fellows. Yet the transition of traditional societies to continuing technological progress seems nowhere to have been led by individuals scattered here and there throughout the society.[6] It seems everywhere to have been initiated, or at least to have become conspicuous, only when innovational activity by many members of some distinctive and disparaged social group occurred. Why have not scattered deviant individuals been the innovators?

[5] See Marion J. Levy, "Contrasting Factors in the Modernization of China and Japan," Kuznets, Moore, and Spengler (eds.), *Economic Growth: Brazil, India, Japan* (Durham, N.C.: Duke University Press, 1955).

[6] This generalization is advanced tentatively. Intensive research in many societies would have to be conducted before one could state certainly that there are no exceptions whatever to the rule stated. One can state with certainty that, at most, contradictions to the rule are few.

Perhaps one simple part of the answer is that, although the action of scattered individuals might eventually have brought about the transition by gradually accelerating change in some societies, in almost any society withdrawal of social recognition has occurred to some elite group from time to time; and, when other circumstances were favorable for the transition, many individuals from such a group were motivated to take hold and bring it about sooner than gradual acceleration would have done.

There is force to this consideration. But probably there is also a more positive reason why scattered individuals have not brought the transition about in the absence of a burst of activity by a group. It lies in the fact that the forces making for conformity in a traditional society are powerful enough to overwhelm isolated individuals.

Since deviance or variance in any social group provokes disapproval, the individual deviant is apt to be treated in a special way in any society. If he is deviant only with respect to his needs, he is simply regarded as having an odd personality; every traditional or primitive society has a place for him—special religious office, institutionalized homosexuality, or as holy man or village fool. He is tolerated, put in his niche; he threatens no one. Poets are honored in any society provided that they sing praises of the values the society holds dear.

But the individual who is deviant with respect to his values is a different case.[7] He threatens the social group by implying a low valuation on things which the group holds high and a high valuation on things which the group holds in low or negative regard. As I have suggested in discussing traditional society, he threatens the identity of the elite. He is therefore ostracized. The pressure of social disapproval on him is apt to inhibit his deviance and to force him into conformist behavior, or, if his inner conflicts are too strong, into one of the roles prescribed for deviants, or in the extreme case into insanity.

The isolated individual under social pressure may indeed be sustained by his image of reference groups who approve his deviant values and behavior. His reference groups may be groups not present in his society, or indeed not alive anywhere else in the world. The closet philosopher may be sustained by a vision of future acclaim such as he himself gives to Plato or Aristotle or Spinoza, the poet by his vision of the approval of all the world's dreamers, the scientist by a dream of being accepted into an immortal band of thinkers. But such reference groups are sufficient only for the most highly motivated of individuals; they will neither make such individuals influential in their society nor provide sufficient support for overt action.

If, however, an entire group of individuals in his society has been un-

---

[7] Of course the distinction between deviance with respect to needs and with respect to values is an arbitrary one. Any deviance presumably involves both. But the distinction made here, though oversimplified, seems valid.

der the same pressures he has been under, the individual will find his values and behavior mirrored in the values and behavior of many individuals around him. In them he will find both confirmation that his view of life is appropriate and good and sanction for new overt behavior. Although he is deviant from the viewpoint of the larger society, he is not deviant in the eyes of his group. He is therefore more apt to innovate effectively. Existence of a deviant group whose members reassure and protect each other in their new personalities greatly increases the prospect of effective innovation in technology or human relations.

There probably has been some innovation by scattered elite deviants. Paradoxically, a deviant is the more apt to be an innovator, the more impregnable the social position of his family; for if he inherits social acceptance that cannot be questioned in spite of odd behavior, he is the freer to follow his deviant bent. Such social acceptance is accorded to the individual who inherits the family title and family estate no matter if his ideas and behavior are odd. A landed deviant is fairly free to act as he chooses. This, rather than the supposed economic necessity for innovation in agriculture before it can occur elsewhere, may be why early scattered innovational activities often are in agriculture.

When a larger flow of innovational activity in trade and industry by members of a disparaged group occurs, it increases the prospect of parallel activity by scattered individuals within the accepted elite groups. For the new wealth gained by the derogated group threatens to rob the established groups of their erstwhile monopoly of some of the symbols of their position. The established groups then feel some of the anxieties of the group from whom social acceptance had been withdrawn. The sense of identity of most members of the top elites will still keep them from engaging in the new activities, but deviant individuals will find themselves freer to follow the model set by the disparaged group, gradually it will come to seem less deviant, and innovation will spread throughout the society.

ALIENS AND ECONOMIC GROWTH

I have referred to withdrawal of social recognition from previously accepted groups as the force leading to personality change and gradually to innovation. It is pertinent to direct attention briefly to the reasons why members of alien groups, who clearly are disparaged but have never been accepted, have not often been leaders in technological innovation. Two reasons suggest themselves.

Inhibitions on an Alien Group

The economic activity of such groups is typically in finance and trade. This may be in part because such activities are repugnant to indigenous individuals and therefore available for the aliens. In part, however, it is because alien groups feel safer in these activities. An alien group always perceives hostility and fears attack. Since industrial activity requires the investment of resources in fixed property, which is conspicuous, easily taxable, and easily confiscated, an alien group is apt to center its activities in finance and trading precisely because in these activities its wealth is in forms that can most easily be concealed. One cause of the lack of innovational leadership in technology by the members of alien groups is undoubtedly their fear of venturing outside this limited area of activity. On the other hand, in societies in which the trading-finance group has been an indigenous one, for example, Japan and Colombia, it has provided many of the leaders in the transition.

Lack of Acceptance of Alien Leadership

A second cause is that even insofar as an alien group does provide leadership in technological innovation in other fields, its lead tends not to be followed by other groups in the society.

A major social change such as the transition from traditional economic behavior to widespread technological progress will not occur simply through the actions of one group that has been affected by withdrawal of status respect. If the society as a whole is to grow, the new behavior of the deviant group must be imitated widely by individuals of other social groups, though it probably will never be imitated by all individuals. As has been suggested above, such imitation will tend to occur because of loss of their relative superior position by the erstwhile leading elites. I suggest, however, that a further condition conducive to such imitation, and virtually necessary for it, is that the initial innovating group shall be one that is not too alien to the society. In Russia the Old Believers were schismatics, but they were Russians. In England the Protestant Dissenters and Scots, though they were troublesome deviants, had roots deep in the culture. In Colombia the Antioqueños were Colombians, as proud of their Spanish ancestry as the elites of other regions. In Japan the innovators of change were integrally Japanese.

If, on the other hand, the innovators are an alien minority group, distaste for many aspects of their behavior is apt to be such that, if through innovation they threaten to gain too great relative power, the defensive reaction will be not to imitate them but to expel or suppress them. Indeed, even apart from the question of power, the fact that an alien group holds technological activity in high value is apt of itself to cause indigenous groups to reject it in defense of their own identity. Like indigenous individuals in a colonial society, they cannot accept the values of the alien group without accepting that group's valuation of them as being unworthy.

All this is not an absolute rule but a matter of degree, since alienness is a matter of degree. But such a reaction is probably an important element in the failure of indigenous groups in Asia and Africa to imitate the economically more effective behavior of immigrant Chinese or Indians; of Latin Americans to imitate immigrants from the Middle East; of medieval Europeans to imitate Jews. The hostility, bitterness, and superiority with which countries of medieval Europe (and modern Germany, not to mention other countries today) regarded Jews, and with which Latin Americans, Africans, and Asians regard the "Turkos," "Syrians," Chinese, and Indians is well known. "Grubby," "pushing," "crafty," "greedy," "vulgar"—the bitterness with which such epithets are applied is the greater because of the superior economic prowess of the groups to whom they are applied.

Any innovating group arouses the same sort of reaction in some degree, for in innovating they are acting in an alien way. The attitude of Bogotanos and Caleños to Antioqueños, and of the landed gentry of England toward the Protestant Dissenters, are cases in point. If it is objected that these attitudes existed before the groups in question became technological innovators, the answer is: Of course; it existed because they were different; and they would not have become technological innovators if they had not been different.

However, if the innovators possess deep and acknowledged roots in the society, then the feeling of repugnance is relatively less and the feeling that their road to improved economic status should be followed, to overcome the inferiority which their success has imposed on other groups of the society, is the greater. The prospect is far greater than if they were alien culturally that a number of individuals throughout the society will feel the pressure of unwonted inferiority or of loss of wonted economic superiority and will follow their lead.[8]

The discussion of the preceding sections may be summarized briefly. The state of scientific and technical knowledge, the size of the market, and the size of the flow of saving may materially affect what individuals who emerge with creative personalities choose to do and are able to do; but change in these three factors is much less apt to be of importance in disrupting the stability of traditional society and initiating a sequence of change leading to economic growth. The degree to which alternative channels are available as means to gain recognition of one's worth is also important in determining the areas in which creative individuals will be able to use their energies and will choose to do so. A number of creative individuals will be much more apt than otherwise to innovate effectively if they are members of a deviant group which protects them from the censure of the larger society. An alien group is not likely to lead the way to economic growth both because its members will be inhibited from investment in capital instruments of types that can easily be preyed upon and because their alienness will inhibit the rest of the society from follow-

---

[8] See Chapter 9, n. 7.

ing their lead. For these reasons, basic social change, especially a transition to economic growth, is apt to involve withdrawal of social recognition from a group well imbedded in the society. The reactions of members of such a group to the disparagement are apt to cause personality changes conducive to innovation, and their reaction as a group plus their place within the society protect them from the inhibiting factors summarized above.

DYNAMIC PROCESSES

In the discussion of the preceding chapters the reader may have noted absence of discussion of a number of influences widely recognized as forces for economic and political modernization. The union of disparate regions into nationhood; urbanization; improvements in transportation and communication; nationalism; the influence of an expanding economic sector on others; the introduction of money, or of marketing, into a self-sufficient subsistence sector; the appearance of religious dogma favorable to modernization—where do all these and other often discussed forces fit into the schema of analysis presented here?

The answer is that all of these developments seem to be primarily of importance as incidents in the process of change once some other factor has caused change to begin but not as initial causal factors in change.

This does not make them less important. It is of no less importance to analyze the course of change than to analyze how it began. These forces are causal in the sense that each event in a sequence, caused by the event before it, in turn causes the next. This section considers each of the events mentioned from this viewpoint.

Increase in the Scale of the Society

One of these events is increase in what is called the "scale of the society," a term which I shall use here in the simple sense of the number of persons who act as members of a common society. Apart from immigration, a community may expand in numbers either by natural increase of population or by an expansion of its boundaries. The latter phenomenon is considered here, especially the phenomenon of change in the attitudes and relationships of a group so that they think of a nation, rather than merely their villages or group of villages, as the community of which they are a part. The boundary between one society and another cannot be delimited precisely. Whether one regards an individual outside one's own immediate group as a fellow or an alien is always a matter of degree. But there is a clear contrast between the attitude of the villager in seventeenth century England or eighteenth century Burma who thought of persons from 50 miles away as aliens, and felt free to stone or rob them, and the attitude of the modern individual who thinks of his basic social allegiance as to his nation. The most important single change in the scale of a society is the appearance of a sense of nationhood replacing purely local loyalties.[9]

An increase in the scale of society tremendously facilitates economic growth. The scale of a society directly influences the advantageousness of some types of technology. Certain methods of production will not be economic unless the market for the product concerned is of a certain minimum size. The scale of the society influences the rate of growth of knowledge. An increase in the scale of society from the local community to a larger area also implies a growth of law and order, increased freedom of travel, increased communication among a larger group, and an ability to engage with trust in economic transactions with persons at a distance who previously were aliens, if not enemies, and considered untrustworthy.

The most important effect of the scale of society is probably its impact on these and other aspects of one's cognition of the world. Technological progress will almost necessarily be by "translocal" individuals, individuals whose background includes acquaintance with more than one community. If the world of an individual includes only a single village or town, the range of facts he has observed is probably so limited that he will hardly have that understanding of the diversity of causes and effects in the world which is a prerequisite to innovation.

Economic growth often occurs first in one region of a country and only later spreads to the entire nation—as is happening in Brazil and in considerable degree happened in Colombia. Hence a full-fledged sense of

---

[9] In an interesting little book, *The Analysis of Social Change* (Cambridge, Eng.: The University Press, 1945), Godfrey and Monica Wilson have suggested that the scale of a society can be measured by the intensity or volume of relations within a group (delimited presumably by geographic boundaries) compared with those between the group and persons outside it. The book is based on observations in central Africa. Chapter 2 relates to "Scale." "By the scale of a society," the authors suggest, "we mean the number of people in relation and the intensity of those relations. . . . In comparing the scale of societies, therefore, we compare the relative size of groups with relations of similar intensity" (p. 25). To measure the intensity of relations, they suggest seven indexes, which they summarize as follows: "the proportion of (1) economic cooperation, of (2) communication of ideas and of (3) feelings within and without the group; together with the relative inclusiveness of (4) value, of (5) dogma, and of (6) symbolism within and without the group, and (7) the degree of social pressure exerted within and without the group." (*Ibid.*, p. 29. I have inserted the numbers.)

Thus one might construct an index ranging from zero to 100 of the proportion of one's economic transactions within a group rather than with persons outside, the proportion of one's communications that are within the group, the fraction of the persons in the group who, averaging the results for various values, share one's values, and so on. If, taking an average of the seven indexes, in one circumstance the composite index was say 85 for a group consisting of the members of one's village, and less for any larger group, whereas in another circumstance the scale expanded to include the entire nation before the composite index fell to 85, then the scale of society has expanded from village to nation. Or perhaps one will find that beyond some group the index drops off rather sharply, and would consider the boundary beyond which it falls sharply as the boundary of one's society, even though for the nation it was never quite as large as it had originally been for the village.

nationhood is not a necessary condition. But economic growth is hardly possible until there has been some expansion of the sense of social unity beyond the local community.

Yet expansion of the scale of society can hardly be taken as a starting point in the analysis of social change except with a frank admission that one is breaking into the middle of a dynamic process without attempting to probe its origin. For such expansion does not occur either by accident or by some inevitable force which can be attributed to nature or to "the nature of things." Something causes it.

The Influence of Urbanization and the Appearance of Mass Media

An increase in the scale of society results partly from an increase in the ability of the individual to put himself in another's place, to experience (or feel) empathy; and an increase in empathy perhaps results from the growth of cities and increased communication and travel. Hence it is tempting to suggest that urbanization and increased use of modern communications media (radio and newspaper) are the prime initiating factors. Daniel Lerner makes this suggestion in *The Passing of Traditional Society*.[10]

Urbanization must have had important effects in western Europe, most conspicuously when the reconquest of the Mediterranean from the Saracens during the eleventh century led to a great increase in trade and the growth of cities in western Europe in the twelfth. It is easy to exaggerate the importance of this "reopening of trade" (a term that is itself an exaggeration) on the historical trends in western Europe. Pirenne, for example, seems to have done so.[11] I have noted in Chapter 2 that technological progress on the manors and the slow growth of cities were going on during the sixth to tenth centuries and that at most the freeing of the Mediterranean for trade accelerated a process already under way. But the earlier growth of cities no doubt was of considerable importance in the earlier process of social change.

In the present context, an important question is: Should urbanization and increase in the availability of communications media be considered as the forces initiating change, or are they incidents in the process of change which follow from other identifiable initial disequilibrating events? Undoubtedly, in a number of cases urbanization and improvement in communication, or unique historical events immediately underlying them, may appropriately be the starting point of analysis. The reopening of the Mediterranean, the construction of a road or railroad, or the establishment of a postal or radio system by a colonial power may be events behind which the complexities of history forbid one to go, and which therefore may be taken as exogenous events for whatever impor-

[10] Glencoe, Ill.: Free Press of Glencoe, Inc., 1958, chap. ii.

[11] Henri Pirenne, *Economic and Social History of Medieval Europe*, trans. from the French (New York: Harcourt, Brace & World, Inc., no date).

tance one sees fit to attach to them. And, although we have little evidence except *post hoc propter hoc* that such changes lead to widening of the scale of society, it is plausible to assume that they do.

But there is an interesting aspect in Professor Lerner's data—which he notes, though only briefly—which suggests that in the general historical case increase in empathy should not be regarded as the result of an initial improvement in communications or an initial increase in urbanization, but rather as one *cause* of these developments. For Professor Lerner's data indicate that whereas cities, use of modern communications media, and literacy ordinarily exist only where empathy exists, empathy exists where none of these three do.

Lerner's volume is based on a number of years of research, including field research in six Middle Eastern countries and interviews with approximately 1,600 individuals in those countries. The interviews included nine questions designed to test the individual's ability to project himself into the position of another and express a judgment concerning what he would do or feel if he were the other person. For example, two of the questions are: "If you were made editor of a newspaper, what kind of a paper would you run?" and "Suppose that you were made head of the government, what are some of the things you would do?" As I have suggested in Chapter 5 in discussing world cognition, many peasants are simply unable to answer some such questions.

Professor Lerner presents a cross-classification of the individuals interviewed, according to whether they scored high or low in empathy, participated much or little in the use of modern communications media (movies, radio, newspapers), lived in a city or elsewhere, and were or were not literate. A schema derived by Lerner from the tabulation is presented below. A plus sign indicates a high degree of the characteristic indicated, a minus sign a low degree. The classification into modern, transitional, and traditional is on the basis of the empathy score.[12]

Type	Literacy	Urbanism	Media Participation	Empathy
Modern	+	+	+	+
Transitional A	−	+	+	+
B	−	−	+	+
C	−	−	−	+
Traditional	−	−	−	−

This illustrative table of course does not reflect every case. For example, there were several cases in which an individual was urban, or was urban and media-participant, but was not yet highly empathic. (These may have been the post-World War II refugees from the countryside who in virtually every low-income country have fled to the cities but are not participants in urban life.) But these are outweighed by those who were

---

[12] The table is presented in Lerner, *The Passing of Traditional Society*, p. 71.

empathic although not urban, media-participant, or literate, so that the characteristics of each group are clearly on balance as indicated in the table.[13]

Thus the table is consistent with the thesis that media participation causes urbanization, and that the two cause increase in literacy. However, usually one is not urban and media-participating unless one is empathic, but a number of individuals are empathic who are neither urban or media-participating.

The implication is clear. Typically, first one becomes empathic through some not yet explained influence. Then one becomes urban and comes to use modern communications media, and then becomes literate. In the process one loses localism and becomes part of national society. As Lerner suggests, there is mutual interaction among these changes. An increase in any of the four variables, urbanism, contact with wider information through modern communications media, literacy, and empathy, probably tends to increase the others; but these data suggest that increase in empathy, rather than urbanization and the increased use of modern communications media, should be regarded as the causal or initiating factor in the sequence. Alternatively, one may suggest that urbanism increases through some extraneous development, and that the presence or absence of empathy in rural individuals determines which ones choose to move to the city. This is Lerner's suggestion. But may not empathy appropriately be regarded as also the cause of growth in cities?

Empathy is a personality trait. An important element in it is need autonomy, for the process of acquiring the perception that one may safely and appropriately think and feel and act alone involves also acquiring the perception that others may do so, and in ways different from oneself. Thus empathy is probably a fairly good index of creativity. This creativity may cause persons to embark on new activities which lead to the growth of cities.

I suggest, therefore, that change in personality is typically the first step in the sequence leading to urbanization, increased media participation, increased literacy, and further change in personality, and that the urbanization and communication aspects of the sequence are steps in the process of change but not its point of departure.

This, I suspect, is sometimes true even where urbanization and improvements in transportation and communication occur because of action by an outside force, for example a colonial power. The tendency to moderni-

---

[13] There were more persons who were classed as urban but low in media-participation than the opposite, suggesting that the plus and minus signs in the third row of these columns should be reversed and the columns interchanged. See *ibid.*, Appendix C, Table 3, p. 442. However, the class "Urban" included all persons in towns above 2,000 in size. A division line at a larger minimum size would be more meaningful, and would presumably show fewer urban persons low in media-participation (and empathy). Hence it is reasonable to arrange the illustrative table as shown. In any event, this reversal of columns does not affect the point being discussed here.

zation caused by such changes may be very slow except in the presence of other factors tending to alter personality. When change in a society largely from internal forces is in point, it is probably true that the changes in communication and so on do not occur until after changes in personality have occurred.

The difference in viewpoint is of importance. To the extent that the appearance of mass communications media is the initiator of change, it is logical to conclude that its artificial introduction as a policy measure will bring about the desired end of modernization. To the extent, however, that in the natural history of change other forces are the more important causal factors, then the introduction of mass media may not, in the absence of more basic changes, have the desired effect. No one would argue that the introduction of mass media has no causal influence, but I suggest that the causal influence sometimes assigned to it is spurious.

Nasser's use of mass communications media is a case in point. Undoubtedly the mere availability of a method of receiving emotion-arousing messages has an impact on social action in Egypt as elsewhere. Yet I suspect that Nasser's influence depends relatively little on the existence of mass media and very much on the social situation which causes the fellahin to rise from their apathy and respond to the symbols he raises. If that social situation did not exist, would the fellahin respond to the news of speeches transmitted by means of the mass media? Or would they ignore them and go about their traditional round of life?

Nationalism

More or less parallel comments are in point concerning nationalism. Nationalism is a set of attitudes, a view of the world; that is, a complex of elements in personality. Nationalism is important in almost any modernization movement, and xenophobic nationalism in many. It is indeed a cause of modernization in the sense in which any event in a sequence causes the next. But one must ask concerning it: What caused it to appear? To regard it as a cause in some other sense involves believing either that a national leader can turn it on or off at will or at least can channel it in one direction or another if only he chooses to do so.

It is not infrequently stated or implied that a national leader can do one or both of these things. This is an engaging set of ideas, appealing to many students of history and politics. For each of us, not knowing the forces in his personality which influence his decisions, thinks of himself as having free will to decide as he chooses and attributes the same free will to national leaders. And likewise, not knowing the forces which cause public emotions, attitudes, and opinions, we tend to assume that the public (of some community other than our own social group, and especially of a peasant society) is a blank slate on which a leader may write whatever he wishes.

And it must be agreed that a leader with charisma has some personal freedom to determine the nation's policies. He gained charismatic hold over the public because of his association with an event or events to which strong emotions attached. Being sanctioned as the agent of satisfaction of a deep-felt public need—the attainment of independence, the overthrow of a tyrannical or corrupt ruling class, perhaps only the assuaging of deep anxieties felt about unknown forces—he is free to make his own choices in matters concerning which the public feels no great emotional involvement, and, at least temporarily, even in matters in which its emotional involvement is countered by its emotional attachment to him. The policies of Tunisia concerning the Algerian question during the period of strife between the Algerian nationalists and France were probably influenced considerably by the personality and choices of Bourguiba.

But the leader's freedom to act is far more restricted than the rather romantic notions of leadership stated above would suggest. This is true both because he is not able to sway the public in matters concerning which it has a deep emotional commitment and because his own personality, which caused or permitted him to become the national leader, by the same token determines the choices he will make. He is no more free than is his public.

The first point is attested to by the fact that history is strewn with the figures of moderate ex-leaders replaced by more extreme ones whose stance or vigor satisfied public emotions better. Naguib's replacement by Nasser and Kerensky's by Lenin and Stalin are cases in point. In each of these the idea that the small group of revolutionaries who made the decision had free will to choose among alternative leaders, and that their personalities, which determined the choice, were not closely interlocked with the national character of their times, is a too shallow reading of history. The idea that the peasantry or the public in general of a traditional society is a blank slate or that it is an inert mass which a leader may mold at will originates in misunderstanding or lack of information. I suggest that as our understanding of personality formation increases, we shall steadily replace these notions of the sway of leadership with an understanding of the forces which do shape public attitudes and the determinism with which they operate.

But perhaps more important in limiting the scope of a leader's choices with respect to such a matter as nationalism is his own personality. It has been suggested that if in the American presidential elections of 1952 and 1956 Eisenhower had said precisely the things Stevenson said, and vice versa, Eisenhower would have been elected by the same voters who in fact elected him, because what they voted for was not policies but the father image cast by Eisenhower, which promised them that they need no longer worry about the vague dangers which made them anxious. But if Eisenhower had in fact believed and stated the more nervous intellectual conceptions of Stevenson instead of his own platitudes, would he have been the person who cast the reassuring father image?

Nasser, because of his association with the overthrow of a corrupt and

hated regime, has great charisma for the Egyptian people. It has been suggested that if he should only choose to extend the hand of friendship to
Israel and lead the energies of Egypt more wholly toward economic
modernization, the Middle Eastern problem would be solved. But I suggest that the reading of Nasser's autobiography with a clinical psychologist's eye will indicate a pattern of response to a fear of vague threatening
forces which, however his specific policies may vary under varying external pressures, makes it impossible for him to take a basic international
position greatly different from the one he has taken.

It is often stated in American historical writings that if only Woodrow
Wilson had accepted Lodge's reservations to the charter of the League of
Nations, the United States would have become a member, and world history might have been significantly changed. But I suggest that the need
for perfect order inculcated in Wilson by his childhood relationship to his
father made it impossible for him to accept such reservations; he had no
free will in the matter.

These more or less random examples might be multiplied. In general,
I suggest that no national leader can create or dispel so emotion-charged
an attitude as nationalism. And although, if he were free to do so, he
might at least in the short run divert nationalism in one direction or another, I suggest also that he himself is a product of the environment
which produced the nationalism and so is not a free agent.

These judgments do not justify the conclusion that foreign nations
should do nothing to influence the course taken by a nationalistic leader.
His choices among alternatives are influenced by the nature of alternatives. My judgments do suggest, however, that it is easy to fail to understand the bases for his choices. And, more directly in point here, these
judgments suggest that both the appearance of nationalism and its influence in channeling a nation's energies into or away from economic
growth are phenomena whose prior causes we shall do well to study.

Religion

More attention needs to be paid to the appearance of changed religious
dogma in the society or in some social group within it. Religious systems are in general a projection of the need structure of the members of
the society, but there is no reason to deny them a reciprocal influence
of their own. The case studies of Part IV illustrate the point that presence
of one or another religious dogma is in no sense a necessary accompaniment of economic growth, to say nothing of being a cause. The presence
of Protestant dissent in England is matched by the presence of pious
Catholicism in Antioquia and of little fervor associated with any religious
dogma in Japan. And in Burma the presumed passivity and renunciation
of the world of Buddhism is hardly a barrier to economic prowess, since
it did not prevent sanguinary and aggressive wars among ethnic groups.
In previous chapters I have suggested that when elite groups in tradi-

tional society no longer provide a satisfactory object to which to attach one's need dependence, there emerges a reinterpretation of religion by which one visualizes a more direct personal dependence on a deity. I have suggested, too, that such a reinterpretation may sanction changes in social values conducive to economic growth. Beyond these marginal observations, however, the question of the relationship to economic growth of "projective systems," and specifically religious behavior and belief, is so complex that its consideration must be omitted from this volume. It merits a volume of its own.

To sum up: increase in the scale of the society, the appearance of cities, literacy, and modern communications media, and the appearance of nationalism are all steps in the transition to economic growth, once it has begun, rather than starting points or causes. This is probably true also of change in religious ethic, though that question is not pursued here.

part **IV**

Transition to

Economic Growth:

Some Cases in Point

England: Continental Values
and Anglo-Saxon Virtues

chapter *13*

PURPOSES OF THE CHAPTER

SINCE THIS BOOK DEALS PRIMARILY WITH SOCIETIES that are still economically underdeveloped or are only now making the transition to continuing economic growth, in the main it treats the first Industrial Revolution as a prologue. However, the theory of social change presented, if it is correct, should apply to the first transition from traditionalism to economic growth as well as the later ones. Hence it seems desirable to suggest the historical developments which constituted withdrawal of status respect for important groups in Britain and then to inquire whether the innovating entrepreneurs were mainly from these groups, as the theory would suggest.

The discussion of English history in this chapter differs from that of Colombia, Japan, Burma, and the Sioux elsewhere in this volume in that the discussion of Britain is more tentative. British history is longer and more complex than that of any of the other societies; it is more difficult to make firm statements concerning the causal links. The sketch below suggests the forces at work in England during the millennium before the Industrial Revolution which may have caused English social and especially economic history to be what it was. It is believed that a more elaborate study would support the analysis advanced here, but the suggestion is made more modestly in this chapter than in others. The analysis applies to English history hypotheses derived from study of a number of societies and from the theoretical considerations presented in earlier chapters. This chapter is addressed to the question whether these hypotheses are consistent with the facts of English history, but it should not be assumed that the hypotheses could have been derived from the facts of English history alone.

Some Comments on Historical Method

An objection likely to be raised by some students of English history is not that the causal analysis suggested is wrong but that it is unnecessary. Each event, each change in trend, seems in retrospect to follow so naturally from the previous ones that a theory which goes underneath the *ad hoc* historical analysis seems superfluous. Trevelyan's fascinating study of English social history from the time of Chaucer to the eighteenth century and Tawney's penetrating study of the relationship between religion and the rise of capitalism are cases in point.[1] Each historical development is seen to flow so logically from the preceding one that to superimpose added theory seems unnecessary depreciation of well-informed and judicious analysis.

However, such analysis is retrospective and rather particularistic, that is, devoted to the explanation one by one of the varied links in a long chain of events. If historical analysis is eventually to have predictive value rather than merely retrospective plausibility, it must discern causal factors of rather general applicability.

It must also avoid the error of assuming that the values of people at an earlier age are similar to our own at a later age. Because we prefer democratic political procedures we are apt to explain an historical trend toward democracy by assuming that "naturally" people prefer democracy. Because we have no repugnance to working with tools and machines we fail to raise the question whether people in another society or at another time may have found such activity repugnant. And so on. This tendency to read our values into another era or society is stultifying to historical analysis.

Consideration of the model of personality and society presented in this volume suggests three principles which historical analysis ought to follow. In this chapter and in the later ones which analyze historical change in Japan, Colombia, Burma, and among the Sioux I attempt to gain insight into the causes of change by applying these principles.

One is that while there may be certain universals in human behavior, the values, motives, and cognitions of people differ so greatly from one place and time to another that the historian must not assume that he can interpret the motives and world view of the people of another era or society from his own or those of his society. Rather, he must infer them by considering what motives and world view are consistent with the historical situation and with each other.

A second is that, in drawing such inferences, there is a *prima facie* assumption that a social structure which prevailed in any society for a considerable length of time, say several generations, was satisfying on balance to each of the groups of the society. In some instances the assumption may prove wrong, but the ready assumption that a set of relationships among the groups of the society may have been maintained for a long period merely through the exercise of force or by virtue of inertia perverts historical interpretation. Even where force is the most conspicuous sanction, the historian must ask whether the continued submis-

---

[1] G. M. Trevelyan, *Illustrated English Social History* (London and New York: Longmans, Green & Co., 1949–51), three volumes; R. H. Tawney, *Religion and the Rise of Capitalism* (New York: Harcourt, Brace & World, Inc., 1952).

sion to force does not suggest that the relationships satisfied certain needs of personality.

The third principle is that except through force people will cause or submit to a change in social structure only as their personalities change so that new relationships become satisfying. A sequence of historical change almost certainly involves as an important causal element (and perhaps also a resultant) a sequence of changes in personality.

Historical analysis, then, must infer both how personality affects society and how society affects personality. To do either it must employ a theory of personality consistent with modern psychology.

Comparative Analysis: England and the Continent

A transition to economic growth was probably implicit in the history of all western Europe as the societies of that area approached modern times. I suspect that it occurred first in England for three reasons. Traditional society may never have been as firmly rooted in England as on the continent. Secondly, during most of the period from the beginning of the Christian era until the nineteenth century the top elite of England were aliens. This was true of the political elite from 1066 to say 1461, and of the religious elite from before 1066 until say the reign of Elizabeth. (The replacement of alien by English elite in both fields was gradual, and no precise date is fully correct.) Their alien ways offended the lesser elite and speeded their rejection of traditional values. Moreover, partly because of England's separation from the continent and perhaps through the historical sequence that led to the Cromwellian absolutism, the values of the society turned against military prowess as a means of self-assertion by socially deviant groups sooner in England than on the continent. This inhibition on military revolt helped to channel energies elsewhere.[2]

The significance of these three factors in England will become apparent as this chapter proceeds. However, I shall not attempt to justify by comparative analysis among societies the assertion that they were the causes of England's priority. Such an analysis, which would be far more complex than one of England alone, is beyond the scope of this chapter. Rather, I shall present merely an analysis of the operation within England of forces causing the decay of traditional society and a transition to economic growth.

---

[2] It may also be true that the textile industry offered more fertile soil than other industries for the type of technical advance that was feasible in the state of knowledge that existed in the seventeenth century. If so, since Britain was a great textile producer, this circumstance was conducive to early advance in Britain. This suggestion does not seem persuasive to me, for advances in the iron and steel industry followed so hard upon those in textiles that one may suspect they were in part independent. A stimulus arising elsewhere than in textiles might easily have tripped them off, or they might indeed have begun the sequence of events. If conditions of the other three types listed had favored some other country, that country might well have led the way in its smaller textile industry or in some other industry.

Scope of the Chapter

In no society was a traditional social structure ever fully stable, and in England the approach to stability was less close than in many other societies. I shall suggest that tensions within the English society caused it to move steadily toward a qualified hierarchical authoritarian structure during the Anglo-Saxon period, and that William the Conqueror acted

TABLE 13–1

PERIODS OF ENGLISH HISTORY, FIFTH CENTURY TO 1688, WITH HOUSES AND DATES OF KINGS

A. *The Traditional Society Takes Form: From the Anglo-Saxon Invasions through 1087.*
    ANGLO-SAXON PERIOD: Fifth century to 1066
    Alfred the Great, 871–99

    NORMAN
    William the Conqueror, 1066–87

B. *Withdrawal of Status Respect and Its Sequels: The First Cycle, 1087–1422.*

NORMAN	Henry III, 1216–72
William II, 1087–1100	Edward I, 1272–1307
Henry I, 1100–35	Edward II, 1307–27
Stephen, 1135–54	Edward III, 1327–77
	Richard II, 1377–99
PLANTAGENET	
Henry II, 1154–89	LANCASTER
Richard I, 1189–99	Henry IV, 1399–1413
John, 1199–1216	Henry V, 1413–22

C. *The Second Cycle, 1422–1688.*

LANCASTER	Edward VI, 1547–53
Henry VI, 1422–61	Mary, 1553–58
	Elizabeth I, 1558–1603
YORK	
Edward IV, 1461–83	STUART
Edward V, 1483	James I, 1603–25
Richard III, 1483–85	Charles I, 1625–49
	(Cromwell)
TUDOR	Charles II, 1660–85
Henry VII, 1485–1509	James II, 1685–88
Henry VIII, 1509–47	

wisely to preserve and strengthen the structure he found, but that during the centuries which followed, new tensions, largely created by the presence of alien elites, caused the society to move progressively away from traditionalism and eventually channeled energies into economic growth. This hypothesis will be best understood if the discussion begins with the Anglo-Saxon period.

The presentation of historical facts is brief and selective. The dates of each king's reign are given the first time he is mentioned, but as an added aid to readers not well versed in English history, Table 13–1 presents a reference list of English rulers, subdivided to correspond to the chapter's discussion.

THE TRADITIONAL SOCIETY TAKES FORM: ENGLAND THROUGH WILLIAM THE CONQUEROR

The Anglo-Saxon Kingdoms

The Romans withdrew from England in the first half of the fifth century, after the loss of Gaul, and in that century and the next the Angles, Saxons, and Jutes invaded and conquered the area that is modern England and settled there. They came not as one large well-organized force but in many small groups. A large number of petty Anglo-Saxon kingdoms developed. Long after their establishment, savage strife continued among many kings and even among the nobles within each kingdom.

Religious Change

However, the elites were not preoccupied with violence to the exclusion of an attempt to gain a more satisfying understanding of the world. Christianity had spread only slowly and incompletely during the centuries of Roman occupation of Britain, and had gained the adherence of only part of the population.[3] But when Augustine and his group of missionaries began their work in England in 597, acceptance of the new religion spread rapidly throughout that country. Within half a century the English were pretty thoroughly converted.

The church became the sponsor of intellectual development. In the seventh and eighth centuries, under the initial leadership of the archbishop Theodore of Tarsus, an intellectual renaissance within the church made famous the cathedral schools at Canterbury, York, and Jarrow, produced the Venerable Bede, and sent Alcuin to the court of Charlemagne.

However, the elevation of spirit did not last. In the ninth century many members of the church hierarchy became conspicuously venal, devoted to secular pleasures, and negligent of their religious duties. (There may have been similar though less conspicuous tendencies earlier.) This corruption of religious office continued through the remainder of the pre-Norman period and beyond.

Evidences of Tension: An Interpretation

I suggest that the continuing strife, the ready conversion to a new religion, the intellectual flowering, and then the corruption within the

---

[3] In the fifth century the Celts of Ireland had become pretty completely Christianized, albeit with the usual survival of pagan beliefs and practices.

church all derive from a common cause: continuing high need aggression and great anxiety concerning it.

Repeated warfare by the members of a social group against other groups may be a sanctioned method of venting need aggression. That it was not in this instance is indicated by the facts that it contradicted the religious ethos that was adopted, that the strife was among groups with many ethnic and cultural bonds, and that it continued within the groups as well as among them.[4] In this case the strife was a disruptive means of releasing aggression and must have caused much anxiety.

That anxiety explains the rapid adoption by these conquerors of England of a new religion containing strong injunctions against the attitudes which they felt in themselves.[5] Perhaps inhibitions against violence which had existed in their tribal relationships on the continent were left behind when they crossed to England, or perhaps, no longer finding alien groups to attack once they had settled in England, they now turned on each other more frequently than before and hence felt new anxiety. In any event, their rapid abandonment of the pagan faith that had seemed a satisfactory world view in previous centuries suggests the presence of new tensions.

I suggest that members of the society who were more anxious than the rest found life within the church satisfying both because it was religious and because it was hierarchical. Intellectual endeavor in the service of religion would provide an obvious means of assuaging their sense of guilt, and I suggest that this motivation explains the renascence of the seventh and eighth centuries.[6] One would need a detailed understanding of the cultural history of the times to know why intellectual achievement ceased to be satisfying to many church officials, or why men to whom it was not satisfying sought church offices. Some general principle of social causation is involved; any one method of relieving anxiety is often abandoned in favor of another after two or three centuries. In any event, the corrupt and grasping behavior of many members of the clergy indicated a high level of both anxiety and need aggression. That church officials

---

[4] The alternative case, in which attacks on outside groups are sanctioned by the religion and provide an effective and socially integrative outlet for aggression, is well illustrated by the Sioux society, which is discussed in Chapter 19.

[5] The experience may be contrasted with that of Burma. When Islam spread over Southeast Asia and later when missionaries carried the message of Christianity to Burma, the Burmese were completely impervious to both, and they have been so to the present time. Virtually the only converts in Burma are members of other ethnic groups. The reason, as I suggest in Chapter 18, is that Buddhism so fits the needs of Burmese personality that a different religion has no attraction. (Now that Burmese society has been disrupted by a century of colonial rule, one would not wish to predict that Buddhism will continue to be as satisfying, but it may.)

[6] Intellectual advance is frequently taken for granted; it seems natural that men should move from one idea to another. However, the process seems natural only to men who are moved by the same needs as the participants, or who have become accustomed to the process in their societies. I suggest that each burst of intellectual advance needs specific explanation.

turned to this channel in the ninth, tenth, and eleventh centuries is evidence of the continuing presence of these qualities in personality.

Social Integration

The little kingdoms of the time were authoritarian; their social structure indicates that personality was authoritarian, and the events sketched above indicate that the need aggression present in personality was high. The need submission-dominance present in such personality will tend to make individuals accept a social structure which binds many small groups into a single hierarchy and thus ends the uncertainties concerning power relationships; yet need aggression will be a barrier to accepting the hierarchy of relationships. A stable societal equilibrium can be reached only if a hierarchy of authority is somehow created which prevents disruptive strife and yet provides and sanctions channels for releasing need aggression. Moreover, the members of the society must gain a world view which rationalizes and sanctions both the social structure and the urges in their personalities. One element of the social structure must be a structure of religious institutions which is consistent with the world view and which persists because it also satisfies the needs of the persons occupying religious roles.

The emergence of a social structure satisfying these interlocking conditions may be impossible. As has been suggested in Chapter 8, fairly high need aggression can be released in muffled but satisfying ways on the persons dependent on one in a hierarchy, including juniors in one's family. However, this release may not be sufficient to be satisfying if need aggression is high. Moreover, need aggression may block the development of the more comprehensive hierarchical social structure. As seen above, it may also lead to behavior by religious officials which conflicts with individuals' views of a good world and causes them to feel that they are not being given sure contact with the spiritual powers. If this happens the social structure will not be stable.

The organization of a stable traditional social structure in these circumstances, if it occurs at all, is apt to be a long halting process. It will proceed only as individuals appear who are creative enough so that they can impose their authority on others whose need aggression is high and yet give those others sufficiently meaningful roles in the hierarchy so that they are satisfied rather than humiliated. No matter how creative the leaders are, they may not be able to accomplish this effect if need aggression in the society is too high.

In England during the sixth through the eleventh centuries these tensions within personality brought a slow uneven movement toward a single society with a traditional social structure and culture. One aspect of this process was the evolution of a nationwide social-political hierarchy. Now and then one king or another was able to build up his strength and force the submission of others or eliminate them and absorb their territory.

Late in the eighth century Danish Vikings made the first of a series of attacks on England, and thereafter for almost a century successively conquered additional bits of the country. Perhaps partly because of the first attacks, not long after 800 the king of Wessex induced or forced all of the other six remaining kings to swear homage to him, and there emerged a more or less united kingdom of those parts of England not controlled by the Danes. By the time of Alfred the Great, 871–99, the unity was solid. Alfred checked the advance of the Danes, and his son and grandson drove them out, though not permanently.

During the same period a clearly feudal structure of political-economic relationships took shape below the king. Until at least the eighth century loyalty to each king consisted almost wholly in willingness to fight and die for him; the rewards were the "simple ones of land, treasure, food, and drink."[7] In the eighth or ninth century the king began to appoint "ealdormen," from among his relatives or from the nobility, to head shires. While no doubt various royal purposes were served by creating these offices, a main purpose was to obtain revenues and fighting men. Under the shires, hundreds and wapentakes were created for similar reasons.[8] The ealdormen gained both power and opportunity for self-enrichment. The office tended to become hereditary, and by the eleventh century the ealdormen had become earls, with expanded geographic area, and powerful landed magnates in their own right.

By the seventh century king's councils, formed of influential laity and clergy from among the king's retainers, had appeared. These councils developed into the rather formal assemblies of the tenth and eleventh centuries. Composed of both clergy and laity, they are not to be distinguished sharply from church synods, for they dealt with both civil and religious matters, which in turn were hardly to be distinguished. The king was God's servant, and there was no sharp distinction between church and state.

Thus a religious-political hierarchy of the sort usually found in traditional societies was steadily taking shape. It extended down to the simple folk. Most of the people were of course engaged in agriculture and lived mainly in villages and hamlets, though some were scattered about on farms. There were only a few larger communities which might be

---

[7] Peter H. Blair, *An Introduction to Anglo-Saxon England* (Cambridge: The University Press, 1956), p. 211. My discussion of political change is largely from Blair. Concerning the development of feudal institutions see also G. O. Sayles, *The Medieval Foundations of England* (2d ed.; London: Methuen & Co., Ltd., 1950).

[8] Blair stresses only the desire of the king for armed men and revenue, and states: "It is probable that the primitive right of exacting tribute from subjects was a far more potent stimulus towards the growth of local units which might share the burdens imposed upon them from above than any popular desire towards sharing in local government." (*Ibid.*, p. 242.) While I agree that popular desire to share in local government may have been slight, I shall suggest that Blair's judgment concerning the motivation is probably incomplete, mainly because it takes account of only conscious motives.

termed towns. "The two major elements in Anglo-Saxon society are comprehended in a jingling phrase which is found in seventh-century Kentish laws—*ge eorle ge ceorle*, 'noblemen and commoners.' "[9] The ceorls (churls) paid taxes, a sign of being "free men." Below them were men with various kinds of servile obligations. Blair suggests that there may have been fewer free men by the eleventh century than immediately after the Anglo-Saxon conquest, many having been driven to surrender part of their freedom in exchange for greater security.[10] Blair refers to economic and especially physical security, but it may be assumed that the motivation also included the need of individuals with authoritarian personality to have a place in a hierarchy.

The feudal social, economic, and political structure that had evolved by the time of the Norman conquest must have offered great satisfactions not only to the nobles who dominated it but also to the lesser nobles and gentry and the simple folk, each of whom depended for guidance on authority above him and in turn controlled many aspects of behavior of the individuals who depended on him.

However, neither the hierarchy of authority nor the doctrines of Christianity were sufficiently compelling to channel the need aggression into acceptable channels. Robbery, murder, rape, and other physical violence were still frequent. Each man had to guard his own property and family except as his village afforded joint protection. More important neither the members of the nobility nor the higher clergy always behaved in ways consistent with the values of the lesser elite and simple folk below them. Simony, plurality, the obtaining of income from religious office without rendering any religious service either useful or symbolic, and other abuses were common in the church, as were extortion and neglect of obligations to their dependents by the nobility. Neither the religious nor the civil elite, therefore, conveyed a consistent perception of the rightness of authority. Badly though the lesser folk needed to believe in the rightness of authority, and willingly though they would undoubtedly have accepted the rightness of arbitrary actions by the authorities above them if there had been no other shortcomings, they must often have been unable to believe fully.

William the Conqueror, a wise man, not only left largely untouched the institutions which might be expected to yield satisfaction and a sense of security to the mass of the people but also acted to reform those that might be expected to offend popular values. Moving quickly to make his power secure, he dispossessed the great lords and assigned the great estates to his Norman followers, reduced the earldoms in size, and retained about one sixth of the land for his own. But he left the feudal positions of the lesser lords untouched, and left the Church undisturbed in its

[9] *Ibid.*, p. 259. The remainder of this paragraph summarizes chap. v of Blair's book.

[10] Trevelyan, *Illustrated English Social History*, notes the fewness of free men in Norman and early Plantagenet times.

feudal control of perhaps one fourth of the land of the country. By making the sheriffs subject to royal removal he took control of an essential link between the native local government and the Norman central government, but he altered Anglo-Saxon laws and the local administration of justice very little. Moreover, removing some especially corrupt or incompetent bishops and replacing others as they died, he appointed reformers who introduced the Cluniac reforms. The perception of the simple folk and lesser nobility alike must increasingly have been of a social hierarchy in which the possessors of high earthly power and the bearers of spiritual power alike respected them and their values, and in which authority extended up to a supreme spiritual power to whom it was good and fit that the greatest mysteries of life should be entrusted. If the social system had functioned so as to produce a series of rulers with the attitudes and abilities of William the Conqueror, it probably would have been highly satisfying to most nobles and simple folk alike and would have persisted without major change.

While we have little direct evidence concerning personality, the nature of the social structure that was found satisfying indicates that personalities of the period must have reflected all of the dominant characteristics of authoritarian personality: a view of the events of the physical world as arbitrary and not understandable; a view of the social world as manageable only by force; need dominance and aggression, and desire to depend on authorities above one for guidance rather than to face decisions on one's own; and a view of physical labor as menial and demeaning. As in all societies, there were exceptional creative individuals. William the Conqueror, who of course came from abroad, was one. However, as will become evident below, they were few even among the higher elite. Until these personality characteristics changed, neither the invention of new political forms nor technological progress would be great.

WITHDRAWAL OF STATUS RESPECT AND ITS SEQUELS: THE FIRST CYCLE, 1087–1422

The next seven centuries of English history witness armed struggles to gain and keep the throne, corruption in the church, religious heterodoxy, outbreaks of popular violence, liberal revolts and repression of them, the gradual seizure of more and more power by a Parliament in which the townsmen were represented more and more strongly, and slow economic change. I suggest that these events should be interpreted as constituting withdrawal of status respect by the higher elites for the lesser gentry and the common folk, followed by a long sequence of reaction to that withdrawal culminating in the appearance of creative individuals who, alienated from traditional values, created new institutions and found new roles in which to demonstrate their worth to themselves.

The behavior of kings, the Pope and archbishops, the higher nobles, and the higher clergy was such as repeatedly to create the perception in the minds of lesser nobles and the simple folk that these higher elite had little or no regard for the public welfare or public standards of morality and decency. Consider first the events up to about 1400 which might have this effect, and the reactions of the lesser folk to this perception.

Withdrawal of Status Respect: The Manifestations

The very alienness of the higher elite must have offended the lesser folk. Alienness always violates native values. To any people who have not become part of an international society the behavior of aliens seems impolite or ungentlemanly or perverted or immoral or rude.

The higher nobles during the first century or more were French, and they imported also a small flood of French or Italian church officials. Like all conquerors, they continued to speak their native language. Even at the end of the twelfth century, a century and a quarter after the conquest, the appellation given Richard I by the nobility was not "lion-hearted," which is a translation, but "coeur de lion." For almost 300 years after the conquest French was the language of pleading and judgments in the courts. For an added 300 years and more English kings were apt to marry French or Spanish noblewomen for reasons of dynastic ambition that had little to do with the welfare of the English people; and many of the queens brought streams of courtiers and church officials in their trains. Trade and finance were long in the hands of foreigners. Though foreign trade was vital to England, through the fourteenth century there were few Englishmen engaged in it except for wool export, in which they did a minor share of the business. Until the end of the thirteenth century, when Edward I no longer needed them and expelled them, the financiers were Jews, and for another half-century, until Edward III repudiated his debts to them, Italians.

The French nobility and later the English nobility, copying continental manners, often behaved in ways that seemed immoral or effeminate to the English. Trevelyan notes how Chaucer's fashionable contemporaries of the last half of the fourteenth century, "especially the younger sort, abandoned the decent gown for a short coat or jacket and displayed the symmetry of their legs in tight-fitting 'hosen.' . . . One leg might be draped in red, the other in blue. Men 'wore their estates on their backs' and flashed in jewels and costly stuffs no less than their wives. . . . Sleeves 'slod upon the earth'; shoes with long toe-points chained to the waist prevented the wearer from kneeling to say his prayers.[11] While this dress was not typical of earlier periods, the sexual morality, dress, and speech of the continental nobility from 1066 on must have seemed somewhat indecent to the simple folk.

---

[11] *Ibid.*, Vol. I, p. 24.

In the church the priests or clerks performing pastoral functions in the village parishes were often devoted to their tasks. Their steadfastness perhaps delayed alienation of the simple folk from the church, but it could not fully offset the impact of misbehavior at higher levels. Corruption and neglect of duty were common among the higher clergy, so that the religious establishment often seemed not a vehicle through which to obtain protection by the spiritual powers against danger or anxiety but an instrument by which the clergy profited by betrayal of one's religious needs. The Pope placed foreign favorites in many rich benefices. Hard pressed for income, he obtained it by scandalous methods, such as the sale of indulgences and sham relics, and the sale of church offices even to persons who thereafter collected the income of the office but performed no function, and even several offices to one individual. Bishops commuted punishment for sins, particularly sexual immorality, in return for money payments. To obtain money, officers of the Bishop's Court often took the initiative in demanding the payments. In Trevelyan's word they "blackmailed" sinners in their homes. Rectors and vicars left their parishes to live in London or Oxford or at a friend's manor house, while a clerk performed the mass and heard confession. Monks became "worldly and well-to-do, living lives of sauntering comfort in the monastery, or roaming the land dressed like laymen, to hunt game or look after their estates."[12] Many persons who had learned to read and write in monastery schools and were in theory ecclesiastics held clerical positions in government or business offices. Some of these clerks robbed or raped or murdered and escaped prosecution in civil courts by claiming "benefit of clergy," but received only light punishment in church courts. While not all of these abuses were recorded in every period, betrayal of the duties of religious offices manifested itself in the church in one form or other at all times.

There was perhaps equal corruption among civil officials. In addition, the king might waste the land's substance and shed the blood of its people in a foreign war conducted to satisfy his dynastic ambitions. At some times the people apparently supported war against the French with enthusiasm, but as the Hundred Years' War drew on, the incompetence with which it was conducted and the absence of any reason for it related to the interests of the nation as distinguished from the personal interests of the king and nobles caused a feeling of betrayal.

Kings and nobility were frequently untrustworthy and cynical as well as corrupt. A summary of relevant events during the period from the death of William the Conqueror through the reign of Richard II will illustrate the point better than any general statement.

William II, 1087–1100, ruled arbitrarily, with little regard for the desires or customs of the people. Henry I, 1100–35, promised as he gained

---

[12] *Ibid.*, p. 44. My account of corruption in the church is mainly from *ibid.*, pp. 39–46.

the throne to return to the good ways of the Conqueror, and, although he repeatedly broke the promise, he did preserve order in the land more effectively than had been done by his predecessor. However, when his sister's son, Stephen, had gained the throne by force, there followed almost 20 years of dynastic war that caused anarchy in the feudal system and economic distress throughout most or all of the country.

The first of the Plantagenets, Henry II, 1154–89, restored feudal order. He also attempted to control the scandalous behavior of "criminous clerks" by obtaining the right to punish them after a church court had convicted them, but the murder of Archbishop Becket by the king's supporters alienated public sentiment and forced the king to yield the point, and benefit of clergy continued to be a scandal until the end of the sixteenth century.

On balance his reign was pleasing and reassuring, but some of the acts of even the best of his successors and many acts of the worse among them created a foul odor. Richard Coeur de Lion, 1189–99, was an adventurer with little interest in the affairs of domestic government. John of Magna Carta fame, 1199–1216, has been characterized briefly as "cruel, mean, licentious, faithless, weak of will, without counterbalancing virtues."[13] Quarreling with the church over the control of appointments to church offices in England, he yielded when baronial revolt threatened. He then made his kingdom over to the Pope as a fief, whereupon the Pope paralleled John's lack of principle by supporting him against the barons. Nevertheless, the barons succeeded in forcing the Magna Carta upon him. Meanwhile through incompetence John had lost all English lands in France except Aquitaine.

During the long reign of Henry III, 1216–72, a revolt of the barons with strong clerical and middle-class support forced him to agree under oath to establish a council of 15, a majority of whom would be barons, with power to veto his decisions. However, in return for Henry's consent to new financial exactions by the church the Pope "dispensed" Henry from his oath and Henry thereupon disregarded it.

Edward I, 1272–1307, a very able ruler, returned the country to temperate, trustworthy, equitable rule. He consulted frequently with knights and townsmen, whether or not they were members of his council, and a Parliament with broadened membership began to take shape. During his reign the Pope offended the public sense of equity by decreeing that the clergy, some of whom were very rich, might not be taxed by lay rulers without the Pope's consent. By refusing the clergy access to royal courts and confiscating the lands of clergy who did not make "presents," Edward forced the Pope to withdraw the decree.

Yet Edward in his turn had his troubles in civil affairs. The barons and townsmen, both seeking security against Edward's pressure for reve-

---

[13] William L. Langer (ed.), *Encyclopedia of World History* (rev. ed.; Boston: Houghton Mifflin Co., 1952), p. 197.

nue, united to force from him the "Confirmation of Charters," a reaf-
firmation of Magna Carta plus a provision that no nonfeudal levy would
be imposed without Parliament's consent. Edward agreed, but arranged
that the actual granting of this concession should be made by his son as
his agent, and later, in exchange for the right to collect their first year's
income from persons appointed to church offices in England, Pope Clement V freed the second Edward from his promise.

The son, Edward II, 1307–27, was controlled by his favorites. Rule
broke down. The Scots regained their independence, private wars broke
out among the English nobility, and once again the maintenance of civil
order was neglected. The barons forced acceptance of a "reform committee" of their members, but since they used it for selfish and cynical
purposes, its creation hardly increased public trust in the social hierarchy.

Edward III, 1327–77, opened his reign with generous concessions to
the barons, and also invited the complaints of the middle class. The need
to obtain financing for the Hundred Years' War, which opened in 1337,
greatly increased the power of Parliament, and the evolution of Parliamentary institutions proceeded.

At the end of his reign, however, the disregard of the nobles for the
lesser folk again manifested itself. In his old age Edward became senile.
His oldest son, the Black Prince, who had on occasion taken charge of
the government and had both won successes in France and improved
governmental administration at home, led Parliament in reforms in 1376,
but after his death before that of his father in 1377, another son, John of
Gaunt, who had misled English armies to defeats in France, packed Parliament with royal supporters and reversed the reforms.

Thus for three centuries the English people had seen the higher elite
behave in ways not sanctioned by popular values, ways not sanctioned,
indeed, by the values of the lesser folk in any society. During periods of
better rule, notably that by William the Conqueror, Henry I, and Edward I, the people had come to expect a measure of equity in government,
as opposed to mere rule by force. Belief that the political hierarchy
should and would rule considerately must have been increased by their
need to believe it. Authoritarian personality dictates such belief. They
had needed also to believe in the spiritual guidance of the church hierarchy. Most of the time, however, they experienced greed and contempt
for moral standards on the part of many civil and religious elite alike. At
the top of the social hierarchy, when the king needed support for violating a pledge of better conduct that had been forced upon him, he often
obtained it from the Pope in return for granting the Pope financial advantages. While the actions of the higher elite, civil and religious, could
be put in a better light than they have been here by noting the motivations that caused their behavior, the impact on the lesser folk is perhaps
not overstated by the brief stark account presented here.

In the terms used in previous chapters, the lesser folk, in order to feel a satisfying identity, had to retain a conception of their own views of life as good and also had to conceive of the elite on whom they depended as good. However, they could not reconcile these two needs, for the higher elite had little regard for them or their values, so that if the values of the lesser folk were good, then obviously the elite were not.

Reactions: Protests and the Search for Flaws

Previous chapters have suggested that the sequence of reaction of a group in whom anxieties are created by such inner conflict is fairly certain. First, they will protest in whatever way the values of their culture permit, and in an attempt to evade giving up either of their irreconcilable views they will blame the failure of the higher elite to meet expected standards on flaws in the social system rather than on the basic structure of the system. As the attempt to remedy one flaw fails to restore goodness to their world, they will find another.

Second, as such stratagems fail to remedy matters and their anxiety persists, the effect on their home environment will be to cause deepening retreatism over a period of generations. And, third, some generations later there will emerge out of this retreatism individuals who are alienated from some traditional values and also are more creative than their forbears had been. These individuals will either try to overthrow existing social institutions and substitute others which counteract the misbehavior of the elite, or they will adopt new forms of behavior, possible within existing institutions, in which they can reassure themselves of their worth and perhaps also gain the social esteem that has been withdrawn from them. The difference between remedying flaws in the social system and replacing old institutions by new is of course a matter of degree; the more creative individuals are, the bolder the changes they will attempt. In a highly traditional society protest at the behavior of the higher elite may be completely inhibited, and neither protests nor even the smallest proposals for change may be made until a group has passed through the sequence of retreatism and then increased creativity.

The detailed history of England from the late eleventh century on reveals many specific instances of protest at the behavior of the new elite. Perhaps, however, it is appropriate to treat the nationalism of the thirteenth century as the first attack in the large on a flaw on which anxieties could be blamed. That attack centered on the aliens who, it was felt, were corrupting the kingship, the social hierarchy, and the church. French and papal influence were indeed great during the reign of Henry III. The bitter public outcry was strong enough so that two agents of the Pope in England were driven from their high governmental offices and Parliament denied Henry's desire to donate one third of his revenues to the papacy.

In the fourteenth century nationalism continued to rise. In 1351 Parliament limited papal appointments to English benefices and two years later forbade judicial appeals to courts outside England, that is, to the papal curia. Both laws were renewed several times. In 1362, by act of Parliament, English was made the language of pleading and judgment in the courts, though "law French" was retained in legal documents to avoid ambiguity. Popular songs with anti-French sentiments appeared, and as the century progressed Langland and then Chaucer wrote the first notable literary works in the English tongue.

Labor unrest in the fourteenth century centered upon economic institutions that were felt to be responsible for the laborers' sense of wrong. During the Middle Ages relationships on the manors had been governed by custom, but for a century or two before 1350 population growth had made land more and more scarce relative to the number of peasants who sought to cultivate it, and landlords had steadily raised rents. Then after the Black Death in 1348 and 1349 labor in its turn was scarce, and in spite of offering lower and lower rents and reducing feudal services landowners were unable to keep all of their land under cultivation; abandonment of land proceeded. The income of peasants rose. But, making their feudal obligations the scapegoat for their sense of uneasiness, peasants were not content with an increasing level of material living. All Englishmen, they declared, should be freemen. Their demands were gradually accepted. Under the economic pressure of labor scarcity, the breakup of the feudal manor and the commutation of serfdom proceeded. Workers already free repeatedly struck for higher wages, and obtained increases greater than the rises in prices. But still unrest continued.[14] The reason, I suggest, was that these economic conditions were not the basic cause of their anxieties but only the scapegoat on which they blamed them.

In government too the search for remedies continued. Here the remedies were directly related to the abuses of kings and the high church officials. By a series of steps Parliament increased its power and checked that of the king. A series of declarations, charters, and "provisions" are landmarks: Magna Carta in 1215, followed in 1258 by the Provisions of Oxford, by which Henry gave a council of 15 veto power over his acts (a pledge from which the Pope excused him); the Confirmation of Charters in 1297; reform ordinances in 1311; restraints on the Church in 1351 and 1353; and so on. Yet somehow no improvement was ever quite enough to bring reassurance and satisfaction.

Reactions: Radical Attacks on Institutions

The social protests of the fourteenth century were not merely a continuation of those of the thirteenth. By the fourteenth century the alienation from old values had proceeded far enough so that it was possible to attack the social institutions themselves rather than merely the individuals who were misusing them, and creative individuals appeared who could

---

[14] See, for example, Trevelyan, *Illustrated English Social History*, Vol. I, pp. 2–10.

conceive of basic changes in institutions. The difference is only one of degree, but it is significant.

The story of Robin Hood appeared; because evil laws were made, the tale implied, he was justified in violating the law in order to help the poor.

Langland's *Piers Plowman* appealed on behalf of the poor virtuous peasant. Amid Langland's attacks on governmental and ecclesiastical corruption, there were more radical notes. When a priest in the story declares invalid a pardon for sin that Piers had received because of his good works, Piers tears the pardon in two and declares that he does not need priestly sanction but can depend directly on God. He bases his stand directly on the Bible. "Though I walk through the Valley of the Shadow of Death," he says, "I will fear no evil, for Thou art with me." In another place one of the poet's characters declares that the emperor Trajan, having been a true knight, was baptized by his deeds and his soul safe in heaven even though he was never baptized at the font.

John Ball and other itinerant preachers not only denounced misbehavior but also preached scriptural equalitarianism that was revolutionary in its implications.

Wiclif, in addition to attacking the "Caesarian clergy" who supported the rich in their suppression of the poor, advocated a propertyless church in which the purely spiritual function would be emphasized, insisted on the direct access of the individual to God and the right of individual judgment in religious matters, and denied that in the mass the bread and wine become wholly converted into the body and blood of Christ. These doctrines, which declared in essence that the enormous wealth of the Church should be taken from it and that there was no religious justification for the existence of the church hierarchy, were known as Lollardy. Wiclif organized wide preaching of them by his itinerant preachers, known as the "poor priests," and their preaching struck a wide response.

I suggest that these radical doctrines could not have emerged until creative individuals alienated from the traditional social system had emerged out of retreatism.

The Peasants' Revolt: Social Reaction

In 1381 occurred the logical sequel to this loss of faith in the social system, the Peasants' Revolt. On the specific occasion of imposition of an unpopular poll tax, in 28 counties peasants arose, invaded manor houses and the abbeys of wealthy monasteries, obtained by force promises of reform, burned oppressive charters and manor rolls, and murdered some especially hated individuals. Then, under Jack Straw and Wat Tyler, they invaded London. Here they murdered a number of lawyers, civil officials, an archbishop, and some foreign artisans, sacked the houses of some of them, burned the house of John of Gaunt, and obtained the surrender of the Tower (a royal fortress, not yet known as a prison). They demanded commutation of servile dues, disendowment of the Church, and abolition of game laws.

Their belief that their hastily organized revolt could have effect against the attitudes and entrenched power of the nobility and landed gentry was as unrealistic as the frenzied behavior of peasants in colonial countries who, unable to endure longer the disparagement of the things they value highly in life, convince themselves that magic will protect them and march with primitive weapons against guns and cannon. In both cases, men believed that their problems could be remedied in this way because they could not afford not to believe.

The English peasants were not starving men driven to violence by physical misery. Their income was rising, not falling, and they were steadily gaining freedom from the restraints of feudal obligations. One must conclude that what they were unable to endure longer was the contempt for their values in life that was implicit in the actions of civil and religious officials and the upper elite during the previous three centuries. The provocation at the time of the revolt was no greater than it had been at a number of previous points in history. To explain the revolt at this time, it is reasonable to believe that generations of conflict between their need to respect their own status in life and their need to respect the position and judgment of the classes above them had created first intense anxiety and then the repressed rage of retreatism in them, and that out of retreatism had emerged some creativity, enough at least to dare contemplate revolt. The conception that revolt was possible was encouraged by the disruption occasioned by the Black Death of 1348–49 and also by the knowledge that various bits of self-assertion had not brought disaster. When these forces had been at work long enough, the explosion occurred.[15]

Richard II, 1377–99, met the peasants, made many concessions to them, and started them back home. Then, with the situation in hand, he had Parliament annul his promises on the ground that they were obtained under duress, had some of the leaders hanged, severely and cruelly punished others, and attempted to restore villeinage. This, however, he was unable to do.

---

[15] Trevelyan says, "In wealth and independence their position was improving fast, but not fast enough to satisfy their new aspirations." (*Ibid.*, p. 12.) Thus he implies that the revolt was due to what has more recently been termed "a revolution of rising expectations." Since I believe that the concept of a revolution of rising expectations as a source of social discontent is a somewhat distorted interpretation of history, it is useful to note a distinction here. I do not believe that violence over 28 counties occurred because a slow trend of improvement made men murderous at not getting faster improvement. Rather, the change that is mistaken for this one is the replacement in the minds of a social group of a frustrating feeling that they are powerless to remedy their humiliation by a perception that the forces oppressing them are not overwhelming and can be opposed. The former could occur only if perceptible improvement had taken place. The latter may occur, and in the twentieth century has occurred a number of times, where there has been no social or economic improvement and the only significant change in conditions is the perception that one is not powerless, that one dares to strike back.

The peasants were disillusioned not only by the repressive action of Richard but also by widespread revulsion against their violence, at least among the classes in power and perhaps among many of the lesser gentry and simple folk as well. Wiclif was discredited by their actions and was forced to withdraw from his vigorous public work, although the authorities did not dare molest him until after his death, when his body was dug up and burned. Henry IV, 1399–1413, obtained from Parliament a statute that increased the authority of the Church to act against Lollardy, and Henry V, 1413–22, hanged a number of Lollards and drove Lollardy underground until Henry VIII separated the national church from Rome more than a century later. One attempt to repair denial of status respect not only had failed but had brought increased repression, increased denial of respect.

Innovation without Revolt

Concomitant with these attempts to reform the system were attempts by individuals to prove their worth to themselves in new statuses. These attempts were possible only as the values of the individual changed, but they did not require the overthrow of existing institutions. The attractiveness of education to many individuals and the development of the monastery schools plus Oxford and Cambridge probably should be regarded as an example. "The medieval student . . . ," Trevelyan says, "was riotous, lawless and licentious. He was miserably poor; he often learnt very little for want of books and tutoring, and left without taking a degree. Yet many were enthusiastically eager for learning or at least for controversy."[16] They were, I suggest, seeking a means of self-justification.

The more conspicuous innovation, however, was economic. The development in the thirteenth century of a method by which cloth was fulled (cleaned, thickened, and felted) by water-power driven hammers rather than by hand was so important in the wool textile industry that it has been termed an industrial revolution.[17] Perhaps its appearance in the thirteenth century is not a mere historic accident, for this was also the century when people felt free enough to think new ideas so that the writings of Langland, Ball, and Wiclif could appear. It is also not a coincidence, I think, that the half-century of the Peasants' Revolt is also the period which Professor Postan has referred to as the "great breeding season of English capitalism."[18] The tensions that motivated peasants to the one type of action motivated some of the lesser elite to the other. These tensions caused a search for new means of increasing one's individ-

---

[16] *Ibid.*, p. 50.

[17] E. M. Carus-Wilson, "An Industrial Revolution of the Thirteenth Century," *Economic History Review*, Vol. XI (1941), pp. 39–60.

[18] M. M. Postan, "Revisions in Economic History: IX, The Fifteenth Century," *Economic History Review*, Vol. IX (1939), pp. 160–67. The quoted phrase is from p. 165.

ual power, and the economic conditions of the Hundred Years' War made trade, finance, and industrial organization the likeliest channels. The war prosperity stimulated luxury expenditures by the upper classes, which caused new opportunities in trade. At the same time the growth of cloth manufacturing created opportunities in industrial organization which ingenious men who no longer felt industry to be beneath them seized upon. And the new moneyed men lent to the king, created new financial institutions, and gained a new sense of their capability and power.

These possibilities, however, were open only to a few, even if there had existed a larger number of sufficiently creative men sufficiently alienated from old values. In any event, in the fifteenth century a secular economic decline occurred, reducing the opportunities. Moreover, perhaps it is not fanciful to suggest that the revulsion of opinion caused by the Peasants' Revolt, a revulsion that led to reactionary measures against the peasants, also inhibited individuals from other unconventional acts and is in part responsible for the economic conservatism of the fifteenth century.

For most men the perception, renewed with increased force, that there was no way out of their derogated positions must have caused renewed or increased retreatism, out of which generations later would emerge a new group of creative individuals who would seek another method of reforming the society and other methods of testing their individual worth.

WITHDRAWAL OF STATUS RESPECT AND ITS SEQUELS: THE SECOND CYCLE, 1422–1688

Behavior by the higher elite that carried with it implicit contempt for the good opinion of the lesser folk continued. A running chronological account of the highlights of this denial of status respect will give the flavor of the three centuries that followed the Peasants' Revolt.

The Manifestations

Henry IV and Henry V offended the nationalist opinion of the fifteenth century by taking French wives. Henry V renewed England's involvement in dynastic war on the continent, the Thirty Years' War, and while English pride swelled at the victory at Agincourt, continued prosecution of the war by Henry VI, 1422–61, at the cost of considerable expenditure and some lives and without benefit to England, was highly unpopular.

Henry VI acceded to the throne at the age of nine months. He was mentally unstable and unfit to rule even when of age. Within the council which did rule, "factions and favorites encouraged the rise of disorder," and again the country was the plaything of nobles seeking personal aggrandizement without regard to the effects on the lesser folk. "The nobles, enriched by the war and the new sheep farming and progress of enclosures, maintained increasing numbers of private armed retainers . . . with which they fought one another, terrorized their neighbors, paralyzed the courts, and dominated the government."[19]

From 1455 to 1485, during the last six years of Henry's reign and the reigns of the two succeeding Yorkist kings, Edward IV, 1461–83, and Richard III, 1483–85, there occurred the Wars of the Roses between the houses of York and Lancaster. It was a private war between small hired armies. Most of the lesser gentry and the simple folk apparently regarded the two sides as equally callous of the public welfare. Others, especially the new middle classes, saw right on the side of York. Whatever one's attitude, the 30 years of strife between private armies must have created anxiety among the lesser folk concerning their own role in such a social system.

The evils included not merely private warfare but also on occasion deceit, robbery, and murder. They included also during the entire period of Lancastrian and York rulers—Henry IV through Richard III—neglect of the maintenance of public order. The slow small gains during preceding reigns were lost, and once again one had little protection for one's life or property except one's weapons and, if one was fortunate, those of one's neighbors in one's community.

The first Tudor, Henry VII, 1485–1509, restored public order, and Henry VIII, 1509–47, maintained it. The change must have been reassuring. Yet other acts of each must have added greatly to public anxiety concerning the rightness of the social order.

Henry VII gained the throne by force of arms. The public's reaction to the brazen act of trickery and murder by which he besmirched his predecessor and supported his claim to the throne illustrates vividly the tensions of the age. The story begins some years earlier in the reign of Edward IV. Edward, a handsome and engaging man who was ever susceptible to feminine charms, and apparently the more so the more difficult the prize, had charmed and conquered many women, noble and other. The nation had become somewhat inured to such behavior in the royal family. However, his royal relatives were surprised and dismayed when he entered into a marriage ceremony with a beautiful commoner, Elizabeth Woodville. When he died in 1483, it was revealed that he had been secretly married to another commoner before his supposed marriage to Elizabeth Woodville. The clergyman who had conducted the earlier ceremony, feeling compelled to keep silence when Edward suddenly placed the Woodville beauty beside him on the throne, belatedly absolved his conscience by confessing in Parliament, with presentation of evidence. Edward's young children by Elizabeth Woodville, being illegitimate, were therefore not legally eligible to succeed to the throne, and Edward's brother, Richard, did so, becoming Richard III.

---

[19] The quoted clauses are from Langer, *Encyclopedia of World History*, p. 270.

However, when Richard was killed at the battle of Bosworth two years later and a son of Henry V captured the throne as Henry VII, he strengthened his claim to the throne by declaring that of Richard III illicit. To make the declaration plausible, he suppressed the documentary record of the pastor's confession in Parliament. Later he substituted in the story of Edward's earlier marriage the name of a woman whom Edward had not married and discredited that story by proving that Edward had not married her. Still later he accused Richard of murdering Edward's two sons, who did indeed disappear from the Tower, but, it is now clear, disappeared after Henry had mounted the throne. Henry then bribed some persons close to the true events and had others murdered, and throughout his reign succeeded in carrying out this amazing fraud on history, a fiction which has been retold down to the present time, so that Richard III is still commonly thought of as the ogre who murdered the young princes in the Tower.[20]

The true events had received sufficient publicity at the time of the confession in Parliament so that there must have been a large number of persons who knew of them. Their sense of humiliation and their alienation from traditional institutions must have been heightened by the need to keep silent. A question of peculiar interest is: Why did the enormous lie smother the truth for so long in spite of the ready availability of the truth?

In explanation it has sometimes been said that the simple folk were so far removed from and inured to the machinations of kings that they were simply not interested. The explanation is not convincing, for they were interested, so interested that they chose to forget the truth and very persistently repeated the lie long after the truth was revealed.

I can think of no plausible explanation except one that testifies to the desperate need of the mass of the population of England to believe in Edward's innocence. I have recorded above repeated gross abuses of the kingship. Yet the kingship was at the apex of a hierarchy in which it was necessary for persons still high in need of submission-dominance to believe. Edward IV was an attractive man, a good and capable king, and like few of his predecessors a peculiarly English king, pure English on both sides of his parentage and in his interest in the welfare of the common English people.[21] After the strife during preceding reigns and the impossibility of believing deeply in the honor and the honorable intentions of many preceding sovereigns, the ability to believe in the goodness of Edward IV must have satisfied a deep need. Here at last was a king whose

---

[20] Soon after Henry's death a substantially correct account was published, and now and then a historian has testified anew to the true course of events. For an amusing imagined reconstruction of the truth by a detective idling away time in a hospital, together with mention of earlier historical accounts which tracked it down, see Josephine Tey, *Daughter of Time* (New York: The Macmillan Co., 1951).

[21] He has been termed the first truly English king, but this characterization has also been made of Edward I.

rule proved that the kingship was good. To believe after his death that this hero had feet of clay, that he would deceive the public by presenting a false queen throughout his reign, would have threatened the entire structure of one's comforting belief in the hierarchy of authority. And so the public, in the days of Henry VII and later, simply refused to remember the evidence. At least no other explanation seems plausible. If this is the true explanation, it testifies both to the need to believe in the institution of the kingship and to the sense of betrayal by previous sovereigns, and illustrates the retreatism of the times. For such withdrawal from reality is a peculiarly impressive type of retreatism.

Henry VIII, driven to six marriages by both his desire for a male heir and a sense of sexual inadequacy to which the record of his personal affairs amply testifies, and unable to obtain the Pope's assent to his marital adventures, in 1534 obtained from Parliament the Act of Supremacy, by which he rather than the Pope was declared supreme head of the Church of England. The church officials whom he appointed then approved his actions.

England did not separate from the Church of Rome merely because of Henry's sexuality or his desire for an heir. I have sketched above the sources of English popular disillusionment with the Church and its alien hierarchy. There were other reasons, reasons of national policy, which need not occupy us here. The separation from Rome was approved by many, probably most Englishmen. Nevertheless, since Henry had no religious quarrel with the Pope, his motives being clearly personal and political, the faithful and unfaithful alike in England must have regarded his actions as cynical.

Thereafter Henry and after him Edward VI, 1547–53, confiscated the property of the monasteries, an act which also was popular. However, their use of the proceeds had little to commend it to the public. The monastery schools, which had been maintained with income from monastery lands, had been the backbone of the nation's school system, but Henry and Edward found it inconvenient to continue the expense of maintaining them. They sold most of the lands at extremely low prices to rich nobles and gentry, both to relieve the extremely straitened royal finances and to bind the purchasers to the new order in defense of their property. "There were probably more schools in proportion to the population at the end of the fifteenth century," Tawney states, "than there were in the middle of the nineteenth. . . . 'King Edward VI's Grammar Schools' are the schools which King Edward VI did not destroy. . . . The end of Popery, the curtailment of ecclesiastical privileges, six new bishoprics, lectureships in Greek and Latin in place of the disloyal subject of the canon law, the reform of doctrine and ritual— side by side with these good things had come some less edifying changes, the ruin of much education, the cessation of much charity, a raid on corporate property which provoked protests even in the House of Commons, and for ten years a sinister hum, as of the floating of an immense land syndicate, with favorable terms for all sufficiently rich, or influential, or mean, to get in on the ground floor."[22]

Edward revised the articles of faith and the Book of Common Prayer. Many of the revisions brought doctrine into line with some Protestant thinking, but some of the radical religious reformers thought the new ritual "like a Christmas game," and a peasant revolt arose in the West in opposition to it.

During Mary's brief reign, 1553–58, she restored Catholicism and involved the country in the war between Spain and France. However, Elizabeth, 1558–1603, repealed the Catholic legislation, re-enacted that of Henry VIII, and had the articles of faith rewritten, many of them ambiguously so that they were acceptable to a broad spectrum of non-Catholic opinion. All but a few hundred of the ordinary parish priests went along with all of these shifts of dogma from before Henry VIII through Elizabeth, perhaps an indication of their greater interest in their parishioners than in dogma rather than a sign of their cynicism. Elizabeth's reign was a long and important era, which in any comprehensive survey of English history, even a summary one, would merit much more attention than is given it here. Private warfare was largely ended and civil order in the country greatly improved. A great national victory over the Spanish Armada was won. England prospered and came to feel united and strong. The responsiveness of her rule to the values and needs of the people must have created intense relief through its contrast to the previous frequent disregard of popular desires and public morals.

However, after Elizabeth came James I, 1603–25, and Charles I, 1625–49. When they attempted to turn the clock back toward absolutism and toward Catholicism, a large segment of the Scottish and English people rose up in arms, and the great Civil War ensued. I shall discuss that war below.

It would be futile to attempt to find ultimate causes for the failure of kings, Popes, and the upper elite during the preceding seven centuries to behave in ways that satisfied the need of the lesser folk for responsible guidance. In part, underlying the surface causes of international intrigue and domestic irresponsibility was a level of need aggression that drove many kings, nobles, and clergy alike to acts whose purpose was individual aggrandizement. Another underlying cause was a view of the world by the upper elite which included little or no regard for the simple folk or even for the lesser elite. The simple folk were simply seen as a different and unimportant kind of people; the impact of one's acts on them was

---

[22] R. H. Tawney, *Religion and the Rise of Capitalism* (New York: Harcourt, Brace & World, Inc., 1952), p. 143. For his information concerning the destruction of the schools, Tawney depends on A. F. Leach, *English Schools at the Reformation, 1546–48* (1896), and for the comparison with the nineteenth century, on Leach's *The Schools of Medieval England* (1915), p. 331.

not of great significance relative to the effect on one's own fortunes. In previous chapters I have suggested the causes of such a world view. The same attitude prevails in many low-income countries today. The peasants and menials are tools; many of the elite do not really see them as individuals. Finally, some acts which lessened faith in the social system were due to tensions within some individual rulers not fully comprehended within the term "need aggression." The sense of inadequacy which drove Henry VIII is a case in point.

As in the earlier historical period, the reaction of the lesser folk to the sense of lacking a secure and respected place in the social system, the sense that they were not regarded as having worth, included protests, attempts to remedy flaws in the system, attempts by individuals to prove their worth in ways that did not involve challenging the system, and, climactically, the evolution of radical new values followed by radical social revolt.

Protests and the Search for Flaws

Throughout the period various groups had raised their voices in protest at acts of the king, the nobles, or the higher clergy. The demands of Parliament for increased powers or for the maintenance of rights granted earlier continued throughout the sixteenth century and in the seventeenth became an increasing stream in protest at the attempts of the Stuarts to restore absolutism. As during the earlier period, many protests centered on foreign involvements of the king and foreign influences in the country. In 1450, when incompetent leadership in the war and at home by the men around Henry VI had inflamed public opinion, perhaps 30,000 men of Kent and Sussex, including both peasants and many small landowners, marched on London to demand the restoration of the Duke of York to power. Ten years later the merchants and craftsmen of London refused entrance to the city to Margaret of Anjou, Henry VI's queen and leader of a Lancastrian army. Distrust by the Londoners of the French elements in the Lancastrian party was certainly an important cause of their stand. Early in the fifteenth century Parliament resisted granting money to the council of Henry VI for use in the continued prosecution of the Hundred Years' War; 200 years later Parliament refused to declare war on Spain at the request of James I; and during the intervening centuries comparable sentiments appeared now and again. While these attitudes may be attributed to the reluctance of the nobles to bear the costs of war, they also reflected widespread public dislike of involvements on the continent when those involvements seemed intended to advance the personal glory of the king or nobles but did not promise to advance the welfare of England.

A sense that one is not regarded as having worth takes the form of a sense that one is threatened by something evil outside one, and many other events of the sixteenth and seventeenth centuries, which are best understood as attempts to find the source of evil and extirpate it, give evidence of this feeling of being threatened. The people found one cause after another on which to blame their persisting anxiety. When attack on one supposed cause failed to allay their sense of unease, they conceived that something else was the cause. During the reigns of Edward VI, Mary, and Elizabeth it was possible for the individual to see the sinister figures of Spain and Popery as causes of his unease. When demolition of these dangers left people still oppressed with a sense of ill, they decided that witches were at work, and the first half of the seventeenth century witnessed that surge of belief in witchcraft which historians have so often deplored. In the economic field, the repeated outcries about enclosures in the later sixteenth and early seventeenth centuries persuaded modern economic historians that this was a period of unusual distress, until further research revealed that the times of most rapid enclosure in many areas where the outcries arose were the reign of Henry VIII and the decades following 1750, and not the period of the greatest protests.[23] The real source of economic trouble, so far as there was one, was the formless force of rising prices, which cannot be made a scapegoat. One must conclude that the intensity of the outcry against enclosures was due largely to the search for a cause of inner unease.

However, the most conspicuous result of this national sense of inner unease, and the distinguishing characteristic of this second great tide of social protest and revolt, was the radical attack on the religious hierarchy and the system of belief supporting it. In the early Tudor period there came a renascence of classical scholarship and Biblical exegesis. It was as though learned men felt that their unrest arose from a failure to understand aright their relationship to God and could be remedied if they could find the truth. Out of these studies a new wave of eloquent criticism of the abuses within the Church emerged. Colet, More, and Erasmus, the former two native Englishmen and Erasmus a continental who spent a large part of his life in England, leveled their pens at the abuses of their day. William Tyndale's rendering of the Bible into beautiful English permitted the mass of the people to read or to hear it and to share in the sense that release from anxiety was there in the true teachings of God.

Then in 1536 Calvin pronounced his new vision of the world, a vision evolved out of those of Wiclif, Luther, Zwingli, and others, but which carried the implications of those earlier visions to a new radical satisfying conclusion. The traditional authorities are evil, so the message ran; a higher authority exists on whose unmediated guidance one must depend. Man owes obligation not to a hierarchy of authority extending up to God but directly to God himself. The goodness of one's life rests not on one's submission to the rituals of the socioreligious hierarchy but on the degree to which one's life glorifies God. New economic activities

---

[23] See Sir John Clapham, *A Concise Economic History of Britain* (Cambridge, Eng.: The University Press, 1949), chap. viii.

are not mere instruments for human aggrandizement but instruments for the glorification of God. Men who pursue them need not be anxious, for if they prove by their righteousness that they are of the elect, then they can be sure that their salvation has been predetermined by God and that they are men of ultimate worth. Lest men have any doubt concerning what was righteous, Calvin announced his readiness to spell it out in every detail, and to enforce it on men; and he called upon the elect in turn to be policemen to prevent evil acts by any man.

Those are highlights of the dogma; now let me restate them to make explicit their significance to men suffering under denial of status respect. One who cannot reconcile belief in the goodness of the authorities of his society with belief in his own worth need not continue to feel anxiety, Calvin said; let him cast aside his dependence on the authorities and satisfy his need dependence and need submission by depending directly on God alone. If dependence directly on God is too abstract a conception to satisfy his need, then let him rest his anxieties on Calvin and the lieutenants whom Calvin would select. If he is seeking to test his own worth in an unorthodox activity, let him no longer be made anxious by lingering belief in old values which declare that the new occupation is demeaning; any occupation which makes the earth productive is a means of glorifying God. If his need aggression is high, let him not be anxious; his aggression will be sanctified if he directs it at the existing evil authorities and at all others who do evil. If the tensions of his childhood have given him a longing to indulge in sensuality and laxity, a longing that fills him with guilt, let him assuage that guilt by denouncing the evil desires in those around him. Denouncing them, he may at the same time inwardly experience the sinful acts he denounced and thus satisfy his own lust; and, scourging them in place of himself, he may find his guilt relieved and the sense of purity he seeks temporarily attained.

Thus Calvinism provided a solution for all those derogated groups whose rage, persisting need submission-dominance, and need for new roles convinced them of the desirability and possibility of overthrowing the old institutions and forcing on society the new similar ones that Calvin visualized.

In England Calvin's views were modified by a small group of men whose need aggression was less and whose personalities in general had moved farther from the traditional. They accepted his view of the new economic endeavors as being sanctified by being devoted to the glorification of God; indeed, this doctrine, which was somewhat incidental in Calvin's theology, became a central aspect of theirs, and they derived it as much from their own English predecessors as from Calvin. Their other major tenet they also drew from a stream of thought that had been flowing since the time of Langland and John Ball, Chaucer, Bunyan, and Wiclif. This was their vision of man's personal responsibility to God and his ability to make contact with grace directly rather than through any hierarchy, whether traditional or Calvinist. Having less rage than the Calvinists, they did not need to visualize the complete over-throw of the old social order, and, having less need submission-dominance, they did not need to visualize creation of a new hierarchy. Hence out of their study of ancient sources they arrived at a quieter doctrine.

These, then, were the two visions that competed for acceptance. In the middle decades of the sixteenth century John Knox preached Calvin-like doctrines in Scotland, where they were seized upon by almost the entire nation. In England only a small percentage of the population actively entered into religious controversy. Of those who did, one group, the Independents or Congregationalists, held the radical view and would root out the Church of England and replace it by a theocracy, while others would merely purify the Anglican Church of its sensuous ritual and relics of "Popery," and when they were persecuted within the Church wished merely to be allowed to go their own way. In the main these religious nonconformists were townsmen—craftsmen and traders. It may be assumed that the same characteristics of personality that had caused them to turn from traditional occupations to these newer ones somewhat detached from the hierarchical structure of society caused them also to reject the traditional religious hierarchy. Many Englishmen who did not actively embrace the new movements responded sympathetically to the emotions they expressed.

Civil War

James I and Charles I, not understanding the significance of the new religions, the new nationalism, or the new self-confidence of the lesser elite and the simple folk, set out to restore the old order so far as they might. During the half-century of their reigns the two kings and Parliament often acted in ways pleasing to the lesser gentry and the simple folk, yet in many ways each king aroused apprehension and dismay. The acts of each again threatened foreign involvement and the re-establishment of alien elites. In 1623 agents of James negotiated a marriage treaty with Spain so favorable to Catholicism that it created great dissatisfaction; even so, the emissaries could not persuade Spain to grant military aid to James and broke off negotiations. In 1625 Charles I married a sister of Louis XIII of France, who brought Catholic priests to England in her train. Charles acted in several respects to improve the economic condition of the poorer classes, but he also dissolved Parliament and without its consent raised revenues by ways which, while not entirely illegal, ran counter to evolving precedents.

Above all, each tried to suppress the new religious sects, James declaring in a famous phrase that if the religious dissenters would not conform he would "harry them out of the land." In 1604, at his bidding, an ecclesiastical convocation enacted a code that bore so harshly upon Puritans that 300 clergymen left their positions rather than conform.

Repeated persecution of Nonconformists ensued, though none were killed. Charles' Archbishop of Canterbury, Laud, forced Puritan clergy to read a royal declaration encouraging archery, dancing on the green, and other diversions which they considered sinful.

These measures succeeded, at least in the sense that they were carried out. However, when Charles attempted to carry the struggle to Scotland and in 1637 sanctioned Laud's order that the liturgy of the Church of England be read in Edinburgh, he ignited a conflagration he could not extinguish. The Scottish Presbyterians took to arms. They defeated Charles' army in 1640 and forced on him an agreement to support their army until a permanent settlement was reached. Unable to raise the necessary funds, he had to call Parliament, a Parliament dominated as Parliaments had been for some time by Presbyterians and Independents. There followed steady seizure of more and more power by Parliament. In 1642 Parliament committed the revolutionary act of issuing a call to arms without the royal seal, and revolt in Scotland became civil war in England.

In that war the king was supported by most of the titled nobles, Catholics, Anglican clergy, gentry, especially the greater gentry, and peasantry, who because of their high need submission tend in almost every society to remain loyal to the traditional regime, however much they have responded earlier to the notion that the authorities are evil. The yeomen and lesser gentry, the urban middle classes of petty manufacturers and shopkeepers, the urban artisans, the great merchants—groups which included the religious dissenters—and many great nobles as well were supporters of Parliament. Social lines coincided in some measure with the religious lines. Not all of the royalists were Cavaliers nor all of the supporters of Parliament Roundheads, as these terms were initially used, but the identification was close enough so that the terms Cavaliers and Roundheads came to be used to identify the two sides. In these terms the disparagement of each group by the other is epitomized.

For this was not a private war between small armies composed of the retainers of noble houses who fought while the lesser folk looked on in indifference and disgust. The Parliamentarian-religious dissenters and the traditionalist Anglicans and royalists each saw in the other the source of that evil of which they had long had an inner sense; and the masses of the people in town and country alike raised armies so that at last they might extirpate the evil and gain peace.

From 1642 to 1646 the war was one between the Parliamentarians, supported by all of the dissenting sects, and the king. In 1645, having obtained an act of Parliament providing for the abolition of bishops and converting administration and forms of the Church of England to Presbyterian ones, the Presbyterians were ready to make peace. But Oliver Cromwell and his troops, the Ironsides, the best troops of the war, had ideas for more basic socioreligious change. In 1646 Cromwell and Parliament came into open conflict. In 1648, in a second civil war, the Presbyterians plus the royalists opposed the Independents and the Roundheads who supported them. Cromwell defeated his opponents, and from 1649 to 1658, purging the Parliament or turning it out if it disagreed with him, Cromwell governed the Commonwealth which he proclaimed. In 1649 he executed Charles I. By 1655 rule was wholly by generals. They censored the press, forbade Anglican clergy to teach or preach, and rigidly controlled arts and morals. That religious state of which Cromwell and many of his supporters had dreamed, devoted wholly to serving God as His will was interpreted by Cromwell, came into existence.

But many Englishmen did not find satisfaction of their anxieties in Cromwell's Protectorate. Even by 1658 Parliament had voted and Cromwell had been forced to accept toleration for all persons who believed in the trinity except Episcopalians and Catholics. In that year Cromwell died; two years later Charles II was called to the throne. Like the Peasants' Revolt, the attempt to reconcile the inconsistencies of life by military establishment of a perfect religious order had failed.

Inner unease persisted; in part it turned on the Nonconformists. As had occurred after the Peasants' Revolt, there was political and social reaction. Charles could not regain the powers the kings before him had lost, but with his co-operation the landed classes gained control of Parliament. Thereupon clergymen who refused to accept the Anglican prayer book were deprived of their offices, and obstacles were again put in the way of dissenting worship. The bawdy dramas, gambling, coarse language, and sexual looseness that Cromwell had sought to extirpate returned to the society of the higher elite with such a vengeance that Restoration society has become notorious in history. The attempts of Charles II and James II to restore rights and privileges to Catholics were, however, unsuccessful; the anti-Catholicism of the nation was too strong. Indeed, it was the birth of a son to the strongly and openly Catholic James II which led to his deposition and replacement by Mary, his Protestant daughter by an earlier marriage, and her husband, William of Orange.

THE ECONOMIC SEQUEL IN THE
EIGHTEENTH CENTURY

It might have been forecast at that time, I suggest, that the religious dissenters, Presbyterians, Puritans, and Separatists alike, would within a few generations provide the leaders of a technological revolution. John Bunyan suggested the reason in 1678 in his famous book:

> I dreamed, and behold I saw a Man clothed in rags, standing in a certain place, with his face from his own house, a Book in his hand, and a great burden upon his back. I looked, and saw him open the Book and read therein; and as he read, he wept and trembled; and not being able longer to contain, he broke out with a lamentable cry, saying, "What shall I do?"

The pilgrim of whom Bunyan had dreamed was all the anxious people of England who had turned to the Bible to find their way. Many attempts to solve their problem had failed. Protest at the unrighteous conduct of civil and religious leaders had been fruitless; efforts to discover and remedy flaws in the social system had not relieved the sense of unease; the civil uprising of the Peasants' Revolt, an attempt to reconcile values and institutions by changing the institutions, had failed; armed revolt in the name of religion had gained control of the country, yet had failed to remedy the social unease; and the trend of the times was such as to bring conviction that none of these methods of remaking the society would succeed in the future. More important, one may reasonably assume that there was an increasing number of individuals whose childhood under retreatist fathers and nurturant mothers had been such that their need aggression was only moderate in degree. Thus, although their bond to many old values was attenuated, they felt no compulsion to overthrow the socioreligious system but only a deep sense of personal responsibility and a need to prove themselves, a need which drove them to cry out, saying, "What shall I do?"

Because their childhood had made them creative they were ready to prove themselves in new ways. Migration, however, was too drastic a severance from their social system except for a few; although the migrations to the New World were of importance for American history, they provided an outlet for only a small fraction of the alienated groups.

Others of these derogated individuals who were free from high need aggression tried to gain a sense of satisfying identity by study of the operations of the physical world, a study that gives deep satisfaction to some creative individuals, to whom intellectual understanding gives a sense of mastery. In Chapter 2 I quoted Sarton's comment that the number of "scientific events" in Europe doubled from the fourteenth century to the fifteenth and tripled in the sixteenth.[24] The acceleration continued in the seventeenth, and almost certainly more sharply in England than elsewhere in Europe (though I do not have quantitative evidence to support this assertion). Professor Merton has presented convincing evidence that the Protestant Dissenters, the social groups most alienated from traditional values, provided a greatly disproportionate share of the men who made the advances in scientific knowledge.[25] Various reasons have been advanced for this disproportionate share of the Dissenters in the intellectual advance, among these being their better education and the probable nature of their childhood training.[26] I suggest a central reason is that these groups were alienated from traditional values, were

---

[24] Chapter 2, note 8.

[25] Robert K. Merton, "Science, Religion, and Technology in Seventeenth Century England," *Osiris*, Vol. IV (1938), pp. 360–632.

[26] The latter by David C. McClelland, *The Achieving Society* (Princeton, N.J.: D. Van Nostrand Co., Inc., 1961).

creative, were under inner pressure to prove to themselves their own worth, and found in intellectual prowess a means of gaining a sense of mastery while removing themselves from the conflicts of their society.

To most individuals of the disparaged groups, however, the satisfactions of intellectual life were too attenuated. To many individuals, the reference groups on whom one must depend for a sense of approval of one's intellectual efforts were too remote to be internalized. The opportunities of venting need aggression, moreover, were indirect and limited; for many individuals with moderately high need aggression they were unsatisfying. To creative individuals alienated from old values who felt thus, economic prowess through entrepreneurial ingenuity was a promising alternative channel.

To some men it had been a promising channel since the twelfth century and perhaps before. Since that time technical advance had occurred now and then in some fields. In agriculture there had been little change. The enclosure movement had gone forward slowly from the fifteenth century onward, and the substitution of horses for oxen had progressed slowly; but even at the end of the seventeenth century both changes were far from complete. And the introduction of new crops, the use of fallow land for fodder or turnips, and better methods of plowing would all wait until the eighteenth century.

In industry, however, a number of changes had been made. I have mentioned the introduction of fulling mills in the thirteenth century. By 1500 they were common in the cloth-making counties. In the fourteenth century occurred the great shift from the export of wool to its use for making cloth. There was a large enough industrial sector by 1450 so that the problem of industrial unemployment was being discussed.[27] By 1500 clothier "putter-outers," men who bought yarn or cloth and contracted with independent craftsmen to process it, were an established part of the economic system.

Slow change in detailed methods of handicraft or manufacturing production went on through the sixteenth and seventeenth centuries. Skilled immigrants from the continent who brought demonstrations of new methods contributed considerably to them, for in these centuries one region or another on the continent was ahead of England in various techniques.[28] The spinning wheel slowly replaced the distaff between say 1500 and 1725 or 1750. In Elizabeth's reign cotton was imported for the

---

[27] Clapham, *A Concise Economic History of Britain*, p. 194. My summary of technological change from the thirteenth to the seventeenth century is largely from Clapham, though I have also used the far more detailed accounts in Charles Singer, E. J. Holmyard, A. R. Hall, and Trevor I. Williams (eds.), *A History of Technology*, Vol. III: *From the Renaissance to the Industrial Revolution, c. 1550 to c. 1750* (Oxford: The Clarendon Press, 1957).

[28] See *A Concise Economic History of Britain*, p. 234, and *A History of Technology*, Vol. III, *passim*.

first time; until then the only materials used for making textiles had been wool in England and flax in Scotland. Through the sixteenth century the yarn spun from cotton was used mainly as the woof for a linen warp; all-cotton goods were few. The stocking frame, a knitting machine invented late in the sixteenth century, spread widely during the next 100 years. In the sixteenth century the gig-mill was invented. It consisted of a water-power driven wheel covered with hooked heads which passed over the cloth and raised the nap to prepare the cloth for shearing. Its use spread over the country during a century or more. Some time after 1600 the "Dutch loom" or "inkle-loom," a loom on which a dozen or more narrow tapes or ribbons could be knit at once, was introduced from abroad, was gradually improved, and spread slowly and then fairly rapidly.

Ships gradually became larger. In metallurgy a number of mechanical (rather than chemical) advances occurred in the sixteenth century. The first small blast furnaces appeared in this century; by 1635 they were common. Lastly, during the period from say 1600 on there began a gradual substitution of coal for wood in both industrial and domestic use. It was not complete until far along in the eighteenth century.

One marvels not at the speed of this sequence of advances but at its slowness. For example, it is not possible to explain solely on technical or economic grounds why once the principle of the application of water power to textile operations had been conceived of in the fulling mill, it took so long for its application to spread to other operations. We must assume, I think, that the anxiety at facing new situations that is characteristic of authoritarian personality kept individuals from seeing the opportunities for profitable change that lay waiting around them, and that the technological advances that appeared here and there were typically made by men whose ancestors had felt withdrawal of status respect and whose family history and childhood environment had alienated them from traditional values and made them more than ordinarily creative. Of course we have no direct evidence one way or the other, for we have no individual biographies as we have of many of the eighteenth century innovators.

However that may be, by the time the Restoration had occurred and the members of the disparaged dissenting groups were seeking rather desperately for fields in which to achieve in order to gain a sense of personal worth, traditional areas were hardly available to them. They were closed partly by social barriers but perhaps even more by the fact that the Nonconformists no longer thought them part of a good life. On the other hand, there were available models of achievement in technology. The market was expanding; economic opportunities were favorable. No other field was as available as the economic one.

As I have suggested earlier, men need a sense that the careers they choose are consistent with their view of the nature of a good life. To some degree, creative children faced with such a problem will somewhere find models which persuade them that a career in which they have an opportunity to achieve is also a good career. They will also find models which show them how to perform in that field. And so the Nonconformists were able to find in their reinterpretation of the Bible evidence that to make the earth fruitful was to glorify the Lord and do His bidding.

For the prevalent Puritan attitudes, one should turn not to the formal theological treatises but to popular Puritan works, of which the best known is Richard Baxter's *Christian Directory, or a Summ of Practical Theologie and Cases, of Conscience* (1664–65).[29] Diligence in one's calling glorifies God, "who calleth thee to labor," Baxter declared. "That which is good materially pleaseth Him, as it tendeth to His glory, and to our own and other's benefit, which He delighteth in." And can one not find the evidence that this is true in the life of Jesus, who was the son of a carpenter, whose apostles were fishermen and similar humble folk, and whose parables spoke of craftsmanship and the earthly things of life: a good foundation, light under a bushel, salt of the earth, the fruit of a tree, by which ye shall know it? Was it not Jesus whose attention to earthly productivity was such that he thought it fitting to turn water into wine and to produce food for a multitude out of a few loaves and fishes? And since Jesus approvingly told the parable of the son who by usury turned five talents into 10, and as a reward was given the one talent of the son who had not used it productively, does it not follow that, "If God show you a way in which you may lawfully get more than in another way (without wrong to your soul or to any other), if you refuse this, and choose the less gainful way, you cross one of the ends of your Calling, and you refuse to be God's steward"?

When this transformation of world view had spread among a large group of individuals, they were able to see economic opportunity all about them. An increasing number of individuals turned from their farm or artisanship to manufacturing, and their sons, each following his father's model but going beyond it, devised new productive processes. As the eighteenth century advanced, the technological revolution gathered increasing sweep.

WHO WERE THE INNOVATORS?

It is universally assumed that the Nonconformist groups provided entrepreneurs of the Industrial Revolution in Britain out of proportion to their numbers. Weber stated his thesis that religious belief and innovation are intimately connected in "Die protestantische Ethik und der Geist des

---

[29] My quotations are all from Baxter, but I have them from R. K. Merton, "Science, Religion, and Technology in Seventeenth Century England."

Kapitalismus" in 1904–5.[30] In the extensive discussion that has ensued from that time until the present there is consensus that the Nonconformists did in fact provide a disproportionate number of the innovators. In the discussion above the supposed fact has also been taken for granted, and I have endeavored to provide an explanation of it.

Yet the assertion that Nonconformists were with unusual frequency innovators has been made merely on the basis of unsystematic observation of the frequency with which the names of Nonconformists appear in the historical accounts. It seemed worthwhile to select a sample of the innovating entrepreneurs of the Industrial Revolution, investigate their religious affiliation or inclination as well as other aspects of their social and economic background, and thus quantify the oft-repeated assertions concerning the peculiar association of religious nonconformity and economic innovation. The results of the study are summarized here, and the evidence is presented and the methods discussed in more detail in the Appendix to this chapter.

To justify any given list of entrepreneurs as a random or representative sample of the innovators of the Industrial Revolution is difficult. Innovation is a matter of degree; no two writers, no matter how well informed, would agree on the names to be included in a list of all innovators. To obtain a complete list is of course impossible. What was wanted was a list representative with respect to religious affiliation and inclination, that is, that did not stress or slight a group of men because of their religion or because of social characteristics with which religion is correlated. *The Dictionary of National Biography* is an illustration of a source that is biased in this respect. It weights heavily not only literary and artistic achievement, which would not matter, but also social distinction and membership in the nobility.

The problem was solved by taking as a source T. S. Ashton's admirably informative little book, *The Industrial Revolution, 1760–1830*.[31] A list of all entrepreneurs mentioned in it, excluding those in trade and finance, and with a qualification discussed in the Appendix to this chapter, was drawn up. Ashton discusses developments in the iron and steel, chemical, and textile manufacturing industries, and in agriculture, mining, and transportation. Technology advanced rapidly in these industries. It also advanced rapidly in some consumer goods industries which he does not discuss, such as brewing; and it is possible that there is some correlation between religion or nationality and entry into one or another manufac-

---

[30] In *Archiv für Sozialwissenschaft und Sozialpolitik*, Vols. XX and XXI. Weber revised it considerably before its republication in 1920. It first appeared in English in 1930, translated by Talcott Parsons, with the title *The Protestant Ethic and the Spirit of Capitalism*. See Parsons' preface to the first English edition, reprinted in the 1956 Scribner's edition.

[31] (London: Oxford University Press, 1948); the Home University Library of Modern Knowledge, No. 204.

turing industry, so that omission of certain minor sectors of manufacturing creates a bias.[32] With this possible qualification, however, Ashton's work provides a list of names selected solely because of their importance in the Industrial Revolution.

Names of persons concerning whom research uncovered no innovational activity were eliminated. A list of 92 names was thus arrived at. Of these, it was possible to obtain information concerning nationality for 91, concerning religious affiliation or inclination for 71, and concerning

TABLE 13–2

THE INNOVATORS: INDUSTRY, NATIONALITY, AND RELIGION

	English or Welsh	Scot	Other	Not Known	Total
MANUFACTURING:					
Anglican.........	21	2	0	1	24
Nonconformist*...	22 (includes 2 Sweden-borgians)	3	1 (German)		26
Presbyterian......		2			2
Calvinist, other....		1	1 (French)		2
Not known........	8 (includes Garbett)	8	2 (Irish)	–	18
	51	16	4	1	72

MINING, TRANSPORT, AND AGRICULTURE (M, T, A):

	M T A	T A		Total
Anglican.........1 5 4		2		12
Nonconformist.... 1 1				2
Presbyterian......		1		1
Calvinist, other....	1			1
Other...........1 (Roman Catholic)				1
Not known.......2 1				3
	16	4		20
Inclusive totals. 67		20	4 1	92

* Anabaptists, Baptists, Congregationalists, Methodists, Quakers, Uritarians.

the industry of the entrepreneur's father for 62. In all but a few cases this last also indicated the socioeconomic class of the father, and for two others the suggestion was obtained that the father's circumstances were "humble," without indication of his industry or occupation.

Table 13–2 classifies the major industry of each entrepreneur's career, his nationality, and his religious affiliation or inclination.

To compare the composition of this group of entrepreneurs with that of the population of England, Wales, and Scotland in general, it seems reasonable to use population estimates for the year 1770. In that year Scots constituted about 17 per cent of the population of England, Wales, and Scotland. Nonconformists and their families constituted about 7 per

---

[32] As Professor Ashton noted in a letter to the writer.

cent of the population of England and Wales. They were negligible in number in Scotland. While the number of Calvinists who were not adherents of the established Presbyterian church was greater, it too was apparently rather small.

The corresponding fractions among the entrepreneurs provide an interesting contrast. Scots form 24 per cent of the entrepreneurs; in proportion to population the number of Scottish entrepreneurs was more than one half greater than that of English and Welsh. While the sample is so small that this difference is not conclusive, it is consistent with the frequent assertion that Scotland provided a disproportionate number of the innovators. It may be true that these entrepreneurs came almost wholly from lowland Scotland. If so, the lowlands provided entrepreneurs in greater relative numbers than these figures indicate for all of Scotland. Firm evidence concerning this point is not available, however.

It is of interest to note that while information concerning religion is available for four fifths of the English and Welsh entrepreneurs, it is available for only three fifths of the Scots. Information is similarly lacking concerning other elements in the social and economic background of the Scots. Moreover, much of the information that is available is from English writers. While English observers of this period were recording the deeds of their fellow countrymen, the Scots were doing so to a far smaller degree. They were, so to speak, too busy acting to write.

The most striking contribution to the number of entrepreneurs, however, is not that of the Scots; it is that of the English Nonconformists. In contrast to their 7 per cent of the population of England and Wales, they contributed 41 per cent of the English and Welsh entrepreneurs whose religion is known, while the Anglicans, who constituted almost all of the remaining population, contributed only 58 per cent. The Nonconformists contributed about nine times as many entrepreneurs, relative to their total number in the population, as did the Anglicans.[33] Why this association between religious attitude and innovational career? The reason is implicit in the discussion of the preceding section. I suggest that the innovators were men who felt strongly a compulsion to understand the problems about them through the exercise of their own capacities. In all the major aspects of their lives they had to prove their own worth by repeatedly meeting standards of excellence within them. This high need achievement and need autonomy operated in their confrontation with the spiritual aspects of life as well as with the material and political. Their nonconformity in religion and in economic activity were common results of their personality traits.

---

[33] This assumes that 3 per cent of the population was of Catholic, Jewish, Presbyterian, or other faith or had no religious faith. This is a rather arbitrary number. If all of the other 93 per cent of the population is assumed to be Anglican, the Nonconformists contributed $9\frac{1}{2}$ times as many entrepreneurs relative to their numbers.

There is of course an alternative thesis, namely Weber's, that industry and hence innovation are directly associated with religious dogma rather than the two being co-results of a third factor. However, the information concerning Scottish entrepreneurs provides as clear evidence countering Weber's thesis as could be provided by a small sample.

It is not easy to know what belief to term conformity in Scotland. Shall Presbyterians be considered Nonconformists? Or, Presbyterianism being the established church in Scotland, shall Anglicans be considered Nonconformists? It would be contradictory to treat them both as conformist. However, Weber's thesis refers not to conformity but to dogma, and if that thesis is correct, the Scottish Presbyterians even more than the English Nonconformists should be the innovators. But of the 12 Scottish entrepreneurs for whom we have information only three were members of the established Presbyterian church. Another three were of dissenting Calvinist sects, two were Nonconformists, and four were Anglicans.

It is clear, I think, that the common denominator is not dogma but independence—in psychological terms, need autonomy. The innovator wants to analyze his problems himself. He is not willing to accept without examination the judgment of any mediator. This conclusion countering the Weberian thesis is perhaps the most exciting addition to previous analysis suggested by the statistical study.[34]

One may ask whether the considerable number of Anglicans present among the innovators is consistent with this thesis.[35] If some degrees of need autonomy, creativity, and alienation from old values are necessary for innovation, and if an untraditional view of the spiritual aspects of life is an element of this set of personality traits, is the number of Anglican innovators readily to be explained?

There is no inconsistency. We know the relevant attitudes of only a small number of the Anglicans who were innovators, but such knowledge as we have is consistent with their being all somewhat variant or deviant individuals. Church membership is after all a formal matter which to some deviant individuals is not of central concern and with respect to which they may follow a conventional course, their view of life being a personal rather than a formal matter. Thus Boulton "was attracted by the Cornish Quakers" and Bramah considered the Old and New Testaments "the only infallible exemplar by which the conduct of life ought to be guided."[36]

Many individuals of the middle or lower social classes who were anxious

---

[34] Tawney questioned Weber's thesis on the ground that the Nonconformist creeds included a variety of beliefs, as well as on other grounds. (*Religion and the Rise of Capitalism*, pp. 315–17, n. 32.) However, while it is true that Weber's discussion may give the impression of a greater uniformity of dogma than actually existed, yet there were fairly general common elements, and the vulgar versions of the beliefs may have had more in common than did formal church statements.

[35] The same question arises concerning Weber's thesis.

[36] Samuel Smiles, *Lives of Boulton and Watt* (London: John Murray, 1865), and Cullen Brown, "A Memoir of James Bramah," *New Monthly Magazine*, 1815, p. 213.

for social acceptance no doubt joined the Church of England or maintained their parents' membership in it for reasons quite separate from matters of dogma. Such individuals may repress their spiritual uncertainties; they are not consciously calculating or hypocritical. A number of innovators who were sons of Nonconformists joined the Anglican church; we may suppose that many of them found relief in the social acceptance which membership in the Anglican church gave and that they were thereby the freer to be bold in other fields.

The deviants within the Church of England also undoubtedly included many members of the higher elite. In any society some members of the dominant social groups will feel a sense of withdrawal of status respect, for such a sense is often felt by a single individual within a family in any social class because of some aspects of the environment of the particular home. In a society as disturbed by internal stresses as England during the centuries under review, the environment in many homes of all classes must have been such as to create such individuals. If such scattered individual cases were the only ones in a society, most of them would withdraw to some conventional niche, such as a life of learning or religion, but with an innovational movement readily at hand because of the activity of other groups, they may join it.

More important, in England the upper classes as a group had felt withdrawal of status respect for several centuries. Whenever the values of one group in a society conflict with those of another, each group, and not merely the one of lower social status, is aware of the disapproval of the other. The status of the higher elite in a society does not seem quite right to them so long as the people under them have the temerity to disapprove of their actions. In a typical traditional society the impact on the higher elite is slight because the opinion of the lower classes is of little importance to them. In England, however, where the opinion of the lower classes had led to important movements in Parliament, a spectacular Peasants' Revolt at the end of the fourteenth century and a number of lesser ones subsequently, and finally the Civil War in the sixteenth century, the sense by the higher elite that their status was not respected was acute and pervasive.

I have noted earlier in this book that when a socially rebellious group has innovated and gains increased possession of some socially important symbol, such as economic power, this makes the erstwhile conventional groups feel a decline in their relative status and will cause some of their members to take up the innovational activity in self-defense. This is one way in which the conventional group feels a change in the respect for its power, if not for its values, which the innovating group previously had. In England, since this sense by the higher elite of a lack of respect for their position was felt long before the lower elites began to innovate, the psychological impact on the higher elites occurred early and they entered into innovation fairly early.

Thus far, I have made no distinction among industries when analyzing the religious affiliation or inclination of the entrepreneurs. When the information concerning manufacturing is separated from that for agriculture, transport, and mining, an interesting difference appears. Of the 43 English and Welsh manufacturing entrepreneurs who were either Nonconformist or Anglican, 22, or approximately half, were Nonconformist; in the other three industries taken together there were only two Nonconformists and 12 Anglicans. Relative to their number in the total population the Nonconformists contributed 14 times as many entrepreneurs in manufacturing as did the Anglicans, but only some $2\frac{1}{2}$ times as many in the other industries; and the total number of cases in those industries is so small that little importance should be assigned to this difference. Why did manufacturing attract relatively so many more Nonconformists than the other industries?

It might be expected that the innovators in agriculture would be men whose families had land and that such men would also be Anglicans. This turned out to be true. Of the five English innovators in agriculture concerning whose religion we have information, three were landed, a fourth is referred to as a farmer, and the fifth was a renter; and four of the five were Anglican. (A Scot and another Englishman, whose religion we do not know, were also landed.) However, the association between landedness and Anglicanism on the one hand and between landedness and a career in agriculture on the other does not explain the dominance of Anglicans in mining and transport. Yet of the eight English innovators in transportation and mining whose religion we know, six were Anglicans, only one a Nonconformist, and one a Catholic.

One might be tempted to assume that the difference in religious distribution in the different industries was associated with a difference in values. The argument would run that a creative Anglican, having rather traditional values, tended to think of manufacturing as a pedestrian and unattractive career, and on the other hand could think of agriculture, transport, and mining as all associated with the land and therefore more attractive. By the same logic one might conclude that the Nonconformists tended to think of mining, transport, and agriculture as traditional and avoided them.

However, another explanation also seems plausible. There is another important difference between manufacturing on the one hand and transport and mining on the other. Manufacturing at the time might begin with no more than a handicraft operation. Even steel mills initially were very small. Ventures in mining and transport tended to require a larger amount of initial capital. Perhaps experimentation in agriculture did also, for the poor agriculturist had little land and moreover may not have dared to run the risk of experimenting. Hence at least part of the reason Anglicans are relatively more prominent in mining, transport, and agriculture probably is simply that more of them were wealthy, and ventures in these fields required greater wealth.

Probably both a difference in values and a difference in wealth influenced the results.

It is not true, however, that all of the well-to-do innovators chose agriculture, mining, or transportation as their field of activity. At least a moderate degree of wealth was an almost necessary condition for innovation in these fields, but it was not sufficient to draw a man of creative bent thither. As Table 13–3 shows, most of the innovators with well-to-do fathers were in manufacturing, though manufacturing also offered a career to sons of very poor men. Obviously such a classification is a very rough one. Attempt was made to use the terms "well-to-do" and "moderate income" as they might have been used at the time; the former includes men well below the economic position of the landed nobility, and the

TABLE 13–3

A ROUGH CLASSIFICATION OF THE INCOME OF THE INNOVATORS' FATHERS

Income Class of Father	Industry of Innovator			
	Manufacturing	Mining	Transport	Agriculture
Well-to-do	12	0	3	5
Moderate income	24	3*	2	2*
Low to moderate income†	12	0	2	
Poor	3	0	2	
Unknown	21	1		

Source: Table 13–5.
* All of the three in mining and one of the two in agriculture may have been well-to-do.
† In these cases the available information did not permit selection between these two income classes. "Low income" and "poor" are identical in meaning.

latter anyone who would have been regarded as "comfortably off" in a town or village.

The entrepreneurs of the Industrial Revolution, the classification indicates, were not typically very poor men who struggled to greater affluence through their creative efforts. Even in manufacturing 36 of the 51 for whom information is available were sons of men of at least moderate income, and in mining, transport, and agriculture the only innovators whose fathers were clearly poor by the standards of the times were Metcalf and Telford, though the uncertain information available suggests that this may also have been true of Brindley and Macadam. In the main they were the sons of men in comfortable circumstances. The data suggest that the historical records have stressed unduly the low income of the families from which the innovators arose.

Our understanding of their socioeconomic background will be increased by an analysis of the industries in which their fathers spent their lives.

Only into transportation and manufacturing was there any shift whatever from other industries in the 64 cases for which there is information. Every agricultural innovator came from an agricultural father; each of the three mining innovators was the son of a mine manager. It was almost inevitable that the innovators in transport should come from families that had been engaged in other industries since until the construction of the toll roads and canals there had been virtually no industry engaged in the construction of transport facilities.

The most striking fact is that even in manufacturing 27 of the 47 innovators for whom we have information were sons of men engaged in the manufacturing industry. More often than not, that is, manufacturing had been accepted as a career before the generation of the innovator; in entering upon activity in manufacturing he was simply following his father's model. Moreover in 17 of the 27 cases the father was a proprietor

TABLE 13–4

INDUSTRIAL AFFILIATION OF THE INNOVATORS' FATHERS

Industry of Father	Industry of Innovator			
	Manufacturing	Mining	Transport	Agriculture
Manufacturing:				
Proprietor..................17	0	1‡	0	
Artisan or laborer...........10	0	0	0	
Agriculture...................12	0	5	7	
Trade...................... 4	0	0	0	
Mining...................... 0	3	0	0	
Professional or allied.......... 4*	0	1†	0	
Unknown...................25	1	2§	0	
Totals..................72	4	9	7	

Source: Table 13–5.
* One civil engineer not attached to any one industry, one artist, one schoolmaster, one clergyman.
† Lawyer.
‡ Pease.
§ Hedley, Metcalf.

of a manufacturing establishment or became one before his death. In some instances the son moved away from his father's specific line of endeavor as a young man and then came back to it, as though he dared not rival his father until he had tested his ability in a line of endeavor not too closely related. Thereafter he much exceeded his father's achievement. The innovator did not make the two bold steps of entering a new industry and devising new methods in it; his father or grandfather had made the first; he made the second.

The fact that many persons shifted from agriculture to manufacturing is consistent with the thesis that many of the lesser elite in agriculture (small landowners, yeomen, renters) sought a new field after some generations of derogation of the family's economic role had caused the necessary changes in values. It is of interest that only a few individuals whose fathers' activity had been solely in trade made a shift to manufacturing and became innovators there. The shift would not have been a great one; even in the eighteenth century an occasional trader was also a merchant capitalist who contracted for the production of his wares. The smallness of the number who shifted from trade to manufacturing is the more remarkable since so many of the Nonconformists were traders; since the seventeenth century the prevalence of Nonconformity among the merchants had been conspicuous. Some merchants of course made an innovational career in trade, but the opportunities were far more numerous in manufacturing. That so few shifted illustrates the assertion so often made that while the liquid capital accumulated in trade may be an important source of finance for investment elsewhere, the trader himself has a view of the world which tends to bar him from making the transition. It is interesting to note that all of the four fathers who had been merchants and whose sons shifted to manufacturing were well-to-do, and all diverted their money in part from trade into another field. The fathers of Cookson, Hutton, and Oldknow, while traders, were also rural landowners, and the father of Lewis Paul acquired considerable property, which may have been either rural or urban. Thus the son moved to manufacturing only if the father had a secure economic base and was himself not wholly wedded to trade. Paul was a Huguenot, Oldknow a Methodist, and Hutton a Presbyterian. We do not know Cookson's religion.

This accounts for four of the 15 innovators in manufacturing whose fathers were well-to-do. One, Gott, was the son of a civil engineer, and another, Nasmyth, of a portrait and landscape painter of some note. The fathers of the remaining nine were divided between manufacturing and agriculture in a proportion which does not differ greatly from that for the entire group: seven in manufacturing, two in agriculture.

Amid these complexities of socioeconomic background, which contradict in part hitherto generally accepted theses, one fact is of importance here. Wherever relevant the evidence provided by the statistical study is entirely consistent with the hypotheses presented earlier in this volume.

APPENDIX: CHARACTERISTICS OF THE INNOVATORS

The purpose of the study of a sample of entrepreneurs was to estimate the prevalence of various national origins, religious affiliations or inclinations, and social and economic background among all innovators in the Industrial Revolution. An attempt was therefore made to obtain a sample that is random with respect to these characteristics.

The sample was selected as follows: T. S. Ashton's *The Industrial Revolution, 1760–1830*, an authoritative work, was selected as the source of names. All names mentioned in Chapters I–IV of Ashton were listed, Chapters V and VI being eliminated because in them the author reflects on the nature of the Industrial Revolution rather than summarizing its events. Names of the following sorts were then stricken from the list:

1. Individuals concerning whom the allusion was not to economic activity, for example, Edward Gibbon.

2. Individuals whose careers were confined to trade or banking. This restriction was made not in the belief that activity in trade or banking may not be innovational but because it is more difficult in those fields to determine whether innovation occurred, and because the sample seemed adequate with this limitation.

3. Individuals listed on pages 17–19 of Ashton who are not also mentioned elsewhere in Chapters I–IV. Since on these pages Ashton specifically discusses the roles of Dissenters and Scots in the Industrial Revolution, inclusion ceases to be random with respect to these characteristics. Six names mentioned only on these pages were deleted, those of the Foleys, Hanburys, and Murrays, Bannerman, Gladstone, and M'Guffog. The deletion itself may have created a bias since, having mentioned certain men here, to avoid duplication Ashton may have omitted mention of them elsewhere, while if these pages of special comment had not been included he might have mentioned them. However, omission of names which appear only on these pages seemed the lesser evil.

4. Individuals concerning whom Ashton's mention conveys no implication of innovational activity and concerning whom research indicated no evidence of such activity.[37] Innovation was defined as bringing into production a new (that is, significantly changed) product or the introduction of new methods of production, the latter term being interpreted to include not only technical methods but also methods of management and organization.

5. One innovator of Queen Elizabeth's day, William Lee.

6. Lastly, decision was made how to handle joint mention of relatives. Where a father and son are mentioned jointly, only one is listed (for example, Wedgewood) unless the evidence clearly shows separate acts of innovation in separate generations, as in the case of the Reynolds. Cases of brothers mentioned jointly as developers of an enterprise caused some difficulty. It was decided to include both George and Thomas Cranage, but to include only Samuel Walker, excluding Aaron, since Samuel seemed to be the driving force.

There remained 92 names. The following table summarizes the information obtained concerning these individuals. The tables in the text were derived from it. Where there is any possible ambiguity concerning how a name was classified to derive the figures presented in the text tables, a note of explanation is appended. The information is from direct statements of writers regarded as reliable, various sources having been checked against each other, or in a few cases from indirect evidence. These cases are noted. Where an entrepreneur's career lay in more than one industry he is classed in the one where his main endeavors apparently lay and his other activity is noted.

The distribution of various characteristics among these innovators was compared with the distribution of the same characteristics in the population of England, Wales, and Scotland as a whole. For this purpose estimates had to be made of the population of Scotland and of England plus Wales, and of the number of Nonconformists in England and Wales. A date was selected as follows. For 78 of the entrepreneurs the date of death is known. For 8 others there are available dates when they were active but not when they died. An assumed date of death was arrived at by assuming that death occurred 20 years after the midpoint of the period of recorded activity. On this assumption the median date of death among the 86 persons for whom information is available is 1810(11). A date early in their career, when their innovational activity had be-

---

[37] This list (the numbers in parentheses refer to pages in Ashton) includes Edward Knight (10), Franklin, Priestley, and Dalton (16), John Anderson (67), John Robison (68), Booth (97), David Dale (114), and Cookworthy and Champion (130).

TABLE 13–5

SELECTED CHARACTERISTICS OF BRITISH INNOVATORS

Name	Dates of Life	Nation-ality	Religion	Industry and Socioeconomic Status of Father
A. ENTREPRENEURS IN MANUFACTURING				
Arkwright, Richard	1732–92	English	Anglican	Yeoman. Humble circumstances.
Bacon, Anthony	b. 1717 or 1718; d. 1784	Manx	Anglican[1]	Humble circumstances.
Barlow		English		
Bell, Thomas	fl. 1783	Scottish	Independent (perhaps Unitarian)	
Blair, Alexander	fl. 1780–94	Scottish		
Boulton, Matthew	1728–1809	English	Anglican[2]	Maker of metal trifles. Possessed considerable property.
Bramah, Joseph	1749–1814	English	Anglican	Agricultural renter. Moderate circumstances.
Brunton, William	1777–1851	English		Clockmaker.
Cameron, Hugh	1705–1817	Scottish		Humble.
Cartwright, Edmund	1743–1823	English	Anglican	Landowner. Family old and affluent.
Clanny, Dr. William Reid	1776–1850	Irish	[3]	Respectable.
Clement, Joseph	1778–1844	English		Handloom weaver.
Cookson, William	1749–1811	English		
Cort, Henry	1742–1800	English	Anglican[4]	Mason and brickmaker.
Cranage, Thomas	fl. 1766	English	Quaker	
Cranage, George	fl. 1766	English	Quaker	
Crawshay, Richard	fl. 1788; d. 1810	English	Anglican	Yeoman. Respectable farming family.
Crompton, Samuel	1753–1827	English	Swedenborgian	Tenant on small farm. Also spinner and weaver.
Crowley, Ambrose, Jr.	1658–1713	English	Quaker (later Anglican)	Nailer and ironmonger. Prosperous.
Darby, Abraham	1677–1717	English	Quaker	Farmer; also locksmith and nailer.
Davy, Sir Humphry	1778–1829	English	Nonconformist	Owned a small farm. Woodcarver for amusement.
Dawson, Joseph	fl. 1799	English	Independent	
Dobson		English		
Dundonald, 9th Earl of (Sir Archibald Cochrane)	1748–1831	Scottish		Earl; major in army.
Ewart, Peter	d. 1842	Scottish		Clergyman.
Gamble, Joseph	fl. 1828	Irish		
Garbett, Samuel	fl. 1746	English		
Gott, Benjamin	1762–1840	English	Anglican[5]	Civil engineer; gentleman.
Greg, Samuel	1804–76	English	Unitarian	Mill owner.
Hargreaves, James	d. 1778	English	Anglican[6]	

TABLE 13-5—*Continued*

SELECTED CHARACTERISTICS OF BRITISH INNOVATORS

Name	Dates of Life	Nation-ality	Religion	Industry and Socioeco-nomic Status of Father
Highs, Thomas	fl. 1741–85; d. 1803	English	Swedenborgian	
Horrocks, John	1768–1804	English	Anglican	Yeoman; owned a small property in a village.
Huntsman, Benja-min	1704–76	German or Dutch	Quaker	
Hutton, James	1726–97	Scottish	Presbyterian[7]	Merchant. Owned farm. Became city treasurer of Edin-burgh.
Johnson, Thomas		English		
Kay, John	1704–?	English	Anglican	Merchant in staple trade; then factory owner. Educated son abroad.
Keir, James	1735–1820	Scottish	Anglican[8]	
Kennedy, John	1765–1855	Scottish	Nonconformist[9]	
Lees, Asa		English		
Lloyd, Nehemiah	1745–1801	Welsh	Quaker	Prosperous maker of iron for nails and bars.
Lombe, Sir Thomas	1685–1739	English	Anglican[10]	Worsted weaver.
M'Connel, James		Scottish	Unitarian	
M'Gregor		Scottish		
Maudslay, Henry	1771–1831	English	Anglican[8]	Artificer in royal artil-lery.
Murdock, William	1754–1839	Scottish		Miller, farmer, mill-wright, gunner in royal artillery.
Mushet, David	1772–1847	Scottish	Anglican	Weaver; of Scottish aristocracy.
Muspratt, James	1793–1886	English	Anglican[8]	
Nasmyth, James	1808–90	Scottish		Landowner, architect, landscape painter of note. Well-to-do.
Neilson, James B.	1792–1865	Scottish	Free Church	Millwright, later en-ginewright.
Need, Samuel	1718–81	English	Congregational	Humble origin.
Newcomen, Thomas	1663–1729	English	Baptist	Freeholder.
Oldknow, Samuel	1756–1828	English	Methodist	Tradesman, landowner.
Owen, Robert	1771–1858	Welsh	Free Thinker	Saddler and iron mon-ger; also postmaster of small town.
Paul, Lewis	fl. 1738; d. 1759	French	Huguenot	Druggist; acquired con-siderable property.
Peel, Sir Robert	1750–1830	English	Anglican[11]	Proprietor of calico printing firm.
Radcliffe, William	1760–1841	English	Anglican[12]	Weaver; inherited small farm, remainder of estate confiscated by Cromwell.

TABLE 13–5—*Continued*

SELECTED CHARACTERISTICS OF BRITISH INNOVATORS

Name	Dates of Life	Nationality	Religion	Industry and Socioeconomic Status of Father
Reynolds, Richard	1735–1816	English	Quaker	Iron merchant.
Reynolds, William	1758–1803	English	Quaker	Factory owner; innovator in iron making (see above).
Roberts, Richard	1789–1864	Welsh	Anglican[8]	Shoemaker and tollgate keeper.
Roebuck, John	1718–94	English	Independent	Prosperous manufacturer of cutlery.
Savery, Thomas	1650–1715	English	Anglican	Scion of well-known family. Himself undistinguished.
Southern, John	1758–1815		Anglican[8]	
Spode, Josiah	1754–1827	English	Anglican[13]	Potter.
Stephenson, George	1781–1848	English	Anglican[8]	Laborer; fireman in coal mine.
Strutt, Jedediah	1726–97	English	Unitarian	Farmer and maltster.
Stubs, Peter	1756–1806	English	Anglican	Currier.
Tennant, Charles	1768–1838	Scottish		Farmer.
Walker, Samuel	1715–82	English	Methodist	Nailer; small-scale farmer. Of moderate means.
Watt, James	1736–1819	Scottish	Presbyterian	Maker of mathematical instruments, carpenter and joiner, builder.
Wedgwood, Josiah	1730–95	English	Unitarian	Potter. Had small entailed estate.
Whitworth, Joseph	1803–87	English	Congregational[14]	Schoolmaster; minister.
Wilkinson, John	1728–1808	English	Nonconformist[15]	Farmer, day laborer, then maker of flat-irons; became fairly well-to-do.

B. MINING

Name	Dates of Life	Nationality	Religion	Industry and Socioeconomic Status of Father
Buddle, John	fl. 1790's d. 1806	English	(son of Unitarian)	Miner, then village schoolmaster, then colliery manager.
Curr, John	1756–1823	English	R. Catholic[16]	
Spedding, Carlisle	1696–1755	English		Chief steward of the Lowthers; became viewer of their collieries.
Trevithick, Richard	1771–1833	English	Anglican[17]	Manager of Dolcoath mine.

C. TRANSPORTATION

Name	Dates of Life	Nationality	Religion	Industry and Socioeconomic Status of Father
Bridgewater, 3d Duke (Francis Egerton)	1736–1803	English	Anglican[18]	Duke.
Brindley, James	1716–72	English	Anglican[8]	Cottier; then purchased small estate.
Gower, Earl	1721–1803	English	Anglican	Earl.
Hedley, William	1779–1843	English	Anglican (?)	Well-to-do.
Macadam, John	1756–1836	Scottish	Scottish Reformed Church	Landowner; lost his estate.

TABLE 13-5—*Continued*

SELECTED CHARACTERISTICS OF BRITISH INNOVATORS

Name	Dates of Life	Nation- ality	Religion	Industry and Socioeco- nomic Status of Father
Metcalf, John	1717–1810	English	Anglican[8]	Poor.
Pease, Edward	1767–1858	English	Quaker	Wool merchant and putter-outer.
Smeaton, John	1724–92	Scottish	Anglican[8]	Attorney.
Telford, Thomas	1757–1834	Scottish	Anglican[19]	Shepherd.
		D. AGRICULTURE		
Bakewell, Robert	1725–95	English	Unitarian	Renter of 440 acres on Dishley Grange.
Coke, Thomas, 1st Earl of Leicester	1754(2)– 1842	English	Anglican: Low Church	Landed gentry.
Elkington, Joseph	1740–1806	English	Anglican[20]	Farmer.
Lovell, Lord	1697–1755	English		Lord.
Sinclair, Sir John	1745–1835	Scottish	Presbyterian	Estate owner.
Townsend, Viscount Charles	1674–1738	English	Anglican	1st Viscount of Rain- ham.
Tull, Jethro	1674–1740	English	Anglican[21]	Well-to-do landowner.

The notes below indicate the evidence on the basis of which religion was deduced, where direct in-formation was not available.

[1] Member of Parliament.

[2] Educated at St. John's Chapel, Deritend, and buried at parish church of St. Mary, Handsworth, both Anglican.

[3] Freemasons attended his funeral.

[4] Names of his 16 children by his second wife are recorded in parish register of Holy Trinity Church, Gosport (Anglican).

[5] Referred to as "stalwart Churchman." Monument to him erected at Armley Church (Anglican).

[6] Death recorded in parish register of St. Mary's, Nottingham (Anglican).

[7] Buried in Greyfriars churchyard, probably Presbyterian.

[8] Buried in an Anglican churchyard.

[9] Buried at Rusholme Road Cemetery, Ardwick, Manchester (Nonconformist).

[10] Member of London Mercer's Company; held office of sheriff in City of London. At this time both were open only to Anglicans. Knighted by George II in 1727.

[11] Member of Parliament, 1790–1818; governor of a school for Anglican children.

[12] Trustee on the board to rebuild St. Mary's Church, Mellor (Anglican).

[13] Contributed £500 to construction of Parish New Church of Stoke (Anglican) and laid cornerstone.

[14] Son of Congregational minister, and educated at a Nonconformist academy.

[15] Has been variously described as a Churchman, a Methodist, a Unitarian, and an unbeliever. Father was Unitarian. Son educated at academy of Dr. Caleb Rotheram, a well-known Nonconformist. Requested that his epitaph read: ". . . Jesus Christ, in whose gospel he was a firm believer."

[16] Has been referred to as Quaker, but he was buried in the churchyard of St. Marie's Roman Catholic church in Norfolk.

[17] Baptized, married, buried in Anglican churches.

[18] Since a duke.

[19] Requested burial in Anglican parish church; actually buried at Westminster.

[20] Stated orally by family historian. Much supporting evidence.

[21] Death recorded in parish register of St. Bartholomew's Church, Basildon (Anglican).

gun, seems an appropriate date for the comparison with the population at large. Since a number of these men were long lived, and since their innovational ac-tivity often was apparent at a fairly early stage in their career, the date 1770 was selected. The date chosen does not materially affect the ratio of Non-conformists to the total population of England and Wales since the rough esti-mates available indicate that between 1750 and 1800 the number of Noncon-formists increased at about the same rate as the population. However, since the population of Scotland was increasing more slowly, an earlier date would show a higher ratio of Scottish population to the total, and a later date a lower one.

The changes would not affect the broad comparisons made here. The population estimates are as follows:

POPULATION (THOUSANDS)

Year	England and Wales	Scotland	Scots as % of Total
1750	6,040	1,403	18.8
1760	6,480	1,363	17.4
1770	7,227	1,434	16.6
1780	7,815	1,458	15.7
1790	8,541	1,567	15.5
1801	9,187	1,652	15.2

The estimates for England and Wales are those of Finlaison, given in M. C. Buer, *Health, Wealth, and Population in the Early Days of the Industrial Revolution* (London, 1926). Those for Scotland are from the 1801 census.

The authoritative work on the prevalence of Nonconformity is that of E. D. Bebb, *Nonconformity and Social and Economic Life, 1660–1800* (London, 1935). He estimates the number of Nonconformists in England for the period 1740–1800 as "between 250,000 and 400,000, tending to rise throughout this period, especially toward the end of the century" (p. 45). I have assumed an increase of 25,000 per decade throughout the 60-year period, thus presumably slightly overstating the number in 1780 and hence the ratio to the total population. Since Bebb's estimates refer only to the number of adult Nonconformists, an estimate of the number of children is necessary. By means of the Carlisle Tables, life expectancy tables built up from the mortality records of the town of Carlisle in Cumberland County for the years 1779–87, plus birth records for the years 1780–99 given in the 1801 census, it may be estimated that persons under 21 years of age formed approximately 35 per cent of the total population. Assuming that Bebb's estimates refer to persons above the age of 21, I increased them by 35/65 or approximately 54 per cent to obtain an estimate of the number of Nonconformists of all ages. The estimate for 1770 is therefore 500,000, or 6.9 per cent of the population. For lack of information, no attempt was made to estimate the number of either Nonconformists or Calvinist splinter sects in Scotland.

Most of the research concerning the entrepreneurs was done by Ruth Alexander Hagen. Gabrielle Fuchs completed the search of sources available in Cambridge, Massachusetts, and Bernard W. E. Alford and Charles D. Cohen checked readily available sources in England. The estimate of number of Nonconformists was made by Charles Cooper.

A list of major sources from which information was obtained is available from the writer.

Japan: History Mocks the Tokugawa

chapter 14

THE PERIOD OF JAPANESE HISTORY THAT OFFERS THE proximate explanation of Japan's entry upon economic growth is the Tokugawa era, 1600–1867. In the last half century of that period the pace of technological progress accelerated, and after the Meiji Restoration of 1868 technical advance was rapid. In the historical record of the Tokugawa era the governmental policies that constituted withdrawal of status respect, the ensuing retreatism, and the later emergence of many creative individuals who no longer held traditional values stand out sharply and impressively; and it is clear that creativity and change in values were important causal elements in the rapid technological progress and accompanying social change.

However, social change and technical progress had been going on much earlier than the Tokugawa era. The Japanese society, which has sometimes been pictured as traditional at the time of the Meiji Restoration, was not that even in 1600. Traditionalism had been disrupted long before, and one will not understand the changes that took place during the Tokugawa era unless one understands the process of change that had been set in motion during earlier eras. Hence this account will begin not in the year 1600 but some 1200 years earlier.

BASIC CHARACTERISTICS OF JAPANESE HISTORY

In interpreting Japanese history I shall follow the principle, already followed with respect to England, that to understand any historical change it is necessary to understand why, in the light of their values at the time, the previous condition was unsatisfactory to the persons experiencing it.

As in other primitive societies, social structure and personality in early Japan were traditional, that is, authoritarian. At times the basic social unit was a clan or other local group, at other times the nation. In either case, the organization of the group was hierarchical, and clearly this type of organization satisfied the needs and values of the people. Until at least the beginning of the Tokugawa era the Japanese world view was largely traditional, so that a social and political hierarchy in which each individual had his place and respected the power and guidance of those above him seemed right and good to almost all Japanese of all classes. Thereafter, new views of the world replaced the traditional one. As in England, they did so gradually over a period of hundreds of years. (It is sometimes stated that Japanese personality and social structure are still authoritarian. I shall indicate that this is only partially correct. In important ways authoritarianism has been modified in many groups.)

The history of Japan falls into periods even more clearly than does that of England, but the periods have a different significance. Each one in Japan before the Tokugawa era consists of a swing from national political integration to localism and back again. After a period of national unity the national government lost its power and local or regional chieftains or lords became largely autonomous, but then one of them gained national hegemony and national rule was restored. Between the earliest historical times, say 400 A.D. and 1600 A.D., there were three such cycles.

The movement was not merely away from and then back to the same position, like the swing of a pendulum. First, each swing was wider than the one before. In each successive period of localism the breakdown of national unity was more complete, and when national unity was again attained, a tighter integration than before was devised. More important, at each period of national integration, and each of localism, the political and social structures differed in complex ways from those of the preceding cycle.

It was as though a raft on a stormy sea repeatedly broke into pieces and after each segment had been steered separately for a time was lashed together again. At each breakup the passengers were uncertain for a time whether their separation meant freedom or danger, but each time they voted for reunion but came to a different conclusion concerning the appropriate nature of the craft and the voyage. Thus at each new lashing both the shape of the craft and the interpretation of the meaning of the voyage were different. Finally a vessel was constructed that for the time being at least seemed durable enough to sail on, but not all the passengers knew even then where it was going.

It is superficially plausible to interpret each period of national integration as resulting primarily from the emergence of a local leader of such military ability that he overcame all resistance, and each period of disruption as due simply to a change in relative military strength. However, this interpretation is inadequate.

It is true that each leader who achieved national integration before the Meiji Restoration succeeded because, as he demonstrated his ability in local wars, other lords fell in under his leadership. Thereafter he gained national power by defeating an opposing alliance. However, no leader after gaining national power dared attempt to end the quasi-autonomy even of the lords who had opposed him, for he knew that if he did so the lords who had formed an alliance with him would turn against him and demolish him.

It is reasonable, then, to suggest that lords and the simple folk under them did not fall in under a vigorous leader merely because they thought that by doing so they would gain more power than they lost. This motivation existed, but if it had been the sole motivation, they would have joined in the complete destruction of the power of opposing groups. Rather, they followed a leader so far as they thought, consciously or unconsciously, that what he was doing was good, and not much farther. It is reasonable to suggest that after each period of localism to many local leaders the absence of a national structure was unsatisfying, and creating a national hierarchy of political power seemed good and right.

It is easy to understand why this should have been true. During periods of localism many local lords pursued programs of self-aggrandizement, often with violence and in disregard of the welfare of the simple folk or even the lesser elite. Most of the millennium preceding the Tokugawa era consisted of periods of feudal strife in which the lesser elite and the simple folk found new rules imposed on their lives by force, or their lord humbled and themselves humiliated by conquest by an outsider, or perhaps found themselves left leaderless by the murder of their lord.

To persons with authoritarian personalities, to whom a hierarchy of social order seemed the natural order of things, this repeated violent disruption or threat of disruption of their places in the society must have been especially shocking. Some generations of such experience must have countered the authoritarian tendency to follow without question the leadership of their immediate chief or lord and must have created instead an enhanced sense of the rightness of a national political structure. Even the quarreling lords themselves must have experienced this same effect, and it must have been an important force tending toward national integration.

However, in each period of national integration the status attained by individuals of the middle and upper elites seemed inadequate to many of them. They could have been satisfied, if at all, only by higher status than was possible in a single national hierarchy; their need aggression was such that only supreme power could have satisfied them. Their self-seeking response to this sense of inadequate status gradually warped the political and social structure, until it was at last disrupted and the nation returned for another unsatisfying period to localism.

If it is asked why the sense of the lower elites and simple folk that a social hierarchy is right did not cause them to oppose disruption of the national structure, the answer is twofold. Because many of the higher elites abused their power during each period of national hierarchy, a sense that something was wrong with that hierarchy must have increased from generation to generation, even though initially it had seemed good. Moreover, authoritarian personality included a sense of the rightness of following the lead of the lord immediately above one in the hierarchy. Hence when he acted to disrupt the national hierarchy, it seemed right to follow him; and in doing so one could hope that he would make right what one felt was wrong.

In short, the inability of the social structure of each historical period to satisfy the needs of the personalities of that period led to an oscillation between national integration and localism. Authoritarian personality need not lead to such oscillation; in some traditional societies autonomous regional power persisted through many centuries, and in others when national unity was once attained it did not again give way to localism. Why the alternation between national integration and localism occurred in Japan but not elsewhere does not directly concern us here, and apart from one passing suggestion later I shall not speculate concerning the difference between Japan and other societies which caused it.

The central point of interest here is that the tensions in Japan which caused the oscillation had another effect as well. The social system in which these events occurred could not have seemed wholly right to members of the society at periods of either localism or national integration. Chieftains or lords who felt that something was wrong might use force or political position to increase their power, but the lesser elite were powerless to remedy the lack of respect for their values and status. Therefore they must have become retreatist. Hence we may expect to find retreatism not merely appearing at some one stage but running throughout Japanese history. We may also expect to find, as retreatism worked its effects, a continuing strain of creativity and associated with it some degree of continuing alienation from former values.

A sense that the old order was wanting and a turning away from an old view of the world to an altered one appeared repeatedly in religious beliefs. When the times had been out of joint long enough to cause the appearance of creative individuals, those individuals asked why the spiritual powers had permitted the evil events of the period, and raised questions also about the true nature of the world. This questioning led to repeatedly altered views of the true nature of a good social and spiritual hierarchy, then eventually to the conclusion that the hierarchy itself was a source of evil and that the individual could make contact with spiritual power directly, either by reaching out directly to the gods or by searching within himself. Some time after this stage was reached, clues were seen in the world about that the individual might increase his power by the exercise of creativity in the performance of his daily work. Probably influenced by these clues, even though unconsciously, persons searching the ancient writings found in them evidence that the gods valued the individual's diligence and effectiveness in his occupation. Creative individuals who in this way had come to feel satisfaction in labor in the everyday world exerted their creativity in technological progress and brought about the Japanese industrial revolution.

The sections which follow illustrate this thesis. Men denied status respect and thus gradually alienated from ancient ways channeled their
energies into work, I suggest, partly because they saw opportunities
for creative effort in it, partly because other methods of satisfying their
unease had been tried one after another by their ancestors and found
wanting, and partly because other channels formerly open had been
closed. Hence to present the thesis it is necessary to survey the earlier
periods of Japanese history, not merely the Tokugawa era. Because the
account discusses successive events in Japanese history briefly, at points
it gives the impression of discontinuity. This is false. The great historical
changes in Japan are better described as evolutions from earlier trends
than as new phenomena.

THE EARLY SOCIAL SYSTEM[1]

The Clans

Concerning the events of Japanese history during the first half millennium of the Christian era we have only uncertain legendary accounts,
but we can deduce something of the nature of the social system. It consisted at first of a number of rather large *uji* or clans.[2] The members of
each *uji* thought of themselves as descended from a common ancestor and
worshiped common deities. As in other primitive societies, sacred and
secular rule were not differentiated; the head of the clan was both the
secular ruler and the high priest.

Like other primitive peoples, the Japanese in their search for an
explanation of the events of life believed the world to be dominated by
forces that had wills like their own. Every element of nature that impressed them—sun, tree, rock, insects—was thought to have a will and
power. Each was called *kami*, which is sometimes translated *god*, but which
also means simply *superior*. The Japanese, apparently believing that if the
spiritual powers did not help them gain their desires it was because they
had not been approached in the proper way, devised rituals which they
thought did reflect the proper way and by which they thought the forces
embodied in nature could be influenced to make their fields fertile,
protect them from disease or disaster, give them strength, and so on.

Such a ritualistic religion arises from a sense of inadequacy rather
than a sense of wrongdoing. The gods are asked not how one can atone for
one's sins or avoid sin in the future but how one can achieve more or
acquire more. The compulsion which drives an individual is the need to

---

[1] Except for some aspects of religious change, my summary of pre-Tokugawa
history is based, more than on any other one work, on Edwin O. Reischauer and
John K. Fairbank, *East Asia: The Great Tradition* (A History of East Asian Civilization, Vol. I) (Boston: Houghton Mifflin Co., 1958). The chapters on early China and
those on Japan are primarily by Reischauer.

[2] *Uji* is both the singular and the plural form; these forms of Japanese nouns are
identical.

avoid the shame of having others observe that he is unable to perform the tasks facing him rather than guilt because of a sense of having sinned or anxiety lest he sin in the future.

The dominance of shame rather than guilt as the force controlling individual action is common in primitive societies; it is almost certainly associated with a certain general type of childhood environment before and during the period of the Oedipal crisis. It is one of the remarkable characteristics of Japanese society that even up to the present time behavior has been controlled by shame far more than by guilt.

Japanese Personality and Japanese History

A sense of doubt concerning one's adequacy and an associated sense of shame arise initially in late infancy if the child finds himself unable to do things that he perceives are expected of him by persons who seem to love him. If certain conditions prevail in the Oedipal and later periods, the sense of shame and doubt will be replaced by one of guilt; in other conditions it will dissolve; and in still others it will persist and color the individual's entire life. The nature of the Japanese social structure and culture must have been such from early times until the recent past as to cause the third sort of childhood environment to be repeated generation after generation.[3] The sense of inadequacy and need to obtain guidance create need submission in the individual, but the pain and anxiety suffered also create need dominance and need aggression, in varying proportions and repressed in varying degrees. In short, one type of authoritarian personality emerges.

A person may also be authoritarian even though his personality includes a somewhat larger component of guilt. Japanese authoritarian personality was characterized by a greater predominance of shame and doubt over guilt than authoritarian personality in most other societies has been. It may be that this difference is a cause of the fact that Japanese social structure oscillated between national integration and localism rather than merely proceeding unevenly away from authoritarianism, but this is a highly uncertain speculation whose logic will not be spelled out here.

Emergence of a National Hierarchy

The need submission-dominance in Japanese personality in early times not only caused a hierarchical political and religious structure to appear within many clans; in addition, a hierarchical order began to be recognized among the clans. Within the clans a hierarchy of hereditary political-religious positions held by relatives of the clan leader evolved. Under these officials were hereditary occupational groups, and under them a small number of slaves. Also, before the middle of the first

---

[3] At present there are evidences of basic change.

millennium of the Christian era one of the clans, the Yamato, had won hegemony over an area stretching from western Japan to the Kanto plain around present Tokyo, and had been accorded religious primacy by the clans of this area. The cults of the Yamato clan became the principal cults of the entire land, the Sun Goddess worshiped by the Yamato was accepted as the chief divinity, and belief in the divine descent of the Yamato priest-chief was general. Belief that a divinely connected family headed the polity continued to provide emotional security through the various shifts and transfers of power throughout Japanese history. So great was the respect accorded the imperial family that the family ruling in Yamato days was never displaced (though often deprived of power). All Japanese emperors to the present time are direct lineal descendants of the Yamato.

NATIONAL INTEGRATION, DISRUPTION, AND REINTEGRATION: THE FIRST CYCLE, EARLY TIMES TO 710

The Yamato suzerainty continued for some generations and, loose though it was, may be regarded as the first interval of national integration. We do not know its precise duration.

Disruption of National Power

The aggressiveness of the Japanese elites was too great for them to find roles within a hierarchy of authority satisfying. In two ways, as time went on, they created political disorder. There was no clear rule of succession, and more often than not in the fifth and sixth centuries the death of an emperor was followed by a war of succession. Moreover, by the sixth century clans other than the Yamato had become so powerful that they dominated the activity of the court. The power of the emperor had declined and had become largely symbolic. The rivalry among the clans became a central fact of Japanese political life. There is no evidence that national government broke down completely, but clearly the power of local lords increased.

These changes must have occurred in spite of fervent pleas to the gods that they be prevented. In these circumstances (presumably after a period of retreatism) the belief of many of the elite in the acceptability to the gods of their traditional rituals broke down, and they searched for new ways of gaining the favors and averting the displeasure of the spirits. It is not strange that they grasped at methods learned from China, for they had had long contact with China and respected its civilization as more ancient, more developed, and more powerful than theirs. Slow cultural borrowing from China had gone on since at least the first century, but in the sixth century it was as if a crisis of faith occurred and the Japanese grasped with special urgency at new religious rituals.

In any event, when the practices of Buddhism, which had earlier reached Korea, were brought from Korea to Japan at about the middle of the sixth century, they were accepted rapidly by the elites of the court and of various clan centers and then by the emperor. While the emperor and some clan leaders gained a scholarly understanding of the Buddhist teachings, most practitioners adopted merely Buddhist rituals, not Buddhist philosophy and ethics. Supposedly the simple folk of a clan followed the lead of their clan chief, but apparently in reality they continued animistic and shamanistic practices as before. The native religion, which had been nameless, became known as Shinto, to distinguish it from the new one.

Governmental Reform

The new creativity, if it was that, affected political structure in the following century. The emperor and the elite no longer took their political structure for granted. They groped for improvement. Reforms introduced by the emperor were gradually accepted in large part by the powerful clan chiefs. Not until the eighth century were they put into effect throughout Japan. Like the new religious rituals, the reforms were adapted from Chinese models.

The reformers adopted the Chinese concept of an omnipotent emperor ruling over the land, adding to it their own concept that the emperor was a priest of divine origin. He began to be called "Tenno" or "Heavenly Emperor." New elaborate rituals were introduced at the court, as though the court felt the need for more efficacious forms. A formal structure of hierarchy among the elite was established. In a simplified version of the Chinese pattern the Japanese created eight ranks of nobles, with subdivisions which provided 26 grades in all, and classed every governmental post in one of these ranks. Imitating the educational system of China, they also set up a central university to which they sent all young men destined to become court officials.

Previously each emperor had established his court wherever he chose. Typically he did so where he had lived before he became emperor. However, the more elaborate court machinery now created could not be moved around readily, and in the eighth century for this and other reasons a permanent court was established. The place was Nara, in central Japan. The period 710–784, when the reforms had their maximum effect, is therefore known as the Nara period.

In 784 the emperor moved the center of government from Nara to a nearby site, probably to escape the powerful influence of the monasteries at Nara, and in 794 set it up at Heian (present Kyoto), and so the long ensuing period, 794–1185, is known as the Heian period.

During the Nara period a far more clearly structured hierarchy than before was imposed on government throughout Japan as well as on the court. The country was divided into provinces, districts, units consisting of about three villages, and at the base units of five families, each responsible for the behavior of its members. Over each province a governor was appointed.

The most important function of the new hierarchy of officials was to administer the land tax. Land throughout the country was declared to be the property of the central government. The holders of each parcel and the legal claims on the produce from it were recorded. The owner's share of the produce was declared due to the emperor, and this interpretation was apparently accepted by local lords. However, as is noted below, the emperor received little of the revenue.

As in China, short-term conscription of peasants to form a national army was introduced. However, since Japan had no need for a large army these troops became primarily a labor corps, and before the end of the eighth century the practice was abandoned.

With the adoption of these reforms, national rule was again strengthened.

THE SECOND CYCLE: THE NARA AND HEIAN PERIODS, 710–1185

Durability of the Reform Government

Even though historical accounts often stress the subsequent breakdown of the governmental structure, it was remarkably long-lasting compared with the duration of governmental institutions in the Western world. After the war over the imperial succession in 672, except for one flare-up in 764 there were no major civil disturbances until after the year 1000; and although the central government gradually lost control over the localities, the civil disturbances that developed later did not directly threaten it until 1156. This period of five centuries without a break in the national administration is amazingly long when compared with any similar period in the history of say the Roman Empire or in the modern world. During this period the total area under cultivation in Japan increased considerably, and the government extended its authority over the southern part of the southern island of Kyushu and over the Ainu people at the northern end of the main island of Honshu.

Since the reforms curtailed the powers of the clan chiefs, and since the emperor had little physical power by which to impose them, their success must be due in large part to the fact that localism made the clan chiefs themselves feel uneasy. They felt the need for restoration of a hierarchy. However, other factors also help to explain the acceptance of the reforms. One of these was their Chinese origin.

Disruption and the Rise of Localism

Another was the fact that the Chinese system had been modified to make it consistent with deeply ingrained Japanese values. Yet the modifications made for this purpose contained the seeds of disruption. Appointment to the Chinese bureaucracy was on the basis of examinations in Chinese literature, but attendance at the Japanese university was only a sort of ritual through which all must pass; appointment to the various grades of governmental positions was on the basis of hereditary social rank, not educational achievement. Also, it was impossible or seemed improper to deprive local aristocrats of their lands, and they were appointed to district positions and their old revenues from their lands allotted to them as salary.

Provincial officials were appointed from the middle social ranks. The status of these positions did not satisfy them, and the appointments were used to gain more power by enriching oneself and one's family out of tax revenues or by means of gifts from families whom one exempted from land taxes. It became common for an influential member of the central aristocracy to obtain appointment to a post as governor of a province and to benefit from the financial advantages of the post without performing its duties and indeed without leaving the capital, a parallel with the holding of benefices by absentee church officials in medieval England, which is only one of a remarkable series of similarities between Japanese and English history.

Thus a central concept of the Chinese system, divorce of the bureaucracy from local loyalties, was eliminated. Instead, many offices were placed in the hands of men whose central motivation was not the success of national governmental administration but increase in their own power at the expense of the national government.

The system progressively weakened the national government in another respect. As has been noted, lands of the local aristocracy were in effect tax free. Moreover, to encourage the extension of cultivation newly developed lands were exempted from taxes. The tax burden fell more heavily on peasants who had not obtained exemption. For this reason and perhaps also because position outside of the structure of the hierarchy made them uneasy, peasants increasingly put themselves under the tax-free estates and paid feudal dues to the local landed class rather than heavier taxes to the government. The landed estates thus grew in number and size, though they remained much smaller than the earlier *uji* had been. These developments progressively deprived the central government of revenues, and its position deteriorated because of progressive financial starvation which it was unable to reverse.

Changes in the Local Governmental Structure

Locally, a classification of four levels of status developed. At the base were the cultivators, who included both the former free men or "good people" and the slaves or "low born," the line between them having largely disappeared. Next were holders of several levels of managerial positions on the estates. Above them were the owners of estates, who were local aristocrats, court aristocrats, or monasteries. Above them, if they were not sufficiently powerful to protect their own interests at court, were persons who were influential enough to do so. In feudal fashion, each of the four classes had its right to receive a fixed share of the annual produce of the estate. As the power and functions of the central government deteriorated, the second and third of these four classes, the managers and owners, became more important. Many of these men now rising in power were descendants of the *uji* aristocracy. In a measure they were regaining the status their ancestors had once had.

As the central government ceased to be able to preserve order, the managers and owners of the estates organized small armies of mounted warriors in order to protect themselves against disorder and encroachment by their fellows. These bands appeared in the eleventh century and possibly earlier and were conspicuous in the twelfth. The leader of each was an aristocrat who because of his position or power or perhaps his personal prowess attracted followers. An individual with sufficient income from land to provide himself with horse and armor swore personal allegiance to the leader and became his samurai, or retainer (the word literally means "servant"), or in the feudal terminology of Europe his vassal. That is, out of the breakdown of central government, the need to organize for local strength, and the role played by claims on land in providing the resources which made the relationship possible there arose the main characteristics of feudal relationships as known in Europe.

Many Buddhist sects had sprung up during the Nara period, and groups within them had established monasteries, especially in the vicinity of Nara. As religious groups they were exempt from taxation. They acquired control of large amounts of land during the following century or two, no doubt by inducements parallel to those by which the secular estates grew. Within each sect there developed a hierarchy of command parallel to that on the estates. Monasteries and perhaps other religious groups established their own armed forces, at least as early as the secular aristocrats, and engaged in feudal warfare. From the late eleventh century until they were crushed late in the sixteenth century the monastic armies repeatedly descended on Kyoto to coerce the government. That formation of armed forces by a monastery and their use largely for aggrandizement of the monastic group involved no conflict with religious principles indicates one of the differences between the shame culture of Japan and the guilt culture of western Europe.

Thus disruption of national government progressed. Armed conflict appeared throughout the country beginning in the eleventh century, and even in Kyoto itself robbery and depredations by outlaws became serious problems.

Social Unease

We have no direct evidence of the unease, the sense of lack of status respect, which these manipulations and conflicts among the higher elite and the widespread civil disorder must have caused. However, during the four centuries of the Heian period basic changes in world view occurred which could hardly have been caused except through retreatism and then emergence from it with the capacity to search creatively for new values and cognitions that might be more satisfying than the old.

During these centuries the observance of Buddhism in the court came to be concerned almost wholly with rituals, magical prayers, and the creation and appreciation of works of art. Outside the court the old was salvaged without sacrifice of the new by a process of interpreting each Shinto deity as a manifestation under a different name of a Buddhist deity. Buddhist traditions thus became blended with Shinto.[4]

However, at the same time a change of far greater import occurred, the beginning of abandonment of belief in the social hierarchy. It appeared first in a new concept of the nature of salvation and the path to it. Buddhism as originally formulated in India by Gautama and his disciples had taught the doctrine of Nirvana, peace gained by divesting oneself of all desire. This concept, however, has little meaning in a shame culture, and so it disappeared from early Buddhism in Japan. Nirvana was converted to a life after death much like the Christian heaven, and reincarnation was converted to a doctrine that after death one would go either to heaven or to hell.

A Pure Land sect in China had been teaching these concepts since the end of the fourth century. (The Pure Land is heaven.) The doctrine of heaven which is easy of access met the needs of the simple folk of Japan who during the Heian period no longer felt emotional assurance that their traditional view of the nature of the spiritual world was a true one. In the tenth century the monk Kuya taught that one can gain salvation by prayer to Amida Buddha. It is difficult to know whether this was a doctrine of faith or one of ritual, but in popular belief it clearly became ritual. By the beginning of the eleventh century it was widely believed that one could attain rebirth into the Pure Land at death, not by the old primitive rituals, it is true, but by a more elevated one which however turns out to be much the same sort of thing, calling on the name of the Buddha in a chant.

This doctrine constituted a partial abandonment of old animistic faiths. It constituted also a turning from traditional emphasis on the group as the source of emotional security toward individualism; for while up to the Nara period one had practiced ritual for the sake of one's village, one's family, or one's dead ancestors, now one practiced ritual for one's own salvation. Far more important than either of these changes, however, it constituted a view of the individual as not needing to depend on a hierarchy. While the efficacy of previous rituals had depended on the inter-

---

[4] That the Japanese gods were regarded as manifestations of the foreign ones, and not the reverse, is evidence of the prestige which attached to the imported religion.

On the Theory of Social Change

cession of religious intermediaries, now the individual himself, unaided, might gain contact with the spiritual powers.

The doctrine of attainment of heaven by calling on Amida Buddha was taught in the monk Genshin's *Essentials of Salvation*, which long circulated orally and was put into print by the early thirteenth century or earlier. Much of Genshin's book is occupied with descriptions of the horrors of hell and pleasures of paradise. Genshin's popularly satisfying reinterpretations of religious doctrine became the central concepts of later Japanese popular Buddhism and are very popular in Japan today.

At the beginning of the twelfth century a singing monk, Ryonin, modified Genshin's doctrine to liberalize the requirements for salvation even more. One man's calling on the name of Amida Buddha, he taught, would benefit others. He attracted followers who formed a new sect. His teaching was in the tradition of the philosophy of all-in-one and one-in-all, which had been taught in Japan from at least the Nara period, and which in turn was a natural outgrowth of traditional dependence of the individual on the group. It is reasonable to suppose that the attractiveness of his doctrine lay in the fact that if one believed it one could seek salvation without compromising one's traditional obligations to the group.

A change in world view also arising out of new awareness of the individual, though on the surface it seems opposed in nature to that just sketched, became conspicuous in the following era but apparently first emerged late in the Heian period. This was the concept of the limitless debt which one owes to one's superiors. The doctrine emerged that one's family, one's lord, one's country, and the gods had conferred on one a blessing infinite in extent by bringing one into being, rearing one, and giving one the opportunity to live. One must recognize the infinite obligation one owes in return and work all one's life to repay it.[5]

This doctrine is a verbalization and rationalization of the individual's sense of inadequacy mentioned above. Its significance lies partly in the fact that for the first time religious thinkers were sufficiently aware of their own unconscious needs to let them come to the surface, analyze them, and make a system of them. This development reflected an awareness of self as a system not previously found in Japanese religious thinking, and although in this case the consciousness of self was fully reconciled with the old hierarchical system, it could be expected to have more revolutionary results in the future.

One radical implication lay in the concept that the individual owed a moral obligation to the superior powers. For this concept could not appear until religious leaders had become sufficiently empathic to conceive of their fellow individuals as having worth. One cannot conceive of in-

---

[5] The infinite blessing was known as *on*, the infinite obligation as *hoon*. In *The Chrysanthemum and the Sword* (Boston: Houghton Mifflin Co., 1946), Ruth Benedict portrays the place which this sense of obligation has in Japanese national character. While her sketch is based mainly on more recent materials, the personality type she outlines seems to be similar in essence to one that began to appear at this time.

dividuals as owing an obligation to the spiritual powers unless one also conceives of individuals as being valuable enough so that the gods care what attitudes they have. Thus although the new concept has often been interpreted as subordinating the individual, in fact it marks the appearance in the Japanese culture of a new sense of the worth of the individual.

Two new elements of religious faith which appeared either at this time or in the following century in the thinking of religious intellectuals must have been fairly closely related to this change in world view. One of these is a change in the meaning of the concept of purity. Purity had long been stressed in the Shinto sects; it had long been believed that the gods would receive a suppliant only if he came with purity. However, purity had been conceived of as physical and ritual purity. Now it was conceived that the purity which pleased the gods was purity of heart and behavior, a concept clearly not unrelated to that of recognizing one's obligations. The second, which appeared among Buddhist teachers, was the concept that faith, not rituals, wins one salvation. Although the concept of purity did not enter into Buddhist doctrine, the closely related one of right attitude did. If the right attitude is an inner matter, not a matter of observance of appropriate rituals, then rituals cannot gain one salvation after death, not even the ritual of calling on the name of Buddha. Neither can one's own deeds if it is impossible even by a lifetime of striving to repay the obligation one owes to the gods for bringing one into being and nurturing one. But faith may do so; and so these reformers accepted the nobler version of the Pure Land doctrine, that salvation comes through faith in the Buddha. The appearance of these doctrines is surely associated with a growing sense of the worth of the individual; an individual who can gain acceptance merely by being pure, or who will be accepted if he has faith, is clearly an individual of more consequence than an individual who gains acceptance by the gods by going through certain forms. The changes are also undoubtedly associated with the appearance of an increased sense of guilt in personality. Only persons who feel guilt will worry about their purity or inner attitude. Thus the appearance of these doctrines must be associated with change in childhood environment in some groups. In the world view underlying these doctrines can be seen the seeds of destruction of traditional social structure. The doctrines themselves were too esoteric to gain wide popular acceptance, but they became important among religious intellectuals.

Reintegration

The social tensions which brought these changes in world view also brought a new movement for national unification.[6] In the twelfth century, after a generation of conflict between two collateral branches of the imperial house for control of the court, two men of great military ability

---

[6] This statement does not imply an ability on the part of the writer to trace the precise relationship between the change in world view and the political change. It merely implies that both changes resulted from the social tensions of the time.

emerged from a provincial family that belonged to one of the branches. In a few years they not merely defeated the other branch and gained control of the court but also established mastery throughout the country. These men, natives of Kamakura, near present Tokyo, were Minamoto Yoritomo and his younger brother.[7] By 1185 Yoritomo was ruler of almost all of Japan. Soon thereafter he established control of the remaining area.

THE THIRD CYCLE: THE FEUDAL PERIOD, 1185–1600

With Yoritomo's ascent to power there began another cycle of integrated national government, decay of national power, localism, and reintegration. Yoritomo had himself appointed shogun, or generalissimo, a title that had been used occasionally before and now was to be used almost continuously until 1867. He arranged the murder of relatives who might become rivals (including his younger brother). The result was the extinction of his line, for when he died his oldest son was seventeen and unable to defend his position. However, one of Yoritomo's retainers defeated rival claimants for power and preserved a unified national political structure. It continued to exist for 150 years. Both Yoritomo and his successors, the Hōjō family, maintained their headquarters at Kamakura rather than moving to Kyoto.

Political Structure of the Kamakura Period

The new period of integration differed from previous ones in several characteristics. One of these lay in the nature of the cement which held the structure together. The Yamato suzerainty had depended primarily on a religious concept of the office of emperor, and the unification of the Nara and Heian periods on an elaborate court structure, national bureaucracy, and tax system imported from China. The first had failed because it was possible to offer reverence to the emperor without granting him power, and the second because Japanese traditional social relationships had eroded the tax and bureaucratic system. In this third attempt to hold the nation together the cement used was the new or newly enhanced sense of obligation of a samurai to serve his lord loyally. The early Kamakura rulers, sharing and taking advantage of this concept of personal obligation, appointed to key positions men who had advanced in power and social position as their retainers and relied upon the dependence of these men on their lord and their sense of obligation to him to keep them faithful. A structure much like that of feudal Europe emerged.

Japanese tradition kept it from becoming fully feudal or fully integrated. Yoritomo and the Hōjō took estates from their rivals and appointed their own warriors as owners or managers. However, it was neces-

---

[7] Minamoto is the family name. Throughout this chapter, in citing Japanese names I shall give the family name first, in the Japanese style.

sary to permit court nobles, the imperial family, and monasteries in the area of the capital to retain their lands. Moreover, the old imperial administration continued to function, and in theory Yoritomo's men received their estates from the court. Thus there was no sharp break with former practices.

Yoritomo established a more closely knit national administration than had existed in the earlier periods of national integration by appointing one of his henchmen to be a steward on each estate except some of the estates, where the claim of imperial privilege prevented their placement. The steward received a share of the estate's produce, saw to the proper division of the rest of the produce, and was responsible for the preservation of order on the estate, the prosecution of criminals, the judicial function, and the administrative activities of local government. As was inevitable in Japan, positions as steward were made hereditary. Hence, even though in theory someone else owned the land, the stewards became much like feudal lords.

Yoritomo also appointed one man in each province to be supervisor over the stewards of the province. This office, called that of protector, also became hereditary. Through these officials and through the supreme court and administrative bodies set up at Kamakura, the Kamakura shoguns administered stern but impartial justice, which is said to be an important element in the acceptance of their rule for 1½ centuries.

The central shogunal administration was notable for the placing of top administrative and judicial power in boards rather than single officials, so that both authority and responsibility were collective rather than individual. Collective decision making became a conspicuous feature of Japanese behavior; it has continued to the present time. Today, even in many large business corporations, no one administrative official either is responsible or receives credit for any given decision.[8] It may be suspected that everyone concerned, including the owners of the business, knows which individuals made which suggestions and are responsible for various actions, but formally individual responsibility is avoided. In a culture in which shame is as important as in the Japanese, so that the danger of awareness by others that one has made a mistaken decision might paralyze the will to act, in retrospect the appearance of collective authority and responsibility seems inevitable; but why it first became conspicuous in the national administration at this time rather than earlier or later is difficult to explain. (It may have existed earlier without being so formalized as to be evident in the historical records.)

Changes in Values and World Cognition

The radical changes in values and world cognition which had budded during the Heian period flowered now. Though three new manifestations

---

[8] This generalization is made on the basis of James C. Abegglen's book, *The Japanese Factory* (Glencoe, Ill.: Free Press of Glencoe, Inc., 1958), and of conversations of the writer with Japanese business executives.

are markedly dissimilar in specific content, each reflects a sense of man's worth and proposes a hypothesis about the relationship between men and the spiritual powers which is far more orderly than that of the old animistic ritualistic faiths. Each, then, reflects the creativity which was gradually to undermine the foundations of the traditional order.

One of these was the adoption by the warrior class of a modified form of Chinese Ch'an (Zen) Buddhism. The new doctrine had two main elements. One was great stress on the virtue of physical bravery and loyalty. This, I think, may be regarded as primarily an intellectualization of need submission-dominance, arising from introspection into the unconscious processes of the mind. The other major element was the precept to meditate or free one's mind from the web of thought in order to gain insight. By doing so, it was taught, one might learn virtue and gain peace and salvation. I suggest that this emphasis also arises from new-found awareness of the unconscious processes of the mind; it is based on recognition that there are powerful unconscious processes that may rise to consciousness if one is able to remove the obstacles one puts in the way. The two strands of Zen Buddhism, then, while superficially little related, in fact are intimately interconnected.

The second important change was the emergence of greater awareness of the simple folk by those above them. This awareness appears in literature, in religion, and, as will be noted in the following section of this chapter, in social structure as well. In the year 1175, a decade before the beginning of the Kamakura period, the monk Honen had founded a Pure Land sect. Together with a True Pure Land sect and lesser offshoots of the two, it gained great popularity among the simple folk during the Kamakura period, popularity which continues today. The new religious leaders, following the logic of direct contact of the simple folk with divinity to its conclusion, taught the undesirability of the clerical structure that had developed in the old Buddhist sects and of the esoteric position and rites of the clergy. They therefore advocated the abolition of monasteries, advocated and practiced marriage for the clergy, and translated the Buddhist scriptures into simple Japanese.[9] These teachings and practices are all remarkably similar to those of the popular religious reformers in England a century later. The abandonment by the Pure Land sects of dependence on hierarchy in favor of the doctrine of direct access to grace is a change which seems eventually to occur wherever the elites of the social hierarchy have denied status respect to those below them for a sufficiently long time, and a change which in England as in Japan was a forerunner of individual action to prove one's worth.

I suggest that deviant individuals made more creative by the social

---

[9] The Pure Land doctrine of salvation by dependence on the power of another (*tariki*) and the doctrine of self-help (*jiriki*) held by all other sects are commonly contrasted. *Jiriki* is stressed in Zen Buddhism.

pressures sketched above preached these new doctrines, for with creativity goes empathy, an ability to appreciate the attitudes of others. On the other hand, the simple folk accepted the new doctrines because their perception that the elites had little regard for them had in time, through retreatism, both alienated them from old values and made a direct contact with grace rather than one through a hierarchy especially attractive.

The True Pure Land sect separated from the parent sect because Shinran, a disciple of Honen, more or less unintentionally advocated new principles. Reciting the name of Amida Buddha, Shinran taught, will not bring salvation. Salvation in this degenerate age, he said, can be attained only by faith. Faith in turn causes one to call on Amida Buddha. Here again one sees evidence that a sense of sin, that is, of guilt, was entering the culture.

A third change in world view was the appearance of the doctrine of the greatness and rightness of Japanese religion freed from Chinese incrustations and truly interpreted. The monk Nichiren, who preached the new faith, denounced the doctrines of all other sects, old and new, as leading only to damnation. He was, so to speak, the Calvin of a shame culture. His sect grew in size and has remained of importance to the present. Following one strain of Buddhist tradition, Nichiren taught that heaven is in this world; there is no other paradise. To him, "this world" meant Japan, and his preaching contained an important element of mystical faith in and reverence for Japan. While he made no attack on the Buddhist system, the logic of his teachings, carried further, would constitute a basic attack on the feudal hierarchy which by its conduct interfered with devotion to Japan as such. Though he spoke in the name of tradition, he too was unwittingly undermining the traditional order.

Collapse of the Shogunate: The Ashikaga Period, 1333–1568

Thus the aggression of the feudal lords was leading at long last to loss of faith in hierarchical organization of the society. The new world view among the warrior class weakened the position of the shogunate, for each warrior felt obligation to his immediate lord and above that in a symbolic sense to the emperor, but certainly not to the Hōjō, who after all had little claim to the shogunate except that they had proved stronger than other nobles. The new world view of the simple folk, even though it pointed to the rightness of national unity, also weakened faith in the Hōjō and had no alternative national organization to suggest. Thus the immediate social change was collapse of the national government and increase in the power of the local feudal lords.

As generations passed, provincial lords grew in independent strength, and in the fourteenth century national integration was disrupted as it had been at the end of the Yamato period and again at the end of the Heian. After warfare among the lords, in 1333 a leader of the Ashikaga family emerged with sufficient power to have himself named shogun, established his government at Kyoto, and the Kamakura period came to an end. The national political structure fell apart, however, for the Ashikaga did not gain control over the lords throughout Japan. The managers and owners of the estates and the stewards and protectors owed nothing to the Ashikaga, and the Ashikaga did not have enough power to coerce many of them. After an outbreak of warfare in the middle of the fifteenth century even the semblance of national government virtually disappeared. For a century local lords intermittently waged warfare among themselves. Localism assumed a more extreme form than it had in either previous cycle; Japan became virtually a group of separate countries.

As national power disintegrated, the local political structure became more tightly knit in some respects and changed in a number of others. The stewards who had been established on the estates by Yoritomo became increasingly squeezed economically by the division of the income of each among multiple male descendants. Their power often declined accordingly, and as it declined that of the provincial protectors rose. A number of them and other individuals who had succeeded in grasping power over considerable areas became veritable little kings whose more powerful status than that of earlier feudal lords earned them the new name of daimyo.

The object lesson of the dilution of power by division of income among a number of children was so persuasive, and the freedom of these more creative individuals from tradition so sufficient, that the daimyo adopted the practice of transmission of property to one son only, not necessarily the oldest if he was not the most competent, and indeed not necessarily a natural son at all. The practice arose of adopting a son if none of one's own sons seemed capable of handling the task which was to be passed on to someone. The preservation of the entity and of the family as a symbol had become more important than the welfare of one's begotten children.

The estates of court nobles and members of the imperial family were gradually absorbed by daimyo. The result was to make the fiefs of the daimyo, which came to be called *hans*, more compact, and at the same time to reduce to nullity the already diminished position and influence of the court.

As these changes occurred, a number of social changes occurred within the fiefs.

The positions of estate managers ceased to have their former importance since the estates were no longer political units of importance but instead had been absorbed within the larger territories of the daimyo. Conversely, the units of a few contiguous villages that had existed since the days of the Yamato reformers became of greater importance since often they were natural units, having a common interest in a source of water, an irrigation system, an ancient shrine, or some other focus of local life. The descendants of many men who had had managerial positions of some level on the estates became more distant from the higher nobility and closer to the villagers than heretofore. They tended to become the village headmen and to hold these positions as hereditary ones, becoming, as Reischauer puts it, "more an upper crust of peasant society than the bottom stratum of the feudal system, as they had previously been."[10]

At the same time the simple folk attained a somewhat new status in society, more important and less detached from the nobility than their position at any previous time.

As in an earlier period the lords turned to mass armies of lightly armed foot soldiers recruited from among the simple folk. Presumably the most adventurous and aggressive members of the simple folk became soldiers. The mounted soldiers now associated with the foot soldiers, not as officers and men, but as cooperating elements in a common army; and the sharp social distinction which had formerly existed between knights and the simple folk was replaced by a gradation within which there was no longer a single clear line. With this blurring of class lines it became possible for able and lucky commoners to rise to high position by demonstration of ability in the army. Though the occurrence was rare, a few became landed aristocrats.

Individual villages or units composed of several villages became largely self-governing, the daimyo being content so long as the village provided its taxes and labor services. Peasants in the villages became freer of feudal restraints than they had been previously.

The new sense of the simple folk that they had some freedom to act in their own interest manifested itself in other ways as well. Village rioting in the fifteenth century against pawnbrokers and moneylenders when the financial situation seemed unjust and unbearable became both fairly common and effective; it led to repeated orders by the shogunate forgiving the villagers their debts. More striking, some towns deposed local petty owners and became quasi-independent. Most though not all of these were communities of religious groups, notably the True Pure Land and Nichiren sects.

A common thread runs through the story of these changes: a new awareness by the elite of the individuals beneath them, and a new awareness by individuals of their own worth and potential.

Economic Change

Thus by the Ashikaga period many men had lost their ancient faith in the hierarchical social order, and, more important, their sense of a need to depend on it. They felt ability to make direct contact with a source of grace, and they looked for new ways to gain satisfactory status and identity. It might be expected that the search would channel the energies of many individuals into economic prowess as well as into prowess of

[10] *East Asia: The Great Tradition*, p. 576.

other kinds, and that their creativity would lead to technical progress. For income and wealth were symbols of status in feudal Japan as elsewhere, and whereas many men might gain a sense of achievement and identity in careers in the armed forces, leadership in peasant movements, or intellectual life, surely for many others these channels were less available than economic achievement. With the important exceptions of a broad base of scientific knowledge and long experience in metallurgy, the major ingredients that later led to the Industrial Revolution in England were present, though in lesser degree.

And the economic change that might have been expected did occur. Reischauer states that through changes in agricultural methods production per acre doubled and even tripled in many places during the Ashikaga period, a period of 125 years.[11] This is an impressive rate of change. The average for the country of course was less, but it was considerable, for the handicraft industries expanded greatly, an indication not only of improvements in techniques but also of a rising level of income with which to purchase handicraft products. Trade flourished; a class of wholesale and retail merchants developed. Between the twelfth and fifteenth centuries the use of money became fairly general. To resist local restrictions and obtain monopoly rights, handicraft workers and traders organized into groups somewhat resembling the guilds of Europe. For the first time towns that were purely commercial centers and not primarily political centers appeared. Trade with Korea and China became of considerable importance, and before the end of the sixteenth century Japanese mariners were sailing regularly as far south as the Malay Peninsula. They brought home both new types of goods and information about the advance of the Europeans around Asia.

A Portuguese ship sailed into a Japanese port in 1543. Thereafter Portuguese ships arrived fairly frequently, and from the Portuguese the Japanese received new plants, such as tobacco and potatoes, mechanical products, firearms, and new techniques of manufacturing, though in their techniques the Japanese were very little behind Europe. Economic change was accelerated by the contact.

This technical progress is impressive evidence that economic growth depends less on modern science and more on the presence of favoring values and motivations than has commonly been supposed. I suggest that the Japanese industrial revolution began not in the Meiji era but in the Ashikaga era. For the progress was not abortive. It continued without serious interruption during the ensuing Tokugawa era. It was not rapid during that era both because Tokugawa rule, which created some incentives, also imposed some barriers and because the development of skills in metallurgy and underlying knowledge of physics and chemistry would in any event have required a long period. It is difficult to know whether

---

[11] *Ibid.*, p. 557.

on balance Tokugawa rule accelerated or retarded the process. During its closing decades it certainly impeded advance. But the rushing tide of technological progress which appeared after the Meiji Restoration of 1868 was not a new current in Japanese life; it was only the surging forth of an old one after it had broken through political barriers.

Acceptance of Christianity

The Portuguese were as interested in missionary activity as in trade. They gained converts to Christianity at a rate that testifies to the continuing tensions within Japanese personality. The number of Christians in Japan has been estimated at 150,000 in 1582, 300,000 by 1600, and perhaps 500,000, or one in 40 of the total population of perhaps 20 million, in 1615.[12]

The central doctrine of Christianity is the death of Christ in atonement for human sin, and that doctrine appeals only to men who feel a sense of guilt. Hence the eager acceptance of Christianity may seem to be evidence of the widespread presence of a sense of guilt in Japan by the sixteenth century. One must be wary of accepting this conclusion, however, for if the Christian doctrine is altered to the idea that Christ died not to atone for sin but to gain salvation for men in spite of their inability to fulfill all of their obligations during life, then Christianity becomes hardly more than another of the popular versions of Buddhism. So, apparently, it was widely regarded. It came with great prestige, as the Chinese religions had earlier, for the Japanese had become well aware of the power of the Europeans through their maritime activity. The new religion, eager individuals might hope, would be more effective than the older doctrines in relieving the sense of inadequacy that tormented them.

Perhaps the greatest social significance of the rapid spread of Christianity is its indication that the Japanese did not regard their world as a good one, and were ready for still another change in social structure.

National Unification, 1568–1600

The trends within Buddhism which were implicitly inconsistent with the dominance of the Hōjō over the emperor were much more sharply inconsistent with localism, for, while the sects were in conflict with each other, the doctrines of all involved a view of Japan as a religious unit. The economic changes too worked against localism, for they created a greater degree of economic contact among the regions of Japan than had ever existed earlier. However, when national integration came, it came with a feudal structure as before, but with new mechanisms which the leaders hoped would make the structure more lasting.

The movement toward integration began in 1560 with the rise of a minor daimyo, Oda Nobunaga. In 1568 Nobunaga captured Kyoto, and

---

[12] The estimates of the numbers of Christians are from *ibid.*, p. 582, and that of population from *ibid.*, p. 629.

thereafter he controlled the adjacent area. Conscious of the trouble repeatedly caused by the monasteries near the capital, he devoted a major
effort to destroying their military strength and temporal power, and by
his death in 1582 he had largely done so. His ablest general, Hideyoshi,
who succeeded him, completed the task, and the monasteries were never
again of political significance.

Hideyoshi had conquered all of Japan by 1590. After his death in 1598
a capable vassal, Tokugawa Ieyasu, won out in a military struggle for
power, the crucial battle being that at Sekigahara in 1600, and the Tokugawa era began.

THE TOKUGAWA ERA, 1600–1867

In 1603 Ieyasu re-established the shogunate, which had been allowed
to lapse by Nobunaga. From then until 1867 members of the Tokugawa
family were shoguns. Ieyasu and his successors maintained as the seat of
their rule the village of Edo (now Tokyo), in which Ieyasu had begun
to build a castle before his accession to national power, and which was
conveniently removed from Kyoto.

The Tokugawa knew well the difficulties of integrated national government in Japan, and they attempted to perpetuate their power by
measures different from those that had failed in the past. Ieyasu took over
some of Hideyoshi's measures, and between 1600 and 1651 Ieyasu and
his son Hidetada and grandson Iemitsu executed a series of further
measures designed to freeze Japan in the existing social mold, prevent
the rise of a local military leader such as had ended each previous period
of national rule, and perpetuate the rule of the Tokugawa.

The Tokugawa System

While the Tokugawa wished to curb the daimyo, tradition prevented
eliminating them. Even though Tokugawa hegemony was conceded by
all, a movement to wipe out the fief governments would no doubt have
provoked a successful rebellion. Instead, the Tokugawa set barriers
around and between the daimyo. They divided them into three major
categories: the *shimpan* daimyo, most closely related by blood to the Tokugawa; the *fudai* or "hereditary" daimyo, with a few exceptions those
who had recognized Ieyasu as their overlord before 1600; and the *tozama*
or "outer" daimyo, those who formally had been co-ordinate with Ieyasu
in 1600. Within this group were former allies, neutrals, and enemies who
might be enemies again. Many of the Tokugawa measures were directed
at holding the *tozama* daimyo forever in safe relationships.

Thus when occasion or pretext permitted, the Tokugawa accused a
too powerful daimyo of disloyalty, executed him, moved his heir to lands
farther from Edo and probably reduced in area, and placed one of the
fudai daimyo on his former lands. They kept the fiefs of *fudai* and *shim-*

pan daimyo small in size so that their power depended on their relationship to the Tokugawa, almost completely filled the region of Japan near Edo with them, and also scattered them among the *tozama* daimyos farther away from Edo to serve as the eyes of the Tokugawa. While the Tokugawa dared not encroach unduly on the internal administration of the fiefs, they did create inspectors who spied upon it. They forbade intermarriage or any mutual contacts among the daimyo, and also forbade them to enlarge their military establishments or engage in any construction without Tokugawa permission.

Payments from the daimyo to the Tokugawa were small, were controlled by custom, and were not increased. However, both to get projects executed and to burden the more powerful *tozama* daimyo, the Tokugawa on occasion conferred on one or another of them the honor of constructing a large civil work or defense project or supporting for a period of years the armed forces defending a section of the coast. An unanticipated effect was to increase the technical capability of these daimyo. To execute these policies the Tokugawa created a large bureaucracy known as the *Bakufu*. It was financed by the revenues from Tokugawa lands, which became very large in area through confiscations of land from various daimyo.

Hideyoshi had moved to prevent the blurring of social class lines by forcing all peasants to surrender their swords, thus establishing a clear line between sword-carrying nobles and non-sword-carrying commoners. He had also prohibited many types of occupational shifts among the four social classes of samurai, peasants, artisans, and laborers. Ieyasu extended this social legislation by decreeing a definite order of social ranking, farmers being next to samurai because agriculture was regarded as the economic basis of life, and merchants being at the bottom because they were regarded as nonproductive. The prohibition against shifts among the occupations of farming, handicrafts, and trade were not strictly enforced, but a sharp line between these groups and the samurai was maintained.

To keep the emperor from becoming the focus of a hostile alliance a development that on several previous occasions had broken the power of a shogunate, the Tokugawa isolated him. They left him and his court at Kyoto, surrounded him, and permitted approach to him only through Tokugawa intermediaries, who carried messages in and replies out.

Of all the domestic measures of the Tokugawa to preserve their power *sankin kotai* was the capstone. This was the requirement that the wife and children of every daimyo live in Edo under Tokugawa supervision, and that the daimyo himself maintain his residence there half of the time, in most cases every other year. Daimyo traditionally had made pilgrimages to present their respects to the current shogun and often had left their families in his care, so that *sankin kotai* was only a generalization and systematization of established usage. Its primary purpose, of course, was to have hostages against revolt. However, in combination with the distant location of some of the major *tozama* daimyo at the western tip of the main island of Honshu and on the farther islands of Kyushu and Shikoku it was also intended to impose heavy expenses on them which would keep them poor.

The remaining danger of a breach in the wall, it seemed, was ingress by foreign power. To prevent alliance with foreigners by hostile groups in Japan, the Tokugawa took steps to cut off any contact with them. In 1613, on the basis of a report that Catholic missionaries were plotting to involve Spain in Japan, or from fear that they might try to do so, Ieyasu ordered their expulsion. By ruthless suppression between 1614 and 1638 he and Hidetada virtually extirpated above-board Christianity in Japan. It ceased to be important either politically or as a religion until the Meiji Restoration.

In 1633 Iemitsu forbade Japanese to leave Japan without Tokugawa permission, under penalty of death if they did so and returned. To prevent foreign contacts by Japanese sailors, he limited construction of ships to ones of a capacity of 2,500 bushels or less, not larger than an enclosed modern American railroad freight car. Three years later he ordered all foreign traders from the country except a few Chinese, Dutch, and Portuguese. Later he excluded the Portuguese. He closely supervised the Chinese and confined the Dutch to one trading post at Nagasaki, on Kyushu Island. Thereafter a series of orders barred all foreigners from Japan except a limited number of Dutch and Chinese traders. Iemitsu and his successors kept the Dutch at Nagasaki partly to obtain desired imports, but partly deliberately to have a channel of information concerning the West. A Japanese official wrote: "To defend ourselves against the barbarians, we must know them and ourselves: the way to know them is through Dutch studies."[13]

Withdrawal of Status Respect

Along with the intended results these measures created in four social groups an oppressive sense of being denied rights and position in the society which they valued and to which they had, so they felt, just claim. One of these groups was the merchants. During the feudal period they had become prosperous and influential. Now, no matter how great their wealth, they were officially declared to be the lowest social class, and the declaration entailed restrictions on their dress, behavior, and relationships to other groups which made their degradation a public matter.

A second was the samurai, who were affected in two ways. The measures providing for a sharp social separation between samurai and other groups had placed in an unhappy position the *ronin* or "wanderers,"

---

[13] Quoted in Thomas C. Smith, *Political Change and Industrial Development in Japan: Government Enterprises, 1868–1880* (Stanford, Calif.: Stanford University Press, 1955), p. 2.

samurai who had become masterless. During the warfare of the Ashikaga period many lords had been killed or deprived of their lands. At the beginning of the Tokugawa era some samurai abandoned daimyo who had compromised their principles to the extent of allying themselves with the Tokugawa. And the Tokugawa policy of executing *tozama* daimyo or reducing their land holdings deprived many samurai of their lords and livelihoods. It has been estimated that between 1600 and 1650 some 400,-000 samurai became *ronin*, largely through the last-mentioned course.[14] In the new order, these men were not samurai, for only nobles serving a daimyo were so classed. Thus they had either to sink into the peasant class or to make an ignoble existence in a town or city. Some wandered in roving bands. Others were spiritually wanderers, men who had abandoned or been deprived of their destined place in life.

The more general depressing effect on the samurai, however, was simply the imposition of national peace by the Tokugawa. At a stroke this "pax Tokugawa" deprived the samurai of their central reason for existence. The function of guarding one's lord against his enemies and of fighting for him no longer existed, or insofar as it did exist consisted of protection against contingencies so remote that they hardly served to maintain the morale of the samurai class. One group must have felt a new social elevation for the time being, namely the foot soldiers who were classed with the samurai and so elevated above the peasantry. However, they like other samurai suffered from lack of a function and were depressed by later developments noted below.

Thirdly, the rigid division of the population into four social classes deprived the so-called "wealthy peasants," the descendents of the estate managers of the Heian period, of their remaining contacts with the lower nobility, and relegated them to the category of peasants. They had been sinking in life during the Kamakura and Ashikaga periods, as the estates became of lessened importance. Now, with a new gap created between samurai and peasants, the erstwhile managerial families found themselves on the wrong side of the social demarcation line.

Lastly, to some followers of the newer sects the new treatment of the emperor may have seemed little short of sacrilege. The isolation of the emperor removed him from his supreme position in a sense in which no previous domination of him had done. The Tokugawa, being practical men, treated him with great deference, but the fact remained that he had no voice whatever in national affairs and was completely inaccessible.

Perhaps a fifth group should be added, all of the daimyo and especially the *tozama* daimyo. While daimyo in the past had been subordinate to every shogun, it is arguable that the restrictions imposed by the Tokugawa constituted new socially humiliating treatment which created a

---

[14] G. B. Sansom, *The Western World and Japan* (New York: Alfred A. Knopf, Inc., 1950), p. 191. Sansom notes that there is no implication that many *ronin* existed at the end of the period.

sense of lack of status respect that previous relationships had not. However this may be, the daimyo would hardly become leaders in social change, for their positions were so interwoven with the old social order that they could hardly become bearers of the new. However, their lieutenants, who rose to political power in the nineteenth century, may possibly have been alienated from the old system by a sense that under that system the traditional position of the daimyo had been destroyed.

The system set up by the Tokugawa to freeze the social and political order caused further great changes as time passed. *Sankin kotai* greatly accelerated the increase in interregional travel and trade which had begun in the previous centuries. Edo, Kyoto, and Osaka became great cities, and the commerce necessary to supply them developed. Modern banking developed; the techniques devised by the merchant-bankers of Japan paralleled the earlier ones of the Fuggers and then the Rothschilds in Europe.

Spending was intensified by the social pressure on each daimyo to indicate by the pomp of his travel to and from Edo and the splendor of his establishment at Edo the exalted level of his position, and also by the rapid development of urban life. To meet their financial needs, the daimyo and their retainers strove with success to increase the productivity of rice cultivation, to introduce other crops, and to expand handicraft production and create new handicrafts. Productivity increased throughout the Tokugawa era, perhaps more rapidly than it had during the Ashikaga era.[15] But the daimyo spent beyond their resources, however much these grew. They attempted to meet the financial strain in three ways: by borrowing from the merchants, squeezing the samurai, and perhaps extorting more from the peasants.[16]

Daimyo's debts to merchants grew cumulatively, and the income, wealth, and influence of the merchants grew in spite of the social restrictions. By the last half of the eighteenth century some of them could violate with impunity the prohibition against change of occupation and purchased from samurai or wealthy peasants their positions as landed intermediaries. Some merchants procured nobility for their daughters. While it would have been disgraceful for a samurai to marry except into the samurai class, a few wealthy merchants succeeded in having a daughter adopted by a samurai class, to be married in a few months or a few hours to another samurai, presumably to the financial benefit of both the husband and the adopting father. But in spite of their new economic power, merchants were still social inferiors, finding a place only where their financial power made it impossible to push them out.

---

[15] Concerning the Tokugawa era, see Thomas C. Smith, *The Agrarian Origins of Modern Japan* (Stanford, Calif.: Stanford University Press, 1959).

[16] Because of the borrowing from the merchants, the merchants' expansion of credit by modern banking methods, and later the debasement of the currency by the Tokugawa to create added money to finance their expenditures, spending increased faster than the supply of goods and services, and with some interruptions prices rose throughout the two and one half centuries of the Tokugawa era.

As the financial position of the daimyo worsened, they found it necessary to reduce successively the stipends they paid their samurai. Some samurai were pushed down to the economic level of peasants. Successive laws were passed for samurai relief, for example, laws canceling their debts, yet the deterioration of their position continued.

It has been asserted that the daimyo collected progressively increasing dues and levies from the peasants, and that the peasant level of living deteriorated during the last of the eighteenth century and the first half of the nineteenth.[17] This, however, may not be correct. The increasing sense of injustice felt by peasants may have been due to exactions which prevented their incomes from rising commensurately with other incomes, and to the impact on them of fluctuations in prices and harvests while their costs remained rigid. Certainly these factors caused many peasants to lose their lands, and there was a steady concentration of landholdings.[18]

In any event, peasant revolts became startlingly frequent. They testify vividly to the extremity to which peasants felt driven, since the revolts were so unthinkable in Japanese culture that on occasion the peasant leaders surrendered voluntarily to death sentences after the revolt, having known in advance that while the protest was imperative this result for the leaders was inevitable.

Thus as the Tokugawa era progressed, the sense of withdrawal of status respect felt by merchants, samurai, and peasants became more acute.

At the same time, through the indirect effect of the Tokugawa measures, the "wealthy peasants" were further demeaned. With the change in the functions of samurai, samurai who had been scattered over the fief gradually withdrew to the central fief town or towns. Thus in their conduct of local government affairs—for they tended to have hereditary possession of the headmanships and other chief local offices—these village leaders were abandoned by the nobles with whom they were wont to associate and on whom they had depended for guidance and prestige.

A clearer case of withdrawal of status respect from many of the higher elite, almost all of the lesser elite, and many of the simple folk than is provided by events in Tokugawa Japan would be hard to find. The results

---

[17] See *East Asia: The Great Tradition.*

[18] George B. Sansom, in *Japan: A Short Cultural History* (New York: The Century Co., 1931), pp. 505–11, stresses these factors while also mentioning increased taxes. Smith, in *Agrarian Origins,* chap. xi, cites evidence which brings the allegation of tax increases into question, and attributes the trouble to the factors mentioned in the text above.

The sense of withdrawal of status respect may have contributed to the inability to adjust to the new economic practices, for an individual concerned about his status may be under such pressure to reassure himself by increasing his level of consumption that he is shortsighted about future contingencies. The absence of saving other than their contributions to the social security program by many American industrial workers whose real incomes are higher than ever before is probably an example of this phenomenon.

provide a classic case of the operations of the social and psychological mechanisms of retreatism and emergence from it with altered values and increased creativity.

Manifestations of Retreatism

The retreatism took the form of a philosophy of "eat, drink, and be merry." It lacked the strain of melancholy which sometimes pervades it in a guilt culture—or perhaps only the flashy surface has been recorded. At any rate, in Osaka, Kyoto, Edo, and on a lesser scale in the castle towns and throughout the country, there occurred a wave of interest in style and form, in the theater, gay life, entertaining art, and romantic or salacious literature which has a common element of flight from the unsatisfactory nature of everyday life.[19] The wave reached its crest in the last two or three decades of the seventeenth century and the first two of the eighteenth, the so-called "Genroku" period, but the characterization of that period which follows applies in only less degree to the generations before and after it.

Many city people, Reischauer says in summary, were frivolous, even dissolute. Feminine fashions and masculine styles were important. Ceremonies were elaborate. Novelty was highly esteemed. To be *chic* and to have *savoir faire* were important. Dress and behavior were often flamboyant, but the flamboyance was tempered by sophistication.

New popular forms of drama developed. The style of play and acting known as *kabuki* was founded. The interest of the early companies was so conspicuously in prostitution rather than drama that the authorities banned women from the stage, and the Japanese tradition of portrayal of feminine parts by men developed. The most famous dramatist, Chikamatsu, wrote both historical plays and pieces about contemporary life. The historical dramas dealt with chivalry and the loyalty to lord and duty of the samurai, the modern ones with thwarted lovers, jealous wives, and the like. Both dealt with the conflict between duty and sentiment, both were romantic, and both were highly popular.

Another popular attraction was the life of the "gay quarters." Sections of Osaka, Kyoto, and Edo all became renowned for the nature of their entertainment. While the purpose of a large part of the activity was prostitution, the quarters also provided gay and frivolous feminine entertainment which men could not otherwise obtain since wives were confined strictly to the home and were not expected to be companions to their spouses. Moreover, the strict social divisions restricted informal social intercourse. In the gay quarters such divisions vanished; samurai could not there act as samurai but went more or less incognito. The life of the gay

---

[19] I have drawn my description largely from *East Asia: The Great Tradition*, chap. xiii; and Sansom, *The Western World and Japan*, chaps. ix and x, and *Japan: A Short Cultural History*, chap. xxii.

quarters symbolizes the entire period. While it is usually thought of as participated in mainly by the townspeople and especially the merchants or their sons, Sansom cites a judgment that "more than half the visitors to the best-known establishments were samurai of all ranks, not excluding the highest."[20] In pursuance of their theory of enforcing class differences, the Tokugawa should have prevented such behavior by the samurai. One reason they did not may be that they desired to have the *tozama* daimyos squander their resources.

For the first time in Japanese history popular art appeared. Paintings and woodcuts depicting portrayals of the passing scene, or, in the Japanese term, the "floating world" (*Ukiyo*), gained a wide audience. The best of them had artistic style and merit though they lacked the refinement, restricted in its appeal to a select trained few, of earlier Japanese art. Critics found them decorative, entertaining, comic, and characterized by gay colors and a light and sensuous touch and by sentiment and fantasy. The wood-block art continued to develop, and a century later there emerged the masters Hokusai and Kiroshige, whose woodcuts have become so well known in the West.

Much of the popular literature of the period dealt with sex, ranging from vulgarly realistic stories to romantic tales of the charms and proclivities of the famous courtesans. *The Man Who Spent His Life in Love, Five Amorous Women, Characters of Modern Sons*—these are some of the titles, the first one freely translated.[21]

It should not be assumed that there had been no artistic or literary flowering in earlier periods of Japanese history. For the sake of economy in narration, I have ignored these aspects of earlier periods. There were earlier cultural efflorescences which undoubtedly had roots comparable in their general nature to those from which the lush Tokugawa growth burgeoned. That of the Tokugawa era, however, was unique both in its content and in the scope of its audience.

We have no record of the impact on family environment of the social tensions which caused the retreat from grappling with problems which the gay life and literature of the Tokugawa cities represent, but we do have a record of the cultural changes which occurred as time passed. In them the revolt against the traditional order which had appeared in the Heian and feudal periods reached its climax and brought a social revolution.

The Sequel to Retreatism: Changes in Values and World Cognitions

Early in the Tokugawa era the samurai perhaps faced a more acute personal problem than other classes. By the middle of the seventeenth

---

[20] *The Western World and Japan*, p. 219.
[21] I have taken these titles from *East Asia: The Great Tradition*, p. 651.

century the military function which had been the central element of samurai status ceased to exist, and the samurai faced the problem of finding a new identity for themselves. It will be remembered that in the systole and diastole of national integration and localism in previous periods the focus of their loyalty had repeatedly shifted, so that their attachment to traditional values was already somewhat confused and they were not without some psychological freedom to search for new values.

Many of them gave up the attempt to understand why evil days had come upon them, and instead turned to the gay quarters for diversion. However, the more thoughtful among them turned to the ancient sources of wisdom, as troubled men with at least a modicum of creativity often do. Early in the Tokugawa era they found in Chinese writing descriptions of the proper activities of warriors, and for a generation or two they turned rather feverishly to practicing medieval military skills now obsolete for use in war, such as archery and fencing, and also became learned in the Chinese writings concerning the rituals and manners of behavior which marked the warrior character.

Their search for the meaning of life caused them to cling to the samurai ethic, *Bushido*, which they derived from Zen Buddhism. It stressed loyalty, filial piety and obedience, courtesy or decency, an aesthetic style of life, and high regard for learning. Many of them strove to observe these virtues and thought of themselves as the preservers of Japanese morality. Tokugawa Mitsukini, 1628–1700, wrote to his samurai:

> What, then is the use of the *shi*, or *samurai*, class? Its only business is to preserve, or maintain, *giri* [right, honor, duty]. The people of the other classes deal with visible things, while the *samurai* deal with invisible, colorless, and unsubstantial things . . . if there were no *samurai*, right (*giri*) would disappear from human society, the sense of shame would be lost, and wrong and injustice would prevail.[22]

On unique occasions a few of them found romantic ways of affirming their identity, a spectacular oft-cited case being that of the 47 *ronin* whose master was goaded into an impossible situation and then killed. They disguised their intention to seek revenge by living lives of dissipation or seeming disregard of honor for two years, and then when they were no longer closely watched avenged their master's death even though they knew they would have to commit suicide thereafter. For most, however, no such heroic role was possible.

After a time the Chinese military ritual, having no relationship to the life of the times, proved ineffective in relieving their anxiety, and gradually they abandoned it. Likewise, the conception that they were the special vessels for the preservation of Japanese honor could not continue to be persuasive to all of them generation after generation in the absence of

----

[22] Quoted from an article by Ernest W. Clement in the *Transactions and Proceedings of the Japan Society*, London, 1898, by Robert N. Bellah, *Tokugawa Religion* (Glencoe, Ill.: Free Press of Glencoe, Inc., 1957), p. 90.

some overt function, and this self-delusion palled on some of them. Many of them turned to the life of the gay quarters.

Then many samurai and others found new meaning in Confucian elements of their religious tradition. They did not abandon Buddhism; they did not think of the two religions as distinct. But Confucian strains in religious thought became more attractive. Confucianism included Zen and the *Bushido* code; in fact it had originally been brought to Japan by Zen scholars; but it also provided some comforting new views. It taught that immutable natural principles create and justify a social hierarchy with sharp class divisions, that everyone has his natural place in society in one of these divisions and should do his duty in it, that a just government which observes these principles has the right to the loyalty of every citizen. Persons who could find these principles acceptable could find increased satisfaction in the Tokugawa social order.

The merchant class in particular adopted much of this Confucian dogma, combined with Zen ethic and the *Bushido* code. If it was the decree of heaven that they should remain within the merchant class and do their duty within it without jealous striving to attain another rank, then their lot in life was after all divinely sanctioned and was not merely an imposition of the Tokugawa.[23]

They found one Confucian teaching and a closely related Zen tenet of especial interest and selected them out for an important place in their view of life. These were the Confucian doctrine of occupation and the Zen teaching of the virtue of work. Confucian philosophy stressed the need of diligent pursuit of one's occupation. Bellah suggests that this concept fused with the Japanese concept of a need to repay limitless *on*. The merchant ethic of the period, in addition to accepting the doctrine of occupation, stressed the Zen teaching of the virtue of simplicity, frugality, and diligence in work as parts of one's filial duty to family and society. The two closely related tenets became central in their version of Zen and Confucianism.

The monk Ishida Baigan, who lived from 1685 to 1744, preached these doctrines. He added frosting to the cake by teaching that all persons are samurai, each class serving in its appointed task just as samurai serve in theirs. Merchants, he asserted, are stewards, who deserve just profits as a just reward. With their social rank thus blessed by being equated to that of the samurai, the merchants found the philosophy singularly attractive.

Logically the concepts of occupation and the duty to work might imply that man's place in life is fixed and he should accept it. Indeed, to avoid this connotation the central doctrines of Confucianism had to be ignored. Yet the merchants managed to subordinate this aspect of the doctrines and instead stressed the aspects of this-worldly asceticism and the need to labor diligently to maximize the product of one's labor, as-

---

[23] The discussion of religion from this point on is primarily from *ibid*.

pects remarkably reminiscent of the ethic of the English Nonconformists at approximately the same time. The point is vividly made by noting that the advice below is that of a Japanese merchant in 1610, not that of an English divine:

> When a man has capital, small though it may be, he must allow himself no relaxation in his attention to household problems or the running of his business, and must continue to make the earning of a living his principal concern. This is his lifelong duty. If, when one has capital, one begins to relax, to buy things one longs for, to behave in a wilful manner, to live in style, and to do all the things which one wishes to do, the money is soon spent. . . . One must set to work from the moment one has capital.[24]

That this interpretation rather than a Lutheran-like one appealed to the Tokugawa merchants results, I suggest, from the needs of their personalities, not from the logic of the religious doctrine.

The peasants too found the doctrines of natural class divisions and the duty and virtue of work somewhat comforting, and doctrines somewhat like those of Baigan spread through the villages.

As life went on and anxieties continued, some persons looked elsewhere for wisdom and found it in the ancient Japanese writings. Out of these writings, two strains of thought were found appealing. One of these, the so-called "Mito" school, was developed, interestingly enough, under the leadership of Tokugawa Mitsukini, a member of a collateral branch of the family who was daimyo of a fief that included the town of Mito. Under his direction a famous and scholarly history of Japan was begun in the seventeenth century. While the members of the Mito school had high regard for the Chinese writings, they taught that Japan was superior to all other nations. They viewed Shinto as the highest religious teaching, and rejected Buddhism. Most important, in their historical studies they proved beyond question that there had been a time when the emperor had ruled the nation; and on the basis of Shinto teachings they concluded that the emperor conveyed the benevolence of the gods, that every Japanese therefore owed limitless obligation to him, that his expressions in political as well as religious matters, being the will of the gods, required complete obedience, and that he was the legitimate ruler of the nation. The moral, though not spelled out, was clear: the Tokugawa shoguns were usurpers, and perhaps the ills of the nation were due to their sacrilege.

The other strain of thinking which developed from the study of ancient Japanese sources entailed extreme rejection of China, intense nationalism, and emotional and mystic devotion to the emperor. This trend developed in the late seventeenth and eighteenth centuries. In an intellectual sense, if not historically, these teachings were derived from those

---

[24] Quoted from *The Japanese Family Storehouse or the Millionaires' Gospel Modernised* (Cambridge, 1959), by Kurt Samuelson, in his *Religion and Economic Action* (trans. E. Geoffrey French; London: William Heinemann, Ltd., 1961), p. vii.

of Nichiren; they respond to the same attitudes and advocate generally similar rules of action.

These two schools of religious thought gained widespread acceptance in the later part of the Tokugawa era. That they did, I think, clearly indicates the emotional need felt by Japanese to find scapegoats for their continuing anxieties. These scapegoats were found in foreigners and in the Tokugawa; finding them enabled the people to see outside themselves causes of the rage and frustration which they felt unconsciously, and so made these seem more rational and more bearable.

We must assume that these anxieties, unsatisfied by any of the new views of the world and so leading on and on to search for other views, were products of the childhood environment in which the tensions of the time resulted. There is no other equally plausible explanation.[25]

Repercussions: Political and Economic Change: The End of the Era

Beginning in say the middle of the eighteenth century, decay in the Tokugawa political system became increasingly conspicuous. The Tokugawa, in their traditional belief in the especial virtue of agriculture, relied almost wholly on the proceeds from their lands for the revenues with which to finance the national government. In the last half of the eighteenth century and the first half of the nineteenth, they found their resources increasingly inadequate. Worse, they faced problems which baffled and immobilized them. The number of landless peasants was increasing, and disorder was rising in the countryside. Merchants were buying their way by one device or another into social positions that were forbidden to them. Merchants and wealthy peasants were hiring impoverished samurai to teach their children forbidden knowledge, such as political theory and the arts of government. The *tozama* daimyo had grown in power and were violating some of the old restrictions. All of these things progressed insidiously; there was no great misdeed one could stamp out. Preventing the eruptions was like trying to hold down with one's bare hands a liquid that bubbled up between the fingers. The basic trouble was that old loyalties were dissolving under the pressure of long-continued withdrawal of status respect, and in the presence of this change the Tokugawa were frustrated and confused.

The nationalist doctrines therefore were not merely intellectual exercises or means of emotional release through pleasant fantasy. The samurai and others who seized upon them perceived the weakening of the national political structure and could visualize the possibility of being

---

[25] A theme of Bellah's book is that the religious doctrines caused the type of behavior found in the Tokugawa era—the merchants' frugality and diligence, and so on. It will be clear to the reader, I think, that in my view this assumed causation is categorically wrong except as a strand in a complex set of relationships. Much more important strands, I suggest, are those by which both the religious beliefs and the nature of behavior flow from the personality characteristics inculcated in individuals, beginning in the early years of their lives.

successful in action to end the evil conditions on which they blamed their unease. Hence the movement gained vitality, and it provided some of the stimulus to the tide of political revolt after 1850.

The possibility of political action satisfied the needs of only certain persons, however. Other individuals and groups saw their personal release in other aspects of the new doctrines they had succeeded in creating out of the old materials, those aspects which stressed diligence and the virtue and nobility of work. In the Ashikaga period many individuals had found satisfaction by applying their energies and creativity to problems of production. Now, technical knowledge was available from the "European barbarians" whose power was so evident. Many ways of gaining economic strength had been repugnant, but an increasing number of individuals now came to believe that if no other route to respect for one's place in the society was available, economic achievement was a good use of one's energies after all.

I suggest that awareness of this possibility influenced the development of religious thought, that the presence of the Dutch and the knowledge of superior Western technology gained from them were of importance in causing eighteenth century students of the Buddhist and Confucian classics to note and stress the strain of thought in those doctrines which asserted that diligence in work is virtuous and noble, a strain of thought that had attracted no attention when life was different. That the presence of the "European barbarians" was necessary for the formation of the new values is doubtful; the Nonconformists of England had been able to arrive at such values in the absence of such models. Other factors causing the change in world view no doubt were the inability to see other solutions to the problem of denial of status respect and the possession by many persons of enough creativity to permit them to look for new solutions. Yet the knowledge of Western achievements and the prestige in which Western power was held must have accelerated the appearance of the new element in religious thought. And once values favorable to economic innovation existed, the presence of the Europeans provided technical knowledge that made those values more fruitful.

And so a movement toward "Dutch studies" took place. Through the Dutch at Nagasaki some samurai and some others painstakingly began to learn the Dutch language even as early as the seventeenth century in order to gain acquaintance with the knowledge of Europe. The number grew slowly, then in the last several decades of the eighteenth century became a rushing tide. Dutch grammars and Dutch-Japanese dictionaries were prepared, language schools opened, and many books or parts of books translated dealing with physics, mathematics, geology, geography, astronomy, navigation, metallurgy, engineering, military tactics, medicine, government, and other subjects. Later, important schools for the "study of barbarian books" were opened—only one by the Tokugawa, several by the outer clans. In the first half of the nineteenth century laboratories were established to perform on a pilot scale the processes described in the scientific books. Some pilot metallurgical processes were performed with the guidance only of Western texts, that is, without any technical advice. Then full-scale enterprises were established—an iron ore smelter, one or more reverberatory furnaces, and an iron foundry, to cast, among other things, cannon. The emphasis was on metallurgy and armament.[26]

The samurai were probably drawn strongly to such studies for an additional reason—because the Westerners were powerful warriors. The study of Western strength was both a symbolic substitute for the vanished power of the samurai and a symbolic protest against the weakness of the Tokugawa. Later the relation of technical studies to the defense of Japan became more and more clear. The threat to Japan from the West grew. During the first half of the nineteenth century Russia and Western powers made a number of "requests" of Japan, which she turned away with difficulty. In seeking the sources of Western strength the samurai were preparing to perform what in their eyes was the noblest of their historic functions, the defense of Japan.

By the first half of the nineteenth century these various forces for change had created almost unbearable tensions in Japanese society. The disintegration of the social order became more and more evident. The merchants, the peasants, and the samurai were breaching old social walls; the *tozama* daimyo were nibbling away at the restrictions that had been placed on them. The Tokugawa became more and more incapable of governing.

At this crucial juncture in Japanese history a foreign power appeared again, this time with force not to be denied. In 1853 Commodore Perry appeared in Tokyo Bay and announced that he would return the next year to obtain a commercial treaty. He reappeared with four small warships, with which he could, if he wished, have blockaded the harbor and starved the city. The Tokugawa signed a treaty which opened two ports to American trade and limited Japan's power to regulate the trade. In 1857 the American consul, Townsend Harris, negotiated a further agreement expanding trade and providing extraterritoriality for Americans accused of crime in Japan. Other Western countries demanded and received commercial treaties similar to that with the United States.

Japan was saved from dismemberment like that of China, perhaps because conditions elsewhere, for example, the rise of Germany, civil war in the United States, and revolt in India, kept foreign powers occupied. For these reasons Japan also had time to conduct a great internal debate concerning the appropriate response to the aggression from abroad.

The Tokugawa cry was: "Open the ports and help Tokugawa." It may be interpreted as meaning, "We do not have the strength to resist

---

[26] For an excellent brief discussion of these developments, see Smith, *Political Change and Industrial Development in Japan,* chap. i.

the foreigners. To prepare for resistance would involve drastic social changes which must be avoided. Therefore we have no alternative to opening the ports." The opposition cry, "Loyalty to the Emperor. Repel the barbarians," was far more than an emotional slogan. It meant, "We must acquire the strength needed to repel the barbarians. To do so will require drastic social action. Let us restore the position of the emperor, thereby preserving a symbolic link with the past. And, rallying around him, let us overthrow the Tokugawa so that we may get on with the job of making the necessary changes." There were bitter divisions among *hans* and within *hans*. There ensued coups and counter-coups by rebellious clans and by the Tokugawa to keep control of the emperor's court at Kyoto. Steadily the support of the Tokugawa dwindled. In 1867, no longer able to punish rebellious *hans*, and no longer morally sure of their mandate, the Tokugawa formally surrendered the mandate of government to the emperor, and the new forces took over the government. They were led by high-ranking samurai of the Choshu, Tosa, and other *tozama* fiefs.

The new leaders promptly ignored the principle of making the emperor the supreme political power, for which they had presumably fought, took matters into their own hands, and made political changes which had not been contemplated in the public discussions of the preceding 15 years. At a stroke they demolished the structure of local political power, which no previous national leader had dared to touch. They simply eliminated the daimyo and the fiefs over which they had ruled, taking over the daimyo's share of agricultural income as governmental revenue and placing the daimyo and samurai on governmental stipends. In the process they removed all local barriers to trade. Soon after, to make all governmental revenues available for other purposes, they replaced the stipends by long-term bonds which provided less income than the stipends and forced the daimyo and other samurai to go to work. Within half a dozen years the new governmental leaders, too impatient for development to wait for the fruits of private endeavors, had entered upon a vigorous program of governmental promotion of new industrial, transport, and financial concerns (and their subsequent sale at bargain prices to friendly individuals).[27] Hardly any large enterprise appeared except with governmental support. Private enterprise also burgeoned in less spectacular but basically important activities, the stream of technical change widened and deepened, and Japan began that remarkable period of economic growth which has continued to the present.

CONCLUDING COMMENTS

That period need not concern us here since we are interested in the causes, not the course, of economic growth in Japan. We may return to

[27] See *ibid.*, chaps. iv–vii.

the question raised in the second chapter of this volume. Why did rapid economic growth begin in Japan sooner than in any other non-Western society except perhaps Russia? It should be clear from even the summary account of Japanese history presented in this chapter that to refer merely to the events after Perry's visit to Japan is superficial and misleading. Likewise, Japan did not develop merely because of her contacts with the West, for she had to draw those contacts, so to speak, through the narrow mouth of a bottle, while other major Asian countries bathed in them. Relevant major differences between Japan and other non-Western societies, I suggest, were both freedom from the negative effects of colonial disruption and the repeated long-continued withdrawal of expected status from important groups in her society which drove them to retreatism, caused them to emerge alienated from traditional values and with increased creativity, and, when other means of regaining self-assurance seemed not available, led them to technological progress.

It has been suggested as another strand in the explanation that elements in the Japanese culture visible since the early periods of Japanese history make the Japanese more ready to accept foreign values than are the people of other societies. I do not reject this hypothesis; but recognition of its possibility should not cause one to lose sight of the great importance of the factors summarized above.[28]

The Japanese political structure, as I have noted, oscillated between national integration and localism. It is reasonable to suppose that technological advance has permanently ended that oscillation, for with modern transportation, communication, and economic interrelations it is difficult to see how political localism could appear again. The fact that this change seems permanent does not, however, give reason to assume that technological progress has brought Japan (or any other society) to a uniquely enduring social phase. There is no reason to suppose that the problem of tensions within personality is solved in Japan; those tensions seem as high at present as they seem to have been in any earlier period. One may speculate, then, that after say two centuries of seeking a solution by directing their energies into this channel some groups in Japan, having passed through retreatism, and emerging creative and alienated from present values, will strike out in some other direction. In this respect Japan

---

[28] Another hypothesis not discussed here is that of Marion Levy that the possibility for a successful trader in China to become a member of the landed gentry and thus elite by buying land constituted a permanent siphon drawing economic energies away from continuing advance, while the prohibition on such a social shift in Japan kept the energies of the urban class concentrated in commerce. See Marion J. Levy, "Contrasting Factors in the Modernization of China and Japan," in S. S. Kuznets, W. Moore, and J. Spengler (eds.), *Economic Growth: Brazil, India, Japan* (Durham, N.C.: Duke University Press, 1955). There was such a difference, but I would not stress its importance, particularly in view of the fact that technological progress in Japan was not concentrated especially in the merchant class either during the Meiji era or previously.

is probably like other technologically progressive countries. Neither in centrally directed nor private enterprise societies has social change ended with the industrial revolution.

Perhaps a further comment on the significance of the Puritan-like ethic in Japan is in order. In English Nonconformism the doctrine that service to God lies in diligent attempt to glorify Him by making the earth fruitful is associated with a deep pervasive sense of sin and guilt. That sense is central in the religious dogma of Puritanism. The same ethic appeared in Japan, associated not with a sense of guilt but rather with a sense of inadequacy and of shame at revealing it, and associated with a sharply contrasting religious dogma. This is persuasive evidence, it seems to me, that the religious dogma as such was not of central importance in the economic behavior, but rather is a reflection and rationalization of unconscious needs which are also the proximate causes of the economic performance.

In conclusion, the paradox of Japanese behavior in recent times may be faced. I have suggested that the disruption of the traditional world view began late in the Heian period and proceeded progressively during the feudal and Tokugawa eras. But has Japan ceased to be traditional? True, there is continuing economic progress, and at a remarkable rate, and the political forms of Western democracy have been adopted. But until World War II public life was dominated by an aristocracy of the political elite and then the military elite; the forms of democracy were empty. And even today the minority party in the Diet feels keenly the injustice of majority decision in the Western style, and feels justified in blocking by violence majority action which does not take adequately into account the views of the minority. Moreover, at least until World War II the religious phenomenon sometimes referred to in the West as "emperor worship" continued. Is this society modern?

Clearly the economic innovators are modern. Beyond question there continues to be a degree of technological creativity in the Japanese society that would be impossible if the needs and values of traditional personality prevailed. Clearly, too, an increasing awareness of the worth and potential of the individual has emerged in Japanese religious thought of the past several centuries. Why, then, has political democracy failed to appear?

I cannot answer that question fully; I can only make certain relevant comments. For one thing, while creative personalities and new values have appeared among the lesser elite and the upper crust of the simple folk—the "wealthy peasants," the merchants, and the former lower echelons of the samurai—they may not have appeared to a corresponding extent among the mass of the simple folk. A very important factor in the development of political democracy in the West was the fact that the common people demanded it. Some members of Western elites would be politically authoritarian also, if they could. In Japan the corresponding demand has been weak and limited, though complex changes are going on at present. Up to the present the simple folk of Japan have remained far more traditional in personality than have the common people of the West. This difference is manifest in their relationships to industrial employers as well as in their political behavior.[29]

However, this is at best only part of the explanation, and perhaps this hypothesis is quite wrong. For technical progress has gone forward in Japanese agriculture since the feudal period, and peasants as well as their masters may have contributed to it. Perhaps the central fact in Japan relevant to the explanation of this puzzling phenomenon is that creativity has been channeled into economic activity, while the political values of the simple folk and elites alike have remained traditional even though not fully authoritarian.

How it can have happened that withdrawal of status respect, retreatism, and emergence from it with new creativity and new values passed over the simple folk to a greater extent in Japan than in the West, or alternatively created more far-reaching changes in economic values than in political ones, is a complex historical and social question to which I shall attempt no answer here. Perhaps it is pertinent to note in conclusion that the values of the Japanese simple folk seem to be changing fairly rapidly at present. Whether the change will lead to political democracy or, running into stubborn resistance from elite individuals in positions of social and economic power, will eventuate in more radical social change is an important question for the future.

APPENDIX:
WHO WERE THE INNOVATORS?

As a postscript, comments may be advanced on the social status of the men who became economic innovators and those who became political leaders in the new regime. The comments are few; the facts available do not permit an analysis comparable to that made in the preceding chapter concerning the English innovators.

In England withdrawal of status respect bore with especial heaviness on the groups who became Nonconformists and on the Scots. In Japan it bore upon virtually all social groups, even on the commoners and samurai of the Tokugawa clans. Hence one would expect the innovators (in economic activity, politics, or other fields) to come from all groups, the proportions from different groups being determined by other factors such as their training and contacts, or perhaps by the severity of withdrawal of status respect. To measure the degrees of severity, however, would require an instrument more refined than can be provided by the analysis presented here.

It would be interesting, nevertheless, to determine the proportions in which the innovators did come from major social groups relative to the shares of those groups in the total population. The comparison cannot be made because not

---

[29] Concerning the former, see Abegglen, *The Japanese Factory*. However, concerning post-World War II changes in attitudes, see also Jean Stoetzel, *Without the Chrysanthemum and the Sword* (New York: Columbia University Press, 1955).

even approximate estimates of the composition of the population are available.
A census was taken in 1869.[30] However, it does not include the officials of the
new central government at Tokyo, it includes or excludes samurai in degrees
which vary from clan to clan, and it reflects a situation when the Tokugawa
clans and clans which had supported them in the final struggle had been sharply
cut down in size.[31] It does not provide an occupational breakdown other than
between samurai and commoners.[32] That census indicates a number of samurai
equal to 3.7 per cent of the total population of 29.4 million. This gives an order
of magnitude. Even assuming gross understatement, the true total can hardly
have been more than say 5 or 6 per cent. This figure may be compared with the
prevalence of samurai among innovators and social leaders in the Meiji era indicated in Table 14–1.[33]

The table includes men who gained eminence in the fields indicated and who
died before 1920. The percentages of samurai shown in the table are overstated,
for in each group except the "Entrepreneurs (small sample)" the father's occupation is not known for between 20 and 25 per cent of the cases, and it is highly
likely that in all of these cases the fathers were nonsamurai. However, even with
allowance for this the table indicates what one would expect, the presence of
sons of samurai among the business and governmental leaders in a proportion
far higher than their number in the population as a whole. It is unfortunate
that it is not possible to distinguish among the ranks of samurai in order to test
the hypothesis that the lower-rank samurai provided proportionately more
innovators than the higher ranks. In the small sample of entrepreneurs such a
distinction was made by rather rough yardsticks. Of the 29 fathers of business
leaders who were samurai, 7 were classed as upper-rank samurai, 5 as middle
class, 16 as lower class, and 1 could not be ranked. Unfortunately we do not
know the corresponding distribution of all samurai, so this classification tells us
only that lower-class samurai were rather well represented.

Sansom states flatly that "the organization of Japan at and following the
Restoration of 1868 was in great measure the work of samurai of the lower
grades."[34] The remark may be true of economic as well as political organization. However, for the time being the generalization must rest on informed
judgment. It is highly plausible, but a systematic empirical investigation of it
has not been made.

---

[30] It is reproduced in *Koydo no Rekishi: Chugokuhen,* ed. T. Yoshida of the
Institute Shiryo Hensanjo (Tokyo: Hobunkan & Co., 1959).

[31] For this information I am grateful to Professor Sakamoto Taro, Director of the
Tokyo University Historiographical Institute (Shiryo Hensan-jo).

[32] Perhaps one could be estimated, since the data are available by geographical
units, but making such an estimate was beyond the scope of the research project reflected in this volume.

[33] Except for the "Entrepreneurs (small sample)," I am indebted for the data to
Dr. R. P. Dore, who kindly provided me with duplicates of punch cards summarizing
data concerning all men whose biographies are presented in the two biographical
dictionaries, *Nihon Jinmei Jisho* and *Dainihon Jinmei Jiten.* I have eliminated not
only those who died in 1920 or later but also those whose major eminence was in
fields other than business or government; namely, artists, scientists, educators, jour-
nalists, religious leaders, and retail merchants, whom I excluded from the merchant
group. The "Entrepreneurs (small sample)" are a group of leaders investigated on
my behalf by Miwa Ryoichi of Tokyo University. The selection of cases was by Mr.
Miwa and Professor Ando Yoshio of Tokyo University. I am indebted to Professor
Fukutake Tadashi and Professor Ando for arranging this research for me. (Earlier
work in this investigation was done by Mr. Kee Il Choi and Miyazaki Isamu.)

[34] *Japan: A Short Cultural History,* p. 514.

TABLE 14-1

SOCIAL ORIGINS OF JAPANESE SOCIAL LEADERS OF THE MEIJI ERA*

(Percentages Are of the Number of Fathers Whose Position Is Known)

Subject's Occupation		Father's Position								Han Affiliation			
		Socioeconomic Class											
		Dai-myo or Court Noble†	Sam-urai‡	Mer-chant or Uni-denti-fied Towns-man§	Head-man or Wealthy Peasant	Peas-ant or Uniden-tified Vil-lager‖	Other	Total Known	Not Known	Sat-suma, Choshu, or other	Ba-kufu	Other	Total
Government official or political leader¶	No.	25	162	2	1	17	22	239	58	65	16	216	297
	%	(10)	(68)	(1)	(5)	(7)	(9)	(100)		(22)	(5)	(73)	(100)
Army or Navy	No.	2	76	0	1	6	7	92	31	45	7	71	123
	%	(2)	(83)	(0)	(1)	(7)	(8)	(100)		(37)	(6)	(58)	(100)
Entrepreneur (including corporate executives)	No.	3	64	28	13	24	12	144	52	26	8	162	196
	%	(2)	(44)	(19)	(9)	(17)	(8)	(100)		(13)	(4)	(83)	(100)
In finance or trade	No.	0	7	8	2	3	1	21	5	3	3	20	26
	%	(0)	(33)	(38)	(10)	(14)	(5)	(100)		(12)	(12)	(77)	(100)
Other	No.	3	57	20	11	21	11	123	47	23	5	142	170
	%	(2)	(46)	(16)	(9)	(17)	(9)	(100)		(14)	(3)	(84)	(100)
Entrepreneurs (small sample)	No.	1	29	11	11	6	4	62	4	13	18**	34	65††
	%	(2)	(47)	(18)	(18)	(10)	(6)	(100)		(20)	(28)	(52)	(100)

* Except for "Entrepreneurs (small sample)," the data relate to all men who followed the careers indicated, and who died before 1920 whose biographies are included in the two biographical dictionaries, *Nihon Jimmei Jisho* or *Dainihon Jimmei Jiten*. Concerning "Entrepreneurs (small sample)," see n. 33.

† Court nobles: *kuge*.

‡ Includes foot soldiers (*sotsu, ashigaru, doshin,* and *yariki*).

§ Excludes known artisans. In the six rows, the numbers unidentified are respectively 2, 0, 5, 1, 4, and 0.

‖ In the six rows, the numbers unidentified are respectively 14, 6, 20, 1, 19, and 2.

¶ Includes government officials, technical ("civil service") personnel, and central and local political leaders.

** Includes court officials.

†† Affiliation of one father not known.

"Wealthy peasants" too were important. Sons of village headmen, "wealthy peasants," and other peasants were a considerable number of the leaders, in combination over one fourth of the business leaders and about one eighth of the civilian governmental leaders. Most of the fathers classed as peasants or unidentified villagers may have been "wealthy peasants," since except in the "Entrepreneurs (small sample)" a large majority were unidentified. It is clear that either sons of "wealthy peasants" were rather generously represented among political and business leaders or that a surprising number of peasants' sons attained eminence.

The data are the more impressive when it is realized that many of the persons classified as samurai were in fact "rural samurai" (*goshi*), who are hardly to be distinguished from "wealthy peasants." This was true of five of the 28 samurai in the small sample of entrepreneurs. Smith, *Political Change and Industrial Development*, Chapter II, notes that among men given court rank posthumously because of their eminence in the restoration movement (1800–1867) more than 10 per cent were admittedly peasants (including "wealthy peasants"), about an added 10 per cent in a large sample he studied were *goshi*, and some among the small number of merchants were rural merchants, that is, perhaps really peasants.

Beyond these general comments concerning origins the table is mainly of interest in indicating the differential degree in which men of various origins selected different occupations. While sons of samurai, including daimyo and high court officials, constituted almost four fifths of the government officials and political leaders whose fathers' occupation is known, they were less than one half of the business leaders. Sons of merchants plus townsmen whose origin is uncertain (some of them may have been artisans rather than merchants) were about one fifth of the business leaders, and almost double that share of those in finance or trade, but there were almost no governmental, political, or military leaders among them. One may suspect that this was due not merely to their selection of career but also to their rejection by the tight-knit group of former samurai who formed the governmental and political club. Villagers are represented among the governmental, political, and military leaders; this was probably because of their local political strength.

The classification by clan origin of fathers selects out only three important *tozama* clans and the *bakufu*. This is because Dore's materials did not include identification of other clans. While these clans contributed only some 13 per cent of business executives in the larger sample, they contributed 22 per cent of the governmental and political leaders and 37 per cent of the military leaders. These data seem to suggest a greater hold of traditionalism on the *tozama* clans than on others. This implication may be correct. The animus of these clans at the Tokugawa may have so turned their energies toward military revolt and the gaining of political power that when opportunity offered they moved in larger numbers than other clans into these fields. Another explanation is possible, however. These clans dominated the new government, and they may appear in greater relative numbers here and in the military simply because they excluded many of the Tokugawa and their supporters.

From the difference in clan origin of the large and small samples of business leaders it is obvious that the principle of selection in the two samples was somewhat different. This being so, the general agreement between the two with respect to the samurai and merchant origins of the business leaders gives some assurance of the general representativeness of the figures.

The Transition in Colombia

chapter *15*

ALTHOUGH THE ECONOMIC GROWTH OF COLOMBIA DURING the past 40 years has gone largely unnoticed by the world at large, one could count on one's fingers, possibly on the fingers of one hand, the countries of the world whose rate of increase in per capita income during this period has been greater. That rise has continued in spite of governmental mismanagement and resulting foreign exchange problems during several years of the 1950's.

In area and population Colombia is the third largest country of South America. Its area is about one seventh that of the United States; its population in 1960 was some 14,000,000. The country's per capita gross national product in 1957 was 1,066 pesos, equivalent in purchasing power to perhaps $265 or more.[1] Thirty years earlier, in the mid-1920's, it was only one half as great. This is the earliest date for which a comprehensive estimate of output and income in Colombia has been made, but partial estimates make clear that 30 years earlier still it was even lower.[2] As I shall note in more detail below, industrial production had been rising fairly rapidly since at least the turn of the century,[3] and agricultural

---

[1] This figure is derived by use of the 1957 free market rate of exchange of four pesos equal to one dollar. Estimates of Colombian economists suggest that, since the purchasing power of the peso in 1957 for capital and consumer goods and services used in Colombia was higher than 25 cents, the dollar figure equivalent in purchasing power to 1,066 pesos should be more than $265. At the rate of exchange prevailing early in 1961, per capita income in dollars would be computed at less than one third as much, or say $80; but the specific conditions which cause that rate make it invalid as a measure of the relative purchasing power of the peso and the dollar.

[2] The earliest year for which an estimate of gross national product in Colombia has been made is 1925. The Economic Commission for Latin America has estimated that from 1925 to 1953 the gross product of Colombia increased at an average rate of 4.6 per cent per year. Since the average annual rate of population growth was 2.1 per cent, output per capita increased at an average rate of 2.4 per cent. Per capita output rose by 5.2 per cent per year during 1925–29, 2.0 per cent even during the depression years 1930–38, 0 per cent during the war years 1939–44, when both exports of commodities and imports of supplies were especially severely curtailed for lack of shipping, and 3.6 per cent during 1945–53. The rate from 1953 to 1960 averaged about 2 per cent. (United Nations Economic Commission for Latin America, *Analyses and Projections of Economic Development, III. The Economic Development of Colombia*, Geneva, 1957. [E/CN.12/365/Rev. 1] Section I, chap. i.)

[3] Many of the leading industrial companies of today, or their predecessors, are listed in the *Anuario Ilustrado de Bogotá y Registro Mercantil de Colombia*, issued

production had been increasing markedly since at least the 1870's.

This economic growth has occurred in three areas barred from the outside world and from each other by rugged mountain ranges and on a humid tropical lowland. One could hardly pick a less likely place in Latin America unless it is Bolivia. Colombia's economic progress is therefore doubly impressive. Why did it occur?

THE SETTING

The Land and the People

Colombia is the northwestern-most country of South America, its coastline interrupted by the Isthmus of Panama. The eastern half of the country's area, the extensive transmontane undeveloped grasslands known as the *llanos*, contains less than 2 per cent of the country's population.[4] It may be neglected for our purposes. In the western half of the country three rugged fingers of the Andes, the western, central, and eastern Cordilleras, thrust northward from Ecuador. The central and western ones taper down and disappear 150 miles or so short of the Atlantic, but the eastern one continues aggressively to the ocean. Between the central and eastern ranges, the Magdalena River runs the length of the country to the Atlantic. The Cauca River flows down through the valley west of the central range, joining the Magdalena perhaps 125 miles from the ocean.

In the eastern Cordillera there lies a high plateau, called the Sabana,

---

in Bogotá in 1921. Of the manufacturing companies listed on the Bogotá stock exchange (Bolsa de Bogotá, S.A.) in 1947, certainly one third and perhaps one half were the companies or the legal successors to companies which were flourishing before 1920. An appreciable number existed before 1900.

If any date should symbolize the beginning of modern industry in Colombia it might be 1901 or 1906. In 1901 a modern sugar refinery began to operate at the La Manuelita plantation near the town of Palmira in the Valley, after more than 1,800 mules and oxen had been employed for some three years in hauling the machinery from Buenaventura over the roadless Cordillera Occidental to the Valley. (According to Phanor J. Eder, in the biography of James M. Eder, *El Fundador: Santiago M. Eder* [Bogotá: Ltda., 1959].) American engineers, laying a pipeline in 1957, on one stretch of which even then they had to haul in pipe and equipment by muleback, uncovered one of the large cogwheels which had been lost en route at some time between 1898 and 1901. In 1906 a modern textile mill began to operate in Antioquia, the machinery for which, transported up the Magdalena by boat and then to Antioquia by mule, had arrived in such shape that it is said in Antioquia that it was built in the repair shops of Medellín. Ex-president Pedro Nel Ospina, exiled in the war of 1899–1902, had decided then to construct in Antioquia a textile mill like one he observed in Mexico. In the financial crisis of 1904 his enterprise became bankrupt. The factory was opened by F. Restrepo y Compañía in 1906. In 1908 a more modern factory, the Compañía Colombiana de Tejidos, which had benefited from Restrepo's experience with technical problems, began operations. This company, known as Coltejer, is now, after several consolidations and great prosperity in World War II, one of the largest manufacturing corporations in Latin America. However, these are symbolic rather than logically significant dates. The development of industry, in Colombia or elsewhere, was a gradually accelerating process.

[4] According to the 1951 census.

some 400 miles south of the Atlantic. On it stands the capital city of Bogotá, at an altitude of 8,500 feet. The two other most important cities lie in the valley of the Cauca, Cali some 150 miles southwest of Bogotá and Medellín some 150 miles northwest, so that the three form an equilateral triangle. Cali lies at an altitude of 3,000 feet and Medellín at 5,000. The area around Cali is known as the Valley of the Cauca, or simply the Valley (Valle); that around Medellín as Antioquia. Between the two, hills and ridges only less rugged than the Cordilleras cross the Cauca Valley and create a formidable barrier to. north-south travel.

The three cities have grown rapidly during the last century. In 1960 the population of Bogotá plus its many suburbs was one million or more, and that of Medellín and Cali may be estimated very roughly at 500,000 each. The fourth city in size, Barranquilla, at the mouth of the Magdalena River, is somewhat smaller. Between Barranquilla and the other cities lie the hot swampy lowlands of the lower Magdalena and then the mountains. It is difficult to overemphasize how removed Bogotá, Medellín, and Cali were from the world and from each other until airlines and improved surface routes over the mountains opened up access in the 1920's. Until some time after 1900 every pound of material which came into any of the three was carried over the mountains on the backs of animals or men; no vehicle could traverse the mountain paths.

Ethnically, except for a handful of non-Spanish immigrants, Colombians are of Spanish, Indian, and Negro blood. The proportion of the population with Negro blood is greater in some parts of Antioquia and the Valley and on some parts of the Atlantic and Pacific coasts than elsewhere. The census of 1918, the last to inquire concerning ancestry, indicated 33 per cent of the population of white, 52 per cent of mixed, and 15 per cent of Indian or Negro blood. The percentage given for pure white blood is undoubtedly considerably exaggerated.

Formally the entire country is Roman Catholic in religion, though in the villages there is a noticeable tendency to identify some saints with pre-Christian gods or guardian spirits. The handful of non-Catholic Christian congregations minister largely to foreigners.

Historical Background

Spaniards first landed on the Atlantic coast of what is now Colombia in 1500. Between 1530 and 1540 they discovered the Sabana, the Valley, and Antioquia, conquered the Indian tribes in each, and established settlements. In all three regions the Spaniards were seeking gold and silver. Here and there throughout Colombia they found gold and silver deposits, a few of them of some size, but on the Sabana and in the Valley they found none. Yet they remained because of the fertility of the soil and the attractiveness of the environment.

Under the decrees of the king each conqueror was permitted to occupy an area of land and to take a number of Indians under his guardian-

ship and require work from them, in return for which he was to assure
their material welfare and to confer upon them the benefit of Christianity. In practice, and in spite of occasional rulings to the contrary from
Spain, the lands became the property in fee simple of the individual
Spanish families, and the Indians became slaves. On the Sabana the land
grants were large and the Indian tribes peaceable and skilled in agriculture, and the conquerors soon became landed gentry. In the Valley a similar development occurred except that the rolling land was less suitable for
farming and the settlers specialized in cattle raising. Yet here and in fertile lands nearby they found it profitable to produce other food as well as
meat for export over the western Cordillera to the miners working in the
jungles along the Pacific coast and in Antioquia. In Antioquia a number
of small gold and silver deposits were found, and attention centered
more than elsewhere on the quest for wealth in gold mining. The Indians
in Antioquia were gatherers, not cultivators, and did not learn to farm
well.

During the first 50 years after the conquest, and to a lesser degree until
the beginning of the seventeenth century, two or three areas in Antioquia
yielded considerable wealth in gold; but as the gold was laced throughout the rock or lay in a lean mixture in river bed sands, much cheap labor
was required to extract it. The methods of extraction were primitive ones
learned from the Indians, and only the Indians knew how to do some of
the aqueduct building required. Through depletion both of the richest
gold-bearing rock and of the labor supply, by about 1630 gold production
had passed its peak. From the mid-seventeenth century until almost 1900
it continued barely on a subsistence basis, and it was increasingly the
descendants of the conquerors, who termed themselves Spaniards, who
did the mining, often with pick and hammer and hand screening of the
crushed ore or the sands. The most prosperous communities of the region after the beginning of the seventeenth century seem to have been
Medellín and Rionegro, which benefited not from the mining itself but
from the trade by which the miners were supplied.

Spain's economic control of her colonies in the New World followed
the usual mercantilist pattern. Trade was permitted only with the mother
country, and on both sales to and purchases from the colony taxes were
levied which greatly burdened the producers in the colony.

Politically the dominance of the home government was complete. Not
only did the colonists have neither representation in Spain nor formal
voice in the administration of the colony;[5] in addition, when in Spain they
had neither the freedom of movement nor the full right to hold property
which a native of Spain possessed, and socially they were looked on as
inferior. In part their exclusion from important political offices may have
been because it was known that many of the original immigrant adven-

---

[5] Though some individuals who could claim pure Spanish blood were appointed
to administrative posts.

turers had been of the lowest Spanish classes, economically and socially, and in part because it was suspected (correctly) that many or most of them were in part of Indian or slave blood; but it was also motivated by a desire to maintain the authority of the crown and hold centrifugal tendencies in check.[6] In any event, resentment at social and political discrimination festered in the colonists. In the New World persons of local birth who could claim pure Spanish blood looked with contempt on the mestizos or "men of color"—contempt the fervor of which may perhaps have been proportionate to the dubiousness of their own blood claim.[7]

In 1810 the colonials of Spanish blood on the Sabana rose up in a movement for reform, then a demand for autonomy. It was harshly put down. During the decade that followed, disturbances and demands rose in several waves, but within the small Spanish group troops loyal to the motherland were able to quell the revolts. Then at the end of the decade, after previously leading two unsuccessful attempts at independence, Bolivar called on the mestizos to rise against the Spaniards. Under this call and the magnetic leadership of Bolivar, the revolution succeeded; in 1819 the leaders of New Granada declared their independence, and thereafter they successfully defended it. But the hopes of the mestizos were not fulfilled; the creoles dominated political life. They called the new republic Grancolombia. But there was little cohesion among the various regions of Grancolombia. In 1830 Ecuador and Venezuela seceded,[8] and throughout the remainder of the nineteenth century, or until 1902, differences within Colombia erupted in a series of civil wars.

ECONOMIC CHANGE: THE HISTORICAL RECORD

The Gradual Expansion of Agriculture and Manufacturing

One of the impressive facts revealed by a detailed study of Colombian economic history is the gradualness of the appearance of technological progress.[9] To identify any given date as marking its beginning would be as absurd as to identify any given point on an exponential curve as the point at which it begins to rise rapidly. Because specific information

---

[6] I am indebted to William P. Glade for this suggestion as well as for refinement of several points below.

[7] Today Colombians insist a little too forcefully that there are no discriminations in Colombia on the basis of color. There are no such legal distinctions, but the persons one meets at the country club tend to be of light skin while those carrying burdens on the street are dark. In at least one recent instance cited to me it was impossible to promote a dark-skinned factory worker over others because two valued lighter ones in the group he would have directed would have resigned.

[8] Colombia included Panama until the secession of Panama in 1903 fostered by President Theodore Roosevelt.

[9] My information concerning economic change before 1900 is mainly from Luis Ospina Vásquez' basic work, *Industria y Protección en Colombia, 1810–1930* (Bogotá: Editorial Santafé, 1955).

concerning the early stages of economic growth is rarely available, it seems useful to narrate that for Colombia in some detail.

During the eighteenth century little economic change is recorded: It is a plausible speculation, though only a speculation, that with the increasing percentage of persons of European blood in the population aggregate output rose more rapidly than did total population. In the nineteenth century, and especially after independence, economic change became slightly more noticeable. The production of unrefined brown cake sugar known as *panela* grew in importance, and, although this growth may have been mainly a displacement of even more primitive sugar production in the home, the change probably increased productivity and income. More important, coffee cultivation, which was known in the first years of the republic in valleys near Venezuela, spread to Antioquia, then to the slopes on the edge of the Sabana, and finally to the department of Caldas, geographically within the Valley but peopled with Antioqueños, and became the nation's largest industry. After 1880 coffee cultivation increased rapidly in Antioquia and Caldas.[10]

New industries gradually arose in the nineteenth century and contributed to the rise in per capita income. Early in the century the textile industry of the Sabana had been injured by the import of foreign fabrics, but the records of 1830–60 indicate a proliferation on the Sabana of consumer goods industries.[11] During the next decade or two production of china and additional textiles began. Steam-powered wheat mills were established. Gas lighting was introduced into Bogotá in 1876.

Meanwhile heavier industry had also been appearing. Early in the nineteenth century an improved gunpowder plant replaced or augmented primitive establishments. At some time after 1810 iron mining methods were improved in three mining areas, with foreign technicians and in part with English capital, and an iron refining plant was established. These enterprises struggled along throughout the century. At some time after 1830 the refinery installed a blast furnace. At about the same time production of some chemicals began.[12] The first commercial bank in Colombia, a branch of an English bank, was established in Bogotá in 1865. Within a year or two the first bank owned by Colombians, the Banco de Bogotá, was opened. After 1875 iron processing developed further. The Sabana felt a sense of great progress as the century drew to a close,

---

[10] By 1913 Antioquia and Caldas together produced 36 per cent of Colombia's growing output of coffee, and by 1940, 50 per cent.

[11] Handicraft and cottage enterprises were numerous, and slightly larger establishments, using newer machine methods, began to produce beer, hats, pottery, porcelain, matches, flour, glass and crystal, paper, and cloth. The paper factory lasted only some 25 years; the glass and crystal plant collapsed after a time, to be revived later. Between 1890 and 1900 a modern brewery, a bottlemaking plant, a new pottery plant, new textile plants, a tannery, and a salt manufactory appeared.

[12] A sulphuric acid plant failed after some years; it was the first of several during the remainder of the century, each failing for lack of demand and being succeeded after some time by another.

and in 1899 an industrial exposition at Bogotá celebrated that progress.

Industrial activity was more impressive on the Sabana than anywhere else in Colombia during the nineteenth century. At the other end of the scale, the Valley continued with very little industry. The region's economy rested largely on general agriculture, the raising of cattle, and the production of sugar and later of coffee.[13]

In Antioquia industry was of intermediate importance. Early in the century the main industries other than agriculture and mining seem to have been production of hats and beer. (A steam engine was first used in mining not long after 1800.) Then, during the last half of the century, economic growth in Antioquia, though starting behind that of the Sabana, seems to show greater vigor. By the 1860's breweries with advanced methods and various other small consumer goods enterprises existed, and during the 1870's and 1880's many others appeared.[14] In the 1870's textile plants began to appear. By the end of the 1880's small plants with machine looms had appeared here and there among the many handloom establishments, though socks were still woven by hand of jute and sisal. Unlike earlier iron works, one established in 1864 survived and 20 years later entered upon production of simple mining and agricultural machinery and especially machinery used in coffee processing. By the end of the century production of this machinery was a flourishing industry in itself.

Of the 42 commercial banks which existed in Colombia in 1881, 12 were in Cundinamarca, 11 in Antioquia, and from one to five in each of seven other regions.[15]

This incomplete listing of consumer goods industries which developed in Colombia during the nineteenth century indicates the trend of events. As in all early development, the picture includes overoptimism, many false starts, and failures together with steady expansion. From Ospina Vásquez' account one gets the impression that the false starts and failures were more frequent in Cundinamarca than in Antioquia—that even in the last half of the nineteenth century business entrepreneurs in Antioquia were less wishful and more capable in their judgments or in their execution of projects, though equally bold. This impression, however, may result from a difference in the extent of the information available to Ospina Vásquez rather than from a difference in reality.

---

[13] Even toward the end of the century, apart from handicraft industries, cottage industries processing agricultural produce, the woolen and Panama hat industry, and the ubiquitous breweries, the only industry in the Valley mentioned in Ospina Vásquez' account is a textile industry specializing in the production of flannel cloth.

[14] A cacao mill, a pottery industry, production of ceramics, half-peasant, half-capitalist in method, and the tanning of hides and making of shoes by primitive methods are reported in the 1860's. By the 1880's, improved tanneries had been opened, and shoes, cigars, cigarettes, and chocolates had become products of some importance.

[15] Camacho Roldán, *Escritos Varios, Segunda Serie* (Bogotá: Librería Colombiana, 1893).

Even in the absence of data concerning aggregate production in the economy it seems fairly certain that per capita income was increasing steadily (with interruptions during the civil wars) during the last four or five decades of the century, and quite possibly earlier as well.

The Development of Transportation

During this period of gradually accelerating economic growth, transportation facilities were remarkably primitive. Before 1850, except in the immediate vicinity of cities, all "roads" apparently were pack trails which only a single beast of burden might traverse. Items too large or heavy to be packed by mule[16] were transported on poles between mule backs or human backs. Extremely heavy ones were drawn up mountainsides by block and tackle. Coffee, sugar, machinery, pianos, even the first locomotives—everything was carried in this fashion out to the rivers or in from the rivers.

Indeed, even trails were not everywhere present. The first "mule road" from Cali over the Cordillera Occidental toward the Pacific was not completed until 1866.[17] In the 1850's there occurred a flurry of building of wagon roads around Bogotá (and perhaps, if one had the local histories, around other cities as well). In the 1870's railroad construction began. Between 1872 and 1880 eight railroads were built, extending a few miles in one direction or another from major cities or closing the first few miles of a link between some city and the Magdalena River. They were built by the national government, by the states, or by individuals with governmental financial aid. By 1890 four had failed financially and had ceased to operate,[18] but the early lines on the Sabana, in Antioquia, and carrying freight for the first leg of the journey from the Magdalena to the one region or the other were successful.[19] The rapid development of coffee cultivation in Antioquia and Caldas came only when railroad and truck transportation to the Magdalena was possible.

Even by 1912 there were only 1,000 kilometers of railroad track in

---

[16] Each mule carried two packs weighing not more than 70 kilograms or about 155 pounds.

[17] And the first mule road from Cali to the important Valley town of Palmira was not completed until 1869. Phanor J. Eder, *El Fundador: Santiago M. Eder*. James (Santiago) M. Eder was a leading force in the construction of both.

[18] Camacho Roldán, *Notas de Viaje* (Bogotá: Librería Colombiana, 1890).

[19] Of the four railroad stretches which survived of the first eight built, one ran from Bogotá toward the edge of the Sabana, one from Medellín northeastward toward the Cordillera Central, and one from Puerto Berrio on the Magdalena toward Antioquia. My historical information is not specific enough to be certain which other road survived.

The first locomotive to be used in Antioquia, which was carried across the Cordillera Central by a gang of from 30 to 50 men, is still on display in Medellín. It is shorter than the smallest American automobile of the 1950's before the advent of the compact car.

Colombia, and it was divided among 14 separate lines, of which the longest was 135.7 kilometers.[20]

Not long after 1900 a wagon road of a sort was completed from Bogotá over the mountains rimming the Sabana down to Puerto Salgar on the Magdalena; thereafter goods were drawn to Bogotá by teams of two, four, or six pairs of oxen.[21] The first wheeled transportation to Medellín from the outside world became possible in 1909, when a yard-gauge railroad was completed from Puerto Berrio on the Magdalena to a point on the Cordillera Central, whence a 27-kilometer road over the ridge joined the section of the railroad running from Medellín.[22]

Not until 1929 was a tunnel completed which achieved a railroad connection direct from Medellín to the river; not until some time in the 1930's did a road over the Cordillera Central permit motor transport into and out of Antioquia to the east and south; and not until 1958 was a railroad connection from Medellín to Bogotá (other than by a long loop to the South) completed.

Cali was similarly mountain-locked until the completion of the railroad from Buenaventura on the Pacific, over the Cordillera Occidental, to Cali in 1914. This plus completion of the Panama Canal in 1915 suddenly made transport between Cali and the eastern United States coast and Europe almost miraculously easy. A motor road from Cali to Bogotá was completed in 1928, and one from Cali to Medellín in 1940 or 1941. The last link of a railroad between Cali and Medellín was completed in 1942. No railroad traverses the mountain ranges between Cali and Bogotá even today. A road across the mountain from Cali to Bogotá was completed in 1928, but even now it is still cheaper for most freight to use a combined road-railroad route—by railroad northeast to the town of Armenia, then across the Cordillera by truck, then by railroad on to Bogotá.

The Twentieth Century

After 1900, while transportation facilities were still primitive, heavier industry began to expand. The first modern sugar refinery began production in 1901 (in the Valley), the first modern textile plant in 1906 (in Antioquia), and the first major cement plant in 1909 (on the Sabana). One after another, others appeared. Then the stream became a widening tide.

---

[20] René Roger, *La Colombie Economique* (Paris: Librairie de la Société du Recueil Sirey et Librairie R. Roger et F. Chernovez, 1914).

[21] But Puerto Salgar was on the upper reach of the Magdalena, above a rapids, and almost dry during the dry season. Above the rapids all goods had to move by small boat and then be hauled by road or rail around the rapids.

[22] From Medellín one could then travel to Bogotá by taking a train to the pass, a cart across the pass, train to Puerto Berrio, boat up the river to La Dorada, railroad around the rapids above La Dorada, smaller river boat to Girardot, 1-yard gauge railroad up to Facatativa on the edge of the Sabana, and 1-meter railroad to Bogotá. With luck, the trip (now one hour by DC-3) could be completed in the greatly improved time of six days; with bad luck, it required twice that time.

Small metallurgical plants increased their output; production of simple agricultural and mining machinery increased in importance. New glass plants were established. Electric light and power plants became numerous and prosperous. Production of pharmaceuticals began. The industrial system became able to manage the construction of larger and larger, more and more demanding structures.

Agriculture steadily declined in relative importance, though its output continued to increase in amount, and manufacturing and tertiary industries steadily and rapidly increased in both absolute and relative importance. Data for 1925, 1945, and 1953 are presented in the table below.

TABLE 15-1

COLOMBIA: GROWTH AND COMPOSITION OF PRODUCTION OF GOODS AND SERVICES

	Composition of the Product by Activities			Average Rates of Growth	
	1925	1945	1953	1925-53	1946-53
Total...........................	100.0	100.0	100.0	4.6	5.9
Agricultural and livestock...........	58.8	47.0	36.9	2.9	2.7
Mining..........................	1.5	3.7	3.7	8.1	5.7
Manufacturing...................	7.6	13.4	17.2	7.7	9.2
Artisan industry.................	2.9	3.1	3.8	5.6	8.4
Construction.....................	2.6	6.1	4.8	7.0	2.7
Transport........................	2.3	4.2	7.4	9.1	13.7
Energy, communications, and public utilities........................	0.4	0.7	1.2	8.7	12.7
Government......................	5.7	5.5	6.9	5.4	8.9
Trade, finance, and services........	8.7	10.2	12.9	6.1	9.0
Personal income from rentals.......	9.5	6.1	5.2	2.3	3.8

Source: ECLA, *The Economic Development of Colombia*, Table 3, p. 16.

Bloodless though the statistics are, detailed estimates by the Economic Commission for Latin America tell the story from the 1920's on impressively. Industrial growth continued during the 1930's after falling in 1930 and 1931. During earlier periods of foreign exchange shortage Colombia was able neither to produce substitutes for the finished products whose importation was cut off nor to cope with the shortage of imported industrial components, and her domestic industrial production probably fell rather than rose; but by the 1930's Colombian entrepreneurs had gained enough technical versatility so that absence of imports provided an opportunity rather than a handicap, and industrial expansion continued.

Since World War II, industrialization has been occurring within agriculture. In the hot lands little above sea level stretching from the middle reaches of the Magdalena between Bogotá and Medellín down to the Atlantic, Colombian entrepreneurs have established large-scale mechanized production of rice and other tropical crops and large cattle ranches. The cattle are of breeds, some imported and some developed in Colombia, which are suited to the hot humid climate. Large unused areas remain; the taming of the hot lowland jungles is continuing. Growth in this sector of the Colombian economy is as important in some ways as the continuing industrial expansion.[23] Technological progress is now so deeply rooted in Colombian behavior patterns that it is a thoroughly safe assumption that economic growth will continue indefinitely.

WHY DID GROWTH BEGIN?

Not for the Economic Reasons Conventionally Advanced

One thing is clear: Economic growth in Colombia did not begin for the economic reasons conventionally cited as causes of such growth.

Foreign companies or individuals did not provide capital and thereby break a bottleneck. Foreign investment in Colombia before World War II was minimal; before World War I it was almost negligible. While there were a very few earlier investments, in the main foreign capital began flowing into Colombia only after economic growth was firmly implanted and the expanding market attracted foreign enterprises.[24]

Contacts with foreign goods and technology were not greater in Colombia than elsewhere where growth has been slower in starting. On the contrary, as I have noted, the Sabana, the Valley, and Antioquia, where growth has centered, were extremely difficult of access until well into the twentieth century. Moreover, the seedbed of growth was Antioquia, which in turn had far less opportunity for contact with Europe and other American countries than did Bogotá, the national capital.

Growth did not wait upon the development of an infrastructure, or social overhead capital, to use the economic terms, which created a national market or otherwise laid a base for progress. The extremely primitive state of transportation until growth was under way has been sketched. Transportation, communication, and power facilities all developed in response to the demands created by growing production rather than as prior steps which laid the basis for it. (As they developed, they in turn stimulated further advance.) Production until say 1910, except for primary commodities, was for small regional markets, not for a national market. It is possible that the protection provided by transportation difficulties stimulated rather than hampered early industrialization. Even today production of cement, steel products, and other heavy products is for regional markets limited by transportation costs.

Thus growth began in spite of the supposed economic barriers, not because those barriers were removed.

---

[23] Perhaps next will come expansion onto the *llanos*, but difficult problems of transportation, or the establishment of a largely self-contained economy on those eastern grasslands, must be solved before development there can proceed.

[24] Concerning earlier United States investment, see J. Fred Rippy, *The Capitalists and the Colombians* (New York: Vanguard Press, 1931).

The Antioqueños

The proximate answer to the question why growth began is: Because of the enterprise of the Antioqueños.

It is a Colombian national myth that virtually all of the nation's important industrial enterprises are run by Antioqueños. "If they did not found them," it is said, "they own them now." "The only person a Turco can't outsmart in a business deal," I was told so often that it is clear that this is a stock statement, "is an Antioqueño." The facts do not support these extreme versions of the myth. Capable and effective entrepreneurs have arisen in every region of the country. Yet the predominance of Antioqueños is impressive.

From the 1956 Census of Industry[25] I obtained lists of all nonfinancial private business concerns in Cundinamarca, in Antioquia, and in the Valley employing more than 100 workers. I then asked informed individuals to identify the founders of these enterprises by nationality, and,

TABLE 15–2

ORIGINS OF FOUNDERS OF LARGER ENTERPRISES IN CUNDINAMARCA,
ANTIOQUIA, AND THE VALLE DEL CAUCA

	Number of Enterprises with More Than 100 Workers in 1956 Founded by Individuals from:							
Department	Antio- quia	Cundi- na- marca	Valle del Cauca	Other Regions	Persons of "For- eign" Origin	Subsidi- aries of Foreign Com- panies	No In- forma- tion	Total
Antioquia............45	1	0	0	5	1	6	58
Valle del Cauca........17	2	8	1	9	7	0	44
Cundinamarca.........13	17	0	6	15	1	7	59
Totals..........75	20	8	7	29	9	13	161

if Colombian, regional origin. This was done hurriedly shortly before my departure from Colombia, but I believe that the margin of error is not great. The results of the survey are presented in Table 15–2. The classification included as Antioqueños entrepreneurs from Caldas of Antioqueño stock.

Of the 148 enterprises concerning which information was obtained, 110, or just under three fourths, were founded by persons referred to as "Old Colombians." Nine, of which at least seven were founded after World War II, are subsidiaries of foreign companies, and 29 were founded by individuals of families termed "foreign" in Colombia. Almost all of the

[25] República de Colombia, Departamento Administrativo Nacional de Estadística, *Directoria Industrial (Provisional), 1956* (Bogotá, 1957).

29 are older companies founded by individuals of non-Spanish stock who had settled in Colombia but whose families are still termed "foreign." Of the 26 identified by origin, 10 were from the Middle East, six were identified as Jewish without other designation of nationality, and the other 10 were Italian, German, French, Dutch, and Russian. The persistence of the label of "foreign" is indicated by the fact that one of the firms so identified (the largest) is Cervecería Bavaria, a major national brewery founded before 1900 by German families which have been Colombian since that time.[26] In general these 29 companies are of the second rank in size and importance, 24 of them in textiles or food products. With due recognition of their role, the relative unimportance of foreign entrepreneurship as a focal point of economic growth and capital and the importance of entrepreneurship of Old Colombians are facts of the Colombian record.

Among the 110 enterprises founded by Old Colombians, 75, or 68 per cent, were founded by Antioqueños. In 1905, a pertinent year for this comparison, the population of Antioquia and Caldas constituted somewhat less than 40 per cent of the population of Antioquia, the Valley, and Cundinamarca.[27] The percentage of individuals of Antioqueño ancestry to the total population was probably slightly higher. Assuming that it was 40 per cent, that per cent of the population provided more than two thirds of the entrepreneurs of large companies, while the remaining 60 per cent provided less than one third. In proportion to population, more than three times as many Antioqueños became entrepreneurs as Old Colombians of non-Antioqueño stock.[28]

Waiving historical precision to make a point vividly, it might be said that if the Bogotanos, in their more favorable economic environment, had been as effective entrepreneurs as the Antioqueños, rapid economic growth in Colombia would have begun half a century sooner than it did, or around 1850; whereas if the Antioqueños had been no more effective entrepreneurs than the Bogotanos or Caleños, rapid economic development would not have begun until half a century later than it did, or around 1950.

Such a statement is subject to misinterpretation. It is an important fact of Colombian history that effective economic innovators arose in every region of the country. There is no difference in kind among regions, but only one of degree. But the difference in degree is so great that it must

---

[26] But the Eder family, of Russian stock, a generation farther back, was termed Colombian. All the other families termed Colombian were of Spanish stock.

[27] Because I do not have complete data from the 1905 census, this estimate is imprecise. I estimate that the percentage was between 38 and 39. In 1951 the population of Antioquia and Caldas constituted 49.1 per cent of that of the three departments, a result primarily of the rapid rate of natural increase among Antioqueños.

[28] Because some persons may have been termed Antioqueños who are of mixed regional origin, these data may overstate the facts. However, with due allowance for a margin of error, the evidence is impressive.

be concluded that factors at work in Antioquia were not present else-where or were much weaker elsewhere. It is of interest to sort out the facts of history to try to decide what those factors were.

Until some time in the nineteenth century Antioquia was the poorest of the regions of Colombia. The romance attached to silver and gold should not mislead one. "Instead of representing the wealth of the Crown," wrote Padre Joaquín de Finestrad in 1783, "the mines seem to have been responsible for the notable backwardness in certain provinces. Antioquia, which is paved with gold, is the poorest and most miserable of all."[29] In 1808 an Antioqueño observer, José Manuel Restrepo, wrote of the mines in Antioquia, "Those in operation today are poor and only make enough profit to keep their owners alive."[30] Until the end of the colonial period (or through the first quarter of the nineteenth century) observers "were struck by the general backwardness, illiteracy, and pov-erty of the province."[31] Then some change gradually became manifest. It was noticeable by mid-century and conspicuous a generation later. In 1883 the German traveler Ferdinand von Schenck wrote:

> There are probably few places of similar size in South America where as many important fortunes are concentrated as in Medellín. The number of families considered as rich is considerable, but with few exceptions they appear so unassuming that their wealth, won mostly by trade and mining, and less commonly through farming and stock-raising, is not apparent. Even the middle classes or artisans are well situated.[32]

During the last half of the nineteenth century the energies which led to these results were exerted mainly in Antioquia. In the twentieth cen-tury they sought new outlets throughout the nation.[33]

Why this burst of creative activity in business and technology by the people of one region?[34]

---

[29] *El Vasalle Instruído*, quoted by Rufina Gutiérrez, *Monografías* (2 vols.; Bogatá, 1920–21), Vol. 1, p. 413. I in turn have this quotation, not from Gutiérrez, but from James J. Parsons, *Antioqueño Colonization in Western Colombia* (Ibero-Americana: 32) (Berkeley and Los Angeles: University of California Press, 1949), p. 55.

[30] José Manuel Restrepo, "Ensayo sobre la Geografía: Producciones, Industria y Población de la Provincia de Antioquia en el Nuevo Reino de Granada," in Francisco José de Caldas (ed.), *Seminario del Nuevo Reino de Granada* (Bogotá, 1808–10). Reprinted in 3 vols. (Bogotá, 1942), Vol. I, p. 257, quoted by Parsons, *Antioqueño Colonization*, p. 55.

[31] *Ibid.*, p. 5.

[32] Ferdinand von Schenck, "Reisen in Antioquia," *Petermanns Mitteilungen*, Vol. XXIX (1883), p. 89, quoted in *ibid.*, p. 6.

[33] When I asked a taxicab driver in Cartagena, on the Atlantic seacoast, whether there were Antioqueños there, he replied, "De aqui a China, Antioqueños." ("From here to China, Antioqueños.")

[34] The economic rejuvention of Antioquia is sometimes attributed to the reforms directed by the royal inspector Juan Antonio Mon y Velarde during his three-year turn of duty in the province in 1784–87 (or possibly 1785–88). He reformed govern-mental administration, directed the establishment of new agricultural towns, pro-vided bounties for the introduction of new crops, enforced vagrancy laws while simultaneously providing opportunities to work in the new towns, and so on. How-

WHY THE ANTIOQUEÑOS?

Not Because of Economic Advantages

The reason does not lie in economic advantage—a larger market, greater access to technical knowledge abroad, better natural resources, greater capital. On the first two of these four counts, a great advantage lay with the people of the Sabana, and they probably had an advantage with respect to the other two as well. The population of the Sabana, throughout both the colonial era and the nineteenth century, was considerably larger than that of Antioquia. The Sabana had the best land and the most prosperous agriculture in Colombia throughout the colonial period. Next most prosperous was agriculture in the Valley and the regions south of it. Per capita income in both must have been higher than in Antioquia. The market available on the Sabana was much the largest in Colombia, one reason why the first attempts at development of industry, during the first half of the nineteenth century, were there.

Further, during the colonial period and the nineteenth century (and indeed with some qualification up to the present) Bogotá was the main point of Colombian contact with Europe and the foreign world in general. Before independence it had been the most important administrative seat. After independence it became the nation's capital. Foreign diplomats, such representatives of the sciences and arts as visited Colombia,[35] and foreign businessmen seeking to establish trade or looking for a new area in which to establish themselves came first of all to Bogotá. Until the late nineteenth century many more families on the Sabana than elsewhere were wealthy enough and sufficiently interested in culture and the foreign world to send their sons and daughters abroad. Through contacts with Peru and Ecuador, the Valley had more lines of communication with the outside world. Of the three regions, Antioquia was the most isolated.

The only natural resource to be noted in Antioquia other than the gold is a number of small waterfalls. These indeed provided the occasion for the location of several textile mills at the turn of the century, but they were of no importance in the subsequent development of the mills. Greater falls, though probably fewer in number, exist on and at the edge of the Sabana.

Creative Personality

One is led to the conclusion that the difference between Antioqueños and others lay not in the external conditions but in the people. And

---

ever, we may reasonably distrust a thesis which assumes that reforms in external institutions over a three-year period fundamentally alter the nature of the people and account for their creativity over the following 175 years.

[35] See Jesús María Henao and Gerardo Arrubla, *History of Colombia*, trans. and ed. J. Fred Rippy (Chapel Hill, N.C.: University of North Carolina Press, 1938), *passim*. Bogotá's rival in this respect was not Medellín but Popayán.

as soon as one considers this possibility, convincing evidence appears.

First, differences appear in psychological tests in which a number of Colombian business and community leaders courteously agreed to participate. The successful economic innovators of Antioquia in 1957 were so different in personality structure from a group of equally prominent community leaders elsewhere in Colombia who were interviewed and studied that they may be thought of as a different breed of men. The differences are discussed in a monograph being written by my colleague, Dr. Louis C. Schaw. Since that monograph is not yet available, let me summarize some of them.

The group of entrepreneurs studied in Antioquia are a group of some 20 businessmen in Medellín whose careers stamp them as effective innovators, entrepreneurs of the Schumpeterian type. Not all are among the wealthiest men in the community; some are men in mid-career who started as poor men and whose wealth today, relative to Medellín innovators in general, is only moderate. The contrasting group is a group of community leaders in Popayán, a city with a present population of some 60,000 which was a cultural and political center in colonial days and the nineteenth century, and which now lives in the past, rather defensively spurning the "crass materialism" of such cities as Medellín.

One of the psychological instruments used in analyzing these men was the "thematic apperception test" or "TAT," in which simple pictures are shown to the individual one at a time. In the series usually used, one picture is of a young man and an older one; another of a young man and woman; another of a group of men around a table; and so on. Others are less commonplace. Concerning each, the respondent is asked to use his imagination to tell out of what situation the scene pictured arose, what the individuals in the pictures are thinking and feeling, and what the outcome of the situation will be.[36] In the process he tells much of his own attitudes toward life, for no interpretations of the pictures come to his mind so readily as ones which arise out of his own view of the world.

Some simple aspects of the differences between the two groups are as follows. The responses of the Medellín innovators typically embodied: (*a*) a perception of a situation as a problem to be solved, (*b*) awareness that to be solved a problem must be worked at (absence of any fantasy of magic success), (*c*) confidence in their ability to solve it (though sometimes tension and anxiety are also present), (*d*) a tendency to take the viewpoint of each individual in turn and analyze the situation as he might see it before suggesting an outcome, rather than to adopt a formula identification with any one type of character—with the old versus the young, the young versus the old, and so on. In the terms used in previous chapters, they manifested high need autonomy, need achievement, and need order; had a keen sense of the realities of a situation; saw the world as

---

[36] He is asked, that is, to tell what themes he perceives in each picture. Hence the name of the test.

manageable with good judgment and hard work. The Popayán leaders gave intellectually more complex responses. They associated a picture with something in literature or the arts, philosophized about the ways of youth, were led into speculation about the course of history—but tended to see no problems in the situations pictured. Or, if they saw problems, they had formula solutions for them ("the old know best; he should listen to his father"), or visualized success without any suggestion that it would entail effort and pain. Frequently they gave the impression of running away from the possibility that they might be facing a problem, as though it made them uneasy; they veered away to some peripheral aspect of the picture. They found it easy to turn to fantasy or reverie not closely connected with reality. They showed low need autonomy, achievement, and order; saw the world as not manageable, one's position as given. These differences of course were matters of degree; there was a range of response within each group with regard to various elements. If the responses were shuffled, without identification, a person examining them would not unerringly separate all of those from Medellín and all of those from Popayán correctly. Nevertheless, the net differences between the groups were striking.[37]

It should be emphasized that what is portrayed is not a difference in personality between all Antioqueños and all Popayanese or other Colombians. The Antioqueños selected were those most apt to have creative personalities. So, however, were the Popayanese, for they were community leaders. There are undoubtedly creative individuals, some of whom have turned their talents to problems of technology and some elsewhere, in every region of Colombia. What is suggested, however, is that the incidence of creative personality is probably much higher among Antioqueños than elsewhere, and that this is an important cause of their greater entrepreneurial success.[38]

Not surprisingly, along with this creativity goes an attitude that any man worth his salt will get into business for himself—"get his own feet wet"—and make his way. A prominent Medellín executive stated that when he came home from college in the 1930's and took a salaried job with a large corporation his action in becoming merely a hired hand was looked upon with raised eyebrows. Many other individuals confirmed the prevalence of such an attitude.

There probably is also a regional difference in the attitude toward

---

[37] Professor William E. Henry, a distinguished analyst of thematic apperception tests, said jokingly when he examined the responses of the two groups to the test, "Of course you made these up, but you didn't need to exaggerate the contrast so sharply."

[38] An alternative explanation may be that creativity is randomly distributed everywhere but that more of the creative Antioqueños chose to exert their talents in problems of business and technology. There is no evidence in Colombian history, however, that in other regions an equal share of the population was creative in other fields.

manual-technical work, though here my evidence is merely impression-istic. An industrialist in Bogotá, hiring 10 college graduates, put them at operating jobs in his factory for training. Within a year eight had re-signed. Underlying the avowed reasons, he felt, were attitudes on the part of the individuals or their families that the jobs demeaned them. (The two who remained, interestingly, were of lower-income families.) "If they had been Antioqueños," he said, only half jokingly, "all of them, having learned the processes, would have resigned within the first year—in order to start their own competing businesses." And the head of an en-terprise with operations in four centers in Colombia, himself neutral so far as regional affiliation is concerned, told me that the learning time for office and clerical detail is clearly somewhat shorter in Antioquia than else-where.

Finally, there is a feeling in Medellín that effective work is a social duty. I did not sense this feeling equally in Cali or Bogotá. It is felt by many Antioqueños that the man who fails to put his capital at work pro-ductively in business is somehow lacking in the best qualities and is failing in a duty to the community. "He neither uses his axe nor lends it" is the Antioqueño phrase of disapproval. And, while the entrepreneurs in all regions are pious Catholics, both Dr. Schaw and I thought we sensed a difference in religious attitude. We thought we sensed a feeling in Medellín, not paralleled in the same degree elsewhere, of a personal involvement with the deity[39] and a feeling that to achieve is a personal moral duty. In short, we thought we found among Antioqueños the "Puritan ethic."[40]

Associated with the personality differences among regions is a differ-ence in procreative behavior. During the past 35 years population growth in Colombia as a whole has been rapid—slightly more than 2 per cent per year, almost altogether from natural increases. The increase in the frac-tion of the total population which Antioqueños constitute is such that natural increase among them must have been at least 0.5 per cent per year faster than among other Colombians, and census data and estimates for periods extending back to 1870 suggest an earlier differential of at least 1 per cent per year.[41] I have no suggestion to make concerning the

[39] Some other Colombians have an image of Antioqueños as "always praying."

[40] Parsons notes a regional difference in religious attitude, though with what authority I do not know since his stay in Colombia was limited to six months and apparently was spent almost entirely in Antioquia. "In piety and devoutness," he states, "the Antioqueños are far ahead of other Colombian ethnic groups, for the Catholic faith is embraced by them with the conscientious passion of their fore-fathers." *Antioqueño Colonization*, p. 6.

[41] The statement is based on a comparison of data for the population of Colombia as a whole in República de Colombia, Departamento Administrativo Nacional de Estadística, *Anuario General de Estadística, Colombia, 1956* (Bogotá, 1957), with the estimates of Antioqueño population in Parsons, *Antioqueño Colonization*, p. 103.

relationship of this greater vigor of population growth to other personality characteristics; it may be observed, however, that more rapid population growth in an innovating group than in the rest of a society has been remarked on by various writers, and that psychologists have commented on the association observed in a number of individuals between creativity and sexual vigor.[42]

Perhaps the innovative activity is also related in some way to need aggression. It may be that Antioqueños are characterized by higher need aggression than the Colombians of other regions, or that they are less afraid of their need aggression and release it more freely in overt activity. However, beyond the general considerations relating some degree of need aggression to economic innovation, which are set forth in Chapters 5 and 6, there seems little to add.

Having asserted that these differences in personality exist, we must attempt to find why they exist. If there is a personality difference, what is its source?

Ethnic Differences

Contrary to one popular fancy, the source of personality differences does not lie in the degree of Jewish blood. Neither early nor later immigrants to the region were in any unique degree Jews.

Concerning later immigration there is no dispute, but the legend dies hard in Colombia that the sixteenth and seventeenth century immigrants to Antioquia were Spanish Jews who forged records of Christian blood to obtain permission to migrate. Dr. Emilio Robledo of Medellín has done a scholarly job of evaluating the legend.[43] The assertion first appears in print, so far as Robledo could determine, in a volume published in 1803 by a Franciscan priest who had taught in Antioquia for a time. But neither early histories nor the voluminous primary materials in archives in Medellín and Bogotá contain any suggestion of this origin of Antioqueños. And although the Inquisition tribunal which held forth at Cartagena for some two centuries found Jews elsewhere in Colombia—68 of its total 767 sentences were against Jews—it found none in Antioquia.

The legend gained wide circulation in the nineteenth century. It was spread among others by the noted Colombian Jewish author, Jorge Isaacs, who was proud of it. It probably owes the credence given it today to its convenience. Bogotano businessmen, for example, look down on their aggressive competitors from Antioquia and at the same time take pride in their own pure Spanish Catholicism. When they say of the Antioqueños,

---

[42] Though there is no clear evidence concerning whether in general greater sexual activity is associated with greater creativity.

[43] He narrates the results of his study in a preface to Gabriel Arango Mejía, *Geneologías de Antioquia y Caldas* (2d ed.; Medellín, Colombia: Imprenta Editorial Medellín, 1942), Vol. I.

"They are *New Christians,* you know," they are at the same time condescending toward them and explaining away the lesser frequency of effectiveness in business activity among Bogotanos.

The other variant of the defensive explanation given for Antioqueño business success is that the Antioqueños are of Basque origin. The Basques, being rugged individualists who have survived in a spare and rugged mountain environment, are presumed to have qualities conducive to achievement in business. This explanation has a better claim to credence. Whether or not the ethnic difference is an explanation of the difference in economic prowess, some difference with respect to Basque blood may exist.

Data presented in Appendix 2 to this chapter indicate that, while only some 15 per cent of those families in Medellín listed in the city telephone directory bear Basque names, between 20 and 25 per cent of the executives and directors of industrial enterprises in Antioquia do.

These facts are not entirely conclusive evidence that persons of Basque blood have been more successful entrepreneurs than have others; subscribers to telephones are not necessarily representative of the entire population, and there are also other possible sources of error (noted in the Appendix).

There is no obvious reason, however, why these sources of error should result in an upward distortion of the proportion of Basque names. Hence the evidence is suggestive that persons of Basque descent in Antioquia tend to achieve business executive status to a greater degree than persons of non-Basque Spanish descent. This does not necessarily demonstrate a regional difference in entrepreneurship within Colombia, for we do not know what fraction of individuals in other regions are of Basque blood and how well they have fared in business careers. However, the argument—often advanced in Colombia—that the Basques, living in mountain mining country, tended to select Antioquia as a destination to a greater than random degree is a plausible one. One must therefore conclude that Basque ancestry in Antioquia may be associated in some degree with the economic success of Antioqueños.

If it is, there is no reason to assume that the greater propensity for business success is biologically inherited. It is much more apt to be inherited culturally. The people of the Basque provinces have long been looked down upon, or at least have been looked upon as different and a little odd, by many other Spaniards. They are rugged hard-working mountain people who have preserved a cultural separateness. These personality characteristics may have been transmitted in Colombia over many generations.

However, even if true, that circumstance hardly seems sufficient to explain the differential entrepreneurial achievement of Antioqueños. The extra margin of entrepreneurship among Antioqueños is much greater than that attributable to Basque ancestry. Of course the Basque example could have motivated all other Antioqueños to more vigorous and judicious entrepreneurship, though why it should have increased their judiciousness is hard to see. With due allowance for the possible influence of Basque blood, some other causal factors must be important.

Mining Experience as a Cause

It is possible that their careers as petty miners prepared the Antioqueños to be industrialists? It seems reasonable to suppose that to some degree it did.

I have noted that from some time in the first half of the seventeenth century the Spaniards themselves were by force of necessity workers in the mines. If we take 1850 as the date when the process of economic growth had its early beginnings, we may say that for three centuries previously Antioqueños had been managing the mines and for two centuries had been working in them with their own hands. The *conquistadores* had come to New Granada with the fantasy of being lords of creation who would make their fortunes romantically and rule over their own little kingdoms. Even though things did not work out just as they had hoped, many of them made this fantasy come true on the Sabana and in the Valley. It may be supposed that, determined to bury their humble past, those who had been of working-class origin turned all the more zealously and haughtily to the values of landedness and gentility. This is a familiar phenomenon.

But in Antioquia that life slipped away from them, and they had to work again with their hands, with tools, at dirty work. There is reason to think that at first they yielded to apathy; but by six or eight generations the need to believe in the worth of the occupation to which one and one's ancestors have voluntarily devoted their lives asserted itself, and the Antioqueños found value in their labor.

The fact that large risks were involved in mining forced a bit of social invention which is of some importance. To the traditional Spaniards, family ties were of great importance, and the logical unit of economic activity was the family. However, a single mining venture might take all the family capital, and by risking it in a single venture one might lose it all and leave the family destitute. Therefore the very regard for the family which is at the base of the family relations elsewhere forced the Antioqueños to divide the risks of mining ventures among a number of families.

Thus there arose in Antioquia a special form of business association, permitted for a mining venture but for no other type of business operation. When a prospector had filed a claim, he might organize a company with 24 shares and invite participation. As the company needed added funds, the shareholders (presumably by majority vote among them) could be called upon to contribute equal added amounts, without limit. If one was unable to do so, reorganization ensued. Legal liability to creditors was limited, as in the modern corporation. In practice, however, it was compulsory for shareholders to contribute equally sums needed to pay the debts of a venture which failed. The essential effect was that a majority of stockholders could decide when to call a halt to a failing venture and divide the losses among them.

At the present time even in Antioquia business corporations tend to be family firms; and in even the largest corporations instances in which the top executives are not closely related by blood are uncommon. But there are more such instances in Antioquia than elsewhere in Colombia; Antioquia has escaped to a greater degree from the identity of family structure and business structure than have the people of other regions of Colombia. The necessity of spreading the risk of mining ventures may be the major explanation of this fact.

One of the essential features of entrepreneurial talent is the ability to assess business risks judiciously. Perhaps engaging in mining ventures gave the Antioqueños experience and judgment in business risk-taking. This point should not be stressed unduly, however, for entering on a prospecting and mining venture often partook more of the nature of gambling than of rational assessment of risks. The companion argument that their mining experience gave the Antioqueños familiarity with machinery and mechanical operations probably has more merit. Perhaps apart from the higher valuation of work with their hands and with machines, their experience in mining gave them more skill, confidence, and judgment in assessing and conducting mechanical operations.

However, only 40 per cent of the gold mined in New Granada was mined in Antioquia.[44] Perhaps within Colombia alone as much gold was mined elsewhere as in Antioquia. In addition, silver mining and mining of other metals was carried on in various regions other than Antioquia in significant amounts. If mining experience were the major influence, it should have produced a relatively larger number of entrepreneurs from the other mining areas. Yet the mining experience of the Antioqueños is certainly one of the causal factors.

Trading and Economic Development

Another possible explanation lies in regional differences at the time of the decline, early in the twentieth century, of large-scale trading in Colombia.

I have noted that until after 1900 the process of getting goods to the Sabana, Antioquia, and the Valley was expensive and risky. In addition to overcoming physical transportation difficulties, the trader had to establish

---

[44] The total gold production of New Granada up to 1886 has been estimated at $639 million (U.S.) in value, of which about $255 million had come from Antioquia. Vicente Restrepo, *A Study of the Gold and Silver Mines of Colombia*, trans. C. W. Fisher (New York: Colombian Consulate, 1886), cited in Parsons, *Antioqueño Colonization*, pp. 58–59.

contacts with traders and sources of finance in London, Paris, New York, or other centers, and to manage the necessary financial accounting and negotiations. For an individual or firm in a Colombian city, far from the foreign financial and industrial centers and without internationally recognized *bona fides*, these processes were not simple. Individuals who possessed both the necessary capacities and ability or luck in carrying on the physical processes of exporting or importing possessed a natural monopoly of importance.

For each family which made a fortune, small or large, in foreign trade there were apparently several who lost the capital they invested. At the turn of the twentieth century there were in each of the three main cities a few families who were doing exceedingly well in trade and whose income and wealth, relative to that of the other families around them and also by most absolute scales, were considerable.[45] A substantial volume of coffee was exported from Medellín, and imports were correspondingly large.

The risks in the trade were great, but for firms that could master them the margin of profit was also great. Then, between 1900 and 1915, improvements in transportation tremendously reduced both the cost and the risk of importing and exporting. In reaction, what did the trading families do?

According to accounts given me in the three cities, the differences in the opportunities open to them are important in explaining their reactions. In Bogotá families who had made fortunes of some size in trading and now foresaw reduced opportunities in that field automatically did one or both of two things. If their sons were so minded, they educated them for the professions. Whether or not they did this, they invested their money in land and entered into the landed elite. The professions and life as a member of the landed gentry were the two social positions of highest status, and by instinctive reaction they turned to them.

In Cali the reactions were more diverse. Two of the families which were prominent in trade at the end of the century are now prominent in finance or industry in Cali. (One was already more in industry than in trade.) One, the Menotti family, has left Colombia. (Gian-Carlo Menotti is a son.) Others have to some degree disintegrated. While perhaps some of the trading money has gone into the cattle business, there has been no general reversion to the land comparable to that in Bogotá.

But in Medellín, it is said, money which had been made in trade flowed into industry because these alternative opportunities were lacking. There were neither cattle ranches nor landed estates to acquire; there was no

---

[45] In Cali, the leading individuals of which this was true included a German named Bomer (perhaps Bohmer), Pedro Pablo Caicedo, Henry J. Eder, Gregorio Gonzalez, Fidel Lalinde, Ulpiano Lloreda, Benito López, and perhaps others. In Antioquia the four most important trading firms were perhaps Alejandro Echavarría e Hijos, Pablo Lalinde y Compañía, Lazaro Mejía y Compañía (or, Lazaro Mejía e Hijos), and Hijos de Fernando Restrepo. I do not have a corresponding list for Bogotá. A little later other families came to prominence who are now prominent in both cities.

landed gentry with the social prestige of that on the Sabana. Neither was there a humanistic cultural *milieu* in which the professions were of quite as high status. Hence, lacking these alternatives, the families with money appraised the opportunities around them and went into industry.

Such an explanation does not explain enough. Industry was not developed in any of the three regions merely by the trading families. The rise of industry had begun both in Antioquia and on the Sabana before the decline of the large trading margins occurred. The tendency to enter the professions existed in Bogotá before the turn of the century. Further, the phenomenon to be explained is not simply the greater entry of Antioqueños into industry but also their greater business acumen, entrepreneurial foresight, and organizational skill. The availability of capital from trade probably accelerated the later growth of industry in Antioquia and is one strand in the explanation we are seeking, but other, sturdier strands remain to be located.

Social Tensions

There remains for consideration an influence affecting personality in Antioquia which is less tangible, less obvious to common sense than those so far discussed above, but which seems of peculiar importance. This is the impact of withdrawal from Antioqueños of respect for their status in the society.

As I have attempted to show above, the Antioqueños, like the settlers in other regions, came from Spanish stock. In Spain they had been of equal status with the immigrants to other regions, and they looked upon themselves as of equal worth in the new land. But they were not looked upon as equals by Colombians of the other regions.

Economically, throughout the colonial period and into the era of independence, they were looked upon as backward; and clearly in fact they were less successful than their fellows in other regions. They were also looked upon by the Bogotanos, the Caleños, and the inhabitants of Popayán as socially inferior. In view of the traditional values of those groups, it is obvious that they would look with some scorn or at least condescension on a group who worked as menials. Perhaps the greater number of Basques among them provided an added reason for condescension toward them. In any event, condescension existed.

It persists today. When the Bogotano of today says, "They are New Christians, you know," he is expressing condescension (and rage at their success) which is like that felt by a New Englander of 1875 at a prosperous gauche Chicagoan (the Antioqueños probably were gauche too) or by an Englishman of the eighteenth century at any American. The sense of this attitude which one gets in Bogotá (or Cartagena, or Popayán) does not depend merely on such verbal comments. It is manifested in tone and attitude in almost any luncheon conversation about business progress in Colombia.

The disparagement is not merely a defensive reaction to the greater economic success of the Antioqueños. It existed before that success was achieved. The pervasiveness in the nineteenth century of the legend that Antioqueños are of Jewish origin was probably a rationalization of the attitude felt then that they were different, that is, alien, and therefore inferior; it certainly is evidence of such an attitude.

Politically and socially Antioquia was a backwater. In a history of Colombia which stresses political events, like that by Henao and Arrubla, one finds Antioquia rarely mentioned in the account of the nineteenth century. Political events took place in Bogotá, Popayán, the Valley, Cartagena, and to a lesser extent Pasto and Santa Marta. Antioquia did not enter conspicuously; it did not count. When technical experts were sent to New Granada to suggest improvements in the mines, they did not visit Antioquia. Schools or scientific institutes were established by the Spanish government of the colonial administration at Bogotá, Popayán, and Cartagena, but not at Medellín.[46] When armies from Antioquia joined in the nation's civil wars, they were markedly less successful than armies from other regions. Apparently they did not fight with fervor. Antioquia was regarded as so much outside the stream of things that in mid-century a political leader exiled in the bitter civil strife or who fled for his personal safety went to Antioquia—as though that were an alien territory which did not count in the rivalry.

In all probability, the Colombians of the Sabana, the Valley, and elsewhere in the nineteenth century were not self-conscious about an attitude that the Antioqueños were of inferior worth (as many of them are self-conscious today); it was just that, as they perceived the world, the Antioqueños were inferior just as the grass is green and the rain wet.

If this sort of social relationship had been the traditional one, and the relative social status taken as a fact of life by both parties to it, then it might have been merely an aspect of a stable social structure, as serfdom and other differences in social level were in the feudal system and the caste system in India. The Antioqueños, however, did not think of themselves as inferior. Today they are as conscious of the attitudes of many other Colombians toward them as an outsider is, and they smart under them. Undoubtedly they did so in the nineteenth and eighteenth centuries. I suggest that this tension, by its effect on family environment, caused changes in personality (in needs, values, and world cognition) conducive to creativity. I suggest, too, that as these changes in personality proceeded, the Antioqueños sought restlessly to prove their worth and, in the world of the nineteenth and twentieth centuries, found what they sought in economic prowess. In other eras they would have found it in some other type of activity, but the availability of advanced techniques to those who sought them out, the importance of economic power, their

---

[46] See Henao and Arrubla, *History of Colombia*. The Antioqueños themselves early established a university at Medellín, but that is a different matter.

economic experience, the noneffectiveness in the Colombian setting of channels such as military or political activity, and the probable aversion they had acquired to aping the humanistic-intellectual activities of their disparagers combined to channel their energies into economic activity.

Over a series of generations the Antioqueños seem to have passed through a period of apathy or retreatism and then become creative. Colombian accounts imply that the Antioqueños in colonial times were shiftless, reckless, gambling, bawdy—all characteristics which may be associated with retreatism as I have defined it. The entire sequence of historical events is consistent with the hypothesis that the Antioqueños reacted gradually over a period of several centuries to withdrawal of status respect, and that this reaction and its impact on their personalities form an important strand in the explanation of the economic growth of Colombia.[47]

I have noted in earlier chapters that a group which rejects traditional symbols of status which it does not possess and cannot attain, and by the yardsticks of which it has been denied the status it feels due it, apparently never rejects them entirely. Even while it suppresses them and overlays them with new values such as the worth of hard work in erstwhile menial occupations, it yet retains also a melancholy longing to attain the old symbols of status for further self-reassurance. So it has been with the Antioqueños. They have turned to business prowess, but when they have attained economic success they replant one foot on the land which their ancestors abandoned by force of necessity. Thus one will find that almost every successful Antioqueño (among those with whom I became acquainted there were no exceptions), whether in Antioquia or elsewhere, has purchased an estate, small or large, in the country and thinks of that estate as his home or his "second home." If his career is elsewhere than in Antioquia, preferably his *pied à terre* is back in Antioquia.

CONCLUSION

These, then, are possible strands in the web of causation which led to Antioqueño leadership in economic innovation. Their activity in this field has more than sufficient causes; it is, in the terminology of logic, overdetermined. Perhaps a higher incidence of Basque blood in Antioquia than elsewhere contributed. Perhaps the mining experience of Antioqueños, even in the absence of other factors, would have caused them to be leaders in economic growth. Perhaps the differences between the opportunities most open to them and those open to the traders of other regions when the opportunities for profit in international trade shrank at the beginning of the twentieth century would have been sufficient. Probably withdrawal of status respect would have been sufficient. No doubt,

---

[47] A far more detailed study of Colombian social history than I have been able to make, to test this hypothesis more comprehensively, would be of interest.

the combination of these factors explains their predominance in economic entrepreneurship.

APPENDIX 1
NEED AGGRESSION IN COLOMBIA

Even though its relationship to economic growth is not clear, need aggression in Colombia is so conspicuous that it should be noted.

It would be rash to refer to the brutal treatment of the indigenous population by the Spanish conquerors as evidence of unusually high need aggression, for indigenous populations which were uncivilized by European standards have been treated brutally by virtually every conquering group. However, unrestrained need aggression is apparent historically both in the civil wars which were so conspicuous in the nation's history from its independence in 1819 until 1902 and in some political behavior since that time. No decade, and hardly any four-year period, from 1819 to 1902 was free from minor or major civil wars, 70 of which in all are recorded. The political differences which were the ostensible causes of civil strife were never great enough to account for the repeated blood-letting except by a people whose need aggression was almost uncontrollable. An estimate generally accepted in Colombia is that in the last great conflict of 1899–1902 some 100,000 persons were killed;[48] and an American authority presents an estimate, which I cannot trace to another source, that in the late 1870's, 80,000 were killed.[49] The 1899–1902 figure is 2.5 per cent of the total population of that time, or one person of every 40 men, women, and children in the country. The estimate of deaths 20 years earlier is a slightly larger percentage of the population. Deaths in the four-year American Civil War were a considerably smaller fraction of the population (about 2 per cent). These are only two of the most spectacular in a series of bloody chapters. They are not chapters in a closed book. It is estimated that rural violence in Colombia during the past 13 years has apparently taken more lives than the civil war at the end of the century. It was exacerbated in 1948 when political violence flared and some leaders of the party in power encouraged bands of peasant thugs to seize the lands of political opponents, but its continuing level, even in 1961, is not explained by the aftermath of those incidents.[50]

The high need aggression is manifested less spectacularly today in urban traffic, in the national beauty contests, and in the prostitution rate. Traffic at major urban intersections is rigidly controlled—so rigidly controlled that one senses awareness of a special need for control. Elsewhere it reflects a sort of tense, proud warfare between driver and pedestrian. In the annual beauty contest the candidates are not, as in the United States, young women of lower or lower-middle income classes who among other attractions see the contest as a path to a possible luxurious future, but include daughters of the most influential "recently arrived" families—though not of the "old" society. Regional excitement is intense. During the several weeks before the national contest late in 1957 the leading metropolitan daily newspapers devoted an average of more than two full pages daily to the contest. Judges for the national contest are brought in from abroad, presumably because no Colombian would be thought to be impartial. When the national champion ("winner" is not an adequate term)

---

[48] See, for example, Henao and Arrubla, *History of Colombia*, p. 519.

[49] J. Fred Rippy, *The Capitalists and the Colombians*, p. 23. He gives the date of war as 1879. This is in error, and renders the estimate doubtful.

[50] *New York Times*, February 14, 1961.

came home to Medellín in the 1957 contest, the expectant crowd milled about the main street in a burst of aggressive release which included a degree of drunkenness, rowdyism, destruction of property, and minor brutality by police attempting to control the most extreme individuals. In Bogotá the automobile carrying the national and regional champions was unable to make its way through a similar crowd to reach a social occasion in the elite section of the city; one of the girls fled into a drugstore, minus one shoe and in fear for her person, while, according to newspaper reports, the crowd stripped hub caps, rear-view mirror, and one headlight from the automobile bearing her.

Licensed prostitution is a more regular outlet for the same need aggression, one tolerated by the arbiters of community morals presumably in an attempt to keep sexual aggression from bursting out of bounds elsewhere. Prostitution is said to be greater in Antioquia than in other regions. Licensed prostitution has been increasing there. In 1930 there was one registered prostitute in the city of Medellín for every 50 males of all ages. In 1946 the number had increased to 4,260, or one for every 30 males of all ages,[51] and I was told by a responsible informant that in 1957 the number was about 12,000, or one to every 24 or 25 males (say one to every 12 to 15 males old enough to be patrons) in metropolitan Medellín.

In noting this I would not suggest that need aggression is higher in Colombia than in other Latin countries. Manifestations of high need aggression in most or all Latin countries are frequently recorded in descriptions of those countries. Neither would I assert that need aggression is higher than in non-Latin Western countries; all that can safely be asserted is that the manifestations are different.[52] Whatever the relative facts may be, it is worthwhile to record that the personality mix out of which the economic and political innovations of recent generations have arisen includes high need aggression which manifests itself in various active ways.

This need aggression in Colombia is probably a result of social tensions that affect the environment in the home. I do not know whether it contributes to or retards economic growth, but because some reader may be more perceptive than I in sensing its significance I record it here.

APPENDIX 2

BASQUE ANCESTRY AMONG ANTIOQUEÑO ENTREPRENEURS

The evidence that persons of Basque blood in Antioquia may be business entrepreneurs in relatively larger numbers than persons of other Spanish blood derives from a notable genealogical volume by Gabriel Arango Mejía, *Geneologías de Antioquia y Caldas*, Vol. I.

This opus lists the names of all the families mentioned in the earlier records of Antioquia and Caldas (excepting perhaps some for whom Arango could not obtain information) and traces them to their Spanish origins. It is the work of most of the lifetime of a man, freed of the necessity of earning a living by the

---

[51] *El Colombiano* (Medellín), January 18, 1947, quoted in Parsons, *Antioqueño Colonization*, p. 108.

[52] Perhaps North Americans are as high in need aggression but because of greater guilt about it release it in less overt ways, for example, in watching the portrayal of brutality in Western and detective stories on television. However, the probable presence in Colombia of a greater degree of authoritarianism in child training makes me suspect that the level of need aggression, insofar as this can be isolated in personality, may be greater than in the United States (or Canada).

earlier success of his family, who turned instead to this particular piece of scholarship.

Clearly many of the genealogical facts stated in the volume are open to question. It is known that some early migrants to the new world bought their family papers, for example, to conceal prison records which would have caused them to be denied permission to join the *conquistadores*. But it is reasonable to assume that in such cases the individual was apt to assume a name from his section of Spain, so that the practice, however rare or common it may have been, probably does not greatly distort the analysis of the regional origins of Antioqueño families.

On this assumption, I had a research worker tabulate all of the surnames listed in the 1957 Medellín telephone directory into three groups: Spanish names listed in the genealogy, Spanish names not listed in the genealogy,[53] and non-Spanish names. Almost 97 per cent of the names listed were of Spanish origin, and of the Spanish names, more than 70 per cent appear in the genealogy. The Spanish names shown in the genealogy were then tabulated according to the region in Spain from which they originated.

The same procedure was then followed for the chief executive officer (*presidente* or *gerente*)[54] and the principal and alternate directors of all companies in Medellín which were members of the National Association of Industrialists (Asociación Nacional de Industriales) in 1957; the president or owner of each company which was a member of the National Federation of Commercial Companies (Federación Nacional de Comerciantes); and the president or owner of each company which was a member of the Association of Small Industrialists (ACOPI, or Asociación Colombiana de Pequeños Industriales).[55]

The terms "principal" and "alternate" director require explanation. The "regular" members of boards of directors are termed "principal directors." In all or almost all companies, for each principal director there is an alternate who serves as a member of the board of directors at any meeting which the corresponding principal director is not able to attend.

It should be noted also that, as in other countries of Spanish culture, every individual has two surnames, that of his father (which is written first, following his given name) and that of his mother (which is written last). The maternal surname is the family name of the mother's father. Most though not all individuals use both names. Thus Gabriel Arango Mejía, author of the genealogy, is the son of a man whose surname was Arango and of a mother whose surname was Mejía. He would customarily be referred to by his father's surname, that is, as Señor Arango. In the study of regional origins the maternal surname of chief executives of the National Association of Industrialists was checked as well as the paternal surname. The results are shown separately.[56]

The results of the research are shown in Table 15–3.

[53] With this group were also included names which according to the genealogy were native to more than one region of Spain, so that from the name it was not possible to assign a Medellín family to one or another region.

[54] As in United States companies, there is some ambiguity concerning the title of the chief executive officer. In some companies the president of the company may be the chief executive; in others, the general manager (or *gerente*). The name used in the tabulation was that of the individual who, according to the knowledge of officials at the National Association of Industrialists in Medellín, was in fact the chief executive.

[55] For this study I am indebted to the very capable and conscientious work of Juan Be Londoño B.

[56] The names of many families are identical. Each name was counted as many times as it appears in the directory except for the elimination of duplication between office and residential listings.

TABLE 15-3
ORIGIN OF MEDELLÍN SURNAMES*

Spanish Region of Origin	Families Listed in Telephone Directory		National Association of Industrialists								FENALCO: President or Owner†		ACOPI: President or Owner‡	
			Presidents:		Presidents: Mother's Family		Principal Directors		Alternate Directors					
	No.	%	No.	%	No.	%	No.	%	No.	%	No.	%	No.	%
Vasconia	1,700	10.4	14	11.1	14	13.5	30	13.0	40	17.8	33	9.9	16	11.9
Andalucia	2,298	14.1	12	9.5	15	14.4	18	7.8	24	10.7	42	12.7	12	8.9
Asturias	2,283	14.0	13	10.6	11	10.6	29	12.6	25	11.1	50	15.1	23	17.0
Castilla	3,355	20.5	16	12.7	15	14.4	28	12.1	34	15.1	63	19.1	23	17.0
Extremadura	1,255	7.7	7	5.5	10	9.6	9	3.9	11	4.9	20	6.5	7	5.2
Aragon							2	0.9			7	2.1		
Navarra							1	0.4	1	0.4				
Galicia	80	0.5	1	0.8							2	0.6		
Region not identified	4,813	29.4	25	19.8	21	20.2	54	23.4	50	22.2	73	22.3	32	23.8
Not Spanish	567	3.5	38	30.1	18	17.3	60	26.0	40	17.8	39	11.8	22	16.3
Total	16,351	100.1	126	100.1	104	100.0	231	100.1	225	100.0	329	100.1	135	100.1

Memoranda:
1. Names of Vasconia origin as percentage of Spanish names:

	Families	Presidents	Mother's Family	Principal	Alternate	FENALCO	ACOPI
	10.8	15.9	16.3	17.5	21.6	11.4	14.2

2. Names of Vasconia origin as percentage of Spanish names whose regional origins are identified:

	Families	Presidents	Mother's Family	Principal	Alternate	FENALCO	ACOPI
	15.5	22.2	21.5	25.6	29.6	15.2	19.8

* Father's family, except for "Presidents: Mother's Family" columns.
† FENALCO = National Federation of Commercial Companies.
‡ ACOPI = Association of Small Industrialists.

The figures which probably are of most interest are those of the second memorandum line at the bottom of the table. Among persons bearing Spanish names whose region of origin in Spain is known a much higher percentage are from the Basque country in every executive group than in the population at large.

The differences are so large that obviously they are statistically significant. That is, they could hardly have come about by chance.[57] It is not equally certain that they reflect a greater tendency for persons of Basque blood than persons of other Spanish blood to be successful as business executives. There are a number of possible sources of error. Perhaps the persons bearing certain surnames in Medellín are not in fact the descendants of persons of the same names in the genealogy. Or subscribers to telephones in Medellín may not be representative of the entire Medellín population; possibly some distortion is involved here. Possibly for some historical reason persons in Spain buying false family names purchased names from one region to a greater extent than from other regions. But there is no obvious reason to assume that these possible sources of error would have a greater tendency to bias the results so as to increase the percentage of Basque ancestry shown among executives relative to that in the population as a whole.[58]

Perhaps one final fact should be noted. In 1951 the estimated population of the Basque provinces was only 3.7 per cent of that of all Spain. If the same ratio prevailed in the sixteenth and seventeenth centuries, persons from the Basque provinces either migrated selectively to Antioquia or formed a much higher percentage of all migrants to New Granada than they did of the Spanish population. However, the difference in the rate of population growth in the new environment and that in the old may in any case have been so great that population ratios now are no guide to those 300 or 400 years ago.

ACKNOWLEDGMENTS

I spent three months in Colombia, and Dr. Louis C. Schaw spent six months there, beginning in November, 1957. The information presented and judgments stated in this chapter rest upon our observations there and upon conversations with many Colombians who had lived through and participated in the economic and political developments of the twentieth century, as well as on printed materials. Among the many individuals in Colombia who were hospitable and extremely helpful I list here a number on whose personal knowledge and generous use of their time in imparting it to me I depend in part for my information concerning developments in the three regions of Colombia with which this study is primarily concerned.

In Bogotá: Salvador Camacho Roldán, Hernán Echavarría, Roberto de J. Herrera, Señor Peñalosa, Jorge Restrepo Hoyos, Julio Samper Ortega, Luis Soto.

In Cali: Ernesto Arango Tavera, Manuel Maria Buenaventura, Hernando Caicedo, Manuel Carvajal, Harold H. Eder, Alfredo Lloreda.

---

[57] The possible sources of error in the analysis are sufficient so that deriving precise numerical measures of significance by applying standard statistical procedures does not seem justified.

[58] A surprising percentage of the executives, especially of the presidents and principal directors of the larger industrial firms, bear non-Spanish names. Presumably this large foreign representation among executives is due in part to the need of larger Colombian firms for foreign capital and financial connections. To get them, they admitted foreign representation into their management.

In Medellín: Luis Echavarría, José Gutierréz-Gómez (then in Washington, D.C., as Ambassador to the United States), Pedro Nel Ospina, Daniel Peláez, Gonzalo Restrepo Jaramillo, and Diego Tobón Arbeláez. I am grateful to Mr. Tobón for reading a draft of the manuscript and correcting a number of errors.

I must acknowledge also my great indebtedness to the National Association of Industrialists, whose aid in guiding me to helpful individuals, in arranging for their co-operation, and in other ways was invaluable.

Social Change and Economic Modernization in Two Indonesian Towns: A Case in Point

by Clifford Geertz

chapter 16

THE TWO TOWNS I SHALL COMPARE ARE MODJOKUTO (A pseudonym), in eastern central Java, and Tabanan, in southwest Bali. Although they are culturally diverse and show certain important differences in social structure, they stem from a common historical tradition, represent approximately the same level of organizational complexity, and are embraced by a single national state and economy. It is this similarity amid difference which gives them their peculiar value for the analysis of Indonesian development. Modjokuto was studied in 1952–54, Tabanan in 1957–58.

MODJOKUTO: A JAVANESE MARKET TOWN

Modjokuto, which is located in the great Brantas River valley, is a typical example of the drab, overcrowded, busily commercial little crossroads which are spaced every 15 or 20 miles apart along the main thoroughfares of the Javanese rice plains. It has a population of 24,000, including some 2,000 Chinese, and is the administrative headquarters for a district of some 170 square miles containing nearly 250,000 people. Its market forms the hub of a far-flung and intensively active trade network through which a fabulous variety of goods flows and from which perhaps a majority of the town population in one way or another draws its living; and it has a fairly large trade in the export of cash crops and the import of manufactures, carried on by the Chinese. As a community, it reflects the elaboration of modern nationalist political life, with a great many parties, labor unions, youth groups, women's clubs, and so on; and there are

385

probably more than 2,000 students enrolled in the various schools of the town.

Modjokuto was founded in the latter half of the nineteenth century. By the early decades of this century it became a rapidly expanding boom town on the basis of Dutch activities in large-scale commercial agriculture, most particularly in cane sugar, in the surrounding countryside. Though the main economic returns resulting from this period of rapid growth went to the Dutch, there were important effects among the Javanese population as well. Native commerce of all kinds expanded and an incipient middle class of traders and landholders appeared, as did a proletarian class of landless workers employed on the plantations and in the mills.

In the early thirties, as a result of the world-wide depression, expansion ceased rather suddenly and rapid contraction occurred. Peasants who now had no income from renting their land to the mills turned to cash crops. The market was flooded with hundreds of very small-scale traders eking out a marginal living where a few large merchants had prospered before. And a certain amount of putting-out, cottage, and small industry appeared as an effort to take up the slack. Paradoxically, though income fell, the town experienced an intensification rather than a slowing down of human effort in economic activity. The over-all trend toward the conversion of the bulk of Modjokuto's inhabitants into small-scale businessmen continued unabated through the Japanese occupation period into the postwar era.

In the pre-1930 boom period the town was composed of four main status groups: the gentry (*prijaji*), consisting of the government civil servants and some of the higher white collar workers from the mills; the traders (*wong dagang*), who were dealers in cloth, tobacco, hardware, and so on; the "little people" (*wong tjilik*), consisting of landless laborers, small peasants, and petty craftsmen; and the Chinese (*wong tjina*), who, although they were almost without exception traders, actually stood largely outside the Javanese social system as a foreign, self-contained, and disliked minority.

The gentry represented the cultural and political elite of the town. They were rather less numerous than in most contemporary towns of equal size because Modjokuto was only a district capital while most of the otherwise comparable towns were regency capitals with consequently much larger civil servant contingents.

However, as an effect of the plantation economy, the commercial, trader class was much larger than normal for a town of its size. The leading figures in this group, the more substantial merchants, were strongly pious Moslems migrant from Java's north coast, for centuries the center of Javanese commercial life and Islamic learning. Thrifty, industrious, moralistically pious, they infused the town with the atmosphere of the bazaar, giving it an almost Levantine tone. And despite the greater cultural prestige of the gentry, the traders were, in this period, the most dynamic element in the society.

There were also probably more "little people" than in neighboring towns of comparable size, but this group played a mainly passive role. For their part, the Chinese lived in a separate quarter, devoted themselves almost solely to business, and maintained an uneasy but nevertheless workable relationship with the mass of the population.

After 1930, and particularly during the Japanese occupation and the immediate postwar period, the lines between the three Javanese groups began to blur. Depression, forced labor, guerrilla warfare, and runaway inflation, following one upon the other over a 15-year period, fundamentally disturbed the entire social system. By the time of the transfer of sovereignty from Holland to Indonesia in 1950, the process of dislocation of the traditional social structure had been accelerated to the point where the need for new patterns of organization was very keenly felt, a need only partially satisfied by the proliferation of political parties and other nationalist organizations after independence.

As a result, the most outstanding characteristic of contemporary Modjokuto social life is its provisional, in-between, "neither-fish-nor-fowl" quality. From a town composed of self-contained subcultural status groups having no more contact with one another than was absolutely necessary, Modjokuto has more and more come to consist of a melange of mass organizations engaged in competitive interaction.[1] Yet not only have the more traditional social loyalties not wholly dissolved and the more modern ones not wholly crystallized; the general economic structure of the town also remains peculiarly poised between the past and the future. The reconstruction of Modjokuto's economic life, like the reconstruction of her social structure generally, is so far but half-begun; it remains tentative, ill-defined, seemingly unable to complete itself. Bustling, fluid, forward-looking, and yet for all that basically undynamic, the town seems stranded between the heritage of yesterday and the possibilities of tomorrow.

TABANAN: A BALINESE COURT TOWN

Tabanan, located in the southwest quarter of the island of Bali, has a population of 12,000, including about 800 Chinese. According to tradition, the Tabanan royal line was founded in 1350. In 1906, 18 generations of theoretically unbroken succession later, the ruling king of Tabanan, tricked into captivity by the Dutch, cut his throat, and the 500-year reign was interrupted. In the twenties, the closest living relative of the dead king was restored to a cardboard throne as a Dutch gesture toward

---

[1] These organizations, though of great political importance, cannot be adequately described in this summary. They include political parties, labor unions, youth groups, peasant organizations, women's clubs, and so on.

Balinese self-government. In 1955 the most recent king in the line abdi-
cated for political reasons. Since then there has been no official king, but
the role of the nobility still remains central. Here it has not been the
bazaar but the palace which has stamped its character upon the town, not
the Islamized trader but the Hinduized aristocrat who has been its distinctive figure.

Compared to Modjokuto, Tabanan has much more of a "just beginning" quality about it in terms of social, political, and economic modernization. One index of this is the striking contrast between the occupational
structures of the two towns.

	Percentage of Population	
	Modjokuto	*Tabanan*
Farmer	6	42
Storekeeper, trader, peddler	41	21
Skilled worker, craftsman	12	9
Unskilled worker	34	20
Civil servant, teacher, clerk	7	8

Despite the lesser detraditionalization of Tabanan as compared to
Modjokuto, the Balinese town is also beginning to change toward a more
modern type of structure. Within the last five years a great number of
Balinese-owned businesses have appeared, the local civil service bureaucracy has expanded, and political activity has become more intense and
involves an increasing proportion of the population. Though still calm,
well-ordered, and in a sense self-contained, the town is not static, and a
fundamental transformation of its social and economic structure seems to
have at least commenced.

The primary moving force in the transformation is the local nobility.
Before 1906 the members of about 15 noble houses, all of them patri-
lineally related to one another and to the royal family at their head,
formed the effective ruling group not only in the town but also in the
surrounding countryside. The peasantry was tied to them by customary
obligations to render corvée and military service, and looked to them for
general leadership in certain supravillage religious matters as well. In addition, though most of the nobles lived in the town, all of them owned
land in the villages (which was worked by commoner share tenants), had
taxation rights, and exercised judicial powers. Although internally riddled
with intrigue, the nobility, which formed an endogamous caste, was
unreservedly accepted by the mass of the population as the legitimate
bearer of regional political authority.

When the Dutch took over South Bali just after the turn of the century
(before this time, the Dutch though nominally sovereign, had permitted
the Balinese kings to rule their bailiwicks largely independently), they
suppressed the traditional political service tie between lord and peasant
and replaced it with a territorialized bureaucratic relationship, transform-

ing the nobles into colonial civil servants. Though they were able to maintain their economic ascendency as landlords and much of their caste-based prestige, the nobles lost a great part of their effective political power.

Since the revolution even this modified pattern of aristocratic pre-eminence has come under attack. Progressive land taxation, laws protecting tenants against displacement and high rents, and the general egalitarian sentiments engendered by nationalist ideology have made landlordism a much less attractive proposition than it was before the war. Further, the opening of administrative posts to talent and to political party patronage has tended to reduce the monopolistic hold of the aristocracy on the civil service.

In such a situation trade and industry, insofar as they can be profitably pursued, become an attractive means to maintain one's threatened status, wealth, and power; so it is perhaps not entirely surprising that it is this group of obsolete princelings which is behind Tabanan's recent economic expansion. The fundamental instability introduced into Tabanan's social system by the Dutch displacement of the indigenous aristocracy from their position at its political center has now begun, 50 years later, to have its effect on the economic structure of the society. The "just starting" quality of the town's modernization is in part misleading, for the sources of the changes now occurring trace back to the reduction of Tabanan in 1906. The suicide of the old king represented in a quite literal sense the death of the old order; and the contemporary movement of his heirs into the yet but partly formed world of trade and industry represents the birth, whether it ultimately proves to be abortive or not, of a new one. In Modjokuto the economic leadership has fallen to the successors of the Islamized commercial elite of the tens and twenties, in Tabanan to the successors of the Hinduized, caste-insulated political elite of the traditional state.

ECONOMIC DEVELOPMENT IN MODJOKUTO

In Modjokuto the problem of economic development presents itself primarily as an organizational one. What the entrepreneurial group of Islamic small businessmen most lacks is not capital, for in terms of the realistic opportunities for innovation which they actually have their resources are not inadequate. Not drive, for they display the typically "Protestant" virtues of industry, frugality, independence, and determination in almost excessive abundance. Certainly not a sufficient market, for the possibilities for significant expansion of both trade and industry stand apparent in Modjokuto on all sides. What they lack is the ability to mobilize their capital and channel their drive in such a way as to exploit the existing market possibilities. They lack the capacity to form efficient economic institutions. They are entrepreneurs without enterprises.

Progress toward more effective patterns of economic activity in Modjokuto takes the form of a movement away from a bazaar type economy
—that is, one in which the total flow of commerce is fragmented into a
very great number of small and disconnected person-to-person transactions—toward a firm economy—that is, one in which trade and industry take place mainly within the framework of a set of impersonally
defined, corporate social institutions which organize a variety of specialized occupations with respect to some particular productive end. It is the
creation of firm-like distributive or productive institutions, of small
stores, service shops, and factories, which represents the process of development in the present state of Modjokuto's economy. Out of the diffuse, individualistic, confused tumult of the bazaar a few of the more
ambitious of the town's established trading class are attempting to organize their activities in a more systematic manner and conduct them on a
larger scale. In the means these men use and in the obstacles they face in
their endeavor to move out of the world of the bazaar and into the world
of the business establishment they display most clearly the characteristic
texture of the problem of economic growth as it appears in contemporary
Modjokuto.

The Traditional Bazaar Economy

The traditional bazaar (*pasar*) is at once an economic institution and a
way of life, a general mode of commercial activity reaching into all aspects of Modjokuto society and a sociocultural world nearly complete
in itself. As agriculture for the peasant, so petty commerce for the trader
provides the concrete backdrop against which almost all of his activities
are set. It is his environment, as much, from his perspective, a natural
phenomenon as a cultural one; and the whole of his life is shaped by it.

To understand the bazaar in this broad sense one needs to look at it
from three points of view: as a patterned flow of economic goods and
services; as a set of economic mechanisms to sustain and regulate that
flow; and as a social and cultural system within which those mechanisms
are embedded.

So far as the flow of goods and services is concerned, one of the most
salient characteristics of the bazaar is the sort of material with which it
deals: unbulky, easily portable, easily storable foodstuffs, textiles, small
hardware, and the like whose inventories permit marginal alterations in
the scale of trading operations rather than demanding discontinuous major changes in investment levels. A second important characteristic is
that, whatever the wares, though volume in any sale is very small, turn-
over is very high. Goods flow through the bazaar channels at a dizzying
rate, not as broad torrents but as hundreds of little trickles, funneled
through an enormous number of transactions. And this flow of goods is
anything but direct: commodities once injected into the market network
tend to move circuitously, passing from trader to trader for a fairly ex-

tended period before they come within the reach of a genuine customer. One piece of cloth may have half a dozen or more owners between the time it leaves the Chinese-owned factory in a nearby city and the time it is finally sold to someone who seems likely to use it. And, third, it needs to be emphasized that most of the processing and manufacturing activities which take place in Modjokuto are also included within the bazaar realm. The bazaar is not merely a simple distributive apparatus; it is a productive apparatus as well. The two elements, the movement of goods and their processing, insofar as this is accomplished in Modjokuto, are wholly intertwined.

As for the set of economic mechanisms which sustain and regulate this flow of goods and services, three are of central importance: a sliding price system, a complex balance of carefully managed credit relationships, and an extensive fractionization of risks and, as a corollary, of profit margins.

To a degree, the continual haggling over terms merely reflects the fact that the absence of complex bookkeeping and long-run cost or budgetary accounting make it difficult for either the buyer or the seller to calculate very exactly what, in any particular case, is a reasonable price. The buyer and seller have to explore the matter through a system of offer and counter-offer.

Even more important, the sliding price system tends to create a situation in which the primary competitive stress is between buyer and seller. In a firm economy the fixed-price system, along with standardization, brand names, advertising, and the other economic customs which accompany it, relieves the buyer-seller relation of competitive pressure and places that pressure on the relation between sellers. Lacking fixed prices, in the bazaar the buyer pits his knowledge of the contemporary state of the market, as well as his stubbornness and persistence, against a similar knowledge on the part of the seller and the seller's nerve and stubbornness.

One result of this kind of competition is that it tends to focus all the trader's attention on the individual two-person transaction. The aim is always to get as much out of the deal immediately at hand as possible; and the bazaar trader is perpetually looking for a chance to make a smaller or larger killing, not attempting to build up a stable clientele or a steadily growing business. His aim is not so much to create a market for whatever he has to sell as it is to be present when a chance to sell appears and to make the most of it. The sliding price system provides the flexibility needed in the fluid economic context of the bazaar, but it does so at the cost of encouraging an essentially speculative, *carpe diem* attitude toward commerce.

The second economic mechanism of importance is a complex and ramified network of credit balances binding larger and smaller traders together. This network is the primary integrative factor in the bazaar, for it creates a hierarchic ranking of traders in which larger traders give credit to smaller ones. These credit balances are only half understood if they are seen only as a means by which capital is made available, for they set up and stabilize more or less persisting commercial relationships. If a buyer owes you too small a balance, it is relatively easy for him to shift his business to some other seller; if he owes you too much, he may default. The margin between these two possibilities is carefully calculated. From the financial point of view, the bazaar consists of a complex of debts carefully managed to keep trade active and yet not disrupt it. Most of everyone's time is consumed in pursuing debtors and dunning them, or in trying to wheedle a little more credit from one's creditors. Such an economy can be seen as a sort of hydraulic system in which the balance of credit pressures at hundreds of larger and smaller couplings determines the speed, direction, and volume of the flow of goods through the system.

Third, despite his aim to maximize his trading activities, the bazaar trader has a tendency to spread himself thin over a very wide range of deals rather than plunge deeply on any one. As a result, even moderately large single deals with only two persons involved are very rare even if the traders involved are large enough to handle such deals alone. Both large and small transactions usually involve a multiplicity of people, each making a small contribution and each taking out a small return, thus fractionating both risks and profits. The bazaar traders are individualists in the sense that they operate independently of any persisting economic organizations, make decisions entirely in terms of their own interests as they conceive them, and relate to each other wholly through separate person-to-person agreements; but this does not mean that alliances among traders are not extremely common. The individual trader is the center of a series of rapidly forming and dissolving one-deal, compositely organized trading coalitions. Further, this tendency to spread risks and profits is so much a habitual reaction of bazaar traders that it would persist for a long time even if capital were to become much more readily available.

Lastly, as a sociocultural system the bazaar is characterized by an interstitial position within Javanese society generally; by a highly developed division of labor which, in the absence of firms, guilds, and so on, provides directly the major basis of social-structural organization for the market as a whole; and by a very sharp segregation of specifically economic from diffusely noneconomic social ties.

From an historical point of view, the main reason for the interstitial position of the bazaar within Javanese society is that it is primarily not a local growth but was introduced from outside after Java had already achieved very high levels of social, political, and religious development. It was only in the fourteenth and fifteenth centuries, when Madjapahit, the island's greatest kingdom, climaxed more than a thousand years of political and cultural evolution under the aegis of Hinduism, that a comprehensive commercial network was forged. Islam was introduced, and the bazaar pattern took its characteristic historical form. A quality of intrusiveness, of incongruity and alienness, clings to the bazaar trader even today. The Javanese word for "trader" still also means "foreigner," "wanderer," or "tramp." The status of the traditional merchant in the wider society is thus ambiguous at best, pariah-like at worst: the peasant tends to fear the trader as a cheat, the gentleman to despise him as a money grubber.

On the social-structural side the most notable characteristic of the bazaar pattern is the hyperspecialized division of labor, of which the folk caricature is the trader who sells only left shoes. This overdifferentiation reflects more than an oversupply of labor. The fact that in what is otherwise an extremely fluid system there is a strong tendency for individuals to persist in a single kind of trading rather than to shift easily among various sorts is evidence of the fact that trading is a full-time, technically demanding, completely professionalized occupation, not the part-time job of a farmer come to market.

Relationships between traders are highly specific: commercial ties are carefully insulated from general social ties. Friendship, neighborliness, and even kinship are one thing; trade is another. The impersonal approach to economic activity which has sometimes been held to characterize only advanced economies is present in the Modjokuto bazaar in marked degree. It is the one institutional structure in Javanese society where the formalism and status consciousness so characteristic of the culture generally are relatively weak: bargaining, credit balances, and trade coalitions, largely free of the constraints of diffusely defined cultural norms, all respond quite directly to the narrow concerns of material advantage.

In sum, the bazaar economy is traditional in the sense that its functioning is regulated by fixed customs of trade hallowed by centuries of continuous use, but not in the sense that economic behavior is not well differentiated from other sorts of social behavior. What the bazaar economy lacks is not elbow room but organization, not freedom but form.[2]

The Developing Firm-Type Economy

The exact nature of the innovational task facing Modjokuto's would-be entrepreneurial class is conditioned by two main determinants: the general character of the bazaar as an economic institution, and the emerging form of postrevolutionary urban society. From an individualistic, speculative, marvelously intricate trading pattern, the entrepreneurs must move to a systematically yet simply organized firm-based "business" pattern dedicated to long-term economic ends. And from an interstitial, vaguely outcast position within traditional society they must

[2] For a full description and analysis of the Modjokuto market, see Alice G. Dewey, *Peasant Marketing in Java* (New York: Free Press of Glencoe, Inc., 1962).

move to an established place as respected shopkeepers and manufacturers, true bourgeois, within the now developing modern type of class structure.

In the light of the theories of Max Weber concerning the role of Protestantism in stimulating the growth of a business community in the West, it is perhaps not surprising that the leaders in the creation of such a community in Modjokuto are for the most part intensely Reformist Moslems, for the intellectual role of Reform in Islam has, at least in some ways, approached that of Protestantism in Christianity. Emphasizing that the systematic and untiring pursuit of worldly ends may be a religiously significant virtue of fundamental importance, Reformism, which swept through the urban trading classes of Java from 1912 to 1920, paved the way for the creation of a genuinely bourgeois ethic. By substituting a progress-oriented self-determinism for classical Islam's ineluctable fatalism it injected into the bazaar context a dynamic which had previously been lacking. Chinese-owned enterprises aside, of the seven well-established stores in Modjokuto, six are run by Reform Moslems; of the two dozen or more small factories of one sort or another, all but three or four are in pious Moslem hands.

Thus, despite marked cultural differences, economic development in Modjokuto is tending to take the classic form we have known in the West. An at least in part religiously motivated, generally disesteemed group of small shopkeepers and petty manufacturers arising out of a traditionalized trading class are attempting to secure an improved status in a changed society through the rational, systematic pursuit of wealth. This sequence of change, occurring several centuries after it occurred in Europe, and taking place in a world which is already partially industrialized, will have a significance and outcome in Java quite different from what it had in Europe, but the general similarities between the two cases are nevertheless quite real.

Leaving aside any detailed descriptions of the enterprises the Javanese pioneers in economic change have in fact created, it is worth noting that they are all either small "Western-type" retail stores or small workplace-type factories, and thus are true firms in the broad sociological sense of well-defined corporate institutions specifically devoted to economic ends. The stores, catering to the modernizing tastes of the new urban classes—school teachers, students, political leaders, civil servants, technicians—are characterized both by a generally better quality of goods, including many that are imported, and a more regularized manner of doing business than is typical of the bazaar. They have fixed (or nearly fixed) prices, a concern with firm reputation and advertising, a steady clientele, and an interest in creating markets rather than merely responding to them. The extreme complications in distributive patterns have been eliminated, and in fact success in such retailing enterprises seems heavily dependent upon the ability of the owner to establish workable relations with stable, reliable distributors (or manufacturers) in one or another of the major cities of the island to complement the growth of sales relationships with the emerging urban public. The factories— cigarette, garment, food processing, furniture—are all small scale (the largest employs about 50 workers), but a number have become at least partly mechanized, follow rigorous work schedules, and produce a cheaper and more reliable product than those of which cottage industry, putting-out arrangements, or individual craftsmen are usually capable. The establishment of these stores and factories is not to be thought of as merely comparable in difficulty with a similar operation by an enterprising American individual. Each involved a set of breaks with tradition which required boldness, judgment, and a certain unconventionality not possible for the traditional bazaar trader. The storekeeper or factory owner is a new type of man. To conceive of the required deviations from traditional purchase, employment, management, and sales practices, and to persuade some of the other parties to the transaction that the new relationships were appropriate and acceptable, required considerable talents. To establish the stores even more than the factories required a set of new relationships each of which would have been more difficult if the conditions permitting the others had not also existed.

A Rising Middle Class and Its Problems

Modjokuto's fitful and sporadic movements toward economic change are but part of her more general movement, also fitful and sporadic, toward a whole new pattern of social life. The movement from territorially based traditional political allegiances toward ideologically based modern ones in the nationalist parties and associations, the transformation of the stratification system from a collection of discrete, more or less closed status groups to across-the-board, culturally heterogeneous open classes, and the development of corporate economic firms out of a background of hyperindividuated bazaar trading are all of a piece. Each of these changes demands the others as its environment for it to flourish, and together they both produce and are the results of fundamental alterations in cultural beliefs, attitudes, and values. It is in this sense that such often vaguely employed terms as "modernization," "urbanization," "rationalization," and "economic development" are really equivalent in their basic meaning; they all point, if from somewhat different directions, to an integral pattern of social change.

Nevertheless, Modjokuto's pattern of development has its own specific quality, as indices of which four points may be mentioned.

First, Modjokuto's entrepreneurs are almost all traders or traders' sons; their activities both grow out of the bazaar context and are a rebellion against it. The traditional trading culture of Modjokuto is both facilitative and inhibitory of economic reform; it is both the source of the innovators' methods and aspirations and one of the major barriers against the employment of those methods and the realization of those aspirations.

Second, the immediately limiting factor on entrepreneurial activity is not lack of capital, shortages of skilled or disciplined labor, insufficiency of markets, or lack of technical knowledge (though these all are problems), but the task of organizing diverse activities into unified institutions—stores or small factories. It is the ability and originality to organize a range of different economic activities in a systematic manner that most distinguishes a Modjokuto entrepreneur from his noninnovative bazaar-trader fellows—not wealth, not education, not even drive.

Third, the entrepreneurial group *is* a group, not a random collection of individuals. Innovators are clearly set apart by both their social origins and their religious intensity, and they represent the sort of generally disesteemed, highly serious petty businessmen who have appeared in the early stages of economic revolution in many countries.

And fourth, Modjokuto's economic growth is dependent on an ongoing revolution in urban style of life—explicitly in the emergence of the postrevolution pattern of politicosocial organization, the new bases of social ranking which have appeared along with this pattern, and the expansion of the school system which sustains it. Together, these have caused a critical shift in taste in the urban masses as against their prewar counterparts.

On the other side of the ledger, there are two main barriers to the success of the Javanese entrepreneurial group in Modjokuto. One is the presence of the Chinese. In the race to be the town's modern middle class the Chinese have the advantages of possessing more capital and greater business acumen; they have more experience and are better organized than the Javanese shopkeepers and factory owners. But they are Chinese, and resentment against them, always great, has mounted rapidly since the revolution. The recent regulation forbidding the residence of noncitizen Chinese in towns the size of Modjokuto may have greatly reduced their role. It is difficult to say whether for the better or the worse so far as the economy is concerned.

Secondly, a middle class, to be successful, will have to be able to move into industry, and there may be some question whether the Javanese shopkeepers will be able to do so because of the so-called "lumpiness" problem. Some recent economic theory has emphasized the discontinuities in economic change, the quantum jumps which are often required in moving from traditional to modern production methods. Steel mills, automobile plants, or even capital-intensive sugar refineries do not come in all sizes; nor do they arise gradually by incremental changes from obscure beginnings. Some observers feel that in the context of this requirement there is about Modjokuto's "shopkeeper revolution" a peculiar air of irrelevancy.

There are, however, a number of counterarguments to this view. In the first place, without the growth of some sort of sturdy, indigenous business class the Indonesian government is likely to find the task of inducing rapid economic growth an insuperable one. Such a class provides the skills, values, and motivations without which industrial development is as impossible as it is without natural resources; and no more than iron or coal deposits can such resources be created by fiat. It is one thing to stimulate, channel, and supplement the growth of a modern economy; it is quite another to create such an economy *ex nihilo* out of an almost wholly traditional culture. Whatever their shortcomings, Modjokuto's shopkeepers and manufacturers are a human resource for the Indonesian government to work with.

Second, the establishment without prior steps of fairly large industrial units, even if it should be a necessary part of the process of economic development, which is not certain, is only a small part. Multiple and unconnected regional expansions, intermittent and self-contained spurts of this industry or that, largely independent, even contradictory, institutional developments—all these too are characteristic of countries in the initial stages of growth. It is necessary neither that everything be done at once nor that maximum integration be maintained at each and every stage of development. And, in any case, in the sort of jammed and disorganized situation Indonesia finds herself in today, no genuine growing point is so small or so peripheral as to be irrelevant. Modjokuto is not Indonesia, but neither is Djakarta.

ECONOMIC DEVELOPMENT IN TABANAN

In Tabanan the nascent entrepreneurial class of displaced aristocrats is concerned not with reorganizing a bazaar economy but with readjusting an agrarian one. They are not trying to give some articulate form to a fluid, individualistic trading pattern but to adapt the intensely collective and long-established institutions of traditional peasant society to novel economic ends. By mobilizing habitual sentiments of loyalty, respect, obligation, and trust they hope to make ancient custom serve modern enterprise.

Such modern enterprise does not yet exist in Tabanan; they must create it. Like their Modjokuto counterparts, they must establish autonomous merchandising and manufacturing firms, institutional forms more or less novel to the society; but the social and cultural building blocks available for the task come not from the bazaar but from the village. Enmeshed, as they have always been, in a complex network of traditional ties both with one another and with the great mass of commoners they once ruled, the town-based aristocracy is attempting to manipulate these ties in such a way as to construct and support modern

economic enterprises. Thus an analysis of social and economic organization in the Balinese village is prerequisite to an analysis of this urban-
based pattern of development.

Rural Social Structure and Economic Organization

The general organization of the Balinese village is best seen as a set
of overlapping and intersecting corporate associations known as *seka*.
A *seka* is a more or less enduring social group, formed on the basis
of a single criterion of membership and dedicated to some narrowly
specified social end. Some *seka* are permanent, others temporary; in some
membership is ascribed, in others more or less voluntary; in all, each
member has absolutely equal rights and duties regardless of what his
general position in the society may be. Every Balinese belongs to from
three to four up to a dozen *seka*, and the Balinese do virtually everything
except make love in *seka*, for they strongly prefer to act in groups rather
than as individuals. This combination of an almost ant-like attack on the
performance of important social activities with a tendency to direct any
one group to a single end rather than employing the same group for
multiple purposes leads to what one might call, paradoxically, a pluralistic
collectivism. The crosscutting of social alliances means that almost no
one is completely engrossed in any single totally comprehensive institution without alternative loyalties to which he may have recourse against
group pressures, and yet no one is ever obliged to operate entirely on his
own, independently of some well-defined social aggregation.

There are, speaking roughly, five types of *seka:* temple congregations,
residential units, irrigation societies, kinship groups, and voluntary associations.

1. *Temple congregations.* Members of each such group are obliged
to worship at a given temple on certain holy days, and to maintain it. The
first duty involves elaborate ritual offerings of food, and so on; the second,
financial support. Both demands are met by collective economic activity
more often than by monetary assessments: harvesting jointly and con-
tributing the harvester's tenth share to the temple; working riceland
bought in the name of the temple; dance and drama performances for its
benefit; and so on.

2. *Residential units:* hamlets of a dozen to a couple of hundred house-
holds centered around a communal meeting house. There are monthly
gatherings at which policy decisions (taxes, fines, exiling wrongdoers,
public works undertakings) are made, and the hamlet can call on members for public services of various sorts. To earn income the hamlet may
form a harvesting group, or sponsor a dance society, or buy riceland.
There are also hamlet-owned enterprises such as coffee shops, retail
stores, and small brick and tile factories. One hamlet even started its own
bus company, financed by selling its riceland, and used the profits to build
a school and pay the teachers' salaries. Other hamlets form the basis for

co-operatives, one particularly successful consumer-producer co-operative being maintained by 16 hamlets in concert. In addition, some hamlets are craft-specialized, concerned with the manufacture of salt, the forging of musical instruments, weaving, pot making, carpentry, tailoring, or some other occupation.

3. *Irrigation societies.* Members of these *seka* are all those whose land is irrigated from a single watercourse. As land holdings tend to be scattered, one man may be a member of several such societies, and the members of any such society come from perhaps 10 to 15 hamlets. The main functions of an irrigation society are management of water resources, coordination of planting, and the performance of agricultural rituals. Within an irrigation society a water *seka* may undertake to keep dams in repair and canals clean for pay. In rare instances wholly professionalized water *seka* composed almost entirely of landless villagers belonging to no irrigation society at all are paid to perform these tasks for three or four irrigation societies.

4. *Kinship groups.* Descent is patrilineal, residence patrilocal, and semiendogamous corporate kin groups play a very important role in village life in some hamlets, often forming the framework for economic enterprise. Thus in one village four such groups were engaged in the competitive manufacture of gamelan orchestra instruments, primarily a smithing job; in others weaving, harvesting, or other activities may be organized in kinship terms.

5. *Voluntary associations.* Membership in such *seka* is through voluntary affiliation, and they often have purely economic functions. They may plant, weed, harvest, carry sheaves from the fields, make house roofing from grasses and palms, transport goods, perform dances, drama, or music, hawk iced drinks or snacks, make tiles and pottery. Sometimes several tasks are performed by a single, well-established, long-persisting voluntary *seka*.

In short, *seka* organization, whether religious, political, irrigation, kinship, or voluntary based, is the heart of Balinese social structure, which can in fact be seen as a set of crosscutting *seka* of various types loosely adjusted to one another. It is on this type of pluralistic collectivism that the aristocratic entrepreneurs of Tabanan town must base their efforts at innovation, reform, and economic growth.

The Tabanan Aristocracy and the Firm-Type Economy

One of the most persistent, most widespread, and most fallacious scholarly stereotypes of Balinese social organization is that it consists, and has for centuries consisted, of almost wholly independent, closed-in peasant communities—socially insulated, self-absorbed "village republics" enduring passively and patiently beneath an equally self-contained and aloof though more unstable gentry ruling class. In this view, kings, dynasties, whole ruling classes have come and gone, but the peasant, the real, original Balinese, for whom such political upheavals merely signify a change of tax collectors, plods on forever in the unchanging paths of uncounted centuries. Between noble and commoner the relations are conceived to have always been ones of pure hostility and a direct opposition of interest.

This view of gentry-peasantry relationships is wholly misconceived. The Balinese gentry were not "outsiders" but, from the very beginning, an integral part of Balinese society. They were not simply tribute takers; they performed altogether crucial interlocal political, religious, and economic functions upon which the supposedly self-subsistent villagers were dependent for their very existence. In traditional times (that is, prior to 1906) nobles gathered commoners into military *seka* for wars. They judged interhamlet legal issues and punished various crimes, such as miscaste marriages. They inherited the ricelands of village decedents without heirs, executed the more serious hamlet-passed punishments, supported exiles from the hamlets; and, of course, they had a very large number of retainer families living in the villages themselves. Further, they conducted important ceremonies, such as cremations and temple consecrations, in which the whole population was involved both as mobilized labor and tribute givers and as audience for the great ritual dramas produced.

The members of the gentry were also landlords maintaining village-dwelling sharecroppers, played a certain role in co-ordinating irrigation societies, monopolized foreign trade, and set up local markets. In politics, religion, art, and economics the rulers and the ruled represented, in traditional Bali, not parallel but intersecting, not independent but complementary, social groups. Though the caste barrier between aristocrat and commoner was almost impermeable, the etiquette of deference extraordinarily well developed, and the lines between local and supralocal concerns very sharply drawn, both the Balinese state and the Balinese village became what they became in great part as the result of the close, multifaceted, long-term, and ever-changing interaction they had with one another, a circumstance too obvious to need special comment were it not so often denied.

It is this heritage of undisputed leadership in supralocal affairs which the Tabanan aristocracy is now attempting to turn to their account in building an urban-based nationally oriented firm economy. In contrast to the Modjokuto small businessmen, whose puristic Islamic piety represents a nonconformist pattern within the local culture, Tabanan entrepreneurs are cultural exemplars. They symbolize the quintessence of indigenous culture, demonstrate its furthest reaches of complexity, refinement, and sophistication. And today, when many of the specific structural arrangements which supported this role of cultural representative have been either dissolved or drastically reorganized, the sentiments which underlay them persist. Thus in their bid to create a modern economy the aristocrats have at their disposal a quantity of cultural capital in the form of traditionalized social loyalties and expectations which Modjokuto's self-made shopkeepers entirely lack. "We have lost control of the government," these disestablished nobles say, "so we'll capture the economy."

Perhaps the most striking case example of the manner in which modern firm-building in Tabanan reflects and depends upon traditional patterns of organization and loyalty is the development of what is today the town's largest and most important business concern, Gadarata (an abbreviation meaning "The People's Trade Association of Tabanan"). Founded in 1945 by four local noblemen plus a long-resident Javanese market trader, who evidently served as a technical advisor, the association amassed its capital of 100,000 rupiah by levying a "contribution" of five rupiah on every household head in the region, each contributor being awarded a voting share in the projected enterprise. Approximately 10,000 villagers bought a share apiece, and the remaining 50,000 rupiah were raised by selling multiple shares to richer individuals, most of them town aristocrats. The plan was to funnel all export trade of the region through this one well-organized, incorporated, upper-caste-managed concern as agent, as well as to launch certain other associated business enterprises. A large two-story warehouse, store, and office building, the town's most imposing edifice, was erected at the main crossroads near the market.

In 1950, after the transfer of sovereignty, the governing board, which by now had had two more strategic members of the ruling family added to it (the Javanese trader had withdrawn), reorganized the firm by changing the value of the shares from five to 100 rupiah each, thereby reducing the total number of shares from about 20,000 to about 1,000 at a single blow. The individual household head shareholders in the villages were thus forced into either selling out their interests to larger holders or banding together into "Gadarata *seka*" of 20 people each and selecting a representative to cast their vote at the annual meeting. Altogether, about 350 such *seka* were formed, covering about 7,000 of the original 10,000 villagers, while the rest of the small owners sold out to the leadership group, which thus consolidated its hold on the firm through this process. By the end of 1957 the enterprise had become worth something more than a half million rupiah and dominated much of the export trade of the area. By almost any measure, Gadarata, which now operates a retail store selling a wide variety of imported goods as well, has been a most successful undertaking.

Over-all management and policy making are by now completely in the hands of seven salaried directors, five of whom, including the chairman and vice-chairman, are members of the ruling family. The process of bringing the firm progressively under the sole control of the "palace" group is now almost completed, a fact recognized and for the most part accepted by aristocrats and villagers alike. Despite some grumbling, most of the peasants do not expect to have any particular say in an institution focused around the nobility simply because they have provided capital any more than they expected to influence state policy simply because they contributed work and material to the lord's ceremonies in the old days. The managerial revolution has come quickly to Tabanan mainly because it involves no revolution.

A number of other stores and industries, some of them differently organized, of course, but also all noble led and dominated, could be cited as further examples—another trading concern, a tire recapping factory, several hotels, a weaving factory, a bus line, a bookstore, a garment-making shop, an ice factory. Thus, though there are also some smaller stores run by commoners, at the heart of Tabanan's postrevolutionary economic expansion has been a very small group of displaced traditional rulers. Tabanan's erstwhile ruling family—about 6 per cent of its population—overwhelmingly dominates the nascent modern economy of the town.

Upper Caste Revolution and the Limits of Tradition

The essential nature of Tabanan's "upper caste revolution" can be summarized, and its longer-run prospects tentatively assessed, by making a fourfold comparison of similarities and differences between development in Tabanan and in Modjokuto.

1. *Business Organization.* The bringing together of hundreds of villagers (as stockholders) into a single firm is not a realistic possibility to a Modjokuto entrepreneur. Not only does he entirely lack the traditional prestige to mobilize people on such a scale, but 300 years of intensive, Western-stimulated social change in Java have eroded the foundations for large-scale collective effort in the villages. And, too, Modjokuto's entrepreneurs emerge directly from a bazaar economy in which individualistic, every-man-for-himself activity is carried almost to an extreme, in constrast to the lineage-like organization of the generally solidary and corporate ruling family from which Tabanan's new men come.

As a result, almost all modern enterprises in Modjokuto are individual or immediate family concerns. Capital must be raised either through personal savings or government loans; selling shares to villagers or large-scale borrowing on the open market is virtually absent. Even partnerships, so easily formed in Tabanan, where strong noneconomic ties of kinship, co-residence, or status deference usually insure their persistence, are almost nonexistent in Modjokuto. When it comes to the organizational problem, the Tabananers have a clear advantage.

Yet there is another side to the coin, which is reflected in the constant complaint of the directors of the popularly based large firms that they are unwieldy and inefficient. In particular, as national political affairs come to have more importance, there is a tendency for the operation of these supposedly specifically economic institutions to reflect them, causing internal disruption, something the individualistic Modjokuto entrepreneur completely avoids. Cast in quasi-political terms to begin with, Tabanan's firms can easily become political in modern terms, a condition which, at least in a democratic, multiparty state, is extremely disfunctional to further growth or even continued solvency.

Second, and perhaps even more important, the popularly based concern has a tendency to behave very uneconomically because of the "social welfare" pressures of its members, who, for the most part, are not basically growth minded. Not only is there great pressure to divide profits rather than reinvest them but there is also a tendency to employ overly large staffs in an attempt by the directorate to appease the rank and file.

Both Tabanan's group-centered approach to change and Modjokuto's individual-centered approach have defects and virtues. Tabanan's method smooths the way to the formation of larger-scale concerns; but traditional values supporting collective benefits as against individual enrichment induce a strong resistance to the rationalization of these concerns once they are formed. Modjokuto's method avoids this problem; but, although bold and rugged, not to say ruthless, individualism has advantages in stimulating creativity and destroying traditional constraints on enterprise, it also imposes severe limitations on the capacity to grow by limiting the effective range of collective organization. Modjokuto firms seem to grow so large and then no larger, because the next step means widening the social base of the enterprise beyond the immediate family connections to which, given that lack of trust which is the obverse of individualism, they are limited. Where Tabanan's approach tends to expand firms beyond their most efficient organizational base, Modjokuto's tends to confine them to too narrow a one.

2. *Religious and Ideological Dynamics.* In Modjokuto the entrepreneur mainly follows a discordant, rationalized, and self-consciously critical Islamic modernism—which sets him apart from his much less devout and zealous fellows and which in its very nature makes economic achievement ethically significant. His countertraditional ideological orientation puts him in the position of being not only an economic but also a religious and ethical innovator. Tabanan's economic leaders, on the other hand, are committed to religious beliefs and values which, far from clashing with those of the general society, are the most elaborate, developed, and systematic expression of the culture's traditionally institutionalized ethos.

Thus both marked deviation from the main stream of traditional religious thought and complete conformity to it seem able to provide an ideological context suitable to growth. What is important as a stimulus to economic enterprise is not whether a creed is revisionist or restorationist, but whether the state of affairs the creed celebrates differs significantly from the entrepreneurs' perception of the actual situation. In both Java and Bali there yawns a gap between the vision of the way things ought to be and the way they seem to be. In Modjokuto the pious shopkeepers see themselves as the vanguard of a truly Islamic Indonesia which must be created out of a community whose religion is now heterodox and outmoded. In Tabanan the nobility sees itself as wrongfully displaced from its true position as cultural cynosure, and as fighting to maintain the traditional patterns of deference, respect, and reverence upon which it feels the intrinsic value of Balinese culture rests.

3. *Political- versus Economic-Based Development.* The Javanese entrepreneurs want mainly to get rich, the Balinese to get (or remain) powerful. Tabanan's entrepreneurs, in contrast to Modjokuto's, have come from a class long used to wielding power; they have not lost the sense of confidence that comes with the effective exercise of political power on a broad scale. The comparable class in Modjokuto—the civil servant *prijaji* —has over 150 years been reduced to a group of nonpolicy-making petty bureaucrats, and has long since lost its original sense of playing a decisive role in its society. Thus in Tabanan the taste of the individual entrepreneur for economic innovation grows out of an aristocratic, even arrogant sense of being a man born to lead, while in Modjokuto it grows out of his sense of his superior shrewdness, toughness, flexibility, and ambition as contrasted to the passive, acceptant traditionalism of the mass of the population.

Again, each movement has its strength and weakness. Modjokuto's is apparently more apt to lead to democratic liberalism and the protection of individual political freedom; but it may be unable to cope with the need for large-scale enterprises which now seems to be faced by latecomer backward nations. The Tabanan entrepreneurs can set up larger enterprises by virtue of their ability to corral larger amounts of capital and also by virtue of being able to get the protection of monopoly situations or other special privileges from the government. But their developmental pattern skates fairly close to totalitarianism, and the development of this politically based sort of pattern into a Japanese-type industrial feudalism, a semitraditional, semimodern capitalism in which a small elite gains most of the advantages of modernization, is a very possible even if not necessary outcome. A traditional elite can make a more integral attack on the multiple problems of economic modernization than can a foot-loose bourgeoisie, which must go at its task haphazardly and piecemeal, but there is the danger of that intense domination of political concerns over all other concerns which is the hallmark of modernized totalitarian states.

4. *Urbanization.* As noted, Modjokuto is much more urbanized than Tabanan. The Balinese town, several centuries older, is only now losing the outlines of a traditional court center. Urbanization, which the growth of the plantations stimulated in Modjokuto, brings a mingling of individuals from all walks of life, greater personal anonymity (and hence greater freedom from traditional constraints and prejudices), a more variegated life. The brisk disorder of Modjokuto, compared to the sedate deliberateness of Tabanan, is certainly conducive to change, flexibility,

and aggressiveness, if only because it is impossible for everyone to stand still very long and continue to survive.

Yet urbanization, particularly when it occurs within a wider society which is economically stagnant, also breeds malaise, discouragement, and aimlessness; and so, though urbanization may be a necessary condition for economic take-off, it is hardly a sufficient one. Tabanan lacks a large commercial class, a developed proletariat, a strong office clerk and school-teacher intelligentsia comparable to that of Modjokuto, but on the other hand it may be fortunate in starting the whole process of modernization at a time when it may prove possible to avoid the sort of change without progress characteristic of the Javanese town since the middle thirties. Everything depends upon what happens in Indonesia as a whole. If over the next decade or so economic opportunities expand significantly, Tabanan's lack of a history of boom, bust, and stagnation may prove advantageous; half an urbanization may prove to have been worse than none.

CONCLUSIONS

Indonesia as a nation is not the village or the small town writ large. One cannot generalize in any direct way from Modjokuto or Tabanan to the country as a whole. What then can be learned from a study of the two towns? The following six propositions are intended as tentative summary hypotheses derived from the above comparative analysis, designed only to point out some possible leads for future research:

1. *Innovative economic leadership (entrepreneurship) occurs in a fairly defined and homogeneous group.*

In both towns the entrepreneurs come neither from the general population in a more or less random way nor from several distinct social groups at once; in both they come almost entirely from a single quite clearly demarcated, set-apart group, the pious Islamic traders in Modjokuto, the ruling family in Tabanan.

2. *This innovative group has crystallized out of a larger traditional group which has a very long history of extravillage status and interlocal orientation.*

In neither area are the peasants leaders in economic change; both leadership groups are primarily interlocal in their outlook, some of their most important ties being with groups and individuals in areas other than their own. In Modjokuto this horizontal orientation originated out of contact with the all-Indonesia trading network which grew out of the internationally based bazaar culture of the fifteenth and sixteenth centuries. In Tabanan horizontality was an aspect of the sophisticated "great tradition" court culture associated with the indigenous Indonesian state structure, which was carried forward through the whole of the colonial period as well.

3. *The larger group out of which the innovating group is emerging is one which is at present experiencing fairly radical change in its relationships with the wider society of which it is a part.*

In prewar Modjokuto the town's traders were a self-contained, set-apart, rather despised group; today they are becoming integrated into a broad and generalized middle class within an uncertainly urbanizing structure. In prewar Tabanan the aristocrats were the unquestioned political and cultural elite of the region; today their position is increasingly threatened by the growth of a universalistic civil bureaucracy and the populist sentiments of nationalist ideology. It is thus neither upward nor downward class mobility or a blockage of these which is necessarily crucial but any kind of decisive change in intergroup relations which, by throwing accepted status demarcations into disarray, stimulates active efforts to anchor social positions to new moorings.

4. *Ideologically the innovative group conceives of itself as the main vehicle of religious and moral excellence within a generally wayward, unenlightened, or heedless community.*

Islamic Reform, a sort of Moslem puritanism, the doctrine of the overwhelming majority of the entrepreneurs in Modjokuto, aims at a radical purification of the prevailing religious and moral syncretism of heterodox elements and is intensely critical of a wide range of established usages of ethics and worship. The ideology of Tabanan's new men, on the other hand, is catholic and restorationist, but they have the same sense of representing the proper against the prevailing. They see abandonment of customary patterns of deference, progressive usurpation of political power by the hereditarily unequipped, and growing failure of the average man to recognize and appreciate the indispensable social and cultural functions performed by those of high status as symptoms of a general cultural decline. Thus both innovative groups tend to see the general cultural level of the whole wider community as almost entirely dependent upon the success of themselves and their activities.

5. *The major innovational problems the entrepreneurs face are organizational rather than technical.*

The specific technical problems so far as development is concerned in the two towns now have mostly been solved; they need only be adopted to local needs. The Indonesian entrepreneur does not have to invent a sugar press, an ice machine, or a tire recapper; he has only to purchase them. It seems likely, therefore, that the organizer will play the central role in stimulating Indonesian take-off rather than the engineer-inventor as in the English and American experience.

6. *The function of the entrepreneur in such transitional but pretake-off societies is mainly to adapt customary, established means to novel ends.*

It is their uncommon ability to operate at once in the traditional world of established custom and in the modern world of systematic economic rationality which is the chief resource of the economic innovators of both

Modjokuto and Tabanan. In Modjokuto the small shopkeepers and manu-facturers capitalize on the knowledge and skills developed in the bazaar economy and attempt to apply them toward the creation of economic institutions better organized and more efficient than the bazaar economy has been able to produce. In Tabanan the businessmen nobles redirect the political loyalties of agrarian society into the support of economic rationalization. Both groups draw much of their strength from this ability to operate on both sides of the line between traditional and modern in economic matters and so form a bridge between the two. As a result, they are able to create transitional economic institutions within which many of the values, beliefs, structure, and skills of a customary trading or peasant culture are integrated with features characteristic of developed and specialized-enterprise (firm) economies.

The degree to which these propositions, or others which might be derived from our two-town comparison, will prove of value to the analy-sis of development generally remains to be seen. But, in more general terms, perhaps this sort of community-study approach to economic growth will help to turn planning in underdeveloped countries away from the rigid, a priori, hypertheoretical, almost dogmatic approach which has often been characteristic of it toward a more pragmatic, concrete, and realistic approach—one which uses general principles, economic or sociological, not as axioms from which policies are to be logically deduced but as guides to the interpretation of particular cases upon which poli-cies are to be based.

part V

The Transition:

The Colonial Case

Colonialism and Economic Growth

chapter *17*

WHILE PHYSICAL CAPITAL USEFUL FOR ECONOMIC
growth was constructed in many areas under colonial rule, colonialism
caused psychological reactions whose continuing effects hamper economic growth. Colonial rule caused rather widespread retreatism, which
might be a stage on the road to creativity, but the severe pressures on the
individual that resulted from the colonial situation also led many individuals to the more extreme reaction of ritualism. Various forms of group
hysteria that may be referred to collectively as Messianism manifested
the intensity of the stresses. Both among the retreatist and ritualist individuals and among others not so severely affected there resulted a rather
compulsive clinging to values inimical to economic growth. After a summary of the pressures exerted on individuals by colonialism, these phenomena will be discussed in turn, and then some reactions that somewhat
alleviated the effects.

THE PRESSURES OF COLONIALISM

Colonial rule, wherever it was imposed, created extreme psychological
pressures on the subject people not only as a result of measures which the
colonial masters adopted as a matter of deliberate policy but also inescap-
ably by virtue of what the colonial administrators were and what their
presence in the colonial area represented.

To begin with, they came unwanted and conquered the society by
force. In doing so they provided an unqualified demonstration that the
structure of the native society was of no importance to them relative to
the satisfaction of their own desires—that in their view the indigenous
structure of political and social power was not worth preserving. In
their administration they disrupted further the overt structure of administrative relationships. They regrouped local governmental areas for the
sake of administrative convenience, provided for choice of legislative or
administrative officials in new ways for convenience or in the name of advance toward democracy, and modified other traditional political mechanisms to control their functioning. They had to do some or all of these

things to prevent the traditional channels of leadership from being mechanisms for the organization of resistance to their rule.

There have been partial seeming exceptions, notably leaving in power the Maharajas in India, local princes in Indonesia, and some tribal rulers in Africa, under policies of indirect rule. But surely in such cases the indigenous population was not deceived. The native rulers were left in nominal possession of their functions and prerogatives only if they submitted their exercise of power to the will of the conquerors and turned over to the conquerors such a share of the material produce of the society as seemed feasible and was desired. The indigenous rulers may have submitted to the humiliating procedures of yielding to alien rule for the sake of their skins, in which case their continuance in authority was a source of shame to their subjects, not an evidence of the grace of the colonial rulers. Even if they continued to function to preserve as much of the traditional life as they could, their ambiguous position must have stirred unease. In addition more detailed investigation would probably show that in all cases the colonial masters found it necessary to intervene repeatedly by physical force or threat of force to effect their purposes; the society was not left intact.

Among the virtually inevitable changes was some disruption of the economic functioning of the native society. The purposes of the conquest included economic ones, and, however important or unimportant they may have been relative to other purposes, they were not ignored. New taxes were imposed so the necessity to earn money should impel indigenous workers to present their produce for sale in the market or to offer their labor to Europeans who wished to exploit the natural resources of the country. In the latter case, traditional family and community relationships of great psychological importance, of whose existence the colonial administrators may not have been aware, were disrupted. Ownership of property in fee simple was often introduced under the guise of economic progress and so that Europeans would be able to enter into business operations in the society. Thereby age-old equities in tribal and family wealth and in the inherited use-ownership of property were destroyed, and the social basis of existence in the villages eliminated. More generally, new codes of civil and criminal law were introduced for at least certain purposes. Their introduction destroyed the moral basis for the settlement of some types of disputes among individuals and made it inevitable that, from the viewpoint of the system of values of the traditional society, in some situations inequity and evil would be done.

In some cases religious customs were left alone so far as it was convenient to do so. However, because the Europeans regarded their own culture as superior, they were apt to forbid practices which they regarded as primitive (human sacrifices, the burial of individuals alive under sacred buildings so their spirits may protect the buildings, suicide by a widow on the bier of her husband) but which to the persons they ruled were either demonstrations of their obedience to the desires of the supernatural forces or necessary precautions against supernatural wrath. Even if the Europeans did not forbid such practices, they themselves literally or figuratively desecrated holy ground, as, for example, when they walked on temple grounds wearing shoes. And, as a minimum, the new rulers did not themselves observe the native religion, thereby offending the supernatural spirits and cutting the ties between the society and the supernatural forces at the highest level.

Perhaps equally important, by their very daily existence the colonial masters indicated in countless ways their contempt for the traditional culture. They built their houses differently, used different furniture, wore different clothing, showed repugnance for traditional methods of preparing food, and so on through every aspect of living.

And finally, if these aspects of the behavior of the new masters did not sufficiently suggest to the indigenous people that they were regarded as of little worth, the Europeans taught the lesson unmistakably in the relationships which they established in personal contacts between the two peoples. They regarded the individuals of the subordinated society as inferior not because of what they might or might not do but purely because they were natives. There could be no better evidence than that the word *native* has become a term of derogation, so that to avoid a connotation of contempt or condescension one must use instead the term *indigenous*. The European colonials would not meet indigenous individuals as social equals (even when those individuals were more liberally educated in Western culture and had better claim to intellectual attainment than the Europeans), excluded them from their homes and their clubs, required them to use terms of address which indicated the inferiority of the speaker, and informed them in a great variety of other deliberate and unconscious ways that they were regarded as unchangeably inferior. The central aspect of the relationship was that the indigenous people were tools being used for the benefit of the Europeans; and no exertion of effort by the individuals at the fringes of European colonial life such as missionaries whose main purpose was to advance the welfare of the subordinated people (or so these individuals believed in their conscious minds) could materially alter this perception.

These results of colonialism are not fortuitous. Many of the acts and attitudes sketched were necessary for the attainment of the avowed purposes for which the colonialists conquered the society: to introduce Western economic practices, to enhance the power and glory of their country, to save the souls of the heathen, and so on. Some which do not seem so are found to be so when we consider the network of actions and relationships necessary to reinforce and secure the effectiveness of certain central actions. The social exclusiveness was justified on the ground that in one's relaxation one wants to associate with one's own kind. The insistence of overt acknowledgment of an inferiority-superiority relationship was said to be necessary to enforce recognition that the Europeans were the rulers and must be obeyed. But, more basically, these acts and attitudes were inescapable because of the nature of the colonial relationship. It would have been psychologically impossible for the European elite to live in the role of unwanted intruders in an alien society if they had not persuaded themselves that they were of their essence superior to the conquered people. That is, to suppress their guilt at their aggression, they had to assure and reassure themselves that their culture was superior, presumably because of the biological inheritance which made them superior persons, and that the values and institutions of the natives were of little worth, so that it was justifiable to impose oneself and one's purposes by force. This is the rationale by which any society must assuage its guilt at conquest and control of alien peoples. In additon, the specific individuals who became colonial administrators and businessmen were in the main self-selected, and one of the bases of self-selection was a need structure which was satisfied by the rule of other individuals, After a generation or so the colonialists assured themselves that the indigenous people were grateful for the benefits which had been conferred and wished colonial control to continue. This self-deception was an added defense against guilt at their aggression.

One exception may be noted to this sketch of the personality of colonialists: the colonial administrator who chose that vocation because he was impelled to try to save the indigenous people from the attitudes of his fellow administrators. There were such individuals, their motivation being some degree of rebellion against their own society, some degree of identification with the underdogs, perhaps humanitarianism in some other sense. They were, however, few. Moreover, individuals who objected to their own social system could have opposed it at home; that some such individuals went to the colonies usually implies that they partook of the perception that they were superiors who would lead the benighted natives to more worthy lives. Certainly this was true of missionaries; though their methods were gentler, their disparagement of the native culture was not less extreme than that of the administrators.

The comprehensive derogation thus expressed or implied by colonialism was tempered somewhat by expressed or implied admiration for some qualities of indigenous individuals—their capacity as fighters, their dexterity, and a few others; but these bits of high valuation were almost insignificant offsets to the virtually all-encompassing disparagement.

The low valuation of indigenous individuals manifested by the conquerors would not have mattered if the conquerors had no prestige in the indigenous society. However, the conquerors did have one characteristic conveying tremendous prestige, their overwhelming power. Thus their valuation counted. And even apart from the disparagement they expressed, their disruption of the traditional sources of emotional security created intense stresses.

RETREATISM IN COLONIAL SOCIETIES

When such pressures had persisted for one or two generations, they induced retreatist personality in most members of colonial societies. Adults responded to their rage and frustration with behavior in the home which led to retreatism in their children.

In many accounts of colonial societies in Asia, in the Middle East, and in North Africa one may read of the apathy of the people, of their lack of interest in affairs beyond the immediate circles of their lives. Leaders of Western countries, seeing this apathy, believed that the people of colonial areas had no thoughts or feelings about matters beyond their immediate ken. They believed that tribal or national leaders in the traditional societies who could not be bought might, without much reaction by the people, be replaced by ones who could, and that it was a matter of indifference to the people whether the kept leader pledged the support of his society to one or the other side of an issue. The Western leaders, conceiving the people of colonial societies to be without important values of their own, thought also that they could recognize Western culture as superior to their own if only, like children, they received enough education; and believed, too, that such people were grateful for the blessings that were being conferred upon them.

In country after country, therefore, the Westerners were shocked when, after World War II, the people voted overwhelmingly for independence; and they were still more shocked at the violence with which mobs in many countries manifested their hatred and rage once the circumstances were such that they dared admit these emotions to themselves. These phenomena, as well as the charismatic appeal of leaders like Castro to the simple folk of many countries, are understandable if we recognize that the apathy was not that of brutish unfeeling but that of retreatism, which always masks intense unconscious rage. For generations adults in the society had perceived the contempt of the colonial masters for the values of the society. The deep belief of the indigenous people in those values had conflicted with their respect for or fear of the power of the colonial rulers. The conflict had caused intense anxiety, as well as rage which it was necessary to repress. Children observing this anxiety and humiliation in adults had learned to repress their values, as a defense against pain, but the process had generated rage, none the less intense because it was unconscious. From generation to generation the effect had deepened; retreatism became more complete.

There may have been other causes of retreatism as well. In the discussion in Chapter 19 of the Sioux on two governmental reservations, it is suggested that because their traditional life had been disrupted, their childhood environment provided many conflicting signals to them, in addition to the conflict of values directly resulting from the behavior of the conquerors. It is suggested also that their childhood environment provided them with many motivations which adult life could not satisfy. Both of these results may occur in other colonial societies. Insofar as they do, they add to the pressure on the individual to repress his conflicting values, that is, to become retreatist.

MORE EXTREME REACTIONS

But though retreatism was the most common reaction of colonial subjects to the tensions which developed in the home environment, the behavior of individuals who came most directly under the pressure of almost complete absence of status respect plus almost complete helplessness led to still more extreme ones.

A Scale of Reactions to Derogation

In any environment a child will perceive that sometimes he is only an instrument; that at times powerful and valued others place their convenience before his and use him or ignore him as needed to suit their purposes. This derogation creates anxiety in the child, and he wonders why he is treated thus. Among his responses to this anxiety in the normal case is identification with his parent of the same sex. By identifying himself with his father the son of say four years of age reassures himself that his father does not hate him, that he does not hate his father, that he is attractive to his mother, that he is big, and so on. In this way a child can cope with an occasional sense of being devalued without great hindrance to the development of needs favorable to creativity, that is, to the ability to solve problems with the most efficient use of one's mental capacities.

However, if the disregard by others of one's purposes and values in life is more frequent and more harsh (or, perhaps, if one is more sensitive to it), personality less attuned to coping with the world emerges. With a certain amount of pressure, and certain other specific characteristics of the environment, high need submission-domination and authoritarian personality result; with more pressure and certain other environmental features, values and needs are repressed and retreatism results. In the extreme case, in which the world seems virtually completely hostile to his urges and initiatives, the individual becomes paranoiac. Finding the real world so terrifying as to be intolerable, he refuses to believe that it exists and in desperate fantasy creates for himself a world in which he has a position that makes his existence endurable. Somewhat short of this extreme degree of pressure is the degree which causes the type of personality termed ritualist and, if the pressures impinge on a group rather than an individual, the group behavior known as Messianism.

Ritualism and Messianism, which were fairly common in colonial situations, may be thought of as standing between retreatism and paranoia in the scale of reactions.

Identification with the Aggressor

A child experiencing extreme derogation may seek to protect himself by a mechanism known as "identification with the aggressor." It will be useful to discuss this mechanism in general terms before applying it specifically to the colonial case.

The term was first suggested by Anna Freud.[1] Among the half-dozen or more examples that she cites, a trivial one will illustrate the term, that of the small girl, afraid of ghosts and therefore afraid to walk across a dark hall, who solved the problem by pretending each time she crossed the hall that she was the ghost. Another example may illustrate more vividly the nature of the inner behavior of the child who tries to protect himself thus. One of Anna Freud's patients, a boy mortally afraid of being hurt, had been caused pain by his dentist. The boy brought a pocket knife to the next session with Dr. Freud and cut up a rubber ball, cut a string into small bits, and sharpened a pencil incessantly; on a later occasion, when his teacher had accidentally injured him, he came to his therapeutic session wearing a military cap, toy sword, and pistol. He said he "just felt like wearing them today." He was protecting himself from destruction by trying to persuade himself that he was the destroyer and therefore obviously would not be attacked by the destroyer. In the same way, some children put under extreme pressure by the self-centered and non-loving care of their parents solve this problem by masquerading, so to speak, as one of the parents.

The child masquerades as his parent, but he is not duplicating with pleasure so far as his capacities permit the behavior of someone he loves. His problem is that he is not loved. He lives in terror. He attempts to relieve his terror by persuading himself that he has characteristics identical with the person who has power over him. If he becomes identical with the aggressor, surely the aggressor will not destroy him. But he is not really imitating the quality but only its appearance. The boy did not imitate the dentist's cutting skill in any way that would give him a useful ability; he cut compulsively, ritually, and uselessly except for the function of assuaging his terror. Of course he patterns his behavior after some model around him in his childhood, for except in cases that become psychotic he learns to walk, to talk, to eat in a conventional manner. Presumably he models himself after the least terrifying individual or individuals among those important to him. He acquired no rich sense of

---

[1] Though she probably had suggested the term earlier, Chapter 9 of her book (*The Ego and the Mechanisms of Defence* [London: The Hogarth Press, Ltd., and the Institute of Psycho-Analysis, 1937], translated from the German) presents the discussion of the concept usually referred to.

nurturance from anyone, for presumably if he had he would have been
saved from ritualism, but he finds someone to model his routine behavior
after.

Since very little regard for him is manifested by the self-centered
father who creates such fear, the child, finding no reason not to believe
that his father willingly hurts him, finds no reason to blame himself.
Hence all of his rage can be turned outward, and it is intense. At the
same time that he slavishly imitates external traits of his father, he hates
him with a consuming hatred. But it would be mortally perilous to admit
his hatred since he is so completely dependent on the aggressor, his
father. Hence he struggles to deny his hatred even to himself. At the
same time he struggles with value conflicts. Thus the boy who used his
knife to cut, cut, cut was actually tremendously afraid of a knife, and
no doubt had to summon up great effort to take the thing in his hand.
To do the things he hates and fears but thinks he must do to prevent destruction requires tremendous effort by the individual. The inner struggle
drains him of vitality and initiative.

The Colonial Case: Ritualism

In the colonial case the parents' frustrations at their disparaged existence caused the behavior which forced the child to this extreme defense.
The father subjected to the most severe withdrawal of status recognition
must have reacted with especial severity in his home. Denied other
channels for his need dominance and his rage, he must have asserted
them in the home with extreme harshness. He must have been so occupied
with his rage, humiliations, and bewilderment that he had no capacity
to respond to persons around him; he merely ruled them and pushed them
out of his way. The perception his children received must have been
almost unrelievedly a stark one of a powerful figure who controlled them,
who valued them little, and who had his own interests and concerns
on which it was dangerous to intrude.

Since we have no direct accounts of such children, we can only re-
construct the childhood behavior from the adult personalities which
emerged. The son must have sought in desperation to duplicate some
overt aspect of his father's behavior, perhaps his withdrawal from the
world and unresponsiveness to things around him. The son dared not
direct at his father the rage which filled him, but in his father's rage at the
disparaging colonial masters he found a permissible target. The images
of the disparaging group that the son perceived at this time in his life
were of course very vague and confused ones, consisting largely of some-
thing-toward-which-my-father-has-an-attitude. Yet even very early in
life he might hate this vague object. He thus served a dual purpose: he
could hate, and, at the same time, here was an aspect of his father's
attitudes he could identify with, thus protecting himself against his
father.

Yet at the same time another motivation impelled him in an opposite direction. If these other persons have more power than his father, perhaps he could protect himself against his father by aligning himself with them instead of hating them. Or perhaps he could do both: both hate them and ape them. His emotional life became confused.

Then, as he moved outside the home and came into more and more actual contact with the power of the colonial elite, he found that in the kind of stimuli they presented to him they resembled his father. They had superior power. And they would no more receive him, regardless of what he did, than would his father. At this point the pattern of behavior he had learned in early childhood suggested to him the threat of complete destruction, complete rejection. But it also suggested a remedy. Using the mechanism of identification with the threatening figures already built into his personality, he now tried to persuade himself that he was just like these new aggressors. By this maneuver he not only warded off this new terror but also lessened his old one; he gained protection from his parents. For he had now become identical with something even more powerful than they.[2]

And so in a Dutch colony in his sports and clothes and speech he might become more Dutch than the Dutch; in a British colony, depending on his social class, he went in for soccer or tennis or golf, and, whatever his class, for physical fitness. If he had the opportunity, he might study in the Western-type schools which the colonial masters established. He might pursue the occupations they approved, becoming, for example, a clerk in their offices. He might become a Christian, a particularly meek and ritualistic Christian.

But even as he masqueraded as one of the aggressors, he was consumed with rage at them which he dared not admit to himself. So, as was true as a child, his energies were forever absorbed in a continuing inner struggle to contain his rage and deal with the conflict within him. The mask-like appearance which characterized many such individuals, presumably the extreme cases, revealed the tenseness of their control; if they gave way an inch to their inner impulses, their self-constraint might break down. Even in the less extreme cases the imitation of Western modes was as if at a distance—as though they did not dare approach too close to being Western. The imitation was a little slavish and intense, a little "tight." Behavior was rote rather than alert. Conflicted and constricted, the individual aped such of the social modes of the colonial masters as were open to him, but with half a heart, no will, bewilderment in his brain, and no initiative and judgment. He would never advance in their world, but he would continue to go through the motions. He is appropriately termed a ritualist.

---

[2] This "overdetermined" characteristic is typical of many psychological mechanisms. They often serve several purposes, including contradictory ones, at the same time.

Many such persons are found in colonial or ex-colonial areas today. They are clerks in the offices of Western businessmen in colonial areas. They are anxious to succeed, so they think, but something is wrong with their performance. Western businessmen in colonial areas are apt to say, "They are all right as clerks, but they have no head for business." The Westerners think that the characterization applies to all indigenous individuals of the society. Believing this justifies that feeling of innate superiority which, as I have noted, they must have to justify their existence as colonial masters. It does not occur to them to look at the history of the country and wonder how this can be if, as is often or usually true, that history indicates magnificent administrative achievements in war, governmental administration, architecture, engineering, or other activities.

Persons whose personalities partake in considerable degree of identification with the aggressors have sometimes become the first leaders of a colonial country after independence. Sufficiently pursuing identification with the aggressors so that they acquired various European values, but just free enough so that they might speak out for independence, they gained a certain degree of charisma as leaders of the independence movement and so have become leaders of the new nation. However, their values are so mixed that they cannot adequately express the nationalist hatred of the foreigner which the mass of the people feel. Because they cannot, those who are still nationalist leaders today are apt to be replaced, as they age or their initial charisma wears off, by less cultured, more raw and emotional leaders who give vent to the nation's attitudes more effectively. This has been the course of events in Ceylon and Egypt. Some of the pro-French leaders of the African nations that are members of the French community are probably of this conflicted type (others perhaps being merely venal or faithful to the interests of a narrow elite group). Mr. Kasavubu and Mr. Mobutu in the Congo may be conflicted in this way. Certainly a number of leaders in Burma, India, and Pakistan are. Even Mr. Nehru, like the British, speaks patronizingly of the Indians. ". . . My legacy to India? Hopefully, it is 400 million people capable of governing themselves."[3]

It will be surprising if the so-called "moderate leaders" in a number of the former French colonies are not replaced by more violently anti-Western ones. It would not be surprising to see a parallel development in Burma when U Nu has lost his hold on the people, though that may not occur for so many years that other social currents may determine the country's course by that time. In the complex cultural circumstances of India many other tensions will also affect the course of events, and it

---

[3] Norman Cousins, "Talk with the PM," *Saturday Review*, May 27, 1961. Mr. Cousins had suggested that perhaps Mr. Nehru was Gandhi's greatest legacy to India, and had asked Mr. Nehru, "Who is your legacy to India?"

would be rash to predict that this sequence will occur; but even there it is a possibility.

Not only the top national leaders but some of their ministers and many of their civil servants at all levels are ritualist in greater or less degree. They entered the civil service in imitation of their European masters. They are excellently trained in European institutions, but many of them are constricted by their inner conflicts. These individuals will faithfully perform routine clerical or ministerial functions, but their lives are essentially imitative and they lack the initiative to meet their countries' complex problems effectively.

Ritualism as Unstable

Ritualism can hardly perpetuate itself. The tensions within the personality of the ritualist are such that the attempts of his children to defend themselves against them may be expected to produce warped, unintegrated personalities in them, but hardly ones with the same malformations as those of the parents. Given a physical environment which in later life confirms the childhood experience, authoritarian personality tends to perpetuate itself since it offers an effective means of coping with interpersonal relationships and the physical world. But ritualism serves a purpose only if there is a harshly dominating personality that must be identified with to avoid self-destruction and that offers a model of power to identify with. The ritualist personality itself does not seem to be such a personality. His personality may be bewildering and confining, and his behavior may cause pain, but he is certainly not powerful.

Ritualism, then, will not produce ritualism. It is an element in a dynamic society, not in a society in equilibrium (though in a society in equilibrium it may appear in an occasional deviant for whom the society has a niche). Ritualism is a characteristic of a process of disruption of equilibrium, a process which may be expected to continue further.

Where the social pressures which led to ritualism continue, retreatism, it seems to me, may emerge.

The ritualist is addicted to order and routine, and his meekness masks inner compulsions. When he becomes a father, the combination, I would suppose, will cause him to dominate his children and to ignore their needs and urges so that they receive the perception, as forcefully as their father obtained it a generation earlier, but not quite in the same way, that the world is unmanageable. While the father of the first generation bludgeoned his children into being merely instruments, the ritualist simply does not respond very much to his children (or to anyone else). He can no more give love freely than he can strike out violently. It seems plausible to suggest that the resulting home environment might readily create a perception in the children that nothing does any good—not obeying, or striking out on one's own initiative, or being aggressive, or identifying with one's parents. This might well be true even if only the father is a ritualist provided that the mother is so submissive in her feminine role that she offers no model of more active (and successful) personality to her children.

It is of particular interest to speculate what the course of change in ritualist personality may be when the social pressures of colonialism have ceased. In ex-colonial societies what personality traits will replace the ritualist ones in the next generation? While the personalities of adults who are ritualist at present will change little, the reduction in social pressures will certainly somewhat alter their behavior in the home. Their children hardly have a traditional personality to fall back on. Will a transition to at least a moderate degree of creativity occur in one generation? Or will the children of these families be ineffective and confused individuals while other families provide the leadership in continuing social change? The latter seems more probable, but the entire subject is so complex that no attempt will be made to explore it here.

Messianism[4]

Even closer to paranoia than ritualism is a group reaction to the psychological pressures of colonialism that I shall term Messianism, though it does not always involve the belief in a Savior who will save one from one's troubles. Messianism, broadly defined, apparently has appeared in most traditional societies in which an alien power has imposed alien institutions. Suddenly a social movement emerges which embodies the belief that by magic the power of the conquerors can be nullified and the good life restored. The belief is characterized by wishful thinking intensified in desperation to the point of fantasy in which the real is no longer distinguished from the wished for. Under some combination of defense mechanism learned as children and inability as adults to tolerate the crushing weight of the colonial environment, men who previously had been rational citizens peacefully (though resentfully) obeying the colonial commands find the frustrations of reality intolerable. Seeing no rational way to restore an identity for themselves, and unable to live without one, they insist on believing that there is one and find it in magic practices which in moments of lesser pressure they know are of no use.

---

[4] For discussions of Messianic movements other than the discussions cited below in specific contexts, see:

N. M. Ames, "Reaction to Stress: A Comparative Study of Nativism," *Davidson Journal of Anthropology*, Vol. III, No. 1 (Summer, 1957).

R. Linton, "Nativistic Movements," *American Anthropologist*, Vol. XLV (1943).

F. W. Voget, "The American Indian in Transition: Reformism and Accommodation," *American Anthropologist*, Vol. LVII (1956).

A. F. C. Wallace, "Revitalization Movements," *American Anthropologist*, Vol. LVIII (1956).

In Burma, in 1930 and 1931, men in the countryside suddenly believed that incantations and charms would make them immune against the weapons of the English. Armed only with primitive weapons, they marched in a solid phalanx against rifles.[5] In Madagascar, protected from rifle-fire by a bit of wood on a string clenched between the teeth, men charged similarly against European guns.[6] In South Dakota, a generation after the Sioux had been subdued and the buffalo had disappeared from the plains, the Sioux gathered to regain their lands and summon back the buffalo by ritual and dances.[7] The Mau Mau movement in Kenya in the 1950's served several psychological ends by combining Messianism with aggression. In the Southwest Pacific, where the islanders had seen ships and planes pour out supplies during World War II, they believed after the war that if they could cast off the Europeans, ships and planes would appear which would return their native goods to them or would bring them an equitable share of the goods which the Europeans who had destroyed their civilization possessed in such quantities. So they organized in various ways, religious intensity everywhere being a characteristic, to obtain these ends. In New Guinea those who lived inland built airstrips in the jungle, and those in shore villages built wharves into the sea and cast their furniture and household equipment into the ocean, waiting thereafter for their magic to bring the ships and planes that should re-equip them.[8] And these are only more or less random examples of what has occurred where the pressure of extreme withdrawal of status respect has made the real world intolerable. It has been suggested to me[9] that a study of the infiltration of European words into native languages has indicated a rough law of the point of cultural pressure at which the life of reality becomes intolerable and Messianic movements tend to appear, but I have not myself seen the evidence in the literature.

It is not unreasonable to suggest that the desire of the leaders of some low-income societies for industrial establishments which are demonstrably grossly uneconomic is a manifestation of the same psychological phenomenon. A steel mill, for example, is a symbol of power. People who have one, it seems, will have power. So the steel mill is built, and the

---

[5] A brief account of the movement of which such incidents were a part is presented in John F. Cady, *A History of Modern Burma* (Ithaca, N.Y.: Cornell University Press, 1958), pp. 309–13.

[6] (Dominique) O. Mannoni, *Prospero and Caliban: The Psychology of Colonization*, trans. Pamela Powesland (New York: Frederick A. Praeger, Inc., 1956), chaps. ii and iv, especially p. 149.

[7] Milton Lott, *Dance Back the Buffalo* (Boston: Houghton Mifflin Co., 1959); and see Chapter 19, below.

[8] For a brief account, see Raymond Firth, *Elements of Social Organization* (London: Watts & Co., 1951), pp. 110–13.

Perhaps not all of these movements should be termed Messianic, for not all incorporate belief in a leader, present here on earth, whose magic will make people invulnerable to deadly weapons.

[9] By the late Clyde Kluckhohn, in conversation.

political leaders of the country are impervious to argument that the country lacks coking coal and iron ore and will soon run out of steel scrap, or that these resources are so situated that under the most favorable circumstances, after maximum efficiency has been attained, the steel produced will cost twice the price at which it could be imported. Add perhaps that the funds invested in the plant could instead have been used to produce other goods that would replace imports or increase exports with an efficiency that would raise the level of living. It is not that the leaders are stupid, or that they simply believe that the analyses available to them are imperialist tricks. Rather, they are somehow unable to receive the analyses in their minds; their need for a quick path out of their humiliation to dignity and power is such that it is not possible for them to believe that they cannot achieve the result quickly by magic.[10]

The belief that one can be rescued from one's troubles by magic of course inhibits intelligent imaginative action to attain economic growth. Messianism is mentioned here both for that reason and because it testifies to the intensity of the psychological pressures created by colonialism.

THE PERPETUATION OF VALUES INIMICAL TO ECONOMIC GROWTH

This analysis of certain extreme reactions of some groups in colonial societies to severe social pressure may make it easier to understand the more general effects of such pressures among colonial and ex-colonial peoples.

A derogated individual tends to attack both the persons who disparage

---

[10] The cultures and personalities of Western societies are not immune to such aberrations. The belief of many Americans after World War II that Senator Joseph McCarthy could save the country from Communism, and was doing so, is a case of Messianism. (The degree of attachment of many Americans to Franklin Delano Roosevelt in the 1930's and to General Eisenhower after World War II are not entirely dissimilar phenomena.) In both the American case and the cases in traditional societies, there were pressures that made many individuals extremely anxious. There was bewilderment about the nature of the threat, and lack of perception of any rational solution. Because acceptance of continued anxiety was intolerable, fantasy and belief in a magical solution were resorted to. Senator McCarthy's followers did not regard themselves as resorting to magic. They believed that Communists in the federal establishment did threaten their lives and that Senator McCarthy could find Communists whom the executive officers were unable or unwilling to discover. But this does not distinguish the two cases. Surely the intelligent individuals in traditional societies who resorted to Messianism perceived equally plausible reasons for believing that the method they followed was logical.

World cognition based on more advanced scientific knowledge excludes or curtails the ability to believe in certain types of magical manipulation of the physical world (though the anxious individual can still believe in an invasion by Martians). Yet even up to the present time peoples with the most advanced knowledge have believed in Messianic remedies if the level of their anxiety was sufficiently high.

An early study of a less extreme form of the psychological mechanism is William James' "The Will to Believe," in *The Will to Believe and Other Essays in Popular Philosophy* (New York: Longmans, Green & Co., 1896).

him and the things they value. For this reason a person with a normal traditional childhood cannot set a high value on using his energies in attacking the problems of industrial production or other varieties of modern business activity. For the Western view that such use of one's energies is a worthwhile way of life and the Western view that the indigenous individuals are of contemptible intrinsic worth are intertwined; the two were associated in the colonialists' scheme of values. Accepting the first involves accepting the European way of life as a frame of reference, and that involves accepting the second. To do so would be self-destruction. Hence the indigenous individual clings to traditional values, not unself-consciously as he would in undisturbed traditional society, but compulsively, to protect himself from the threat to his identity which acceptance of Western values would constitute. By holding to the idea that physical labor is demeaning, that an elite individual is interested in humanistic learning, that one's status determines one's worth, a member of the traditional elite can protect himself after a fashion from the derogation of the Westerner. He can tell himself (unconsciously) that the powerful Westerner's view of the indigenous individual's worth is not so important after all, since the Westerner by violating the traditional values proves himself to be of inferior worth. And for the same sort of reason the nonelite indigenous individual clings with equal compulsiveness to his religious belief, his view of what type of social structure is good, his traditional methods.

This is the reaction of the normal traditional individual in a colonial or newly ex-colonial society toward Western values. That of a retreatist or ritualist person is similar. The retreatist individual has internalized traditional values even though the conflict among them is so painful that he has repressed them from consciousness. Thus the values of the colonial masters threaten him just as they do the traditional individual, and he responds to that threat with the same defensive maneuver. The ritualist individual is prepared to ape Western behavior, just as earlier he aped some threatening characteristic of his father, so that he can try to persuade himself that since he is like the Westerner, the Westerner does not really feel contempt for him. However, beneath that external aping he fears the person who derogates him, just as in infancy and childhood he mortally feared the person or persons who showed no love for him. The values he holds to are the ones he found least dangerous in early life. He cannot productively imitate the persons who threaten him.

Sometimes the controlled appearance of a ritualist is deceptive to casual observation. Thus it is not always apparent at first glance whether the diligent colonial student of Western learning is a person high in need autonomy and need achievement who is acquiring a useful tool or a ritualist busily but uncreatively strengthening his defense. The similarity, however, is superficial.

Because of the threat posed by the attitudes of Western colonial masters to the identities of indigenous individuals, it is often difficult for a member of a colonial or ex-colonial society to receive technical advice from a Westerner. In the case of American technical aid the problem is intensified by the fact that since World War II American actions that affect the underdeveloped countries have been such as repeatedly to rearouse the sense of humiliation and resentment in the peoples of those countries. In some of our economic aid programs, and even more in our military assistance programs our support of repressive established ruling classes in some countries and our intervention to displace legitimate rulers in one or two others, we have conveyed forcefully to the peoples of those countries the perception that we have no regard for their purposes, even no interest in inquiring what those purposes are, but rather feel justified in flouting their purposes to serve ours.[11]

As a result, with the fibers of their nervous systems, not merely with their minds, many individuals in underdeveloped countries must fear Americans and other Westerners and unconsciously distrust their advice even while apparently listening or watching closely. Would a person who feels contempt for them advise them except in his own interest? And can any action in his interest also be in theirs? Perhaps they fear him especially as he bears gifts, for the colonial administrator often tried to bribe the colonial subject to serve administrative purposes. The defense mechanisms built into the indigenous individual's neural processes rise up to block the processes of his mind when the European advises him. Obviously this sort of attitude is not an absolute bar, but the inhibiting quality of this behavior pattern is no doubt one cause of the ineffectiveness of much technical aid.

Many indigenous individuals, it is true, seek employment in Western business organizations, but close observation will indicate that their behavior is usually ritualist. They seek to identify themselves with European externals; but when they try to function in these positions, their hatred of the underlying European values and the perpetual conflict within them prevent them from functioning successfully. They have "no head for business." It is plausible to believe that unconsciously they deliberately sabotage the European-type operation. They make mistakes, misunderstand instructions, fail to anticipate needed actions. They do so, I suggest, because they need to protect their identity by demonstrating to themselves that they would not wholeheartedly function as aliens. Or they impose on the operation the traditional interpersonal relationships which one aspect of their value and need structure demands, and the operation fails to function well. Reconciling traditional relationships with the economic and technical requirements may be possible, but it would require an order of creativity which in their conflicted condition they do not possess.

----

[11] See the Appendix to this chapter.

Thus, although colonial rule has laid a material base for economic growth in many countries, it may have created psychological barriers more important in their effects.

A QUALIFICATION: RIFTS IN THE TRADITIONAL SOCIAL STRUCTURE

One important qualification should be noted to the inability of individuals in traditional societies to share the values of their colonial masters except in a constricted ritualist way. Because of domestic power shifts before any European intrusion, in some traditional societies groups who had once held an accepted place in the society were later denied recognition of the status which they believed was rightfully theirs. When Europeans overthrew the dominant traditional group, the members of some such subordinated groups greeted the Europeans as deliverers. If they did, they may have accepted Western values fairly readily. This reaction occurred in some degree among the Karens, Shans, and Arakanese in Burma, in the Shia sect in Saudi Arabia, among tribal groups in a number of African countries, among important groups in India, and perhaps among groups in many other areas as well. Moreover, if the groups from whom status recognition had been withdrawn have passed through the phase of retreatism and become creative, they may enter effectively upon technological progress.

However, they will not necessarily do so, for two reasons. One is that status recognition may not have been withheld from them for a sufficiently long period to arouse creativity in them. The other is that under the rule of the colonial administrators and businessmen opposing pressures will weigh on them. For the colonial masters indicate extreme disparagement of the values of the subordinated group as well as those of the erstwhile dominant group. Hence the subordinated group is simultaneously attracted and repelled. The resultant impact on them depends on a balance of influences concerning which no general statement can be made, but it is clear that in some situations the subordinated group may seize upon not only Western values but also Western techniques with speed and ingenuity and set economic growth on its way.

India provides an example. Successive waves of invasion and conquest of parts of India and resulting migration and cross-migration within the subcontinent have resulted in complex centuries-old patterns of withdrawal of status recognition, varying over time. Today, as for centuries past, a linguistic-ethnic group that is the dominant elite in one area may be a somewhat derogated minority in another, and a group which by general consensus is the top elite in an area may nevertheless find some aspects of their behavior disparaged by other individuals or groups whose opinion weighs upon them. The situation in India has seemed to me too complex to lend itself to analysis in terms of the analytical model presented in this volume without more intensive examination than it has been possible to give it, but the general observation seems justified that this situation may have produced creative personality in individuals of a number of different groups. India may be ripe for continuing technological progress even though it has very recently come out from under the ordinarily impeding influences of colonial rule; the pertinent question is whether the number of creative individuals produced by the various pressures is great enough.[12]

Even if this is the case, it would be difficult to decide whether on balance colonialism hastened the process of economic growth in India. It may be expected that creative Indian individuals seeking new routes to achievement and status would have established contacts with the West in any event, as they did in Japan and Colombia. Under colonialism they had more extensive contact with many Westerners. Did the greater access to knowledge offset the psychological barriers which the colonial relationship created and the tendency of Western administrators to hamper developments which might compete with their own interests? No one can say with certainty. To the writer it seems likely that even in India colonialism delayed economic growth, but this is a subjective judgment for which no conclusive evidence can be adduced.

IMPLICATIONS FOR THE FUTURE

If colonial rule has had the effects that have been sketched above, what may one conclude concerning the prospects for economic growth in colonial areas, either while they remain colonial or after they obtain their independence?

If the derogation of colonial rule results in retreatist personality after several generations, some individuals with creative personality may emerge in still later generations by the process already sketched by which retreatism leads to creativity. It is to be expected that creative individuals who do emerge while the area is still colonial will not imitate the economic activity of the colonial masters for the same reason that repelled earlier generations: assumption of the master's values will carry with it self-condemnation. They may carry on economic innovation of a distinctly different type, but the situation in which they live is more apt

---

[12] Even if the number is great enough and economic growth proceeds, that fact alone will not assure smooth social change. The creative individuals leading the technological change are members of the elite. The question remains whether they will act so as to convey to the simple folk a sense that they are valued and will do so before the continued derogation of their status to which the simple folk are still subjected, and their suspicions of the European values of national leaders, cause radical political change. (These forces, and not the impression one gains from much popular writing that the Indians will be unhappy if they do not do as well as China, seem to me to be at the core of the political-social problem of India.) While the prospects for social stability seem reasonably good to many observers, one would not wish to make unqualified forecasts.

to direct their innovational energies into other activities, such as the attainment of independence.

Even after colonial rule ends, economic growth is not apt to become vigorous until change in personality has occurred. However, it does not follow that a sequence of several generations of personality change must lapse before economic growth will begin. Rather quickly, say in the period between infancy and maturity of one generation, creativity may emerge out of retreatism on a fairly large scale, and the creative individuals may see in economic prowess their best opportunity to prove their worth.[13]

If this analysis is correct, it suggests a minimum lag of say 30 years between the time when independence is assured and the time when economic growth becomes vigorous, and a typical lag somewhat longer. India, however, might be an exception to this generalization because of the quantum of innovational personality channeled toward technological advance that already existed when the British established themselves in the country. Because of it, economic prowess no doubt had a place in the value system of some groups at that time. Hence it was not necessary to react against this value of the conquerors; other values could be identified as the alien and threatening ones. If so, there may have persisted throughout colonial days a stream of economic innovational personality large enough to initiate vigorous economic growth sooner.[14]

APPENDIX:
AMERICAN FOREIGN POLICY AND THE UNDERDEVELOPED COUNTRIES

One of the results of the derogation of individuals of colonial and ex-colonial societies by the colonial rulers is the rage which lies latent in the personalities of many or most individuals in those societies. They do not feel rage in general (there is no such thing) but specifically rage at being used by some person or nation to serve its purposes without regard for their purposes. They rage at being treated as instruments rather than as human beings with their own purposes and values worthy of respect.

Like other important personality characteristics, this tendency to rage must have originated in childhood. Indigenous parents, preoccupied with their frustrations under colonial rule, presumably acted arbitrarily and inconsiderately in the home without conveying the perception of the rightness of their actions which is conveyed in the traditional situations, and their behavior engendered in their children rage at being treated with disregard of their needs and pur-

---

[13] In Chapter 19 the emergence of creativity among some American Indian leaders is discussed. While their condition is in a sense the archetype of complete colonialism, it differs from the usual case in such important respects—notably immersion in an alien society of overwhelming size, many of whose leaders support their cause—that it would be hazardous to generalize from the American experience to other and more usual colonial situations.

[14] This is admittedly *post hoc* theorizing. It is included to make clear the limits of the generalization stated in this section.

poses. As the children grew to adulthood, they experienced again from their European masters the same treatment as instruments, with little regard for their purposes in life. Their rage was confirmed and intensified.

It is appropriately termed an allergy. The reference is of course figurative, but the figure of speech is singularly apt, so close is the parallelism between the reaction of colonial peoples and the physiological one. Most of the societies involved are now free of colonial control, but they are subject to the impact of diplomatic policies of foreign nations; and when any event suggests to the people so sensitized that they are being used by a foreign power to serve its purposes with disregard of their own, a sense of humiliation and rage is re-aroused. The tendency exists among Latin American peoples and in a number of other countries which have long (or always) been free of colonial control, where, as has been noted in Chapter 10, the elites of these countries have treated the classes below them in a colonial manner.

Since World War II many American actions have aroused this sense of humiliation and resentment in the peoples of most of the economically underdeveloped countries of the world. The result has often been unwitting; in our egocentricity we have not understood that they had purposes different from ours; but this has not lessened the impact. Although this is not the place for a documented account, a brief summary will make clear the nature of the American actions referred to.

In addition to military agreements with countries whose people wanted them, we have made agreements with many whose people did not. For a time we encouraged almost any government that would take our money and munitions to create armed forces of a size that served our purposes and the purposes of that government and the elite classes, but for which the other people of the country saw no need, an undertaking which disrupted families, brought rich and rather arrogant foreigners into the country, and brought on the people danger of a war in which they felt no concern. (That they should feel no concern is shocking to some Americans, but consideration of the history of ex-colonial countries suggests they should be as suspicious of us as the Soviets.)

By our aid we seated more firmly in power ruling groups not selected by the will of the people, some of which groups are in Western terms corrupt, reactionary, insensitive to the needs of the people they rule, and actively oppressive. We supplied these governments arms without pressuring them or effectively helping them to alter the nature of their domestic rule. If we were aware of this effect of our military aid, we regarded it as of less importance than our short-run interest in military security.

In some instances our intervention has been more positive and specific. Because he avowed allegiance to us, we supported a prince in Laos who has no base of popular support; because he was leftist we aided in the deposition in Guatemala of a president legitimately elected who promised eagerly desired land reform; and we aided a plan to overthrow Castro in Cuba because we, and not the people of Cuba, dislike his Communist ties. (We criticize Castro's denial of freedom of speech and action and confiscation of property, but to peasants and workers in Cuba and throughout Latin America denial of these freedoms to elites with whom they feel no empathy must mean little. To them Castro apparently symbolizes primarily social reform and self-respect. And in any event the fact of American intervention probably has more emotional significance to them than any substantive question in Cuba.) Offering economic aid does not offset the rage which these actions arouse; the rage of people who feel humiliated is not dissipated by offering them money. Moreover, in our aid programs we have sometimes put the pocketbook interests of our citizens or our enterprises above what underdeveloped countries regard as their national interest.

Of course this is our prerogative, but they feel that we flout their dignity for our profit. Perhaps the example that arouses most emotion in Latin America is our refusal to aid the Brazilian national petroleum enterprise. Latin Americans commonly regard this not as a matter of principle but as a result of the influence in our government of our oil companies and as evidence of our contempt for Latin American wishes.

These comments of course imply no predictions concerning the stability of Castro's position. His internal errors may alienate the people, though his original charisma should survive many errors.

In most of these respects our policies have now been reversed or modified in ways lessening their offensive impact. However, persons who are psychologically allergic remember past humiliations, and react strongly to a few present incidents.

This perception by underdeveloped peoples that we, like their colonial masters, have contempt for their purposes in life or at least have not bothered to understand them has great political and diplomatic significance. It explains actions which have bewildered Americans—some anti-American riots, coolness to Western aims, tendencies to ally with Communist powers. By using countries for our purposes in disregard of theirs we have very probably generated throughout the countries affected and the continents of which they are a part suspicion and hostility vastly greater in significance than the shorter-run purposes we were pursuing. Our actions have helped to assure that if the peoples involved cannot resist these indignities with their own power they will look for support from our enemies, who are not tainted with our historical association with colonialists and who wear the halo of having themselves risen up to overthrow oppressive force. (Their more recent colonialism does not touch the emotions of the peoples of underdeveloped countries, partly because it is repression of peoples with whom the underdeveloped peoples have no empathy and partly because the emotional commitments of the underdeveloped peoples, caused by the Western actions sketched above, predispose them not to believe that it exists.) These reactions of the peoples of underdeveloped countries, rather than the diabolical cunning of Communist agents, are probably the basic reason why the trend in the sympathies of those peoples during the 1950's seems to have been against the United States and the West and toward the Communist powers.[15]

These repercussions of our policies of course strengthen the psychological blocks to effective participation in Western-type economic activity.

---

[15] The evidence of this trend is scattered. I believe, however, that the consensus of responsible reporters who have been in positions to sense the attitudes of the lower classes and the intellectuals in South and Southeast Asia and in Latin America is that the trend is as I have stated it.

To solve their purely domestic problems, people may turn to Communist ideology or leadership even if we do not thus pave the way. The actions I have sketched in the text above are by no means the sole explanation of trends in the attitudes of the people of underdeveloped countries. They are, however, of great importance.

A Case in Point: Burma*

chapter 18

I HAVE SKETCHED IN CHAPTER 8 CHILDHOOD ENVIRON-
ment in Burma and its effects on Burmese personality. In this chapter I
shall relate that information to the course of the country's development
before, during, and after its colonial period. I shall suggest the causes of
the actions of Burma's leaders during the 1950's and shall speculate concerning Burma's future. As a basis for the discussion there is available unusually complete knowledge of political and especially economic events
in Burma since her independence and the role of national leaders in them,
since the writer headed a group of economic consultants to the government of Burma from 1951 to 1953 and a critique of the government's
actions concerning economic development such as is possible for few
countries has been prepared by Louis J. Walinsky, who headed a team of
economic consultants from 1953 to 1959.[1]

The men who have been leaders of Burma since she gained independence avow an earnest desire for rapid economic development. The central
questions of the chapter will be why they have acted repeatedly in ways
that appear so ineffective and irresponsible, and how it happens that
the economy has made moderately good progress in spite of the bumbling
and wasteful actions of the national government. The answers will be
found in the impact of colonial rule on the traditional Burmese society,
and it will therefore be necessary to devote considerable attention to
both the Burmese kingdom and the period of colonial rule.

THE TRADITIONAL SOCIETY[2]

Early History

Burma's history has been governed to an exceptional degree by the
inner workings of her own society rather than by external contacts,

---

Note: As this book goes to press, U Nu has just been ousted for a second time
by a military government. References to U Nu as prime minister have been left in
the present tense.

[1] Mr. Walinsky and I served as directors of a field staff of Robert R. Nathan
Associates, Inc. The scope of his responsibilities was greater than mine had been
during the earlier period. Walinsky's book is *Economic Development in Burma,
1951–1960* (New York: Twentieth Century Fund, forthcoming 1962). Since my references to this work are to the typescript, not the printed version, I can identify them
only by chapter.

[2] My main source of information concerning traditional Burma is the writings of
J. S. Furnivall cited here and conversations with him. I rely also upon conversations

since she had little contact with her neighbors and the rest of the world during the thousand years before the British came. In early days traders who sailed along the southern coast of Asia visited Burma and penetrated up her rivers, but after the art of navigation developed sufficiently to permit long voyages out of sight of land most traders bypassed Burma, sailing directly from the eastern coast of India across the Bay of Bengal to the waist of the Malay Peninsula or around the Peninsula. Burma borders on Pakistan, India, China, Laos, and Thailand, but she is walled off from all of these nations by rugged mountain ranges, and her historic isolation was increased by the fact that when the Burmese conquered the country they established their capital well up country, first at Pagan and later at Mandalay. These towns are in the higher land called the dry zone, though it is dry only relative to the lowlands. An east-west line drawn across Burma at the southern edge of the dry zone divides Upper Burma from Lower Burma. The latter term, however, does not include the hilly lands in the southeast.

Hostilities among Burma's indigenous ethnic groups (all Mongoloid) occupy much of Burmese history, cause some of Burma's present problems, and, paradoxically, give rise to hopes for the future. The Burmese[3] make up almost two thirds of the present population of some 21 million.[4] The Karens constitute perhaps two million or about 10 per cent; the Shans, the Arakanese, who occupy the coastal strip facing Pakistan and India, and the Mons progressively smaller fractions; and various hill tribes a few per cent. There are altogether probably somewhat more than a million Indians, Pakistanis, and Chinese—say 5 or 6 per cent of the population.

In early times the Mons, moving into Lower Burma from the east, found the less aggressive Karens on the plains and scattered them, driving many into the mountains of eastern Burma. In the ninth century A.D. or earlier the Burmese, driven south across the Himalayas by the Chinese, occupied Upper Burma. By the middle of the eleventh century they had established dominion over virtually all of Burma. Later an ethnic group related to the Chinese expanded west and southwest from the Yunnan plateau of southeast China onto the tablelands in east and northeast Burma, where they are called Shans. From the end of the thirteenth century to the middle of the sixteenth the Shans, Mons, and Burmese disputed the control of Burma. Then the Burmese established

---

with informed Burmans, the standard historical works, and two works which attempt to interpret Burmese personality and culture, Shway Yoe (Sir James George Scott), *The Burman: His Life and Notions* (London, 1910), and Harold Fielding Hall, *The Soul of a People* (reprint; London: The Macmillan Co., 1946).

[3] Perhaps the most common but by no means the invariable usage of the words "Burman" and "Burmese" as nouns is to use "Burman" with reference to any Burma national, and "Burmese" as an ethnic term. As an adjective, however, the term "Burmese" is commonly used to refer to the entire country, for example, "the Burmese government." I shall follow these usages.

[4] Since estimates of the present population are projections of prewar data, they are far from precise.

supremacy again, retaining it until the end of Burmese independence except for a Mon revolt which interrupted it briefly around 1750.

The periods of Burmese supremacy as well as those of divided rule were filled with savage tribal warfare. One reads of an entire court city carried off into captivity, cities razed or ravaged and looted as punishment for resistance, and of mass executions; and one can imagine the ruthless individual acts which accompanied these official deeds. The last vicious Burmese-Mon war in the eighteenth century largely depopulated Lower Burma, and much of it returned to jungle. After the 1750's the country gradually became more peaceful, but memories by each group of the depredations and cruelties of the others surely remain even to the present day.

Nevertheless, when the British absorbed Burma in the nineteenth century there existed a prosperous viable national socioeconomic system with which all of the peoples of Burma except minor hill tribes identified themselves. The Mons had absorbed Buddhism and other elements of Hindu culture from early Indian traders, and the Burmese had integrated these into their own culture in modified form and had spread them throughout Burma.

The Traditional Society: Personality

As has been noted in Chapter 8, the personalities of the members of the dominant ethnic group in that society were highly authoritarian. The childhood of girls prepared them to bear more responsibility and act with more independence than men, yet to acknowledge men's superiority. Like authoritarian men everywhere, Burmese men were not certain of their manliness. Their fear manifested itself in much extramarital testing of their sexual virility, combined perhaps with infrequent approach to their wives, resort to the celibacy of monkhood by one man in 30, great anxiety about frictions in interpersonal relationships, and resolution of that anxiety by meticulous attention to relative social rankings and extreme deference to the judgment and will of persons of superior rank. The frustrating experiences that gave rise to the fear also caused rage, which was vented in rigid dominance over subordinates, aggressiveness when interpersonal relationships permitted it or were not well defined, and on occasion an orgy of violence which in Gorer's phrase was a "romantic, orgasmic ecstasy."[5] As protection against the danger that these impulses might get out of control, the Burmese clung to Buddhism with its doctrine of self-abnegation; forbade themselves to ask gifts or material aid from others or to assume any responsibilities for others' affairs; and adopted the veneer of placidity which has caused them to be referred to as carefree and happy-go-lucky. The extreme deference to persons of

---

[5] Geoffrey Gorer, "Burmese Personality" (typewritten; rev.; n.p., 1945), p. 37. (The copy examined, a mimeo, was in Peabody Museum Library, Harvard University.)

superior rank was also no doubt a defense against their own need aggression.

The personalities of the Arakanese, who are closely related ethnically, were very similar. Karen personalities differed somewhat. Concerning other minority groups we have less information.

Social Structure and Culture: Variant Features

The society was similar in basic respects to traditional societies everywhere. Here there need be discussed only the variant aspects of the social structure and culture—for like every society it differed from all others in some respects. The variant aspects in Burma related to the position of women, the techniques in use in production, the absence of landedness, a strain of egalitarianism, and the emphasis on relative rank even in the absence of inherited class differences. Taken as a group, they suggest that traditional social structure and culture were less firmly rooted in Burma than in other traditional societies,[6] so that if some stimulus to economic growth had appeared before the time of British colonial rule, the resistances to it would have been fewer and weaker than in the typical traditional society. Indeed, such a stimulus did appear, and the first shoots of economic change seemed to be flourishing when they were uprooted by historical developments that will be examined below.

Though the Burmese found Buddhism an invaluable complement to other aspects of their culture and adopted it wholeheartedly, it did not override an attitude toward women also present in their culture. In all of Southeast Asia, even in Muslim Java, women had great personal freedom, and this was even greater in Burma than elsewhere although somewhat inconsistent with the Buddhist ethic. Buddhism implies that women are of inferior worth. No woman can attain Nirvana; she must first be reincarnated as a man. Moreover, the wishes of a Burmese girl are subordinate to those of her brother, as is common in authoritarian societies, and a Burmese woman follows her husband down the street. Yet when a Burmese girl marries there is no change of name or mode of address to indicate subordination to a spouse, or even that she is no longer single or who her husband is.

Furthermore, women in Burma are often the decision makers. Burmese women historically have played important and often dominant roles in family decisions. During British days they were said to be the proprietors of virtually all retail stores operated by Burmese. These roles of women are no doubt closely associated both with the sex fears of Burmese men, which make them reluctant to test whether their symbolic superiority over women corresponds to reality, and with the training of girls in

---

[6] Perhaps because the society had existed as a settled agricultural society for only a few centuries before the colonial period.

childhood to bear more responsibility and have more initiative than boys.

Even though the Burmese traditional society was a young one relative to other traditional societies, its techniques of production were not primitive. (It picked up many aspects of Hindu culture rapidly.) Irrigation systems were in operation in some areas of the dry zone that made possible production of two or even three crops per year. While the only industry was handicraft industry, there were specialists who may appropriately be termed engineers, and many pagodas show great engineering skill. In the port village of Rangoon, on the terminal hill of a finger of mountains running down the length of the country from the Himalayas, the Mons built a pagoda not long after Buddha's death. The Burmese repeatedly enlarged it, and it became known as the "great golden pagoda" or Shwedagon. It is said that early British engineers in Burma observed with admiration the elevation, to cap a structure already 280 feet in height, of a 1¼ ton finial 47 feet high. There were also schools for medical training, and there is testimony in British records that for some time after the British came to Burma native doctors were more successful than European ones in the treatment of native diseases.

Since land was plentiful relative to population, it had no scarcity value; and, although the better land might have had a premium value, the institutions of land alienability and land rental had not developed and there was no landed class. Instead land was held by the cultivating family in inherited use-ownership. The only person other than the cultivator and the members of his family who shared in the produce was the king.[7] Before World War II the most common size of landholding was some 15 acres, and this may well have been the approximate size centuries earlier. In comparison to landholdings in the larger Asian countries, these holdings were remarkably large, and the Burmese level of living was higher than that of India or China.

The family was rather similar to the nuclear family of the West. Extended family ties not known in the West existed, but they were so weak that they did not prevent migration of part of a family group; and if the population of a village grew uncomfortably great in relation to the amount of land available nearby, a group of village members might migrate and start a new village.

Egalitarianism and Rank

The absence of landedness was no doubt associated with a peculiar strain of egalitarianism with which the authoritarianism of the culture and social structure was interlaced. Traditional Burma has been called

---

[7] While land could be mortgaged in a sense, at least in some parts of Burma, it could always be redeemed, after no matter how long a time, for a sum not exceeding the principal of the loan plus an equal amount of accumulated interest. (This was the usual rule. There were variations.) Such mortgages were apparently uncommon.

a "community of equals."[8] Economic manifestations of the egalitarianism may have derived in part from fear of the aggressiveness which the acquisition of wealth might unleash. In addition, there was not much point in amassing wealth.

Since there was no costly productive equipment and land was so plentiful that most of it had no value, the only objects of wealth that might have been amassed were consumer goods. The headman of the village sometimes had a house with teak floor and walls, but since this was less cool than the usual hut, building a pretentious home had no point. Families whose piety did not interfere accumulated finer textiles than ordinary, and women of the average family accumulated jewelry bearing precious stones and ornaments perhaps in excess of those possessed by the typical American family even today; but beyond this accumulation one gave away one's income to gain merit. One gave it not to the poor, for it was sinful for them to receive it, but to the monastery. Construction of a monastery yielded especial merit. (Curiously, maintenance did not, and Burma is full of small monasteries falling into ruin.)

Egalitarianism in the political field may have been rooted in customs of earlier life in Central Asia. There the Burmese had probably lived in authority-resisting migrant bands. There may have been no single leader in these bands except as an able man was given authority temporarily in time of emergency by consensus of the elders. Elements of continuing authority such as exist in traditional agricultural societies everywhere emerged in Burma, but the Burmese rejected the role that an individual should inherit office without undergoing a test of ability.

The largest cohesive unit of government was the *myo* or "circle," consisting of say 10 to 50 villages. Each circle was led by a headman.[9] As in other traditional societies, his powers were limited by the restrictions of custom and the degree of his ability to lead; but when he had observed the consensus of the elders and reached a decision, his decision was final. So poorly integrated was the office of a circle headman into the culture that there was no protection against abuse of power by a headman except an extreme one: on occasion an arbitrary headman was assassinated. The position of headman descended within the family of the previous headman, but, although the oldest son usually succeeded, a younger son or nephew might if by the informal consensus of the villagers he was more able. Each village was led by a village headman chosen by the circle headman usually from within the family of the predecessor but with care as to his actual position of influence in the village.

In theory each circle headman was responsible to a lieutenant of the

---

[8] H. F. Hall, *The Soul of a People*, p. 54.

[9] His jurisdiction was tribal rather than territorial. If an individual moved to another circle (a rare occurrence until recent times), his tribal headman retained jurisdiction over him.

king. In theory also the powers of the king were absolute; as a conspicuous example, he had the right not only to punish offenses against him in any way he chose but also to take the lives of citizens innocent of any offense for ritual purposes which custom sanctioned. He controlled all foreign trade and carried on in his own name the tiny amount he permitted. In practice his powers were limited by the degree to which he had captured the imagination of the people. Unlike feudal nobles of Europe who gained control of a country, he had no land from which to recruit an army. His armed forces were quasi-feudal levies which he was able to summon only if the people responded to his leadership, or if enough of them responded so that he could coerce the rest.

Like the position of headman, the kingship was hereditary but only within the king's family broadly defined. Here the concept of succession according to ability worked especially badly, for the only test was ability to seize and keep the throne. Intrigue within the court concerning the succession was intense, and since the culture of the society gave the successful claimant freedom to execute all potential rivals, the tension of life in the court was so great that it frequently warped personalities, and psychotic or near-psychotic individuals fairly often became king, with tragic consequences for the country.

In spite of the king's absolutism, he had a council of advisers whose position was so firmly rooted in custom that they often vigorously questioned the king's proposed policies.[10]

Though there were no inherited differences in class except for headship and membership in the king's court, which however was also open to individuals not born to it, there were differences in rank which were vital to the operation of authoritarian interpersonal relationships. Within the family, differences in status rested on sex, age, and position as parent, and within the village on age and headship. Throughout the society they rested on monkhood, religious learning, and preferment by the king. An instance of the strictness of age-ranking within the extended family in present-day Burma occurred at a gathering at which the writer was present. A high-school educated Burmese man from an outlying town addressed his cousin two years younger, who had a foreign university education and held a professional position, by the term of address one applies to inferiors, and since he was addressing a younger cousin the usage seemed not to attract the attention of anyone present. Elders of a village were regarded with deference. Hanks notes of contemporary Burma that "at a gathering in a house an elderly small landholder in a

---

[10] Concerning the work of the king's council, see H. Gouger, *A Personal Narrative of Two Years' Imprisonment in Burma* (London, 1864), quoted by J. S. Furnivall, *Colonial Policy and Practice* (Cambridge, Eng.: The University Press, 1948), p. 19. Other evidence of the position of the council is provided by the record in standard Burmese histories of the attempts by its senior members to dissuade several of the last Burmese kings from foolhardy acts, and to manage the succession to the kingship for the good of the country.

village may outrank the headman when the elderly man is a kinsman of the host and the headman is unrelated."[11]

The positions of status, except for those as headman and king, were of course open to anyone through ability and luck. At about the age of eight every boy served as a novice in a monastery for at least one week and usually for three months, and thereafter he was required to attend monastery school for from six to eight years to attain minimum literacy in the scriptures. Any boy might elect a religious career by remaining in the monastery or returning at any time and might learn as much as his mental capacity permitted. The king might select advisers from any class, and a peasant girl to whom the king was attracted might become not a concubine but one of his queens and mother of a king. And as noted above, even succession to positions as headman and king depended in part on ability and cunning. Emphasis was thus "on relations between individuals of relative ranks rather than on membership in a group of superior or inferior status."[12]

But the emphasis on relative rank was great. Today, as has been noted in Chapter 8, an individual dealing with a person of higher rank is often so inhibited against independent thought that he is literally unable to come to a conclusion in his own mind until the superior has rendered a judgment.[13] As has also been noted, where no structure of ranks is manifest, aggression may be extreme; the individual may go out of control. In Burma as everywhere, the system of ranks is in large part a defense against such release of unconscious rage. In the novitiate each boy was subjected to the severest discipline and required to do the most menial work. The discipline was much more severe than that necessary to get the work done, and it is reasonable to assume that it evolved as a corrective to the egocentric aggressiveness stimulated in the boy by his earlier environment. No doubt it brought relief to the boy, whose interpersonal relationships must have caused him anxiety.

Resistances to Technical Change

Lastly, in this listing of traits of personality and culture that were of especial importance in Burma, it should be noted that they included some of the resistances to technological innovation that have been discussed earlier with reference to other traditional societies. Specifically, they included the perception that phenomena of the natural world dominated human life, that these phenomena were the result of arbitrary actions by unseen spirits, parallel to human acts of will, and that the safest defense against misfortune was to appease these spiritual powers

---

[11] L. M. Hanks, Jr., "The Quest for Individual Autonomy in Burmese Personality with Particular Reference to the Arakan," *Psychiatry*, Vol. XII (1949), p. 287.

[12] *Ibid.* Hanks' reference is to modern Burma, but the statement is equally applicable to old Burma.

[13] According to repeated observation by the writer during his two years in Burma.

and avoid offending them. This concept exists in refined form in Buddhism, and in more primitive form in the animist religion that exists interwoven with popular Buddhism.

It has sometimes been suggested that Buddhist doctrine or the culture traits associated with it constitute a unique barrier to economic progress. I believe that this is not correct. True, Buddhism preaches the evil of aggression and sensual desire, but this is not a stronger injunction than that it is easier for a camel to pass through the eye of the needle than for a rich man to enter the kingdom of heaven, or the injunction to "sell what thou hast, and give to the poor." The Buddhist injunctions do seem to reflect traits that are imbedded more deeply in the Burmese culture than the Christian ones ever were in European cultures. The fact that Burmese will not beg even if literally starving testifies to the power of inhibitions against one type of interpersonal relationship. Yet Buddhism did not prevent Burmans from fighting savage wars for the conquest of their neighbors or from building systems of irrigation canals in the dry zone. Neither did they deter Mindon, the next to last Burmese king, from introducing new industries or from sending Burmans abroad to study European techniques. They have not deterred the present Prime Minister of Burma, U Nu, a devout Buddhist, from leading a program for economic development.

In other respects the forces making for stability of the traditional society and thus constituting barriers to technological change were weaker than elsewhere. Notably, the hierarchy of authoritarianism had not become frozen into inherited class differences, and there was no distinction between a landed class and a working class.

The latter fact does not mean that there was no attachment to landedness. There was. Landedness was the basis of membership in a village; except possibly for a goldsmith in some villages, there was virtually no village family without land. (The monks abandoned family existence and form a special case.) Existence in a village except on a base of land seemed strange to the Burmese. After the introduction into Burma under the British of land ownership in fee simple, and the loss of their land by many Burmese either because they did not understand the new rules or because the ease of obtaining money by mortgaging land seduced them, the unlanded were apparently bewildered and demoralized. A position as agricultural laborer was regarded as so inferior to one as agricultural proprietor (which in turn was a substitute for ownership) that cultivators trying to rent land bid up rents to a point at which the net income of a renter was typically less than the wages of the laborer.[14] There was a Burmese saying that at the end of a year there remained to a renter "only his winnowing tray and his fan." Today it is not uncommon for an owner of agricultural land to sign after his name the title, Land-

---

[14] J. S. Furnivall, *Introduction to the Political Economy of Burma* (Rangoon: Burma Book Club, Ltd., 1931), chap. vi.

owner. These various facts attest to the attractiveness of landedness in traditional Burma.

Thus, there must have been an inhibition against leaving the land to try a new career in industry or trade. However, there was not the added barrier of a need of a landed man to justify his inherited eliteness by having an aversion to the manual-technical activities of the simple folk. The Burmese cultivator, that is, virtually every Burman except the king's courtiers and the monks, had pride in his own craftsmanship and presumably regarded a skilled handicraftsman with respect. (This respect for craftsmanship did not imply an experimental spirit. Fear of infringing on the domain of the spiritual powers was also present. That fear inhibited experimentation.)

In summary, then, it would appear that resistance to technological change was not so many-layered in traditional Burma as in societies in which the traditional relationships had evolved more fully. It should have required less stimulus to set economic growth in motion in Burma than elsewhere.

MODERN POLITICAL HISTORY

As a backdrop against which to sketch the problems of socioeconomic change, it will be useful to outline the recent political history of Burma.

The Colonial Period

In 1824–25, partly to end repeated border troubles, the British moved from India to occupy the Arakan, the strip of Burma adjoining India, and the Tenasserim, the long tail extending down the Malay Peninsula. The ease with which they defeated Burmese forces did not cause a rational revision of Burmese policies. Three kings in succession, all apparently insane before their reigns ended, chose to deny the inadmissible fact of superior foreign power and remained remote and difficult of access. In 1852 the British occupied Lower Burma. The war brought a palace revolution in the Burmese kingdom, and a remarkably able king, Mindon, came to the throne. Under him the government of Upper Burma was stable and her relations with Britain satisfactory to both. Unfortunately, at his death in 1878 his attempt to prevent intrigue over the succession failed, and an incompetent of doubtful sanity, Thibaw, succeeded him. Thibaw created conditions in which the British found it expedient to occupy Upper Burma, and in 1885 the Kingdom of Burma came to an end.[15] The pieces of Burma that were successively annexed were ad-

---

[15] At his wife's instigation Thibaw murdered many rivals by having them tied in sacks and trampled to death under the royal elephants. (The spilling of royal blood was forbidden, a prohibition which earlier kings observed by having rivals drowned but which Thibaw violated, though in such a way that the spilling of blood was concealed.) Six years later he followed this group murder with another. The two events caused a wave of revulsion in England, but the British deposed Thibaw

ministered by the British as part of India; not until 1937 was Burma treated as a separate colony.

Under colonial rule the Burmese lapsed into the apathy which observers have noted in colonial lands everywhere. From the end of the nineteenth century Burmese groups agitated for some measure of national self-government and then for independence, and in response to this agitation an advisory council was created in 1923 and a legislature with limited powers in 1937. Yet only a small minority of eligible voters participated in the elections of these bodies, and the British administrators were usually able to control them by attracting the votes of minority ethnic group representatives, by personal influence, and by a fairly generous use of appointments to governmental positions that were fabulously well paid by Burmese standards. Because of this control it may seem retrospectively that Burmese political apathy was justified; but if a majority of the voters had participated vigorously, they could have elected representatives whom the British could not have controlled.

As has proved true in so many other places, the apathy was only superficial. When an opportunity appeared, intense opposition to British rule emerged. By prior secret agreement with the Japanese, a "Burmese Independence Army" of 30,000 helped the incoming Japanese in 1942 in return for a promise of immediate independence. However, the Burmese were disillusioned by Japanese postponement of independence until the war's end and by the nature of Japanese wartime rule; and two resistance groups, one Communist-led, helped the British and American armies which attacked the Japanese from India. Stung and distrustful because of Burmese "treachery" early in the war, the British in 1945 revoked many of the powers of self-government that had been granted in 1937.

Independence

The Anti-Fascist People's Freedom League or AFPFL, a party formed by merger of the two resistance groups, threatened guerrilla resistance. However, the Labor Government that came into power in Britain consented to Burmese independence if it was desired, and a constituent assembly that met in 1947 voted overwhelmingly to leave the Empire. Burma became independent on January 4, 1948.

The government of the nation thus formed is parliamentary. It is also federal in part. So-called "autonomous" states were formed for the Shans, Kachins, Kayahs, and Karens, and the central government shares powers with these states. Over the remainder of the country the national

---

not for this reason but to prevent Thibaw's negotiations with the French from developing into a situation that might cause friction leading to war in Europe. The immediate occasion for annexation was a dispute concerning a fine levied by Thibaw on a British lumbering firm which had a franchise to extract teak in Upper Burma and which was accused of falsifying its accounts and bribing Burmese officials.

government exercises all authority. The Karen State is unsatisfactory to the Karens, who form a large minority in many areas not included within it and claim that they form a majority in some. Even though the Arakanese predominate in an easily distinguished geographic area, no state was granted them, perhaps because they lie at one edge of the country and it was feared they might seek full independence.

The wartime leader, General Aung San, was assassinated by a rightist fanatic before independence. U Nu, who assumed leadership of the new government, had been his lieutenant.

Rebellion

A few months after independence Communist leaders who had seceded from the AFPFL and gone underground instigated a rebellion. The revolt did not seriously threaten the government, and the government talked of obtaining peace through welfare rather than arms until, toward the end of the year, a Karen army and some splinter forces from the other minority ethnic groups mounted rebellions of their own. These rebellions, though they were not expected, are easy to explain in retrospect. During the colonial period the British had given preferential treatment in selection for civilian and army positions to Karens and other minority groups and thus re-aroused ethnic tensions. After independence Burmese groups retaliated in various ways against minority groups, especially Karens, in spite of official government policy and exhortations to the contrary. In one incident a group of Karens was disarmed and then shot down by Burmese troops who were out of control. The depth of resentment felt by the Karens was not suspected until the insurrections; the Burmese were as much surprised at it as the British had been at the depth of Burmese desire for independence.

Fortunately, the rebel groups did not unite. The government came within a hair's breadth of loss of Rangoon and overthrow early in 1949, but during the following two years increased its armed forces and reduced the rebellions to haphazard guerrilla activity. To the present time it has not completely suppressed guerrilla warfare, dacoity, and disorder in the countryside. (The three are sometimes hard to distinguish.) Indeed, large areas of the countryside, especially wooded and hilly areas, are out of government control today except when the army moves in to control them, and the army cannot control all areas at once.

Because of the insurrections no parliament could be elected until 1954. The constituent assembly that had voted independence served as a legislature until that time. The AFPFL, which held a large majority both in the constituent assembly and in the 1954 parliament, continued in power until 1958. It was a one-man party; because of his charismatic hold over the voters as Aung San's lieutenant and as a national Buddhist leader, U Nu dictated its policies. He is well intentioned and personally honest beyond question, but he was ineffective and even irresponsible as a

leader; he neither managed an effective economic development program nor prevented ruthless political machinations and corruption by
party officials.

In the autumn of 1958, reflecting popular disenchantment, the army
took over control of the government. To preserve legality, the com-
mander-in-chief, General Ne Win, arranged his own election as prime
minister. The initial reaction reported publicly in Burma was satisfaction
and relief. The army officers who assumed key governmental posts
were more vigorous than their predecessors, and they ended many
abuses and improved the operations of many government agencies and
enterprises. But they injured many groups: squatters whom they moved;
political leaders and the persons who had been beneficiaries of their
patronage and corruption; unneeded civil servants threatened with dis-
missal and others asked to observe discipline. They transgressed traditional values such as respect for seniority and noninterference with
individuals not directly harming one. And junior officers in the districts
abused their authority. Altogether, the country became restive after a
year or so and seemed relieved when Ne Win, keeping his promise to the
people, arranged for election of a civilian government. The election took
place in April, 1960.

The AFPFL had split, and the army reputedly favored the anti-U Nu
faction in that election. However, U Nu demonstrated that he still retained a considerable hold on the imagination of the people. With a confession of past errors and promise of reform, plus promises of autonomous
states for the Arakanese and Mons and establishment of Buddhism as a
state religion, he gained a clear majority for his wing and formed a
government termed the Union Government. Within his government there
is a split between a faction favoring governmental reform and a faction
favoring politics as usual. Despite his campaign promises, up until the
time this is written late in 1961 U Nu has held himself aloof from the
struggle, with a resulting victory for politics as usual. Abuses ended by
the army have reappeared. The discussion below of the economic development program will illustrate some of them.

ECONOMIC DEVELOPMENT BEFORE INDEPENDENCE

Technical Advance during Mindon's Reign

There was little reason to expect technological progress in Burma,
however receptive the culture may have been, until the nineteenth century, for contact with the outside world before that time had been sporadic
and not conducive to conveying a perception of European technical
superiority. However, humiliating military defeat in 1852 shocked King
Mindon and his lieutenants into a decision to modernize, and a remarkable brief spurt of economic change occurred.

Mindon sent a small stream of court officials and other young men to Europe for training. They learned English thoroughly, and a few of them also came to speak French well. He introduced coinage. He built a fleet of river steamers. At his direction Burmans adapted the Morse code to the Burmese alphabet and erected telegraph lines for communication between the capital at Mandalay and Lower Burma. He stimulated an increase in the cultivation of rice in Upper Burma, erected factories with European machinery and in some cases under European management for the manufacture of cotton and silk piece goods and also of lac, cutch, and sugar, and vigorously and successfully promoted increased export and import trade. He also introduced fixed salaries for his officials, introduced a new equitable tax which worked so well that the British continued it after taking over Upper Burma, and convened the Fifth World Buddhist Council (the fifth held since the death of Gautama) to purify the Buddhist scriptures. He arranged for the erection of the new finial on the Shwedagon which has been mentioned above. If he had lived longer, this remarkable ruler might have accomplished great changes in Burma.[16]

It is possible that Mindon's son Thibaw was not interested in his father's new enterprises and that some of them decayed or were abandoned during his seven years on the throne. Others may have been dissolved by the British or absorbed into British firms. In any event, they came to an end as Burmese-operated firms, and with them a fascinating episode in Burmese history.

A parallel between developments under Mindon and the economic development of Japan after 1868 suggests itself, but for two reasons it would be fallacious to draw conclusions from that parallel concerning the possible speed of westernization if the British had not occupied Upper Burma. One is that King Mindon's program was not remotely comparable in scope or intensity with that of the Japanese leaders. The other is that certain preconditions of rapid technical progress which existed in Japan in 1868 did not exist in Burma—notably a rather broad base of interest in and advanced knowledge concerning the physical sciences, mathematics, and engineering, and the presence of innovational personality in many individuals. Under the most favorable of circumstances, the road ahead would have been long and progress slow.

It is interesting, however, to speculate about the deductions concerning

---

[16] These incidents constitute one of the interesting "might have beens" of history. Their potential significance is little noticed. My information concerning them is from a brief summary by Furnivall, in *Colonial Policy and Practice*, pp. 64–65; Furnivall has it from Annual Reports on the Administration of Burma and Annual Reports of Maritime Trade and Customs (or Navigation) for various years, issued by the British administration of Lower Burma. Modern Burmese historians have paid little attention to this aspect of Mindon's career, and I have been unable to obtain further information by inquiry of a leading historian at the University of Rangoon. Historical records available in English likewise give no information concerning what became of the few Burmans in Thibaw's court with knowledge of English and of Western business.

Burmese culture and personality to be drawn from Mindon's success.
The members of the king's court, it is obvious from the account above,
were not reared in traditional circumstances. Clearly there were among
them a number of men with innovational and entrepreneurial ability
and with values such that new enterprises sponsored by the king stimulated their energies and initiative. Among the types of personality that
might evolve in the rather bizarre conditions of the court this obviously
was one. Moreover, it would have been easy to recruit staff and labor
force for enterprises sponsored by the king since serving the king had
high value in the Burmese culture. However, it is idle to speculate concerning the possible impact of continued royal sponsorship of modern
enterprises on the personalities of individuals outside the court and
on Burma's economic development. When independence ended, the court
was dispersed and this small leavening stream of creative personality
either came to an end or was suppressed by colonial rule.

The Colonial Period: Exploitation of Burma's Resources

Under British rule, development of Burma's physical resources proceeded rapidly and the British laid down the transport, communications,
and urban facilities which economists are wont to refer to as a necessary
base for economic growth.

The first resources to be exploited were the rich soil of the Delta
and the teak forests. Burma's teak was the best in the world, and British
firms extracted and milled it and exported it throughout the world.
After some early destructive cutting, government supervision insured
perpetual forestry.

The British were eager for the rice which the Delta might produce,
and both to facilitate settlement of the Delta and for other reasons
introduced Western institutions of land ownership, land transfer, and
mortgage. Burmans, attracted by rising rice prices, and no doubt also
remembering the productivity of the Delta before the fierce war in the
seventeenth century between the Burmese and the Mons had depopulated
it, borrowed money for sustenance during the clearing period and
swarmed onto the Delta in an increasing stream. Some 400,000 tons of
rice were exported annually by the early 1870's, almost two million tons
at the end of the century, and three million just before World War II.

The rice trade together with a general expansion of internal commerce
created an increasing need for improved transport. The British bound the
country together with railroad and river transport systems and later a
road system. The river steamship lines were products of private investment. In the 1890's the railroad too was leased to a private company.
It made the entire country except the Arakan strip adjoining India
accessible by land from Rangoon and permitted Rangoon, which had
been a British administrative center since 1855, to become the economic

heart of the country as well. The postal system was improved and telegraph and telephone lines constructed between the main cities.

Apart from transportation and communication facilities, teak extraction and milling was the only domestic industry operated primarily by foreigners until the last decade of the century. British interest in other indigenous products was limited to exporting them. Thereafter, however, the exploitation of previously little-developed natural resources proceeded rapidly. In the 1890's Burma became one of the world's oil exporters. During World War I large-scale exploitation of a tin and tungsten deposit in southeastern Burma began, and in the 1920's large-scale mining of a rich ore body in the Shan states of Upper Burma containing lead, zinc, silver, and other metals.

Before World War II Burma produced about 2 per cent of the world's tin, 3 per cent of zinc, 5 per cent of lead, and 17 per cent of tungsten. Yet in the 1920's rice still constituted 60 per cent of exports in value. In the 1930's, because of both a sharp fall in the price of rice and an increase in oil production, agricultural products constituted 46 per cent of exports and oil 35 per cent, but mineral products still constituted only 9 per cent, forest products 7 per cent, and other commodities 3 per cent. Export of the major commodities was predominantly in British hands, but an increasing number of other European, Chinese, and Indian firms had also established themselves in foreign trade.

Almost no modern manufacturing had appeared, unless rice and teak milling are included in this category, and apart from trade and finance the economy was still basically agricultural and extractive. In 1931 agriculture employed two thirds of the nation's workers, forestry and mining together with fishing and hunting 3 per cent, manufacturing and cottage industry 11 per cent, and all service industries 19 per cent. Data concerning the distribution of the labor force just before the war are not available because almost all records of the 1941 census were destroyed during the war, but the percentages had probably not changed much since 1931.

The Role of Burmans during the Colonial Period

Except in agriculture and perhaps forestry Burmans did not participate greatly in the new developments even up to the beginning of World War II. Government administration became largely British and Indian, though as time went on Burmans participated more and more in clerical and other lower level positions. The first Burman gained entry into the select Indian Civil Service, from which higher level administrators were recruited, only in 1922, and not very many of his fellow countrymen equaled his success thereafter. As Furnivall has noted, oil and mineral extraction and processing were done by Indian and Chinese workers directed by European technicians to the profit of British shareholders; virtually the only interest of Burmans in the operation was the depletion of their country's resources.[17] As time went on Burmans were squeezed out of unskilled urban employment and some crafts such as carpentry by Indians and later also Chinese. Burmans of course participated in the general expansion of economic activity, but apart from agriculture and forestry they did so mainly in traditional types of trade, transport, finance, and other services.

It is easy to understand why this was true initially. When the British annexed Burma, the Burmans were first enemies and then subjects whose loyalty there was as yet no reason to expect. Except for the few individuals educated and trained in Europe at the initiative of Kings Mindon and maybe Thibaw, they spoke an unknown tongue, had no training in Western techniques or professions. They knew nothing of British administrative procedures or practices. On the other hand, Indians spoke and wrote the English language or could be spoken to in their own language by Englishmen with experience in India. They had Western-type training and were experienced in British administration. British governmental officials brought them along from India to fill the administrative, professional, and technical posts below the top levels filled by Britishers. Burma became "doubly colonial," as the Burmese say; below the layers of Britishers were layers of Indians.

Until perhaps the 1920's, moreover, most administrative procedures were an extension of those current in India. The telephone, telegraph, and postal departments were administered from India. Postal clerks and postmen were Indians, perhaps because initially it was easier for the British to communicate with Indians and because they understood the forms on which reports to India were required. Telegraphy, then and until some years after independence was gained in 1948, was in English. A Burman might send a telegram if he had his message translated into English, but until some time in the 1930's, unless he could speak Hindustani or English, it was not possible for him even to use the telephone system, much less be employed in it.

Just as it was convenient for government administrators to employ Indians, it was convenient for British businessmen and for the European, Chinese, and Indian firms which entered Burma as traders and brokers to import Indian assistants, technicians, foremen, skilled workers, bookkeepers, and clerks.

Indian craftsmen and unskilled workers were employed for a different reason. The level of living in India was markedly lower than that in Burma, and Indian workers could be obtained at a lower scale of pay than that which prevailed for comparable work in Burma. Indian coolies would work servilely under conditions which Burmans rejected, and for wages on which Burmans could not live. Initially private companies

---

[17] J. S. Furnivall, *An Introduction to the Political Economy of Burma* (2d ed.; Rangoon: Burma Book Club, Ltd., 1937).

paid the cost of bringing Indians to Burma. Later, when the replacement of sails by steam brought the cost of passage down to an amount that coolies themselves could scrape together or borrow, one of the world's great migrations began. In the peak year 1918, 300,000 coolies entered Burma. In British eyes, since Burma was still being administered as a part of India, this was internal migration.

In competing with Indians for jobs at a somewhat higher level Burmese were handicapped until well into the twentieth century by the difficulty of obtaining the necessary preparation. It was difficult to obtain a good primary education in Burmese, more difficult to obtain a good secondary education in English, and even more so to obtain university training. However, this situation gradually improved, and it does not explain the almost complete failure of Burmans to advance far in business or government administration even by the 1920's and 1930's. Even at the time of independence only a small fraction of upper-level government administrative officers were Burmans; and in private industry apparently no Burman had ever held a high administrative or executive position in rice exporting, in the extraction, large-scale milling, or exporting of teak, or in oil extraction or mining—that is, in any of the important industries. The testimony of British businessmen is that they lacked the necessary capacities. So universal is this judgment that one would be rash to put it down to mere prejudice, but on the other hand, Burmese history indicates no lack of innate capacity. Some influence must have been at work which needs more analysis; I shall return to the point later.

In passing it may be noted that Burmans certainly shared in the rising level of living in Burma.[18] The evidence is threefold. First, additional Burmans moved from Upper Burma to the higher-income commercial agriculture of the Delta each year. Renter and farm laborer alike on the Delta lived better in purely material terms than did individuals in Upper Burma.[19] Secondly, most of the noncultivating landlords and many if not most of the money-lenders in agriculture, who received a large share of gross agricultural income in the Delta, were Burmans. Thirdly,

[18] I avoid the question whether they shared adequately in some ethical sense. In 1938–39, the first year for which there are data, at least 20 per cent of the gross national income was profits of foreign-owned companies or flowed abroad as remittances by foreigners to their families elsewhere. In the 1920's and 1930's foreign exchange receipts were half again as large as payments. The difference—one third of the value of exports—was profits and remittances.

[19] By the 1920's Indians were providing seasonal labor in agriculture. By the 1930's a number of them had learned how to grow rice efficiently in the conditions of Lower Burma and were invading agriculture as tenants. Both for this reason and because of the world depression, in the 1930's incomes available to Burman agricultural laborers and cultivators fell temporarily, it would appear, to the coolie level. If colonial administration had continued unaltered, Burman levels of living would have been depressed permanently and racial conflict more serious than the riots of the early 1930's might have occurred, but World War II and independence intervened.

the steady expansion of internal commerce in Burma up to the 1920's caused a continual increase in the demand for nonagricultural services, and at such a rate that in spite of the influx of Indians petty trades and services continued to provide expanding opportunities for Burmans. Income in these occupations was much above the agricultural level.[20] But these increases in income were due to increased demand for traditional sorts of activity. Burmans did not participate except passively in the technological change that was going on.

In summary, then, during the colonial period a physical base for continuing economic development was laid, and Burmans participated in the rise in the level of income caused by the increased exploitation of Burma's natural resources; but Burmans were not drawn into new occupations, entrepreneurial positions, or other aspects of the process of technical change.

ECONOMIC PARADOX IN INDEPENDENT BURMA: DESIRE AND PERFORMANCE

During the war the country's physical plant suffered great damage. The British forces destroyed productive facilities as they retreated in 1942, the Japanese bombed cities and communications facilities fairly heavily as they advanced, and British and American forces bombed them more heavily as they reoccupied the country. Altogether, perhaps one third of the country's man-made capital was destroyed. Burma suffered destruction of a greater share of her man-made productive equipment than say Germany, Belgium, or Russia—more indeed than any country except Greece. Restoration by both foreign and indigenous capital and effort proceeded rapidly in 1946 and 1947, but during the insurrections railroad lines, the pipeline from the oil fields to the refinery near Rangoon, and much other capital was destroyed for a second time. Not until 1950 could reconstruction begin again, and even then rebellion was still smoldering.

The government leaders, dedicated to attaining rapid economic advance, proceeded not so much on the premise that economic advance required an integrated economy-wide process of reconstruction as on the theory that modernity could be achieved by a few large and rather spectacular steps.

The Statistical Evidence

Let us examine the facts concerning the progress they have made. Table 18–1 presents estimates of production in Burma before the war, im-

---

[20] The 1931 data on the labor force and the 1938–39 national income estimates in combination permit an estimate that per capita income in all nonagricultural occupations was between three and four times as high as in agriculture. Although non-Burmans shared heavily in these incomes, with maximum allowance for their share it remains true that the nonagricultural incomes of Burmans must have been much higher than the agricultural.

TABLE 18-1

GROSS DOMESTIC PRODUCT IN 1947–48 PRICES
(MILLIONS OF KYATS)*

	1938–39	1947–48	1951–52	1953–54	1955–56	1956–57	1957–58	1958–59	1959–60
Agriculture, fisheries, and rice processing	2,089	1,576	1,559	1,646	1,748	1,897	1,744	1,944	1,989
Forestry	360	273	266	289	314	344	347	347	376
Mining and quarrying	273	29	34	49	66	84	101	115	120
State marketing (mainly rice exporting)	633	286	248	278	460	482	413	429	486
State transport, state banking, and other public utilities	148	78	59	92	115	119	125	126	155
General government	153	229	314	412	461	487	535	570	600
Rental value of housing	165	151	162	177	194	203	210	215	230
Other industry and services	1,124	935	994	1,103	1,092	1,292	1,223	1,274	1,312
Gross domestic product	4,945	3,557	3,636	4,046	4,450	4,908	4,698	5,020	5,308†
Index (1938–39 = 100)	100	72	74	82	90	99	95	102	107

* One kyat = approximately U.S. $0.21.

† There is an error in this column of the table. The total of the items shown is 5,268.

Sources: 1951–52: Government of the Union of Burma, *Economic Survey of Burma* (Rangoon: Superintendent, Government Printing and Stationery, 1957), Table 2. Other years: *Economic Survey of Burma*, 1960, Table 2. Quoted in Walinsky, *Economic Development in Burma 1951–1960*, chap. xx.

mediately after the war, and for selected years of the 1950's. It indicates production in 1951–52 was 26 per cent below the prewar level and in 1959–60, 7 per cent above. Some components of the estimates are subject to a wide margin of uncertainty, and in particular the increase shown in "general government" (the general administrative services of government) is partly fictitious, but on balance it is likely that output in 1959–60 was at least as high relative to its level before the war or in 1951–52 as is shown.[21] Production, then, increased at an average rate of approximately 5 per cent per year from 1951–52 to 1959–60. This would be a rapid rate of increase for a country that was fully utilizing its productive capacity at the beginning of the period, but it is not impressive for Burma during this period since the starting point was so low. In 1951–52 output per capita was more than 35 per cent below that before the war. In 1959–60, according to the official estimates, it was still 20 per cent below prewar.[22]

Burma of course was handicapped by the destruction of capital noted above. However, at the low level of production indicated a rapid increase occurs more or less spontaneously, both because of the desire of individuals to get at work again and because, since repair or replacement of a relatively small amount of equipment often restores a larger unit to production, the gain in production from a modest amount of reconstruction may be great.

Unless the estimates grossly understate the true increase, Burma's failure to increase output faster in these circumstances indicates either a high degree of lethargy and lawlessness in the population or a striking degree of mismanagement by national leaders. The latter, which was clearly present, I shall consider first.

The Failures of Leadership and Management

True, the army organized itself with reasonable efficiency to suppress rebellion and reduce disorder in the countryside. But beyond these measures of self-preservation, if one investigates the positive action to promote economic development by the men who avowed fervent desire for

---

[21] The general services of government are shown as having increased fourfold from 1938–39 to 1959–60, and this estimate no doubt reflects accurately the change in the number of persons employed by the government, but the increase in payrolls without corresponding increase in services rendered has been so great that the estimate of 1959–60 may merit reduction by one fourth or more. However, the estimate for "other industry and services" rests on a rather fragile statistical base, and there is reason to suspect that it considerably understates the increase in private manufacturing and related activity. Some evidence concerning that increase is presented later in this chapter. The writer was responsible for preparation of the national income estimates during 1951–53 and devised the method of estimating "other industry and services." Limitation of data has prevented much improvement in the method of estimate of this sector since that time.

[22] These estimates assume an increase of 1.3 per cent per year in the population. Even if the increase in the population was in fact faster, that in the labor force may not have been.

development, one's judgment must be harsh. Many major governmental actions purportedly taken to further development were harmful to the country and deleterious to development. A number of national leaders were corrupt, and many others were indolent, naive, or irresponsible.

Performance of this quality is not unique to Burma. I discuss it here because it is typical of the performance of societies in which traditional social structure and culture have been disrupted by certain types of pressures. To give content to the generalization that persons who have been subjected to the pressures of colonial rule may be incapable of effective judgment and action, I shall cite the relevant facts in Burma at some length.

In many of the departments administering economic affairs there was a near-complete breakdown of capacity to make and execute decisions. A few examples will illustrate:

Burma now receives low prices for her rice because it is broken and dirty. It has been of this inferior grade since the war. Wartime destruction and wear and tear on machinery could have been repaired rather quickly, but since the State Agricultural Marketing Board pays millers almost as much for poorly milled rice as for better grades, there is no incentive to rehabilitate the country's milling machinery. The difficulty may have lain originally in reluctance to give large British-owned mills assurances that would induce them to restore operations, the political influence of Burmese with inferior mills, and perhaps the added trouble of arranging for the separate shipment of different grades of rice. While the last suggestion may seem frivolous, in view of the low quality of management of the State Agricultural Marketing Board it may have been a factor even though a minor one. In any event, in a decade the causes of the inertia have not been overcome.[23]

When the outlet pipes of two irrigation dams being constructed by the Irrigation Department collapsed in the mid-1950's because of faulty construction and had to be rebuilt, the Department neither replaced its engineers nor obtained consultants; it simply ceased to execute other large projects.[24]

At the beginning of the decade the government appropriated funds to provide low-interest loans from planting to harvest time to cultivators. Collections were never higher than about 70 per cent of the amount loaned; they declined to 50 per cent. It soon became public knowledge that local officials of the AFPFL used the funds as political largesse and successfully exerted pressure against vigorous collection. As a remedy, the loan function was transferred to the State Agricultural Credit Bank, a subsidiary of Burma's central bank, the Union Bank of Burma. Here it

---

[23] Instances of government maladministration for which Walinsky is not cited as the source of information are from the personal knowledge of the writer.

[24] This example and the four which follow are from Walinsky, *Economic Development in Burma, 1951–1960.*

was well managed, but the old lending process, with its old evils, was also continued on a reduced basis.

A village development and agricultural extension program was established under a competent administrator, and by 1958 some 400 to 500 village workers were being trained annually and some 1,700 were in the field. But no transportation, not even bicycles, had been provided for most of them.

A very promising program of grants-in-aid by the central government to local communities was inaugurated in 1952 to encourage local initiative in the rehabilitation and improvement of community facilities. Local committees dominated by local officials of the AFPFL were set up to allocate the funds. Within two or three years their use for local political machinations became flagrant, and public resentment increased. The prime minister did not take steps to reform the program; he simply abolished it.

Imports were put under controls both to save foreign exchange and to aid Burmese nationals in entering foreign trade. But under the direction of AFPFL officials the agency controlling import licenses granted them to party officials, friends of ministers and government officials, and others to whom special favors were due, and with few exceptions the recipients then sold them to the Indians, Chinese, and Europeans who had been importers all along. During the military regime, licenses were limited pretty much to bona fide importers, but after U Nu resumed power in 1960 the old practices recommenced.

Some of these events were due at least in part to greed and a desire for party advantage. No such simple explanation is possible for the quality of administration of various governmental enterprises. Again, a few examples will give content to the statement.

The Union of Burma Airways is a governmental airline that came into existence in March, 1948, and began operations in September. The condition of the Union of Burma Airways accounting records in 1956 will illustrate the level of public administration that was found acceptable. The financial operations of UBA were studied in September of that year by economists who were consultants to the government. "Its accounts for the fiscal year 1952–53," Walinsky states, "were reported as final but not yet verified. The accounts for 1953–54 were still provisional. Operating and traffic statistics were on an actual basis only through the first nine months of 1953–54, and were estimates for the fifteen months thereafter. Even estimated data were not available for 1955–56. Costs by major expenditure categories (flight operations, ground operations, services and general administration) had been analyzed only through the year 1952–53 and were unavailable for the three years following. Aircraft utilization data had been computed through 1952–53. Data on load factors on domestic flights were available only through January 1956."[25]

---

[25] *Ibid.*, chap. xxix.

This was not an isolated case. The State Agricultural Marketing Board "could not establish its holdings [of rice] within a couple of hundred thousand tons, and took its first physical check of stocks only in 1958. As of September 1960, the inventory position of the Civil Supplies Management Board, a merchandising agency, was available only as of September 30, 1958."[26]

The most striking cases of ineptness and negligence, however, occurred in the planning and execution of new manufacturing projects.[27] Perhaps one twelfth of net governmental capital formation—governmental investment minus the amount needed to replace depreciation of existing facilities—during the nine years 1951–52 to 1959–60 consisted of construction of 10 major state manufacturing plants: factories for the production of pharmaceuticals, rolled steel products, jute twine and gunny sacks, brick and tile, silk, and tea, two sugar refineries, and expansion of a cotton spinning factory and a cement plant. The total cost of the 10 was equivalent to some $52 million at the official rate of exchange.

The pharmaceutical plant and steel rolling mill together cost almost half of the total of the 10. The pharmaceutical plant was constructed because of an impression the prime minister had gained earlier in his life that the consumption of yeast tablets would ensure the health of the populace. At his instructions a team of three laymen negotiated a contract with a foreign firm to erect a plant to produce or to mix and package all pharmaceuticals except antibiotics. No analysis by medical or public health experts, no estimates of production costs or markets, and no plans for distribution of the products underlay the project, and no engineering consultants were obtained to aid in the negotiation. It required daily consumption of 10 or more of the yeast tablets produced to provide the desired beneficial effect; this also produced flatulence and discomfort. When the production process was revised to concentrate the tablets, they cost almost as much to produce as far superior vitamins. The public enterprise running the plant suffered large losses. (The military government reduced its losses by reducing its production and gave it revenues almost equal to its reduced costs by granting it a monopoly of import of all drugs and pharmaceuticals.)

Planning for the steel mill was based on a highly optimistic estimate of the amount of steel scrap remaining in Burma after the war and disregarded the country's lack of coking coal or limestone. In 1960–61 production of wire was stopped at least temporarily because of its high cost, and some other sections of the mill were closed down for alterations. If the mill continues to run, it will presently be running on imported coal, flux, and ingots and producing at costs greatly above import costs.

Except for the pharmaceutical and steel plants, the projects are probably economically advantageous if sensibly administered, though the lo-

---

[26] *Ibid.*

[27] *Ibid.*, chap. xvii.

cation of at least two of them, one because of political considerations and
one apparently because of negligence, is not optimum. But in the cases of
most and perhaps all of the 10 the nature of the administration testifies to
the irresponsibility of the policy makers. A summary of events concerning the sugar mills and the brick and tile plant will illustrate.

One of the two sugar mills has functioned well technically. The other
was obtained at a lower price from a Japanese supplier who had not previously produced sugar mill equipment. During the period of construction, to save foreign exchange the Burmese negotiated changes in design
and reductions in the quality of the equipment. Perhaps as a result, "the
plant suffered serious flood damage during its first producing season and
later experienced difficulties with its water supply. It also experienced
serious difficulties with its production machinery."[28] Expert management
advice was not obtained. In 1959–60 the mill was not yet producing as
much as 60 per cent of its rated capacity.

One of its chief difficulties, however, lies not in these technical aspects
of operation but in the procurement policy foisted on it by party officials.
The price for sugar cane was set at K 42 per ton (the kyat, whose par
value is about 21 cents, is the Burmese unit of currency), about 50 per
cent higher than the price in the private market. This price was offered
for cane at the point of production regardless of distance from the mill.
More cane was tendered than could be used, and local farm and co-operative organization officials determined whose cane should be accepted.
The cane selected included some grown at a distance from the mill, whose
sugar content fell before it reached the mill, in preference to cane grown
nearer the mill. Whatever may have been the initial reason for the pricing
policy, its continuance is associated with the fact that, in Walinsky's
words, the officials responsible "reaped their own 'harvest.' Farmers
were forced to reward these officials with a sizeable share of the uneconomic price differential they received."[29]

The procurement policy was altered under the military government,
but after U Nu's Union Government took office in 1960 the K 42 per ton
price for cane and arbitrary selection of buyers was resumed.

The brick and tile factory provides an example of maladministration
not explainable by cupidity or corruption. Good clay lands near Rangoon
were purchased in 1951 and equipment ordered. The ship carrying it sank
and it had to be reordered, but when it arrived in July, 1953, building
construction had not yet begun. It was begun in March, 1954.

When it had proceeded some distance it developed that the factory,
kilns, staff residences, and auxiliary buildings were being constructed directly above the most accessible clay deposit. (I do not suggest that their
location was due to mere inadvertence. If the reason were to be un-

[28] *Ibid.*
[29] *Ibid.*

covered, it might turn out to be frivolous rather than venal.) A road approximately two miles in length was built across wet land to reach another supply.

Construction proceeded casually. In October, 1955, it was found that the tile presses would have to be taken out and reset because their foundations were not adequate to carry the load. A year later elaborate housing for the staff was complete but the main kilns had not yet been built. They were completed in 1957, but on their first use their brick linings cracked and had to be replaced because in the name of economy ordinary brick rather than fire brick had been used to line them.

Production began in 1958. The brick produced sold readily. The roofing tile, however, was priced high relative to alternative roofing materials. The nine authorized distributors, who were allowed a 5 per cent discount, which apparently seemed reasonable to the factory management, did not promote sales. Even at a lower price the margin of profit would, it seems, have been greater than on brick,[30] but instead of exploring the market the management reduced tile production almost to zero and concentrated on brick.

"Early in 1961," Walinsky states, "the general attitude within the government with respect to the brick and tile plant seemed to be one of general satisfaction!"[31]

These instances of mismanagement relate to governmental enterprises. While failures of performance in governmental actions affecting private enterprise have been less spectacular, they are not difficult to find. Import controls were erratically administered. Granted in a pattern designed as much to result in personal gain for influential persons as to benefit the nation, and applied and relaxed as foreign exchange exigencies required or administrative expediency suggested, they caused repeated shortages and then gluts of some goods and wide fluctuations in their prices. A chaotic structure of freight rates on the government river steamship lines, established to achieve monopoly gains for the steamship corporation during the insurrections, when other transport was impossible, was left without basic change thereafter and seriously hampered some interregional trade. Major roads continued to decay throughout the 1950's, apparently simply because the Roads Department of the Ministry of Public Works was incapable of administering their maintenance. And so on.

Underlying these specific examples of governmental malfunctioning was a fairly general failure of the administrative mechanism to cope with any but routine matters. As Walinsky states, throughout the administrative apparatus "decisions of all kinds floated inevitably to the top for determination. These comprised not only the major and the important but also the minor and even the trivial. The resulting necessity for a multi-

---

[30] So Walinsky suggests, *ibid.*
[31] *Ibid.*

plicity of decision making at the very top led to overcentralization, to intolerable delays followed by hasty decisions, to a lack of perspective and to the pre-empting of a disproportionate amount of the time of the top policy makers with the unimportant, the procedural, and the irrelevant, while many matters of great moment never got considered or decided at all."[32]

A cabinet subcommittee, the Economic and Social Board, formally had top responsibility for the economic development program. It found little time for discussion of questions of general policy. Apart from its discussions of trivial current matters, it spent its time largely deciding whether to approve specific new projects or new contracts. Typically, the prime minister would make a decision in the absence of objections, but if even one serious question was raised there was a tendency to avoid decision. When discussion had gone on for a time without decision, the chairman often turned abruptly to the next item. The previous one was simply left undecided, and the existing state of affairs continued.

The Board paid virtually no attention to the execution of its decisions, the management of government departments or the public enterprises, or the implementation of projects. Thus questions such as the sugar cane procurement policy, the rate of progress of the brick and tile factory and the reason for its improper location, or why the jute, cotton, and sugar mills were all failing to produce the anticipated output per shift did not come before the Board.

Successes—The Exception

Yet there were, as I have said, a few exceptions to the record of mismanagement. Both in governmental enterprise and in actions to facilitate and stimulate private enterprise some things were done rather well. The central bank has managed its affairs with technical competence, and its subsidiary, the State Agricultural Credit Bank, has operated rather effectively, as noted above. In fact, throughout the fields of fiscal and monetary policy the government, following the advice of economic consultants, has acted responsibly and rather effectively apart from its erratic handling of import controls. The extraction and refining of petroleum and the mining of lead, zinc, and silver in the northern mining district proceeded well, each in a joint venture managed by the private British company that had conducted the operation before the war. Elsewhere, things went well here and there where an effective individual was given command. After half a decade of inaction, the program to install small electric generators in the towns and that to restore teak production made modest progress. In 1956 capable and vigorous men were installed as director-general and chief executive officer of the Land and Resources Development Corporation, and thereafter a number of the projects of the

---

[32] *Ibid.*, chap. xxxi.

corporation were carried forward effectively.[33] Examples are the program to expand paddy (that is, rice) acreage, that to expand peanut acreage, the construction of curing barns to handle the increase in tobacco production stimulated by incentives offered by the private cigarette industry in co-operation with the Department of Agriculture, and construction of rice storage facilities (which would not have been necessary if marketing procedures had been adequate).

A hospital was erected here and there, though in some places without adequate provision for doctors and nurses to man it. Several public housing projects were capably executed. As Table 18–2 indicates, the number

TABLE 18–2

SCHOOLS AND SCHOOL ENROLLMENT

	1952	1956–57	1959–60
Number of State Schools			
Primary............................	3,335	10,226	11,557
Middle.............................	150	415	520
High...............................	n.a.	220	273
Technical high school..............	—	33	52
Agricultural high school...........	—	11	37
Enrollment in State Schools (000's)			
Primary............................	462	1,003	1,544
Middle.............................	n.a.	144	173
High...............................	n.a.	55	48

Source: L. J. Walinsky, *Economic Development in Burma, 1951–1960*, Tables 67 and 68.

of state schools in existence and the number of pupils in them were increased rapidly. Many of the schools were bamboo and thatch huts, and the quality of the education and length of the school term minimal; nevertheless, the advance was great. In 1955 the percentages of the eligible children attending primary, middle, and high school respectively were 31, 5, and 1; in 1959, they were 51, 9, and 3.[34]

As one more example, the government invited UNESCO, UNICEF, and the United States Public Health Service to initiate campaigns in Burma against malaria, tuberculosis, venereal diseases, and other diseases that are common causes of death. Perhaps it is more accurate to state that the government agreed to the proposals of these organizations to initiate the campaigns. At any rate, Burmese officials co-operated, and some striking reductions in morbidity and mortality were achieved. No comprehensive statistics are available, but it is indicative that sample censuses of 252 towns found 34 per cent of their population under 15 years of age in 1953 and 36 per cent in 1957.

The effective actions of which these are examples are only tiny bits of leaven in the sodden mass of inaction and irresponsible behavior in the

---

[33] *Ibid.*, chap. xvi.

[34] *Ibid.*, chap. xx.

government's economic development program as a whole. Even so, their presence is somewhat surprising in view of the prevailing norms of public behavior. An explanation of the behavior of the majority of national leaders will not be satisfactory unless it is also consistent with this contrary behavior of a small minority.

The Paradox

The question which on the surface is most puzzling is not, however, the coexistence of these two contrasting kinds of behavior. It is the existence of an apparent dedication to economic development by intelligent leaders side by side with their irresponsibility or worse in the execution of measures affecting development. Adding to the seeming confusion is the complaisant acceptance by the public of the irresponsible behavior. True, there was some restlessness in the country by 1958, after almost a decade of maladministration, and the accession to authority of the army was welcomed; but the brusqueness of army rule and the army's lack of respect for seniority and position seemed more offensive than the malfeasance of the AFPFL administration. U Nu's admission of error in 1960 seemed to the electorate to atone for any shortcomings, and he was returned to power with a large majority in the parliament. We must account both for the bad management and for the lack of concern about it.

If we can understand this behavior of national leaders and the public's complaisance concerning it, we may have the key to complex forces at work in the Burmese society. It is not to be explained by an assumption that the Burmese as a people lack industry or technical capacity or leadership ability. They have evidenced the first in agriculture, the second in their traditional architecture and engineering, and the third in many achievements in their military and religious history. While some party hacks of mediocre ability are included among the ministers, it is the judgment of various individuals who have known them or observed their careers, including the writer, that the more influential of the ministers are men of superior intelligence.

Neither is it helpful to characterize the political elite as corrupt and cynical. Some rob the public till, but they are not knowingly committing evil in doing so. Rather, they seem to regard personal gain as the prerogative of a leader. It is of little use simply to call them corrupt. One must ask how their attitude came to persist in the modern political system and why the system threw such men to the top. And in any event, such corruption is true of only few of the top leaders. Not only is U Nu's personal financial integrity beyond question; his hatred of corruption among his associates is also well known. The phenomenon to be explained is that a man with such attitudes and associates of equal integrity perpetrated one irresponsible act after another more damaging to the nation than large-scale personal graft would have been and permitted gross venality by officials not immediately associated with them. This is a far more puzzling and significant phenomenon than the venality itself.

Much of the behavior I have sketched might be explained superficially simply by stating that the personalities of the individuals are traditional. Devoting energies to the technical and economic problems of planning and running a brick and tile, pharmaceutical, sugar, or spinning factory or steel mill would be impossible for individuals with traditional personalities. For to do so involves continuing problem solving, with all the anxiety that facing a series of problems entails. Further, involving themselves with technical problems would demean them, put them on a level with menials. The delegation of authority necessary for the effective management of industrial enterprises would involve sharing their eliteness with subordinates. Lastly, to check on the implementation of projects and the operation of enterprises by their associates would be to interfere with someone else's prerogatives, to challenge someone else's status, and so would arouse the deep anxieties which such interpersonal challenges arouse in the Burmese culture.

However, to state that personalities are traditional is not a convincing explanation. For if their personalities were simply traditional, the individuals would not have concerned themselves with industrial projects in the first place. The phenomenon to be explained is such behavior by intelligent individuals who intensely desire, so they avow—and there is no reason to question their sincerity—to achieve economic modernity as rapidly as possible.

The behavior that resulted in the record indicated was complex. It is probably fair to state that administrative officials throughout the ranks of the bureaucracy as well as at the top were not aware that things were being done badly. Honest and dishonest officials alike seemed unaware that inaction, irresponsible action, political party manipulation, and corruption had any effect on growth or the public welfare. The objective economic problems that confronted them did not seem to be the central realities of their lives. They acted, so it seemed to observers, as though the substance of those problems had at best only a shadowy significance to them. With a few exceptions, they seemed preoccupied with inner concerns that caused them to live in a dream world in which economic realities did not intrude. One felt as though there were a glaze through which one's analysis concerning current economic problems and policies did not penetrate. Indeed, they gave the impression of avoiding critical analysis for fear it would disrupt that dream world. This, rather than indolence or venality, seemed to be the central problem.

To understand this behavior, it seems to me that we must go back to examine relationships between conquerors and conquered during the colonial period, relationships which also explain the failure of Burmese to enter into Western-type occupations during that period. The impact of colonial administration on a subject people has been discussed in general terms in Chapter 17. Here it will be illustrated in more detail in Burma.

THE SOCIAL AND PSYCHOLOGICAL IMPACT OF COLONIAL RULE

British administrative policy in her colonies in the nineteenth century was dominated by the enlightened liberalism which every cultured Anglo-Saxon felt to be the climax of the world's intellectual development. When Bentinck left to be governor-general of India in 1828, he wrote to the utilitarian philosopher Jeremy Bentham, "I am going to India, but it is you who will be Governor-General."[35] Guided by libertarian philosophy, British administrators in Burma proceeded to impose upon the society the principles and practices of contract, rule by impersonal law, and separation of church and state. They had no concept of each culture as having its own yardsticks which influence what will work well; the social sciences were not sufficiently advanced. What was good in England they thought would be good in Burma. To the measures dictated by these principles were added others necessary to keep the subject people under control. The imposing of these principles involved direct rule; the British directly supervised the internal administration of their colonies rather than leave it to a local chieftain who might preserve barbarous customs as well as foci of resistance.

In the process of imposing direct rule British administrators abolished the inheritance of circle headmanships. They appointed circle headmen and made them responsible for enforcing central government laws and orders. Individuals who refused these assignments were replaced by others who accepted them to save their skins and their salaries. The British found circles of various sizes; to increase administrative efficiency they pretty completely redrew circle boundaries. Indeed, successive commissioners with differing ideas concerning administration did so several times. Later in the century village headmen were made directly responsible for enforcing the orders of the colonial administration, and the position of circle headman was gradually abolished. Villages were then repeatedly redefined in geographic area. Then gradually the authority of various specialized central government officials, many of them Indian, was extended directly to the villages.

These successive steps increased administrative convenience. They also had the unintended effect of destroying the political and social basis of Burmese community life. When circle and village headmen became agents who enforced the arbitrary orders of an alien regime, and community boundaries became arbitrary, communities were left without effective forms through which consensus could be reached and the moral-

---

[35] Furnivall, *Colonial Policy and Practice*, p. 29.

ity of the group could function. Many villages became "crowds of strangers."[36] Villages ceased to function as social organisms. Common lands, necessary for wood supply, grazing, and village gatherings, disappeared, in some places because the community they served was no longer the governmental unit and in others because the headman no longer had the authority and prestige necessary to protect them from the private encroachment which the new institutions of land ownership made possible. Village wells fell into disrepair and became contaminated, and village streets deteriorated. Community apathy set in.

An equally drastic alteration of legal institutions was carried out. Clearly defined uniform legal codes and procedures were necessary to facilitate the entry into Burma of finance, commerce, and large-scale industry. Burmese court decisions in any event seemed too nonuniform for other civil purposes and for criminal prosecutions. The headmen who had presided over the settlement of disputes and offensive acts by a process of mutual accommodation were replaced by judges bound by a code of law. British administrators mistakenly thought they were applying a Burmese code of law except where it conflicted with British law, but such a code did not exist.

An important example of legal change that seemed evil to the Burmans was that in landownership. Land throughout Burma was made alienable. In Lower Burma the change consisted merely in recognizing as a deed of sale the Burmese mortgage instrument, which from the wording on its face seemed a deed of sale and which British administrators may have mistakenly thought to be so. The result, however, was to permit money lenders to gain possession of land by trick.

Land tenure in Upper Burma was unclear to the British and in any event was inconveniently complicated. Therefore at the time of the institution of British land administration there the person then engaged in cultivation of each plot of land was declared to be its owner in fee simple. Land not in cultivation was made available for settlement. In some cases unscrupulous individuals seized village common land and land lying fallow, and such an individual found by the administrator to be the cultivator of a piece of land and therefore declared the owner could deprive his relatives of the fruits of land that had been the basis of family life from time immemorial. The regulations were disregarded for a long time in many areas in Upper Burma, but villages and families that disregarded them were in danger of depredations by unscrupulous individuals. Thus British rule broke down the basis of family life and for individuals who

---

[36] Furnivall describes the deterioration of community life most clearly. See *ibid.*, chaps. iii and iv. Though they did not understand the causes, a number of other British administrators have noted the effects. See F. S. V. Donnison, *Public Administration in Burma* (London: Royal Institute of International Affairs, 1953); G. E. Harvey, *Burma, 1852–1918: British Rule in India* (The Cambridge History of India, Vol. VI) (Cambridge, Eng.: The University Press, 1929); and G. E. Harvey, *British Rule in Burma, 1824–1942* (London: Faber and Faber, 1946).

were now legally landless the basis of community life, and it encouraged the corruption of family and village relationships. The courts sanctioned the land regulations, and the colonial administration used its physical power to enforce them.

As a result, in Burmese eyes the courts ceased to be agencies of justice. They denied protection to deep-seated traditional moral and ethical principles and gave sanction to acts of trickery and skulduggery. "As the law had no roots in the community, [the judges] applied it literally, mechanically."[37] ". . . There were no high courts in the British Empire where the atmosphere was so unreal."[38]

Even if there had been no other causes for the decline of morality, in view of these practices it is no wonder that life became corrupt. A Corruption and Bribery Enquiry Committee was appointed by the colonial administration to investigate and report at the end of the 1930's. The majority of the committee doubted that in the two lower grades of the general and judicial services (there were three grades in all) more than 30 per cent of the personnel were honest. "Most of the subordinate officials, even, and perhaps especially, those charged with welfare activities, were regarded as agents of oppression to be propitiated by petty bribes."[39] Judges of the lower courts "were usually corrupt; even sympathetic observers did not think more than one in three could be honest."[40] Dacoity and murder increased steadily throughout the colonial period in spite of repeated enlargement and reorganization of the police force.[41] This is not surprising in a society in which it was felt that a framework of morality no longer guided life.

The colonial administrators showed equal disregard for traditional religious values. Under Burmese rule a patriarch selected by the king had advised him, and an ecclesiastical commission had enforced high standards of morality on the monkhood. Otherwise each monastery had a high degree of local autonomy. With the termination of the kingship the function of the patriarch ceased to exist, and judicial decisions gradually transferred from the ecclesiastical commission to secular courts the power to hear criminal cases involving monks. The power to unfrock a monk thus ceased to exist, and since citizens refused to testify against monks in the secular courts, monks became largely outside the law.

In the disorder that prevailed in Lower Burma following annexation and during the rush to bring the land under cultivation many communi-

[37] *Ibid.*, p. 135.

[38] G. E. Harvey, *Burma, 1852–1918*, p. 443. For harsh judgment of the court system, see the section from which this sentence is quoted, or for briefer comment see G. E. Harvey, *British Rule in Burma, 1824–1942*, pp. 33–37.

[39] The Report was published in Rangoon, by the Superintendent of Stationery and Printing in 1941. My summary and the comments quoted are however from Furnivall, *Colonial Policy and Practice.*

[40] Harvey, *British Rule in Burma, 1824–1942*, p. 39.

[41] Furnivall, *Colonial Policy and Practice*, pp. 137–41.

ties developed which had neither monk nor monastery. Furnivall estimates that perhaps only one in three or four had a monk, and fewer had monastery schools. Autonomy within the Buddhist organization and the Burmese trait of not involving oneself in another's affairs prevented the development of channels by which monks might have been directed to new villages, and the British destruction of the ecclesiastical structure insured even further that the leadership to do so would be missing. The level of culture of monks declined; the permanent monkhood came to include many rather ignorant and ignoble men and some criminals.

The lack of concern of the administrators with this decline in the purity of Buddhist life indicated their lack of regard for the Burmese religion. The British indicated it even more clearly by their individual behavior. Many of them treated monks with some contempt, exercising their prerogative as rulers to refuse to remove their footwear when walking on monastery grounds—the equivalent of spitting on the symbols of Christ at the altar in a Christian country.

These modes of indicating disparagement for almost everything that was Burmese were capped by individual relationships to Burmans. As a general rule Britishers addressed all Burmans by titles that one uses in talking to an inferior, and many if not all insisted on being addressed by Burmans not merely by the term one uses in addressing a respected senior person, "U," but as "Thakin," which means master. Very few Britishers had social relations even with the most cultured Burmans. The entire tone of personal relationships indicated that in the view of the colonial masters the Burmese were an inferior race and their beliefs, values, and personal characteristics lacking in worth. The colonial rulers said, in effect, "We will rip apart your family and community relationships, desecrate your channels of contact with the spiritual powers, and deny you individual dignity. Insofar as your persons and the things you value interfere with our convenience, they are worthy of little consideration."

The derogation had its greatest impact on the Burmese ethnic group. While all ethnic groups must have felt the disparagement rather deeply and been affected by it, still it was possible for other groups to think that it was really directed at the Burmese and that the rest were only innocent bystanders who were injured because of their propinquity. For the British favored the minority ethnic groups, either deliberately to align them against the Burmese or because those groups reacted more favorably to British control. First by formal rule and then informally Burmese were barred from the army even while Karens and Shans were vigorously recruited. Minority ethnic groups seem to have been preferred in appointments to civil service positions as well. The destruction of traditional social institutions went less far for other ethnic groups than for the Burmans, Karens, and Mons since the other groups were farther removed from the geographic regions in which the British had most interest. For some deep-seated cultural reason, associated with but perhaps not fully explained by their previous suppression by the Burmese, many Karens took readily to Christianity (evangelical Baptism) and became faithful supporters of the British. Moreover, all minority groups could feel that in some degree the British had liberated them. Hence, whereas the derogation was unrelieved for the Burmese, it was possible for other groups to persuade themselves with some success that it was only the Burmese whom the conquerors thought of no worth.

AN INTERPRETATION AND FORECAST

Results of the Colonial Pressures

The impact of these colonial relationships on traditional Burmese personality, it seems to me, explains various aspects of Burmese behavior that are otherwise inexplicable.

I have noted early in this chapter that the Burmese were politically apathetic under colonial rule, but that the apathy was only superficial. Burmese acts during World War II demonstrated the hatred of colonial rule that lay under it. Their behavior, in short, was retreatist. The rage must have been associated with humiliation at the derogation of many things that were valuable to them, a need to cling to traditional identities in order to avoid accepting the contemptuous British evaluation, and hatred of everything associated with the conquerors. I suggest that these attitudes and needs created aversion in Burmans to European-type occupations, and that this aversion is an important causal element in the failure of Burmans to enter into the new occupations in large numbers during the colonial period.

It explains, too, I believe, the acquiescence of Burmese in the actions of their leaders. The Burmese still feel aversion to identification with the view of life of the colonial administrators and businessmen, which included contempt for their culture and behavior. Therefore they do not feel indignation when their leaders behave ineffectively in modern business roles. It is far more important to them that their leaders reflect respect for traditional values and interpersonal relationships. This U Nu does in high degree. The fact that as Prime Minister he has been responsible for many acts of mismanagement in economic development therefore detracts little from his hold on the public imagination.

The impact of colonial relationships, I think, also explains the behavior of Burmese national leaders during the decade of the 1950's. I believe that their behavior reflects ritualism or "identification with the aggressor" as I described that phenomenon in the preceding chapter. To persuade themselves that the powerful and threatening European thought well of them, they had to persuade themselves that they were identical with him. Wanting industry was an important instrument of this self-persuasion, for obviously Europeans want industry. Since to prove to themselves that they wanted industry they had to build factories—the kinds of factories that most symbolize modernity—they adopted decisions to have factories. In turn, they refused to consider analyses which might show that their natural resources are not suited to some types of factories that give prestige because they dared not admit the possibility that some of the factories they needed in order to reassure themselves were not desirable.

At the same time, having reassured themselves by these decisions and by visions of the prestige associated with them, they continued to hold desperately to ways of life and interpersonal relationships reflecting the identities which the aggressor challenged—so desperately, in fact, that their behavior was not merely normally traditional. Rather, their behavior was compulsive; the common sense of a normal traditional individual would not have permitted him to behave so irresponsibly as they have done. This set of circumstances, I think, constitutes the reason for the irresponsible action manifested by many national leaders in Burma.

A Further Explanation

As a postscript to this explanation of Burmese attitudes and behavior, let me suggest that the aversion to entrepreneurship, manual-technical work, and in general participation in the operations of industry may have a still further cause in Burma, and that the same added mechanism may also operate in many other ex-colonial countries. Even while the Burmese leaders identified with the aggressors they looked for someone against whom they might dare to vent their rage, and they found a possible target because of the divergence in values between British governmental administrators and British businessmen. Many British colonial administrators themselves placed a low value on technological knowledge or competence. They had little interest in natural science or its logic; they were products and exponents of a cultural and humanistic education not entirely unlike the education which Buddhism valued highly. Nor did the administrators place great premium on initiative. Too much probing into problems sometimes made an official suspect. To many colonial administrators as to the Burman the concept of government office involved rote administrative paper work, correct attitude, and pride of position rather than effective entrepreneurship. Further, the administrative group regarded business as an inferior function and the business group as an inferior group. Finally, like the traditionalists they too felt physical labor beneath them. Some of them asserted that one had to keep the distinction between oneself and the "natives" clear by giving orders to get lowly work done rather than doing it oneself. Perhaps in fact some of them were separating themselves a little anxiously from their own humbler origins. In any case, the typical British official did not so much as carry his papers from office to automobile or automobile to residence; this lowly act was performed by his office errand-boy or his houseboy.

This split in British attitudes provided the Burmese with a life-saving opportunity. They could give themselves a greater shell of protection by observing that in following traditional values they were identical with their conquerors; they could persuade themselves that they were really identical with their masters (and thus could not be thought worthless) by asserting and believing that they admired British parliamentary, legal, and administrative institutions. Today these institutions are rather scrupulously adhered to in Burma in form though not in substance. Thus identifying with one set of aggressors, the Burmese could more safely channel their rage at the invading businessman, associating "colonial imperialism" with him, and with less danger could feel aversion for his values and his behavior.

The Effective Deviants

Against this background it is not difficult to understand the presence of a few effective leaders. First it may be noted that not all individuals in colonial society are under such pressure that they adopt identification with the aggressor as a defense. Those who come under the most acute disparagement during infancy and early childhood in their homes and during adolescence in the larger community may feel most deeply both the need to overthrow the oppressors and also the need to identify with those aspects of the behavior of the oppressors that are threatening. They will cry most intensely for independence and may become leaders of the independence movement and later of the national government. And because of their resort to identification with the aggressors they will behave in the irresponsible ways sketched above. However, other individuals who escaped the most severe pressure will be less conflicted individuals.

A second explanation is related. In Burma persons of the Burmese ethnic group, as has been noted, were under the most severe pressure. In some degree members of the other ethnic groups could feel that the British were releasing them from subordination to the Burmese and did not derogate them. One would therefore be more likely to find capable entrepreneurs in the other ethnic groups, not because they are more capable by heredity but because they have not been subjected to as severe psychological pressures.

And when one notes the individuals who have done outstandingly effective jobs of governmental administration, one finds that many of them are wholly or partly of non-Burmese blood. To draw a line between competent and ineffective or irresponsible top administration in order to name individuals would be invidious, but I think it is a common judgment of informed observers that a majority of the capable top administrators are wholly or partly of Mon, Shan, Chinese, or Pakistani blood, and that the fraction is much larger than the fraction of individuals belonging to these ethnic groups among government administrators as a whole or in the population as a whole.

Private Entrepreneurship

If this analysis is correct, one would expect to find more traditionalism among the entire population of the Burmese ethnic group than among other groups, and more innovating entrepreneurship among other groups. That is, the contrast noted above should be found not merely among national leaders but more generally. Sufficient evidence to indicate the facts without doubt does not exist, but such information as is available is consistent with the hypothesis.

First, private entrepreneurship has apparently been much more effective than that in government. This is suggested by information concern-

TABLE 18-3

THE GROWTH OF PRIVATE INDUSTRIAL PRODUCTION IN BURMA
1953–57

	1953	1957	1957 as Per Cent of 1953
Number of establishments	65,365	97,530	149
Cottage and home	62,900	93,600	149
Manufacturing*	2,465	3,930	159
Employment (000's)	276	393	142
Cottage and home	174	239	137
Manufacturing*	102	154	151
Value of output (K million)	65	159	243
Cottage and home	21	68	320
Manufacturing*	44	91	207

* Roughly adjusted to deduct government establishments and employment.
Source: *Economic Development in Burma*, chap. x, Table 54.

ing manufacturing and cottage industry. In 1953 and again in 1957 a census of industry was taken in Burma. Since the censuses covered only the towns, and these could be reached by government officials, they may be reasonably complete and their coverage may be comparable though this is not certain.

The results are shown in Table 18–3. Prices of manufactured goods rose somewhat between 1953 and 1957; the 143 per cent increase in the value of output apparently indicates roughly a doubling of the volume of output.[42] One may guess that this doubling represents more than postwar reconstruction, for that had already progressed some distance in the

---

[42] The increase of 143 per cent may be compared with an increase of 28 per cent in "value added" in manufacturing and cottage industry, indicated in Government of the Union of Burma, *Economic Survey of Burma* (1958), Table 1. Insofar as the two figures have the same coverage, they ought to change in roughly the same ratio. The "value added" figure includes work in government railroad repair shops and timber mills, which increased greatly during the four-year period; on this account the "value added" figure might be expected to be slightly higher than the other. The comparison gives increased reason to believe that the official national income estimates understate the rise in private output in areas in which no direct bases of estimate were available.

towns by 1953. If the rapid rise in employment and output was real rather than merely a statistical artifact, and continued beyond 1957, no doubt it brought with it a related rapid rise in activity in supplying, transporting, and trading industries. That this has occurred seems probable because of a phenomenon that would otherwise be very puzzling, the lack of more evidence of acute economic distress in Burma than has appeared. That production per capita in 1960 was actually 20 per cent below that before World War II is difficult to believe. But if it was higher than this, the rise must be in the output of varied small private enterprises, for the measurement of the output of the government enterprises and the large joint government-private ventures is fairly accurate.

The growth of cottage industry and small-scale private manufacturing which seems to have occurred probably indicates expansion of activity to new levels and activity in new fields by thousands of self-reliant entrepreneurs. It is interesting to relate this series of conjectures to the judgment of two visitors to Burma in recent years, both men interested in economic development who had also visited Burma earlier in the decade, who state that from personal observation they believe that there has been a much geater expansion of manufacturing activity than the national income estimates suggest,[43] and that many of the entrepreneurs in this activity seem to be Sino-Burmans and other non-Burmese.

The evidence is so incomplete that one cannot state with certainty either that the expansion in private activity has occurred or that the ethnic participation in it is as suggested above. Both seem probable, however. If true, they provide an interesting illustration of the hypothesis that groups derogated within a traditional society are apt to be psychologically ready to accept new values and turn to nontraditional activities.

That the minority ethnic groups seem to be providing leadership in economic growth also provides a suggestion of possible trends in Burma. As has been noted earlier, a dominant social group whose relative status is threatened by the rise in power of individuals from other groups reacts in one of two ways. If the group threatening its status is sufficiently alien, the dominant group may eject or suppress it. But if the group rising in relative status is sufficiently well-rooted in the society so that suppression is not sanctioned by the culture, then the dominant group is apt to turn in self-defense to the activities by which the other is rising. Members of the conventional majority in England followed the Puritan Dissenters into industrial entrepreneurship, and men from other areas are following the Antioqueños into entrepreneurship in Colombia. In like manner the Burmese ethnic group may follow individuals of the indigenous minority groups into economic entrepreneurship in Burma. Burma may then advance into economic growth sooner than one would otherwise predict.

---

[43] Because they visited Burma in official capacities and may do so again, they wish not to be identified.

A Case in Point:
Sioux on the Reservations[1]

chapter 19

RESERVATIONS AS COLONIAL SOCIETY

TO ILLUSTRATE THE IMPACT OF COLONIAL CONTROL ON economic development by citing the experience of American Indians is not as strange as it may seem at first glance. The essence of the colonial situation is that a people has been conquered, the functioning of its culture and social structure disrupted and suppressed in some degree, and alien control imposed with such force that resistance is futile. By this definition the position of American Indian tribes is the archetype of colonialism, for their social structure and culture have been disrupted and suppressed more completely than those of any people conventionally regarded as colonial.

One who has visited both low-income countries and American Indian reservations is impressed with their similarity—in the political relationships between the indigenous people and the governing power, in the personalities of the conquered peoples, in the lack of economic progress. Yet there is a difference. What one notes in Asia, one notes in South Dakota intensified. In some respects the problem of economic, political, and social development of the American Indians is that of underdeveloped countries distilled, concentrated, raised to a power. Thus in the American microcosm one may perhaps understand some aspects of the macrocosm more readily than in the more complex macrocosm itself.

Few of the American Indian societies, it is true, were agricultural. Almost all were nomadic hunting groups. They were nonetheless traditional societies, and it is all the more impressive that the generalizations made in earlier chapters about traditional agricultural societies apply to them with

---

[1] This chapter reports on a study conducted by the writer and Dr. Louis C. Schaw. It draws heavily on E. E. Hagen and L. C. Schaw, *The Sioux on the Reservations* (mimeo; Cambridge, Mass.: Center for International Studies, Massachusetts Institute of Technology, 1960). The language here and there is closely parallel. For data concerning the reservations and information concerning the work and policies of the United States Bureau of Indian Affairs, I am indebted to officials of the Bureau in Washington, the Aberdeen Area Office, and the agencies at Pine Ridge and Rosebud, and especially to Mr. Glenn L. Emmons, former Commissioner of Indian Affairs, and Mr. Benjamin H. Reifel, former director of the Aberdeen Area Office.

nonessential modifications. Two other characteristics distinguish them from most other colonial societies, their small size and the blood mixture that has occurred. These differences, however, do not seem to distort the parallelism. At the two Sioux reservations studied almost 60 per cent of the individuals have some fraction of non-Indian blood, and about 7 per cent have more than three fourths non-Indian blood. But the non-Indian trappers, traders, and soldiers responsible for the blood mixture have disappeared from the tribal area, and the Indians remain as a distinct cultural group. And though the populations of the two tribes are small—one of them 5,300, the other 8,200—the boundaries between them and the white society around them are sharp.[2]

They proved to be informative examples of colonialism in the small.

RIDERS ACROSS THE PLAINS

To understand the relationship of the Sioux society to the white, which in its working out has brought the present situation, it is necessary to understand the Sioux society before the whites came.

Early History

The Indians whom most Americans call the Sioux refer to themselves as the Dakotas. I shall use the two terms interchangeably. At some time before the seventeenth century a group of Indian tribes including the Dakotas pushed up the Mississippi River. The Dakotas, who pushed to the headwaters in north central Minnesota, were reputedly the most aggressive. Nevertheless, some time after 1650, when an enemy tribe to the north obtained firearms, the Dakotas were forced to leave their lands. They retreated southwestward. The more conservative then veered north to stay in wooded country, but the bolder Tetons struck out westward onto the grasslands of South Dakota, where buffalo roamed in large herds.

This migration was not the bold advance of a powerful tribe. It was a wandering advance by small bands of individuals related by blood and marriage who were as apt to beg or steal food as to fight for it and who only occasionally came together in an encampment and formed a large war party. It was on foot; the Sioux did not yet have horses. Women, girls, and dogs carried the minimum necessary supplies and equipment on their backs, while the men kept themselves free for hunting and fighting. The Sioux killed rivals they could master, and through cunning, skill, and endurance evaded those they could not. The buffalo they killed provided meat, clothing, bone for implements, hides for tents and thongs, and indeed virtually all of their needs except for some foods.

---

[2] All data cited here and below concerning the two reservations are from the Aberdeen, South Dakota Area Office of the United States Bureau of Indian Affairs. The data for total population are for 1960. Most other data are from a 1956 census conducted by the Bureau of Indian Affairs.

In the eighteenth century, as the descendants of horses which had escaped from Spanish explorers in Florida or the lower Mississippi valley became plentiful on the great plains, the Tetons began to acquire horses by theft and capture. After the middle of the century they acquired them in large numbers. Armed with guns they had obtained in barter with white traders, they then became the bold, savage, powerful "riders across the plains" of whom we read in literature.

By the end of the century trade had become important in their lives. They exchanged furs, hides, and delicacies such as buffalo tongues not only for guns and ammunition but also for other European products, especially colorful textiles and trinkets, which provided so easily the prestige earlier provided by dyed materials and elaborate beadwork painstakingly prepared by women. But they were not drawn to the white way of life. They obtained the new instruments of power and symbols of prestige by the fruits of their traditional types of prowess, and these had never seemed sweeter to them.

Personality and the Social System

In a brief summary of some essential qualities of their way of life the basic features of their culture may be seen. Their hunting-fighting life required certain types of behavior for its success and their survival, and it succeeded so well for a period because the web of their culture and the personalities bred into each successive generation led without deliberate planning to behavior patterns consistent with it.

Cunning and daring appealed to them. This was at least one of the reasons that for fighting effectiveness they chose the high mobility of small bands rather than the strength of large ones. However, as they grew in strength they came together in brief large encampments each year in late spring unless warfare or catastrophe prevented.

In the small bands it was essential that the men be always free to fight or hunt at short notice. They thought any form of labor demeaning. The only men who did camp work were sexual inverts, known as *berdaches,* who had chosen to wear the dress and live the life of women. For them, work was appropriate.

Mobility also required that the goods of the band be held to a minimum. The possession by a family of unnecessary goods, an extra burden to transport, might have made it impossible for an individual to escape from a dangerous situation and might have caused his death. If it did, it would also have weakened the band. But this requirement of minimum possessions caused no problem, for any tendency to accumulate was regarded as a sort of perversion. Moreover, there was no unnecessary duplication of possessions among families. The words *my* and *mine* denoting possession apparently do not exist in the Dakota language. Every family of the band offered to any other member any item in which he showed interest. (It was bad form to express interest in fighting equipment or

minimum equipment for camping and cooking.) No family carried a reserve supply of meat; all shared in the kill of any member of the band.

Personal rivalries which might lead to friction were a danger to the
group. Individual vying in skill therefore held dangers. It was sanctioned
only in the areas where individual skill was of supreme importance to
the group: shooting, tracking, and other skills related to killing, and persuasive advocacy in tribal councils. Even in these areas it was surrounded
by religious ritual to safeguard it from abuse. Argument in council was
limited to braves who had proved their ability. Any competition in areas
other than these was a sign of personal untrustworthiness.

Finally, the hunting-fighting life required that the braves be ready to
kill an enemy or a suspicious stranger "at the drop of a hat" without compunction and without inhibiting guilt. They felt none, and killed without
hesitation and with pleasure.

A brief discussion of childhood environment will indicate how successive generations of Sioux came to have these characteristics of personality.

To Sioux parents, love of children demanded that children receive all
they desired of everything they desired. Nothing, for example, was allowed to interfere with nursing. The baby fed whenever he wished. In
other ways also he received his mother's unending attention. Strapped in
a cradle board, he was close to her even while she worked, either attached
to her back or lying close by.

There was no weaning; the child nursed at his mother's breast until
gradually he chose not to. If the arrival of another child interfered, he
was nursed by other women. Mother's milk, like other possessions, was
community property. Perhaps typically the child gradually abandoned
nursing in his third to fifth years, but Erikson tells of a mother who came
to school during recess to nurse her eight-year old boy, who had a bad
cold.[3] Children were given any object that attracted their attention; delicate objects were put outside of their range of attention, but if this failed
to be done, the child was given what he desired even if he destroyed it.
Even in recent reservation years, Erikson related, "the traders never tire
of repeating stories of Indian parents who came to town to buy long-
needed supplies with long-expected money, only to smilingly grant their
children their every whim, including their wish to take new gadgets
apart, and then to return home without supplies."[4] Nothing was denied
to the child, and nothing was taken from him.

This paradise of receiving and of plenty must have provided the basis
for the individual's lifelong unconscious assumption that one will always
get things from those who have them; that therefore one not only does

---

[3] Erik H. Erikson, *Childhood and Society* (New York: W. W. Norton & Co., Inc.,
1950), p. 119.

[4] *Ibid.*, p. 124.

not need to accumulate for oneself but also can always safely share all that one has.

Not only were children denied nothing. No restrictions were placed on them by parents (for example, they were not toilet trained by their parents), and so there was never any occasion for punishment. Children must have acquired a deep-seated sense that only unlimited goodness came from the powers above them.

But there was one exception to this parental permissiveness—a traumatic exception. A child in teething bites to relieve his pain, and when a Sioux child bit his mother's breast while nursing she withdrew it abruptly and rapped him on the head. He must have been startled, terrified, and angered. His rage amused and pleased his mother, for she believed that the vigor of his cry indicated his future prowess as a warrior. She offered him her breast again; if he bit, she rapped his head sharply again. Not until he learned to repress his rage, endure pain without outcry and without striking out, and approach the source of nourishment with humility and self-control could he again obtain nourishment.

I have suggested earlier that in every culture the child experiences pain, and finds his life incomplete until he has found a satisfying reason for the existence of pain. Perhaps the context in which pain is first experienced differs somewhat in each culture. To the Sioux child the severe trauma of the teething experience and the extreme self-control he had to learn even as an infant to re-establish his contact with the source of goodness must have raised the question in a form that required a unique answer.

Apart from the tremendous self-control required in nursing, the requirement of self-discipline was imposed on the child by his peers, not his elders. For example, they trained him in his toilet habits. When he was old enough to walk about and to follow and imitate other children and to control his eliminative functions, he was taken in hand by slightly older children who led him to the appropriate places and told him to imitate them. At first their requests were benign and permissive, but soon if the child did not do these things in the right place and at the right time he was teased and taunted. Defiance was futile; it resulted only in humiliation and alienation which he could not endure. No doubt the older children unconsciously found in this coercion an outlet for the rage generated in them by the teething-suckling trauma. As soon as he complied, the child would find the same outlet against slightly younger children and also those of his own age who had not yet complied.

Thus, the child, facing the imperious demands of his peers, learned that he dared not exert his autonomy in this matter any more than in nursing, and dared not exert it against the group any more than against the powers that conferred good on him. To avoid the scorn of the group and continue to be accepted in it, he must offer the group what it asked of him.

This childhood experience was by no means unique. There were many subsequent occasions on which the attitude of the group taught the individual to conform to its standards and when, in turn, he gained satisfaction by retaliating with the same pressure on others. The posture which gave him security in the group was not being superior to others but being as good as others, not differing from others but doing as they did. The individual would ever after be uncomfortable if he attempted individual achievement except on behalf of his group. Even then his action had to be surrounded by religious sanctions to free the group and perhaps the individual from anxiety concerning it.

The childhood experience of the Sioux must have left its imprint on the personality of the individual in the form of two questions to which he would have to find answers if life was to be satisfying. Why must he suffer pain and summon up great self-control to keep his contact with the source of goodness? Why must he submit to the will of his group?

He learned an answer to the second, I suggest, by observing adult life. His father did not always gain for the family all the necessities of subsistence in the high adventure of craft and aggression in the hunt. Rather, the group of peers of which his father was a member collectively embarked on each adventure. On one occasion one man made the kill, on another occasion another; and on each occasion every member of the group shared by virtue of his membership in the group. Since in due time the boy would be a member of such an adult group, I suggest that in yielding to his group in childhood play he experienced an anticipation of the security he would obtain from his group when he himself became a warrior and hunter.

Meanwhile, good came to him from above, from the band of adult providers, and this knowledge must have provided some justification for enduring pain. However, the full justification, which gave complete meaning to life and made his whole culture and social structure satisfying, must have come only as he understood the significance of his tribe's annual religious festival.

All power in the world, according to the elders, existed in a pervasive supernatural force, and all good came from that force. The force was manifest in the sun and in the buffalo his comrade; in the sky, the male principle; the earth, the female principle; and rock, the spirit of action; in animals and birds and all the elements of nature. It was responsible for victory and defeat, life and death, and all natural events, and some human beings had more skill and power than others because this almighty supernatural force conferred it on them. Skill depended on long and diligent practice, but that man gained it by practice on whom grace had been conferred. This force the Dakotas termed Wakan Tanka. They believed that from Wakan Tanka the success of their society came.

To receive grace from Wakan Tanka, man must prove himself worthy. At each annual encampment, held "when the buffalo were fat, the wild

berries ripe, the grass tall and green,"[5] the tribe resolved its lingering uncertainties concerning its worthiness and sought grace from Wakan
Tanka anew. The religious ceremony "started with ritual feasting, the
expression of gratitude to the Buffalo Spirit, the demonstrations of fel-
lowship among fellow men. Fertility rites followed, and acts of sexual
license such as characterize similar rites in many parts of the world. Then
there were war and hunting games which glorified competition among
men. Men boisterously recounted their feats in war; women and maidens
stepped forward to proclaim their chastity . . . the mutual dependence
of all the people would be glorified in give-aways and in acts of fraterni-
zation."[6]

The climax was the Sun Dance. On behalf of the tribe, chosen braves
thrust skewers through the muscles of their breast. The ends of the skewers were attached to the sun pole by long thongs. Facing the sun in day-
long dances, the braves backed away until they tore the skewers loose
through the muscles and flesh. By their self-inflicted suffering and their
fortitude they purified themselves and proved their worthiness on behalf
of the tribe and assured for the coming year the grace of the sun, the
buffalo spirit, and the other manifestations of Wakan Tanka.

Even as a young boy, if his conduct during boyhood impressed the
elders and earned him the honor, a child may have participated in the
ritual by having his ear pierced, the symbolic equivalent of the purposeful
supreme pain of the Sun Dance. I suggest that in his observation of this
ceremony and the intense beliefs of the elders that surrounded it the child
learned the meaning of pain and his life became meaningful and complete. The belief that grace is conferred by Wakan Tanka and is earned
by enduring pain stoically seemed immediately plausible to him because
of his need to find justification for his early experience of pain. The pain
he had experienced in isolation as an infant was preparation for his re-
experiencing of pain as an adult, pain that would integrate him with his
tribe, earn goodness for the tribe, and give meaning to all of life.

In the Sioux society as elsewhere elements of culture were seized upon
by each succeeding generation because they satisfied deep-seated needs,
not merely because the words were heard at an impressionable age. I
suggest too that in some unconscious way the perception by the parents
that each individual must learn to endure pain on behalf of the group
caused them to see good in imposing the requirements for self-control at
teething. Neither element in the behavior pattern was uniquely the cause
of the other; these and other elements fit, and as a result the culture was
stable.

Both the teething experience and that of toilet training left rage pent
up in the child. The childhood play which trained him in the skills of

---

[5] Quoted by Erikson, *ibid.*, p. 131.
[6] *Ibid.*, pp. 131–32.

the adults around him also provided him with outlets for aggression which no doubt made the play the more attractive. Small boys lassoed tree stumps and killed small animals and birds with small bows and arrows. Boys of three or four were taught to destroy hornets' nests and escape without being stung. If they failed, they learned the penalty of insufficient stealth and too slow escape.

Boys played with "bone horses," bones three or four inches long gathered where buffalo had been killed. When not in use in games of horse racing or buffalo hunting they might be fingered continuously in the boys' pockets. Erikson, noting the phallic shape of these bones, suggests that they may have been the medium by which boys in the stage of infantile genitality and the early use of their locomotor capacities cultivated competitive and aggressive daydreams.[7]

During the same years boys heard tales of cruel and dangerous enemies against whom the heroes of the tribe had performed deeds of great valor and cunning. Knowledge of the presence of such enemies was probably necessary for a continuing feeling that only nurturance comes from above. For certainly in the Sioux lives there were periods of anxiety and peril, and unless there were external enemies on whom they could be blamed, one could not continue to believe in powers that provided only good and safeguarded one from danger. Thus at the same time that the tales provided models for future behavior which added point to the childhood games, they made the world consistent.

As equally fascinated auditors in other groups the boys heard adolescents boast of their sexual exploits. A boy might attack any girl whom he caught outside of a defined area in the camp. And if a young man should touch any girl's vulva, even by stealing upon her as she slept, and would swear later under ritual conditions that he had done so, the girl was cast out of the circle of the elect and had to spend her life as a prostitute unless she chose to commit suicide. Young men vied in the number of such coups they could count. Their accounts of their successes were not tales told surreptitiously around corners; they were open boasts of manly feats and had the approval of the adults. Soon the young boys who heard these tales began to ride horses and gained exhilarating knowledge of the power thus transmitted to their bodies, and then later they themselves entered upon sexual aggression. In these ways throughout childhood and adolescence sexual aggressiveness and the aggressiveness of the warrior became equated. Few inhibitions existed in the sexual area which by diffusion might interfere even minimally with aggressiveness in the other area. The prime responsibility for sufficiently restricting aggression against young women rested with the young women, who to preserve the family and band structure were expected to remain within the safe camp areas and to sleep with a rope tied around their thighs.

---

[7] *Ibid.*, p. 126.

Yet a young man approached the girl whom he sought as his wife tenderly, calling to her with the love flute. Simultaneously he safeguarded himself by ritual against the danger that tenderness would destroy his manliness.

The girls' games stressed homemaking and sharing. But vicariously women shared in the males' aggression and in their fortitude. A brother brought his sister his best prey for butchering and the corpses of his worst enemies for mutilation.[8] Maidens helped in preparation for the ordeal of the Sun Dance, and a virtuous sister bathed her brother's self-inflicted wounds.

During childhood and adolescence, while the boys were learning the skills needed for hunting and warfare and were learning unadulterated pleasure in aggression, they were also learning that hunting and fighting are the roles of the man and that other activities are beneath him. They learned this in legend, in precept, and in the models set by the adults. Before adulthood they had as strong a repugnance for other forms of labor as the repugnance of the elite in any traditional agricultural society for the manual-technical labor of the simple folk.

Because it was believed that the exercise of power is dangerous and might both corrupt the individual and contaminate the group as a whole unless ritually controlled, no youth might become a brave who had not first been cleansed. Hence each youth at puberty sought to prove his worthiness by purifying himself until he received a vision. He left camp alone, naked except for loincloth and moccasins, and unarmed. Exposed to the dangers of nature, he fasted for several days until the vision appeared. When he related his vision to the medicine man, the medicine man told him his future role.

Even this brief sketch indicates the way in which the elements of Sioux behavior throughout life fitted together: The view of life of the adults determined the nature of their training of the children, the training of the children in turn created needs that were satisfied by the pattern of adult life, and the nature of the physical world fitted with both and made both reasonable.

Like all social-cultural systems, this one did not work perfectly, and its stresses produced deviants for whom the society had to find niches. The deviant male roles were sanctioned in dreams. Thus a boy or young man who saw a thunderbird in a dream would have to behave in a clownish fashion until his weakness had been relieved. A man who received the wrong vision on the Vision Quest was doomed to live as a *berdache*, wearing women's clothes, doing women's work, and in some cases becoming a male homosexual prostitute. As has been noted, a woman who failed to protect her virginity had to live as a prostitute, aggressively seeking out men. No doubt in almost all such cases the role satisfied a

[8] *Ibid.*, p. 130.

conscious or unconscious need of the individual. The roles also solved for the group the problem of what to do with individuals whose personalities did not come out as the culture decreed that in general personalities should, and solved it in ways that contributed to the life of the group rather than burdened it.

Defeat and Captivity

How long the Sioux social system had possessed the form sketched above is not known. Probably its elements had been much like this for generations before horses began to be important, the use of horses accentuating certain already existing relationships among elements of the culture. Thereafter the internal evolution of the society might have produced continuing change. However, there was little time for this evolution to work itself out, for the impact of external events caused change sooner. By 1800 trade had become very important to the Sioux, and during the next quarter century they ceased to be primarily hunters and gatherers with a self-sufficient economy and became mainly providers of raw materials who obtained manufactured goods in exchange. In 1835 the Oglalas, one wing of the Tetons, moved south to be near a trading post on the Platte River and completely adapted their lives to the requirements of trade. By mid-century, in their greed for whiskey and for colorful textiles and trinkets, the Sioux were slaughtering many times as many buffalo as did the settlers moving West and were killing off their food supply and the base of their trading activity.

The federal government established a number of agencies throughout the area west of the Mississippi to deal with the Indians, and in 1852 or shortly before established a military post at Laramie Fork on the Missouri to protect settlers moving West. Violence by the Indians thereafter brought quick reprisal with power that gave the Indians a new perception of the strength and intention of their new enemies. Soon after this date the Sioux, or at least a group of Sioux chiefs, accepted a treaty in which they were granted rather extensive land bases and rations of food and supplies during part of the year in return for their promise not to molest other areas. Subsequently, however, Congress opened to settlement large tracts of land that had been granted the Sioux by the treaties, tracts that seemed empty and unutilized to the land-hungry whites. Prospectors in search of gold poured into the Black Hills, the Sioux' "holy mountain, game reservoir, and winter quarters."[9] The Sioux themselves repeatedly violated the treaties, whose terms they often did not understand and the authority of whose signers they often challenged. The warfare continued.

In a famous battle in 1876 several bands of Sioux and Cheyenne under Sitting Bull defeated and killed General Custer. Most of them, amazingly, then headed back to their agencies in the belief that the government

---

[9] *Ibid.*, p. 100.

would feed them as usual during the winter and allow them to hunt as usual the next summer. The government, however, presented the Sioux with a treaty by which they were to give up the Black Hills and choose lands on which they were to settle. In the face of overwhelming force[10] their chiefs accepted the terms. The two wings of the Tetons, the Brulés and Oglalas, chose the adjacent areas along the southern boundary of South Dakota which became known as the Rosebud and Pine Ridge reservations. They moved to these areas in 1878, some 200 years after they had been displaced from the headwaters of the Mississippi by the impact of Western technology and had begun to move southwestward.

THE RESERVATION PERIOD: IMPOSING EUROPEAN VALUES

The Early Phase: Messianism

At first the reservations were essentially concentration camps. The Sioux, disarmed, were prevented from attacking settlers. The buffalo were gone; the Sioux lived on rations provided by the government, or, in the recent phrase, on relief. In MacGregor's telling phrase, they became warriors without weapons.

The bands were forced to live continuously in moderately close proximity. They had never done so before except for the few weeks of the annual encampment. They had no practices for regulating life in large groups other than the strict regimentation adopted to make close contact workable for the period of the encampment, the longest period for which they could endure such control. The aggressiveness so thoroughly built into them chafed at continued close relationships beyond the band.

In these humiliating and bewildering circumstances they needed more than ever before the reassurance that their religion might give. However, one of the first acts of their new masters was to forbid the annual pagan ceremonial with its sexual license and the self-mutilation of the Sun Dance. The whites, moved by their own values, unwittingly removed the last vestige of meaning from lives whose external base had already been destroyed.

The reaction, as in other cultures when reality is too intolerable to permit the conviction that there is no way out, was Messianism. In 1889 the prophet of an Indian Messiah who had come to liberate the Indians from slavery emerged at the Shoshoni reservation in Wyoming, and in 1890 the new faith and ritual reached the Sioux. Groups of dancers would engage in hypnotic dances which resulted in trance-like states. Believers in these

---

[10] In the Dakota version of the treaty signing each of 30 chiefs was given a blanket and a bottle of whiskey and signed the treaty when drunk. However, in view of the white predominance of force and determination to disarm the Indians and confine them to a limited area, whether the chiefs were drunk made little difference in the outcome.

states were thought to be dead; they were reborn from death after having visited the promised paradise.

The new religion attracted among others the hard core of rebels who still preached revenge and liberation. Soon the government became alarmed and decided to jail the most vocal of the leaders, and a catastrophe occurred which ever since has colored Sioux memories of white rule. The strongest individual among the rebels was Sitting Bull, who had returned from exile in Canada to live in a reservation north of Pine Ridge. He was killed while resisting arrest. The Ghost Dancers of several communities interpreted his death as the start of wholesale repression and possibly massacre by the troops and began to move in groups with vague plans of seeking refuge in the Black Hills. In the vicinity of Wounded Knee, eighteen miles from Pine Ridge, a large group of dancers was cornered by the cavalry, who started to disarm them. A shot was fired, nobody is sure by whom, and the troops opened fire point blank on the crowd, pursuing men, women, and children as they ran away and killing 128.

Thereafter, according to Sioux memories, and there is documentation of some of the alleged facts, the whites repeatedly cheated the Indians in a variety of legal and illegal ways, but after Wounded Knee the spirit of the Sioux was broken; they offered no further organized resistance.

Even before Wounded Knee the government had begun positive acts to make the Sioux into self-sufficient Americans possessing standard American values. Apparently even before the Oglala and Brulés were forced to settle at Pine Ridge and Rosebud the government had included cattle in the rations to Indians in these areas with the hope of inducing them to become ranchers. Other programs attempted to make them into farmers. By the Allotment Act of 1887 each head of a family was to receive for operation 80 acres of farming land or 160 acres of grazing land. Eventually it was to be released from trust into full individual ownership. Some reservation lands remaining after allotments had been made were declared surplus and opened to non-Indian settlement—further evidence of bad faith in the eyes of the Indians. The law was not applied everywhere immediately; in Pine Ridge and Rosebud, lands were not allotted until after 1900.

The Sioux did not respond by becoming farmers, for they considered farming beneath the dignity of males. They did gradually adopt ranching, which had similarities to their previous horse-riding hunting life. Their herds grew, and at the beginning of World War I they were again almost self-supporting. However, the demand for beef during the war years raised the price of cattle to record heights, and in response the Sioux sold their herds. By 1916 there were hardly any cattle left.

The government then allowed the leasing of the land to non-Indians. Most of the lands were quickly taken over by white cattle operators, and the Indians derived some benefits from lease money, but during the depression of 1921 many operators were forced to abandon their leases and most of this revenue stopped. Soon after came the opportunity to sell land which had been released into full individual ownership. The agency encouraged its sale. In 1951 Pine Ridge had shrunk from its original size by one third and Rosebud by two thirds, and much of this loss of land had occurred in the 1920's. By 1930 drought, the collapse of cattle and grain markets, and the quick expenditure of the money received from land sales wiped out the economic basis of the reservations for a second time. The Indians lost their income from leases and their own farming operations, and most of them became completely destitute.

Ranching did not reappear. Probably cowboy life no longer had its former appeal to the Sioux. Probably also they were influenced by the deep-seated general conviction they had acquired that, whatever they attempted, the whites would see that they failed. Apathy had developed. Apart from these influences, however, there were others. Their land was so divided up through sales and leases to non-Indians that it was difficult to assemble an area large enough for ranching. There was no source from which to obtain the necessary capital. Few individuals skilled in cattle raising remained. And the pressure of poverty was such that the need to obtain immediate income, which leasing to non-Indians gave, outweighed other considerations. Most of the grazing land and all but a bit of the cultivable land (which is only one ninth of the total in any case) is now in enterprises run by non-Indians to whom it has been leased.

The efforts at acculturation were not confined to the adults. After the attempt to make ranchers and farmers of the Indians had begun, an attempt was begun to make the Sioux children replicas of white Americans by educating them in federal schools. What Erikson has termed the "guerrilla war over the children" ensued.[11]

"Children were virtually kidnaped," MacGregor notes, "to force them into government [boarding] schools. Their hair was cut and their Indian clothes thrown away. . . . Those who persisted in clinging to their old ways and those who ran away and were recaptured were thrown into jail. Parents who objected were also jailed. . . . Where possible, children were kept in school year after year to avoid the influence of their families."[12]

Revulsion at the inhumanity of this policy caused it to be ended. Day schools replaced the boarding schools. They continued to teach, as best they could, white knowledge and white values, and they continue to this day. Under new policies adopted after World War II administration of the schools at a number of reservations has been made part of the educational systems of the states in which they are located, though the federal government continues to bear the cost.

What have been the results of these attempts to induce culture change?

---

[11] *Ibid.*, p. 101.

[12] Gordon MacGregor, *Warriors Without Weapons* (Chicago: University of Chicago Press, copyright 1946 by the University of Chicago), p. 36.

RESERVATION LIFE TODAY:
RETREATISM AT ITS HEIGHT

My colleague Louis C. Schaw and I visited the Pine Ridge and Rosebud reservations during the winter of 1960–61.[13]

As I drove about the reservations in mid-winter my first impression was one of extreme rural poverty. Clearly the Sioux are not participating in the advance of the American economy. The large majority of homes were light frame structures unsuited to keep out the cold, or worse. Many, especially at Pine Ridge, were makeshift shacks, and one small community was living, as apparently they normally lived, in tents. A few old automobiles were parked in front of a café, and more of these plus newer ones belonging to Bureau of Indian Affairs officials in front of the government office buildings. A few persons moved about, bundled up against the cold.

Statistics confirmed the first impression of economic conditions. A census in 1956, a prosperous year in the United States, indicated that 58 per cent of the family heads and single adults had cash incomes below $1,000 per year and almost one third below $500. These data suggest a median income per family head or single earner of say $850 or $900, equivalent to a median income per capita well below $300 per year. Experience elsewhere indicates that such a census enumeration is apt to understate incomes since some items of irregular income are apt to be forgotten. Further, there was a small amount of production of items for one's own use. But with allowance for these facts, the income levels shown are miserably low.

They are due to both unemployability and idleness. More than one fifth of the family heads and adult males were hospitalized, institutionalized, otherwise unemployable, or females with minor children, and more than an added one fifth were fully employable but had little or no work. This was the situation in June. No one regarded these percentages as unusual. This is the normal economic situation at Rosebud and Pine Ridge. It bespeaks a maladjustment of major dimensions between the conquered groups and the conquering white society.

As my attention passed beyond the economic externals, another evidence of social malaise pressed upon me, a sense of heaviness or sluggishness, as though the villages of Rosebud and Pine Ridge were seized with an inanition due to something more pervasive than malnutrition and more penetrating than the cold. The Dakotas seemed as ghosts walking about— withdrawn, passive, lifeless—or bodies from which the breath of life has been (almost) removed. They gave the impression that what they do

---

[13] Dr. Schaw spent three months on the two reservations. I spent one week in January, 1961. My interpretation of the incidents and conditions I observed often rests upon discussion of their significance with Dr. Schaw.

visibly during the day—their trips about the village, their huddles on street corners, their waiting in line to see a Bureau official who controls a segment of their destiny—are measures merely to keep alive or to help time move around the clock. What one missed most was vivacity. Only in small children did one note it. The quietness and boisterousness of teen-agers both seemed somehow forced.

An observer of the 1930's noted feeling at Pine Ridge "as if he were part of a slow-motion picture, as if a historical burden arrested the life around him."[14] The burden has not lifted since he was there.

The general apathy may be illustrated by countless instances relating to community activities. Dr. Schaw and I heard of gardens, begun at the initiative of a government teacher, which were remembered with warmth but which somehow had not been continued; of recreation programs begun with outside leadership which had provided diversion of a summer but which after a year or two had not been renewed; of community movies, remembered with pleasure, which had no continuance beyond the visit of the visitor who introduced them—of these programs dying, not because efforts to continue them met obstacles but because no Sioux seems to have made any effort. In the report of an American Friends Service Committee worker we read of the ease with which, under his leadership, $15 had been raised by community action in the isolated village of Potato Creek to replace a hydrant which had been taken out because it had frozen, but we read also that the community had gone without this source of water for several years because no reservation resident had solved the problem.[15] In the accounts of MacGregor and Thompson we read of the experiment in co-operative economic enterprise at the Red Shirt Table community in the 1940's of which so much was expected by way of social as well as economic revival; but the enterprise has died. The assets have been sold and the proceeds divided among the members; today they are as poor as they ever were.[16] Many problems—real problems, creating real privations—could be solved with a bit of initiative but go unsolved because that bit of initiative and organizational effort is lacking.

The formal community institutions seemed to bear little relation to Dakota life. At a political rally in Pine Ridge village the evening before the election of members of the tribal council some candidates promised resistance to the last breath against the overwhelming power of government. Others appealed for votes in the jocular hail-fellow-well-met manner of the precinct leader. But no candidate discussed specific present-day community problem. These seemed to be regarded as beyond the ability of the Indians to influence.

---

[14] Erikson, *Childhood and Society*, p. 103.

[15] *Final Report of the American Friends Service Committee Pine Ridge Reservation Program, South Dakota, January, 1955–December, 1958* (mimeo; Philadelphia: American Friends Service Committee, July, 1959).

[16] Gordon MacGregor, *Warriors Without Weapons*, pp. 212–14.

The relationship between the tribe and Bureau administrators seemed especially unreal. We attended a meeting of the group termed officially "the executive committee" of the tribal council at Pine Ridge. The composition of the committee was determined some years ago in accordance with a suggestion of the agency superintendent, and, as he had suggested, it includes him. It functioned not as the executive agency of the tribe but as an advisory group to the agency superintendent. But it did not decide things with him. Its discussions (and his) tapered off vaguely and inconclusively; they seemed only remotely related to action.

At the tribal council meeting which followed, a representative of the United States Bureau of Reclamation stated that if the council desired, that Bureau at its own expense would further analyze a moderately promising irrigation project. The council seemed unable to focus its energies on the question. It required pulling and prodding by the agency superintendent and the area director of the Bureau of Indian Affairs, who was also present, before the council could energize itself to cast a vote in favor of this action which would cost it nothing and might bring some benefit. Or at least this was the surface picture. Private conversations later indicated that some council members feared that the project would be used either to reward favorites of the Bureau or "white farmers in Nebraska." One wondered how many other unspoken questions underlay the seeming formlessness of the two meetings.

The only sparks of life came when someone arose to poke fun at the government's program to help Indians find jobs in American cities and when several council members rose in sequence to denounce the callousness of the Bureau division administering relief funds in not granting sufficient relief funds to an aged woman, so they said, to permit her to purchase enough firewood for warmth in below-zero weather. "We can't understand why they [Bureau officials] do this," they said, "except they don't like Indians."

Yet behind this facade there was life. There are sometimes lively individualists in the intimacy of private conversations, we were told. Eloquence is a traditional Sioux virtue, and sometimes individuals speak eloquently in self-initiated community meetings. And we observed that under cover of darkness the reservation came alive. During the night people emerged in almost frenzied activity removed from the world of the whites: visiting, going and coming from wakes, dances, or religious meetings, or just traveling around. The Sioux behaved as if they were dreaming while the non-Indian society was awake and became active only when members of the white society withdrew into their sleep and abandoned reality for the Sioux to enjoy as a private possession.

Alcoholism, theft, family disorganization, sexual delinquency—all of these manifestations of personal disorganization are much more common among the Indians than among whites. The function of warrior-hunter which the father once served has disappeared, and the father is in fact either a mere drudge or a mere drone. He often has no way to assuage his lost pride and dignity except in drink. There is now no outside group on which he may vent his hostility and rage, and often after tensions have produced frustration and hostility he vents it on his fellows (in theft, destructiveness, personal attack) or on his wife. In the old days his wife, happily serving her function in the band, was submissive to her warrior husband. Today if her husband, no longer a warrior, abuses her in his frustration, she may and often does leave him and go to live with another man.

The historic small bands within the tribes, composed of families related by blood and marriage, still have some cohesive force. A common ancestor is a band hero; a historical exploit is remembered. But the ancestors are much less heroes of the tribe as a whole; one kinship group is apt to speak with disparagement of the leader acclaimed by another. Among the bands there are frictions: bickering, recrimination, sometimes drunken fights, on occasion physical injury or even a murder. Running through the inter-band dissensions are mutual accusation of co-operating with the government for their selfish gain. These antagonisms, little related to present realities, seem to provide some of the little emotional stimulus available to the tribal members.

The Sioux come closest to unity in their suspicion and hostility toward the Bureau of Indian Affairs. There are few Indians who accept the attitudes of Bureau officials toward Indian problems as reasonable. The conspicuous reality in relations between the Sioux and the Bureau officials who rule most aspects of their lives is the antagonism that pervades the contacts. A discussion between tribal and Bureau officials or between an individual Indian and an official is not a discussion among persons co-operating in attacking a mutual problem; it is a cautious negotiation between antagonists. The tribal members feel that the Bureau officials are cold and indifferent to their needs; the Bureau officials feel that they cannot trust the tribal members to tell them the truth, but that instead the Indians will deceive them to get added income. Indeed, the Indians may, for they do not trust the officials to deal with them generously or justly if they know the truth, and in dealing with an enemy one will protect oneself as one can. If a member of the tribe becomes an employee of the Bureau, the attitude of his fellow Indians toward him changes; he has sold his group membership for silver, and thereafter he is an "outsider."

The Sioux fear many ills at the hands of the whites. Perhaps most of all they fear abandonment. They regard the Congressional resolution of 1953 calling for dissolution of reservations as soon as possible, the subsequent transfer of health services from the Bureau of Indian Affairs to the United States Public Health Service, the transfer of responsibility for education at Rosebud from the federal government to local school authorities, and the program to help Indians move to cities all as steps in a design to abandon them and leave them to destitution. Yet after conversations with a number of reservation residents an observer feels that their anxiety is not so much concerning the material results of abandonment as concerning abandonment itself, the state of being abandoned.

What has gone wrong?

WHY DID IT HAPPEN?

It is easy enough to perceive, in a vague way that may be termed intuitive, that social disorganization and personal demoralization might result from the disruption of Sioux life. But this indefinite statement is not adequate for social analysis; it is necessary to attempt to identify the mechanisms by which the precise effects on personalities and the social structure occurred.

Conflicting Signals

The first of these mechanisms, then, probably is that the signals conveyed to infants and children by their environment concerning the types of action that will give satisfaction in life are now confused and contradictory.

Certainly there is a tendency for the traditional signals to be given. The persistence of cultural tendencies in the face of external change has often been noted. Perhaps it is due in part to the fact that the roles of women as mothers are private affairs which they carry little changed into a new way of life long after the old roles of men have been destroyed. Old men and women, withdrawing from community life to spend their last years in the comfort of the home, reinforce the continuance of traditional practices with their manifest approval and their tales at the fireside. It is not that mothers plan the personalities of their children and design their activities to these ends. Rather, they know what babies are like, what they need, what is good for them, what maternal behavior is decent and respectable, and act accordingly. In the case of the Sioux, even though a degree of blood mixture appeared, the non-Indians were usually the fathers; maternal care continued much as before.

Thus Sioux children are still raised in an atmosphere which at least intermittently is highly permissive and supporting. They are given as much nurturance and for as long a period as the parents can provide, except as the frustrations of the parents and their hostilities toward the outer world so consume them that their love of the children is momentarily submerged. In the 1930's visitors still observed no weaning process. The child nursed as long as he wished. Within the limits of the parents' capabilities, children are still given free access to food, toys, and other items. To an extent, then, the attitude of the parents still creates in the child's earliest experience a perception of a source from which all good and only good comes. The parents convey the perception that their capacity to provide is limited by an inimical and depriving outer world, against which one's rage may appropriately be directed. The niggardliness of the government and the hostility of all outsiders are blocks to complete satisfaction.

However, even in very early life the perceptions suggested above are contradicted by others. Having promised the infant unlimited goodness, the parents are now unable to provide it. Their inability to do so is not clearly understood by the young child as due to limiting outside factors, and the Sioux child must often perceive it simply as a limitation on the love being offered him. It may be suspected that the requests of Sioux children for toys, candy, and their parents' possessions today are often a compulsive and hostile attempt to force from the parents nurturance which in their present impoverished unhappiness and anger the parents cannot freely give. And of course children who seek to gain nurturance thus are forever unsatisfied.

Moreover, the human world outside the group cannot be seen as a totally hostile force, as was the outside world by the child in the traditional Sioux band, at least until trade became important. From the people of the outside world today come the things on which the life of the family depends and which the parents cannot produce. The child's later experiences with white teachers are not all disappointing or nonnurturant.

Hence the child's perception of where good comes from and what attitude toward the outside world will give him security and satisfaction must be confused.

Secondly, peers still exercise demands, but the relationship of the group of peers to each member is now such that the child learns neither automatically to yield to the group's will nor that it is safe to disregard it. He is left uncertain and anxious. Certainly with the dispersion of homes on the reservations, toilet training is not by the entire group of peers who will be the individual's lifelong associates, as it once tended to be, but one may take for granted that children and not parents are still the socializers in this respect, and that some group compulsion is felt.

Group controls, though less stringent than traditionally, continue to operate in other respects as well. Teasing and shaming continue to be powerful tools, and they are still used by children to impose traditional values. The Sioux boy still fears to be thought of as trying to be better than others in his group. He enters vigorously into competition as a member of a group team against outsiders, but he shrinks from individual rivalry with his peers. Individual achievement in school, even in the traditional Sioux art of persuasive oratory, brings looks and jeering noises from his fellows which cow and subdue him.[17]

The tales and model of adults still inculcate the idea that a decent individual shares his goods. Erikson mentions that the play of girls in the 1930's still included loading toy wagons with "rations" and setting out

---

[17] According to the head of a mission school at Pine Ridge.

to distribute them to relatives. Even when relatives are widely scattered over the reservation, to share with them is still a matter of honor for many Sioux, and failure to comply still draws community censure on the individual.

But neither in childhood nor later in adulthood is the child able to give much to the group. In traditional Sioux society his childhood play was imitation of adult life, and in it he exercised his skills and dreamed fantasies of future life as a brave in which he provided food for the group and killed his enemies. On the reservation there is no such play. The group has little to ask of him.

Neither does it promise to give to him. He observes that his family does not recieve goods through the joint endeavor of the group. The old mutuality is destroyed even more completely by the fact that the great majority of the Indians on the reservation are chronically poor and unemployed and have nothing to offer. The individual adult has opportunities and reasons for having and concealing individual goods and individual purposes. And so in this respect too the child must learn a confused and anxiety-creating set of cues.

Finally, he perceives no clear model in his parents or the other elders of what he shall be and do later in life. His parents' life surely is not fully satisfying to him, and equally surely he perceives that it is not fully satisfying to them. Like the parents in other traditional societies who suffer withdrawal of status respect, Sioux parents are torn between their allegiance to the old values and the pain which the contempt of their conquerors for those values causes them. The child perceives that conflict, and while he partially internalizes his parents' values because his parents are the source of love and power close to him, yet he also fears the pain which seeking to satisfy his parents' values would cause him and cannot fully identify with them.

In these circumstances of confused cues the child has three possible courses of action. Even in childhood he will begin to some extent to try to persuade himself that he has no goals, so that hoping for little he will not be disappointed. That is, he will become retreatist. Or he will follow contradictory courses of action, one type in one circumstance or at one moment, another at another. Each will be anxiety-creating as well as partially satisfying, and his life as a whole will seem incomplete. These are his only possible solutions so far as his current activity is concerned, but so far as he is searching for models for his later life, he may be able to refrain from identifying himself too firmly with persons around him, hoping that he may later find models that will make life more satisfying.

Meaninglessness of Life

This ambiguity and contradictoriness of the lessons his environment is teaching are not the only difficulty faced by the Sioux child on the reservation. Perhaps his most searing and crippling difficulty is that he does acquire certain fairly unambiguous unconscious tendencies in infancy and childhood but later can find no social purpose or rational justification for them.

No doubt in infancy he still learns the need to endure pain with great self-control to maintain his contact with a source of goodness, but life no longer provides him with a justification for that pain. He no longer endures pain with stoicism in later life as an incident to victory in the hunt or the fight, and he no longer can have the glorious experience of enduring pain on behalf of his tribe to insure the grace of the supernatural power from which all good comes.

Put in another way: he has learned to endure pain with self-control in order to receive, but while the pain endures within him, the receiving stops. Neither his father nor the group of which his father is a member has much to give to him, and though he seek and seek and seek he will not be able to receive enough to assure himself that the self-control has meaning. The early pain remains an isolated individual experience, whose only meaning is that he is not valued. The opportunity to re-experience that pain on behalf of his group, thereby sanctifying it and making it a bond of integration, no longer exists. So he fails to find meanings in life; life is forever incomplete. What he will retain from his pain is an unconscious angry desire to retaliate on someone or something in the world that has caused him such pain.

Some Sioux still seek meaning in traditional religious belief or rituals or variants of them. Almost all Indians on the reservations except a few elderly ones consider themselves members of a Christian denomination; Christianity does after all provide an explanation of pain. However, it is not one that fits the Sioux experience, for the early experience of the Sioux individual does not give him a sense of sin. So the Sioux also cling to other religious beliefs. They still believe in the supernatural power of medicine men and resort to them when modern medicine fails, or seek revelations from the priests of the Yuwipi cult, who perform feats of magic and divination while in a trance. Some induce visions by partaking of the mescaline of the peyote cactus; at night the peyote drums of the Native American Church can sometimes be heard. And in the summer of 1960 and again in 1961, an eyewitness informed me, Indians of various reservations gathered again in a pallid version of the old Sun Dance. Braves danced the old dances routinely, as they are apt to dance other dances in high school cheerleader fashion at political gatherings. And while assembled tribesmen looked on, perhaps more in curiosity than out of faith, a few men bared their breasts, thrust skewers through the flesh in the traditional fashion though probably not so deeply, bound thongs to the ends of the skewers and to a pole, and, facing the sun, danced an imitation of the old ritual dance and drew back until the skewers tore through the flesh. No ecstasy was aroused; apparently life has moved too far for this ceremony to seem meaningful. After all, what is it that Wakan

Tanka will now give even if the purity and worthiness of the tribe or at least the individuals have been proved?

Similarly, while the child accedes to some demands on him by the group of his peers, there is no mutuality in life to justify his submission to the group. So, I suggest, he feels an angry and ever-unsatisfied demand that the group shall compensate him, and an angry and unsatisfied demand that none of those who insisted on leveling him shall become better than he. And so sharing, which used to be an automatic, pleasurable, prestige-giving recognition of the mutuality of the group initiated by the individual with goods to share, has become coercive demand by those who will be the receivers. What was mutual support has become exploitation.

An individual with steady income finds that all of his relatives and his wife's come to live with him. One individual with a college education who obtained a relatively well-paying position at the agency of the Bureau of Indian Affairs resigned after a time and returned to poverty in the tribe; he could neither afford financially to support the relatives who came to live with him nor endure the censure of refusing them. Young men and women and even married couples with children will come to stay with elderly relatives living on old-age pensions, remaining as long as supplies last, then leaving the old people to fend for themselves until the next monthly check arrives. An old man came home from the hospital where his wife had died to find his home stripped of all its contents. Neighbors and relatives had taken it upon themselves to anticipate the traditional expression of grief in which the individual divested himself of all earthly possessions.

Models in the Non-Indian Society

Insofar as the child holds his values in abeyance, a possible course of action in his search for models of a satisfying role in life is to turn in adolescence to models in the non-Indian society outside his reservation. One must be careful, however, in making reference to holding one's values in abeyance; this is a phenomenon that can occur only in limited degree. A child with certain values and with a fairly high degree of need autonomy and need achievement, and lacking good models in childhood of how to proceed as an adult, may hold in abeyance his concepts of how to proceed and may seize upon effective models that he encounters only in adolescence or even later. But to hold values in abeyance is a different matter. A child will always react to the sources of love and power near him in his early life. The Sioux child on the reservation learns that he is individually inadequate and receives goodness from above. He learns anxiety at competing with other individuals and at excluding others from sharing goods he has obtained. He learns suspicion of persons outside his group, and aversion to manual-technical labor. These tendencies do not give him happiness, for he can find no way of life in which they function well. Yet he can identify with the values of white Americans only at the cost of lifelong tension between these tendencies and the conflicting requirements of the white American society.

The tension will be the greater because in addition to his conflicting earlier tendencies there is a further barrier to accepting white values wholeheartedly. The whites show a degree of contempt for the Sioux, and by accepting white valuations of the world the Sioux will be granting credence to the charge of his own intrinsic worthlessness. I have discussed this mechanism earlier and need not repeat the discussion here.

This tendency is much less extreme than the parallel tendency in most colonial societies. For the Indian will learn as he grows that Indians have advanced to respected positions in the larger American society; there is no absolute derogation of Indians. Yet he has learned in the tales told to him when he was small of the white man's destruction of the Sioux economy and disruption of Sioux religious life. And in the stories he hears of the current relationships of fellow Sioux to the Bureau of Indian Affairs officials, the people of the neighboring towns in South Dakota and Nebraska, and the farmers who hire Indians for summer work, he recognizes contempt for Indians. Hence even though this barrier to the adoption of white American values is not absolute it is powerful.

Faced with these grim choices, each child as he grows up must decide what he will be. More often than not, he makes the choice in late adolescence, and more often than not his choice is to fall back into the hopeless unreality of the disrupted Sioux culture.

The head of a mission school on the Rosebud reservation said to us in effect: "The children come here, and in the lower grades they gradually unfold and bloom and do well. Then in high school, something happens. Many of them somehow seem to shrivel and fade away; they go back to their homes, and I hear nothing more of them." A man sensitive to human needs, he was puzzled and a little saddened at a disappointing phenomenon he did not understand and could not prevent.

What had happened was that the adolescents had decided to remain Sioux and to withdraw into the disorganized life within the tribe. The extended kinship group even as it survives today provides the individual with a modicum of protection and support, a sense of an identity that is his by right of birth. This is a precious commodity for an individual as torn by conflicting values and drives as is the Sioux. Yet the individual must recognize that the tribal community is a demoralized demiworld; that he chooses it testifies to the terrors of the alternatives which seem open.

About one half of the men and women who make the opposite choice in adolescence or later and go to city jobs under the government-aided program return to the reservations, some of them after an interval of several years. Bureau of Indian Affairs officials think that many of the young men and women who have entered a vocational training program that was begun in 1958 have done so experimentally and will return to the reservations. In view of the tensions which undoubtedly prey on these individuals, it is no wonder that many of them succumb to alcoholism and many others simply give up and return to reservation life.

No Sioux child of the last few decades, it may reasonably be assumed, has escaped rather severe inner conflict of the sort described. Mac-Gregor has sketched the personalities of a sample of children from Pine Ridge.[18] None of them was a happy child. Artichoker and Palmer studied the problems of a number of Sioux students in South Dakota colleges.[19] Their report portrays the usual problems of college students with inadequate funds, but it also portrays something additional. Virtually all of the Sioux students showed a deep sense of being inadequate. They blamed it on their lack of funds, inadequate preparation, limited background. These inadequacies are real enough, but the pervasiveness of the feeling suggests a deeper source. These Sioux boys and girls who go to college are unusually driven and determined individuals. Some of them will go on to overtly successful lives in non-Indian communities, but they will probably do so at the cost of a lifelong feeling of quiet desperation.

The individual who retreats into the reservation must make his choice with despair also, for he knows the limited horizon of the life he has chosen. Nothing he can do can give meaning to the impulses bred into him early in life, can give satisfying answers to the insistent questions that his early experience of pain and compulsion raised. And so one common solution is to reject goals. Like individuals everywhere who face a parallel problem, he becomes retreatist. It seems dangerous to strive for even the smallest goal. Buildings decay and are not repaired; a hydrant breaks and is not replaced; a playground gradually falls into decay. Life is benumbed, and it seems to a visitor as though a historical burden arrests life.

But here as everywhere, underneath the apathy is rage. Life has taught the individual no sanctioned channel for rage except the occasional and pallid one of coercing fortunate fellows to share their goods, but it has indicated almost everyone around him as the source of some pain or frustration. So his hostility and aggression turn on his family, surrogates for the parents and peers who let him down; on his neighbors, who failed to fulfill the early promise of group mutuality; on the members of other bands, whom his forbears always regarded as unsafe to live with in close quarter, and with whom he no longer has a religious union.[20] The

---

[18] In *Warriors Without Weapons*.

[19] John Artichoker, Jr., and Neil M. Palmer, *The Sioux Indian Goes to College* (Vermillion, S.D.: Institute of Indian Studies and State Department of Public Instruction, March, 1959).

[20] The boys have learned to be aggressive sexually as well as otherwise. The girls, however, no longer learn the need to circumscribe their conduct rigidly. The cohesive band that held the girl unqualifiedly responsible for any sexual misadventure under penalty of ostracism is gone. In adolescence the girls see instead the freedom of dress and social life of girls in the non-Indian society around them, and many of them imitate it. But boys see that freedom as an invitation. Moreover, in their child-

reservation is divided into hostile and suspicious groups unable to unite in a common purpose.

There is no conspicuous identification with the aggressor, as there might be expected to be in the circumstances. Perhaps this is because the traditional Dakota culture is such that even under the pressures of reservation life parents do not behave in the home in a way that would arouse this defense. If it is not learned in childhood, it will not be used in adulthood. On the other hand, perhaps some individuals who quietly assent to Bureau of Indian Affairs policies are practicing identification with the aggressors in a way too unobtrusive to be noticed, and perhaps many individuals who migrate to cities and attempt to hold industrial jobs are doing so. One could settle the question only with considerable research.

Pending such research, I suggest that identification with the aggressor is probably rare, and that present-day Dakota childhood plus the nature of later life tend instead to induce another type of defense mechanism, one that may not be found anywhere else in as intense degree as among the American Indians.

In traditional Sioux life the individual, having learned stoic self-control, found justification for it in the good life which, as he saw it, the power above and around him gave him. Now he suffers pain in infancy with self-control in order to receive nurturance, and throughout his life he searches for its justification. The overwhelming power over and around him is now that of the white man or specifically the Bureau of Indian Affairs. And so, unconsciously, he seeks desperately to be given and given and given by this power, in the forever disappointed hope that being given enough will permit him to believe that his pain is justified and he will gain peace. He endures misery now as he endured pain to prove to the all-powerful Wakan Tanka the worthiness of his tribe to receive grace. His early pain and his adult misery are justified only insofar as through them he has gained a right to sustenance and support. And so, as Erikson says, "He is now comparable to what in psychiatry is called a 'compensation neurotic'; he receives all his sense of security and identity out of the status of one to whom something is owed. Yet it must be suspected that even if the millions of buffaloes and the gold taken from the Black Hills could be returned, the Sioux would not be able to forget the habits of dependence or manage to create a community adapted to the present-day world. . . ."[21] Mutuality with his group, the ability to interpret his pain as being on behalf of his group, and the ability to find a group against whom the venting of his rage was socially sanctioned—these

---

hood Sioux girls saw their functionless fathers quarreling with their mothers and no doubt longed for greater male strength and nurturance, a longing that in adolescence causes them to find satisfaction in yielding to male strength. A combination of cultural and social circumstances more conducive to sexual freedom would be hard to find, and sexual delinquency with its resulting problems is common.

[21] *Childhood and Society*, p. 103.

things and others would still be missing. Each individual's pain would still be a lonely act separating him from his group rather than binding him to it, and life would still be without adequate meaning.

However, it seems to me that Sioux behavior is not fully described by the comparison with compensation neurosis. It goes beyond this. The Sioux in their helplessness have adopted toward the officials who manage their destinies a type of behavior comparable to that termed in psychiatry "hostile dependence." This means that they are hostile and also that they are dependent, but it also means more; it means that they act as if they were using their dependence, the only weapon they have perceived available to them until very recently, as a weapon against the government officials.

This relationship sometimes emerges between a child and a mother who does not give him nurturance responsive to his needs, and refuses to let him act as his developing capacities and his reactions to the world lead him to act. Instead, to satisfy the inadequacies of her own childhood, she swamps him with attention, manages his every act, and refuses to let him do what every child needs to do, give her something in return. Sometimes such a child, in an unconscious attempt to punish his mother, becomes completely passive in externals and incapable of helping himself—learns to walk and to speak late and slowly, cannot feed himself, cannot learn to spell or to read—so that through his failure to develop his mother will feel her failure and will be punished. Having no other weapon, he makes his dependence one which operates with excruciating keenness against both individuals.

The Sioux seem to act similarly—to act as if by being completely passive, by leaving in the hands of the white society complete responsibility for their problems, they would remind the white of his incapacity to solve the problem he had so arrogantly set out to master. Before the white society for some reason chose to spare them, it first destroyed their life, and now it insists that in every detail of their lives they shall act as the white society thinks best. Their passive hostility in response is as if they were using the one weapon they have to injure an enemy in the only way open to them—co-operating, as it were, in their own paralysis. Every case of economic need, every individual delinquency, is as if intended to make Bureau officials feel a sense of their personal failure, to cause them to feel guilt and defeat. And so it does. The Sioux are gaining the same crippled and crippling success as the dependent child often does.

Such hostile dependency was certainly learned in infancy and early childhood, for a behavior pattern involving such intense emotional conflict within one is certainly not followed in adulthood unless it was learned very early in life as a desperate measure against external pressures that threatened one then. With this clue, it is not difficult to see the circumstances of early life that forced adoption of this defense. The elders do not manage every detail of his behavior, and thereby thwart his development, as does the neurotic mother discussed above, but the circumstances of his life accomplish the same effect: they prevent him from developing as his earliest perceptions of life had taught him to develop, and especially they prevent him from giving in reciprocity for what was early given him. And so, forbidden to develop as he feels he must, and unable to earn security by giving of his talents, he tries to punish his elders, and to force them to give to him what they do not have to give, by being dependent. In adult life his rage need not be sheathed as subtly as in childhood, and the hostility associated with his dependency becomes more obvious in his relationships with his white masters than it was in his relationships with his parents.

Any Sioux presented with this analysis would deny it in bewilderment and probably with indignation, for the Sioux is not conscious of any desire except to improve his lot. These are interpretations not of conscious decisions but of the unconscious forces which determine human behavior. But the passivity of the Sioux, their inability to take the small actions necessary for small but real improvements, and the tension in their rather unreal relationships to Bureau officials cannot be explained except in terms of such unconscious forces. This is why the problem is so baffling and frustrating to Bureau officials in the field. The endless words of discussion of problems and decisions somehow do not get at the causes of behavior. To the writer of this report, the evidence of an emotional state more or less parallel to "hostile dependence" is strong; no other explanation fits all the facts of the case as convincingly.

WHERE NOW?

However, this state did not always exist, nor will it always exist in the future. Change is occurring. Some of it seems for the worse. Over several generations the apathy of the men has deepened. Before World War I they had turned to cattle raising with sufficient vigor to be largely self-supporting. The present apathy could not have existed at that time; it must have appeared or deepened in the intervening decades. On the other hand, as noted above, some Indian mothers on the reservations now take command of the family. I have suggested earlier that if the apathy of men in a traditional society deepens and the nurturance of women increases, creativity may begin to appear out of retreatism. We do not know that Sioux women who dominate the home are nurturant during the child's early years, but some of them may be; if they are, they may be breeding innovational leaders.

The Sioux child who learns initiative from his satisfying experiences with a nurturant mother is handicapped in becoming creative. He lacks models of effective men. But in the tales his mother tells of old-time leaders he may find enough promise so that he rejects the ineffective models immediately around him and a little later in life finds adequate ones in his broader contacts.

Even if he learns a style of effective action in this way, he is not apt to become an individualistic entrepreneur like his white counterpart. For he is a Sioux, in whom have been imprinted Sioux values from his mother's model and the nature of his early training. He is apt to feel a need for mutuality with his group not paralleled by any need his white counterpart acquires; and if he does burst out of the shallows which surround his early life and become creative, he may use his energies not in individual escape into the larger American society but in defying, surmounting, and manipulating the restraining forces of that society for the betterment of his people.

Perhaps some measures of the Rooseveltian New Deal will help him. In the 1930's there was a general review of governmental policy toward the Indians. In Washington high-minded humanitarianism and a desire to transfer initiative to the Indians replaced the authoritarianism which had intervened since the days when Carl Schurz as Secretary of the Interior had recommended the Allocation Act with high hopes. The new humanitarianism was somewhat more enlightened than the old; the social sciences had advanced since Schurz's day. But not enough; social policies still proceeded pretty much by trial and error. Many experiments entered into hopefully on the reservations died out without apparent effects. But two changes were made which may deserve some of the credit for the hopeful bits of change in Indian attitudes that are now appearing. These were establishment of Indian tribal councils and the execution on the reservations of work projects large enough to provide all able-bodied Indians with income through work.

Perhaps the latter created home environments in which it was more likely that less anxious and, in favorable circumstances, even creative children might appear. The establishment of tribal councils provided a vehicle which leaders, if they appeared, might find useful. The Indians put little faith in the councils, just as colonial peoples everywhere expect little from the pseudolegislative bodies which their masters permit them. And indeed, as noted above, the actions of the tribal council at Pine Ridge seem to have little meaning. Yet if leaders appear, here they have useful instruments.

The relationship of Bureau of Indian Affairs field officials to Indian tribes is still paternalistic. Like colonial field services everywhere, that of the Bureau attracts many men with authoritarian personalities. But their personalities have little relevance to the social change going on among the American Indians. Out of retreatism an effective American-Indian type of personality may be arising even while the administrators are trying to control the Indians paternalistically until they shall have become imitation white men.

Indeed, this seems to be happening, not only within the Sioux but in other Indian tribes whose histories are rather parallel. In New York leaders of the Tuscaroras for two years blocked action by the New York State Power Authority to condemn tribal lands for use in the Niagara Falls power project, and, though ultimately defeated by a United States Supreme Court decision, obtained a settlement much better than Robert Moses had first offered. In the process no doubt they set before thousands of young Indians new models of possible initiative.

In northern South Dakota Frank Ducheneaux and Anthony Rivers, successive chairmen of the tribal council of the Cheyenne River Sioux reservation, acting for the tribal council, have obtained generous compensation for land flooding, defeated a move to divide the money among tribal members, and used it to establish tribal members in ranching projects and various small businesses. The tribe itself, acting as a business enterprise, is providing improved public utility services. It is too early to note the degree of success, but it is not too early to note that the individual leadership is of a quality not found until recently among reservation Indians.

On the Rosebud reservation tribal council chairman Robert Burnette, aided by council secretary Cato Valandra, has provided impressive entrepreneurship. Under his leadership the tribe has begun a ranching enterprise. Some small improvements along the shores of reservation streams and ponds have been made to attract tourists. Burnette obtained from private sources gifts which made possible the purchase of a nucleus herd of cattle, free bus service for reservation residents among the reservation towns, and ambulance service to the central hospital.

These are only conspicuous examples of the new leadership. Probably less well known ones exist elsewhere. In each of these the actions were for tribal benefit, not individual gain. In each they used the tribal council as a vehicle to surmount divisions within the tribe and obtain tribal agreement and support. And they operated not through the Bureau of Indian Affairs but around it and beyond it. Perhaps it would be suggestive to state that they recognized the Bureau as an enemy and defeated it by associating themselves with a higher power.

There has existed since the 1930's a national pan-Indian movement. Annually the National Congress of American Indians holds a meeting of representatives of all United States tribes. In the past this Congress, like the political rally at Pine Ridge, has beeen a forum for grandiose statements on large and diffuse issues. The reality of national unity and effectiveness is still to be built. But the younger leaders, impatient of the mouthings of the past, are using the organization to come together in more earthy and useful discussions. It is reasonable to suppose that American Indians are at the beginning of a transition from retreatism to effective innovation and that the tribes will emerge, preserving their ethnic identities, as vigorous and productive units within the larger American society. If they do, their success on their own terms will probably lessen, not increase, the barriers which keep individual Indians from merging in the larger society, and a long process of amalgamation may go forward. If such a trend is in fact emerging, the number of effective leaders will probably increase until by a generation from now, or say in 1980–90, a process of social and economic innovation that has uniquely Indian aspects will be in full swing.

CONCLUDING GENERALIZATIONS

The case of the Sioux, with its suggestion that the child is troubled both by contradictory experiences in early life and by inconsistency between his early experience and his later life, provides richer detail concerning the causes of retreatism than do the other cases studied. The case of the Sioux also raises the question whether retreatism always contains an element of compensation neurosis or hostile dependency. It seems doubtful that this is necessarily the case, but the possibility should not be ruled out.

The alternative explanation of the presence of compensation neurosis and hostile dependency in the Sioux case seems more plausible. The experience of the Sioux suggests that the appearance of identification with the aggressor depends not only on the harshness of the derogation of the parents but also on the specific features of the previous culture. Even under extreme derogation Sioux parents probably do not behave in the home in such a way as to cause identification with the aggressor by their children. They do, however, behave in such a way as to cause compensation neurosis and hostile dependency, and these reappear in more extreme form in adulthood. If this analysis is correct, it suggests that the one effect may tend to appear generally when extreme derogation presses on a traditional society of a hunting-fighting type and the other when it presses on a traditional society of an agricultural type. This generalization might be tested by determining whether the religions and the early childhood environment of other hunting-fighting societies are parallel in relevant ways to that of the Sioux.

It is possible to draw some broader generalizations tentatively. The Sioux have not completed a transition from traditionalism through retreatism to innovation. If, however, we project their social development boldly, and assume, as has been done in the preceding section, that by a generation from now a stream of innovation will be in full course among them, we shall conclude that the general pattern of change is the same regardless of the economic base or precise cultural characteristics of the traditional society involved.

We may conclude also that the continuance of a colonial situation does not impose absolute psychological barriers to innovation. That is, innovation may appear before the colonial masters leave. However, judging by the first few examples of conspicuous innovation among the American Indians, it will always be of a type directed against or designed to circumvent the colonial masters rather than an imitation of their behavior.

Lastly, perhaps the experience of the Sioux considered in relation to that of other societies gives us a clearer idea of the likely, if not the necessary, time span involved in the transition from traditionalism through retreatism to innovation and also of one of the forces that may determine the time span.

In the abstract, it might seem that the entire process could occur in four generations or say a century. Two generations may be the minimum time for the emergence of retreatism; the values of the adults from whom status respect is initially withdrawn are too sharp and strong for their children to become fully retreatist. Anxiety by a daughter of the third generation at the weakness of her retreatist father may make her a nurturant mother in the fourth, and in that generation nurturance in the mother plus retreatism in the father may inculcate creative personality in the children. To determine whether in fact the likely minimum is this or somewhat more than this requires, it seems to me, both further theoretical analysis and added empirical study.

The period in the Sioux case is closer to this minimum than in others studied. The earliest date that may reasonably be taken as marking the beginning of the breakdown of traditional Sioux society is a date soon after 1800, when trading had assumed importance. If innovation appears among the Sioux in a considerable stream in another 25 years, then the elapsed period will have been about 175 years. In Colombia the comparable time was 400 years or slightly less, in Russia some 300 years.[20] Perhaps we may conclude that the period will be the shorter the more intense the pressures that impinge on the traditional society. For the pressures in Colombia were not great, since the various geographic regions were not in close contact, and the pressures in Russia were more intense, though not nearly so intense as those on the Sioux from 1850 on. Possibly the abrupt imposition of intense pressure, as in some areas in Africa, may cause the entire period of transition to be even shorter than it may be for the Sioux. Whether this is true will interest social scientists during coming decades.

The speed of transition from traditionalism through retreatism to innovation depends also on other factors. Important among them are whether the society was fully traditional before withdrawal of expected status occurred, the size of the group on which withdrawal of expected status im-

---

[20] The cases of England and Japan are ones of less extreme psychological pressure and progressive alteration in the traditional social structure over eight centuries or more. No period comparable to those in Colombia, Russia, or the Sioux society can be identified. In the case of migrants to an alien society, for example, immigrants to the United States, the period may be much shorter than in the case of the Sioux. Application of the hypotheses presented in this volume to the immigrant case might be illuminating.

pinged, its position in the society, and what channels of action and models of behavior were open to its members in successive generations. The hypotheses presented in this volume do not provide a guide to the speed of the transition in the societies of the world which are now traditional, or those in which traditionalism has recently been disrupted, for it does not incorporate estimates of the relative importance of these factors.

It does, however, suggest that a transition will occur in all these societies, that is, in all of the societies which are now termed underdeveloped. For in all such societies, whether or not they have been colonial, the events of modern history have caused withdrawal of expected status from the lesser elite and the simple folk. We may therefore expect that the transition to economic growth and a new political structure will occur, even though we cannot yet forecast its speed.

Appendixes

Analytical Models in the Study of Social Systems[1]

appendix I

As judged by the history of the physical, biological, and social sciences, study in any field is apt to begin with a none-too-ordered description of phenomena in the field, followed by a cataloguing of them on bases that seem to make sense. As understanding grows, the systems of classification become more closely related to the functioning of interacting elements. Gradually, generalizations about functioning are reached which are useful in predicting future events. As the generalizations gain rigor, they take the form of analytical models of the behavior of the elements being studied. An analytical model is a mental construct consisting of a set of elements in interrelation, the elements and their interrelations being precisely defined.

The first stage in the analysis of functioning is usually study of processes at narrowly defined points within the general area of the science. Attention is focused on how the elements at the point being examined would function in the absence of change elsewhere. Then a mental model of the processes at this point is formed, which is a simplification of reality that retains only the features essential for predicting similar processes elsewhere. Such analysis of a narrowly defined point in a system may be termed "partial analysis."

Later comes the development of more comprehensive analytical models, which in some sense encompass a complete system rather than simply one point in relationships. Such a model is termed a "general system" or "analytical model"; its construction and use are "general analysis" or "system analysis." There is no sharp distinction between partial and general models, for analysis of a general system also holds in abeyance change beyond certain boundaries. As a science is able to move to more and more comprehensive systemic analysis, its power increases greatly.

In the evolution of theory, concepts found useful at various stages are later discarded as analysis grows in rigor. In the study of social systems, many early concepts, for example, those which reified society, have been sloughed off. But certain concepts and methodologies remain which are incompatible with rigorous analysis of causal relationships.

LOGICAL REQUIREMENTS OF GENERAL SYSTEM ANALYSIS

The following requirements of general system analysis are of most interest here:

---

[1] This Appendix reproduces with slight adaptation an article bearing the same title published in the *American Journal of Sociology*, Vol. XLVII, No. 2 (September, 1961); copyright 1961 by the University of Chicago. I am grateful to Robert Solow for comments on the first draft.

1. An analytical model is defined by defining the elements and their interrelations.[2] The relationships among the elements of a system are statements of the alternative values (magnitudes) or states of one of the elements associated with alternative values or states of one or more of the other elements. Because the elements are assumed to vary in magnitude or state, they are termed variables—which, broadly, includes constants—that is, the variation in some may be zero. If two variables are related in this way, each is said to be a function of the other without regard to the direction of causation between them. While the flow of causation between any two elements may be in one direction and not the other, among all of the elements taken as a group, apart from the impact of forces from outside the system, all depend on all. Let it be noted clearly that this concept of mutual interdependence or interaction does not involve circular reasoning or indeterminacy.[3]

2. The variables of a system must exist either in conceptually measurable amounts, or in one or another set of definable states. It is impossible to conceive of variation in one element associated with variation in another if the two cannot be conceived of as varying by measurable amounts, or from one state or structural form to another. If a variable (such as "community spirit" or "love of family") is not defined so as to be conceptually measurable or as existing in one or another set of definable states, it cannot have a precise reasoning, in an analytical model or otherwise.

A variable is a single dimension of an entity, not the entity itself. Thus a variable is not a physical body but one of its qualities, for example, length; in a model of society, it is not an individual, but, say, each value and each need (motive) attributed to him and each component of his perception of the nature of the world. The individual as a group of interacting elements may be a subsystem within the model.

3. A system which is interacting with its environment is an open system; all systems of "real life" (concrete systems) are therefore open systems. For analysis, it is necessary to assume in the intellectual construct that the operation of the system is affected only by given conditions previously established by the environment and not changing at the time of analysis, plus the relationships among the elements of the system. This condition is sometimes regarded as identical with the condition that contact with the environment is cut off.[4]

---

[2] Physical scientists refer to a set of elements in interaction as an "analytical system" or simply a "system." They include as systems entities of the real world. I use the term analytical model to emphasize that the concept relevant in theoretical analysis is one of an intellectual construct.

For definitions of systems and discussions of their properties, see the following articles in *General Systems*, Vol. I (1956): Ludwig von Bertalanffy, "General System Theory," pp. 1–10; Kenneth Boulding, "General System Theory—the Skeleton of Science," pp. 11–17, reprinted from *Management Science*, Vol. II (April, 1956), pp. 197–208; and A. D. Hall and R. E. Fagen, "Definition of System," pp. 18–28. See also W. Ross Ashby, "General Systems Theory as a New Discipline," *General Systems*, Vol. III (1958), pp. 1–6; and R. M. Thrall, C. H. Coombs, and R. L. Davis (eds.), *Decision Processes* (New York: John Wiley & Sons, Inc., 1954).

[3] Henderson's mechanical example provides a beautifully simple visual illustration of mutual dependence or interaction: Lawrence J. Henderson, *Pareto's General Sociology* (Cambridge, Mass.: Harvard University Press, 1937), p. 14.

[4] Technically, that there is no exchange of energy in any form, in the broadest definition of the term energy, to include, for example, information. For this reason, Ashby (*loc. cit.*) suggests that instead of being termed "closed," such a system should be termed "energy-tight," "information-tight," or "noise-tight," the last term of course coming from the terminology of the modern study of communication. There has been much discussion among psychologists concerning whether person-

Such a statement, however, is ambiguous. The requirement is merely that the impact of the environment on the system shall not be changing. Thus it may be assumed in a system in physics that pressure is being exerted on the system by the environment, or in a system in economics that demand for goods is being transmitted to the system from the environment. In neither case is there any impediment to rigorous analysis, provided that the pressure or the flow of demand is not changing. I shall define such a system as closed, though some other term might be less subject to misinterpretation.

Elements of the system whose magnitudes are wholly determined by the environment, and which are therefore constant rather than variable so long as the system is insulated from change in the environment, are termed *parameters*. For example, in some analyses in economics the size of the population and per capita income are parameters, that is, it is assumed that they remain constant.

In the process of analysis a closed system is not assumed to remain closed. Only extremely limited analysis is possible except as the theorist opens the system to a change in the environment, and observes its effect. Thus in this volume, the sequence of effects of certain changes in the relationships among groups in a society has been analyzed. The model was opened to permit such a change, and was then closed again.

4. It is often useful to construct a model which is in equilibrium, and in stable rather than unstable equilibrium.

Equilibrium in its simplest sense refers to a condition in which the variables in the system are in such a relationship to each other that all remain constant in value, not by assumption, but by their interaction.

Suppose that some external force that directly affects one variable in the system changes in magnitude temporarily, then reverts to its previous magnitude. The change this temporary disturbance causes in one variable will necessarily cause at least temporary changes in the magnitudes of other variables, because of the functional relationships among them. (If change in one variable affects no other variable, then that one variable is not in any significant sense a part of the system.) These changes will in turn react on the magnitudes of the variable which first changed, and on each other. The equilibrium of the system is stable if the final result of this interaction is a return to the initial values. The equilibrium is unstable if a temporary disturbance causes the values of some or all variables to move cumulatively farther from the initial equilibrium.

The equilibrium of a system may, of course, be stable with respect to one type of disturbance and not with respect to another. Further, the equilibrium of a system may be stable with respect to a small disturbance ("stability in the small") but not with respect to a large disturbance ("stability in the large"). Stability of equilibrium, moreover, implies only that the equilibrium values of the variables will remain unchanged as long as the system remains closed except for temporary "disturbances." If permanent changes in the environment are communicated to the system, there will be corresponding permanent changes in the equilibrium values of variables in the system (that is, the values they will have when the system has settled down into the new equilibrium), even though the equilibrium is stable.

---

ality should be analyzed as a closed or open system. See, for example, Gordon W. Allport, "The Open System in Personality Theory," *Journal of Abnormal and Social Psychology*, Vol. LXI (November, 1960), pp. 301–10. Allport refers to many previous publications. This controversy relates in part to the question whether the system need be closed in the sense defined by Ashby (it need not, as the text indicates), and in part to the nature of the relationship between personality and the environment, and not to the question of method discussed in this paragraph, which is not subject to controversy.

To illustrate equilibrium and related concepts, suppose that deposits in a certain commercial bank are at a "normal" level, and a rumor that the bank is unsafe (a "disturbance") arises. The rumor causes a few depositors to withdraw their money (a movement away from equilibrium). If the total network of circumstances is such that the withdrawals do not lead to a spread of anxiety, but instead the outflow stops, and the funds are redeposited, then by definition the equilibrium was stable; if the initial withdrawals cause a run on the bank so that it fails, the equilibrium was unstable. The bank's equilibrium might be stable with respect to a rumor that a nearby bank was about to close, but not with respect to the unexplained disappearance of the cashier.

The stability of equilibrium is caused not alone by (*a*) the degree of confidence depositors had in the bank, nor by (*b*) the magnitude of the net demand for withdrawals by depositors, nor by (*c*) the ability and willingness of the bank to supply funds taken, but by the interrelationships among the three: the magnitude of rise in net demand for withdrawals caused by a given decrease in confidence; the ability of the bank to supply an increase of this magnitude in the demand for funds, and the seeming lack of concern with which it does so; the effect of withdrawals of this magnitude in causing further decline in confidence; and the effect of the bank's readiness to supply funds (and the attitude of its officers) in increasing confidence.

Suppose total income in the community increased because of the opening of a new factory. With this change in one of the parameters, deposits in the bank may be expected to rise to a new higher level, at which their value will be in a new stable equilibrium.

Comparison of the equilibrium positions of the variables of a model under two differing values of one or more of the parameters—in the example above, comparison of the level of bank deposits at the two different levels of income—is termed *comparative statics* in economics. There is no comparable term in the other social sciences.

If one or more of the parameters of a system goes through a process of continuing change—for example, if total income in the community steadily increases—the values of the variables at which they are in equilibrium may be expected to change continuously. We may then refer to a "moving equilibrium."

It is especially important, in the application of models to the study of societies, to note that the presence or absence of equilibrium in a system and the stability or instability of equilibrium are results of the interrelationships among the variables. Equilibrium or its absence, and its stability or instability, cannot be caused by the nature of one variable considered without relation to the others. If we knew the interrelationships accurately we could tell in advance whether equilibrium would be restored after a given temporary disturbance. Stability of equilibrium is not merely an *ex post facto* fact.

5. It may also be fruitful to study a system which is not in equilibrium.

Often we are concerned only with the conditions for equilibrium. We may solve a set of equations to determine the value each variable will have in equilibrium. But we may also be interested in a sequence of change, in time, in the values of the variables. A change in the position of one variable has an effect on one or more other variables only after a time interval.[5] For example, a change in birth rates will affect the age composition of the population through-

---

[5] It is sometimes said that, when we consider only the conditions of equilibrium, our analysis is as though the causal effect of change in each variable on each other were instantaneous. This statement may give some "feel" of the nature of analysis of equilibriums, but it is not literally correct. Nothing happens instantaneously, and analysis does not really assume so.

out many generations. A change in the environment in which the children of a group are brought up will affect their personalities as adults only after the lapse of years necessary for them to become adults, and through their impact on their children, will continue to cause alteration in adult personality for generations thereafter.[6]

A new equilibrium will be reached only after a time interval.

In contrast to comparative statics, analysis may be made of the path of change of the several variables of the system (presumably from one equilibrium to another) when a change in a parameter occurs. Such analysis is termed "dynamics," and a model whose process of change is being analyzed is said to be a dynamic model. The term "diachronic analysis" in anthropology is apparently identical in meaning with dynamic analysis.

It is unfortunate that the terms *dynamic* and *dynamics* are used in this sense with reference to analytical models and in quite a different sense in contemporary psychology. Both usages are so well entrenched that they must be lived with. Freudian psychology introduced, or gave increased emphasis to, two elements in psychological theory. One was the study of the formation of personality, that is, change in personality. This is a study of "personality dynamics" in a sense precisely analogous to that in which the term "dynamics" is used above; hence, the terms "personality dynamics" and "dynamic psychology" came to be applied. The other new element was emphasis on unconscious motivation. These two new elements appeared at once, and by terminological inaccuracy, "dynamic" became a synonym for "motivational." Thus the terms "personality structure" and "personality dynamics" are sometimes used interchangeably, and the term "personality dynamics" is also used to refer to the study of the influences which cause a person to behave as he does.

Sociology has taken over, somewhat out of context, this extension of psychological terminology. Parsons, for example, frequently refers to dynamic factors or processes in any social system, including one which is in stationary equilibrium. And, on the other hand, sociology has no technical terms for the distinction between a social system in equilibrium and one in movement not in equilibrium. Parsons discusses such movement; he entitles the relevant chapter of *The Social System* simply "The Processes of Change in Social Systems."[7]

6. When the system moves to a new position of equilibrium, not all the variables necessarily change in value. The interrelationships of the system may be such that, in spite of permanent change in one or more parameters, some of the variables, after being temporarily disturbed, will return to their initial magnitudes. This is the condition termed "homeostasis"; it is usually illustrated by organic or mechanical examples. If the temperature in the environment of an organism falls, the fall will cause heat to drain more rapidly from the organism, which, in turn, will activate a mechanism which will increase the body's generation of heat, so that unless the fall in external temperature is too great, the temperature of the organism, after a temporary fall, returns to normal.

Homeostasis (or an analogue, if it is preferred to reserve the term for reference to biological or mechanical cases) may also be illustrated by an example from economics. Suppose that in a certain city, the price charged for putting

---

[6] We select a length of time in which we assume one step of change occurs and treat this as the unit time period. Where the value of a variable is determined by values of other variables in past periods, and not by the values of other variables in the same time period, the value of the variable is said to be "predetermined," and the variable is said to be a "predetermined variable."

[7] Talcott Parsons, *The Social System* (Glencoe, Ill.: Free Press of Glencoe, Inc., 1951).

new rubber heels on a pair of shoes is 75 cents. Suppose that the city now grows rapidly; because shoe-repair shops find themselves flooded with business, they can and do obtain 90 cents for putting new rubber heels on shoes, and obtain similarly increased prices for other shoe repairing. The increased profit margin, however, draws more artisans into the shoe-repair business, so that after a time the supply of these services increases so much that it is no longer possible to obtain more than 75 cents for putting on heels. The new equilibrium of the price of equipping a pair of shoes with rubber heels is the same as the old: a "negative feedback mechanism" has restored the former price.

Note, however, that one variable (the body temperature or the price for supplying a pair of rubber heels) could return to its old value only if another one (the bodily consumption of energy and generation of heat, or the quantity of shoe-repair services available) changed permanently in magnitude. This is an aspect of homeostasis sometimes overlooked. Homeostasis with respect to one variable necessarily implies an altered position of another—"heterostasis"— for as long a period as the changed external condition that brought the homeostatic mechanism into play prevails.[8]

CONCEPTS AND METHODOLOGY

It will be obvious that these requirements of analytical models are necessary characteristics of the interrelationships within any set of variables in any field. Hence concepts concerning society which contradict them are either logically mistaken or, at best, not useful. Concepts which either contradict the logical requirements or, at best, are ambiguous are found, however, in the writings not merely of lesser students but of some of the most creative and influential of recent theorists.

Some of these errors or instances of imprecise formulation of concepts may have arisen originally from a state of mind characteristic of the early stages of anthropology and sociology, social constancy being regarded as good, and social change (perhaps because it created tensions, or because it was imposed, willy-nilly, from without), as bad. Some may have arisen from concentration on social structure rather than on social processes. Perhaps the explanation of their persistence is that the study of societies has not yet fully reached the stage of precise definition of variables. In any event, the social sciences are now moving toward greater precision in the definition of variables, analysis of functional relationships, and creation of models, and in this transitional phase it may be useful to call attention to some concepts that seem obsolescent.

1. In much sociological writing, the concept of society is viewed as necessarily involving stable equilibrium (either static or moving). Thus in *Toward a General Theory of Action*, Parsons writes, with Shils:

"The most general and fundamental property of a system is the interdependence of parts or variables. Interdependence consists in the existence of determinate relationships among the parts or variables as contrasted with randomness of variability. In other words, interdependence is *order* in the relationship among the components which enter into a system. This order must have a tendency to self-maintenance, which is very generally expressed in the concept of equilibrium. That is, if the system is to be permanent enough to be worth study, there must be a tendency to maintenance of order except under exceptional circumstances. It need not, however, be a static self-maintenance or a

---

[8] The term "heterostasis" is from R. C. Davis, "The Domain of Homeostasis," *Psychological Review*, Vol. LXV (January, 1958), pp. 8–13.

stable equilibrium. It may be an ordered process of change—a process following a determinate pattern rather than random variability relative to the starting point. This is called a moving equilibrium and is well exemplified by growth. Furthermore, equilibrium, even when stable, by no means implies that process is not going on; process is continual even in stable systems, the stabilities residing in the interrelations involved in the process."[9]

Note that the word "stable" here is used to refer to static as distinguished from moving equilibrium, and not to stable equilibrium in the sense in which the term is defined above. Parsons presents a similar formulation, though one which may be interpreted as presenting stable equilibrium as a basis for Parsons' work rather than as a general theoretical requirement, in *The Social System* (see p. 481).

In this statement, it is not entirely clear whether the reference to moving equilibrium is to that concept as defined above (continuing shift in equilibrium caused by continuing change in an exogenous force) or to a dynamic process (change in time in the values of variables in the system caused by the relationships within the system). However, in the latter case the statement is tautologous, and means merely, "Do not study a system unless it is a system," for the only possible states of a system are equilibrium and dynamic. Hence, and because his own analytical models are purely static,[10] I conclude that Parsons is warning against formulation of models not in equilibrium.

Related is the implication in the use of the terms "function" and "dysfunction" by Merton that tendency toward equilibrium is somehow good and toward disequilibrium somehow bad. In using the terms "eufunctional" and "dysfunctional," Levy explicitly disavows this connotation.[11]

Parsons does not assert, it should be noted, that a society necessarily possesses stable equilibrium, but only that it is not worth studying unless it does. The restriction is thus logically permissible. It also has empirical relevance. Some societies certainly have had a tendency toward stability of equilibrium; their internal dynamics have at best brought rather slow change. But adherence to this model as the general case unnecessarily limits the domain of sociological theory, and excludes from sociological theory important problems that ought to be treated within it. First, it tends to exclude from the theoretical system consideration of what kind of force is necessary (and sufficient) to push the society away from the equilibrium and lead to the disruption of the social system. Second, it excludes study of the relationships within the society which will determine the nature of the sequence of change in time, once the equilibrium has been disturbed—or the nature of a sequence of change in time in a society conceived of as never having been in equilibrium, but rather under continuing change from its own dynamics. Virtually all societies in the world at present are in a process of change which, however it began, is best analyzed as continuing partly by virtue of the dynamics within the system itself. A model of stable equilibrium is not a satisfactory theoretical analogue for use in study-

[9] Talcott Parsons and Edward A. Shils (eds.), *Toward a General Theory of Action* (Cambridge, Mass.: Harvard University Press, 1954), p. 107.

[10] Parsons discusses social change, not only in specific "empirical" discussions, but more generally in chap. xi of *The Social System*, and in chap. vii of Parsons and Bales, *Family, Socialization, and Interaction Process* (Glencoe, Ill.: Free Press of Glencoe, Inc., 1954), but in each case this discussion is an addendum, not a part of the analytical system which he presents in *The Social System* and in *Toward a General Theory of Action*.

[11] Robert K. Merton, *Social Theory and Social Structure* (rev. ed.; Glencoe, Ill.: Free Press of Glencoe, Inc., 1957), p. 51; Marion J. Levy, Jr., *The Structure of Society* (Princeton, N.J.: Princeton University Press, 1952), pp. 76–78.

ing their behavior. If sociologists are to analyze change in a society as a whole, rather than merely to describe it loosely, they must go beyond models in equilibrium and construct models involving dynamic processes.

Further, even with regard to a society—or a model—in stable equilibrium, or changing only very slowly, study of the relationships that bring about the stability or quasi-stability may be extremely fruitful. It is illuminating to isolate the network of relationships which, if a temporary disturbance brings change within a society, determines whether the change will be cumulative or whether the system will return to the initial equilibrium. Out of studying precisely this question great advances in the understanding of societies, even of societies in stable equilibrium, may come.

2. Perhaps underlying these difficulties are undesirably vague definitions of "function." The question of the meaning of the concept has been much speculated upon since Radcliffe-Brown's essay of 1935,[12] yet in 1954 Parsons had not yet arrived at a precise meaning. Referring to testing the significance of processes, he states "That test of significance takes the form of the 'functional' relevance of the process. The test is to ask the question, what would be the differential consequences for the system of two or more alternative outcomes of a dynamic process."[13]

And in 1957, Merton defined function as "the observed consequences" of "a sociological item" for "the social or cultural system in which it is implicated,"[14] a statement which in addition to being vague suggests that the nature of a single "item" can lead to stability or instability.[15]

These statements are not incorrect, only vague. In them precisely what does the word "consequences" refer to?

These writers have made great contributions to sociological theory, as Radcliffe-Brown did to anthropology. It implies no lack of appreciation of their work to suggest that, in the most fruitful usage, only a quality can be a variable; only a variable has a functional relationship; a functional relationship consists of the change in the magnitude (or state) of one variable (not in a

---

[12] A. R. Radcliffe-Brown, "On the Concept of Function in Social Science," *American Anthropologist*, Vol. XXXVII (1935), reprinted in his *Structure and Function in Primitive Society: Essays and Addresses* (Glencoe, Ill.: Free Press of Glencoe, Inc., 1952).

[13] *The Social System*, pp. 21–22. The term "dynamic" here does not refer to change in the equilibrium of the system, but to a process of action by an individual or a group in a role. In neither *The Social System* nor *Toward a General Theory of Action* does Parsons define "function."

[14] This definition is arrived at by joining phrases from two sentences, on the assumption that "function" and "dysfunction" as contrasting concepts are subcategories of the general concept "function":

"We have observed two prevailing types of confusion enveloping several current conceptions of 'function':

"(1) The tendency to confine sociological observations to the *positive* contributions of a sociological item to the social or cultural system in which it is implicated; . . .

(2) . . . "Functions are those observed consequences which make for the adaptation or adjustment of a given system; and dysfunctions, those observed consequences which lessen the adaptation or adjustment of the system." *Social Theory and Social Structure*, p. 51.

[15] Levy avoids this error by noting that adaptation of a unit *to its setting* is involved. *The Structure of Society*, pp. 76–83. However, his discussion of eufunctional and dysfunctional tendencies would be clearer and more efficient if he abandoned the viewpoint of one unit altogether and referred to the set of relationships among the variables as eufunctional or dysfunctional.

system) associated with change in the magnitude (or state) of another; and no single variable, but only the entire set of functional relationships among the variables of a system can lead to stability (adaptation, adjustment) or instability in the system.

It follows, of course, that these writers do not present a model of a system, for to do so is impossible without a precise statement of the functional relationships in the system. They have presented insightful observations concerning the behavior of some segment of a social system, or useful classifications of various characteristics of a social system. By doing so they have prepared the way for the next step, the analysis of societies as systems.

George C. Homans' 1950 volume, *The Human Group* (New York: Harcourt, Brace & Co.) is a path-breaking scholarly application of system analysis to the theory of societies. Homans failed to arrive at a complete and adequate system simply because he was not able to derive from his information all of the necessary functional relationships, especially not those relating to the behavior of the system through time. Writers following him have likewise not been entirely successful.

Though system analysis is used more in psychological theory than in that relating to societies or communities as wholes[16] failure to state theory relating to social systems in terms of variables, functions, and a general system has not been for lack of sophistication. Rather, the difficulty has been one of substantive complexity. The applicability of functional analysis, in the mathematical sense, in any science does not become apparent to students of that science until they have been able to arrive at a certain precision and breadth of understanding of causal relationships. This is why each discipline slowly and stumblingly rediscovers concepts concerning method already discovered long ago in other disciplines—why, for example, economics clumsily and painfully groped its way to the concept of marginal productivity and only subsequently realized that it was merely applying elementary calculus to its problems; and why anthropologists groped toward the concepts of synchronic and diachronic analysis, and not all anthropologists realize fully even today that they are referring to static and dynamic analysis of an analytical system. Scholars are not apt to realize the applicability of the concepts of variable, function, and general system until they understand functional relationships in their field of study well enough so that their images of the phenomena in their field of analysis begin to resemble variables in interaction.

Freudian and post-Freudian analysis of personality formation has made it possible to formulate plausible and useful models of individual personality and its formation. If we incorporate these subsystems in models of society, it should be possible to formulate useful though heroically simplified models of society in equilibrium and of societal change. In this volume, of course, I have attempted to present such a model.

---

[16] For a recent discussion by a psychologist which takes aim beyond the boundaries of his discipline, see James G. Miller, "Toward a General Theory for the Behavioral Sciences," *American Psychologist*, Vol. X (September, 1955), pp. 513–31, reprinted in Leonard D. White (ed.), *The State of the Social Sciences* (Chicago: University of Chicago Press, 1956).

The Rostovian Schema

appendix II

IN 1960 PROFESSOR ROSTOW'S BOOK, *The Stages of Economic Growth*, appeared.[1] His conception of the stages of economic growth almost immediately captured the attention of laymen throughout the non-Communist world who are concerned with the problem of growth. It was given serious though not generally favorable attention by social scientists as well.[2] It seems desirable to indicate the relationship of his discussion to the analysis presented in this book.

In moving to economic growth, Rostow suggests, any society passes from a traditional stage through four added stages, those of developing the preconditions for take-off, the take-off, the drive to maturity, and high "mass-consumption." This division of the process of growth into five stages is a heroic simplification. This is not a defect, but rather a quality of any fairly general theory. My own models of society and personality involve simplifications no less drastic. In analyzing the Rostovian conceptions I shall inquire not whether they ignore some complexities of reality but whether they are congruent with reality in respects which make them useful for its analysis.

The concept of a succession of stages is useful only if each stage is characterized by a set of empirically testable qualities resulting in processes that lead to the next stage. The initial stage may be one of equilibrium whose qualities do not cause a sequence of change, but then the analyst must indicate what forces break the equilibrium and initiate change. Although any individual quality may be present in more than one stage, the set of qualities characterizing a stage must be unique to it; otherwise the stage is not distinguishable from some other.

A model may be useful even though the qualities which characterize each stage are not measurable at the time the model is constructed. The model

---

[1] W. W. Rostow, *The Stages of Economic Growth* (Cambridge, England: Cambridge University Press, 1960). Rostow also discusses the "take-off" in "The Take-Off into Self-Sustained Growth," *The Economic Journal*, Vol. LXVI, No. 261 (March, 1956). However, since his ideas were obviously developing rapidly (the 1956 article, for example, divides the growth process into only three stages, while the book divides it into five), I shall refer only to the recent book.

[2] Among reviews by economists and economic historians, the following present fairly typical (adverse) analyses:

A. K. Cairncross, "Essays in Bibliography and Criticism. XLV: The Stages of Economic Growth," *Economic History Review*, Vol. III (April, 1961), pp. 450–58.

J. H. Habakkuk, Review in *The Economic Journal*, Vol. LXXI, No. 283 (September, 1961), pp. 601–4.

S. S. Kuznets, "Notes on the Take-Off," a paper presented at the September, 1960, meeting of the International Economic Association.

Goren Ohlin, "Reflections on the Rostow Doctrine," *Economic Development and Cultural Change*, Vol. IX, No. 4 (July, 1961).

builder, analyzing a set of phenomena, may conceive that certain qualities and functional relationships among them must underlie and cause the phenomena, and if the qualities are conceptually measurable the explanatory model may provide illumination even though identification and measurement are not possible until new appropriate instruments have been devised.

With this qualification, a useful model of stages will permit prophecy. While Rostow's characterization of the processes of growth is sometimes metaphorical (the take-off, compound interest, and so on), he identifies specific conditions whose presence or absence can be tested. Undoubtedly one of the causes of the wide popularity of Rostow's book is the perception conveyed by it that there is order in this uncertain world; that once a certain sequence is entered upon, economic growth will follow; that the earnest efforts of men to bring about economic growth will be rewarded and anxieties relieved. Thousands of readers must have gained a feeling of relief from the brilliantly portrayed doctrine of neat and rather rapid stages of progress to economic success.

THE SCHEMA

Rostow identifies a traditional society as one in which methods of production are limited, the view of the world is "pre-Newtonian," a high proportion of productive resources is devoted to agriculture, there is little vertical social mobility, and the value system is fatalistic.

The period of establishment of the preconditions is the period when the idea spreads that economic progress is possible and good, education broadens and changes, new types of enterprising men appear, banks appear, investment increases, especially in transport, communications, and the extraction of raw materials, the scope of commerce widens, and an occasional manufacturing establishment appears. Three changes are of especial importance: creation of an effective national government (a "decisive aspect"), an increase in agricultural productivity, and establishment of a substructure of "social overhead capital."[3]

The period of take-off is the "decisive interval in the history of a society when growth becomes its normal condition" (p. 36), "the interval when the old blocks and resistances to steady growth are finally overcome" (p. 7).[4] All three of the following conditions must occur: a rise in the rate of investment "from, say, 5 per cent of the national income to 10 per cent or more" (p. 39), the development of one or more manufacturing sectors of substantial size with a rapid rate of growth, and the "existence or quick emergence" of a favorable political structure. Income flows into the hands of persons who save and invest a high fraction of it, the economy probably also becomes an attractive place for the investment of foreign capital, the number of entrepreneurs expands, and insofar as they have not done so during the previous stage people become prepared to accept a new way of life.

The pattern of growth of any new industry is one of rapid expansion and then deceleration; this continues to be the pattern throughout later stages. An industry which expands provides stimulus both to industries which provide the capital goods and raw materials it needs (a "backward linkage") and to those which use its new or now cheaper products (a "forward linkage"). Such an industry may be termed a "leading sector."

---

[3] The characteristics of this stage are summarized in *The Stages*, pp. 6–7, and discussed at more length in chap. iii. Concerning "social overhead capital," see my Chapter 3, above.

[4] The take-off is discussed on pp. 7–8 and in chap. iv.

The take-off occurs within "a decade or two" or at least within a "quarter-century" or "several decades." The dates given for nine countries cover periods ranging from 17 to 30 years.[5]

A drive to technological maturity follows the take-off. It occupies about 60 years from the time take-off begins. Maturity is the stage at which an economy has the technological versatility to produce anything it chooses to (though obviously if small in size it may lack the resources).

At some time after it has reached maturity a nation enters upon the age of high mass-consumption (though Canada and Australia are portrayed as reaching high mass-consumption first). An identifying mark of this stage is that durable consumer goods and services become important among the leading sectors. A society which has reached this stage may choose among pursuing external power and influence, the development of a welfare state, and further increase in levels of consumption. Western societies, stressing consumption rather than production, have allocated increased amounts of resources for social welfare and security.

In his discussion of the stages, Rostow notes that in some respects one shades into the next; the lines are perhaps less sharp than is suggested in this summary sketch. The emphasis of his discussion, however, is on contrasting characteristics of the several stages, as of course it must be if the concept of stages is to have meaning.

Obviously Rostow's description of the traditional stage is consistent with the model of traditional society presented here. I shall be concerned primarily with the second and third of his stages, those of developing the preconditions and the take-off, since these relate to the type of social change which is the subject of this volume.

If at one time the techniques in use in a society are constant or little changing, and if at a later time the society is experiencing economic growth, then there must have been a transition from the one state to the other. Hence the concept of a transition is commonplace in discussions of growth. Moreover, there is common agreement that traditional and economically growing societies differ from each other in the ways which Rostow summarizes. The novel feature of Rostow's conception is the notion that first there is a period when the conditions for growth are established, then one or two or three decades within which certain distinctive and necessary transitional events begin and are completed, and thereafter self-sustained continuing growth. An airplane leaves the ground in such a sequence; it is an attractive idea that our mechanical age provides an appropriate analogy for social change. Is it correct as well as attractive?

EMPIRICAL VALIDITY OF THE CONCEPTS

If there is a period of transition as abrupt as that which Rostow suggests as typical, this is not necessarily inconsistent with the model presented in the present study, but the abruptness would require additional explanation. Rostow does not explain it; he simply asserts it as a fact. There have been periods of rapid acceleration of growth in some countries. In the Soviet Union, for example, steps were taken after the Bolshevik Revolution of 1917 to accelerate economic growth. However, as I have noted earlier in this volume, economic growth had begun long before. Rostow himself dates the Russian take-off as

---

[5] The quoted phrases concerning the duration of the take-off are from pp. 8 and 9, the dates from p. 38.

ending in 1914. In both England and Japan there were also dates when the pace of economic growth accelerated rather abruptly, in England perhaps because of the clustering within a short period of several key inventions, in Japan because institutional barriers were demolished and favorable governmental action initiated. But in these countries also, economic growth, and not merely the conditions for it, had certainly begun earlier. Even accepting the periods in England and Japan as ones of take-off, as Rostow does, to accept these cases as typical one would have to assume either that powerful institutional barriers were broken through abruptly in every case of growth or that technological creativity and values and motives conducive to a high rate of saving and investment suddenly appeared rather widely in the population in every transition to economic growth. It is difficult for me to conceive of reasons why either development should be typical, and certainly the logic of the sequences I have posited earlier in this book does not lead easily to the conclusion that an abrupt change would be typical.

However, it is not necessary to seek the reasons for such abrupt change, for the available empirical evidence suggests that Rostow's concept of a period which is merely preparatory and then one of abrupt transition does not have great empirical relevance. Empirical evidence indicates that in the typical case the events which Rostow assigns to the stage of establishing preconditions and those which he assigns to the period of take-off all become perceptible in an early period and all continue to develop, interwoven, throughout the transition to economic growth. There are variations; one development or another may become evident only when the transition is well advanced; but this is as apt to be true of the supposed preconditions as of the events which Rostow assigns to the take-off. Moreover, while there are sometimes abrupt changes in political institutions, all other changes tend to be gradual. In short, the division into stages and assignment of some events to one stage and others to another is too far removed from reality to be useful for explanation or prediction.

I shall refer briefly to relevant data and the conclusions concerning the facts presented in earlier chapters or reached by other students of the process.

The Preconditions

Among the preconditions, Rostow suggests, is the establishment of effective national government, and among the events of the take-off the quick emergence of a favorable political, social, and economic framework. Anyone must agree that economic growth will go forward more effectively if favorable rules of the game are established and enforced. Yet the terms Rostow uses in describing institutional change are qualitative and ambiguous ones, so that it is impossible to determine when they have been satisfied; and a survey of the historical evidence suggests that rather than certain institutional conditions being absolute requisites whose attainment can be assigned to one stage or another, institutions and government gradually became more favorable to growth as the groups interested in new economic activities gradually gained more success, influence, and power.

A study I have summarized in Chapter 2 presents relevant evidence. This is the study which relates the political structure of African, Asian, and Latin American societies to their economic status. The reader may remember that it does not show a certain political structure emerging before economic growth proceeds. Rather, it suggests a continuing transition from authoritarian to competitive governmental structure as economic growth proceeds. The emergence of competitive political structure and of institutions favorable to economic growth are closely related; in general, the more competitive the political structure, the more fully are the interests of the groups concerned with economic growth reflected. Thus the study suggests gradual intertwined economic and political change, not stages of the one requisite for the other.

Specific case studies show the same emergence of more favorable political, social, and economic institutions by degree, while economic growth also proceeded by degree and without waiting upon any given institutional structure. The gradual appearance of favorable institutions from the late Middle Ages through the nineteenth century is common knowledge and may be referred to without being cited. Even effective national government in the minimum sense of that term seems not to have been a necessary condition for growth. In Colombia economic growth slowly began during the closing decades of the nineteenth century while the various regions of the country were politically autonomous and bitter civil wars rent the country; and during the period when economic growth gradually gathered speed after the turn of the century peace prevailed not through national union but through exhaustion.

Rostow's two other supposed preconditions, a rise in agricultural productivity and the establishment of a base of social overhead capital facilities, are equally suspect. In Chapter 3 I suggested some logical deficiencies of the concept that investment in social overhead capital must precede rather than accompany other types of technological advance. Increase in productivity in agriculture must of course accompany the shift of workers from agriculture to processing activities and other urban pursuits, but it need not precede these. Indeed, it can precede them only if the increasing productivity in agriculture results in expanding output without saving labor and if the increased supply of agricultural products is exported, for otherwise there will not be an adequate market for either the released labor or the added produce.[6]

Increasing productivity in agriculture probably began almost everywhere before the appearance of manufacturing, but simply because we define as manufacturing only fairly large-scale industrial activity, which appears only after handicrafts have undergone a considerable process of technological progress. Although I shall not attempt to survey the historical evidence, it is probably true that technological progress in agriculture and in handicrafts have typically begun and proceeded together. They have continued side by side, if, as we should, we regard handicrafts and manufacturing as a continuum, during the periods termed by Rostow "the preconditions," "the take-off," and "the drive to maturity."

In my discussion of economic growth in Colombia I indicated that transportation and power facilities developed only as other advances were proceeding, not before them. Concerning several other societies, Habakkuk's statement about the timing of changes in agriculture and in social overhead capital provides a convenient summary:

"The first requirement of a precondition is surely that it should occur first in time. But in England the principal changes in transport and in agriculture took place during rather than before the period of accelerated growth; in Russia the relevant agricultural developments occurred late in the decade after the take-off had got under way, and in China they are occurring in the middle of the period to which Professor Rostow assigns her take-off. In many cases the increase of agricultural output and the creation of overhead social capital are

---

[6] This assumes what is a well-known fact, namely that the "price elasticity of demand" for agricultural products is not sufficiently high so that an added supply will be disposed of at a price covering the cost of production even though there is no increase in nonagricultural income.

not conditions whose pre-existence explains the acceleration of growth; they are part of the acceleration which needs to be explained."[7]

The Events of the "Take-Off"

Thus again the evidence suggests that the various aspects of the transition from a traditional state to one of economic growth proceed in an interwoven manner throughout the entire transition rather than emerging *seriatim* in stages. If this is true of the supposed preconditions, one might suspect that the events assigned to the take-off will also resist being fitted into a single stage in time. This turns out to be true.

Rostow suggests that during the period of the take-off capital formation rises from say less than 5 per cent of the national income to 10 per cent or more. The significance of these percentages is that a rate of 5 per cent is not much more than enough to offset population growth and hold per capita income constant, while a rate of 10 per cent is presumed to be enough to permit a satisfactory rate of rise in per capita income. Professor Kuznets recently prepared a summary of available information concerning long-term trends in the ratio of capital formation to national income.[8] Estimates for early periods are not available except for England. With this exception, no one can know how low the rate of capital formation was during periods before those which Rostow designates as the take-off. Data for later periods are available for seven of the 13 countries for which Rostow gives "tentative, approximate take-off dates."[9] In Canada ("take-off, 1896–1914"), the percentages behave as Rostow's schema would suggest. For the United States, data are available only beginning in 1869, after the take-off had ended according to Rostow's dates (1843–60). In Germany ("take-off, 1850–73") the ratio of "net domestic capital formation" to "net national product"[10] had reached 11.6 per cent by 1871–80, but was already 8.4 per cent in the earliest period for which data are available, 1851–60; and on a reasonable assumption concerning economic trends in prior decades, the rise in capital

---

[7] *Economic Journal*, Vol. LXXI (September, 1961), pp. 601–2.

[8] Simon S. Kuznets, "Quantitative Aspects of the Economic Growth of Nations. VI: Long-Term Trends in Capital Formation Proportions," *Economic Development and Cultural Change*, Vol. IX, No. 4, part II (July, 1961). This is the sixth of a series of monographs on economic growth prepared by Kuznets, each published in separate covers as the second part of an issue of *Economic Development and Cultural Change*. The data cited below are from the Appendix of this monograph.

[9] *The Stages of Economic Growth*, Table 1, p. 38.

[10] Domestic capital formation is that occurring within the country whether financed from domestic saving or from investment from abroad. National capital formation differs in that investment from abroad is subtracted, and saving within the country which is invested abroad is added. Domestic product is production within the country; national product is this plus the flow of income into the country from production abroad (for example, dividends or interest on investments abroad), and minus the flow of income out of the country to claimants abroad (for example, dividends or interest paid to foreign holders of securities in domestic companies). The most appropriate ratio for the present purpose is that between net domestic capital formation and net domestic product. Where this is not available, the ratio between net national capital formation and net national product is used. In England, the ratio between the *national* magnitudes exceeded that between the domestic ones in the nineteenth century, since Englishmen were investing abroad in large amounts. In Sweden, the opposite was true from 1870 to 1900, because of foreign investment in Sweden. In Japan, this was true from the 1890's until World War I. There are also differences in other countries. None of them affects the conclusions drawn here.

formation from 5 per cent to 10 per cent of national income required a much longer period than the assumed take-off period.

Consider at slightly greater length the other four countries for which Rostow gives take-off dates and for which Kuznets had more complete estimates of capital formation and national product.

For Great Britain ("take-off, 1783–1802") estimates for periods before 1800 are available only for England and Wales. The ratio of net national capital formation to net national product for periods in the eighteenth century is estimated as follows: 1700–40, 4 per cent; 1740–70, 5.5 per cent; 1770–1800, 6.5 per cent. For the United Kingdom the ratio continued to rise slowly. It did not reach 10 per cent until 1860–69. The change posited by Rostow thus required about a century.

For Sweden ("take-off, 1868–90"), data are available only on a "gross" basis, that is, without deduction of the using up of capital in existence which must be subtracted to arrive at an estimate of the net addition to the stock of capital equipment. On the assumption (used by Kuznets in the paper cited in note 2 of this Appendix) that net capital formation was 9/10 of gross, capital formation was already 5.5. per cent of the national product in the 1860's, rose very slowly and unevenly during the next 80 years, and did not become 10 per cent until the 1930's, 70 years later.[11]

Data for Japan are available beginning only in 1887 ("take-off, 1878–1900"). Including capital formation for military purposes, the ratio to national product was 8 per cent in the decade 1887–96, but it did not reach 10 per cent until the decade 1912–21, which included World War I, when it was 11.6 per cent. Excluding military capital formation, the ratio was 6.7 per cent in the early decade, and it did not reach 10 per cent until after World War I.[12]

Lastly, in Argentina ("take-off, 1935–   "), except during World War I the ratio of capital formation to national product was far above 10 per cent from 1900 to 1930, before the supposed take-off period, then fell to below 10 per cent during the depression of the 1930's and World War II, and rose to 11.5 per cent in the decade 1945–54.

It is not possible to interpret these data in a way that offers support for the take-off thesis. Similarly data for other countries presented by Kuznets conflict with the thesis.

The reason the trend in capital formation is thought by Rostow and almost all other economists to be important is that, since technological advances are embodied in capital formation, an adequate rate of capital formation is necessary for rapid improvement in techniques and rise in per capita income. Direct evidence concerning trends in technological progress and per capita income is therefore pertinent to the point at issue. The evidence available, like that above, suggests gradual change from an early period onward, not movement in stages. Data are rarely available. Kuznets cites Phyllis Deane's estimates of the trend in per capita income in England in the eighteenth century. Her estimates suggest an average annual rate of rise in per capita income of 0.3 per cent during the period 1700–40, 0.9 per cent during 1740–70, and 1.5 per cent during 1770–1800. In Chapter 2, I cited estimates that per capita income rose gradually in Russia from 1860 on. No early estimates are available for other countries, but the accounts in previous chapters of economic growth in Japan and Colom-

---

[11] This is true of both the ratio between the domestic magnitudes and that between the national magnitudes.

[12] The ratios are those for net domestic capital formation to net national product. The ratios for net national capital formation to net national product are slightly lower in the decade 1887–96 and considerably lower after World War I.

bia indicated clearly the gradual nature of the acceleration of technological progress. Like the data cited above, these facts will not fit the Rostovian concept of stages.

A second of Rostow's three necessary conditions for the take-off is the existence or quick emergence of a favorable political, social, and institutional framework. This has been discussed above. The third condition is "the development of one or more substantial manufacturing sectors, with a high rate of growth."[13] It is of some importance in Rostow's schema that some sector in which innovation is proceeding expands rapidly and thus creates both expanding demand for materials and capital goods and an expanding supply of products at reduced costs. These linkages, he suggests, are an important engine of continued growth. The expansion of a leading sector must sometime decelerate, but other sectors take its place. Thus this behavior of sectors is not unique to the take-off; "growth proceeds by repeating endlessly, in different patterns, with different leading sectors, the experience of the take-off."[14] Thus this behavior does not distinguish between the take-off and later stages.

If economic growth is occurring at all, some sector must be expanding faster than others except in the unlikely contingency that growth is proceeding at precisely the same rate throughout the economy. Hence to state that the phenomenon of leading sectors occurs is to state no more than that growth does occur, that opportunities for growth at times are greater in some sectors of the economy than in others, and that one industry creates demand for the products of another. If the rapid expansion of one leading sector and then another began suddenly in a previously traditional and quiescent society, it would mark an important dividing line in time, justifying in itself a concept of at least two stages. However, the evidence cited above that improvement in technology and rise in per capita income begin gradually and gradually accelerate is also evidence that the phenomenon of leading sectors emerges gradually, interwoven with the other developments.[15]

Having concluded that Rostow's arrangement of events into stages is of little empirical relevance, shall we conclude that no other definition of stages is

---

[13] *The Stages,* p. 39.

[14] *Ibid.,* p. 53. The discussion of leading sectors occupies pp. 52–57.

[15] It may be noted parenthetically that a linkage between a technically progressive and expanding industry and another industry will not necessarily lead to technical progress in the second industry. Whether it does so depends on many factors other than the nature of the leading industry and whether linkages exist. The linked industry will progress rapidly in response to such stimulus if the general state of science and technical knowledge are such that advance is incipient in that industry, and less rapidly or possibly not at all if it is not. Thus whether a given sector is a leading sector depends partly on whether the sectors linked to it are ready to be led. If the relevant aspects of science and technical knowledge are ripe enough, those sectors will advance without waiting to be led. Moreover, if there are individuals with lively minds interested in technology here and there throughout the society, technical progress will appear somewhere in the processes of production, and the locus of initial advances plus linkages among sectors will determine where it appears far more than at what rate it appears. Thus it is easy to exaggerate the importance of leading sectors and linkages as causal factors. However, from a short-run viewpoint unquestionably they influence the pace of growth as well as its pattern. There is much truth in the statement that the state of technical and scientific knowledge will be important in influencing both where initial advances appear and where linkages lead subsequently. From this viewpoint, the locus of initial technical progress and the technical structure of production become of secondary and only proximate importance in accounting for the pace of economic growth.

likely to be tenable, and that there are no stages in the transition from traditionalism to economic growth? This, it seems to me, is a matter of terminology which is without substance. If a division into stages is to be made, it must, I think, be made on the basis of rates of change. If the advances in technology per time period are somehow rendered commensurable with each other and aggregated, a diagram portraying them would take the shape of a Gompertz curve or "growth curve." Are stages discernible as one moves along a Gompertz curve? Certainly different portions of the curve have different shapes. One may find corresponding differences among periods of the transition from traditionalism to economic growth, even though giving precise dates to the passage from one to another is an arbitrary procedure. If, however, one does not regard movement along a Gompertz curve as involving stages, it seems doubtful that one would find stages in either the pace of technical change or other aspects of the transition. And no substantive issues of importance seem involved in this choice of terminology.

Although Rostow is in error in arraying the events of the transition from traditionalism to economic modernism into a sequence, as though one was completed before another began, this fact should not obscure the perceptiveness of his analysis in other respects. His brief account is an insightful summary of the complex changes which must occur, from which any student of the process may obtain provocative suggestions and an awareness of aspects he had not fully appreciated before.

Bibliography

Bibliography

BECAUSE THIS VOLUME HAS A SOMEWHAT COMPLEX ANA-
lytical structure and in addition presents six case studies, it seems desirable
to divide the bibliography under a number of headings. No bibliography
is presented for four units of the volume: Chapter 1 because it is introductory, and Chapters 2 and 3 and Appendix II because they are brief surveys
of broad fields not centrally related to the argument of the book. A few
works, relevant to two topics, are listed under both of those topics.

It should be emphasized that the bibliography is not comprehensive.
For example, it does not include all standard anthropological descriptions
of peasant villages or all discussions of social structure. It would be in-
appropriate to refer to all of the rich historical literature concerning the
period of English history summarized in Chapter 13; rather, only two general summary accounts and a number of specialized discussions are listed.
And so on. The principle followed was to include all works used specifically in preparing the manuscript, others which seem most useful to
readers wishing to explore further topics suggested by the text, and a
number representative of analyses alternative to that presented here.

TRADITIONAL SOCIETY

(Including a few relevant works on primitive society)
Chapters 4 and 8

ARENSBERG, C. M. *The Irish Countryman*. New York: Macmillan & Co., 1942.
———, and KIMBALL, S. *Family and Community in Ireland*. Cambridge,
Mass.: Harvard University Press, 1940.

BAILEY, F. G. *Caste and the Economic Frontier: A Village in Highland Orissa*.
Manchester, England: Manchester University Press, 1957.

BANFIELD, EDWARD C., and BANFIELD, LAURA FASANO. *The Moral Basis of a
Backward Society*. Glencoe, Ill.: Free Press of Glencoe, Inc., 1958.

BOURNE, GEORGE (pseud. of George Sturt). *Change in the Village*. London:
Gerald Duckworth & Co., Ltd., 1912, 1955.

COULBORN, RUSHTON H. (ed.). *Feudalism in History*. Princeton, N.J.: Princeton University Press, 1956.

DUBE, S. C. *Indian Village*. Ithaca, N.Y.: Cornell University Press, 1955.

EMBREE, JOHN F. *Suye Mura: A Japanese Village*. Chicago: The University of
Chicago Press, 1939.

FALS-BORDA, ORLANDO. *Peasant Society in the Colombian Andes.* Gainsville, Fla.: The University of Florida Press, 1955.

FEI, HSIAO-TUNG. *China's Gentry.* Chicago: The University of Chicago Press, 1953.

——. *Peasant Life in China.* London: Kegan Paul, Trench, Trubner & Co., Ltd., 1947.

FIRTH, RAYMOND. *Elements of Social Organization.* London: Watts & Co., 1951.

FRANCIS, E. K. L. "The Personality Type of the Peasant According to Hesiod's Works and Days," *Rural Sociology,* Vol. X (September, 1945), pp. 275–95.

FREYRE, GILBERTO. *The Masters and the Slaves,* trans. from Portuguese. New York: Alfred A. Knopf, Inc., 1946.

FURNIVALL, J. S. *Colonial Policy and Practice: A Comparative Study of Burma and Netherlands India.* Cambridge, England: The University Press, 1948.

GEERTZ, CLIFFORD. "Form and Variation in Balinese Village Structure," *American Anthropologist,* Vol. LXI (December, 1959), pp. 991–1012.

——. "The Javanese Kijaji: The Changing Role of a Cultural Broker," *Comparative Studies in Society and History,* Vol. II (January, 1960), pp. 228–49.

——. *The Religion of Java.* Glencoe, Ill.: Free Press of Glencoe, Inc., 1960.

GEERTZ, HILDRED. *The Javanese Family.* New York: Free Press of Glencoe, Inc., 1961.

——. "The Vocabulary of Emotion: A Study of Javanese Socialization Processes," *Psychiatry,* Vol. XXII (August, 1959), pp. 225–37.

GRAS, N. S. B. *The Economic and Social History of an English Village.* Cambridge, Mass.: Harvard University Press, 1930.

GLUCKMAN, MAX. *Custom and Conflict in Africa.* Glencoe, Ill.: Free Press of Glencoe, Inc., 1955.

HAGEN, E. E. *The Economic Development of Burma.* Washington, D.C.: The National Planning Association, 1956.

HANKS, LUCIEN M., JR. "The Quest for Individual Autonomy in Burmese Personality with Special Reference to the Arakan," *Psychiatry,* Vol. XII (1949), pp. 285–300.

HANSSEN, BORJE. *Fields of Social Activity and Their Dynamics.* Translations of the Westermarck Society, Vol. II. Copenhagen: Ejnas Munksgaard (1953), pp. 99–133.

HITSON, HAZEL MARIE. "Family Patterns and Paranoidal Personality Structure in Boston and Burma" (Ph.D. dissertation, Radcliffe College, April, 1959).

HUGHES, EVERETT. *French Canada in Transition.* Chicago: The University of Chicago Press, 1943.

KARDINER, ABRAM. *The Individual and His Society.* New York: Columbia University Press, 1939.

——. *Psychological Frontiers of Society.* New York: Columbia University Press, 1945.

KEESING, FELIX M., and KEESING, MARIE M. *Elite Communication in Samoa: A Study in Leadership* (Stanford Anthropological Series 3). Stanford, Calif.: Stanford University Press, 1956.

KLUCKHOHN, FLORENCE ROCKWOOD. "Dominant and Variant Value Orientations," *Personality in Nature, Society, and Culture* (eds. Kluckhohn, Murray, and Schneider), chap. xxi. 2d ed. New York: Alfred A. Knopf, Inc., 1955.

Kroeber, A. L. *Configurations of Culture Growth.* Berkeley and Los Angeles: University of California Press, 1944.

Landy, David. *Tropical Childhood.* Chapel Hill, N.C.: The University of North Carolina Press, 1959.

Leighton, Dorothea, and Kluckhohn, Clyde. *Children of the People.* Cambridge, Mass.: Harvard University Press, 1948.

Lerner, Daniel. *The Passing of Traditional Society: Modernizing the Middle East.* Glencoe, Ill.: Free Press of Glencoe, Inc., 1958.

Lewis, Oscar. *Life in a Mexican Village: Tepoztlán Restudied.* Urbana, Ill.: University of Illinois Press, 1951.

———. "Peasant Culture in India and Mexico," *Village India: Studies in the Little Community* (ed. McKim Marriott).

Maine, Sir Henry. *Village Communities East and West.* New York: Henry Holt & Co., 1889.

Makal, Mahmut. *A Village in Anatolia,* trans. Sir Wyndham Deedes. London: Vallentine, Mitchell & Co., Ltd., 1954.

Malinowski, Bronislaw. "Magic, Science, and Religion," *Science, Religion, and Reality* (ed. Joseph Needham). New York: George Braziller, Inc., 1955.

Marriott, McKim (ed.). *Village India: Studies in the Little Community.* Chicago: The University of Chicago Press, 1955.

Mead, Margaret (ed.). *Cultural Patterns and Technical Change,* chap. iii. Paris: United Nations, 1953.

Merton, Robert K. *Social Theory and Social Structure,* chap. i. Rev. ed. Glencoe, Ill.: Free Press of Glencoe, Inc., 1957.

Miner, Horace. *Saint Denis: A French-Canadian Parish.* Chicago: The University of Chicago Press, 1939.

Moore, Wilbert E. *Industrialization and Labor.* Ithaca, N.Y.: Cornell University and New School for Social Research, 1951.

Murdock, George P. (ed.). *Social Structure in Southeast Asia.* Chicago: Quadrangle Books, 1960.

Murphy, Gardner. *In the Minds of Men.* New York: Basic Books, Inc., 1953.

Nash, Manning. *Machine Age Maya: The Industrialization of a Guatemalan Community.* Glencoe, Ill.: Free Press of Glencoe, Inc., 1958.

Norbeck, Edward. *Takashima: A Japanese Fishing Community.* Salt Lake City: The University of Utah Press, 1954.

Parsons, Talcott. "The Theoretical Development of the Sociology of Religion," *Essays in Sociological Theory* (ed. Talcott Parsons). Glencoe, Ill.: Free Press of Glencoe, Inc., 1954.

Piers, Gerhard, and Singer, Milton B. *Shame and Guilt.* Springfield, Ill.: Charles C. Thomas Co., 1953.

Pitt-Rivers, J. A. *The People of the Sierra.* New York: Criterion Books, 1954.

Pitts, Jesse L. *The Bourgeois Family and French Economic Retardation.* Cambridge, Mass.: Harvard University Press, 1957.

Power, Eileen. *Medieval People.* New York: Doubleday & Co., Inc., 1954.

Radcliffe-Brown, A. R. *Structure and Function in Primitive Society.* Glencoe, Ill.: Free Press of Glencoe, Inc., 1952.

Radin, Paul. *The World of Primitive Man.* New York: H. Schuman, 1953.

Redfield, Robert. *The Folk Culture of Yucatán.* Chicago: The University of Chicago Press, 1941.

REDFIELD, ROBERT. *The Little Community*. Chicago: The University of Chicago Press, 1955.

———. *Peasant Society and Culture*. Chicago: The University of Chicago Press, 1956.

———. *The Primitive World and Its Transformations*. Ithaca, N.Y.: Cornell University Press, 1953.

———. *Tepoztlán: A Mexican Village*. Chicago: The University of Chicago Press, 1930.

SANDERS, IRWIN T. *Balkan Village*. Lexington, Ky.: University of Kentucky Press, 1949.

———. *Rainbow in the Rock: The People of Rural Greece*. Cambridge, Mass.: Harvard University Press, 1962.

SJOBERG, GIDEON. "Folk and Feudal Societies," *American Journal of Sociology*, Vol. LVIII (November, 1952), pp. 231–39.

———. *The Preindustrial City, Past and Present*. Glencoe, Ill.: Free Press of Glencoe, Inc., 1960.

SRINIVAS, M. N. *Religion and Society among the Coorgs of South India*. London: Oxford University Press, 1952.

———. "The Social Structure of a Mysore Village," *Village India: Studies in the Little Community* (ed. McKim Marriott), pp. 1–35.

TAX, SOL. *Penny Capitalism: A Guatemalan Indian Economy*. New York: Smithsonian Institute of Social Anthropology, 1953.

TEY, JOSEPHINE. *Brat Farrar*. London and New York: Macmillan & Co., 1949.

THOMAS, ELIZABETH MARSHALL. *The Harmless People*. New York: Alfred A. Knopf, Inc., 1959.

TURNEY-HIGH, H. H. *Chateau-Gerard: The Life and Times of a Walloon Village*. Columbia, S.C.: University of South Carolina Press, 1953.

WAGLEY, CHARLES. *Economics of a Guatemalan Village*. Menasha, Wisc.: American Anthropological Association, 1941 (Memoir No. 58).

———. *The Social and Religious Life of a Guatemalan Village*. Menasha, Wisc.: American Anthropological Association, 1949 (Memoir No. 71).

WARRINER, DOREEN. *The Economics of Peasant Farming*. London: Oxford University Press, 1939.

WYLIE, LAURENCE. *Village in the Vaucluse*. Cambridge, Mass.: Harvard University Press, 1957.

YANG, MARTIN C. *A Chinese Village, Taitou, Shantung Province*. London: Kegan Paul, Trench, Trubner & Co., Ltd., 1948.

PERSONALITY AND PERSONALITY FORMATION

Chapters 5–7

ADORNO, T. W.; FRENKEL-BRUNSWIK, ELSE; LEVINSON, DANIEL J.; and SANFORD, R. NEVITT. *The Authoritarian Personality*. New York: Harper & Bros., 1950.

ANDERSON, HAROLD H. (ed.). *Creativity and Its Cultivation*. New York: Harper & Bros., 1959.

BARRON, FRANK. "The Disposition toward Originality," *The 1955 University of Utah Research Conference on the Identification of Creative Scientific Talent*. Salt Lake City: The University of Utah Press, 1956.

——. "The Needs for Order and for Disorder as Motives in Creative Activity," *The 1957 University of Utah Research Conference on the Identification of Creative Scientific Talent.* Salt Lake City: The University of Utah Press, 1958.

——. "The Psychology of Imagination," *Scientific American,* Vol. CXCIX (September, 1958), pp. 150–66.

BENEDICT, RUTH. "Continuities and Discontinuities in Cultural Conditioning," *Personality in Nature, Society, and Culture* (eds. Kluckhohn, Murray, and Schneider), chap. xxxiii.

BOWLBY, JOHN. "The Nature of the Child's Tie to His Mother," *International Journal of Psychoanalysis,* Vol. XXXIX (1958), pp. 350–73.

CARON, ALBERT J., and WALLACH, MICHAEL A. "Personality Determinants of Repressive and Obsessive Reactions to Failure-Stress," *Journal of Abnormal and Social Psychology,* Vol. LIX (September, 1959), pp. 236–45.

——. "Recall of Interrupted Tasks under Stress: A Phenomenon of Memory or Learning?" *Journal of Abnormal and Social Psychology,* Vol. LV (November, 1957), pp. 372–81.

CHILD, IRVIN L. "Socialization," *Handbook of Social Psychology,* Vol. II (ed. Gardner Lindzey).

DICKS, HENRY V. "Observations on Contemporary Russian Behaviour," *Human Relations,* Vol. V (1952), pp. 111–75.

ELLIOTT, OSBORN. *Men at the Top.* New York: Harper & Bros., 1959.

ENGEL, LEONARD H. "The Troubled Monkeys of Madison," *The New York Times,* January 29, 1961, Section VI, pp. 62 and 64.

ENGLISH, O. SPURGEON, and PEARSON, GERALD H. J. *Emotional Problems of Living.* New York: W. W. Norton & Co., Inc., 1955.

ERIKSON, ERIK H. *Childhood and Society.* New York: W. W. Norton & Co., Inc., 1950.

——. "Growth and Crises of the 'Healthy Personality,'" *Personality in Nature, Society, and Culture* (eds. Kluckhohn, Murray, and Schneider), chap. xii.

——. *Young Man Luther.* New York: W. W. Norton & Co., Inc., 1958.

FROMM, ERICH. "The Creative Attitude," *Creativity and Its Cultivation* (ed. H. H. Anderson), chap. iv. New York: Harper & Bros., 1959.

GERARD, R. W. "Your Brain and Your Behavior," *Saturday Evening Post,* Vol. CCXXXI (May 30, 1959), pp. 22–23.

GORER, GEOFFREY. "The Concept of National Character," *Personality in Nature, Society, and Culture* (eds. Kluckhohn, Murray, and Schneider), chap. xiv.

HALL, C. S., and LINDZEY, G. *Theories of Personality.* New York: John Wiley & Sons, Inc., 1957.

HARLOW, HARRY F. "Mice, Monkeys, Men, and Motives," *Psychological Review,* Vol. LX (1953), pp. 23–32.

HENRY, WILLIAM E. *The Analysis of Fantasy.* New York: John Wiley & Sons, Inc., 1956.

——. "The Language of Fantasy—A Problem in Instruction and Supervision," *American Journal of Orthopsychiatry,* Vol. XXIII (1953), pp. 315–21.

HITSON, HAZEL MARIE. "Family Patterns and Paranoidal Personality Structure in Boston and Burma" (Ph.D. dissertation, Radcliffe College, April, 1959).

HOMANS, GEORGE C. *The Human Group*. New York: Harcourt-Brace & Co., 1950.

INKELES, ALEX, and LEVINSON, D. J. "National Character," *Handbook of Social Psychology*, Vol. II (ed. Gardner Lindzey), chap. xxvi.

KELLY, FRED C. "They Wouldn't Believe the Wrights Had Flown," *Harper's Magazine*, Vol. CLXXXI (August, 1940), pp. 286–300.

KLATSKIN, ETHELYN H.; JACKSON, EDITH B.; and WILKIN, LOUISE C. "The Influence of Degree of Flexibility in Maternal Child Care Practices on Early Child Behavior," *American Journal of Orthopsychiatry*, Vol. XXVI (1956), pp. 79–93.

KLUCKHOHN, CLYDE, *et al.* "Values and Value-Orientations in the Theory of Action," *Toward a General Theory of Action* (eds. Parsons and Shils), pp. 388–433.

———; MURRAY, HENRY A.; and SCHNEIDER, DAVID M. (eds.). *Personality in Nature, Society, and Culture*. 2d ed. New York: Alfred A. Knopf, Inc., 1955.

KRIS, ERNST. *Psychoanalytic Explorations in Art*. New York: International Universities Press, Inc., 1952.

LEE, DOROTHY. "Are Basic Needs Ultimate?" *Journal of Abnormal and Social Psychology*, Vol. XLIII (1948), pp. 391–95, reprinted in *Personality in Nature, Society, and Culture* (eds. Kluckhohn, Murray, and Schneider), chap. xx.

LEIGHTON, DOROTHEA, and KLUCKHOHN, CLYDE. *Children of the People*. Cambridge, Mass.: Harvard University Press, 1948.

LINDZEY, GARDNER (ed.). *Handbook of Social Psychology*, Vol. II. Cambridge, Mass.: Addison-Wesley Publishing Co., Inc., 1954.

McCLELLAND, DAVID C. "Some Social Consequences of Achievement Motivation," *Nebraska Symposium on Motivation, 1955*. Lincoln, Nebr.: University of Nebraska Press, 1955.

———; ATKINSON, JOHN W.; CLARK, RUSSELL A.; and LOWELL, EDGAR L. *The Achievement Motive*. New York: Appleton-Century-Crofts, Inc., 1953.

———; BALDWIN, A. L.; BRONFENBRENNER, U.; and STRODBECK, F. L. *Talent and Society: New Perspectives in the Identification of Talent*. Princeton, N.J.: D. Van Nostrand Co., Inc., 1958.

———; RINDLISBACHER, A.; and DECHARMS, R. C. "Religious and Other Sources of Parental Attitudes toward Independence Training," *Studies in Motivation* (ed. D. C. McClelland). New York: Appleton-Century-Crofts, 1955.

MERTON, ROBERT K. *Social Theory and Social Structure*, chaps. iv, v. Rev. ed. Glencoe, Ill.: Free Press of Glencoe, Inc., 1957.

MORRIS, CHARLES. *Varieties of Human Value*. Chicago: The University of Chicago Press, 1956.

MURPHY, G. *Personality: A Biosocial Approach to Origins and Structure*. New York: Harper & Bros., 1947.

MURRAY, HENRY A., *et al.* *Explorations in Personality*. New York: Oxford University Press, 1938.

PARSONS, TALCOTT. *The Social System*. Glencoe, Ill.: Free Press of Glencoe, Inc., 1951.

———, and SHILS, EDWARD A. (eds.). *Toward a General Theory of Action*. Cambridge, Mass.: Harvard University Press, 1952, 1954.

PENFIELD, WILDER, and ROBERTS, LAMAR. *Speech and Brain-Mechanisms*. Princeton, N.J.: Princeton University Press, 1959.

PIAGET, JEAN. *The Child's Conception of Physical Causation,* trans. Marjorie Gabain. London: Routledge & Kegan Paul, Ltd., 1951.

―――. *The Child's Conception of the World,* trans. J. and A. Tomlinson. New York: Harcourt-Brace & Co., 1929.

―――. *The Child's Construction of Reality.* New York: Basic Books, Inc., 1954.

PIERS, GERHARD, and SINGER, MILTON B. *Shame and Guilt.* Springfield, Ill.: Charles C. Thomas Co., 1953.

ROGERS, CARL R. "Toward a Theory of Creativity," *Creativity and Its Cultivation* (ed. H. H. Anderson), chap. vi.

ROSENBLITH, WALTER A. "The Quantification of the Electrical Activity of the Nervous System," *Quantity and Quality* (ed. Daniel Lerner). New York: Free Press of Glencoe, Inc., 1961.

Scientific American, Vol. CXCIX, September, 1958.
    The entire issue is devoted to the study of innovation in science. An argument which runs through the several articles is that "an innovation in either [science or art] occurs only when a single mind perceives in disorder a deep new unity."

SPIRO, MELFORD G. *Children of the Kibbutz.* Cambridge, Mass.: Harvard University Press, 1957.

STEIN, MAURICE R.; VIDICH, ARTHUR J.; and WHITE, DAVID MANNING (eds.). *Identity and Anxiety.* Glencoe, Ill.: Free Press of Glencoe, Inc., 1960.

SULLIVAN, H. S. *The Interpersonal Theory of Psychiatry.* New York: W. W. Norton & Co., Inc., 1953.

WALLACH, M. A. "Art, Science, and Representation: Toward an Experimental Psychology of Aesthetics," *The Journal of Aesthetics and Art Criticism,* Vol. XVIII (December, 1959), pp. 159–73.

WARNER, W. LLOYD, and ABEGGLEN, JAMES C. *Big Business Leaders in America.* New York: Harper & Bros., 1955.

―――. *Occupational Mobility in American Business and Industry.* Minneapolis: University of Minnesota Press, 1955.

WATSON, ROBERT I. *Psychology of the Child.* New York: John Wiley & Sons, Inc., 1960.

WHITING, J. W. M., and CHILD, I. L. *Child Training and Personality.* New Haven, Conn.: Yale University Press, 1953.

YOUNG, J. Z. *Doubt and Certainty in Science.* Oxford: The Clarendon Press, 1951.

SOCIAL STRUCTURE AND SOCIAL CHANGE

Chapters 9–12 and 17

(Works specifically relating to the social structure of traditional society are excluded here and included above)

Social Change: General

ALMOND, GABRIEL A., and COLEMAN, JAMES S. (eds.). *The Politics of the Developing Areas.* Princeton, N.J.: Princeton University Press, 1960.

BALANDIER, GEORGES. *Sociologie Actuelle de l'Afrique Noire.* Paris: Presses Universitaires de France, 1955.

BARAN, PAUL A. *The Political Economy of Growth.* New York: Monthly Review Press, 1957.

BARNETT, H. G. *Innovation: The Basis of Cultural Change.* New York: McGraw-Hill Book Co., Inc., 1953.

BATESON, GREGORY. *Naven.* Cambridge, Eng.: Cambridge University Press, 1946.

BECKER, HOWARD. "Sacred and Secular Societies Considered with Reference to Folk-State and Similar Classifications," *Social Forces,* Vol. XXVIII (May, 1950), pp. 361–76.

BELL, DANIEL. *The End of Ideology.* Glencoe, Ill.: Free Press of Glencoe, Inc., 1960.

BELSHAW, CYRIL S. *Changing Melanesia: Social Economics of Culture Contact.* Melbourne, Australia: Oxford University Press, 1954.

BENEDICT, RUTH. "Continuities and Discontinuities in Cultural Conditioning," *Personality in Nature, Society, and Culture* (eds. Kluckhohn, Murray, and Schneider). 2d ed. New York: Alfred A. Knopf, Inc., 1955.

BRINTON, CRANE. *The Anatomy of Revolution.* New York: W. W. Norton & Co., Inc., 1938.

———. *The Shaping of the Modern Mind.* New York: Mentor Books (paperback), 1953. The concluding half of *Ideas and Men.* New York: Prentice-Hall, 1950.

CAMUS, ALBERT. *The Rebel.* New York: Alfred A. Knopf, Inc., 1956.

COCHRAN, THOMAS C. "Social Attitudes, Entrepreneurship, and Economic Development: Some Comments," *Explorations in Entrepreneurial History,* Vol. VI (February, 1954), pp. 181–83.

DEVEREUX, GEORGE, and LOEB, EDWIN M. "Antagonistic Acculturation," *American Sociological Review,* Vol. VIII (April, 1943), pp. 133–47.

DODDS, E. R. *The Greeks and the Irrational.* Berkeley: University of California Press, 1956.

DOOB, LEONARD W. *Becoming More Civilized.* New Haven, Conn.: Yale University Press, 1961.

DURKHEIM, EMILE. *Suicide,* trans. John A. Spaulding and George Simpson. Glencoe, Ill.: Free Press of Glencoe, Inc., 1951.

EPSTEIN, T. S. *Economic Development and Social Change in South India.* Manchester, England: Manchester University Press, 1962.

ERIKSON, ERIK H. *Young Man Luther.* New York: W. W. Norton & Co., Inc., 1958.

FURNIVALL, J. S. *Colonial Policy and Practice: A Comparative Study of Burma and Netherlands India.* Cambridge, England: The University Press, 1948.

GERSCHENKRON, ALEXANDER. "Economic Backwardness in Historical Perspective," *The Progress of Underdeveloped Areas* (ed. B. F. Hoselitz).

———. "Social Attitudes, Entrepreneurship, and Economic Development," *Explorations in Entrepreneurial History,* Vol. VI (October, 1953), pp. 1–19.

HAGEN, E. E. *The Economic Development of Burma.* Washington, D.C.: The National Planning Association, 1956.

———. "How Economic Growth Begins: A General Theory Applied to Japan," *Public Opinion Quarterly,* Vol. XXII (Fall, 1958), pp. 373–90.

———. "The Process of Economic Development," *Economic Development and Cultural Change,* Vol. V (April, 1957), pp. 193–215.

HOSELITZ, B. F. (ed.). *The Progress of Underdeveloped Areas.* Chicago: The University of Chicago Press, 1952.

———. *Sociological Aspects of Economic Growth.* Glencoe, Ill.: Free Press of Glencoe, Inc., 1960.

HUNTINGTON, ELLSWORTH. *Mainsprings of Civilization.* New York: John Wiley & Sons, Inc., 1945.

KARDINER, ABRAM. *Psychological Frontiers of Society.* New York: Columbia University Press, 1945.

KERR, CLARK; DUNLOP, JOHN T.; HARBISON, FREDERICK H.; and MYERS, CHARLES A. *Industrialism and Industrial Man.* Cambridge, Mass.: Harvard University Press, 1960.

KLUCKHOHN, CLYDE. " Have There Been Discernible Shifts in American Values during the Past Generation?" *The American Style: Essays in Value and Performance* (ed. Elting Morison). New York: Harper & Bros., 1958.

KROEBER, A. L. *Configurations of Culture Growth.* Berkeley and Los Angeles: University of California Press, 1944.

LANDES, DAVID S. "Social Attitudes, Entrepreneurship, and Economic Development: A Comment," *Explorations in Entrepreneurial History,* Vol. VI (May, 1954), pp. 245–72.

LERNER, DANIEL. *The Passing of Traditional Society: Modernizing the Middle East.* Glencoe, Ill.: Free Press of Glencoe, Inc., 1958.

LEVY, MARION J. "Contrasting Factors in the Modernization of China and Japan," *Economic Growth: Brazil, India, Japan* (eds. Kuznets, Moore, and Spengler), chap. xvii. Durham, N.C.: Duke University Press, 1955.

———. "Some Social Obstacles to 'Capital Formation' in 'Underdeveloped Areas,' " *Capital Formation and Economic Growth* (ed. National Bureau of Economic Research). Princeton, N.J.: Princeton University Press, 1956.

———. "Some Sources of the Vulnerability of the Structures of Relatively Nonindustrialized Societies to Those of Highly Industrialized Societies," *The Progress of Underdeveloped Areas* (ed. B. F. Hoselitz), pp. 113–25.

———. *The Structure of Society.* Princeton, N.J.: Princeton University Press, 1952.

LEWIS, OSCAR. *The Children of Sanchez.* New York: Random House, 1961.

———. *Five Families: Mexican Case Studies in the Culture of Poverty.* New York: Basic Books, Inc., 1959.

LIPSET, SEYMOUR M. "Some Social Requisites of Democracy: Economic Development and Political Legitimacy," *American Political Science Review,* Vol. LIII (March, 1959), pp. 69–105.

MAINE, SIR HENRY. *Ancient Law: Its Connection with the Early History of Society and Its Relation to Modern Ideas.* London: Lardon J. Murray, 1861.

MALINOWSKI, BRONISLAW. *The Dynamics of Culture Change.* New Haven, Conn.: Yale University Press, 1945.

MANNONI, O. *Prospero and Caliban: The Psychology of Colonization,* trans. Pamela Powesland. New York: Frederick A. Praeger, 1956.

McCLELLAND, DAVID C. *The Achieving Society.* Princeton, N.J.: D. Van Nostrand & Co., Inc., 1961.

MEAD, MARGARET. *New Lives for Old.* New York: William Morrow & Co., 1956.

MERTON, ROBERT K. *Social Theory and Social Structure.* Glencoe, Ill.: Free Press of Glencoe, Inc., 1957.

MILLIKAN, MAX F., and BLACKMER, DONALD L. M. (eds.). *The Emerging Nations.* Boston: Little, Brown & Co., Inc., 1961.

MOORE, WILBERT E. *Industrialization and Labor: Social Aspects of Economic Development.* Ithaca, N.Y.: Cornell University Press, 1951.

NEF, JOHN U. *Cultural Foundations of Industrial Civilization*. Cambridge, England: The University Press, 1958.

PARSONS, TALCOTT. *Essays in Sociological Theory*. Rev. ed. Glencoe, Ill.: Free Press of Glencoe, Inc., 1954.

————. "Some Reflections on the Institutional Framework of Economic Development," *The Challenge of Development*. Jerusalem: The Hebrew University, 1958.

————, and BALES, ROBERT F. *Family, Socialization, and Interaction Process*. Glencoe, Ill.: Free Press of Glencoe, Inc., 1954.

PETTEE, GEORGE SAWYER. *The Process of Revolution*. New York: Harper & Bros., 1938.

PHELPS-BROWN, E. H. *Economic Growth and Human Welfare*. Delhi: Ranjit Printers & Publishers (English Agents: Students Bookshops, Ltd.), 1953.

POLANYI, KARL. *The Great Transformation*. New York: Farrar & Rinehart, Inc., 1944.

PYE, LUCIAN W. "The Non-Western Political Process," *Journal of Politics*, Vol. XX (August, 1958), pp. 468–86.

————. *Politics, Personality, and Nation Building: Burma's Search for Identity*. New Haven, Conn.: Yale University Press, 1962.

RADCLIFFE-BROWN, A. R. "On the Concept of Function in Social Science," *American Anthropologist*, Vol. XXXVII (July–September, 1935), pp. 394–402.

RIESMAN, DAVID; DENNY, R.; and GLAZER, N. *The Lonely Crowd*. 2d ed. New Haven, Conn.: Yale University Press, 1961.

SAWYER, JOHN E. "In Defense of an Approach: A Comment on Professor Gerschenkron's 'Social Attitudes, Entrepreneurship, and Economic Development,'" *Explorations in Entrepreneurial History*, Vol. VI (May, 1954), pp. 273–86.

SCHUMPETER, JOSEPH A. *The Theory of Economic Development*. Cambridge, Mass.: Harvard University Press, 1934.

SMELSER, NEIL J. *Social Change in the Industrial Revolution: An Application of Theory to the British Cotton Industry*. Chicago: The University of Chicago Press, 1959.

SOCIAL SCIENCE RESEARCH COUNCIL. "Acculturation: An Exploratory Formulation," *American Anthropologist*, Vol. LVI (1954), pp. 973–1002.

SPICER, EDWARD H. (ed.). *Human Problems in Technological Change: A Casebook*. New York: Russell Sage Foundation, 1952.

THOMAS, W. I., and ZNANIECKI, FLORJAN. *The Polish Peasant in Europe and America*. Boston: Badger, 1920.

TÖNNIES, FERDINAND. *Community and Society (Gemeinschaft und Gesellschaft)*, trans. and ed. Charles P. Loomis. East Lansing, Mich.: Michigan State University Press, 1957.

USHER, ABBOT PAYSON. *A History of Mechanical Inventions*. Rev. ed. Cambridge, Mass.: Harvard University Press, 1954.

WEBER, MAX. *The Protestant Ethic and the Spirit of Capitalism*, trans. Talcott Parsons. New York: Charles Scribner's Sons, 1930; 1958 paperbound.

WHITEHEAD, A. N. *Science and the Modern World*. New York: Macmillan & Co., 1929.

WILSON, GODFREY and MONICA. *The Analysis of Social Change*. London: Cambridge University Press, 1945.

ZENKOVSKY, SERGE A. "The Russian Church Schism: Its Background and Repercussions," *Russian Review,* Vol. XVI (October, 1957), pp. 37–58.

Social Structure

COULANGES, FUSTEL DE. *La Cité Antique.* Paris: Hachette et Cie., 1905.

DURKHEIM, EMILE. *The Division of Labor in Society,* trans. George Simpson. Glencoe, Ill.: Free Press of Glencoe, Inc., 1947.

FIRTH, RAYMOND. *Elements of Social Organisation.* London: Watts & Co., 1951.

LEVY, MARION J. *The Structure of Society.* Princeton, N.J.: Princeton University Press, 1952.

MURDOCK, GEORGE P. *Social Structure.* New York: Macmillan & Co., 1949.

PARSONS, TALCOTT. *The Social System.* Glencoe, Ill.: Free Press of Glencoe, Inc., 1951.

——; BALES, ROBERT F.; and SHILS, EDWARD A. *Working Papers in the Theory of Action.* Glencoe, Ill.: Free Press of Glencoe, Inc., 1953.

——, and SHILS, EDWARD A. (eds.). *Toward a General Theory of Action.* Cambridge, Mass.: Harvard University Press, 1952, 1954.

——, and SMELSER, NEIL J. *Economy and Society: A Study in the Integration of Economic and Social Theory.* London: Routledge and Kegan Paul, 1956.

Religion and Social Change

BOULDING, KENNETH. "Religious Foundations of Economic Progress," *Harvard Business Review,* Vol. XXX (1952), pp. 33–40.

FANFANI, A. *Catholicism, Protestantism and Capitalism.* New York: Sheed and Ward, 1935.

MERTON, ROBERT K. "Science, Religion, and Technology in Seventeenth Century England," *Osiris,* Vol. IV (1938), pp. 360–632.

ROBERTSON, H. M. *Aspects of the Rise of Economic Individualism.* Cambridge, England: The University Press, 1935.

SAMUELSSON, KURT. *Religion and Economic Action,* trans. from Swedish by E. Geoffrey French. London: William Heinemann Ltd., 1961.

SOMBART, WERNER. *The Quintessence of Capitalism: A Study of the History and Psychology of the Modern Business Man,* trans. and ed. M. Epstein. London: T. Fischer Unwin, Ltd., 1915.

TAWNEY, R. H. *The Acquisitive Society.* New York: Harcourt-Brace & Co., 1920.

——. *Religion and the Rise of Capitalism.* New York: Harcourt-Brace & Co., 1952.

WEBER, MAX. *The Protestant Ethic and the Spirit of Capitalism,* trans. Talcott Parsons. New York: Charles Scribner's Sons, 1930; 1958 paperbound.

ENGLAND

Chapter 13

ASHTON, T. S. *Economic Fluctuations in England, 1700–1800.* London: Oxford University Press, 1959.

ASHTON, T. S. *An Economic History of England: The 18th Century.* London: Methuen & Co., Ltd., 1955 (New York: Barnes and Noble, 1955).

ASHTON, T. S. *The Industrial Revolution, 1760–1830.* London: Oxford University Press, 1948, 1954.

BARLOW, FRANK. *The Feudal Kingdom of England, 1042–1216.* London and New York: Longmans, Green & Co., Inc., 1955.

BEBB, E. D. *Nonconformity and Social and Economic Life, 1660–1800.* London: Epworth Press, 1935.

BLAIR, PETER HUNTER. *An Introduction to Anglo-Saxon England.* Cambridge, England: The University Press, 1956.

BOURNE, GEORGE (pseud. of George Sturt). *Change in the Village.* London: Gerald Duckworth & Co., Ltd., 1912, 1955.

BRINTON, CRANE. *The Shaping of the Modern Mind.* New York: Mentor Books, 1953.

BUER, M. C. *Health, Wealth, and Population in the Early Days of the Industrial Revolution.* London: Routledge, 1926.

CAMPBELL, MILDRED. *The English Yeoman, under Elizabeth and the Early Stuarts, 1560–1642.* New Haven, Conn.: Yale University Press, 1942.

CARUS-WILSON, E. M. "An Industrial Revolution of the Thirteenth Century," *Economic History Review,* Vol. XI (1941), pp. 39–60.

CHAMBERS, R. W. *Man's Unconquerable Mind.* Philadelphia: Albert Saifer, Publisher, 1953.

CLAPHAM, SIR JOHN. *A Concise Economic History of Britain.* Cambridge, England: The University Press, 1949.

COULTON, G. G. *Medieval Panorama.* New York: Macmillan & Co., 1938.

———. *Social Life in Britain from the Conquest to the Reformation.* Cambridge, England: The University Press, 1918.

FRENCH, ALLEN. *Charles I and the Puritan Upheaval.* London: George Allen & Unwin, Ltd., 1955.

GRAS, N. S. B. *The Economic and Social History of an English Village.* Cambridge, Mass.: Harvard University Press, 1930.

HAYES, CARLTON J. H.; BALDWIN, MARSHALL W.; and COLE, CHARLES W. *History of Europe.* New York: Macmillan & Co., 1950.

HODGEN, MARGARET T. *Change and History.* New York: Wenner-Gren Foundation for Anthropological Research, Inc., 1952.

HOFFMANN, WALTHER G. *British Industry, 1700–1950,* trans. W. O. Henderson and W. H. Chaloner. Oxford: Basil Blackwell, 1955.

HUIZINGA, JOHAN. *The Waning of the Middle Ages.* New York: Doubleday & Co., Inc., 1954.

KUZNETS, SIMON. "Quantitative Aspects of the Economic Growth of Nations: I. Levels and Variability of Rates of Growth," *Economic Development and Cultural Change,* Vol. V (October, 1956), entire issue.

———. "Quantitative Aspects of the Economic Growth of Nations: V. Capital Formation Proportions: International Comparisons for Recent Years," *Economic Development and Cultural Change,* Vol. VIII, Part II (July, 1960).

LANGER, WILLIAM L. (ed.). *An Encyclopedia of World History.* Rev. ed. Boston: Houghton Mifflin Co., 1952.

MANTOUX, PAUL. *The Industrial Revolution in the Eighteenth Century.* Rev. ed. London: Jonathan Cape, 1961.

MERTON, ROBERT K. "Science, Religion, and Technology in Seventeenth Century England," *Osiris,* Vol. IV (1938), pp. 360–632.

NEF, JOHN U. *Cultural Foundations of Industrial Civilization.* Cambridge, England: The University Press, 1958.

NUSSBAUM, FREDERICK L. *History of the Economic Institutions of Modern Europe.* New York: Crofts, 1933.
   A summary and interpretation of Sombart: *Der Moderne Kapitalismus.*

PIRENNE, HENRI. *Economic and Social History of Medieval Europe,* trans. from French. New York: Harcourt-Brace & Co., 1937.

POLANYI, KARL. *The Great Transformation.* New York: Farrar & Rinehart, Inc., 1944.

POOLE, AUSTIN LANE. *Obligations of Society in the XII and XIII Centuries.* Oxford: The Clarendon Press, 1949.

POSTAN, M. M. "Revisions in Economic History: IX. The Fifteenth Century," *Economic History Review,* Vol. IX (1939), pp. 160–67.

ROBERTSON, H. M. *Aspects of the Rise of Economic Individualism.* Cambridge, England: The University Press, 1935.

SARTON, GEORGE. *Six Wings: Men of Science in the Renaissance.* Bloomington, Ind.: Indiana University Press, 1957.

SAYLES, G. O. *The Medieval Foundations of England.* 2d ed. London: Methuen & Co., Ltd., 1950.

SINGER, CHARLES J.; HOLMYARD, E. J.; HALL, A. R.; and WILLIAMS, TREVOR I. (eds.). *From the Renaissance to the Industrial Revolution, c.1550–c.1750.* A History of Technology, Vol. III. Oxford: The Clarendon Press, 1957.

SMELSER, NEIL J. *Social Change in the Industrial Revolution: An Application of Theory to the British Cotton Industry.* Chicago: The University of Chicago Press, 1959.

STEPHENSON, CARL. *Mediaeval Feudalism.* Ithaca, N.Y.: Cornell University Press, 1942.

STRAYER, JOSEPH R. *Western Europe in the Middle Ages.* New York: Appleton-Century-Crofts, Inc., 1955.

TAWNEY, R. H. *Religion and the Rise of Capitalism.* New York: Harcourt-Brace & Co., 1952.

TEY, JOSEPHINE. *Daughter of Time.* New York: Macmillan & Co., 1951.

TREVELYAN, G. M. *History of England.* 3d ed. London and New York: Longmans, Green & Co., Inc., 1945.

————. *Illustrated English Social History.* London and New York: Longmans, Green & Co.:
   Vol. I. Chaucer's England and the Early Tudors, 1949
   Vol. II. The Age of Shakespeare and the Stuart Period, 1950
   Vol. III. The Eighteenth Century, 1951.

WARNER, W. J. *The Wesleyan Movement in the Industrial Revolution.* London: Longmans, Green & Co., Inc., 1930.

WEBER, MAX. *The Protestant Ethic and the Spirit of Capitalism,* trans. Talcott Parsons. New York: Charles Scribner's Sons, 1930; 1958 paperbound.

JAPAN
Chapter 14

ABEGGLEN, JAMES C. *The Japanese Factory.* Glencoe, Ill.: Free Press of Glencoe, Inc., 1958.

ALLEN, G. C. *A Short Economic History of Modern Japan 1869–1937.* London: George Allen & Unwin, Ltd., 1946, 1958.

———, and DONNITHORNE, AUDREY G. *Western Enterprise in Far Eastern Economic Development: China and Japan.* London: George Allen & Unwin, Ltd., 1954.

BEARDSLEY, RICHARD K.; HALL, JOHN W.; and WARD, ROBERT E. *Village Japan.* Chicago: The University of Chicago Press, 1959.

BELLAH, ROBERT N. *Tokugawa Religion: The Values of Pre-Industrial Japan.* Glencoe, Ill.: Free Press of Glencoe, Inc., 1957.

BENEDICT, RUTH. *The Chrysanthemum and the Sword.* Boston: Houghton Mifflin Co., 1946.

BORTON, HUGH. *Japan's Modern Century.* New York: The Ronald Press Co., 1955.

———, et al. *Japan Between East and West.* New York: Harper & Bros., 1957.

CRAIG, ALBERT M. *Chōshū in the Meiji Restoration.* Cambridge, Mass.: Harvard University Press, 1961.

DORE, R. P. *City Life in Japan: A Study of a Tokyo Ward.* Berkeley and Los Angeles: University of California Press, 1958.

EMBREE, JOHN F. *Suye Mura: A Japanese Village.* Chicago: The University of Chicago Press, 1939.

FAIRBANK, J. K., *et al.* "The Influence of Modern Western Science and Technology on Japan and China," *Explorations in Entrepreneurial History,* Vol. VII (April, 1955), pp. 189–204.

HAGEN, E. E. "How Economic Growth Begins: A General Theory Applied to Japan," *Public Opinion Quarterly,* Vol. XXII (Fall, 1958), pp. 373–90.

HEARN, LAFCADIO. *Japan: An Attempt at Interpretation.* New York: Macmillan & Co., 1904.

JANSEN, MARIUS B. *Sakamoto Ryōma and the Meiji Restoration.* Princeton, N.J.: Princeton University Press, 1961.

KEENE, DONALD. *The Japanese Discovery of Europe: Honda Toshiaki and Other Discoverers, 1720–1798.* London: Routledge and Kegan Paul, 1952.

KUZNETS, S. S.; MOORE, W.; and SPENGLER, J. J. (eds.). *Economic Growth: Brazil, India, Japan.* Durham, N.C.: Duke University Press, 1955.

LANGER, W. L. *An Encyclopedia of World History.* Rev. ed. Boston: Houghton Mifflin Co., 1952.

LEVY, MARION J. "Contrasting Factors in the Modernization of China and Japan," *Economic Growth: Brazil, India, Japan* (eds. Kuznets, Moore, and Spengler).

LOCKWOOD, WILLIAM W. *The Economic Development of Japan: Growth and Structural Change, 1868–1938.* Princeton, N.J.: Princeton University Press, 1954.

MORGAN, KENNETH W. *The Path of the Buddha.* New York: The Ronald Press Co., 1956.

NORMAN, E. H. *Japan's Emergence as a Modern State.* New York: Institute of Pacific Relations, 1940.

OHKAWA, KAZUSHI, with SHINOHARA, M.; UMEMURA, M.; ITO, M.; and NODA, T. *The Growth Rate of the Japanese Economy since 1878.* (Institute of Economic Research, Hitotsubashi University, Economic Research Series I.) Tokyo: Kinokuniya Bookstore Co., 1957.

REISCHAUER, EDWIN O. *Japan, Past and Present*. 2d ed. New York: Alfred A. Knopf, Inc., 1953.

————. "Japanese Feudalism," *Feudalism in History* (ed. Rushton H. Coulborn). Princeton, N.J.: Princeton University Press, 1956.

————, and FAIRBANK, JOHN K. *East Asia: The Great Tradition*. A History of East Asian Civilization, Vol. I. Boston: Houghton Mifflin Co., 1958 and 1960.

SANSOM, GEORGE B. *Japan: A Short Cultural History*. New York: The Century Co., 1931. Rev. ed.; New York: Appleton-Century, 1944.

————. *A History of Japan to 1334*. Stanford, Calif.: Stanford University Press, 1958.

————. *The Western World and Japan*. New York: Alfred A. Knopf, Inc., 1950.

SHELDON, CHARLES D. *The Rise of the Merchant Class in Tokugawa Japan, 1600–1868*. Locust Valley, N.Y.: J. J. Augustin Inc., 1958.

SMITH, THOMAS C. *The Agrarian Origins of Modern Japan*. Stanford, Calif.: Stanford University Press, 1959.

————. *Political Change and Industrial Development in Japan: Government Enterprise, 1868–1880*. Stanford, Calif.: Stanford University Press, 1955.

STATLER, OLIVER. *Japanese Inn*. New York: Random House, 1961.

STOETZEL, JEAN. *Without the Chrysanthemum and the Sword: A Study of the Attitudes of Youth in Post-War Japan*. New York: Columbia University Press, 1955. (A UNESCO publication.)

TAKAKUSU, JUNJIRO. *The Essentials of Buddhist Philosophy*. 3d ed. Honolulu: Office Appliance Co., Ltd., 1956.

COLOMBIA

Chapter 15

CAMACHO ROLDÁN, SALVADOR. *Escritos Varios, Segunda Serie*. Bogotá: Librería Colombiana, 1893.

————. *Notas de Viaje*. Bogotá: Librería Colombiana, 1890.

CISNEROS, FRANCISCO J. *Ferrocarril de Antioquia*. New York: Ponce de Leon, 1880.

CRIST, RAYMOND. *The Cauca Valley, Colombia*. Baltimore: The Waverly Press, 1952.

EDER, PHANOR J. *El Fundador: Santiago M. Eder*. Bogotá: Autores, Ltda., 1959.

FALS-BORDA, ORLANDO. *Peasant Society in the Colombian Andes*. Gainesville, Fla.: University of Florida Press, 1955.

ARANGO MEJÍA, GABRIEL. *Geneologías de Antioquia y Caldas*, Vol. I. 2d ed. Medellín, Colombia: Imprenta Editorial Medellín, 1942.

HENAO, JESÚS MARÍA, and ARRUBLA, GERARDO. *History of Colombia*, trans. and ed. J. Fred Rippy. Chapel Hill, N.C.: University of North Carolina Press, 1938.

ORTEGO, ALFREDO. *Ferrocarriles Colombianos*. Biblioteca de Historia Nacional, Vol. XXVI. Bogota: Imprenta Nacional, 1920.

OSPINA VÁSQUEZ, LUIS. *Industria y Protección en Colombia, 1810–1930*. Bogotá: Editorial Santafé, 1955.

PARSONS, JAMES J. *Antioqueño Colonization in Western Colombia.* Berkeley and Los Angeles: University of California Press, 1949.

REPÚBLICA DE COLOMBIA, DEPARTAMENTO ADMINISTRATIVO NACIONAL DE ESTADÍSTICA. *Anuario General de Estadística, Colombia, 1956.* Bogotá, 1957.

REPÚBLICA DE COLOMBIA, DEPARTAMENTO ADMINISTRATIVO NACIONAL DE ESTADÍSTICA. *Directoria Industrial (Provisional), 1956.* Bogotá, 1957.

REPÚBLICA DE COLOMBIA, DEPARTAMENTO DE CONTRALORÍA. *Censo de Población de la República de Colombia.* Bogotá, 1924. (The 1918 Census.)

RESTREPO, JOSÉ MANUEL. "Ensayo sobre la Geografía: Producciones, Industria y Población de la Provincia de Antioquia en el Nuevo Reino de Granada," *Seminario del Nuevo Reino de Granada* (ed. Francisco José de Caldas). Bogotá: 1808–10. (Reprinted in 3 volumes; Bogotá, 1942.)

RESTREPO, VICENTE. *A Study of the Gold and Silver Mines of Colombia,* trans. C. W. Fisher. New York: Colombian Consulate, 1886.

RIPPY, J. FRED. *The Capitalists and Colombia.* New York: Vanguard Press, 1931.

ROBLEDO, EMILIO. *Bosquejo Biográfico del Señor Oidor Juan Antonio Mon y Velarde Visitador de Antioquia, 1785–1788,* Vols. I and II. Bogotá: Publicaciones del Banco de la República, Archivo de la Economia Nacional, 1954.

ROGER, RENÉ. *La Colombie Economique.* Paris : Librairie de la Société du Recueil Sirey et Librairie R. Roger et F. Chernovez, 1914.

UNITED NATIONS ECONOMIC COMMISSION FOR LATIN AMERICA. *Analyses and Projections of Economic Development, III. The Economic Development of Colombia.* Geneva, 1957 (E/CN.12/365/Rev.1).

BURMA

Chapter 18

ANDRUS, J. RUSSELL. *Burmese Economic Life.* Stanford, Calif.: Stanford University Press, 1947.

BA U. *My Burma: The Autobiography of a President.* New York: Taplinger, 1958.

BUTTWELL, RICHARD. "The New Political Outlook in Burma," *Far Eastern Survey,* Vol. XXIX (February, 1960), pp. 21–27.

CADY, JOHN F. *A History of Modern Burma.* Ithaca, N.Y.: Cornell University Press, 1958.

CHRISTIAN, JOHN L. *Burma.* London: Wm. Collins Sons & Co., Ltd., 1945.

COLLIS, MAURICE. *The Great Stone Image.* New York: Alfred A. Knopf, Inc., 1943.

———. *Trials in Burma.* London: Faber & Faber, Ltd., 1938.

CROZIER, BRIAN. *The Rebels: A Study of Post-War Insurrections.* Boston: Beacon Press, 1960.

DAW MYA SEIN. *Administration of Burma: Sir Charles Crosthwaite and the Consolidation of Burma.* Rangoon: Zabu Meitswe Pitaka Press, 1938.

DONNISON, F. S. V. *Public Administration in Burma.* London: Royal Institute of International Affairs, 1953.

FURNIVALL, J. S. *Colonial Policy and Practice: A Comparative Study of Burma and Netherlands India.* Cambridge, England: The University Press, 1948.

———. *The Governance of Modern Burma.* New York: International Secretariat, Institute of Pacific Relations, 1958.

———. *An Introduction to the Political Economy of Burma*. Rangoon: Burma Book Club, Ltd., 1931. 2d ed., 1937.

GORER, GEOFFREY. "Burmese Personality" (mimeographed; rev.; n.p., 1945). Photocopy at Peabody Museum, Harvard University.

GOUGER, H. *A Personal Narrative of Two Years' Imprisonment in Burma.* London, 1864. (Cited in Furnivall, *Colonial Policy and Practice.*)

GOVERNMENT OF THE UNION OF BURMA. *Burma and the Insurrections.* Rangoon, 1949.

———. *CBC. Report of the Bribery and Corruption Enquiry Committee.* Rangoon, 1941.

———. *Economic Survey of Burma, 1958.* Rangoon, 1958.

———. *Is It a Peoples' Liberation: A Short Survey of the Communist Insurrection in Burma.* Rangoon, 1952.

HALL, D. G. E. *A History of Southeast Asia.* New York: St. Martin's Press, 1955.

HALL, H. FIELDING. *A People in School.* New York: Macmillan & Co., 1906.

———. *The Soul of a People.* New York: Macmillan & Co., 1898, 1946.

HANKS, L. M., JR. "The Quest for Individual Autonomy in Burmese Personality with Particular Reference to the Arakan," *Psychiatry,* Vol. XII (1949), pp. 285–300.

HARVEY, G. E. *Burma, 1782–1852: British Rule in Burma.* The Cambridge History of India, Vol. V. Cambridge, England: The University Press, 1929.

———. *British Rule in Burma, 1824–1942.* London: Faber and Faber, 1946.

———. *Burma, 1852–1918: British Rule in Burma.* The Cambridge History of India, Vol. VI. Cambridge, England: The University Press, 1929.

———. *History of Burma from the Earliest Times to 1824.* London: Longmans, Green & Co., Inc., 1925.

HITSON, HAZEL MARIE. "Family Patterns and Paranoidal Personality Structure in Boston and Burma" (Ph.D. dissertation; Radcliffe College, April, 1959).

LOCKWOOD, AGNESE N. *The Burma Road to Pyidawtha.* International Conciliation, No. 518 (May, 1958), pp. 385–450.

KNAPPEN, TIPPETS, ABBETT, McCARTHY ENGINEERS (with Pierce Management, Inc., and Robert R. Nathan Associates, Inc.). *Economic and Engineering Development of Burma,* Vols. I and II. New York: Knappen, Tippets, Abbett, McCarthy Engineers, August, 1953.

MAINE, SIR HENRY. *Ancient Law: Its Connection with the Early History of Society, and Its Relation to Modern Ideas.* London: Lardon J. Murray, 1861.

MAUNG MAUNG PYE. *Burma in the Crucible.* Rangoon: Khittaye Publishing House, 1951.

MENDELSON, E. MICHAEL. "Religion and Authority in Modern Burma," *The World Today,* Vol. XVI (March, 1960), pp. 110–18.

MI MI KHAING. *Burmese Family.* Calcutta: Longmans, Green & Co., Inc., 1946.

ORWELL, GEORGE. *Burmese Days.* New York: Harcourt-Brace Co., 1930.

PYE, LUCIAN W. *Politics, Personality, and Nation Building: Burma's Search for Identity.* New Haven, Conn.: Yale University Press, 1962.

RICHARDS, C. J. *Burma Retrospect and Other Sketches.* Winchester, England: The Cathedral Press, 1951.

SHWAY YOE (pseud. of Sir James G. Scott). *The Burman: His Life and Notions.* London: Macmillan Co., 1882.

THAKIN NU. *Burma under the Japanese.* trans. and ed. J. S. Furnivall. London: Macmillan & Co., 1954.

TINKER, HUGH. *Foundations of Local Self Government in India, Pakistan and Burma.* London: University of London, Athlone Press, 1954.

TINKER, HUGH. *The Union of Burma: A Study of the First Years of Independence.* New York: Oxford University Press, 1957.

TÖNNIES, FERDINAND. *Community and Society (Gemeinschaft und Gesellschaft),* trans. and ed. Charles P. Loomis. East Lansing, Mich.: Michigan State University Press, 1957.

TRAGER, FRANK N. "Political Divorce in Burma," *Foreign Affairs,* Vol. XXXVII (January, 1959), pp. 317–27.

——. "The Political Split in Burma," *Guardian,* Vol. VI (January, 1959), pp. 13–16.

UNESCO EDUCATIONAL MISSIONS—III. *Report of the Mission to Burma.* Paris: UNESCO, 1952. (E.D. 51.VIII.3A.)

WALINSKY, LOUIS J. *Economic Development in Burma, 1951–1960.* New York: Twentieth Century Fund, 1962.

WOODRUFF, PHILIP. *The Men Who Ruled India.* 2 vols.; New York: St. Martin's Press, 1954.

THE SIOUX

Chapter 19

AMERICAN FRIENDS SERVICE COMMITTEE. *Final Report of the American Friends Service Committee, Pine Ridge Reservation Program, South Dakota, January 1955–December 1958.* Mimeographed; Philadelphia, July, 1959.

ARTICHOKER, JOHN, JR., and PALMER, NEIL M. *The Sioux Indian Goes to College.* Vermillion, S.D.: Institute of Indian Studies and State Department of Public Instruction, March, 1959.

BETTELHEIM, BRUNO. "Individual and Mass Behavior in Extreme Situations," *Journal of Abnormal and Social Psychology,* Vol. XXXVIII (October, 1943), pp. 417–52.

CARDWELL, WARREN. *An Introduction to the Modern Oglala Sioux.* Washington, D.C.: Department of Health, Education, and Welfare, Public Health Service, Division of Indian Health, 1958.

CARMICHAEL, L. "The Experimental Embryology of Mind," *Psychological Bulletin,* Vol. XXXVIII (January, 1941), pp. 1–28.

CATLIN, GEORGE. *North American Indians.* Edinburgh: John Grant, 1926.

DORNER, PETER PAUL. "The Economic Position of the American Indians: Their Resources and Potential for Development" (Ph.D. dissertation in economics, Harvard University, February, 1959).

DORSEY, JAMES O. "A Study of Siouan Cults," *Annual Report of the U.S. Bureau of Ethnology,* XI.

EASTMAN, M. H. *Dahcotah.* New York: John Wiley, 1849.

ERIKSON, ERIK H. "Childhood and Tradition in Two American Indian Tribes: With Some Reflections on the Contemporary American Scene," *Personal Character and Cultural Milieu* (ed. Douglas G. Haring), pp. 255–86. 3d ed. Syracuse, N.Y.: Syracuse University Press, 1956.

——. "Hunters across the Prairie," *Childhood and Society,* chap. iii. New York: W. W. Norton & Co., Inc., 1950.

————. "Observations on Sioux Education," *Journal of Psychology*, Vol. VII (January, 1939), pp. 101–56.

FEY, H. E., and McNICKLE, D. *Indians and Other Americans*. New York: Harper & Bros., 1959.

HAGEN, E. E., and SCHAW, L. S. *The Sioux on the Reservations*. Cambridge, Mass.: Center for International Studies, Massachusetts Institute of Technology, May, 1960.

HEBB, O. *The Organization of Behavior*. New York: John Wiley & Sons, Inc., 1949.

HYDE, GEORGE E. *A Sioux Chronicle*. Norman, Okla.: University of Oklahoma Press, 1956.

————. *Red Cloud's Folk*. 2d ed. Norman, Okla.: University of Oklahoma Press, 1957.

LINCOLN, T. S. *The Dream in Primitive Cultures*. London: Cresset Press, 1935.

LOTT, MILTON. *Dance Back the Buffalo*. Boston: Houghton Mifflin Co., 1959.

MacGREGOR, GORDON. *Warriors Without Weapons*. Chicago: The University of Chicago Press, 1946.

MALAN, VERNON D. *The Dakota Indian Family*. Bulletin 470. Brookings, S.D.: Rural Sociology Department, South Dakota State College, 1958.

————, and JESSER, CLINTON J. *The Dakota Indian Religion*. Bulletin 473. Brookings, S.D.: Rural Sociology Department, South Dakota State College, 1959.

MEAD, G. H. *Mind, Self, and Society*. Chicago: The University of Chicago Press, 1934.

MENNINGER, KARL. *A Psychiatrist's World*. New York: The Viking Press, Inc., 1959.

MORGAN, C. T., and STELLAR, E. *Physiological Psychology*. New York: McGraw-Hill Book Co., Inc., 1950.

PARKMAN, FRANCIS. *The Oregon Trail*. New York: A. L. Burt Co., 1910.

POND, GIDEON H. "Dakota Superstitions," *Minnesota Historical Collection*, Vol. II (1890).

RADIN, PAUL. *The Story of the American Indian*. New York: Henry Schuman, 1953.

SCHUSKY, ERNEST. *Politics and Planning in a Dakota Indian Community*. Vermillion, S.D.: Institute of Indian Studies, 1959.

SELYE, HANS. *The Physiology and Pathology of Exposure to Stress*. Montreal: Acta Inc., Medical Publishers, 1950.

SULLIVAN, H. S. *The Interpersonal Theory of Psychiatry*. New York: W. W. Norton & Co., Inc., 1953.

THOMPSON, LAURA. "Attitudes and Acculturation," *American Anthropologist*, Vol. L (April–June, 1948), pp. 200–15.

————. *Personality and Government*. Mexico, D.F.: Ediciones del Instituto Indigenista Interamericano, 1951.

UNDERHILL, RUTH. "Religion among American Indians," *Annals of the American Academy of Arts and Sciences*, Vol. CCCXI (1957).

WALKER, J. R. *The Sun Dance and Other Ceremonies of the Oglala Division of the Teton Dakota*. New York: American Museum of Natural History, 1917.

WILSON, E., and MITCHELL, JOSEPH. *Apologies to the Iroquois*. New York: Farrar, Straus & Cudahy, Inc., 1959.

WISSLER, C. "Societies and Ceremonial Association in the Oglala Division of the Teton Dakota," *Anthropological Papers of the American Museum of Natural History*, Vol. II, Part I (1912).

THE USE OF ANALYTICAL MODELS IN
THE SOCIAL SCIENCES
Appendix I

ARROW, KENNETH J. "Mathematical Models in the Social Sciences," *The Policy Sciences* (eds. Daniel Lerner and Harold D. Lasswell), chap. viii. Stanford, Calif.: Stanford University Press, 1951. Reprinted in *General Systems*, Vol. I (1956), pp. 29–47.

ASHBY, W. Ross. "General Systems Theory as a New Discipline," *General Systems*, Vol. III (1958), pp. 1–6.

BERLINER, JOSEPH S. "The Feet of the Natives Are Large: An Essay on Anthropology by an Economist," *Current Anthropology*, Vol. III (February, 1962), pp. 47–77.

BERTALANFFY, LUDWIG VON. "General System Theory," *Main Currents in Modern Thought*, Vol. LXXI (1955). Reprinted with footnotes added in *General Systems*, Vol. I (1956), pp. 1–10.

BOULDING, KENNETH. "General System Theory—The Skeleton of Science," *Management Science*, Vol. II (1956), pp. 197–208.

HALL, A. D., and FAGEN, R. E. "Definition of System," *General Systems*, Vol. I (1956), pp. 18–28.

HENDERSON, L. J. *Pareto's General Sociology*. Cambridge, Mass.: Harvard University Press, 1935.

LERNER, DANIEL. "Model Construction in the Social Sciences," *Public Opinion Quarterly*, Vol. XIV (1950–51), pp. 710–28.

MCKINNEY, J. C. "Constructive Typology and Social Research," *An Introduction to Social Research* (ed. J. T. Doby). Harrisburg, Penn., 1954.

MILLER, JAMES D. "Toward a General Theory for the Behavioral Sciences," *The State of the Social Sciences* (ed. Leonard D. White), pp. 29–45. Chicago: The University of Chicago Press, 1956.

SAMUELSON, PAUL A. *Foundations of Economic Analysis*. Cambridge, Mass.: Harvard University Press, 1948.

Index

Index

547